John Erickson was ed[...] [...]ollege [...]ambridge, and served in British Army I[...] [...]ence from 1946 to 1949. He has been Fellow in Soviet military affairs of St Anthony's College, Oxford, and Lecturer at the University of St Andrew's and the University of Manchester. He has been Visiting Professor at Indiana University, Yale University, Texas A & M University, and the US Army Russian Institute. He is currently Professor and Director of the Centre for Defence Studies at the University of Edinburgh.

John Erickson is the author of numerous books and articles about the Soviet Army. He has contributed biographies of Soviet commanders to *The Warlords* (edited by Field Marshal Lord Carver) and *Stalin's Generals* (edited by Harold Shukman). *The Road to Berlin*, the second volume in his authoritative history of the Soviet-German war, is also available as a Cassell paperback.

JOHN ERICKSON

THE ROAD TO STALINGRAD

STALIN'S WAR WITH GERMANY:
VOLUME ONE

CASSELL&CO

Cassell & Co
Wellington House, 125 Strand
London WC2R 0BB

First published in Great Britain
by Weidenfeld & Nicolson in 1975
This paperback edition published in 2000

Copyright © John Erickson 1975

A CIP catalogue record for this book is available from the
British Library

ISBN 0-304-35375-2

Printed and bound in Great Britain by
Butler & Tanner Ltd, Frome and London

Contents

Preface

A lengthy book stands most urgently in need of a short preface and this is no place to discourse on a wide range of Soviet contacts, but obviously such circumstances have directly affected the scope, content and organization of this study. The object of the present work can be set down briefly enough: it is designed to investigate the kind of war the Soviet Union waged, the nature of command decisions and the machinery of decision-making, the course of military operations, Soviet performance in the field and the economic effort behind the lines, the emergence of Soviet 'war aims' – beyond mere survival – and, finally, the Soviet style of war. In sum, it is an attempt to probe how the Soviet system functioned under conditions of maximum stress: from this point of view it is less military history *per se* and might more properly be regarded as a form of social history. That this is no fanciful extrapolation is perhaps demonstrated by the nature of Soviet investigation of the 'Great Patriotic War' of 1941–5, for recollection of past tragedy and triumph is closely connected with present preoccupations about the efficacy of 'the system' and the image of a future war. The role of the 'surprise factor' springs to mind at once: both the military and the Party had their reputations as guarantors of the nation's security both to salvage and to reinforce, yet inevitably this proved to be the source of mutual recrimination. Simple assertions on the part of crude propagandists that the system worked were as unconvincing as they were irrelevant, if only because the military and operational technicalities of 'surprise attack' made nonsense of such *sancta simplicitas*. The Soviet military, on the other hand, found themselves in the unenviable position of claiming knowledge and awareness of the impending attack in 1941 yet thereby merely reinforcing criticism of them that it should have been met more energetically and effectively. Nor did Khrushchev's tactic in 1956 of heaping all the blame on Stalin – with the caricature of the man sniffing earth and spinning a globe to divine an operational decision – solve much: in the long run it served only to confuse the issue of the culpability and ineptitude of one man, the failings of the 'system' and performance in the field.

To put it somewhat differently, for almost two years the Soviet Union tried to fight the formidably modern war machine of Germany with a pattern or model of organization drawn from the far-off days of the Civil War, for this was the only one known at the outset to be viable. Such a *modus operandi* produced a specific and initially disastrous relationship between doctrine, technology and tradition (under which I include that Soviet amalgam of 'revolutiónary will' with orthodox military professionalism – but the 'discipline of the revolver', to use a Civil War phrase, could not of itself fuel stranded tank columns, compensate for plain tactical incompetence and operational ineptitude). It was to take virtually three years of war before these elements were brought more effectively into balance – the doctrine was adjusted but more important implemented with requisite 'norms' of armament and equipment (not simply sheer numbers) and the relationship of 'will' to professional competence substantially re-fashioned. It is, I believe, a great error to think only of the Russian emergence from near catastrophe in terms of numbers alone and here I would insist that one must listen to Soviet explanations that 'numbers' do not tell the whole story: reduced to their essentials, Soviet explanations do turn on this triad of 'doctrine-technology-tradition'. To dismiss or to ignore this basic theme in Soviet military-historical writing (and reminiscence) means simultaneously missing what lessons have been derived from the last war and what signs have been discerned for the future. Nor is it a matter of that tired joke about generals preparing to fight the last war all over again: no doubt some aged senior Soviet commanders would like to, but the younger military technocrats turn less emotionally to their computers and to their studies in modern weapons technology, loss rates and cybernetics, using the war as a vast data base.

It is nonetheless true to say that a huge and persistent mythology still pervades the history of the 'Great Patriotic War', or the Russo-German war (even this search for a separate identification is revealing). It was in many respects, not least in its unbridled and atavistic savagery, a war set apart and here German attempts to minimize (or rationalize) their defeat combined with Soviet efforts to magnify their own victory have increased the general obfuscation. The obsessive cultivation of the 'heroic image' in the Soviet Union is itself designed to hinder rational explanation and effective investigation of military and civilian responses, yet such explanations are to hand – the consequences of technological inferiority (the 'quality and quantity of armaments'), the failure to exploit existing resources, the anachronism of the 'revolutionary' theory of morale, the inefficiency of the Party as an administrative instrument, the shortcomings of Stalin's 'super-centralization' and so on. And at the eye of the storm is Stalin – are these his shortcomings or those of Soviet society, or where, if at all, do these divide? It is not surprising that Soviet historians have been unwilling to grasp such political live wires, which still carry a dangerously high charge.

What, then, is the case for relying primarily upon Soviet sources and materials? With some 15,000 volumes now published on the 'Great Patriotic War' (including many invaluable items dating back to wartime days, though these are sometimes difficult to obtain) there is no immediate shortage of material. Add to these also the immense holdings of the captured German military documents, which contain a whole 'sub-archive' of items originally captured from the Russians as well as contemporary material on Soviet military

performance – operational documents, intelligence appreciations, PW inter-
rogations and data on the Red Army at large – plus information on the whole
Soviet war effort. While these German collections provided both an additive
and corrective to Soviet studies, let me hasten to add that my approach to many
of these Soviet works was conditioned by contact and discussion with either
the author or with the research group responsible for much of the work. Again,
this is no place for a disquisition on the technicalities of Soviet sources, but I
would stress the professionalism of the military researchers – the teams behind
military histories bearing the names of Marshal Sokolovskii, Rokossovskii or
Malinovskii, for example – or individual officers such as Colonel Proektor, or
yet again such leading historians as Corresponding Member of the Academy of
Sciences Professor A.M. Samsonov, himself the author of a major study of the
Stalingrad battle. Though it would be impertinent and improper to associate
Professor Samsonov with any of my findings (or my views), it would be
churlish not to acknowledge my debt to him for much professional aid and
counsel in making my way through a small mountain of books. Equally I was
the beneficiary in discussions of Soviet findings with Soviet officer-historians,
who displayed very considerable professional competence and a scrupulous
regard for the integrity of source material (with ill-concealed criticism for those
who did not). All this is to say that much Soviet work is far from 'propaganda'
in the blatant or simplistic sense (though a somewhat perfervid patriotism is
never entirely absent), an observation borne out by the reputation enjoyed by
Voenno-istoricheskii Zhurnal (Military-Historical Journal) which is the vehicle of
the professional military and its professional historians.

In an attempt to display this material in its widest possible context I have
elected to compose the supporting notes to the chapters not in terms of single
references but rather as summaries of and comparisons between Soviet accounts
– a device which breaches some of the conventional practices but to which I
have resorted in the hope that the reader unfamiliar with the Russian language
may gain some insight into the substance of these Soviet studies and memoirs.
Finally, the format of the notes notwithstanding, I have allowed myself no
licence with the material and any descriptive point or passage, be it of persons,
places or circumstances, is derived directly from participants' accounts or the
document of the day: I do not pretend to the skill or to the special accomplish-
ment of writing a 'war book' in the sense of any literary re-creation of the
drama and the agony experienced by both sides.

My debt to persons and to previous publication are legion. In the composite
bibliography destined for the final volume of this present work I hope to make
my indebtedness to a multitude of monographs and articles plain, but at this
juncture I would like to acknowledge that personal and private aid which is
indispensable to a work such as this. In recording my thanks to the late
Cornelius Ryan, with whom I worked in Moscow in 1963, I would like also to
pay tribute to the man and his work: mention of Moscow impels me to record

my thanks to all those Soviet officers, some of the highest rank, and to the specialists in military history who helped me unstintingly with their own verbal evidence and with materials culled from their own collections. Major-General E.A. Boltin was kind enough to read and comment on these first chapters: Professor A.M. Samsonov took great pains to keep me abreast of Soviet writing. Beyond the borders of the Soviet Union Professor Alvin D. Coox gave so generously of his vast expertise in Japanese military affairs and Soviet-Japanese relations, while I came to rely heavily on the writing and comments of Professor Alexander Dallin and Dr Matthew P. Gallagher, to mention but two of my American colleagues in the field of Soviet affairs. The late N. Galai of Munich, a man of rare experience and discernment, gave me enormous help over the Vlasov affair, while it was from Germany that I received such munificence in the form of papers, diaries and personal accounts. Nor can I fail to mention the reliance I have placed on Colonel Albert Seaton and his major studies of the Soviet-German war.

Finally, I owe a special debt to Mr Andrew Wheatcroft and Mrs Susan Loden of Weidenfeld and Nicolson: in this University Miss K.U. Brown and Miss T. Fitzherbert have laboured long and hard on my behalf, while my colleagues never stinted in their help. All this company, stretching from Moscow to the United States, made positive and essential contributions: as for the blemishes and the shortcomings, the responsibility for those is mine alone.

John Erickson
University of Edinburgh
1974

It is exactly thirty years since this book was conceived and planned in Moscow and work immediately started upon it.

Since then greater access to Russian archives and printed records, welcome as it is, has not appreciably altered the essentials of this narrative, serving only to magnify the horror, to deepen the riddle of the 'surprise attack' of 1941 and Stalin's behaviour, to etch more sharply the detail of the subsequent tragedy and to confirm the scale of unparalleled human losses.

John Erickson
University of Edinburgh
April 1993

Introduction
On War Games, Soviet and German

In the winter of 1935, Marshal of the Soviet Union M.N. Tukhachevskii, First Deputy Commissar for Defence, Chief of Red Army Ordnance and potential commander-in-chief in the event of war, presented his own proposals for a special war-game to the General Staff. Tukhachevskii's intention was to investigate the situation arising out of a German attack on the Soviet Union. From the outset this suggestion received only little support and encouragement, but in the end the idea was taken up. G. Isserson, deputy head of the General Staff Operations Section (Mezheninov was the head of the Section and *ex officio* Deputy Chief of the General Staff) was therefore assigned to draft an initial plan for the war-games and to prepare the briefings. To Tukhachevskii himself, by common agreement, went command of the 'German party', while Army Commander Yakir (commander of the Kiev Military District) was nominated to control '*the armies of bourgeois Poland*', presumed co-belligerent with Germany.

What he thought of Germany's war potential Tukhachevskii had already made plain in an article in *Pravda*, printed on 29 March 1935. He pointed to Marshal Pétain's argument in the *Revue des Deux Mondes* (for March 1935), that no longer could the French Army rely on time to mobilize before the enemy engaged powerful forces. The French Army, in Tukhachevskii's opinion, was incapable of active opposition to Germany, whose basic aggressive design lay to the east of Europe. By the summer of 1935 Germany would have an army of 849,000 – 40 per cent greater than the French and almost equal in size to the the Red Army with its 940,000 effectives. A powerful and expanding air force added to an already powerful army. In spite of the menace conveyed by these figures, however, they were hardly a guide to German strategic-operational intentions. This was one of the first difficulties encountered by Isserson in his formulation of the game, for the head of Red Army intelligence, S.P. Uritskii, could offer little by way of concrete data on German intentions. In particular, it was virtually impossible to predict how the Baltic states and Poland would converge in a joint attack, with Germany, on the Soviet Union. To assume that Germany would erase Poland as an independent state seemed, in 1936, to be a somewhat unrealistic proposition, for the Polish Army disposed of some fifty divisions, a threat which the Red Army itself had never been able to ignore.

What was more likely was that by intrigue and pressure, Germany would inveigle Poland into a 'military union' and thereby draw her into war with Russia. Tukhachevskii was prepared to admit this possibility; nor was it one which impeded or neutralized his preoccupation with a completely secret concentration of German forces in the east. Thus, the 'German party's' main strategic and political context was set.

Army Commander Uborevich (commander of the Belorussian Military District) took control of the 'Red party's' forces, for whom a plan of strategic deployment from the Western Dvina to the Pripet Marshes was in process of being worked out. This 'Western Front' was deemed all-important. It met with no opposition, unlike Tukhachevskii's design, which was held up for a month until 'higher authority' cleared it for the purposes of the war-game. Clearance having been finally gained, the problem of the actual strength of the 'German party' still remained. Hitler's own statements spoke of a 36-division Wehrmacht; in addition, there were the unconfirmed reports of 3 Panzer divisions and an air force of some 4,000–5,000 machines. Little else could be adduced. Assuming that the German mobilization co-efficient was 1:3, then some 100 German divisions had to be accounted for; Isserson's planning staff therefore assigned 50–55 German divisions in an eastern concentration from the north to the Pripet Marshes. With 30 Polish divisions which could be assumed to be deployed against the Soviet western frontier from the north to the marshes, this gave a round total of some 80 divisions.

For the purpose of the war-game, the German concentration was divided into two armies and a high command reserve, deployed between the river Narew and the mouth of the Niemen along the line Ostrolenko-Kaunas; its main strength was on the left flank. No operational plan and no predetermined axis of advance had been set for these forces, which were to operate strictly to the requirements of Tukhachevskii – a requirement upon which the marshal strenuously insisted. Only the objective had been pre-set, and it was the destruction of the 'Red party' from the north to the Pripet Marshes, with the seizure of Smolensk as a jumping-off area for an offensive against Moscow. Accepting this, Tukhachevskii reserved his objections for the actual strength of the 'German' forces placed at his disposal. He argued that if, in the opening phase of the First World War Germany could dispose of ninety-two divisions, then at the outset of a second this would be more than doubled, giving some two hundred divisions; without such a margin of superiority, it would be impossible for Germany to embark upon a major war. He was therefore disposed to think that in the area from the north to the Pripet Marshes all of eighty divisions would be deployed, and that these would be entirely German. At this juncture, such an idea was considered to be ill-founded or worse – for it established a relationship of forces severely, if not inadmissibly unfavourable to the Red Army at the beginning of military operations. Tukhachevskii, however, had not finished. What the war-game envisaged was merely a preliminary deployment after detraining from the railway networks; he suggested that his operational plan – operative in terms of the real time of the game – would forestall the 'Red party's' concentration and he would initiate military operations. The 'German party' would, therefore, initiate its operations with a surprise blow.

At this point, Marshal of the Soviet Union Yegorov, Chief of the General Staff, intervened. As director of the war-game, he proposed a different notion, based on the preliminary mobilization of the 'Red party'. He was in no way inclined to accede to Tukhachevskii's views, since he no doubt wished to see the war-game fully validate the deployment plan for the Red Army which was then being worked out by the General Staff. As director, he categorically ruled out any German superiority either in terms of numbers or in time-margins; the 'German party' was to appear on the Soviet frontiers only after the concentration of the main Soviet forces. Tukhachevskii's proposals, which in Isserson's own phrase 'met powerful opposition', were rejected in their entirety. The war-game now proceeded on the assumption of the equality of opposing forces at the frontier, with no consideration of the problem of forestalling an enemy concentration and no digression into the actual initiation of military operations. The surprise factor was ignored. Stripped of any strategic acuity, the war-game represented nothing but a frontal, meeting engagement in the form of the frontier battles of 1914 – of indecisive outcome. Tukhachevskii was 'deeply disillusioned'.

Neither at this time, nor presumably later, did Marshal Tukhachevskii have 'direct access' to the Red Army deployment plans, illustration enough of the dissension and division within the Red Army command, split as it was by long-standing rivalries and Stalin's penetrations. To the Defence Commissar, Marshal of the Soviet Union Voroshilov, whose competence had more than once been called into question, Tukhachevskii directed a stream of papers on strategic problems. Nor did he confine himself to the major problems of war-making, but subjected to rigorous scrutiny the new formations – mechanized, mobile and airborne – which he had been largely instrumental in creating. After the Moscow Military District manoeuvres of September 1936, he submitted these criticisms of the exercises:

Mechanized corps made frontal breakthroughs of enemy defence positions without artillery support. Their losses would have been enormous. Mechanized corps operations were jerky, the direction bad. Mechanized corps operations were not supported by aviation. Aviation was employed somewhat aimlessly. Signals, communications worked badly. Airborne drops must be covered by fighter aircraft. Staff work, in particular intelligence, was very weak in all units. Parachutists jumped without weapons. This must be changed.

To the theme of the German threat Tukhachevskii returned publicly in his address to the second session of the TsIK (Central Executive Committee) in November 1936; the scale of the German preparations for war on land and in the air made it imperative that the defence of the Soviet western frontiers be undertaken in all seriousness. Publicly and privily he appeared to lose no opportunity to stress the growing danger, though this can only have grated upon a Stalin who, at this same juncture, was sending his personal emissaries to Berlin, ostensibly to discuss trade but primarily to talk of possible political agreements. The 'Kandelaki mission', dispatched by Stalin, was about to settle down to its real business in Berlin.

At the close of 1936 also, when the work of the newly founded General Staff Academy was just beginning, Isserson (who held the Chair in Operational Art) and Pavel Vakulich (in the Chair of Higher Formation Tactics) approached Tukhachevskii to consult him about the work of the Academy. Isserson had three basic questions to put to the marshal: against which potential enemy should the operational assignments of the Academy be directed? What would be the operational situation in the opening phase of a war? What would be the nature of operations in this initial phase and what types of operations should be envisaged? To the first question Tukhachevskii returned unambiguous answer: Germany. The second was a much more complex problem, since the international situation did not lend itself to forecasts of the 'concrete strategic situation' in which war might begin. Nevertheless, it was clear that the 'classic' form of entry into war with phases of concentration and deployment was a thing of the past. War could begin with large-scale operations with sudden, surprise initiation, conducted by the belligerents on land, at sea and in the air. It followed that an enemy could, under certain unfavourable conditions, forestall the Russians and be the first to initiate military operations. And for this reason special 'operational and mobilization measures' would have to be enforced during peacetime; frontier forces would have to maintain secret operational groupings and sustain operationally-readied formations (covering armies), fully capable of going over to a decisive, offensive engagement on various axes. As for the aim of these operations, they must reckon on the complete destruction of the enemy and yet resolve only the problems connected with the initial period – namely, to seize and invest favourable strategic lines as a preliminary to the concentration of the main forces. The general operational plan could be nothing more – in time of peace – than a definition of general aims, and the assignment of strategic tasks in a given theatre. The investment of the strategic line, however, was a prime object of the initial period, and this in turn depended on the operational groupings which should be established secretly within the frontier forces. Much depended on the disposition of the 'fortified districts' (UR: *ukreplennyi rayon*) and the selection of the frontier forces' operational groupings, so that they might take up flanking positions on those axes where enemy penetrations were thought most likely to occur. Tukhachevskii put it this way; that the 'fortified districts', the URs, should be the shield, absorbing the enemy offensive, and the 'secret operational groupings', the hammer, driving in the flank blows.

Early in 1937, during the General Staff Académy's first large-scale operational assignment (devoted to a study of offensive operations at army level during the initial period of a war), Tukhachevskii was further able to refine his point. On the critical question of the nature of military operations in the initial period of a war – having rebuked Isserson for his excess of optimism, wherein the 'peal of victory' was too readily heard – the marshal went on to sketch it in outline:

Operations will be inestimably more intensive and severe than in the First World War. Then, frontier battles in France lasted for two to three days. Now, such an offensive operation in the initial period of the war can last for weeks. As for the Blitzkrieg which is so propagandized by the Germans, this is directed towards an enemy who doesn't want to and won't fight it out. If the Germans meet an opponent who stands up and fights and takes the offensive himself, that would give a different aspect to things. The struggle would be bitter and protracted; by its very nature it would induce great fluctuations in the front on this or that side and in great depth. In the final resort, all would depend on who had the greater moral fibre and who at the close of the operations disposed of operational reserves in depth.

And again, would these operations assume a positional or manoeuvre form? Since one of his fundamental ideas was that the time-factor is decisive in war, Tukhachevskii's response was hardly surprising:

In general, operations in a future war will unfold as broad manoeuvre undertakings on a massive scale, massive also in their time scale. Even so, against the background of these operations and as part of the process of their development there will be separate phases of stalemate, which will produce positional warfare which cannot be excluded and which will be very rapidly quite inescapable.

For two hours Marshal Tukhachevskii enlarged on his strategic and operational ideas, in a talk confined to the directing staff of the General Staff Academy. The officer-students of the very first intake of the Academy knew nothing of it. The General Staff had the responsibility for laying down the study-courses of the Academy, but Tukhachevskii, at least on Isserson's own evidence, had much to do with formulating the operational problems which the Academy undertook to examine.

In less than six months, in June 1937, Tukhachevskii was dead, shot together with Uborevich, Yakir, Primakov, Putna and Eideman for 'treasonable' activity. Stalin had unleashed the military purge, which slashed and tore at the Soviet armed forces for months, which began to creep into years. Marshal Yegorov vanished into the whirl of these murky and persistent murders in 1938. Marshal Blyukher, commander of the Soviet Far Eastern forces, was shot down in November 1938. The decimations snaked back into past enmities; Tukhachevskii himself had incurred the hatred of Stalin, and Voroshilov as far back as 1920, during the crisis of the Soviet-Polish War. Army Commander 2nd Grade Vatsetis, a former Bolshevik commander-in-chief in the Civil War, at this moment a lecturer at the Frunze Military Academy, was rudely seized. During the break in his lecture, Vatsetis failed to make an appearance. Military Commissar Kascheyev, commissar to the course, made a brief announcement: 'Comrades! The lecture will not be resumed. Lecturer Vatsetis has been arrested as an enemy of the people.' Corps Commander Gorbatov, who made no 'confession' during his interrogation and this in spite of being beaten bloody, after a brief appearance before 'grinning judges', was sentenced to fifteen years' imprisonment. In two minutes, his life and career were crudely amputated. The list of the doomed men, distinguished and undistinguished alike, lengthened as the military purge gathered its dreadful momentum. The highest command echelons were hit hardest and longest; three out of five Marshals of the Soviet Union vanished, leaving only Voroshilov and Budenny to survey the wreckage. The Military Soviet attached to the Defence Commissariat was thinned out of existence. Army and corps commanders disappeared at no less a rate. In operational units there was, to use a Soviet euphemism, 'severe shortage' of trained commanders. The military purge, which remains even now a goad to the Red Army's sense of its own honour, was no short-lived spasm, but a political process, years in its duration, of basic if perverse importance to Stalin's rule in Stalin's fashion. The killings continued, the threat and then the actual advent of war notwithstanding. Colonel-General Loktionov, until March 1941 commander of the Baltic Special Military District air force, was arrested and put to death in June of that same shattering year. His was no isolated case. Major-General (subsequently Marshal of the Soviet Union) Govorov, Deputy Inspector-General of the Main Artillery Administration of the Red Army was posted in May 1941, as head of the Dzerzhinskii Artillery Academy; he came perilously close to failing to take up his new appointment. The NKVD had him high on their arrest list, and only the personal intervention of M. Kalinin saved him. The 'crime' which brought this near-disastrous turn to Govorov's fortunes was not less than being a former officer of Kolchak's White armies – in 1919. Though still alive, many more Red Army officers languished, and would now continue to do so for many months, in distant penal settlements. Gorbatov, victim of a two-minute trial, was more fortunate; in March 1941, 'rehabilitated', he returned to Moscow, ultimately bound for the 25th Rifle Corps in the Ukraine but bound to explain his absence by reference to a 'long and dangerous mission'. Though it was an officially enforced prevarication, it was no less than the truth.

Suppose, however, Marshal Tukhachevskii had lived. It is too much to presume that he alone, or even in the company of his able colleagues who were put to death more or less at the same time as himself, would have been able to turn back the German army at the frontiers in 1941, for all the prescience displayed in his 1936 predictions. Tukhachevskii, Yegorov, Blyukher, Yakir and Uborevich, to mention only the most famous, were able men, professionals who worked and studied hard, aware of developments in foreign armies and quick to seize upon the possibilities offered by Soviet innovations in weapons but they, too, would have had to make war under all the handicaps imposed by Stalin: Tukhachevskii in 1920 learned in the Polish campaign, where his own errors were not small, what Stalin's political meddling could do. It was also beyond the competence of one man to remove that disparity between sophisticated theory as displayed in the 1936 *Field Service Regulations*, and the cumbersome tactical performance of the Red Army in the field. No special magic was destroyed along with the men decimated in the military purge, but the Red Army lost what it needed most at a time of major technical and tactical innovation, a command group which could have maintained effective continuity in military thinking and in military training; this group had shown a lively awareness of what was needed to improve the Red Army and would certainly not have needed the horrifying lesson of the Soviet-Finnish War in order to learn elementary lessons in troop handling. The men who followed Tukhachevskii lacked also that insight into the probable forms of modern mobile war which had so preoccupied the purged commanders; they lacked any intellectual curiosity simply because they disposed of no intellect, either singly or as a group. They mouthed slogans but understood nothing of principles, they paraded statistics about fire-power without grasping any of the implications of the new weapons their own designers were developing, they were martial in a swaggering sense without the least grasp of the professionalism necessary to the military. For this doltishness, by no means confined to the Soviet command but less excusable and explicable after it had seen the blitzkreig in action, the Red Army paid a staggeringly high price in men and machines in 1941.

At the end of 1940 and the beginning of 1941 there were more war-games, involving assumptions about attacking the USSR. Within weeks of each other, as if in some shadowy show-down, the German and Soviet commands played out their prescriptions for victory: this time, however, the reality of war was not very far away. On 21 July 1940, at one of his 'Führer conferences' in which he bestrode the world with whim and word, Hitler directed that preliminary studies for a campaign against the Soviet Union be set in motion.

It was now the turn of the German commanders to puzzle over piercing the Soviet western frontiers: Colonel-General Halder passed the Führer's assignment to the *Operationsabteilung* of the General Staff, and by 1 August Major-General Marcks, chief of staff to the Eighteenth Army, had produced a preliminary operational outline, *Operationsentwurf Ost*. At the beginning of September Lieutenant-General von Paulus took over this project. By 23 November 1940, the first war-game to test possible Soviet responses, *Kriegsspiel O Qu I – rote Partei*, was ready. In December the supply question was thoroughly examined in war-game exercises which demonstrated beyond any doubt that supply must be as thorough and flexible as the combat arm of the Wehrmacht. The day after the opening of those games, on 18 December, Hitler signed the super-secret directive, of which only nine copies existed, setting out the instruction 'to crush Soviet Russia in a rapid campaign': the war plan for the east emerged from under its humble wraps of 'Fritz' and 'Otto' to assume its final and flamboyant code-name, arrogant in its recall of medieval splendours and menacing in its hints of medieval cruelties, Operation 'Barbarossa'.

Meanwhile in Moscow the Soviet command was making a belated and somewhat haphazard attempt to bring itself up to date in matters of contemporary military theory and practice. The Soviet-Finnish war of such recent and lamentable memory had shown up a number of glaring deficiencies in the Red Army, above all in its inferior tactical performance: to these lessons Soviet commanders also had to add the implications of the German victory in the west, a triumph for the armoured forces which had earlier been pioneered by the Russians and which had enjoyed pride of place in the Red Army until their dismemberment after 1938. Late in December 1940 a high-level study conference convened in Moscow to discuss the present organization and main tactical ideas of the Red Army: in line with current Soviet thinking, a great deal of attention was paid to offensive operations and to a relentless insistence on the attack, with little heed for defensive forms. General Zhukov himself presented the paper on contemporary offensive operations, in which armour figures prominently, but it was left to only one critic – Romanenko – to point out that masses of tanks did not mean 'armoured forces' in the cogent sense of that term: Romanenko pleaded for the creation of 'armoured armies' consisting of at least three/four mechanized corps and with proper command and control facilities, as well as effective rear echelons. Zhukov simply brushed this aside and the meeting went along with him: some, in the light of the subsequent Soviet creation of no less than six full tank armies after 1942, have tried to interpret their own utterances in 1940 as support for the 'tank army', but this is wholly convenient hindsight, for the prevailing view of the use of armour was more akin to mechanized cavalry than the complex operational and logistical characteristics of the Panzer division.

The conference adjourned at the end of December 1940 and resumed in somewhat different form, as a major war-game which began at the end of the first week in January 1941. Under the supervision of the Defence Commissar, Marshal S.K. Timoshenko, and the Chief of the General Staff, General K.A. Meretskov, General Zhukov took command of the 'Western' forces opposing the 'Eastern' forces under Colonel-General (Tank Troops) D.G. Pavlov, sometimes described as 'the Soviet Guderian', though a calamitously misplaced comparison that proved to be. The general aim of the war-game involved Pavlov's 'Eastern' forces putting up a stubborn resistance in the fortified regions and thus blunting the 'Western' attack north of the Pripet Marshes, thereby establishing the necessary conditions for his 'Eastern' forces to go over to a 'decisive offensive'. The 'Soviet Guderian' went to work with a will, but much to his consternation the 'Western' forces under Zhukov mounted three powerful concentric attacks, 'wiped out' the Grodno and Bialystok concentrations of the 'Eastern' armies and smashed their way through to Lida.

In a fury Stalin dismissed General Meretskov out of hand and replaced him with Zhukov: Meretskov was installed as Chief of Combat Training and, though momentarily disgraced, lived to fight for many a day. Nor was this sheer blind malice on the part of Stalin. He was not impressed by the explanation that 'victory' in the war-game had been won by skilful manoeuvre: indeed, that was exactly his point, and he urged greater realism on Soviet commanders, who ought not to be deceived by propaganda statements about the capabilities of their divisions. Mobility and regrouping was not a monopoly of the enemy, even on paper as in this case and in spite of the primacy which the commitment to the offensive enjoyed, Soviet commanders should rein in their recklessness. Finally Stalin recommended that Pavlov, who commanded the Special Western Military District, should pay close heed to the lessons of the war-game.

Bloodless though these 'battles' on both sides were at this juncture, and though not a single soldier moved for the moment, the duel between Hitler and Stalin was already engaged. The German war machine had begun to click and whirr as its weight shifted to the east, while the Soviet apparatus seemed for the present to grind on almost mindlessly. Shadowy and symbolic these battles might have been, but as if in some giant mystic projection they showed, albeit dimly, the shape of catastrophes to come.*

---

* For a detailed analysis of the Soviet operational-strategic war game (*operativnostrategicheskaya igra na kartakh*) see Colonel P.N. Bobylev, 'Repetitsiya katastrofy', *Voenno-istoricheskii Zhurnal* 1993 No. 6, pp. 10–16, No. 7, pp. 14–21 and No. 8, pp. 28–35. Also *The 1941 War Game of the Soviet High Command: An Archival Record*. Moscow, Russian State Military Archive, (RGVA: fond 37977), East View Publications, Minneapolis USA: 35 documents, planning, participants, basic directions 'Western' and 'Eastern' sides, First and Second War Game, analytical documents. On 1941 war plans P.N. Bobylev, '*K kakoi voine gotovilsya General'nyi shtab RKKA v 1941 godu?*', *Otechestvennaya istoriya* 1995 No. 5, pp. 3–20.

BOOK I

On Preparedness:
Military and Political Developments
Spring 1941

The Soviet Military Establishment: Reforms and Repairs (1940-1)

The Red Army emerged battered and bleeding from the brief but arduous winter war with Finland. So severely had Soviet military reputations been mauled in the earlier stages of the war that the final episodes took on the character of revenge for and restitution of a badly tarnished honour. Massed Soviet artillery tore open and often quite literally tore out of the ground the Finnish concrete forts of the 'Mannerheim line'. The Finns were forced to fight it out on their timbered barricades, upon which rolled almost a thousand Soviet tanks. Soviet bombers, loosed initially against civilian targets, eliminated technical deficiencies, navigational ineptitude and operational inefficiency sufficiently to provide more effective support for ground operations. As the Red Army laboured to smash in the Finnish defences, Timoshenko in February 1940, prepared for the last major operation, the drive on Viipuri. From 7th Army reserve, the 28th Rifle Corps was specially assembled and ordered to cross the frozen ice of Viipuri Bay, there to establish a bridgehead on the north-western shore, west of Viipuri itself. The tanks, infantry and armoured sledges would be launched across the ice as mobile columns. The few bombers left to the Finns caught the Soviet troops on this terrifying journey, but blowing the ice and strafing the infantry failed to halt the inexorable movement. Early in March, the position for the Finns in Viipuri Bay was critical. The Finnish forces of the Isthmus Army had been ground to pieces, with battalions denuded and weapons smashed. The fighting ceased on 13 March, with a peace which perhaps more than any other was served at the point of a bayonet.

More than one million men, mountains of ammunition, mazes of artillery and powerful armoured formations, supported by a numerically formidable air force, had suffered reverse, humiliation and even annihilation at the hands of a Finnish army never more than 200,000 strong. In the earlier stages of the fighting, Soviet formations had been split into small pockets and then destroyed piecemeal. In December 1939, the 44th Rifle Division, strung out in its five-mile length as it advanced to assist the 163rd Rifle Division, was literally chopped to pieces by the Finnish mobile groups. The result was the hideous battlefield of Suomussalmi. The Soviet relief columns sent out to rescue the encircled were themselves often encircled. North of lake Ladoga, the 18th Rifle Division (8th Army) was encircled; the 168th Rifle Division (also 8th Army) was similarly encircled. Sent out to relieve the 18th Division, the 34th Tank Brigade, with its supply lines amputated, was itself encircled; it was besieged for 54 days until it was stormed and destroyed. Such was the havoc that at the end of December 1939, the entire Soviet effort was reorganized. The mass infantry attacks, which had presented the Finnish machine-gunners with such persistent and generous targets, were to be discontinued. The aimless artillery fire was to be directed henceforth against enemy fire-points. Newly arrived divisions or reinforcements were not to be committed to action without some acquaintance of the conditions under which they would have to fight. The *Model 1939* rifle was issued to the infantry; the new KV tanks were brought into action. Armoured infantry sledges and electric digging machines were rushed to the front. The operational command was reorganized by 7 January 1940, when the North-Western Front was established under Timoshenko; this modified Marshal Voroshilov's control and displaced General Meretskov (commander of the Leningrad Military District) far more completely.

The world at large combined with the Soviet command to view the war with Finland as a test of the Red Army as a modern military instrument. The winter war was not, however, the only military enterprise initiated in 1939; during that tense summer, when the final crisis had engulfed the west, Soviet troops had been engaged in heavy fighting against the Japanese on the Khalkin-Gol, the disputed zone on the Soviet-Manchurian border. The execution of the Soviet counter-stroke was entrusted to corps commander Zhukov; in mid August, 1939, he had some five hundred tanks at his disposal, some of them the latest A-1 (experimental T-34) type. In spite of heavy losses, the Red Army had scored an undeniable success against a formidable enemy in this Mongolian *place d'armes*. The armour, having accomplished its mission against the Japanese, was then hustled on its way to the west, for the Soviet invasion of Poland waited on a speedy and successful outcome in the east. The Soviet 'liberating march' into Western Belorussia, part of the noxious deal of the Nazi-Soviet Pact, appeared to impose no great strain on the Red Army. Yet appearances were deceptive. In his report on the westerly advance, the Chief of Staff of the Western Special Military District, General M.N. Purkayev, stressed that the 'new situation' was one in which 'the negative considerably outweighs the positive'. Barrack-building resources were low. The network of operational aerodromes was still as it was, and there was a lack of concrete runways. The railway network was exactly what it had been on the eve of the First World War; road transport could use only two roads, going from east to west. In the event of a German attack, the military district forces had no 'fortified districts' upon which to fall back. To register positive gain would require a huge expenditure of time and effort, to say nothing of materials.

This was a serious note to strike at this early stage. It was to say that the westerly movement of the Red Army, advancing itself to confront the Wehrmacht, did not confer any automatic advantage. On the contrary, it put the Red Army at a temporary disadvantage, and one which was to be much intensified in the summer of 1940 when the Red Army moved into the Baltic states and into Bessarabia. At a point when the German Army was savouring all the triumphs of shatteringly successful blitzkreig, the Red Army was engaged on a serious, if not desperate, attempt to remedy the operational deficiencies revealed by war with Finland, and to make its new forward areas militarily useful. To make the Red Army fit to fight, and to have it fight in the right place, was the task, massive in its implications, assigned to the chastened Soviet command.

Although he held as yet no military rank or appointment, Stalin was indisputably master of the Red Army. As a result of the military purge, which had only very recently swept away whole echelons of officers, the new command was his creature. Among those senior officers who had survived the military purge – this far at least – one distinguishing feature was very apparent, namely association with the First Cavalry Army which had been raised during the days of the Civil War. Commanded by Voroshilov and Budenny the First Cavalry Army had aided and abetted Stalin in his insubordinate struggle with Trotsky in the far-off days of Tsaritsyn (Stalingrad). For his part, Stalin had encouraged both Budenny and Voroshilov to defy the military directives of the Central Committee, an activity which had a disastrous outcome in the 1920 Soviet-Polish War. From this time forward the enmity of Stalin and Tukhachevskii was firmly sealed, and contributed not a little to the latter's eventual destruction. It was as Stalin's man that Voroshilov had come to command the Soviet military establishment, although he was – until the 1937 purge – much overshadowed by Tukhachevskii and the group of highly talented officers associated with him. In the days of the Civil War, Trotsky had formed an abysmally low opinion of Voroshilov's military abilities; subsequent events seemed to confirm this pessimistic assessment. His incompetent leadership had been forcefully criticized by senior Soviet officers in 1928. During the period of experiment with mechanized formations, early in the 1930s, Voroshilov had spoken out against their establishment. In 1932 he was prepared to envisage only the mechanized brigade. Two years later, during the special meetings of the Military Soviet attached to the Defence Commissariat called to discuss mechanization, he made his opposition even more explicit: 'For me it is almost axiomatic that such a powerful formation as the tank corps is a very far-fetched idea and therefore we should have nothing to do with it.' Voroshilov had to wait five years before the mechanized corps were disbanded, although even in 1934 he succeeded in slowing down the rate of mechanization. To his military cronies of the Civil War days Stalin could also add the military commissars with whom he was associated at that time. The erstwhile tailor Shchadenko was one such commissar who came to wield great power in the Red Army; another, commissar on the Southern Front, was Mekhlis, who seems to have combined a monumental incompetence with a fierce and unbending detestation of the officer corps. Both of these men played vital parts in securing the success of the 1937 purge, not least in taking control of the Red Army Political Administration at a time when the military commissars had become, at least in Stalin's eyes, too readily identified with the command staff. Mekhlis evidently played a lamentably successful role in stalking and finally bringing down Marshal Blyukher, the legendary Soviet Far Eastern commander, who was put to death in November 1938. Stalin did not deny himself the wolfish pleasure of issuing personal arrest orders; to Army Commander Yakir, who wrote a death-cell letter affirming his loyalty to the Party, Stalin returned only curses. Mekhlis rooted out 'treason' in commissar and officer alike. Shchadenko watched the commissars. Beria and his NKVD officers compiled their own lists. Voroshilov stayed silent. In a welter of complicity and denunciation, private vengeance and public humiliations, the Soviet officer corps was bent and broken to the will of Stalin.

Yet even Voroshilov could not escape the upheaval which followed on the war with Finland. It was painfully obvious that public, and possibly private bombast about the Red Army's 'invincibility' would no longer suffice. Voroshilov, moreover, was plainly implicated in the disastrous defeats of the preliminary stages of the war with Finland. If the Leningrad Military District had miscalculated, so had the Defence Commissariat. While Voroshilov retained the general direction of operations after December 1939, the burden of real command had fallen on Timoshenko as front commander. In what can only have been acrimonious sessions, the Main Military Soviet (*Glavnyi Voennyi Soviet*) attached to the Defence Commissariat had examined the reasons for the failures in Finland. This inquest on the dead divisions followed immediately after the cease-fire and lasted throughout April. At the beginning of May 1940, the 'new' Soviet command began to emerge. Marshal Voroshilov was removed from effective day-to-day control of military affairs by being appointed deputy chairman of the Defence Committee (*Komitet Oborony pri* SNK). His post of Defence Commissar went to Timoshenko, though this marked no break with the 'tradition' of the First Cavalry Army, in which Timoshenko had been a cavalry commander attached initially to Budenny. Although by no means a military intellectual, Timoshenko had at least passed through the higher command courses of the Red Army and was a fully trained 'commander-commissar'. During the critical period of the military purge, Stalin had used Timoshenko as a military district commander who could hold key appointments while their incumbents were liquidated or exiled. His services in the war with Finland had been considerable, for Voroshilov had shown that he was incapable of handling large-scale operations. If anything Timoshenko was a realist, impressed by the idea that the Red Army would have to be retrained as a combat force.

At the same time, Timoshenko was appointed Marshal of the Soviet Union, together with Shaposhnikov and Kulik. These appointments of the 7 May 1940, restored the number of marshals·to the 1937 figure of five, although there could be no comparison in capacities. Shaposhnikov was a career officer of the Imperial Russian Army, who volunteered his services to the Red Army in 1918. As a trained and obviously able staff officer, Shaposhnikov had taken part in planning many of the major operations of the Civil War. His subsequent career kept him closely aligned with the development of Soviet strategic doctrine and staff functions, though not until 1930 did he become a member of the Communist Party. After 1937, his was the main hand on the General Staff; in this capacity he took part in the abortive negotiations with the British and French in Moscow in the late summer of 1939, he drew up the plans for the occupation of Eastern Poland by the Red Army, and his was evidently the brain behind the revised Soviet operational plans used in the later stages of the war with Finland. His experience was vast, even if his power was less substantial. He had obviously been unable to prevent the disbanding of the large mechanized armoured formations in which the Red Army had come to specialize. Of even greater consequence was the disregarding of his advice on the deployment of the Red Army after the advances to the new frontier lines in the north and south-west. His professionalism manifestly failed to compete with the brash and idiotic opinions purveyed by men like Lev Mekhlis.

G.I. Kulik, artillery specialist, was altogether a different case. While Shaposhnikov had much to recommend him by way of seniority and services already rendered, Kulik was a nonentity. His prime qualification was that Stalin had known him during the days of the defence of Tsaritsyn in 1918. It was this which ultimately transformed him, in 1937, into the overlord of Soviet artillery, head of the Main Artillery Administration, Deputy Defence Commissar. There is no other evidence of his fitness for this post. He had held hitherto no position or responsibility which might have prepared him for these new duties. Almost at once he tangled with the Defence Industry Commissar B.L. Vannikov over the 1938 artillery developments plans; Kulik demanded 'handsome guns', a requirement which Vannikov, occupied with the complexities of the draft artillery plan, dismissed as mere foolishness. When, however, Vannikov somewhat later ventured to oppose one of Stalin's own ideas, he was forthwith arrested. N.N. Voronov, as Head of Artillery (*Nachal'nik artillerii* RKKA), first deputy to Kulik, has composed an unflattering verdict on him:

Disorganized but with a high opinion of himself, Kulik thought all his actions infallible. It was often difficult to know what he had in his mind, what he wanted and what he was aiming at. Holding his subordinates in a state of fear was what he considered to be the best way of working.

Voronov, Head of Artillery, with his committee, had had a rough passage over the new designs. The 76-mm *Model F-22* field piece, for example, had proved unsatisfactory; when Voronov approached the Defence Commissariat, he found no encouragement, so he turned to the Central Committee. Here he found even less support. He was told that quantity production was in progress and the gun would have to be put right – not scrapped. Finally, the *Model USB* was modified; the issue was partially solved only to be overtaken by that of mechanical towing equipment for artillery. Kulik opposed this, as he opposed the suggestion that special factories should be built to supply this equipment; he had the support of the armoured specialist, Pavlov, who was in charge of mechanization-motorization. In fact, two special factories were built in the Urals by 1939, but more were needed.

In 1940, Kulik embarked on another 'experiment'. He abolished the post of *Nachal'nik artillerii*, no doubt to cow the resistance, and operated this key position himself, assisted by a triumvirate of three deputies: N.N. Voronov, G.K. Savchenko and V.D. Grendal'. It was an impossible and pointless arrangement, although it deprived the specialists of their power. Grendal' was both specialist and commander. He had served as deputy to Rogovskii, who had done much to reorganize Soviet artillery before 1937. Rogovskii had been liquidated. Grendal', *dozent* of the Artillery Academy, survived to work on the 1938 artillery development plan and to continue his technical work as president of the Artillery Committee of the Main Artillery Administration. During the Finnish war, he was brought in to take command of the 13th Army which in February-March 1940, smashed into the 'Mannerheim line'. Twice Grendal' attempted to get Kulik to change his mind over the artillery 'triumvirate'; Kulik refused. Interference with the structure and functions of the Main Artillery Administration had, moreover, repercussions felt far beyond the field of artillery, for the Administration played a leading role in organizing military-scientific research. In that also, Kulik appears to have blundered ominously. In the June 1940 promotions Grendal' became a Colonel-General of Artillery, a consolation perhaps even though he was dying of cancer. In November he was dead.

The May revolution meanwhile continued. In sum, it was to amount to nothing less than the reconstitution of the Red Army after the agonies of the military purge. The formal ranks of general and admiral, hitherto shunned as symbols of the *ancien régime*, were brought into new use. And the men, to assume these novel splendours, the 'Army Commanders 1st Grade' transformed into 'colonel-generals' (a rank unknown in the Imperial Russian Army), were found. One of the immediate consequences of the 'Timoshenko era' was the release of some 4,000 officers from their servitude or disgrace to take up command positions in the Red Army. In all probability, the officer losses of the Finnish war, if nothing else, provided one army lever against the political bosses who pushed the armed forces around. There was the case of Colonel K.K. Rokossovskii, an example of that limbo to which invaluable officers were too often consigned. Rokossovskii, veteran of the Civil War, divisional commander in the Soviet Far East and a specialist in modern, mobile operations, had been accused of participation in an 'anti-Soviet conspiracy'. At his trial, before mocking judges, he was faced with the 'evidence' obtained from one Yushke-vich; this fully implicated Rokossovskii. The defendant, however, confessed not his guilt but his astonishment: Yushkevich had been killed in action at the Perekop in 1920. Colonel Rokossovskii's case was held back for 'investigation'. But he survived, to become in June 1940, one of the new 479 major-generals of the Red Army. In a few months he was to take over command of one of the newly-constituted mechanized corps.

The June promotions involved some 1,000 senior officers. G.K. Zhukov (the victor of the Khalkin-Gol), G.K. Meretskov (much less than victor in Finland) and I.V. Tyulenev (stalwart of the First Cavalry Army) were appointed full generals of the Red Army. Apanasenko and Gorodovikov (Civil War cavalry commanders) took the new rank of colonel-general. Among the new lieutenant-generals were a number who had distinguished themselves in Finland – Kirponos (70th Rifle Division commander) was one – as well as corps or military district commanders of some repute: Koniev, Vatutin, Yeremenko, Malandin, Remizov, Reiter, Sokolovskii, Chuikov (soon to be nominated for duty with the Soviet mission in China), Tsvetayev, Romanenko and Golikov. Recent graduates of the General Staff Academy, of the Frunze Academy and graduates – in a more rigorous sense – of the prison camps and interrogation chambers were crammed into this emergent command group. Prominent among the major-generals were armoured commanders: Rotmistrov, Rokossovskii, Lelyushenko, Panfilov. Shaposhnikov's protégé, A.M. Vasilevskii, was promoted, as were Biryuzov and Antonov. There were parallel promotions in the arms and services: Ya.N. Fedorenko became a lieutenant-general of tank troops, A.F. Khrenov a major-general of engineering troops, V.I. Kazakov, L.A. Govorov and K.S. Moskalenko major-generals of artillery. Like V.D. Grendal', N.N. Voronov, first deputy to Marshal Kulik of the Main Artillery Administration, was promoted to Colonel-General of Artillery.

The Soviet Navy (VMF), which had had a tortuous history and suffered severely during the purge of the officer corps, now acquired admirals. N.G. Kuznetsov (chief of the naval forces), L.M. Galler and I.S. Isakov (both of the Naval Staff) were the new Soviet admirals; V.F. Tributs (commander of the Baltic Fleet) and I.S. Yumashev (commander of the Pacific Fleet) became vice-admirals, and A.G. Golovko (Northern Fleet commander) and F.S. Oktyabrskii (Black Sea Fleet commander) appeared now as rear-admirals. The Soviet Air Force (VVS) received a new batch of lieutenant-generals, P.F. Zhigarev, G.P. Kravchenko, S.F. Zhavoronkov among them. The former commander of the Air Force, Ya.I. Alksnis, received nothing but the final death sentence at this time, which put an end to his languishing in prison. The purge and the restitutions, plus the promotions, hardly balanced out. Promotions did not bring experience with the generals' stars, and behind the generals came the brand-new colonels with their regiments. The Inspector-General of Infantry (Red Army) discovered, in his samplings of autumn 1940, that of 225 regimental commanders, not one had attended a full course at a military academy, only twenty-five had finished a military school and the remainder, 200 in all, had merely passed a junior lieutenant's course. It was, therefore, no wonder that Marshal Shaposhnikov dragged in from all military highways and by-ways officers by the score to attend high-pressure training courses on staff work, and to sit on the rigorous, protracted study-sessions of the failures in Finland.

The Red Army, officer and man alike, had to be retrained. On the surface, it appeared that this was being done in all seriousness. April saw the beginning of a positive turmoil of conferences and meetings which ran on until the end of the year. The first of these gatherings, and clearly one of the most important, was that summoned by the Central Committee of the Communist Party, when senior military commanders were to discuss the results of the Finnish operations. This was, however, no 'discussion' in the normal sense of the word. Stalin took this opportunity, which he had manufactured himself, to refurbish the image of the Soviet armed forces. He announced that the Red Army was striding along the road leading to its being a new, modern army; in the course of its operations in the winter war, the Red Army had mastered not only the Finnish forces, but also the equipment, tactics and the strategy of those leading European powers which had schooled and armed the Finns. It was an extravagant claim, to say the least, for an army which had been so severely mauled, and whose imperfections had even earlier been exposed – admittedly, rather more gently – in the 'liberation drives' into eastern Poland in 1939. It was a claim which Soviet historians record rather sourly today.

There were, in effect, many debates but few decisions, and even those were questionable. That is the burden of retrospective Soviet criticism. Closer inspection of the 1940 'reforms' tends to give credence to these views. After Stalin's April address, the Main Military Soviet turned its attention to the problem of training, most immediately that for officers. The syllabuses and programmes of the military academies were renovated, with greater emphasis on exercises in the field. In the military schools, junior officers were trained more rigorously in controlling their units as well as being taught to handle a variety of weapons and equipment. The general training directive, Order No. 120 (May 16 1940), *On combat and political training of troops for summer period 1940*, laid great emphasis on realistic programmes, to teach the Red Army what it would need to know in war, and only that. The basis task was to implement that condition of being 'ever ready to administer a rebuff to an aggressor'. All-weather training, day and night training, close combat training, infantry-tank-artillery-aviation co-operation training, assault training (storming field and prepared fortifications) – the overriding need was for well-trained infantry. The wasteful, murderous and repetitive mass attack, which had been swept away by Finnish machine-guns, the disorganized battalion or the unco-ordinated division were to be eliminated by strenuous exercise. The weight of concern was directed to the individual soldier, to the small unit and its control in operational conditions. Timoshenko himself had admitted frankly that 'We've got to work at it';.in the particular conditions of the Finnish war, where the robot-soldier was at a loss, the point was plain to see. Yet something had gone wrong on a grand scale, for which the Red Army soldier had had to pay a merciless price. Even if the retraining of the lower ranks had been the only problem, too soon that gave evidence of being no startling success. By the end of the year, the 'intensive' training programme was in real trouble.

At the same time, the Red Army soldier was subject to a new disciplinary code, which marked an important departure from the established path of what might be called the Soviet 'theory of morale and discipline'. Although the Red Army, from its inception, had always wielded a heavy authoritarian hand, the idea of 'coercion' (*prinuzhdeniya*) had been officially eschewed. In line with the general theories of the role of communist 'consciousness', that is, political consciousness, the soldier was 'educated' to his battlefield duties and to his responsibilities towards the socialist motherland. The work of the military commissars, with their responsibility for political education, the utilization of Party members as 'stiffeners' in combat formations, the function of 'political education' in the widest sense were all elements of an official voluntaristic approach. While egalitarianism and the military profession had long since been discerned as incompatibles, the formalism of 'bourgeois armies' – the obligatory salute, for example – had been kept out. Now this was changed, first with the introduction of a deliberately rigid military discipline, strongly coercive and avowedly punitive, and second with the innovation of military forms and courtesies demonstrably 'bourgeois'. Clearly what was at stake was the authority of the officer, which had suffered severely during the most searching period of the military purge; in the same way, the military commissar had lost face, for the purge had fallen on commissar alike. Discipline had broken down during the war with Finland. It was going to be restored quite drastically.

In July 1940 the Supreme Soviet rubber-stamped the decree on increased penalties for 'voluntary absence' and desertion. The revised disciplinary code, *Distsiplinarnyi Ustav*, was promulgated in August. Far from being a monument to 'communist morality', the code represented, in the view of at least one Soviet historian, a reactionary move in the literal sense. It embodied to a large extent the opinions of 'certain officers' who had begun their military careers in the Imperial Russian Army, and who, whatever their persuasiveness in 1940, idealized the relationship between officer and man in the tsar's forces. The pre-1917 Russian officer corps was assuredly not that model of enlightenment, competence and charity which these erstwhile 'Imperials' had come to think it; the Russian soldier did not enjoy either his punishment or his murder by incompetence. The 1940 code visibly increased the number of punishable offences for rank and file. Obedience was henceforth to be unconditional, the execution of orders prompt and precise, Soviet discipline to be marked by 'severer and harsher requirements than discipline in other armies based upon class subjugation'. The 'liberal commander', the officer who fraternized with his men, was declared an official menace. The officers themselves, subject also to the formal disciplinary requirements, were henceforth liable to the strictures of the Honour Court, an institution which went right back to the Imperial Russian Army. All this deliberate, even archaic formalism seemed to run counter to Timoshenko's public protestation: 'We are all for individual initiative!' How much this punitive approach actually smothered it, the political officers were soon to discover.

The breakdown in discipline was testimony also to the degeneration of the Political Administration, which, during and after 1937, became a powerful repressive agency within the armed forces. The relationship between commander and commissar had never been easy. The military commissar, as a watchdog over the commander, inhibited command; as an 'assistant' to command, he merely confused it. When the reliability of the armed forces was in doubt, 'dual command' – commissar-commander control – was enforced; in the interests of military efficiency, and as some recognition of the general adherence of the armed forces to the regime 'unitary command' (edinonachalie) – command exercised without commissar control – had been instituted. The Red Army flourished under 'unitary command' from 1925–37. In 1937, 'dual command' was hammered on with the purge. 'Military Soviets', the command-and-control device of a senior officer flanked by 'political members', blanketed the major commands and institutions. The bearded and brilliant Army Commissar 1st Grade Yan Gamarnik, head of the Political Administration, had, allegedly, shot himself in May 1937. In his place came Lev Mekhlis, now promoted to senior Army Commissar and Deputy Defence Commissar. Like Kulik, Mekhlis was an old acquaintance of Stalin; after serving as a military commissar to a division on the Civil War Southern Front (against Wrangel), he had worked in the Workers-Peasants Inspectorate (Rabkrin) with Stalin, and operated subsequently as one of Stalin's special group dealing with the Party political apparatus. He stepped in as Stalin's man to edit Pravda. In 1937 he had every opportunity to wreak his private vengeances on the Red Army command. At the head of a brigade of new commissars, he arrived in May 1938 in Khabarovsk to do his master's bidding. The first occasion for him to show his military incompetence came later that year at lake Khasan in the Soviet Far East, when Soviet and Japanese forces clashed. Mekhlis showed an almost criminal predilection for frontal assaults; the Soviet troops were charging Japanese machine-guns on the heights. Stupid and self-deceiving bombast about Soviet 'valour' accompanied snide and sinister denunciation of the field commanders. Shortly after Mekhlis's Far Eastern 'inspection', Marshal Blyukher was recalled to Moscow and killed. Mekhlis and Kulik had worked together during the Finnish war, to what sum of Soviet casualties can only be guessed. In the late summer of 1940, Mekhlis was appointed to the State Control Commission, a general inspectorate with wide powers. In this capacity, and as a Deputy Defence Commissar, his responsibilities were very considerable and his influence on Soviet military planning great. His military commissars, however, were under considerable fire for their work during the Finnish war.

In July 1940, the Political Administration of the Red Army (*Politupravlenie* RKKA) was reorganized as the Main Administration for Political Propaganda of the Red Army (*Glavnoe upravlenie politicheskoi propagandy* RKKA), a change in name which coincided with a modification in the nature of political work within the armed forces. (In August, the same institutional modification was carried out in the Soviet Navy, where the Political Administration was replaced by a Main Administration for Political Propaganda.) Political and tactical training were more closely linked, even in the physical sense by taking the political work into the field. The July decree dealing with shortcomings in local Party organs attempted to correct the abuses in the admission of new Party members; the principle of 'voluntary application' had been persistently infringed, especially during the war with the Finns. In the place of 'hurrah-patriotism', the political agitators now switched to amplifications of the military achievements of Red Army divisions, so that, as M.I. Kalinin suggested, the Red Army soldier should know not merely the number of his regiment but its revolutionary achievements. Nevertheless, although 'hurrah-patriotism' (which was a sarcasm coined in the reports of senior political officers) had been somewhat displaced, the propaganda 'line' had not been altered in any basic sense. One set of clichés replaced another. Drawing the political staff more and more into military training inevitably cramped their 'ideological-educational work'. And although the vacuous nonsense about easy victory over a weak enemy had been dropped right out of the propaganda schedules, there was no mention of how tough the potential enemy might turn out to be. Like the discipline which began to turn more and more to open coercion, 'political education' ran itself into the sands of shibboleths.

Hard on the heels of this reorganization of the political departments came the August decree on the restitution of 'unitary command' in the Soviet armed forces. This relieved the military commissar of his control functions, a move justified in official explanations by reference to the 'development' of the officer corps. In practice, it was not as simple as it looked. The 'theory' of 'unitary command' involved the political officer becoming 'deputy commander for political affairs', thus eliminating a complicated intermingling of functions. The 'theory' also extended to envisaging under 'unitary command' the consolidation and co-ordination of 'military and Party-political leadership'. There were also the three levels of activity to be considered: the tactical, operational and strategic. At the tactical level, the commander was freed from the direct control of the commissar. At the operational level, however, involving military districts, fleets, and major military institutions, the 'military soviet' was retained, and at the highest level, the strategic, 'collective organs of direction' (such as the Main Military Soviet) were effectively strengthened. In brute practice, the

R.T.S.—B

'collectivity' of this higher leadership was crippled by Stalin's personal inter-ventions and relentless grip on military affairs, in matters both great and small. The higher commands made no appreciable gain in freedom of action. What contradicted Stalin's own views was jettisoned or disowned. To innovate was dangerous, to oppose was not infrequently fatal.

Also in August 1940, Marshal Shaposhnikov withdrew from his post as Chief of the General Staff. His health had deteriorated sharply. During the late summer, he worked as an inspector of combat training and supervised the compilation of the new field service regulations which were about to be poured on the Red Army. At the close of the year, Shaposhnikov took over the super-vision of the frontier fortification programme, which was organized through a series of 'construction administrations' (*Upravlenii Nachal'nika Stroitel'stva*: UNS), plus 'construction sectors'. Stalin brought in General of the Army K.A. Meretskov to replace Shaposhnikov. The new Chief of the General Staff came of peasant stock and made upon some observers a generally uncongenial impression. Trained in Germany for a while in 1931 under the terms of the secret pre-1934 Soviet-German military collaboration, Meretskov had shown application (though some reluctance to speak German) and now enjoyed a certain reputation as a tactician. Kirponos meanwhile assumed command of the Leningrad Military District.

The times had little to commend them when Meretskov took up his duties. The Red Army was in the throes of a contorted, contradictory reorganization, pressing a new technical stamp on an awkward and warped organizational structure. While the protagonists of a mythical Russian military virtue worked on the Soviet soldier, and as Stalin cut up the political departments to satisfy his own ideas and private priorities, staffs and arms commanders had to face a fresh and evidently unexpected lesson in the methods of waging war. The German blitzkrieg, slicing up the British and French armies, made revision of Soviet views on the organization of armour suddenly essential. More than that, it gave real urgency to the need for coherent and comprehensive military doctrine.

Not that Stalin intended to go to war, or even to run the risk of it. At the end of June, Winston Churchill seized the opportunity presented by the appointment of Sir Stafford Cripps as ambassador in Moscow to warn Stalin of the dangers of German hegemony in Europe. This menaced the Soviet Union no less than Great Britain. Stalin was unimpressed, or at least proclaimed himself so in the account of this retailed by Molotov to the German ambassador. Quite the most important phrase in this conversation was the Stalinist insistence that 'basic national interests' not mere 'transient circumstances' bound Germany and the Soviet Union. If he rebuffed London, Stalin did so by an inverted assurance to the Germans:

Stalin observed the policy of Germany, and knew several leading German statesmen well. He had not discovered any desire on their part to engulf European countries. Stalin was not of the opinion that German military successes menaced the Soviet Union and her friendly relations with Germany.

Nor were the Germans unaware of Stalin's own engulfments. Lithuania, Estonia and Latvia had been reduced by Soviet ultimata in mid June. On the 17 June, after an unhindered 135-kilometre march, Yeremenko's 6th Cavalry Corps entered Kaunas. Troops of the Leningrad Military District moved into Estonia and Latvia. Stalin now swung south, forcing on Rumania an ultimatum (26 June) demanding the northern Bukovina and Bessarabia for the Soviet Union. Anxious not to see Rumania, rich in oil and food, fall in its entirety to Stalin, Berlin forced acquiescence in the Soviet demands on Bucarest. In Kolomea, top-secret *Order No. 001* dated 26 June and timed 22.00 hours had already been issued by the 12th Army commander, Lieutenant-General Cherevichenko; a 'mechanized-cavalry group' would undertake the advance into the new territories. The tank brigades attached to 12th Army's rifle corps were assigned first-day objectives, after which they came under separate corps and divisional commands. In all, two cavalry corps, six tank brigades and a motorized rifle division were used in this operation. Within less than a year, and by a series of bounds, the Red Army had reached the line running through Riga-Kovno-Brest-Czernovitz. The Soviet Navy, appreciably unlocked, could run its bases into the Baltic. Soviet aircraft and airfields could be deployed westwards in this fresh strategic 'front'.

By German reckoning, in late July 1940, the Red Army disposed of 20 armies, a minimum of 30 corps, 151 rifle divisions, 9 cavalry corps, 31–2 cavalry divisions, 6 'motorized-mechanized corps' and 36 'motorized-mechanized brigades'. They were deployed after this fashion:

Finland: 15 rifle divisions
Baltic: 14 rifle divisions, 3 cavalry divisions, 12 mechanized brigades
Poland: 22 rifle divisions, 4 cavalry divisions, 2 mechanized brigades
Bukovina, Bessarabia: 15 rifle divisions, 6 cavalry divisions, 8 mechanized brigades
Kiev, Kharkov, Odessa, Crimea: 20 rifle divisions, 5 cavalry divisions, 2 mechanized brigades
Caucasus: 3 mountain divisions, 1 cavalry division
North Caucasus: 4 rifle divisions, 3 cavalry divisions
Moscow: 10 rifle divisions, 4 mechanized brigades
Volga: 4 rifle divisions
Urals: 3 rifle divisions.

Assuming that Rumania and Finland would contain a number of Soviet divisions, and allowing for the 34 rifle divisions, 8 cavalry divisions and 8 mechanized brigades deployed in the Soviet Far East, the Red Army, by this reckoning could commit against the Wehrmacht 70 rifle divisions, 23 cavalry divisions and 28 mechanized brigades. At no very distant date, prodded by the wary Finns and Japanese, *Fremde Heere Ost* would see fit to raise this estimate.

Sobered by the Finnish war, and shaken by the swift results brought by blitzkreig in the west, the Soviet command had now urgently to look at its own ideas. Colonel-General D.G. Pavlov, armoured warfare specialist at the Stalin Academy of Mechanization and Motorization, the expert who had reported in person to Stalin on his observations in Spain, could not disguise that his ideas were ill-conceived. The Panzer divisions were no figment of the imagination. Thus Lieutenant-General Yeremenko, 6th Cavalry Corps commander, found himself suddenly in July ordered from Lithuania to Minsk, where he received orders to organize the 3rd Mechanized Corps. The large armoured formations were coming back. Colonel-General Pavlov's earlier recommendations were reversed.

Too many of the makers of military doctrine had fallen in the first, fierce decimations of the 1937-8 purge. The research, experiment and discussion ground to a grimly abrupt halt. Much tactical doctrine stood virtually un-developed beyond the point of Tukhachevskii's 1937 introduction to the 1936 *Field Service Regulations* (*Vremennyi Polevoi Ustav* RKKA: PU–36). In general terms, a future war was envisaged as an 'imperialist coalition' directed against the Soviet Union, bringing a protracted conflict necessitating total mobilization. The importance of the 'technical factor' would continue to grow, facilitating mobile operations on an increasing scale, although periods of positional warfare could not be ruled out. The political premises apart, that had been the burden of Marshal Tukhachevskii's outline of things to come in his talk with Isserson in 1937. In line with Soviet traditions, the offensive occupied pride 6f place in the attentions of the theorists; the primacy of the offensive was an article of faith. During the early 1930s, Soviet experts persisted with their investigations of the 'operating art' under modern conditions, in particular, with the operating forms of operations in depth. The 'operating art' (*operativnoe iskusstvo*) lay between strategy and tactics, by general definition 'the theory and practice of conducting operations of all types and scales'. For all practical purposes, this involved investigation of offensive breakthrough operations at army and subsequently 'front' (army group) levels. From the outset, it provoked argument and discussion about force structures; under Tukhachevskii, the Red Army had begun to evolve into two armies in one, the first a powerful, mobile striking force, the second more traditionally 'steam-roller' in aspect. Tukhachevskii was acutely aware of the need to close the gap between technology and tactics, an issue which provoked bitter criticism from Voroshilov. In November 1933, after a particularly ferocious attack on the idea of 'operations in depth' (*glubokii boi*) by Voroshilov, Tukhachevskii pointed out the consequences:

... after your remarks at the plenary session of the Revolutionary Military Soviet (RVS) many have gained the impression that, in spite of the army's new equipment, tactics must remain as of old ... I decided to write this letter, since after the plenary session there has been great agitation in the minds of the commanders. They are talking about doing away with the new tactical forms, or of any development of them, and because, I repeat, that completely conflicts with what you yourself have frequently maintained, I decided to give you this information about the confusion which has resulted . . .

The argument, which had its counterpart in many other armies, was cut brutally short in 1937. The dilemma, however, remained.

German military observers pointed to what they called *Schematismus* (which present Soviet commentators brand as 'dogmatism') as one of the principal failings of the Soviet commanders. What was prescribed in the manuals and regulations was too literal a gospel. Even so, what was propounded in the 1936 regulations – described as late as 1941 in German reports as *neuzeitlich, klar und bestimmt* – formed a by no means inadequate basis for the understanding of modern operations. Unfortunately, the tactical ideas and forms proved to be too advanced for the average Russian soldier and for the officer corps as a whole. Now, in 1940, the problem had grown in intensity. A revised version of the 1936 regulations was under preparation – the 1939 draft regulations – which, not unexpectedly, assigned the offensive a dominant role. In the event of enemy attack, the Red Army would itself take the offensive, and carry the war to the enemy. Victory would be achieved by the complete destruction of the enemy, 'decisive victory at low cost' (*dostizheniya reshitel'noi pobedy maloi krov'yu*). The confidence engendered by this formula had led, even in 1937, to Stalin closing down the work being done to prepare effective partisan warfare in the event of enemy attack and invasion.

It was at the beginning of the 1930s that the Central Committee formally instructed the People's Commissariat for War and Naval Affairs (streamlined in 1934 into the Defence Commissariat) to consider plans for blocking lines of communication, organizing special Party cadres to act as partisan nuclei and building powerful 'rear bases' (which were to remain secret). In the Ukrainian Military District, with its staff headquarters at Kharkov, Yakir instructed his commanders to elaborate training programmes and to prepare special equipment for 'partisans'. One of the items of special attention concerned training with foreign weapons, for it was assumed that partisan armament may well consist of captured weapons. While Yakir, Uborevich and Blyukher played their own parts in these plans, it was inevitable that the chief of the Intelligence Administration of the Red Army Staff (the Fourth Section), Yan Karlovich Berzin, should have taken a special interest in these undertakings. Berzin (whose real name was Piotr Kuizis), was by origin a Latvian, who spent a hazardous youth engaged in revolutionary activity and who after 1917 stayed to serve with the Red Army as a career officer. During the 1920s, he came to head the Fourth Section, the Red Army's intelligence administration, and it was he who was responsible for, among other things, the handling of the outstanding Soviet agent Richard Sorge. In 1936–7 Berzin was sent to Spain in charge of Soviet intelligence and sabotage operations. and in 1938 he was, on Stalin's orders, sent to his death before a firing squad. Meanwhile, the plans for partisan warfare had been taken a stage further; there had been a certain amount of experimentation with the secret 'rear bases' and the use of high-speed means of communication, including courier aircraft and parachutists. In an early lecture, Yakir had underlined the importance of the 'partisan-parachutists' and emphasized that technical improvement had done much to increase the general significance of 'partisan war'. On the western frontiers, at the same time as the 'fortified districts' were being built, a chain of 'partisan bases' was established with them. Already in 1935–6, however, the influence of Stalin, fond of propounding the notion of the 'inviolability' of the Soviet frontiers, was making itself felt; one of the Soviet specialists on partisan trainings and on mines, in particular, noticed the great reluctance of Tukhachevskii to speak openly on the relevance of partisan warfare to Soviet defence preparations. A little more than a year later, the matter became purely academic, as Stalin shot and imprisoned the men responsible for the defence programme, and thereafter had his own way. The most pertinent commentary on this change of course is perhaps that in June–July 1941, when partisan warfare became an obvious necessity, the first 'operating instructions' were nothing more than a reprint of the 1919 Civil War directives, for which there was much scrabbling in the archives.

The same brash and ignorant conceit, the notion of 'easy victory', had equally deleterious effects on the consideration of defensive operations, which were regarded as temporary phenomena, incapable of being sustained for the whole length of a strategic 'front'. For this reason, defence was officially accorded a 'supporting role', with no attention whatsoever being paid to strategic defence, or, for that matter, to the counter-offensive. Colonel Sandalov, lecturer at the General Staff Academy and one of the officers who helped to prepare Tukhachevskii's 'invasion war-game', discerned this weakness at the 1937 manoeuvres. 'Defensive forces' were totally at a discount, until they fitted into the offensive design. The Academy in its work ignored the problems of 'operational defence', much as it ignored any persistent study of the initial period of a war. This, combined with the gross underestimation of the 'potential enemy' and the lack of any examination of the problems of strategic deployment, put the Soviet command at a major disadvantage.

At an earlier stage, the principle of 'depth' had been applied to the consideration of defensive operations; prepared positions, obstructions and anti-tank obstacles were mandatory. The operational form of a defensive front came to consist of the 'support army' (single echelon), with front reserves deployed in depth. This was thought adequate enough to halt an opponent 'along the axis of the main blow'. The army operating defensively should have up to 10–12 rifle divisions, 1–2 tank brigades, 5–6 artillery and mortar regiments of the High Command Reserve, 5–6 engineer battalions and 1–2 'mixed' (fighter and bomber) aviation divisions. Without the operational zone itself, the depth of the defence was set at 40–60 kilometres, divisional frontages in main sectors being 6–10 kilometres (and 12–16 in secondary sectors). The few exercises devoted to this nevertheless resulted in the adoption of a linear defence, where the majority of the divisions were committed to the major zone of resistance, and reserves were skimmed away to one division. Yegorov had chosen this solution in the abortive war-game of 1936. Wasteful and inefficient 'doorstep defence' resulted; for the moment, weakness was concealed by predicating the most favourable operational conditions for the Soviet forces, in defence and attack alike. Although the 1936 regulations emphasized that 'modern defence is essentially anti-tank defence', in 1940 plans and proposals in this field crept along; anti-tank defence (PTO) in theory disposed of artillery and air attack on enemy tanks, of passive mine barriers, of air – and artillery – supported tank counter-attack, and finally of the 'anti-tank reserves'. Nothing like this worked in practice. The density of anti-tank guns (ten per kilometre) hardly corresponded to a situation where 100 tanks could be massed; the remaining artillery was operated from concealed positions, which minimized its effectiveness. As the culmination of this 'defence', the front commander was supposed to retain sufficient operational reserves to mount a 'powerful counter-stroke', specifically a flank blow on an already weakened enemy.

The offensive did not lack its theoretical configurations. Although echeloning in depth was stipulated, in fact only two echelons were considered, for attack and for exploitation. Since aviation and reserves had to be reckoned with, a 'four-echelon' composition operated:

1st echelon: 'forward aerial echelon'
2nd echelon: 'attack echelon' (reinforced rifle corps of shock armies)
3rd echelon: 'breakthrough exploitation echelon' (one or two mechanized corps, or cavalry corps)
4th echelon: reserves.

The 'shock army' (*udarniya armiya*), of which one or two would be assigned to a front, undertook the major breakthrough role. Formations lacking that special reinforcement which characterized the 'shock army' were designated 'holding armies' or 'support blow armies'. A 'shock army' would have up to 4 rifle corps (12–15 rifle divisions), 1–2 mechanized or cavalry corps, 3–4 aviation divisions, 10–12 artillery regiments, infantry support tanks, engineer and chemical warfare battalions. Operational norms for a breakthrough prescribed a density of 50–100 tanks per kilometre of breakthrough (and the same number of guns). A simple reversal of their own requirements for the offensive could have persuaded Soviet commanders how unrealistic was their defensive anti-tank idea. Front offensive operations would have a depth of 150–250 kilometres, those of the 'shock armies' up to 100 kilometres, with a potential of a 10–15 kilometre advance (up to 50 kilometres with mobile forces) per day.

The Finnish war resulted in some innovations. The significance of artillery, which Tukhachevskii had heavily underscored in 1936–7, was demonstrated in the assaults on the 'Mannerheim line'. Small assault groups had proved invaluable, improvised though they were. 'Tank raids' (*tankovyi desant*), used against particular obstacles, had been found effective in speeding up advances. But tanks and artillery, the indispensable support of the infantry, were still far from giving it adequate co-operation. All this obviously prompted the tactical retraining of the Soviet infantry, while the wider lessons were incorporated, in part, in the draft field service regulations which superseded the 1939 draft. The aim of the offensive operation, multi-echeloned as before, was now defined as the encirclement and destruction of the enemy, as opposed to the previous object of 'constraint', merely pushing him back. Here was a fair compliment to Zhukov, for his operations at Khalkin-Gol, although not a complete consummation, had aimed at encirclement. The 'shock' and 'supporting' division of roles was retained, but to maintain the necessary attack momentum, the infantry formations were to increase their echelons, to some two or three. In the organization of defence, special attention should be directed to anti-tank obstacles, in the entire depth of the defensive position. Tanks and anti-tank guns provided the basic anti-tank measures.

The revised regulations stood ready in August 1940, yet they needed still further revision. A special commission carried out one more review, but at the end of October Timoshenko transferred all this work to the Main Commission for Manuals (*Glavnaya ustavnaya komissiya*), presided over by Marshal Budenny, First Deputy Defence Commissar. Meretskov's deputy, Lieutenant-General N.F. Vatutin, Kulik's deputy, Colonel-General of Artillery N.N. Voronov, Deputy Inspector-General of Artillery, Major-General L.A. Govorov, and the senior lecturer of the General Staff Academy, Lieutenant-General (Engineers) D.M. Karbyshev sat down to finalize the draft regulations – a task which never reached completion. At least the naval and aviation manuals appeared in 1940, which temporarily closed one gap.

Soviet naval policy had already proved the undoing of many good men. The purge of the Soviet armed forces worked also to the detriment of the navy. Stalin, bent on acquiring an ocean-going fleet, rid himself in his usual fashion of these who insisted on a defensive force, based on the submarine. The old Soviet naval command toppled into oblivion. Orlov, Muklevich, Ludrii, together with the fleet commanders and the ship designers were shot. Temporary replacement to Orlov was P.A. Smirnov, an officer of the Naval Inspectorate; real power concentrated itself in the Main Naval Soviet, the collective organ of the newly constituted, independent naval force, which was directly under Stalin's own minute scrutiny. Zhdanov presided over the deliberations of the Main Naval Soviet (*Glavnyi Voennyi Soviet Voenno-morskovo Flota*); L.M. Galler, deputy commander of the naval forces in 1937, rose to be chief of the Main Naval Staff (*Glavnyi Morskoi Shtab*). An officer of the Imperial Russian Navy, Galler cannot have entered with wholly unmixed feelings into his new assignment; very quickly he had to screw his courage up, fearful as he was of the purges,* to insist that the training and intelligence administrations should be concentrated in the Naval Staff and not decentralized in the naval commands. He won. And Galler was pressed by constant demands from Stalin to examine ship designs and plans; the construction programme went ahead even without final technical testing. The new cruisers (*Chapaev*-class), *Leningrad*-class flotilla leaders and destroyers were laid down, but so were more submarines (forty-seven in 1938). In 1939 came the battleship programme – and more submarines. Galler at this time was discussing with N. Kuznetsov, who finally came to head the Soviet naval forces in March 1939, the new manual on Soviet naval operations. Before the formalities of official doctrine, several practical issues obtruded themselves, one in particular being naval aviation. Stalin doubted that the navy needed its own aviation arm. The Main Naval Staff had no illusions, especially after the beginning of the Second World War, that it did. Much depended on Galler's final position, and Kuznetsov was able to persuade Stalin of the need for a naval air arm, though strike aircraft, such as torpedo-bombers, were as yet not forthcoming. The Soviet Navy was technically and operationally responsible for the defence of the Soviet coasts; Galler, having analysed First World War and early Second World War experiences, was convinced that coastal defence (*Beregova oborona* vmf) needed a complement of marines, AA guns and land forces (artillery, tanks and rifle units) in addition to the shore batteries. Marshal Shaposhnikov did not think so. With the possibility that the dispute might be referred to Stalin, the Naval Staff prepared its case. 'With great respect', Galler approached Shaposhnikov; sticking literally to more than his guns, Galler got his way. In October 1940, Admirals Isakov and Galler changed places, with the latter heading the Naval Construction programme, of which he became Deputy People's Commissar. Galler left behind him the manual on naval operations (*Vremennoe nastavlenie po vedeniyu morskikh operatsii 1940*). In spite of Stalin's 'big ship' megalomania, the doctrine turned out to be eminently sensible; the naval forces would be committed to sea support of the land flank, to amphibious and anti-amphibious operations, to attack on enemy coastal bases and positions. In operations against enemy sea lanes, the submarine would be the principal weapon. The Soviet Navy remained committed to an essentially defensive role, such as had been conceived before 1937. Stalin, at the price of a shattered command, got his prestige major surface units, or at least the plans for them. The navy, thanks to the June 1940, smash-and-grab raid in the Baltic provinces, got its bases.

The refurbishing of 'doctrine' notwithstanding, the fundamental issue involved the organization and structure of the Soviet armed forces; above all, the command had to make effective decisions about re-equipping the Red Army and its air arm. With Marshal Kulik, Lev Mekhlis and E.A. Shchadenko at the

* L.M. Galler was finally arrested after 1947, 'tried' after the standard Stalinist fashion and sentenced: he died in prison on 12 July 1950.

head of a special commission appointed by Stalin to supervise the procurement of new equipment, the probability of sound decision diminished sharply. The reconstitution of the mechanized corps provided an unfortunate example. The first mechanized brigade in the Red Army (commanded by B.T. Volskii,*) formed up in 1930–1, and was rapidly expanded into the first mechanized corps with two mechanized brigades and one rifle brigade. Two more mechanized corps, in Kiev and Leningrad, were formed in 1932. As the pace of mechanization increased, Voroshilov's opposition to it also increased. From the Spanish Civil War, Pavlov brought Stalin first-hand evidence that large armoured formations had no future; this lay with tank battalions incorporated into the rifle divisions and corps, and with tank brigades, organized independently but available to the rifle formations should the situation warrant their use. By 1939, the mechanized corps had been disbanded, and the highest armoured tactical unity was the brigade. For more than two years, the Soviet armoured forces had stagnated. Now the mechanized corps hurriedly formed up. Commanders like Yeremenko had no margins to play with. For the 3rd Mechanized Corps, Yeremenko selected the Vilno-Alitus-Ukmerg area as his formation points. 3rd Corps staff, and the 84th Motorized Rifle Division remained in Vilno; the 5th Tank Division (Brigade Commander Kurkin) assembled in Alitus and the 2nd Tank Division (Colonel Krivoshein and deputy commander Lieutenant-Colonel Chernyakhovskii) formed up in Ukmerg. Engineer, infantry, cavalry and artillery battalions jostled about, waiting for the new equipment and their assignments to the 'tank' and 'mechanized' components of the corps. In Moscow, Lieutenant-General Romanenko worked to pull the 1st Mechanized Corps into shape, while commanders were selected for or posted to the dozen or so formations which were projected.

The Soviet tank park, bigger than the entire tank forces of the world put together, made a less impressive showing in terms of modernity. The T-26 light-medium tank and the BT (*bystrokhodnyi tank*) models – BT-7 (1935) and BT-7M (1938), highly mobile armoured fighting vehicles for use with the mechanized brigades – predominated. The T-26, the T-27 tankette, the T-28 medium tank and the T-35 heavy tank dated back to the mid 1930s. The BT-7M marked the end of the evolutionary line for these models, although in 1939 the BT-7M, with a V-2 diesel engine, went into quantity production, serving the Red Army at Khalkin-Gol and in the advance into eastern Poland. The T-28 medium tank, triple-turreted, and designed for breaking through fortified positions, underwent modifications to its armour after the Finnish war; 1940 marked the end of its seven-year production run. The 50-ton, five-turreted (one 76.2-mm, one 45-mm gun, five machine-guns) heavy tank T-35, although never mass-

---

* In 1941, as a Major-General, he occupied the post of deputy head of the Stalin Academy of Mechanization and Motorization. After June, he was sent to command Soviet armoured forces on the South-Western Front: in the autumn of 1942, he took command of the 4th Mechanized Corps, formed out of the 28th Tank Corps, and operated on the Stalingrad Front. He died in 1946.

produced, lingered on past 1939. In 1936, work had begun on more advanced models, and two years later the prototypes were ready; already in 1937 the model T-45-6 (T-111) had been used to introduce armour capable of standing up to the new anti-tank guns. The two design studies for heavy tanks envisaged multi-turreted models; in evaluating and improving the twin-turret versions, vehicles of some 58 tons with 60-mm armour and two guns (76-mm and 45-mm), Kotin's team concluded that these monsters – types SMK and T-100 – were less promising than the single-turret machine. Work began in 1939 on the KV-1 heavy tank, single-turreted, diesel-engined, and by December the tank had been accepted for the Red Army. A little earlier, in August 1939, Stalin and the Main Military Soviet, after inspecting various designs, had decided to proceed with the development of the integrally tracked medium tank. Koshkin's design team had been working on a track-and-wheel medium tank, the A-20 which was a modified version of the BT-7M; Tarshinov produced the redesigned and distinctive hull, with the well-shaped sloping frontal armour. The A-20 gave place to the A-30, with a 45-mm gun, and Koshkin and Morozov worked on a further version, the T-32, operating entirely on tracks. The end product was the famous T-34, with its A-20/A-30/T-32 lineage.

These were excellent machines (although the KV-2, with its 152-mm howitzer in the slab-sided turret, was less so). It was, therefore, a blunder of considerable proportions not to have produced them. In 1940, only 243 KV and 115 T-34 tanks were produced. The real danger lay in stopping the production of the old machines without ensuring the production of the new. No final decision had been taken at the Defence Commissariat on the T-34 and the KV machines, for there were other models in the offing (which subsequently enjoyed no great success). The previous mechanized corps, with their three brigades, had an establishment of 500 tanks; the new formations, with their three divisions (two tank, one motorized rifle) had a *paper* establishment of no less than 1,031 tanks. Organic artillery and transport, wireless sets and motor-cycles, tractors and lorries all had to be found, and these quickly.

The Motor-Transport and Motor-Highway Service (*Avtotransportnaya i dorozhnaya sluzhba*) was at this time on the point of being closed down. During the war with Finland, this service organized 100-lorry convoys to shift ammunition and supplies to the north. The GAZ lorries, in response to a General Staff Directive, ran loaded from Gorkii-Moscow-Kalinin-Leningrad and on to the Karelian front. Young drivers under training, severe frost and inaccessibility of spare parts slowed these columns down, as vehicles fell out. Somewhat understandably, the driver aware that he carried a full load of high explosive took so much care to avoid a collision that he frequently ended up in the ditch. To speed the supply columns, spare parts were put in dumps for easy access; hot water for de-frosting was laid on and detachments of ten 'tug-trucks' trundled about to tow out the over-cautious or the under-experienced. Sokolovskii, chief of staff to the Moscow Military District, had less cause for complaint as the trucks moved northwards. Unfortunately, at the end of the Finnish war, largely at the prompting of the head of the armoured forces, D.G. Pavlov, the 'motor-transport service', as a separate administration, was wound up. Henceforth, the armoured forces command would deal with all matters pertaining to motor-transport. A meeting with the Deputy Chief of the General Staff (before August 1940), I.V. Smorodinov, with Major-General N.I. Chetverikov in attendance, made the formal decision. Only the General Staff retained its Motor Transport Section, and that merely for mobilization purposes. Clearly the armoured forces administration (which very shortly emerged as the Main Administration of Armoured Forces: *Glavnoe Upravlenie Bronetankovykh Voisk*, under Major-General of Tank Troops Ya.N. Fedorenko) needed transport, but in the absence of any general rear organization, this was a dangerous decision. It also saddled the armoured forces commander at military district (or front) level with the additional responsibility of procuring, manning, repairing and operating the motor transport available.

A similar problem of aligning technical progress with organizational modification existed in the area of Soviet military aviation. The Soviet Air Force (VVS:RKKA), which unlike the navy never attained an independent service status, suffered not unlike the navy in the period of the purges. The pre-purge air force had been distinguished for the development of long-range strategic aviation forces (TBS), of which the Aviation Chief of Staff, Khripin, was an enthusiastic advocate. Soviet designers supplied a whole series of massive, if monsterish machines, multi-engined potential bombers – in particular the ANT (Tupolev) versions. But the Spanish Civil War, in which the Soviet Union lent considerable air aid, seemed to show little future for the long-range bomber. This was presumably the burden of the report which Smushkevich, Soviet 'aviation commander' in Spain, made to Stalin on his return. Both the Germans and Russians realized the need for special aircraft to be used in immediate support of ground operations; what was particular to the Russians concerned also the problem of a Soviet equivalent to the Me-109, which emphasized the need for more powerful aero-engines. In 1938, the search for the new Soviet fighter aircraft went ahead with all speed, although the aviation industry felt the shocks and perils of the purge. Tupolev, the bomber designer, was 'framed' in 1938 on a charge of passing technical secrets abroad and jailed; he was kept there for some years. Petlyakov stepped ahead of Tupolev, just as Lavochkin moved up when his chief Kalinin was purged. Like the Soviet tank park, the aircraft holdings were massive, amounting even in 1938 to some 5,000 machines, with an annual production of 4,000 to 5,000 to boost this. Yet the same blight of obsolescence crept over tank and aeroplane alike.

The rationalization of organization in the defence industries in 1939 brought some benefit to Soviet aviation. The People's Commissariat for Defence Industry, established in 1936 and headed then by Rukhimovich, was broken up, and the People's Commissariat for Aviation Industry – run initially by one of

Stalin's 'strong men', M.M. Kaganovich – emerged. Kaganovich did not survive, at least in that post, the immense pressure to re-equip the Soviet air force; in September 1940, his post went to A.I. Shakurin. By that time, a greater degree of industrial co-ordination was being achieved by the earlier, general industrial reorganization (April 1940), when six Economic Councils were set up under the Council of People's Commissars (*Sovnarkom*). One of these six, the Defence Industry Council, came under the direction of Voznesenskii; as a co-ordinating body, it had four sections, aviation industries, weapons, munitions, and shipbuilding. The Defence Committee (*Komitet Oborony*) had already in September and October 1939, turned its full attention to increasing the number of aircraft factories and aero-engine plants, and the aircraft-production facilities in the east began to grow. Assembly plants for airframes and engines were scheduled for greater expansion in the period 1939–41. Yet the old machines predominated. Most common of all was Polikarpov's fighter, the I-16, which had undergone combat evaluation in the Spanish Civil War and fought thereafter in the Soviet Far East and in China, and again in Finland. (It continued to battle on until 1943, having absorbed the first fury of the Luftwaffe.) The I-153 Schcherbakov biplane fighter, evolved from Polikarpov's I-15, first saw the light of day in 1935. New fighters and ground-attack machines waited in the workshops and test-stations. The MiG-1 (I-61) fighter made its first flight in March 1940; this open-cockpit single-seat fighter, with a speed of 373 mph, was transformed ultimately into the MiG-3 (I-200). Lavochkin's LAGG-1 (I-22), an all-wood single-seat fighter, had already taken the air in March 1939; in 1940, the LAGG-3, a somewhat strengthened LAGG-1, went into production. Yakovlev's Yak-1, another single-seat fighter, originally designated I-26, flew in the summer of 1940 on its test flights; it went at once into quantity production (Yakovlev collected the Order of Lenin), although only sixty-four machines were rolled out in 1940. Petlyakov's light bomber, the Pe-2, which proved to be an outstanding machine, rolled even more slowly out of the factories; only two were built in 1940. Ilyushin's IL-2, the ground attack *Shturmovik*, had also come into being though not yet into full quantity production. Even so, reconnaissance machines, heavy bombers, transports and naval aircraft had not such an encouraging record of design successes.

Of the defence of cities and military objectives against air attack, the Russians learned much in Spain. Anti-aircraft defence was handled by an administration of that name (*Protivovozdushnaya oborona*: PVO), which, in association (and also in competition) with the Main Artillery Administration (GAU), had investigated the problem of the location of aerial targets. In the early 1930s, the 'infra-red' and the 'acoustical' solutions were found wanting. In January 1934 the GAU had concluded an agreement with the Central Radio Laboratory (TSRL) work on 'radio-technical means' of aircraft detection; both the TSRL and the Leningrad Electro-Physics Institute (LEFI) set to work on behalf of the GAU. Meanwhile PVO engineers, principally Engineer P.K. Oshchepkov, were also investigating 'radio means', though the PVO in 1934 drew the Academy of Sciences into its work; in 1936, the PVO enlisted the aid of the Physico-Technical Institute of the Ukrainian Academy of Sciences. In 1935, however, the Chief of the Signals Administration of the Red Army protested to Tukhachevskii about the pointlessness of the work of the Scientific-Research Test (Signals) Institute of the Red Army (NIIIS: RKKA). Tukhachevskii managed to save NIIIS programmes, but only for the moment. Meanwhile, Professor Bonch-Bruevich at NII-9 (the new designation for LEFI) managed to produce in 1936 a prototype search radar, the *Burya-1* set, but neither range, reliability nor accuracy of angular co-ordination were satisfactory. *Burya-1* lacked the wide polar diagram essential for a search radar. Army Commander Sedyakin (so soon to be liquidated), the successor in 1936 to S.S. Kamenev as head of the PVO, undertook to press the research programme, and, if necessary, 'to go to the government'; already a prototype pulse radar set, with a seven-kilometre range, had been produced for possible use in conjunction with the visual observation service (VNOS) of the anti-aircraft commands.

In 1937, the scientific activity of NII-9 underwent 'investigation'; Director Smirnov was arrested, Engineer Shembel' was 'relieved of his duties'. The tribulations of NII-9 were reported to Kulik, the new head of the Main Artillery Administration; Kulik offered no help. Professor Bonch-Bruevich appealed to Zhdanov, but the Red Army Signals Administration was now stepping in to 'take over' the 'radio-location' work. The *Zenit* set was developed, but the range was only three kilometres, and since the target co-ordinates were given at intervals rather than continuously, this set could not be used with the automatic fire-control system (PUAZO) for AA guns – thirty-eight seconds being needed with *Zenit* to adjust the measurement of the target. NII-9 finally staggered back to its scientific feet; in 1939, the *Komitet Oborony* and GAU approved the production of three sets from the series *Burya-2* and *Burya-3* (the latter with a high accuracy of angular co-ordination – 1° – and a range of seventeen and a-half kilometres). The Signals Administration engineers also enjoyed greater success with the prototype set *Revan*, which was improved and adopted for preliminary service as *Rus-1*; NIIIS RKKA could also point in 1939 to the model *Redut*, which was satisfactorily tested at Sevastopol.

At this point, the directorate of the Chair of Acoustics of the Dzerzhinskii Artillery Academy broke into the dispute on the air-defence problem. The charge of the directorate was that 'radio means' were an irrelevance in air defence; to discuss this, and other issues, a study-conference was called for the summer of 1940, with the radio-physicist, Academician N.D. Papaleksi, Professor of Acoustics N.N. Andreyev, the president of the Artillery Committee (*Artkom*) of the GAU Colonel-General of Artillery, V.D. Grendal' and a Defence Committee inspector, Military Engineer 2nd Grade Kornetskii. In the absence of formal or particular resolutions, but having witnessed the complete demolition of the 'acoustical case' by professors Papaleksi and Andreyev, the conference adjourned. On 4 June 1940 NII-9 received instructions from the Defence Committee to submit to GAU that radar set, from *Burya-2* and *Burya-3*, which best survived the tests. The deadline for selection rested at 1 October 1940.*

Throughout the whole of the Soviet military sector, from research and development to tactical training, the pressure was on, but its application was uneven, unco-ordinated and in parts uncomprehending. The procurement system had broken down and the production system needed speeding up. As for the recognition of priorities, this depended upon a clarification of fundamentals – a risky, if not impossible business under Stalin. Stalin, behind whose wilfulness and incompetence many lesser but widespread incompetences bred and flourished, remained the final arbiter.

In the autumn of 1940, its summer manoeuvres having been delayed by the frantic rush into the Baltic states and into Bessarabia, the Red Army went out to exercises. The marshals were out in force:

Under Marshal Timoshenko
Western Special Military District, 2–3-day exercises, to regimental level.
Kiev Special Military District, 3-day exercises, 'attackers' at reinforced regiment level, 'defenders' reinforced battalions, and 3-day exercises of the 99th Rifle Division.
Staff exercise, 3-day, with 6th Rifle Corps and 97th Rifle Division, on the theme: 'Rifle corps breakthrough of fortified area with subsequent exploitation by mechanized formations.'

Under Marshal Budenny
Odessa Military District, 2-day exercises, sharp-shooting.
Trans-Caucasus Military District, 4-day exercises, with sharp-shooting, 3-day staff exercises (involving parachute troops), 2-day attack exercises at regiment level, 3-day mountain troops training.

Under Marshal Kulik
Trans-Baikal Military District, 4-day river crossing exercises, 2-day attack exercises, reinforced regiment and battalion Siberian Military District, 1-day staff exercise.

Under General Tyulenev
Moscow Military District, 3-day exercises with sharp-shooting.

Lieutenant-General M.P. Kirponos
Leningrad Military District, 2-day sharp-shooting, river-crossing exercises.

* According to General Lobanov, the Soviet air defence command had 25–30 radar installations operating in European Russia, while 45 were sent to the Soviet Far East and to the Trans-Caucasus. The State Defence Committee (GKO) after June 1941, issued *Instruction No. 129* for the manufacture of radar sets, but the evacuation of the factories made production impossible. In June 1943 the 'Radar Soviet' was set up under GKO direction, and the set SON-2A went into quantity production.

Lieutenant-General F.N. Remisov
Orel Military District, 1-day exercise.

Under Colonel-General Apanasenko
Central Asian Military District, 2-day mountain exercise, and cavalry formations with tank units to study the meeting-engagement with cavalry.

Under Colonel-General Shtern
Soviet Far Eastern forces, 3-day exercises, forced crossing of the Amur and 2-day sharp-shooting exercises.

In the Volga Military District, the Chief of Staff, Major-General V.N. Gordov, conducted a two-day staff exercise on the reduction of a fortified sector, while the district commander, Lieutenant-General V.F. Gerasimenko, supervised a rifle division exercise involving reinforced battalions as 'attackers' and 'defenders'.

The exercises followed the recently formulated 'line' that commanders must concern themselves with the training of the individual soldier and with the operation of small tactical units. 'Realistic' training in intelligence, signals, the security of flank and rear, rapid and clear orders, and the 'co-operation of all arms' was the keynote of all of these tactical exercises. 'Without exception' (in the view of German intelligence), the basic notion of the attack and defence of prepared positions predominated. The dangers of encirclement, so vividly displayed in Finland, had obviously begun to make more impression on the Soviet commanders; the 'defenders' were instructed to 'wear the enemy down' in the forward positions. The 'defence zone' would consist in its depth of numerous 'intermediate zones'; one form demonstrated during the exercises involved a rifle company, reinforced with artillery, engineer and 'chemical weapons' sections, investing a thirteen-kilometre 'barrier' with five defensive sectors.

In the staff exercises, signals came in for great attention. Marshal Budenny took the opportunity to praise the work of the Inspector of Red Army Signals Troops, Lieutenant-General Naidenov, for the improved performance. In the movement exercises, convoys and columns operated under strict discipline. The weather, by its general inclemency, added more 'realism' to Timoshenko's programme. The exercises over, the Defence Commissariat handed out its prizes; Major-General A.A. Vlasov's 99th Rifle Division, which its skilful commander had turned from an ill-trained bunch into a first-class formation, came in for high commendation, while the officers of the 6th Rifle Corps received gold watches and the 97th Rifle Division won the General Staff 'challenge trophy'. Also at the close of the exercises, the director of the Red Army Training Administration, Lieutenant-General Kurdyunov, took the opportunity to issue a short 'address' on the revised manuals and regulations which were in the course of preparation and which would supersede the PU-36.

The rank and file were being retrained, the mass of senior-lieutenant battalion commanders had undergone some kind of 'realistic' exercise in handling their units, the divisional and corps staffs had been quickly tested in various military districts. Now, as the winter drew on, it was time for the senior command to learn its lessons.

In this same September, as the Red Army finished its training plan and prepared now to analyse its results, Stalin had cause to consider just what his ally, Adolf Hitler, was engaged upon. A German *Heeresmission*, a suspiciously numerous 'military mission' to Soviet eyes, was on its way to Rumania. German troops moving to northern Norway passed through Finland; a German note explained to the Russians that the 'German-Finnish agreement . . . involved a purely technical matter of military communications without political implications'. Ribbentrop promised to explain all to Stalin in a personal letter. Ribbentrop duly explained, in a long and vapid piece of prose, which could scarcely have satisfied Stalin, whose preoccupation – put a little earlier through the mouth of Molotov – was very mundane: 'How many troops are you sending to Rumania?' Ribbentrop, however, dangled a bait, that of a 'natural political coalition', one which 'if intelligently managed' could serve 'the best advantage' of the powers concerned. These powers read off as Germany, Italy, Japan and the Soviet Union. A *'delimitation of their interests'* on *'a world-wide scale'*, issues of 'decisive importance', needed high-level discussion. Molotov should come, on the terms of 'a most cordial invitation to him in the name of the Reich Government', to Berlin. Stalin, on 22 October, accepted for Molotov, who would arrive in Berlin between 10–12 November. Duly on 12 November, Ribbentrop and Molotov met; to Ribbentrop's bait about a new division of 'spheres of interest', Molotov refused to rise, except to snap angrily at the vagueness of it all. He waited to face Hitler later in the day; during this conversation, Molotov virtually halted an Hitlerian spate of words with his reference to the 'exact instructions' which Stalin had given him before leaving Moscow. The questions came thick and fast, ploughing into the verbosity to which Ribbentrop and Hitler had treated Molotov. Virtually stalled on the 12th, the talks were renewed on the 13th; Molotov here got his teeth into the Finnish problem, tearing away at Hitler's 'interjections'. Ribbentrop attempted, somewhat fruitlessly, to calm the discussion. Hitler took the offensive, remarking on the critical nature of Soviet relations with Finland; only a change in subject prevented the conversation getting wholly out of control. Even this, the not unbeguiling topic of the dismemberment of the British empire, and one to which the Führer warmed, failed to slide the corrosive Molotov from his position. Molotov permitted himself one ironic luxury – to speak 'bluntly' about the German guarantee to Rumania; his speech till then had been hardly silken. Ribbentrop and Molotov conducted the next stage of the conversation in the *Auswärtiges Amt* air-raid shelter; here, in this slightly bizarre setting, Ribbentrop produced for Molotov's inspection a draft agreement which transformed the German-Japanese-Italian tripartite pact into a four-power agreement, the Soviet Union becoming an adherent. The inflexible Molotov stone-walled, never moving a fraction from his brief. Molotov, having stung with the remark that he thought that 'the Germans were assuming that the war against England had already been actually won', left with the sentiment that 'he did not regret the air raid alarm'. It had provided the occasion for an 'exhaustive' talk with Ribbentrop, though the latter could be excused for thinking it more exhausting than exhaustive. The draft treaty, suggested by Ribbentrop, Stalin accepted (on 26 November) but with four ferocious conditions, to be embodied in five (instead of the original two) secret protocols, plus – Stalin's appetite waxed, as it had done in June 1940 – the consideration that if Turkey refused to grant to the Soviet Union the bases for 'light naval and land forces', then the four signatories should take 'the required military and diplomatic measures'. That additional demand would be incorporated by separate agreement. In less than a fortnight the Führer called for the war plan against the Soviet Union.

The closing months of the year, within the Soviet military command, witnessed an attempt to draw up the balance sheet of progress and short-comings. As Hitler issued *Weisung 21*, the directive for Operation 'Barbarossa' (18 December 1940), senior Soviet commanders assembled in Moscow for a special, enlarged meeting of the Main Military Soviet (just as the Soviet naval command gathered for a similar set of meetings with the Main Naval Soviet). What prompted this somewhat unusual step had been no doubt the very critical report submitted by the Central Committee's 'authoritative commission', set up to supervise the hand-over between Voroshilov and Timoshenko. The commission, concerned particularly at the unsatisfactory state of the Red Army armoured and mechanized formations, observed with some asperity:

The People's Commissariat for Defence lags behind in the development of questions concerning the operational utilization of forces in modern war. There are no agreed opinions on the utilization of tanks, aviation and parachute troops . . . The development of tank and mechanized forces within the general framework of the Armed Forces lags behind the contemporary requirements of the mass employment of armour. . . . The ratio of mechanized forces is low, and the quality of tanks in the Red Army – unsatisfactory.

That was to the point, and perfectly true.

The command conference, which ran from mid December 1940 until early January 1941 divided its proceedings into five sections, to run consecutively. Red Army training came first, both the summary of the present year and the consideration of training assignments for 1941. In the presence of the chiefs of administrations, arms commanders and select formation commanders, the Chief of the General Staff, General K.A. Meretskov, introduced the summary of results in training. The chief object had been to increase, during this transitional phase, the combat manoeuvrability of the infantryman. In defensive tactics, Soviet attention fixed itself on the forward zone of defence, in order to 'guide' the enemy offensive into directions favourable to the defender, and there to destroy the opponent, before he erupted into the main defensive zone, with artillery and aircraft. While Soviet troops were being trained to establish these forward zones, Meretskov emphasized that they were not being trained in how to deal with an enemy forward zone, nor was the command giving enough attention to reconnaissance training. As for the separate arms, the artillery had measured up to what it had been assigned (with the best performance from the artillery of the Kiev Special Military District under N.D. Yakoblev). Soviet aviation had meanwhile received a great deal of experience in ground-support operations. This experience showed quite clearly that aircraft could attack enemy forward positions and support an infantry attack. In this respect, Meretskov noted an 'improvement'; whereas before aviation commanders had exhibited a 'superfluous enthusiasm' for independent air operations against the enemy rear, independent of operations by other arms, this tendency had been curbed.

Now, after lists of facts and figures, came the problem of the 1941 training programme. Meretskov suggested that the main problem concerned working out the tactical instructions and regulations for operations in depth, for all types of operations and for all arms; in this way, it should be possible to establish a 'unified view' of training methods and priorities. In the subsequent discussion, twenty-eight Soviet generals, including the Inspector-General of Infantry and the chief of the Training Administration spoke up to add their proposals for the 1941 training programme.

The second part of the conference dealt with theoretical problems of the 'operating art', to which five study-reports were devoted:

General G.K. Zhukov: *The nature of the modern offensive operation.*
General I.V. Tyulenev: *The nature of the modern defensive operation.*
Colonel-General D.G. Pavlov: *The utilization of mechanized corps in the offensive.*
Lieutenant-General (Aviation) P.V. Rychagov: *Combat aviation in the offensive and in the struggle for air superiority.*
Lieutenant-General A.K. Smirnov (Inspector-General of Infantry): *The rifle division in the offensive and in defence*

Four days (25-9 December) were assigned to discuss these questions. Zhukov, whose encirclement operations at Khalkin-Gol in 1939 had enjoyed considerable success, provoked quite a violent reaction. Colonel-General Shtern, who had been Blyukher's successor in the Soviet Far East, criticized Zhukov's ideas on the timing of the introduction of the tank corps into the breakthrough area. Major-General M.A. Kuznetsov, chief of staff in the Far East, disagreed with the idea of introducing front and army 'breakthrough exploitation echelons' (according to operational norms, the third echelon) on multiple axes. As for what Zhukov actually said, this can be more readily estimated by the comment of Romanenko, 1st Mechanized Corps commander:

I venture to express some doubts relating to the study by Comrade Zhukov on the nature and dynamics of the modern offensive operation. It is my view that the study would have been perfectly correct for the years 1932–4, since it reflects the level of military thought of those days, based on a relatively weak saturation level of equipment in formations. But a great deal has changed since then. The experience which we have been having in the west calls into question the analysis of the report, but the conclusions drawn from it are, in my view, incorrect. The lecturer has correctly affirmed that the German Army fulfilled its offensive operations on the basis of mechanized and aviation formations but he has not shown how in actual fact [konkretno] they did this. First and foremost, I think it vital to direct the attention of commanders to the fact that the decisive factor in the success of German operations in the west was the mechanized army group of Reichenau. That mobile formation was committed in the direction of Namur, to the north of Sedan, cut the front of the French and Belgian armies and then carried out the encirclement of the Allied armies operating in Belgium. This in the final analysis played a decisive role in the ultimate destruction of France.

Because of this, in my opinion, it is necessary to come to this conclusion, that the Germans – disposing of considerably less tanks than us – understood that the shock force in modern war should be composed of mechanized, tank and aviation formations, and they assembled all their tanks and motorized troops into operational unities, they massed them and assigned them [the mission] of fulfilling independent, decisive operations. In this manner, they scored major successes.

In this connection I therefore think that it is essential to set out and to explore the problem of the establishment of a shock army with 3–4 mechanized corps, 2–3 aviation corps, 1–2 parachute divisions, 10–11 artillery regiments. I submit that if two such armies were to operate on the internal and external flanks of two fronts, they would in this way smash in the enemy front, give him no chance to pull himself together until the completion of our operation and lead to operational success at the strategic level.

Romanko came to his conclusion:

My proposal will bring criticism, but I ask you to take into consideration that I have worked many years on this problem, and, as it seems to me, examined it fundamentally. If we desist from using shock armies made up of mechanized formations with powerful aviation support, then we will find ourselves in a grave situation and expose our country to a threat.

Prophetic words indeed. Other aspects of Zhukov's lecture Romanenko found equally unacceptable, for example, the short preparatory period for offensive operations, set at two to three days – demonstrably too short, to judge by the fiasco over the Soviet 7th Army offensive against the Finns in the Karelian isthmus in 1939. Romanenko stipulated a ten- to fifteen-day preparatory period. As for committing the mechanized corps to breakthrough operations, it had to be borne in mind that their thrusts could attain a depth of some 200 to 250 kilometres.

Romanenko made no mistake when he predicted opposition to his ideas. F.I. Golikov, for one, came out strongly against the notion of massing the mechanized forces.* Neither Zhukov in his summing-up, nor Timoshenko in his final address, made any reference to Romanko's proposals – as if corps commanders should be seen but not heard. The 'agreed version' of Zhukov's paper, which amounted to a summary of conclusions on offensive operations, remarked on the technical-operational revolution (tanks, aircraft and general motorization) which facilitated an offensive form in which tanks, aircraft, artillery and rifle troops could not only reduce enemy troops in field fortifications but also neutralize modern fortified multi-zone defence systems. The shattering of the tactical zone of defence, and irruption of powerful mobile forces could produce a decisive elimination of operational reserves and lead an 'operational success' into one with strategic implications. A powerful, surprise blow by ground forces, parachute troops and aircraft could similarly eliminate enemy air strength throughout the whole depth of an 'operational-strategic blow' and establish air superiority. (In eerie fashion, the Soviet commanders here prescribed the dimensions of the catastrophe which fell upon them in June 1941.)

General Tyulenev's lecture on defence subscribed, in theory at least, to 'modern' ideas, emphasizing multiple echelons deployed in depth, 'multi-field' defensive positions with numerous tank and infantry barriers. The 'anti-tank barrier' occupied a particularly important place, though defence should be 'anti-aeroplane' as well as 'anti-tank'. Colonel-General D.G. Pavlov, tagged somewhat prematurely as 'the Soviet Guderian', and now installed as commander of the crucially important Western Special Military District, raised much more of a flurry with his exposition of tank corps operations. Lieutenant-General Yeremenko, who joined in the discussion, hastened to add that Pavlov's theoretical ideas on the nature of modern operations were correct; the tank is the most 'stylish' of modern weapons by virtue of its fire-power, mobility, armour, speed and manoeuvrability, making it the supreme offensive weapon yet investing it with valuable counter-attack properties. Yeremenko insisted on the division of armour into two types, the 'general purpose' and the 'operational-strategic' (unities which had been prescribed in PU-36); the former, infantry-support tanks, would assist in the breakthrough of enemy defences, destroying, with infantry in its wake, enemy mortars, machine-guns and artillery. It was about the latter group, however, that Yeremenko wished to talk at length. To shatter enemy dispositions, it was necessary to break in both frontally and in

---

* This is Yeremenko's version. General V. Ivanov, however, has made some important reservations (*Voenno-Istoricheskii Zhurnal*, 6, 1965, pp. 73–4) on Yeremenko's account. Golikov, according to General Ivanov, only criticized Romanenko for saying that Zhukov's ideas dated back to 1932–4; there was more emphasis throughout the study-conference on defence, there was substantial agreement on large-scale armoured operations. General Ivanov also wholly repudiates the idea that Zhukov and Timoshenko showed themselves to be unacquainted with 'basic changes in waging modern war'. Both Marshal Yeremenko and General Ivanov are nevertheless in agreement about the importance of this study-conference.

depth, a task suited to tanks operating with 'mechanized infantry, cavalry and aviation'. There was the question, nevertheless, on what breadth of front the armoured formations would be committed. The mechanized corps moving up with two divisions would employ 14 kilometres of frontage to deploy its first echelon (16–20 kilometres with intervals). The depth of this deployment, with divisional columns reaching for 100 kilometres, could be considerably compressed; with four divisional columns, 100 kilometres could be reduced to 25, and since the second echelon of the mechanized corps (motorized infantry) would by diversification of approach marches take up some 16 kilometres, then the total depth would be some 40 kilometres – this for a frontage of 20 kilometres.

When should the mechanized corps be committed? Some had argued for the point after the breaching of the second enemy defensive line. Yeremenko thought that this hazarded all success; once a six-kilometre breach had been opened in the defensive position, then the mechanized corps should be committed in order to be in an advantageous position to deal with the second line of defences. Even so, just as important a consideration was that of controlling the armour once it had penetrated the enemy positions in depth. Yeremenko pointed to the German experience. German mobile formations, moving on Cambrai after breaking into the Franco–Belgian defences, met and engaged more than 100 tanks, in a battle lasting more than eight hours. The Germans won, thereby demonstrating the superiority of their mobile formations, organized not only into corps but also into army groups. The Allied forces lacked unity, unified command, and a 'concrete doctrine' of 'mechanized operations'. Here was the moral for the Red Army:

> I would like to emphasize that we need to prepare at once an administration of this type, so that in time of war there will be no repetition of the troubles such as those at Novogrudek and Volkovysk during the liberating advance into Western Belorussia, when the cavalry-mechanized group got separated from the other mobile formations and we had a hell of a time to bring order back into the administration.

Yeremenko proceeded to rub this in, pointing out that the supply of fuel was one of the principal problems in regulating the operations of armoured and mechanized troops:

> We have been talking here about supplying mechanized troops with fuel by air. The Germans also adopted this measure. We have tried it. I remember that when we got to the area of Bialystok, we had empty fuel tanks and they brought in fuel to us by air. The same thing happened to Comrade Petrov's corps near Grodno. They dropped him fuel by parachute. From practical experience of the problem, I have come to the conclusion that this is not its solution. The method is an exception. We need 'trucks' of 20 ton petrol-carrying capacity, and we should think of tankers which could be towed along behind the units for 180–200 kilometres. That is the way to do it, and we must plan the organization of our fuel supply.

Recognition of the versatility of the armoured formations was not lacking, but, as subsequent events demonstrated, Yeremenko was right to stress the practical operational-administrative aspect, which Pavlov seemed either to ignore or to hazard with improvident solutions.

Now came the turn of the air force, whose commander, Lieutenant-General P.V. Rychagov, introduced the operational lecture. Rychagov concerned himself with five topics: the struggle for control of the air, air support for ground operations (tactical support), air cover for troops and targets against enemy aviation, air strikes against enemy tactical and strategic reserves, parachute operations, aerial reconnaissance and aerial supply for ground troops. Both air force and ground force officers disputed Rychagov's formula that 'strategic air superiority' over the battlefield could be assigned to 'tactical-operational' levels, such as army. Major-General (Aviation) Kozlov made this point, as did Lieutenant-General M.M. Popov, who stressed that 'strategic superiority' came within the responsibility of the 'supreme command and the front command' and passed out of the range of army commands. The decentralization of air power, the splitting up of the aviation corps and divisions came in for resolute criticism from Major-General (Aviation) G.P. Kravchenko (who, as a major, had taken an extensive and distinguished part in the air fighting at Khalkin-Gol in 1939). Kravchenko had undoubtedly hit the aviation nail right on the head, although a number of ideas hitherto stubbornly held began to go more speedily into the melting-pot. If the 'enthusiasm' for independent air operations had been 'curbed', the idea that attack on enemy air power applied against aerodromes and airfields yielded little result and cost too much had begun to lose its aura of official sanctity. The importance of air superiority had become increasingly recognized, although the 'tactical' and 'strategic' aspects seemed to be tangled and confused. This was clearly the point of Kravchenko's intervention.

Inspector-General of Infantry, A. K. Smirnov, brought up the rear with his lecture on rifle division operations. In defensive operations, Smirnov emphasized that 'the basis of the defence is the battalion defensive area', and that the training of small unit commanders was essential to ensure successful defence in positions deployed in depth; the section and company commanders had an increasingly important role to play, and hence they must be trained for it. The rifle division in attack faced its most formidable task in breaching the main defensive position, although reinforced with two artillery regiments, a rifle division should be able to break through on a front of anything up to four kilometres. Smirnov broke no new ground and merely enunciated the general principles of tactical doctrine, embodied in 1940 in *Obschaya Taktika* (*General Tactics*, I-II). If the mainspring of defence was the battalion sectors, then the foundation of all, the fire-system, found its best expression at divisional level. In spite of the 'official' insistence that anti-tank defence had become critically important, infantry tactics evolved from the principle 'the main opponent of the defending infantry is enemy infantry'. The divisional anti-tank artillery armament of 45-mm and 76-mm guns failed to provide sufficient fire-power against a massed tank assault; in the space of 3-4 minutes (with 45-mm guns firing a maximum of 60 rounds per minute and the 76-mm a maximum of 10), and assuming that 10 hits were necessary to destroy a tank, each gun was required to destroy 3–6 tanks in a 'massed' tank assault (more than 100 tanks to 1 kilometre). None of this had had any practical testing, and it proved, in the event, to be the most fallible of all Soviet assumptions.

The lectures had come to an end. To test the commanders, a series of 'improvisations' – two-party war-games conducted with maps – were to follow; the exercises, like the lectures, covered principally front and army offensive and defensive operations. According to Yeremenko, who took part in the 'front offensive operation', they showed what might have been guessed, that those with some senior command experience 'survived', while the more junior adherents to the *generalitet*, the majors and colonels so recently turned into major-generals, showed their lack of experience. Marshal Timoshenko, who addressed the conference at its conclusion – marked by an inspection of the new equipment on the Moscow training grounds and tank stations – made no reference to the disparities and discrepancies which the lectures and exercises had clearly brought to light. His speech, full of phrases about 'further progress' and 'objective and sound views' was innocuous enough to appear in the open press. No effort, however, was made to disseminate any of the conference work among the Soviet officer corps as a whole. The unified and progressive views, the lack of which had been the cause of criticism on the eve of the command conference, had still not materialized; on the surface, Soviet military thinking had been dragged into a more modern orbit, but while the theory had been brushed up, there seemed to be a marked reluctance to discuss its implementation. Obviously, much depended on the quality – and the quantity – of the new equipment. While some purpose had been served by discussing such matters as modern armoured operations, the new mechanized corps commanders laboured with more immediate matters, the circumventing of the shortage of equipment, the lack of motor-cycles, lorries, organic artillery, radio sets, engineer equipment – even ammunition; they were obliged to bear in mind, as they pondered the German military spectacular in the west, the limitations of ageing tanks with engines of so brief a mechanical mortality, a four-hour life in many cases. Training presented its hazards and anxieties; battle, which came with a swiftness sufficient to overwhelm all this officer-audience, degenerated into a mindless, fuelless and staggeringly disordered nightmare.

'Die [Rote] Armee ist führerlos': 'The Red Army is leaderless'. This observation, together with many more on Soviet equipment and general preparedness, Colonel-General Halder delivered in the course of the four-hour *Führervortrag*, convened on 5 December 1940, to consider the state of preparations and planning for the campaign against the Soviet Union. Still shrouded in the code-name *Otto*, the attack plans envisaged May 1941, as the operational deadline. Success with the offensive operations depended not only upon favourable weather conditions, but also upon the relative strengths of the contestants, not only again in men, but also in weapons and equipment. The Russians, Halder remarked, were as inferior with respect to weapons as the French had been. The lack of modern Russian field batteries gave the German Panzer III, with its 50-mm gun, a free hand; to oppose German armour there existed only a 'badly armoured' Soviet force. Within a leaderless army operated the 'inferior' (*minderwertig*) Russian, a military version of the racist, Nazi notion of the 'sub-human', the *Untermensch*, which unleashed so much fiendishness in the east. Yet German officers, who had fought in Russia in the First World War and who now commanded German formations, had cause to ponder what they had known at first hand of the tenacity of the Russian soldier. On the other hand, the 're-orientation' of the Red Army would not bring any substantial improvement by spring 1941, thereby ensuring German superiority in leadership, equipment and fighting troops. Once this Russian army had been broken, disaster would swiftly overtake the Soviet Union; avoiding the danger of merely 'shoving' the Russian army in front of it, the Wehrmacht would split the Russians into separate pieces, thereupon strangling (*abwurgen*) them by encirclement. Slicing through the traffic and communication networks would induce the same chaos which engulfed Poland.

The study *Die Kriegswehrmacht der UdSSR* (compiled by the General Staff intelligence section *Fremde Heere Ost* (*II*), 'Foreign Armies East', under Colonel Kinzel), dated for 1 January 1941, enlarged in much greater detail on Soviet military posture and preparedness. This was the latest volume in a series of 'Background books' (*Orientierungshefte*) and assessments of the Soviet armed forces and particular military developments. The acquisition of reliable and extensive intelligence data proved to be a formidable task. A vital responsibility, therefore, fell on the crews of the high-flying, camera-equipped German He-IIIs, Do-215-B2s and Ju-88Bs which began their reconnaissance 'over-flights' into the Soviet Union. The German camera-planes were not the first which had prised Soviet secrets open in this manner; British aircraft* conducted an aerial monitoring of the Baku oilfields, whence fuel flowed to Germany under the terms of the German–Soviet agreements. In the course of 1941, the cameras furnished unique and invaluable stocks of information not only along the line of the Russian positions but within their depth also, from the Baltic to the Black Sea. Meanwhile, more orthodox methods contributed to swell the files of *Fremde Heere Ost*. This current survey of Soviet military power painted in the general outlines without any substantial elaboration. The absence of precise

* Paul Carell, *Hitler's War on Russia* (London 1964), p. 60 claims that the idea for the 'experiment with the U-2s' came from German success with Colonel Rowehl's secret aerial reconnaissance. Yet the Germans may have been prompted by earlier British success: in March 1940, a British Lockheed flying from Habbaniya photographed Baku and in April Batum (where the plane was fired on). These photographs, plus detailed interpretation were handed over to the French; undestroyed, they fell into German hands when Paris was occupied. The German command thus had some first-rate prompting in how to 'U-2'. See Constance Babington Smith, *Evidence in Camera* (London 1957), Chapter 6.

information on the composition of the Soviet armies was freely admitted; to date, the existence of eleven Soviet armies in the west could be confirmed after this fashion:

North Russia	3 armies (7th, 14th, 15th)
Baltic	3 armies (3rd, 8th, 11th)
Western MD	2 armies (4th, 10th)
Lemberg	1 army (6th)
North Bukovina	1 army (12th)
Bessarabia	1 army (5th)

The peacetime strength of the Red Army hovered about the two-million mark (giving 30 rifle corps and some 100 rifle divisions); with war and general mobilization, that figure would climb to 209 divisions:

107 rifle divisions	1st wave
77 rifle divisions	2nd wave
25 rifle divisions	3rd wave

The expanded wartime army, with support troops, would probably look like this:

Field army	approx.	4 million men
Rear services	„	0·6 million
Internal troops	„	1·6 million

Since the men mobilized in the Soviet Union in the autumn of 1939 still remained in the army, it would be safe to assume that some 121 rifle divisions were at the disposal of the Soviet command for deployment in the west.

The Soviet air force came under closer scrutiny in this report. After noting the apparent aerial colossus represented by 12,000–14,000 machines, the German analysts concluded that, due to losses in Finland and to general wastage, only 4,000 first-class machines were available, of which two-thirds were fighters (1–15 and 1–16), and that only 160 of the 1,100 airfields could be used for 'tactical purposes'. Inefficient ground-services and unsatisfactory intelligence-reconnaissance systems added greatly to general operational weakness. In general, the Soviet air force was inferior to the Luftwaffe. Of the new machines, the Germans had heard rumours of a new ground-attack plane, but lacked any precise details.

On 18 December 1940, when in Directive No. 21 Hitler unfolded the grand design of the campaign against the Soviet Union, the outlines of 'Otto' gave way to the definitiveness of 'Barbarossa'. Based on planning already far advanced, Directive No. 21 was no mere sketch or proposal, but nine pages of formulated intent. Like Tukhachevskii's war-game, the Pripet Marshes formed the division of the deployment, and, once more akin to Tukhachevskii's concepts, the main blow would be delivered *to the north* of the Pripet, with two army groups. After accomplishing the destruction of the Soviet troops fighting in the Baltic area (and having seized Kronstadt and Leningrad), then and only then would offensive operations be continued with a view to capturing Moscow. South of the Pripet, a third army group, aimed at Kiev, would drive into the flank and rear of the Soviet forces, destroying them west of the Dnieper; further to the south, German and Rumanian units would protect the main operational flank, advancing at the same time along the Black Sea coast and to the industrial concentrations of the Donets basin.

Keeping the plan secret, yet proceeding with the massive and involved preparations, placed a strain at the outset on German ingenuity. For the moment, only a minority in the command actually knew what was intended; the subsequent disclosure of the plan to other senior commanders went under the guise of mere precautionary thinking. The inevitable movement of German troops into Poland, a noticeable accretion in strength, proceeded under an elaborate deception plan. Already on 19 December, Halder, who later confessed himself no champion of the campaign in the east, noted crossly that the *Aufmarsch*, the initial concentration and deployment, would suffer from the slowness of the railways. Divisions in the west, and those at this juncture resting, frontier defence units, Panzer division and Luftwaffe formations, carefully but deliberately, in a massive war-train in its final assembly, all were steadily alerted for and moved in the direction of their new assignments in the east.

In the last days of 1940, the Soviet Defence Commissar, Marshal Timoshenko, worked on the preparation of the two-party war-game which was to take place in the Defence Commissariat early in January 1941. The exercise, in which members of the Politburo showed uncommon interest, aimed at testing Soviet ideas about the conduct of large-scale strategic operations (offensive and defensive), examining some potential theatres of operations, exposing the senior command to further probing into their capabilities, and attaining that 'unified view' on the mass employment of armour, artillery and aviation in modern offensive operations. While Halder and his officers conferred over the details of *Aufmarsch Ost*, the Soviet command laboured on the drafting of its directives – *Order No. 30* on troop training and a Defence Commissariat instruction on officer training, 'operational training'.

In a little more than twenty weeks, the word 'operational' was ripped ferociously, and for many fatally, out of its training context.

2

'Don't Panic. The "Boss" Knows All About It'

When the first stage of the December study-session finished, the corps and divisional commanders returned to their units, but army commanders and Military District staffs remained in Moscow to pursue the second part of these studies, the war-games which were to begin on 8 January 1941, and which Marshal Timoshenko proposed to direct in person. These 'operational-strategic games' played out on maps were concerned with two possible theatres, the Western and South-Western, and the participants changed their roles in the various phases of the game: in the first game the Western Front (The 'Eastern party') was commanded by Pavlov and Klimovskikh, opposed by Zhukov and Kuznetsov (Baltic district commander). In the next game, these men changed sides: Zhukov commanded the 'Eastern party' for the South-Western Front, Pavlov the 'Western party' in that theatre. The games went on without sense of great pressure; the parties and their staffs had ample time in which to make decisions and to work on their documents, both sides concentrated on offensive operations in depth to deal a decisive blow at the main 'enemy' forces. Each front had 50–80 divisions at its disposal, deployed over a wide area from East Prussia to the Pripet Marshes, with only marginal superiority on the part of the 'enemy' (10–15 divisions). But neither party had a powerful second echelon or reserves; it was assumed that operations would be conducted with a single echelon and that superiority 'along the line of the main blow' would be attained by stripping so-called 'passive sectors'.

Stalin himself had not appeared at the sessions of the study-conference, but the analysis of the war-games he evidently decided to make something of an occasion. Only Zhdanov had followed all the previous sessions, intently and purposefully. As the senior officers made preparations to leave Moscow, their orders were suddenly changed and all, the Defence Commissar, his deputies, the Chief of the General Staff, commanders of arms, commanders of military districts, members of the Politburo and Stalin's henchmen in the administration were summoned to the Kremlin at noon on 13 January. The change of plan involved General K.A. Meretskov in a clumsy fiasco, for he had had no time in which to digest the results of the war-games so that he had to speak from memory, blundering and digressing to the overt dissatisfaction of Stalin and the assembled Politburo. An unnerved Meretskov, never incidentally noted for his coolness, came face to face with the displeasure of Stalin and the scorn of Mekhlis. Meretskov began by referring to the conclusions about the revised *Field Service Regulations*:

In working out the *Ustav* [regulations] we have been proceeding from the fact that our division is appreciably more powerful than those of the German-Fascist Army and that in a meeting engagement it would undoubtedly smash up a German division. In defence also one of our divisions could handle the assaults of two-three enemy divisions. In the offensive one and a half of our divisions overwhelmed the defences of any enemy division.

Passing to the war-games somewhat abruptly, Meretskov announced 'results': the 'Eastern', Red party with 60–65 divisions overwhelmed the 'Western' party defending with 55 divisions. At this point, Stalin put a question: what about superiority of forces? Meretskov explained: 'Without a general superiority in forces, the commander of the Western Front was able to take troops from the passive sectors and use them in the assault formations. This established local superiority, which secured the success of the offensive operation.' Stalin took the greatest exception to this, pointing out that 'in these days of mechanized and motorized armies, local superiority does not guarantee success in the offensive'; rapid manoeuvre and regrouping could put paid to this superiority in a very short time. In desperation, Meretskov turned to the South-Western Front war-game, but here he was brought up sharply by the question: 'Who won here?' Meretskov tried to hedge, but was reminded that the members of the Politburo wanted a definite answer. He could give none, and the report fizzled out, whereupon Stalin summed up:

Perhaps the *Ustav* do state with a certain propagandistic emphasis that one of our divisions in a meeting engagement can deal with one division of the German-Fascist forces, and that in the offensive one and a half of our divisions can break through the defence of one of their divisions, but among this group of people assembled here, within the circle of present Front and army commanders we have got to discuss practical possibilities.

At this, the floor was thrown open to discussion, an occasion seized at once by the aviation commanders to criticize the shortcomings in the structure of their forces and the training of their personnel. Much of this was brushed aside, and the heroes of the Spanish Civil War were somewhat trampled, but a first-class row burst out when Marshal Kulik took the floor to argue for the establishment of the 18,000-man division with horse-drawn transport – the complete reversal of the 'mechanized army'. Tanks and motorization simply did not enter into Kulik's calculations. Fedorenko, chief of the Armoured Forces Administration now that Pavlov was in command of the Western military district, had already put his plea for more modern tanks, which the Red Army currently lacked: the decision to increase the production of the new KV and T-34s should be taken without further delay. If this meant exceeding what had been allocated in the defence budget, Fedorenko suggested that this could be overcome by adjustment in other arms, particularly artillery production. This brought Kulik to his feet: 'The artillery will shoot all your tanks to pieces. Why produce them?' This failed to silence Fedorenko, who pointed out that the tank also had a gun and could engage artillery – in fact, it was a superior weapon, being mobile and having not only a large-calibre gun but also machine-guns. 'In mobile war, the tank is the more powerful weapon.' Kulik flatly rejected Fedorenko's idea of any cut at the expense of the artillery: not for nothing did someone in the hall let slip the punning proverb, 'Each snipe [kulik as an ordinary noun also means snipe] praises its own marsh.'

Kulik's remarks created a minor sensation, and he was therefore asked a straight question: how many mechanized (or tank) corps does the Red Army need? Kulik, quite unable to answer positively, hedged by saying that this depended on how much industry could produce, whereupon Stalin rounded on him and told him it was none of his business to argue about production potential. When Kulik failed to answer a second time, Stalin turned on Timoshenko: 'Comrade Timoshenko, as long as the army is so vague in its views on mechanization and motorization, you will never get any mechanization and motorization.' Timoshenko protested that – Kulik apart – there was unanimity of opinion about the need to mechanize, and by simply reckoning up what district commanders had asked for, this was plain: Kirponos asked for one or two mechanized corps, Kuznetsov for two or three, Pavlov for three or four, Zhukov for four or five, Cherevichenko (Odessa) for a couple, and Apanasenko (central Asia) for one.

Stalin had already intervened once to terminate the discussion about resources; in his view the Soviet armed forces were developing 'harmonically', and any dispute about resources amounted to much 'empty talk', the allocations for weapons corresponding to specific proportions and 'to the harmonic development of the armed forces'. Nevertheless, Stalin dealt with Kulik's remarks on the structure of the rifle division a little more fully, comparing his attitude to mechanization with that of the opponents of the collectivization and mechanization of agriculture:

Kulik defends the massed 18,000-man division with horse-drawn transport, he has spoken against the mechanization of the army. The government is pressing on with the mechanization of the army, it is bringing the motor to the army, but Kulik is against the motor. This is just about the same as if he had spoken against the tractor and the combined harvester, defending the wooden plough and the economic independence of the village. If the government adopted Kulik's position, I should say that in the years of the collectivization of agriculture we should have stayed with the single operators and with the wooden plough.

Progressive though Stalin sounded, some officers had certain if secret reservations, mainly because of the well-known 'tug-of-war' between 'the government'

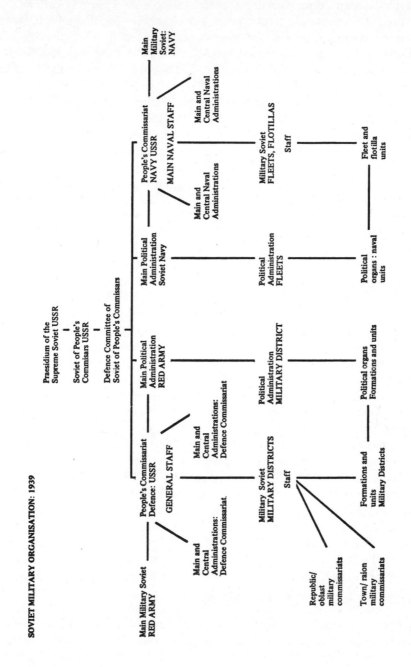

SOVIET MILITARY ORGANISATION: 1939

Praesidium of the Supreme Soviet USSR

Soviet of People's Commissars USSR

Defence Committee of Soviet of People's Commissars

People's Commissariat Defence: USSR

GENERAL STAFF

Main Military Soviet RED ARMY

Main and Central Administrations: Defence Commissariat

Main and Central Administrations: Defence Commissariat

Military Soviet MILITARY DISTRICTS

Staff

Republic/oblast military commissariats

Town/raion military commissariats

Formations and units Military Districts

Main Political Administration RED ARMY

Political Administration MILITARY DISTRICT

Political organs Formations and units

People's Commissariat NAVY USSR

MAIN NAVAL STAFF

Main and Central Naval Administrations

Main and Central Naval Administrations

Military Soviet FLEETS, FLOTILLAS

Staff

Fleet and flotilla units

Main Political Administration Soviet Navy

Political Administration FLEETS

Political organs : naval units

Main Military Soviet: NAVY

and the Defence Commissariat over mechanization. And Stalin himself had also participated in the session of the *Glavnyi Voennyi Soviet*, a similar meeting, which on 21 November 1939 decided to disband all the tanks corps as rapidly as possible. Stalin was also directly responsible for promoting men like Kulik to very senior posts. One officer at least felt that Stalin here was almost defending himself.

In his summing-up, Stalin stressed that 'modern war will be a war of engines'; a future war might well be on two fronts, in the west with Nazi Germany, in the east against imperialist Japan. That governed the disposition of Soviet forces. He made no statement, however, about the imminence (or lack of it) of any future war – merely repeating that a future war would be highly mobile in nature. As for the rifle divisions, Stalin suggested cutting their 'tail' and increasing their mobility; in the future war of mass armies, then a superiority of at least two or three to one must be attained over a potential enemy. And with these mass armies, fully fitted out with automatic weapons and a wide range of equipment, particular attention would have to be paid to their supply requirements: supplies in the widest sense 'must flow to the front from all parts of our country'. Stocks of food should be laid in, and here Stalin referred to the 'wise decision' of the tsarist government which stockpiled rusks. About these Stalin waxed almost lyrical – they were light, they kept for long periods; 'A sip of tea and a rusk,' he said, 'and you've got a hot meal.' On this note, all the way from armoured fighting vehicles to crusts of bread, the Kremlin conference drew to a close, but not before Molotov fired off his stinging rebuke to the commanders of the military districts that they did not know their tasks in the event of war. This was a shot which went wide of the mark, for without a coherent war plan these 'tasks' were inevitably a mystery to the officers concerned and no such plan existed.

The meeting broke up in some confusion. Most of the officers were depressed at the prospect for rapid mechanization in the light of Kulik's sallies. The officers of the General Staff were mortified at the shambles of Meretskov's report on the war-games; the Operations Section had carefully prepared all the material and Lieutenant-General Vatutin, assisted by Vasilevskii and Anisov, had done a thorough job for the report. What had been very striking was the treatment of Marshal Shaposhnikov, who sat silent and depressed during these sessions. He looked only in the direction of his immediate neighbours or stared straight ahead at the row of Politburo members, only his expression and a slight shaking of the head marking his dissatisfaction with and agitation at the turn of the discussion.

There were, however, further repercussions which hit the senior officers straight away. Stalin had already decided to regroup the district commands, but first he replaced Meretskov by Zhukov as Chief of the General Staff. Meretskov was posted as chief of the Military Training Administration, while Kirponos (who had held Meretskov's previous command in Leningrad) went to Kiev, now vacated by Zhukov. To replace Kirponos, Lieutenant-General M.M. Popov received orders to turn over his command of the 1st Special Red Banner Army in the Far East and move westwards; Lieutenant-General P.A. Kurochkin was selected as the new commander of the Trans-Baikal Military District now that Koniev was being transferred from that command to take over the North Caucasus. Koniev and Yeremenko came to be involved in rather a complicated cross-posting, which indicated that though certain moves had been contemplated, nothing quite as drastic as this total reshuffle had been planned; on the eve of the study-conference, Yeremenko had been told that he would be going eventually to the North Caucasus, but on 9 January he discovered that his destination was now the Far East, where he would take command of the 1st Special Red Banner Army, which was about to be converted into a 'Front'. After an interview on 15 January with Timoshenko, Yeremenko made his final preparations for departure.

Yeremenko acquired a new staff, among them Lieutenant-General I.V. Smorodinov, so very recently Deputy Chief of the General Staff; like Meretskov, he had been displaced, and Zhukov turned to an old friend, Sokolovskii, for his deputy at the General Staff. Colonel N.A. Lomov travelled out as the Chief of the Operations Section of the staff of the embryonic 'Far Eastern Front'. The fortunes of Colonel-General Shtern, Marshal Blyukher's successor in the Far East, were on the wane, disastrously so, as his eventual disappearance proved. Thus transplanting a 'little general staff' in the Far East failed to bring Yeremenko any great measure of comfort. He bumped up against the barrier separating the 'General Staff officers' from the field commanders; nor did his visit to the General Staff help to quieten his misgivings. The General Staff accorded him a reception, when he came to talk over problems of operational planning, which was markedly cool and completely unsatisfactory from the operational point of view. Yeremenko failed to receive any answer to his question – relevant enough – about the role of the 1st Special Red Banner Army in the event of war: would it fight offensively or defensively? Such highly secret information, he was given to understand, could scarcely be imparted to a formation commander.

The Soviet forces in the Far East had received no small amount of attention, even as the Red Army dashed into the Baltic republic and the Rumanian provinces in the summer of 1940. On 9 June 1940 the Soviet Union and Japan officially terminated the trouble which produced large-scale military operations on the Manchurian–Outer-Mongolian borders; this, fought in the summer of 1939 on the Khalkin-Gol, was the biggest and bloodiest of the 'incidents' which flourished at a variety of locations along the vast frontier which Japan and the Soviet Union shared. After the Japanese investment of Manchuria, and up to 1935, Soviet strength in the Far East tripled; from the six rifle divisions in 1931, the Soviet command could count on some twenty rifle divisions (with over a thousand tanks and a similar number of aircraft) by 1936. The Khalkin-Gol fighting produced an inevitable build-up in Soviet divisions, and this 1939 peak lasted until the spring of 1941. At the same time, command and deployment underwent marked changes. As far back as 1935, the Special Far Eastern Army (ODVA), the massive military command ruled by Marshal Blyukher, had lost its westerly elements with the creation of the Trans-Baikal Military District. That innovation had both military and political overtones; if the Red Army adopted an offensive plan in the Far East, the Trans-Baikal forces could be used to mount mobile operations directed against the Japanese rear in Manchuria, and at the same time it prevented Blyukher's forces growing too large in what was the only independent military concentration in the Soviet Union. In 1938, with the conclusion of the lake Khasan (Changkufeng) fighting against the Japanese and with the murder of Blyukher, Stalin abolished the Special Far Eastern Army, which had hitherto controlled both the Amur and the Ussuri areas. In its place two armies were established, the 1st Special Red Banner (responsible for the Ussuri area and with its HQ at Voroshilov), and the 2nd Red Banner Army (responsible for the Amur area and with its HQ at Kuibyshevka). Both armies were directly subordinated to the Defence Commissariat, which now held all three Far Eastern commands in a tight grip. In Outer Mongolia, the administration of the 57th Rifle Corps moved in, while the 36th Motorized Rifle Division moved up from Chita to Ulan-Ude. During the Khalkin-Gol fighting, in the summer of 1939, the Far Eastern armies coalesced – temporarily – into a Front (under Shtern), bringing the Amur and Ussuri regions under one command. When the fighting died away, the Front disappeared, to be replaced by an area headquarters at Khabarovsk, a 'co-ordinating command' for the Amur and Ussuri regions. On 10 July 1940 the decision to raise the 16th Army in the Trans-Baikal Military District went into effect. Lieutenant-General M.F. Lukin, Chief of Staff of the West Siberian Military District, took command of this new formation, which was given three days in which to form up, in an area of some 19,000 square kilometres. To the south, the 57th Rifle Corps in Outer Mongolia became the 17th Army, and as such, was also subordinated to the Trans-Baikal Military District.

Lukin, apart from a brief absence to attend the December study-conference, worked hard to push his force into shape; the presence of Major-General I.P. Alekseyenko's 5th Tank Corps (subsequently converted into a mechanized corps, with the 13th and 17th Tank Divisions, plus the 109th Motorized Rifle Division) with 300 tanks testified that this was no paper army. Yeremenko, who arrived in Voroshilov at 8 o'clock on the evening of 4 February 1941, found less cause for satisfaction; a meeting with his divisional and arms commanders on 6 February revealed all manner of shortcomings in training and in discipline. What Yeremenko had inherited was a bloated and inefficient organization, an army stretched out over a virtual Soviet 'front', reaching all the way from Khabarovsk to Vladivostok. Five weeks later (18 March), the 25th Army was carved out of the 1st Red Banner, a rationalization which Yeremenko welcomed in spite of its tardinesss; no longer did he assume responsibility for the entire length of this vast sector, as the 25th Army took station on his left. Some eight months previously, the 2nd Red Banner Army had undergone a reorganization of this kind, when the 15th Army took over its left sector in the Amur area. Finally, Lieutenant-General P.A. Kurochkin arrived in Chita, as Koniev moved to his new command in the Northern Caucasus.

In the first weeks of 1941, however, in the Red Army as a whole, no change in momentum could be detected as these scurryings within the command continued. The training plan, issued five days after Stalin's address to the commanders, made absolutely no mention of the likelihood of war. Stalin himself had made only the vaguest reference to such an eventuality. Mikoyan and Schnurre had signed, on 10 January, an economic agreement regulating 'reciprocal deliveries' – Soviet raw materials, German machines – in 'the second treaty period'. A week later, Molotov used this agreement, with its hint of amicability, to suggest to the German ambassador in Moscow, Count von Schulenburg, that the time had come 'to turn to purely political issues again'. In a ponderous thrust, Molotov reminded the ambassador that Moscow still waited for a reply to its 'statement of position', the same 'statement' delivered with such obdurate and persistent bluntness by Molotov himself during the November conversations in Berlin. Turning to the most recent events, Molotov, inquiring exactly as the Soviet ambassador Dekanozov was doing in Berlin, asked about the significance of German movements in the Balkans. Molotov now insisted that 'Bulgaria and the Straits', which he listed together with Greece as possible German objectives, constituted a 'security zone of the USSR'. The Soviet ambassador in Berlin received a reply to his representations on 22 January; von Schulenburg, on the 23rd, delivered the same reply to Molotov in Moscow. Berlin, now heavily entrenched in Rumania and with Bulgaria within its grasp, brushed the Soviet objections aside; German military concentrations in the Balkans were aimed at the British, and, so ran the insolent German phrases, to forestall the British would serve Russian as well as German interests. Molotov, who had shown himself to be not over-impressed with the wordy lunges of Hitler and Ribbentrop, mentioned in his reply the need to study the situation: thereafter, he would 'take a stand, if necessary'. That plaintive conditional made it plain that no decision of any kind had as yet been taken; the import of German encroachment on his own preserves Stalin failed, or refused to discern.

The German attack on Greece (Operation 'Marita'), mounted from bases in Rumania and Bulgaria, had been decided upon by Hitler and his commanders in November 1940. British victories in Libya early in 1941 necessitated further German military interventions in support of the Italians, so that Operation 'Sonnenblume', a revised version of the original scheme to reinforce the Italians in North Africa, assumed immediate significance. The prospect of British success being used to strengthen the Greeks necessitated modifications to Marita, including detaining formations originally intended for the campaign against the Soviet

Union. For its success, Marita depended on agreement with Bulgaria over German bases and passage for German troops; while the movement of German troops into Rumania evoked Russian suspicions, the approach to Bulgaria brought downright Russian opposition. Hitler rolled across this, flattening the Soviet objection. He had cause enough to argue basic Soviet compliance; although the Soviet Union had fulfilled its obligations under the trade agreements concluded in 1939 and 1940, Germany, committed to satisfy Soviet requirements, had failed to do so. German arrears grew in size. If in November 1940 political co-operation between Germany and the Soviet Union seemed to be on the verge of collapse, the same held for economic relations. Yet Stalin chose the beginning of 1941 to make a gesture of conciliation, if not of actual appeasement in the January trade-agreement; German arrears were abuptly halved (in monetary terms) by Soviet compensation for a strip of Lithuanian territory acquired from the Germans. Soviet deliveries to Germany, that 'substantial prop to the German war economy' as Schnurre himself described them, although virtually halted at the end of 1940, began to flow once more – the indispensable grain and petroleum. That the January agreement marked a particular Russian initiative is emphasized by Molotov's reference to it and his remark that political issues could be discussed *again*. On the one hand, Stalin indicated resistance, and on the other, he indicated compliance and concession. In all previous Nazi-Soviet dealings, the trade lever had been used to force the political door. Stalin appeared to be trying a repetition of this hitherto successful technique. His concessions at the moment were real enough, the resistance vague or formal. It was the latter, however, upon which Hitler battened; Stalin's perfidy the Führer proclaimed with passion, denouncing him, ironically enough, as a 'cold-blooded blackmailer', at the Naval Conference of 8 January.

Obviously suspicious of German moves in the Balkans, Stalin, through Molotov, put the best possible construction upon them. Yet news of 'Barbarossa', passed through a route at first devious and then circuitous, was by January 1941 on its way to him. Since August 1940, very soon after the inception of the first plans for operations against the Soviet Union, the American commercial attaché in Berlin, Sam E. Woods, had been the recipient of the confidences of an anti-Nazi official privy to the inner secrets of the German military. Woods also learned of the German plans for tearing the Soviet Union to pieces in search of economic loot. The incongruity of such explosive military and political intelligence falling into the hands of a commercial attaché, and Woods in particular, led inevitably to scepticism and downright disbelief. Woods dispatched his news, loaded with the details of the German attack plans, to Washington early in January 1941; alert to the possibilities of German 'dis-information' Cordell Hull embarked on a lengthy evaluation of Woods' report, which finally emerged from the hands of the FBI fully vindicated as to authenticity. In due course, the State Department made all this known to the Russians, the first recorded case of the acquisition of reliable information on German intentions in the east.

Not that Stalin lacked the services of an intelligence community in Berlin or further afield; in one sense, it was difficult to see where 'diplomacy' left off and 'intelligence' began, and nowhere was this truer than with respect to personnel. Ambassador Dekanozov (quite recently arrived in Berlin) and Counsellor Kobulov of the Soviet embassy in Berlin were, in the literal sense, lieutenants of the reptilian Beria, the Georgian who succeeded Yezhov (himself a victim of the massive purge which he had done most to implement) as head of the NKVD. Dekanozov had worked before his plunge into 'diplomacy' as chief of the Information Department of the NKVD. Like Beria, like Stalin, Dekanozov was a Georgian. So was Kobulov. This was no innovation; Stalin had long shown a preference for conducting his private diplomatic ventures with Georgian special agents. Kobulov, assisted by the 'press men' of the Soviet news-agency TASS, set about building up an active espionage network, reaching into Poland and Czechoslovakia. These operations came under the aegis of a leading echelon of the NKVD, with the status of a Main Administration, in this case, State Security: *Glavnoe Upravlenie Gosudarstvennoi Bezopasnosti GUGBEZ.* At the end of January 1941, presumably as a measure of further centralization in the intelligence services, the NKVD (under Beria) was separated from these agencies, which emerged as a separate entity, the NKGB (People's Commissariat for State Security) under V.N. Merkulov. 'Military intelligence', the GRU (Main Intelligence Administration: *Glavnoe Razvedyvatel 'noe Upravlenie*), charged also with the external intelligence operations and included in the General Staff organization, had suffered severely from Stalin's purge. Nevertheless, it continued to operate a network of external agents, in addition to the more 'normal' channels of attachés and evaluators, among whom was no less a person than Richard Sorge. The information obtained by these two main intelligence agencies, the external arm of the security services (NKVD) and the foreign operations of the General Staff GRU, passed finally to the massive Central Information Department, under the direct control of the Politburo, but even more specifically fused into the secret secretariat which served Stalin alone. The stream of information which flowed in from a multitude of sources Stalin could dam, divert or choke as he pleased; what he wished hidden, he could and did, in the phrase of present Soviet criticism, 'wall up in a safe'. Before many weeks were out, the safes began to bulge.

In February 1941, at the Eighteenth Party Conference, Malenkov proceeded with a wearying verbal thoroughness to denounce the bureaucratism and inefficiency of Soviet industry as a whole. It was not enough to pass resolutions: the decision had to be taken to act upon them. The Stalinist system, however, was hardly conducive to the operation of any initiative, or the assumption of authority by any but the foolhardy. The Conference, in its dutiful way, while emphasizing that the defence industries were developing faster than the industrial sector in its entirety, pointed to the shortcomings in the production of raw materials, fuel, instruments; the Party pledged itself to eliminate 'loafing', and while assimilating the results of economic activity in 1940, adopted the new assignments for 1941 (to raise pig-iron production to 18 million tons, steel to over 22 million tons, rolled metal to over 15 million tons). This more intensive industrial effort dated back to the autumn of 1940, when stricter labour regulations and longer working hours had been decreed – hence the conference's war on 'loafing'. In the spring of 1940, a much needed 'rationalization' of industry had been attempted with the introduction of the six Economic Soviets, one of which was for the consolidated organization of war industry and run by Voznesenskii, who introduced the report on the 1941 economic plan at the Party Conference. The talk, and indeed the semblance of action, centred on a much publicized 'mobilizational preparedness', yet at the December military conference, the commanders kept asking for their new tanks and aircraft.

Since the beginning of the war in Europe, greater attention had been paid by Soviet administrators to the state of Soviet stockpiles, to the 'state reserves' of fuel, food and strategic raw materials, the object of special decrees on 'mobilization reserves' formulated in August 1940 (and repeated in June 1941). The 'state reserves' were designed to facilitate the transition to a war economy in industry and transportation by stockpiling fuel and raw materials; the 'mobilization reserves' covered stocks of strategic raw materials, not least non-ferrous and rare metals – copper, zinc, lead, cobalt, ferro-wolfram and ferro-molybdium, and cadmium. Stocks of ferrous metals, petroleum and coal grew by the year. A four- to six-month supply of foodstuffs secured the Red Army its nourishment: general food stocks totalled 6,162,000 tons on 1 January 1941.

For a full decade or more, under the gigantic banner of the Five Year Plans, the Soviet Union had been preparing for total war. The Soviet armed forces had had first call on the resources and the capacities of the state; the 'primacy of heavy industry' became a policy precept and a practical implementation of autarky which could never be challenged. The establishment of a Soviet industrial base, was, demonstrably, an achievement of formidable dimensions: the metallurgical plants at Magnitogorsk, Kuznetsk and Novo-Tagil, the Chelyabinsk and Novosibirsk factories, the eastern coalfields (Kuznetsk and the Karaganda, plus the opening up of the Pechora fields), the Baku oilfields and the 'second Baku' (the Urals-Volga district), seventy chemical plants since 1930, the Volkhov and Dniepropetrovsk aluminium works (and the initial exploitation of the Urals mineral supplies), plus the expansion of the industrial facilities of the north-west, the Moscow region and the mineral-loaded southern regions, such as the Donbas. Slowly the figures of the relationship of the output of the eastern regions, the Urals and beyond, compared with that of western and more vulnerable plants, mines and factories, began to climb, but only slowly; in 1940, the Donbas produced 94·3 million tons of coal, the Urals 12 million and the Karaganda fields 6·3 million. Dispersal aside, the grievous weak spot remained transportation, a theme which Malenkov had laboured at the recent Party conference. The expanding east needed extensive investment in new railway lines: Novosibirsk-Leninsk-Kuznetsk, double tracking at Magnitogorsk-Chelyabinsk-Orsk. The construction of the Turkestan-Siberian track aimed to link two treasure houses, Siberia and Central Asia. At the same time, however, the newly acquired territories in the west, in the western Ukraine, and in the Baltic area, demanded much improvement to their rail facilities. This clearly impeded Soviet deployment, if nothing else; the railway lines leading up to the Soviet frontier from East Prussia could take 228 trains per day, but the Lithuanian railway facilities (now controlled by the Russians) which ran up to the German frontier would accommodate only 84 trains. Elsewhere, as in the Urals or Siberia, with a less immediate military relevance, the lack of correspondence between network capacity and traffic did nevertheless represent a real loss, one which Soviet planners hoped to eliminate by technical improvements to track and traffic handling.

Soviet industry had not, to all intents and purposes, been strategically dispersed to the east; the Leningrad, Moscow and Ukrainian industrial regions embodied a vital, not to say overwhelming element of Soviet industrial power, any threat to which could only have the most dire consequences. Considerations such as these evidently played a significant part in the 1940 discussions on 'mobilizational reserves', which took a somewhat critical turn. According to General Khrulev, Stalin refused to entertain any ideas or proposals put forward by the heads of production agencies and by the General Staff that these same 'mobilizational reserves' should be stockpiled behind the Volga, far beyond the reaches of any invader. This Stalin refused absolutely to countenance; on the contrary, the reserves were left intact far to the west of the Volga or actually moved forward into the very vulnerable western frontier districts. Although the final responsibility is laid at Stalin's door, General Khrulev singles out Lev Mekhlis for specific criticism in urging this disposition upon Stalin. The reference to the 'General Staff' makes it likely that this whole subject was discussed by Shaposhnikov, whose recommendations were for a more rational defence deployment based fundamentally on the old pre-1939 frontier lines. Although Stalin has served as an immensely convenient scapegoat in Soviet discussions of the 1941 disasters, there can be little doubt that the most serious charge (and the one most difficult to probe) concerns his overruling of 'expert military opinion' in matters of military preparation and deployment. Here, for once, yet documented so thinly that Soviet commentators still complain, is a specific case; the weight of expert opinion, military and military-industrial, lay with strategic dispersal eastwards. Quite the opposite went into effect, with no evidence of any contingency planning in the event of the western areas being attacked or disrupted. Once the decision was taken, presumably in the summer of 1940, to do almost the opposite of what Marshal Shaposhnikov suggested, to adopt a 'forward strategy' even in the face of the manifest deficiencies of the frontier areas in transportation, communications and military facilities, and to advance the Red Army which lacked any proper rear organization, much of the Soviet Union's security had been put in jeopardy. Ironically enough, Marshal Shaposhnikov late in 1940 was made responsible, as head of the defence construction administration, for the fortification of those lines which he had earlier pronounced as the least suitable for Soviet defensive purposes. The Red Army would have to stand and fight on a line of nothing more than un-completed battalion positions.

In the early spring of 1941, as the re-equipping of the Soviet armed forces entered its supposedly intensive stage, the industrial effort and attempted co-ordination acquired considerable significance. First, ammunition: at this time, Soviet industry was already working on the ammunition requirements laid down by the plan for the 1941 period, although even now industry had been unable to satisfy the full military demand; the ammunition plan, adopted at the beginning of 1941, established the requirements for the *second half* of 1941 and for 1942. In July 1941, as a critical ammunition shortage afflicted the Red Army, the figures underwent drastic revision; the planned figure (for artillery ammunition) in the first half of 1941 must have been in the region of some 14 million rounds, since in the second half of 1941 26 million rounds were pro-duced (only slightly more than half of the new production target but twice the total for the first six months of 1941). Infantry ammunition was produced in 14 factories, but the greatest arsenal was the Tula works, south of Moscow; artillery ammunition came from an estimated 50 plants (17 of which were in Leningrad), and German intelligence assumed that the production of light and medium artillery ammunition amounted to some 4½ million rounds per month. Soviet gun barrels rolled out of plants in Dniepropetrovsk, Mariupol and Kolomna.

In March, the second stage of the formation of the Red Army's mechanized corps began; in 1940, only a small number of the new T-34 and KV tanks had been produced (115 and 243 respectively), but now serial production was organized. In the first six months of 1941, over 1,000 T-34s were produced and 393 KV tanks. Unfortunately, no attempt was made to form up the new machines into proper units; instead of equipping the mechanized formations in systematic fashion, the new tanks merely dribbled into the armoured units, from which old equipment was meanwhile being withdrawn. In this way, there were armoured formations with few or even no tanks in their component units, while the same units were manned to an increasing extent by recruits called up under the spring draft, or by junior commanders brought in from the infantry and the cavalry. Major-General Rokossovskii, commander of the 9th Mechanized Corps (Kiev Special Military District), made this point un-mistakably plain in his report on the 1940–1 training programme; junior officers who had had only February and March in which to learn their new duties could hardly be called trained. Throughout the Soviet armoured forces, tank-drivers obtained little more than, on average, an hour's practice with their machines, many of which urgently needed repair; almost one-third (29 per cent) needed major overhaul and almost half (44 per cent) required sizeable refit. But there were no reserves of spare parts or concentration of repair facilities. Armoured fighting vehicles apart, the situation with motor-transport was hardly less serious; tractors, lorries and motor-cycles were in grievous short supply. The organic artillery units, if they had guns, faced a critical shortage in their ammunition stocks, especially for the 45-mm anti-tank guns (the Leningrad, Baltic and Odessa Military Districts had practically none, and only the 4th and 8th Mechanized Corps of the Kiev district had supplies). Only one-tenth of the necessary 76-mm ammunition had been supplied, and the new tanks, with their 76-mm and 152-mm guns, stood with empty magazines. Radio sets were in equally short supply. In sum, the score or so of mechanized corps in the late spring of 1941 were, from an operational point of view, in a deplorable condition. On average, and including the older tanks, they had some 50 per cent of their complement of armoured vehicles: several, the 13th, 17th, 20th and 24th corps, by virtue of their lack of tanks, could not be called mechanized formations in any effective sense of the word. The eight mechanized corps re-formed in the autumn of 1940 were still not complete; the new ones were in an even more parlous state. Owing to the shortage of trained officers, four of the new corps, the 15th, 16th, 19th and 22nd, could not form operations and intelligence sections of their staffs. The revised establishment for the mechanized corps now envisaged not less than 1,003 tanks (as opposed to 500 for the earlier formations); what the formations received, split up among more than a dozen of them, was 508 KV tanks and 967 T-34s by June 1941, trickling in among the BTs and the T-26s.

In January, in front of the Politburo, Fedorenko had fought the big battle for more tanks – and lost. Marshal Kulik saw to that, while he supervised, together with Mekhlis and Shchadenko, the general re-equipment programmes: it was (by current Soviet condemnation) this incompetent trio which cut back the old procurement programmes but failed to decide on the new. It was Kulik who appraised automatic infantry weapons as mere 'policeman's arms', who failed to authorize any procurement programme for the Red Army – and who later 'confessed' his blunder. Somewhat stranger is the case of the 76-mm field gun, which was taken completely out of production, in spite of its versatility; responsibility for that has been attributed variously to Stalin and to Kulik. B.L. Vannikov, the head of the armaments commissariat (*Narkomat Vooruzheniya*) before June 1941, is rather more specific: he ascribes the decision to cut back the production of anti-tank guns to Stalin, who had been advised to do this by Kulik and by Zhdanov. The cancellation of the anti-tank gun and ammunition programme is the more incomprehensible in the light of the decision to form High Command Artillery Reserve 'anti-tank brigades', composed of two regiments and equipped with 76-mm and 107-mm guns, 85-mm anti-aircraft guns and 37-mm anti-aircraft guns (the latter for the air-defence sections). Yet the production of anti-aircraft guns was already being curtailed, as was that of machine-guns. Soviet infantry weapons came from some thirty factories, the majority in central Russia; German intelligence put the production figures at the beginning of 1941 at 50,000 rifles and 6,000 machine-guns per month. The production of small calibre guns (anti-tank, anti-aircraft and tank guns) reached, in the same assessment, a monthly figure of 1,800 with 400 heavier anti-aircraft guns and howitzers per month. In fact, however, the Red Army in 1940 and in the first half of 1941 received less machine-guns than in 1939; even so, it possessed more machine-guns than the Wehrmacht, although it was impossible to match the Germans in machine-pistols.

That demonstrative pleading on the part of the air force officers in January before the Politburo had, however, produced some effect. On 25 February, the Central Committee approved the new plans, 'On the reorganization of the Red Army aviation forces', which aimed to establish a modernized force with the requisite support and servicing facilities. The aviation rear services would be organized henceforth on the territorial principle, and would consist of two basic types, regional aviation basing, and aerodrome service battalions. New aviation regiments would be formed, half to be equipped with new machines (although only nineteen existed by June); by that time, 1,946 MiG-3, LAGG-3 and Yak-1 fighters had gone to the first-line forces, 458 Pe-2 light bombers and 249 IL-2 ground-attack aircraft. The German estimate of the Soviet air force stressed its inferiorities in training and equipment to the Luftwaffe; tactical training, in particular, was out of date, reconnaissance and close-supprt aircraft were largely obsolete, ground facilities were not of the best (of 1,100 airfields, only 200 were operationally serviceable). Soviet aircraft were turned out in forty-six plants, with three of the main fuselage building factories in Moscow; aero-engines came from fifteen factories, although production was in fact concentrated in four main plants, Zaporozhe, Moscow, Rybinsk and Molotov (in the Urals).

Aircraft and aero-engine manufacture had been an object of Soviet attention since 1939, or more exactly, since the acceleration of 1937; new fuselage factories and engine plants were, however, specifically mentioned in the 1939 decrees and the fashion of creating more plants in the industry as a whole continued. Aero-engines, however, could not keep pace with the airframe plants, for which reason it was proposed to double engine production; at the same time, the rate of assembly for both engine and airframe production was stepped up, with new aggregated factories for weapons, radiators, carburettors, pumps and turbo-compressors being established. The immediate result was a 20 per cent increase in aircraft production (for 1939–40), although all in the older type of machine. In what was deliberate and planned dispersal, the new aircraft plants were sited mainly in the east, in Tashkent, in Irkutsk and Omsk, and further east in Novosibirsk and Komsomolsk; by 1941, these easterly factories accounted for more than half the production in the western areas, although the engine plants of the west still predominated in output and importance. No doubt by design, in the spring of 1941, even when the Soviet Union could no longer anticipate much in the way of technical assistance in aviation from Germany, a group of German experts were shown the eastern factories; back in Berlin, no one chose to believe their reports. Dispersed in the east, modernized in the west, Soviet aircraft plants now operated the flow system of production, which, with improved mechanization, increased output; above all, it laid the essential foundation for rapid wartime expansion.

Meanwhile, the Soviet parachute troops underwent a revival. The Red Army command, prompted largely by Tukhachevskii, had formed the first parachute brigade in any army. After the purges, however, the Parachute Troops Administration (*Upravlenie vozdushnodesantnykh voisk Krasnoi Armii*) under Gorbatov had been disbanded; now, in 1940–1, no doubt impressed by German successes with their parachute arm, the Soviet command reconstituted the Administration and formed out of the parachute brigades one or two corps, whose major strength, with transport aircraft, was concentrated in the Ukraine. The parachute corps consisted of three brigades and specialist units, the brigade of four battalions; the transport aircraft available were the TB-3, carrying a load of six tons, the Li-2 and the PS-84. Not that the parachute training of the new corps was far advanced; in the 4th Parachute Corps, only the men of the 9th Brigade had completed two umps, in the 8th just over half had completed one jump and in the 214th more than half had never jumped at all. Soviet parachute troops, however, had fought as ground infantry before now; at the Khalkin-Gol, in 1939, the 212th Parachute Brigade operated as ground infantry against the Japanese, and Soviet parachute troops would do so again after June, under Colonel Rodimtsev, with his 5th Parachute Brigade and his 1,700 paratroopers. For the moment, Soviet parachute formations came under the command of Major-General V.Ya. Glazunov, and his chief of staff, Major-General (Aviation) P.P. Ionov.

Late in March, German reconnaissance aircraft, loaded at this juncture with cameras and primed with film, began their systematic aerial survey of the frontier districts and middle interior of the Soviet Union. Little of this escaped Soviet attention; if they had not known before, the Soviet command could not ignore the evidence taken from a crashed German machine, which landed near Rovno on 15 April, carrying its camera and exposed film. Soviet anti-aircraft defences and fighter planes were, apparently on the direct order of Stalin, forbidden to open fire on the German intruders. Since the beginning of 1941, the air defence command had been overhauled; the territory of the Soviet Union was divided into air-defence (PVO) zones, the boundaries of which corresponded to those of the military districts, and the PVO zones were subdivided into districts. The zone controlled all the available means of anti-aircraft defence – fighters, anti-aircraft guns, the 'visual sighting and observation services' (VNOS), and barrage balloons; the fighter aviation came under the operation direction of the commander of the military district, but the general air defence was entrusted to the Red Army aviation command, the vvs. The system was cumbersome and, when put to the test, failed to work. Shortage of anti-aircraft guns for the defence of special objectives (such as naval bases) and the. lack of high-speed fighters made this inevitable, although a special fighter aviation corps was being assembled to cover Moscow. Soviet anti-aircraft strength was set by German intelligence in the spring of 1941 at 300 medium and 200 light (including machine-gun) anti-aircraft batteries.

The weapon procurement system, if it can be dignified with that name, was plainly disordered and disorganized. The arbitrary and ill-conceived decisions taken by Stalin and his advisers augmented the shortcomings which derived from industrial sluggishness and confusion. From Yeremenko's observations, it was clear that many senior commanders realized how far present preparations fell short of real operations requirements, most particularly in the field of armour. At the same time, this perceptiveness was relatively restricted, and none of the dissidents had the ear of Stalin. General Zhukov, in his Red Army Day address (23 February 1941), while repeating the formula about the 'mightiest army in the world', went on to enlarge about the work of reform and reorganization, the foundation of which had been laid in the 1940 restoration of 'unitary command'. Zhukov quoted the experience of the Khalkin-Gol and of Finland as proof that the Red Army had learned the necessary lessons by actual battle experience. The 'acid test' had been the war with Finland – how corrosive an experience that had been, in fact, Zhukov declined to point out. At this stage, a long-term transformation of the Soviet armed forces appeared to be the solution contemplated; what the short-term measures had brought so far consisted of little else but a limited rationalization of the Red Army, a formal acceptance of the requirements of modern war but no implementation of the needs of mobility and flexibility, and an arbitrary, often contradictory order of priorities. Nor, apart from stubborn flying in the face of facts, was there any proof in the early spring of 1941 that the Soviet Union would enjoy an extended breathing-space to accomplish long-term designs. Quite the contrary: German encroachment in the Balkans, with German troops by early March in Hungary, Bulgaria and Rumania, replaced the probable by the inevitable, the open collision of German and Soviet interests.

In the circumstances, it was hardly surprising that German military intelligence displayed an early interest in Soviet military preparations. While all previous studies of the Soviet Union were being conned and combed, the high-flying reconnaissance aircraft were filling the gaps with their photographs. In the very early weeks of 1941, there was little enough to be observed, although in February there were signs of increased activity. The *Angaben über die Roten Armee* (15.1.1941) set Red Army strength at 20 armies, 30 rifle corps, 150 rifle divisions (of which 15 were motorized) and 6 mechanized corps. The supplement, dated 6 February 1941, to the January study *Die Kriegswehrmacht der*

UdSSR pointed to the Soviet preoccupation with their newly acquired air and naval bases in the Baltic area, and emphasized the presence of strong Soviet forces to the west of the river Dvina; in the event of an unfavourable outcome to meeting a German attack here, then the Russians would be obliged to halt the attack on the line of the Dvina. Not much could be gleaned from Timoshenko's order of the day (22 February), issued to commemorate the anniversary of the creation of the Red Army; it merely exhorted officers and men to maintain their vigilence and alertness to deal with any 'incidents' which foreign conspiracy might hold in store for the Soviet Union.

German intelligence was correct in emphasizing the intensity of Soviet effort in the Baltic area. Although no definite Soviet 'plan' existed at this stage, and certainly the *Defence Plan for the State frontiers 1941* had not yet been drafted, orders had gone out to Colonel-General Kuznetsov, commander of the Baltic Special Military District, to concentrate on 'defence construction' and he was further informed that this was his most important assignment for 1941, for the completion of which he would be held personally responsible. The assumption shared by most of the General Staff was that any major German attack, which might take the form of a surprise blow, would come from East Prussia, for which reason Pavlov was instructed to make provision for covering the East Prussian frontier and for completing the Grodno 'fortified district'.

Vice-Admiral Panteleyev, serving with the staff of the Baltic Fleet, mentions that by February also the activity of the German photo-reconnaissance planes, busy over the Soviet naval bases, was not lost on the Soviet command. The Russians had cause enough to worry. By the beginning of 1941, the fitting out of the Soviet naval base at Tallinn was almost finished, the Vyborg and Hogland shore battery sectors were also ready, as were many of the installations in the Libau and Hango naval bases. On the Moon Sound islands, the 'Baltic region coast defences [BOBR]', batteries and installations, were being fitted out, but no effective system of artillery collaboration had as yet been brought into existence. On 26 February 1941 the Baltic Fleet received its directive of assignments in the event of war: the enemy was to be prevented from making landings on the coast and denied access to the gulfs of Finland and of Riga, while the Baltic naval forces would also co-operate with the Red Army (naval protection of the land flank). To inhibit possible enemy operations, the naval command was to establish mine barriers at the mouth of the Gulf of Finland and at the Irbensk peninsula, with additional mine barriers to cover the Libau naval base. To increase the effectiveness of these measures, the Baltic Fleet was also assigned a limited number of offensive purposes, related to the entire defensive strategy; enemy bases would be mined, his transports attacked at sea and in their bases by aircraft, with submarine operations aimed at his lines of communication. The attack on enemy lines of communication was not envisaged as an independent undertaking, even though the Soviet naval command was well aware of the importance of the shipment of Swedish iron ore to Germany. The land-sea co-operation was to be worked out between the Baltic naval command and the staff of the 8th Army (defending the Baltic coast). The plans may have looked well enough on paper (though retrospectively, Soviet commanders criticized them for lack of 'concrete orders'); on the ground, the situation looked less promising, for many of the artillery batteries were far from operational, and a large number lacked ammunition both now and in the weeks to come. There were only five rail-mounted batteries, and no tractor-towed artillery whatsoever. Although extensive mining schemes were called for, there were too few mines, and as for enemy mines, no way as yet of dealing with the magnetic type. Minesweepers and small craft were also in short supply. The difficulties were not wholly confined to the new naval bases. It was on 16 December 1940 that Voroshilov called for the preparation of a land-based defence of the naval base at Sevastopol, although this made very slow progress; meanwhile, the base was inadequately protected by too few anti-aircraft guns and by a small fighter force.

Further to the north, the Northern Fleet (established in May 1937) had been committed by Stalin to the command of Rear-Admiral A.A. Golovko, who, at the time of his appointment, had thought himself destined for the Amur Flotilla. On the river Amur, Stalin assured him, there was little to do but 'fight with fishermen',* while in the north much remained to be done. The northern Soviet naval forces were, in 1941, small in number, disposing of coastal defence and anti-aircraft defence forces, a small number of aircraft and a submarine force of medium and coastal types. Its operational zone, which included the Barents, White and Kara seas, was one of ferocious weather conditions. Its operational commitments included co-operation with the 14th Army, which covered the Soviet-Finnish frontier in the north and the coast.

It was undoubtedly in the early spring of 1941 that Zhukov and the General Staff embarked, more or less seriously, upon a defensive plan for the Soviet frontiers. One of the prime decisions, however, had already been made. Shaposhnikov had in 1940 formulated a deployment plan for Soviet forces in the west which would have maintained the bulk of the formations of the frontier military districts in the area of the old (1939) frontiers, where powerful 'fortified districts' did exist, and where a three-week supply of fuel, ammunition and food had always been stocked; in Western Belorussia, in the Western Ukraine and in the Baltic provinces Shaposhnikov suggested the stationing of covering forces only, the function of which would be to secure the mobilization of the main forces *in the event of surprise attack*. Zhukov was well aware of Stalin's dislike of Shaposhnikov's proposals and therefore took care to let them lie unexplored. Consequently, Zhukov's name has become associated with the disastrous 1941 'plan', though if Shaposhnikov could not prevail upon Stalin to deploy cautiously in the west, then it is unlikely that Zhukov could have done it.

The 'defence plan' was based, from the outset, on an advanced deployment of

---

* A reference to the protracted Soviet-Japanese disputes in the Soviet Far Eastern borderlands: both sides shot up small craft 'violating' the frontier.

Soviet forces in European Russia in five military districts, running from the Barents to the Black Sea: Leningrad, Baltic (Special), Western (Special), Kiev (Special) and Odessa military districts. The designation of 'Special' to a military district signified that these were operational groupings capable of carrying out operations for a limited period without the mobilization of additional reserves; ordinary district armies were, for all practical purposes, administrative organizations. The Special Military Districts had their headquarters in Riga, Minsk and Kiev (running north to south); in time of war, they would be converted into 'Fronts' (the equivalent of Army Groups) and indeed in the Soviet-Finnish War the North-Western Front had been established as an operational entity. As for the actual frontier defence itself, this responsibility devolved upon the eleven 'frontier commands' of the NKVD, each command under the equivalent of a divisional officer, and thence subdivided into districts and regions, with the NKVD frontier troops (lightly armed, with a three-day supply of food and ammunition) kept at immediate readiness. These troops were not under the operational control and command of the Red Army, but subject to Beria and his NKVD officers.

The Red Army now stood on the line Vipurii-Kaunas-Bialystok-Brest-Lwow-Kishinev, a massive, undulating frontier, with its complement of dangerous salients and exposed sectors. In considering the defence of this line, with its vast regional subdivisions, two tendencies seemed to conflict; the first was the pre-occupation with 'traditional' threats and possible responses to them, the second the problem of dealing with a German thrust against the Soviet Union. At no time does either of these appear to have been clarified, and it is this which gave the 1941 'plan' its curious aspect and fatal disproportion. In the north, the forces of the Leningrad Military District were assigned the defence of the frontier with Finland and the shore of the Gulf of Finland as their principal task; the threat of Leningrad was thought to emanate from the north and at no time was the possibility of the collapse of the Baltic Military District defences and the appearance of a threat from the south-west entertained. The only force available for any defence of the city in a north-westerly direction consisted of the few regiments assigned to coastal defence duties on the southern shore of the Gulf of Finland. All this presupposed that the recently established Baltic Special Military District, which was responsible for the defence of the southern and south-western shores of the Gulf of Finland, for the naval bases at Osel and Dago, and for the protection of the coast of the Baltic from Riga to Memel as well as the frontier of Soviet Lithuania with East Prussia, would in no way crumple or fold. The Soviet intention was to buttress this military district with fixed fortifications, and so far work had begun on a line running from Kaunas north-westwards along the river Dubissa and on a second line in the region of Panevezyz, intended to cover Dvinsk and to provide defensive positions in front of the river Dvina. But on the border with East Prussia, only rudimentary field fortifications existed so far, while much remained to be done to protect the junction with the Western Special Military District at Kopzovo, to the north-west of Grodno. The harsh and prolonged winter of 1940–1 had delayed much of this construction work, but in the spring of 1941 the construction battalions moved in to set up the reinforced concrete block-houses and fire-points.

The Western Special Military District, with a frontage of 450 kilometres, ran from Grodno to Vlodava. Soviet forces here were provisionally deployed to cover the approaches to Minsk and to Bobruisk, while carrying out the general protection of the frontier. At the moment, engineer troops, assisted by units detached from the rifle formations, took up the construction of field fortifica-tions on the frontier itself; an enormous amount of work remained to be done on the airfield network in Belorussia, on increasing the capacity of the railways (which were being changed over to broad-gauge), on expanding the signal net-works and on fitting out the 'fortified districts' with weapons, supplies, signal facilities and roads. Until such time as these were ready, the troops assigned to man them were housed in temporary barracks and the officers lodged in peasant huts and houses. Both in the Baltic area (in the direction of Riga) and in Belorussia a certain amount of Soviet reinforcement, which did not escape German notice, took place in March 1941. The command of the Western Special Military District had been instructed in February to cover a section of the frontier with East Prussia and to complete construction work on the Grodno fortified district'; on 26 March under *Order No. 008130*, the Military Soviet of the Western Special Military District instituted a 'state of readiness' under the revised '1941 Mobilization Plan', confined however only to units coded as '7490' and with a termination date of 15 June. Nevertheless, the most urgent instruc-tions sent to the Baltic and Western Military District commands concerned the fortification of the frontiers with East Prussia. In March, the same instruction went out to the command of the Kiev Special Military District: maximum concentration on the fortification system.

The magnitude of this effort is apparent from the figures by the spring of 1941; 138 construction sectors were in existence, with 84 construction battalions and 160 engineer battalions earmarked for work in the frontier military districts, and 41 for the interior districts. In an effort managed by the several Chief Con-struction Administrations and under the supervision of Marshal Shaposhnikov 58,000 men in the Baltic, 35,000 in the Western and 43,000 men in the Kiev military districts worked daily on these projects. Many of them, however, were held up by shortage of materials, concrete, timber and cable; another source of friction was the control exercised by the NKVD over labour for construction projects, labour drawn in many cases from its pool of prisoners. In what were presumably designed as interlocking defences, the gaps continued to stare out; these ranged from ten to eighty kilometres. In particular, in the Grodno UR, a pivotal 'fortified district' of major importance, the right flank on the Niemen-Sonichi sector lay open and exposed; to close this breach, two 'support points' were planned but these were never finished. The defensive positions which had been completed in 1940 did receive their complement of weapons, but under the re-equipment programme, much was withdrawn pending the arrival of new items. And, in the final resort, the URS could be manned operationally only on the special orders of the military district commander, who, in turn, would be obliged to wait on higher authorization.

The fortifications of the old, pre-1939 frontiers (installations which had been built during the years 1929–35, under the first major fortification scheme) had been by now stripped of their weapons and denuded of their garrisons; the main 'system' consisted of a belt of fire-points, some two kilometres in depth, with artillery emplacements specially reinforced to resist heavy shell-fire. This was the backbone of the so-called 'Stalin line', which, although neglected at the moment, together with the Karelian, Polotsk, Koroshten and Kiev 'special defensive sectors', was activated in a desperate rush after June 1941.

In contemplating the defence of the frontiers, the Soviet General Staff had some forty rifle divisions and two cavalry divisions, as a first echelon, upon which it could reckon; strictly speaking, the *troupes de couverture* amounted to nine Soviet armies, although the five military districts immediately involved disposed of somewhat larger forces:

Leningrad MD: 14th, 7th, 23 Armies
sector: from the Barents Sea to the Gulf of Finland.

Baltic (Special) MD: 8th, 11th Armies
sector: 300 kilometres of frontier with East Prussia.

Western (Special) MD: 3rd, 10th, 4th Armies
sector: 470 kilometres of frontier, Belorussia.

Kiev (Special) MD: 5th, 6th, 26th, 12th Armies
sector: 865 kilometres of frontier, Ukraine (from Vlodava to Lipkany).

Odessa MD: 9th Army (administration only)
sector: from Lipkany to Odessa (defence of the Crimea assigned to independent rifle corps).

The average divisional frontage was some 50 kilometres, although in the broken country to the south this reached 120 kilometres and more. The covering armies had each two echelons, the first made up of rifle formation, the second of mechanized corps. In addition to fortifications, labour and materials were required to build the barracks and fitments for the covering forces, which were strung out at any distance from 20 to 150 kilometres from the frontier itself (with only rifle units actually within the vicinity of the frontier, together with NKVD border guards and engineer troops). The majority of the mechanized formations, still in the process of forming up, were drawn back deep into the rear of the military districts. In the Kiev Military District, first and second echelons were scattered over a distance of some 400 kilometres, while in the

Western Military District that dispersion reached 250 kilometres. The rifle divisions, even those being newly moved in, were by no means up to strength (falling as low in some cases to 6,000 men, which was less than half of the normal complement); although this was now coming to an end, many of the troops had been busy building barracks, while the completion of actual installations (supply dumps, fuel and ammunition stores, signal centres and the like) was entrusted to the personnel of *Voenstroi*. To speed up the work on the field fortifications, rifle units were detached for a month at a time in the frontier military districts; a whole design of tank barriers, ditches, obstacles, wire traps and artificial ravines was contemplated, but all this required time.

It was, therefore, a dangerous piece of mismanagement to have neglected the role of the mine in all this haste for barring the means of access to the Soviet Union. This was connected with the lost ground which the Main Military-Engineering Administration (*Glavnoe Voenno-inzhernernoe upravlenie*) was obliged to make up. The Red Army had paid for the neglect suffered by this service in the Soviet-Finnish war. Now under the command of A.F. Khrenov, the administration in the autumn of 1940 took up the question of mining and de-mining, which Khrenov considered to be the prime task of his officers. He established two new departments in his administration, one of electrotechnics and the other of minefields. An *Instruction on Operational Minefields/Obstacles* was accepted by Timoshenko, who henceforward permitted the distribution of demolition materials to units and the stockpiling of necessary explosives. All the old dumps, dating back to the 1930s, had been long ago emptied; in the engineer and railways troops of the Red Army only a very few men were trained in demolition techniques (the special demolition battalions, envisaged in early 1938, had never got off the ground). Marshal Kulik was persuaded, perversely, as ever, that mines were the weapon of the 'weak'; the Red Army engineers, revising Kulik's estimates, set their requirements (for a six-monthly period of operations) at 2,800,000 anti-tank, 4,000,000 anti-personnel, 120,000 delayed action and 350,000 trip mines. In early 1941, the Red Army had exactly 1,000,000 anti-tank mines at its disposal, but lacked any delayed-action or other types of mine. At a later and far more critical date, the Military-Engineering Administration could issue Red Army railway troops with precisely 120 delayed-action mines.

Behind the great plans for fortification lay such involved 'technical difficulties'. Of even greater import was the lack of preparation in matters of signals and communications. In the Red Army as a whole, and especially in the mechanized formations, radio equipment was in short supply; the same situation applied in the Soviet Air Forces. From the overloaded factories, new equipment slowly seeped into the formations: RAT, RAF and RSB sets, RSMK, 9R and 10R tank radio sets, the RSB-3bis, RSR-M and RSI-4 sets for aircraft. There was never enough. The basis of the communication network consisted of the landlines (and cables) operated by the People's Commissariat for Communications, the civilian network which it was thought would suffice to handle operational traffic.* To maintain contact between the General Staff and the staffs of the prospective 'fronts', a small number (possibly some twenty-five) of 'High Command Radio Communication Units' existed, which operated under the direction of the signals Administration (*Upravlenie svyazi*) entrusted to Major-General (Signals) N.I. Gapich. Only in one command, that of Leningrad, had the system of radio nets reached any effective degree of development, and it was this, as special German 15-kilo bombs dropped from low level threw the overland wire system into massive confusion after June, which helped to stave off total disaster. What the entire military system lacked was any systematic organization of rear services, and the unsatisfactory state of affairs in signals and communications remained part of a much wider deficiency, which the Red Army rushed to rectify a few months later. Although new fuel dumps were being set up, it so happened that the armoured commanders scarcely knew where these were. The lack of motor transport, which most inhibited the artillery units, was felt by infantry and armoured forces alike; much of the available transport was diverted to the building work in the military districts. The plight, which General Klich, artillery commander of the Western Special Military District, bewailed, was far from uncommon: 'They have taken the lorries from many of the artillery regiments for works on the URs. They have even dragged the towing tractors there. You hear that – guns without haulage. No means to tow them.'

In *Lagebericht Nr. 1*, Colonel Kinzel, head of *Fremde Heere Ost* noted (15.3.1941) the Russian movement near Riga, the activity in the Minsk–Smolensk region, the practice air-alarms and the black-outs; this 'partial mobilization' was, nevertheless, defensive in nature, *Defensiv-Massnahme*, and the concentration of troops merely for the protection of the frontier. Five days later (*Lagebericht Nr. 2*), German intelligence sketched out the main Soviet concentrations, reported an unconfirmed conference held by Timoshenko with Kuznetsov of the Baltic Special Military District (on 15 March) and noted the reinforcement of Soviet troops on the Venta–Dubissa–Niemen line. The Germans were too sanguine in their talk of 'concentration'. Yet they were right in noting the nervousness exhibited by the Russians, and for which, as the crisis in the Balkans exploded, there was every reason.

By the beginning of April, the Soviet commands in the frontier military districts were fully aware of the existence of the German troop concentrations facing them, if as yet they lacked precise details of order of battle. Stalin, meanwhile, did not lack warnings of impending disaster. Moscow had bubbled with rumours in late March, though the Soviet leader had no need to depend on gossip and diplomatic talk. On 1 March, the American ambassador in the Soviet Union was

---

* The signals of the 22nd Tank Division, for example, were operated through the local post office, where the formation 'plugged in' to the civilian telephone network and telegraph service (*22.Tk.Div.* record, 7.6.1941: captured document).

instructed to seek an interview with Molotov, in order to pass on 'orally and confidentially' this message: 'The Government of the US, while endeavouring to estimate the developing world situation, have come into the possession of information which it regards as authentic clearly indicating that it is the intention of Germany to attack the Soviet Union.' Ambassador Steinhardt, for reasons full of insight into Stalinist attitudes, asked to delay his call upon Molotov. In the event, his mission was rendered superfluous by the conversation between the American Under-secretary, Sumner Welles, and the Soviet ambassador in Washington, Umanskii, a conversation which 'took such a turn as to render it opportune for the under-secretary to convey to the ambassador the information which the Department had suggested that you pass on to Molotov'. On hearing this 'information', the confirmation of the existence of 'Barbarossa', Umanskii had gone white. Some three weeks later, on 20 March, Umanskii asked Sumner Welles whether there had been any 'further information in confirmation' of what had been told to him earlier; Sumner Welles intimated that this was indeed so, and one such item of confirmation was a Greek government communication (19 March) that the Swedish government had learned through its missions in Berlin, Bucarest and Helsinki of German intentions to attack the Soviet Union.

It was not long after this that the British prime minister now intervened, sending on 3 April a personal message to Stalin, which emphasized the significance of the movement of German Panzer divisions from Rumania to southern Poland (a transfer at once reversed when the Yugoslavs failed to toe the German line, but in no way invalidating the significance of the earlier move). Hitler, due to complications in the Balkans, was obliged to delay his action against the Soviet Union; this, Churchill suggested to Stalin, presented an opportunity for the Soviet government to consider common action against German designs, and possibly to thwart them completely. That could not fail to benefit the Soviet Union. Sir Stafford Cripps, British ambassador in Moscow, who had recently sent a long letter in similar vein to Vyshinskii, completely blunted the point of this intervention by failing to act promptly on Churchill's instructions; only on 19 April, when Yugoslavia had been ripped to pieces by German aircraft and armour and when Greece was in desperate straits, did Vyshinskii receive the original message.

Bulgaria had already passed into the Axis camp. Three weeks later in Vienna, on 25 March, as Hitler and Ribbentrop looked on, the Yugoslav Prime Minister Cvetković and Foreign Minister Cincar-Marković signed away the soul of Yugoslavia with formal adherence to the Tripartite Pact. But what the Yugoslav ministers had signed in Vienna Yugoslav patriots in Belgrade disavowed with a sudden coup on the night of 26-7 March. This action, engineered by senior Yugoslav Air Force and Army officers, sent Hitler into a delirium of rage only a few hours later, when the Führer swore vengeance, duly exacted with a bestiality which only he could conceive. On 6 April, the Wehrmacht went into action against Yugoslavia, while the Luftwaffe, roaming for three days over defenceless Belgrade, left 17,000 dead. It was maniac revenge (and continued to be), but at a price – the postponement of 'Barbarossa' from 15 May, for four weeks.

Stalin indicated his dissatisfaction with the turn which events had taken in Bulgaria by communicating his disquiet to Sofia, though not to Berlin directly. While the Germans invested Bulgaria, the Russians looked to Turkey; any German-Turkish agreement would have put the Germans in the position to attack the Caucasus. Stalin and Molotov attempted to stiffen the Turkish attitude, with some momentary success, but Stalin was still obliged to face the consequences, at the end of March, of German intervention in Yugoslavia. The air was thickened with rumours of a German attack on the Soviet Union. Reports from Soviet agents confirmed the concentration of German troops, and a Czech in the service of Soviet military intelligence reported that the Skoda works must henceforth decrease its deliveries of war material to the Soviet Union. Stalin's reaction was reputedly to scrawl 'English provocation' across reports of this nature.

The rapidity of events in Yugoslavia obviously overtook Stalin, and though he never abandoned extreme caution, something akin to a definite anti-Nazi stand was allowed to peep out for the first time. The officers who had engineered the March coup in Belgrade sought Russian support; in Moscow, the Yugoslav Minister, Gavrilović, was tantalized by hints, though no actual aid was forth-coming, a point put bluntly by Vyshinskii on 5 April; what Stalin committed himself to was a non-aggression pact, grimly ludicrous in the circumstances. Although signed on the 6th, the pact was dated for the 5th, a diplomatic sleight of hand which removed any overt and declared sign of resistance to Germany. (German operations began at dawn on 6 April.) The only concession which Gavrilović could extract, after stubbornly struggling for it, was that in the event of war, Yugoslavia might anticipate 'friendly relations' rather than formal neutrality on the part of the Soviet Union. It was, even with this flicker of resistance, a shabby piece of diplomacy which Vyshinskii had managed for Stalin.

The most pertinent commentary on this belongs to Milan Gavrilović himself. With the increase in anti-Soviet activities in Finland, the Baltic states and the Ukraine, and with German plans to bring the Balkans under their control, the Soviet government had decided 'to come out of its shell'. Moreover, in his view,

the Soviet Government endeavoured to impede German action in the Balkans by its assurance to Turkey, by its statements relative to Hungary and Bulgaria, and by the signa-ture of the Non-Aggression Pact with Yugoslavia . . . The Soviet leaders had thought that the Yugoslav resistance would keep the Germans involved in the Balkans for about three months, which would give the Soviet Union another year for its military preparations, since it would then be too late for Germany to begin this year an attack upon the Soviet Union.

The rapid collapse of this resistance led to an immediate revision of policy, which aimed at placating Germany – the Neutrality Pact with Japan (13 April), the removal of Molotov (6 May). Dr Gavrilović mentioned Stalin's views on the 1939 talks between the British, French and Russians:

Stalin had stated that the fact that the Allied negotiators were subordinate officials not vested with full powers, the attitude of Poland in refusing to consent to the passage of Russian troops or the flight of Russian aeroplanes over Poland, the attitude of the French Military Offices which indicated that France was planning to remain behind the Maginot Line and not undertake any offensive operations against Germany, made it clear to the Soviet Government that the conclusion of any pact with the Allies would result in the Soviet Union having to bear the full brunt of the German attack at a time when the Soviet Union was in no position to cope with a German attack.

And yet, though Stalin might justify his policies in this way, and proclaim his own foresight in having evaded a capitalist manoeuvre, still the Soviet Union was 'in no position to cope with a German attack'. A few days after the conclusion of the pact with Yugoslavia, on 10 April, Stalin learned from his intelligence reports of the Führer's talk with Prince Paul, which indicated that the blow against Russia would now fall at the end of June. Molotov learned from Gavrilović of this exchange and made the terse reply: 'We are ready' – this at a time when complaints were reaching Stalin of the lamentable state of the Soviet frontier defences.

Stalin duly made his accommodation with Japan, a considerable diplomatic coup, preceded by probing and prodding over economic questions, and consummated on 13 April with the signing of the Soviet-Japanese Neutrality Pact. To Stalin, it might have appeared that he had driven a wedge into the Axis; Matsuoka had been clearly beguiled by Stalin's talk about his opposition to Britain and America. Nor were Soviet gains slight; in return for nothing but words, not even the price of the curtailment of Soviet aid to China, the immediate Japanese threat against the Soviet Far Eastern borders was diminished. In an unprecedented piece of protocol, while seeing Matsuoka off from the railway station, Stalin sought out the German ambassador, Count von Schulenburg, and publicly pressed him over the need for continuing Soviet-German friendship. To the acting German military attaché, Colonel Krebs, he added: 'We will remain friends with you – in any event.'

In his service, Stalin had one of the most brilliant of all intelligence agents, Richard Sorge, operating from Tokyo; Sorge had already rendered important service to the Soviet Union, though he had yet to render his greatest. While the Russians were able to intercept some of the German diplomatic wireless traffic from Tokyo, Sorge, with access to the secrets of the German ambassador, Ott, supplied many more minute details. Early in April (though the exact date remains unspecified), Sorge transmitted a report to Moscow, to the effect that Germany might begin military operations against the Soviet Union at any time after Matsuoka's return to Tokyo from Moscow. It may well have been this

item of information which accounted for the preliminary alert which Timoshenko instituted on 10 April in the frontier military districts, although there was
nothing the Soviet forces could have done, for they had no orders. Although
Berlin professed to see a stiffening of the Russian attitude in the crisis over the
Balkans, this had produced little perceptible result. That (non-Soviet warnings
excluded) Stalin possessed continuous and accurate intelligence of German
intentions cannot seriously be doubted; such information, however, was not
circulated and was marked, in order further to restrict its impact, 'For archives'
or simply 'File'. Vyshinskii had hinted to Gavrilović that there did exist some
over-all Soviet design, and the Japanese, somewhat rapidly disillusioned after
the conclusion of the Neutrality Pact, were not far off the mark in rounding on
Stalin for counting on the eventual exhaustion of the Axis. Clearly, Stalin
viewed with the most jaundiced eye any attempts by London or Washington
to influence his attitude, suspecting no doubt the converse of the Japanese
argument – an Anglo-American *complot* to involve the Soviet Union with
Germany. Up to April 1941 Stalin's policy did make a certain amount of sense,
abject though it might have appeared; Soviet weakness, even if Stalin was the
last to admit it, required semi-appeasement and, until quite recently, it had paid
handsome dividends. The crisis over the Balkans nevertheless marks a major
turning-point in Soviet-German relations, and it led to a policy of total appeasement on the part of Stalin, an attitude which is more difficult to explain.

Very shortly, Berlin noticed 'a return of Russia to the previous correct
attitude'. Reporting from Moscow, Tippelskirch commented on the situation
produced by the Neutrality Pact with Japan: 'Members of the Japanese embassy
here maintain that the Pact is advantageous not only to Japan but to the Axis,
that the Soviet Union's relations with the Axis will be favourably affected by it,
and that the Soviet Union is prepared to co-operate with the Axis.' Much of
that was Matsuoka's own imagining, but Tippelskirch went on to remark
about the extraordinary scene at the railway station:

The view is frequently expressed that Stalin had purposely brought about an opportunity to show his attitude toward Germany in the presence of the foreign diplomats and
press representatives; this, in view of the persistently circulating rumours here of an imminent conflict between Germany and the Soviet Union, is considered to be especially noteworthy. At the same time the changed attitude of the Soviet Government is attributed to
the effect here of the success of the German armed forces in Yugoslavia and Greece.

In Berlin, von Schulenburg, German ambassador in Moscow, talked with
Hitler on 28 April about Soviet motives:

The *Führer* thereupon asked . . . what the devil had possessed the Russians to conclude
the Friendship Pact with Yugoslavia. 1 [Schulenburg] expressed the opinion that it was
solely a matter of the declaration of Russian interests in the Balkans. Russia had done
something each time that we undertook anything in the Balkans . . . The *Führer* said that
upon the conclusion of the Russo-Yugoslav Friendship Pact he had had the feeling that

the Russians wanted to frighten us off. I denied this and repeated that the Russians had only intended to serve notice of their interests, but had nevertheless behaved correctly by informing us of their intention.

Hitler continued to press his charges of Russian perfidy, but von Schulenburg exploded these one by one; as for the suspicion of Russian encouragement to the Yugoslavs, von Schulenburg cited Gavrilović's attempts to 'interest the Soviet Union in the Yugoslav cause' which remained abortive until the very last minute, while the British had been even more brusquely handled: 'Cripps had not succeeded until 6 days after the conclusion of the Russo-Yugoslav Treaty in even speaking to Molotov's deputy, Vyshinsky.' The German ambassador there concluded:

In 1939 England and France had taken all conceivable means to win Russia over to their side, and if Stalin had not been able to decide in favour of England and France at a time when England and France were both still strong, I believed that he would certainly not make such a decision today, when France was destroyed and England badly battered. On the contrary, I was convinced that Stalin was prepared to make even further concessions to us. It had already been intimated to our economic negotiators that (if we applied in due time) Russia could supply us up to 5 million tons of grain next year.

In this, von Schulenburg was incontestably right.

Such a course Stalin chose while possessing not only the warnings of German attack which emanated from abroad (from Soviet and non-Soviet sources alike) but also the count of misgivings which came to him from Soviet military and military-political organs. Soviet nerves had been badly shaken by the Yugoslav crisis; if Stalin retained his imperturbability, then others did not, least of all in the frontier commands, where the evidence of German troop' concentrations could not be wished away. And yet Red Army soldiers were in no way acquainted with their 'potential enemy', who was so uncomfortably close. In February 1941, A.A. Zhdanov, who at that time was carrying out a review of 'ideological questions', wrote in forceful terms about the whole mistaken tone and content of Soviet propaganda:

The whole of the propaganda which is being undertaken in the country bears a peaceful tone, it has a weak emphasis on the military spirit, reminds the Soviet people but little of the capitalist encirclement, of the inevitability of war, of the indispensability of strengthening in every way the defence of our motherland, and of being always ready for battle.

The Main Administration of Political Propaganda/Red Army (*Glavnoe upravlenie politicheskoi propagandy Krasnoi Armii*) made a complaint of a similar nature to Zhdanov, that the propaganda and even the political work was wholly unrealistic and bore no relation to the true situation:

Many propagandists and certain organs of the press proceed from the over-simplified thesis that we are powerful and therefore the capitalists fear to attack us . . . In the propaganda there is no sober assessment of the strength of the Red Army, so that an unhealthy attitude of 'hurrah-patriotism' or 'hats in the air' is inculcated. Frequently in reports and articles for no reason at all the adjectives 'great and invincible', 'invincible force' crop up. All that confuses the troops, contributing to the blunting of their vigilance.

A.I. Zaporozhets, head of the Political Propaganda Administration, who had impressed on Zhdanov the need to follow a realistic propaganda course, and with whom Zhdanov had agreed, took up the shortcomings in defence work with some energy. In April, he submitted a report on the effects of the new Disciplinary Code, which led to an increase in the number of military offences; the increase was steep enough for the Political Propaganda Administration to complain that the discipline had become too often and too much a matter of merely threatening subordinates with punitive action. At the same time, in an act of some boldness, Zaporozhets sent to Stalin, Molotov and Malenkov a report, based on the information supplied by formation commanders and substantiated by personal observation, dealing with the slow rate of progress with the 'fortified districts' being built in the frontier areas:

> The fortified districts located on our western frontiers, are for the most part not opera-tionally ready . . . The fortified districts are not manned by the requisite number of specially trained troops . . . The lack of completed work in the fortified districts not only in the permanent positions but also in the field fortifications aggravates the entire situation.

Not content with this, Zaporozhets sent a second letter immediately in the wake of the first, bitterly criticizing the work of the Main Artillery Administration: 'Throughout the whole of its artillery systems, the Red Army is not properly supplied with shells. . . . To date, the Main Artillery Administration has no plan worked out for supplying the Red Army with ammunition in time of war.' This was not isolated protest; in the same month, Khrushchev as Secretary of the Central Committee of the Ukrainian Communist Party and the Military Soviet of the Kiev Special Military District sent his own special report to Stalin, commenting on the slow progress being made with the 'fortified districts' and offering 100,000 workers so that the work could be brought to a more advanced stage of construction by 1 June. The February Party Conference (Eighteenth Conference) had made a small adjustment in those numbers of the members and candidate members of the Central Committee, who were military men; seven new names, including Zaporozhets, were added to this 'military' roster (bringing the total 'military' representation to eighteen), but this had no real effect on policies and attitudes. One small step forward was the drafting of instructions on the role of Party organs in the armed forces in the event of war, but nothing specific had been done. Obviously, both military commanders and political officers were worried about the whole menacing situation, and some did what they could to induce a response to it. The results were, by and large, minimal, though many were fully persuaded of the increasing urgency of the situation, not least the command of the Soviet 4th Army, a frontier army of the

Western Special Military District, by now fully aware that across the river Bug
lay the German Fourth Army, with twelve infantry and one cavalry divisions,
Panzergruppe 2 under Guderian, and *Luftflotte II*. By 7 June the 4th Army
possessed even more comprehensive and terrifying intelligence of German
concentrations.

Stalin, apparently convinced of his own brilliance in avoiding 'provocations',
British and American, designed to entangle him in war with Germany and
immovably persuaded that Germany would not breach the Nazi-Soviet pact
merely to become involved in a two-front war, dismissed the dangers. To
Gavrilović, who pointed out that Nazi Germany would soon turn upon the
Soviet Union, Stalin returned the confident reply: 'All right, let them come.'
This confidence was not feigned, for already in January Stalin had dismissed as
unnecessary discussions fundamental to the restructuring of the Soviet armed
forces. Locked up in the Kremlin, the master of a world which he had created
by his own selective killings and which reflected back upon him only those
images he had himself ordained, steeped in his own 'genius' and fed on its
outpourings, Stalin could rage away dissension and doubt, from whatever
quarter it came. Even now he kept his soldiers hard under the heel of NKVD
repression: Beria's arrest lists included L.A. Govorov, Inspector-General of
Artillery, who was marked down because of his service as a 'White' officer
under Admiral Kolchak – in 1919. (Govorov, on the eve of his appointment
in May as head of Dzerzhinskii Artillery Academy, was only saved from destruction by the personal intervention of Kalinin.) Within these very weeks,
the aviation commander of the Baltic Special Military District had been
brought to Moscow, from which he never emerged alive. There were officers
enough languishing in prison camps; one who returned was Gorbatov, instructed
on his release in the spring of 1941 to say that he had been absent on 'a dangerous
mission', but otherwise sworn to silence.

Supported by the incompetent and blundering advice of men like Kulik and
Mekhlis, Stalin chose to defend the forward frontiers of the Soviet Union.
Zhukov, deprived of any basic strategic choice, was charged with producing a
plan, which emanated from the General Staff at the end of April and beginning
of May 1941. The plan, 'State frontier defence plan 1941' (*Plan oborony
gosudarstvennoi granitsy 1941*), consisted of a general definition of assignments
for the forces of the frontier areas, plus an operational deployment plan
delivered as the 'Red packets' to the Military Soviets of the individual armies.
As far as can be determined, there were no operational orders to accompany
the plan: the Military Soviets of the frontier military districts received two
instructions,

    (i) to prevent ground and aerial intrusion by hostile forces upon Soviet
        territory;
    (ii) to conduct a stubborn defence in the fortified districts to cover the
        mobilization, concentration and deployment of Red Army troops.

The 'cover plan', in so far that that really existed, envisaged the destruction of hostile forces which broke through by the use of the second echelon of the covering armies – the mechanized corps, anti-tank artillery brigades and aviation. After the destruction of any 'treacherous' enemy attacks in the frontier areas, upon the receipt of *special instructions* from the High Command, operations would be carried on to enemy territory. This plan, which in fact contained no variants or appreciation of contingencies, had been drawn up at a time when the General Staff possessed, through the reports of the frontier commands, substantial evidence of German concentrations on the frontiers. Nevertheless, the whole organization of the frontier defence rested on the assumption that the Red Army would not be taken by surprise, that decisive offensive actions would be preceded by a declaration of war, or that enemy operations would be initiated with *limited* forces only, thus giving the Red Army time to fight covering actions to facilitate mobilization. Soviet forces were deployed along the entire length of the frontier, occupying even those salients which jutted westwards and thereby weakening the flanks. The reserves assigned to deal with hostile penetrations were far from adequate; nor did any provision exist for co-ordinating the operations of the first and second echelons. Finally, and it is this which calls into question the whole notion of a 'plan', no operational or tactical groupings (much less the 'secret concentrations' which Tukhachevskii had envisaged) were brought into being to deal with enemy attacks. It was, as Marshal Biryuzov subsequently observed, a case of preparing for the wrong war, for 1914, not 1941.

Early in May, Stalin emerged from his self-chosen official anonymity – until now, though master of Russia, he had run his empire from behind the modest mask of Secretary-General of the Communist Party – to become head of government, Chairman of the Council of People's Commissars (*Sovnarkom*). Molotov remained as Stalin's deputy and as Commissar for Foreign Affairs. The drama of this move of 6 May could not be contained, either at home or abroad. Shrewd and perceptive as ever, von Schulenburg reported it as an act 'of extraordinary importance'; he continued,

No other reason for this action could have applied than a revaluation of the international situation on the basis of the magnitude and rapidity of German military successes in Yugoslavia and Greece and the realization that this made necessary a departure from the former diplomacy of the Soviet government that had led to an estrangement with Germany. Probably, also, conflicting opinions that were noted among the party politicians and high-ranking military men, confirmed Stalin in his decision to take the helm himself from now on.

Signs of uneasiness among military commanders and political officers had not been lacking in April; the occasion of the May Day review in Moscow provided the opportunity for assembly, when the perils of the present situation might have been a persistent, if guarded topic of talk. At the parade of 1 May, the Soviet ambassador in Germany, Dekanozov, took up a position conspicuously close to Stalin; in the tortuous language of the Byzantine protocol of the Stalinist court, this signified high favour and personal confidence. For the military men, Stalin delivered a forty-minute speech to the graduates of the military academies. This remains even now a highly controversial topic. At the time, German diplomatic sources were 'informed' that the speech emphasized Russian military weakness in the face of Germany, and that a 'new compromise' was in the offing. A second version (compiled from post-June 1941 Soviet statements made to Alexander Werth) attributes much cool calculation to Stalin, who emphasized Soviet military deficiencies and who hinted at the inevitability of war in 1942, even through a Soviet pre-emptive act. This is not what other commentators record; the soldiers had to sit silent while Stalin, much as in January, described the Red Army as wholly reorganized both in weapons and structure, and insisted that the Soviet Union disposed of enough forces, in particular, mechanized and tank troops, as well as aviation, to fight successfully against 'the most modern army'.

The Germans meanwhile continued to puncture the 'inviolate' Soviet frontier, of which Stalin was so proud, with increasing regularity and sinister persistence. Half-way through April, in the thick woods round Augustovo, a German reconnaissance detachment of sixteen men, disguised as Red Army engineers, crossed into the sector controlled by the Soviet 86th Frontier Guards detachment; the result, which was to be repeated in subsequent weeks, was a shooting-match. The German *Abwehr*, utilizing General von Lahousen's *Special Regiment 800*★ and organizing a special intelligence unit out of anti-Soviet Ukrainians (the Nightingale [*Nachtigall*] formation) had begun work in systematic fashion; German operational intelligence busied itself in early May with completing reconnaissance assignments on Soviet signals networks, frontier defences and installations, and formulating sabotage tasks, the *Sabotage-Aufgaben* to be executed only on special orders from the High Command. From disaffected and hostile national groups, Balts and Ukrainians in particular, the Germans tried to form up 'Fifth columns' to work in the German cause.

With the stepping-up of tactical air reconnaissance, the over-flights continued, in spite of diplomatic flurries on both sides. Colonel-General Voronov, who took command of the Anti-Aircraft Defence Command (PVO) in May, discovered with fascinated horror that Soviet AA guns and fighter units had no orders to interfere with this German traffic over Soviet airspace. The tracks of the German photo-reconnaissance flights Voronov saw plotted in red on special maps, the lines looping over the Baltic naval bases, the Belorussian airfields, dumps and

---

★ The *Abwehr* had first used its 'special force', ' "K" troops', against Poland in 1939; the men were either Sudeten Germans or *Volksdeutsche* from the Polish areas. This 'special force' was continued as the 1st Training Company (German Company for Special Missions) and since its depot was at Brandenburg-am-Havel (3rd Brandenburg Artillery Regiment Barracks), the company expanded into a battalion (and finally a division), became known as 'the Brandenburgers'. Similar in some respects to the British Commandos, this force came under the control of *Abwehr II*, and a battalion was detached to operate specifically against the Russians.

troop concentrations and the Ukrainian frontier defences. If he could not shoot at the intruders, Colonel-General Kuznetsov, commander of the Baltic Special Military District, thought at least that he might, by night, remain more hidden; on his own initiative, he instituted partial black-out measures over naval bases and airfields. This the Germans had already perforce noticed. Voronov praised Kuznetsov's precaution and recommended to the General Staff that it be generally adopted. This commendation, however, merely had the effect of drawing attention to Kuznetsov's activities, whereupon the black-out orders were specifically countermanded from Moscow.

In the Tallinn naval base, which had been involved in the earlier black-out precautions, the lights shone out into the darkness from the ships and the multistoreyed naval headquarters, from which by day, as Admiral Panteleyev recalls, the staff officers looked on to the Tallin streets 'filled with greenery and the scent of flowers'. Round-the-clock work went into increasing the readiness state, as new weapons and new squadrons came in: light coastal forces under Rear-Admiral V.P. Drozd, a motor-torpedo-boat squadron under Captain Cherokov, submarine flotillas under Captains Egipko and Orel and Rear-Admiral A. T. Zaostrovtsev. Naval air squadrons under the command of Major-General V.V. Ermachenkov (and later Major-General M.I. Samokhin) were at something of a disadvantage, since they were obliged to operate from aerodromes almost entirely in the distant eastern rear areas, far behind the advanced bases and far beyond potential operational sea areas. The naval staff readily appreciated the threat to the vital Tallinn–Kronstadt communications, which needed many more minesweepers and patrol boats to secure them than the Baltic Fleet possessed. Some weeks earlier Lieutenant-Colonel Frumkin, chief of intelligence, reported that German naval units had increased their readiness state, and German submarines were already on station by the Soviet base at Libau. Admiral Tributs, Baltic Fleet commander, decided in mid May to disperse some of his units to guard against a surprise blow; light coastal forces (including a cruiser and a minelayer), most of the submarines and their depot ships were moved from Libau to Ust-Dvinsk, where the anti-aircraft defences were better than in Libau. The battleship *Marat* moved, much for the same reasons, from Tallinn to Kronstadt. Under orders from Tributs, Panteleyev and a group of naval staff officers went first to Riga and then to Libau, to discuss with their Red Army opposite numbers problems of operational co-ordination and, in particular, the defence of the naval bases, all this at a time when the German deployment was taking its final form.

Formed up opposite these hapless Russians in the north-west was Army Group North (*Heeresgruppe Nord*) under Field-Marshal von Leeb, disposing of its armoured striking force, Panzer Group 4 under Hoepner, and two armies (the Eighteenth and Sixteenth), supported by *Luftflotte* – in all, 29 divisions (including 3 armoured and 3 motorized), assigned to the destruction of the Soviet forces in the Baltic area and the seizure of Leningrad. Neighbour to Army Group North was Field-Marshal von Bock's Army Group Centre (*Heeresgruppe Mitte*), the most powerful of the German Army Groups with its 50 divisions (9 armoured and 6 motorized); on its left flank lay Hoth's Panzer Group 3 and on its right Guderian's *Panzergruppe 2*; a formidable striking force made the more fearful by the presence of large Stuka concentrations in Kesselring's *Luftflotte II*. This mailed fist was to fall on the Soviet forces in the area Brest–Grodno–Vilno–Smolensk, and having smashed these to pieces, to wait upon a further decision after the capture of Smolensk. Army Group South (*Heeresgruppe Süd*) under Field Marshal von Runstedt was to destroy Soviet forces in Galicia, and the western Ukraine, cross the Dnieper and strike at Kiev. Von Runstedt would strike between the Pripet Marshes and the Carpathians with 41 divisions (5 armoured and 3 motorized); in addition, the German Eleventh Army and the Rumanian Third Army were at his disposal. The German command held 26 divisions in reserve, while Germany's ally Finland would commit 12 divisions in support of the attack on Leningrad after 11 July.

The general aim, upon which success and safety hung in this colossal but risky enterprise, was the destruction of the Red Army as an effective fighting force west of the Dnieper. In the choice of objectives, however, Hitler and his generals did not see eye to eye; Hitler aimed for Leningrad and the Ukraine, the military concentrated on the possibility of a blow against Moscow. What was in effect a compromise plan evolved out of this divergence, and one which envisaged the seizure of the Leningrad–Orsha–Dnieper line as a first phase, to be followed by a reconsideration of opportunities and objectives. For planning purposes, the German command anticipated that after some four weeks von Leeb's forces would have reached the high ground to the south-west of Riga, that the two striking forces of Army Group Centre would have linked up across the main highway behind Smolensk and before Moscow and that von Runstedt, having taken Kiev, would deploy his forces southwards to smother the Red Army in the Ukraine. The regrouping of German forces at this juncture would involve Army Group Centre's striking forces joining von Leeb to accomplish the capture of Leningrad, the utilization of Army Group Centre infantry to eliminate the Russians trapped by the first envelopment and the commitment of von Rundstedt to an advance upon the Donets Basin and the Black Sea coast.

The German appreciation of Soviet capabilities and intentions lighted at once on the absence of 'operational groupings'; in the north-west, the frontier defence forces looked thin, and the bulk of the troops of the Leningrad Military District were reckoned to be 'tied up' against Finland. It was assumed that the Red Army would defend its positions to the west of the Dvina–Dnieper line, and in the north-western sector the Russians would fight on the line of the Dvina. The comprehensive survey of Soviet strength, deployment and intentions, the *Feind-beurteilung* of 20 May, identified three main Soviet concentrations: in the south at Czernovitz–Lemberg (Cernauti–Lwow), in the centre at Bialystok and in the Baltic area to the north. Each had apparently strong operational mobile reserves, those in the south at Shepetovka–Prostkurov–Zhitomir, those in the centre south-west of Minsk and those at Pskov in the north-west. In the event of an attack from the west, an '1812-type retirement' was unlikely and for these reasons: the naval and air bases of the north-west and south-west could not be abandoned lightly, the armaments plants of the Leningrad–Moscow–Ukraine region could also not be abandoned, and, not least, the lack of transportation facilities made rapid re-deployment and large-scale movement unlikely. A Soviet 'preventive blow' in the direction of East Galicia or East Prussia, or a drive into Rumania and Hungary, was also ruled out. Bearing in mind the length of the frontier to be defended, the Soviet command in contemplating defensive operations would inevitably seek to establish 'defensive concentration points' (*Verteidigungsschwerpunkte*) lest their forces be 'frittered away'. Three of these 'concentration points' could be readily identified: both sides of the line Lwow–Berdichev–Kiev in the Ukraine, both sides of the line Bialystok–Minsk–Moscow in Belorussia and round about the rising ground in the north-west. Should the Russians use the defences of the 'deep frontier zone' (up to fifty kilometres), then limited offensive thrusts mounted from these 'concentration points' might well be anticipated.

This crisp and competent document did nonetheless impute to the Soviet command a competence and comprehension which was far from being the real case. At least it brushed away the contrived myth about Soviet offensive intentions which Hitler had used to bemuse his incredulous commanders and frighten his reluctant allies; the 'Massierung sowjetischen Angriffstruppen' did not, in fact, exist. There was a moment of genuine fright, but Colonel-General Halder, having conceded on 7 April that the Russian dispositions 'provoke thought', concluded finally that an offensive design did not exist. A rapid re-deployment appeared out of the question, in view of Soviet weakness in signals and communications; nor did the evidence of German reconnaissance in any way support the notion of Soviet re-deployment to this end. On the contrary, the significance of the German deployment, with its two massive armoured claws set to tear away at the centre, seemed to be quite lost on the Soviet command, which concentrated its gaze on the north-west and the south-west. The defence of the Ukraine and the prevention of the development of a threat to the Moscow–Kharkov line of communications had always preoccupied the Red Army command; northwards, where forest and swamp predominated, the defence problem appeared easier, but to the south there was only the barrier presented by the Dnieper – and once that fell, there was little to impede an advance on the industrial centres of the Donets basin. Concentrating strong forces to the west of Kiev (which before 1939 meant manning the 'Stalin line') therefore contributed to the defence of both Moscow and the Ukraine.

Running from north to south, there was a formidable tally of Soviet armies. In the Leningrad Military District, commanded by Lieutenant-General M.M. Popov, the 14th Army (V.A. Frolov) held the Belomorsk–Murmansk sector, the

7th Army (F.D. Gorolenko) the northern and north-eastern sectors of lake Ladoga and the 23rd Army (P.S. Pshennikov) the Viipuri-Keksholm sector. Kuznetsov's Baltic Special Military District, with its 28–30 rifle divisions and 1,000 tanks, had the 11th Army (V.I. Morozov) covering the East Prussian frontier and the 8th Army (P.P. Sobennikov) protecting Riga and the Baltic coast; deeper in the interior, N. Berzarin's half-formed 27th Army was drawn back by the western Dvina. In the Western Special Military District, Colonel-General Pavlov had taken it into his head to re-deploy the 4th Army (Major-General A.A. Korobkov), one of his three covering armies, (the others being the 3rd and the 10th); as early as January 1941 Lieutenant-General Chuikov had suggested some adjustment in the deployment of the 4th Army, with the object of improving its position. Pavlov, however, having won the approval of the General Staff, decided to shift the 12th Rifle Division of the 4th Army into Brest itself, and located the administration of 14th Mechanized Corps – at that moment being raised from Krivoshein's and Bogdanov's tank brigades – at Kobrin; the net result was to deprive 4th Army simultaneously of its reserve and its second echelon. In Kirponos's Kiev Special Military District, where a more healthy state of affairs reigned, the situation with the covering armies was still decidedly bad. Rifle divisions of 5th Army were assigned to cover the Lutsk-Rovno approaches to the western Ukraine and were to man the Kovel, Strumilov and Vladimir-Volynsk 'fortified districts', which unfortunately were unfinished and unfitted for operations. On the two main sectors singled out as the most likely avenues of enemy approach, a stretch of some 100 miles, four rifle divisions were deployed, supported by a reserve of one rifle division and a mechanized corps to deal with any enemy breakthrough. Yet 5th Army, currently in training, was scattered in barracks anything up to forty miles from the frontier, and needed 3–4 days to take up its designated positions. The cover plan for 6th Army depended partly on that of its neighbour, 5th Army; 6th Army units would man the Strumilov and Rava-Russki defences, to prevent an enemy breakthrough in the Krystynopol-Grabovets sector. To defend a 75-mile sector, 6th Army deployed two rifle divisions and a cavalry formation, which were to co-operate with the garrisons of the 'fortified districts'. It was little wonder that the Kiev district command pressed urgently for completion of the frontier defences, for otherwise the covering operations were hopelessly compromised.

Russian strength lay substantially in the Ukraine, with its mass of more than 60 available rifle divisions; in the centre upwards of 40 divisions to hand and the 30 divisions of the north-west. That a massive German shock wave of 20 divisions would fall instantaneously and in all their entirety on the flimsy covering forces, and that the Germans planned to rip their way through the Soviet centre in no way dawned upon the Red Army command. Yet there were signs which should have 'provoked thought', as Colonel-General Halder had been stimulated to think about Soviet dispositions. The Soviet 4th Army, half-doomed already by Pavlov's amputation of its echelons, reported in April on the presence of appreciable German strength; on 7 June, transmitting figures of German strength up to 5 June, 4th Army confirmed that 40 German divisions were on the Belorussian frontier, and identified 15 infantry, 5 tank, 2 motorized and 2 cavalry divisions. For good if alarming measure, the same report mentioned what looked like German bridging preparations on the river Bug.

Almost at the same time, Richard Sorge sent Moscow, in an astonishing compilation of data about 'Barbarossa', the objectives, the 'strategic concepts', the strength of the German troops to be committed and the opening date for the attack on the Soviet Union.

On the day when Stalin assumed formal control of the Soviet government (6 May), the Soviet military attaché in Berlin, Captain Vorontsov, sent a report to Moscow that the deputy naval attaché understood a German attack was pending, scheduled possibly for 14 May; this attack would take place through Finland and the Baltic states, preceded by heavy airborne landings in border areas and raids on Leningrad and Moscow. The day before this Stalin had received (from a source unspecified in Soviet accounts) an intelligence assessment of German preparations and intentions:

Military preparations in Warsaw and on the territory of Poland are proceeding quite openly and German officers and men speak with complete frankness about the coming war between Germany and the Soviet Union as something already decided upon. War is to begin after the completion of the springtime work in the fields.

Early in April, Sorge had sent a supplementary radiogram from Tokyo on German intentions: 'According to the German ambassador, the German General Staff has completed all its preparations for war. In Himmler's circles and those of the General Staff there is a powerful trend to initiate war against the Soviet Union.' At the beginning of May, yet another supplementary report from Sorge underlined the reality of the threat of war:

1 Hitler is fully determined to make war upon and to destroy the USSR, in order to acquire the European area of the USSR as a raw materials and grain base.
2 The critical dates for the presumed initiation of hostilities:
   (a) the completion of the destruction of Yugoslavia
   (b) completion of the spring sowing
   (c) completion of the talks between Germany and Turkey
3 The decision about the initiation of hostilities will be taken by Hitler in May.

In a conversation with the Japanese ambassador in Moscow, the American ambassador on 16 May learned that Molotov on 14 May dismissed talk of a Soviet-German collision as 'British and American propaganda' and emphasized that relations were now 'excellent'. Economic supplies for Germany had been stepped up and those from the Far East, transhipped across the Trans-Siberian Railway, speeded up; in fact, the delivery of 'oil seed, non-ferrous metals,

R.T.S.—D

petroleum and the transit of raw rubber from East Asia' had just been amicably settled between German and Soviet negotiators, and, as Dr Shnurre pointed out in his memorandum, 'the status of Soviet raw material deliveries still presents a favourable picture.' His conclusion was optimistic:

... we could make economic demands on Moscow which would go even beyond the scope of the treaty of 10 January 1941 ... The quantities of raw materials now contracted for are being delivered punctually by the Russians, despite the heavy burden this imposes on them, which, with regard to grain, is a notable performance, since the total quantity of grain to be delivered ... amounts to over 3 million tons up to 1 August 1942.

Lieutenant-General Yoshitsugo Tatekawa, Japanese ambassador in Moscow, put forward his own assessment: 'Germany now has 140 fully trained and equipped divisions on the Soviet frontier, the Soviets have 110, of which only 34 are fully trained and equipped. I think the co-operation will steadily increase.' The German military preparations and the rumours of impending war evidently appeared to Stalin as evidence of Hitler's intention to squeeze every ounce of profit from the Soviet Union, but were not conclusive proof of his actually going to war. Nevertheless, for all the miniscule relaxation in tension which came in mid May, the warnings of impending German attack continued to roll in upon Stalin.

Of the relative abundance of warnings passed to Stalin there can be no doubt: Soviet and non-Soviet sources amply confirm this, though the fate of these messages has remained a point of considerable obscurity. What did Stalin himself believe and what was he led to believe? For almost a year F.I. Golikov had occupied the key post of chief of the General Staff Intelligence Administration (GRU) and through his hands – by his own admission – passed the bulk of the key reports dealing with the German preparations for an attack. Golikov subsequently denied that the first intimations received by Soviet intelligence of an impending German attack came through the interview between Umanskii and Sumner Welles (in March 1941):

The first warning was received through Soviet Intelligence much earlier than March 1941. The Intelligence Administration did a vast amount of work in obtaining and analysing information received through various channels about the plans of Hitlerite Germany, especially and in the first instance about those directed against the Soviet state. In addition to analysing extensive data from agents, the Intelligence Administration carefully studied international information, the foreign press, public opinion, and the military-political as well as the military-technical literature of Germany and other countries and so on. Thus the American information was not and could scarcely have been news for the political and military leadership of our country, from Stalin himself and going on down.

Stalin, however, did not receive this data raw. Before it reached his hand, it had been processed apparently by Golikov himself, who was directly responsible to Stalin and to none other. The intelligence data went to Stalin under two classifications, from 'reliable sources' and from 'doubtful sources'. According to the officer who actually handed over the reports to Stalin and Molotov, Stalin fell at once upon what was classified as 'doubtful', the better to buttress his policy of inactivity and the more to feed his fancies of 'doing a deal', and thereby eventually tricking Hitler. All and anything which confirmed that Hitler had marked down Great Britain as his real target, for which the easterly deployment of German forces was merely a huge feint, Golikov – with full consciousness of what his master thought and wanted to go on thinking – classed as 'reliable'. Richard Sorge's information, vital as it was from the outset and increasingly detailed as it became, inevitably came under the 'doubtful' column and was thence banished to the limbo of 'on file'. The detailed exposition of 'Barbarossa', the German operational plan, was certainly submitted by Golikov to Stalin but presented (according to the Soviet historian who read the file) as merely the work of *agents provocateurs* aiming to embroil Germany and the Soviet Union in war. That there was indeed 'provocation' afoot, nothing less than British incitement to Germany to make war on Russia, was driven in on Stalin's mind by the flight of Rudolf Hess to Scotland, in whose baronial halls the anti-Soviet plot was hatching and thickening during May, when Hess's 'proposals' were woven into London's great *complot*.

While Stalin received Golikov's 'disinformation', the doctored reports and the disparaging files, neither Zhukov at the General Staff nor Timoshenko at the Defence Commissariat was favoured even with this. The Intelligence Administration data on German plans and rumoured attack dates were not disclosed to the military command: they remained dependent on the reports of the frontier district commands, though these were also becoming alarming. Yet the margin of doubt remained legitimately wide. Not for nothing had Barbarossa been planned with elaborate deception measures built into it. Stalin fed on his fancies, his conceit and doctored information, and what he hoped for was what indeed the British Joint Intelligence Committee predicted in late May; in an extensive review of Soviet-German relations, the conclusion stood out that 'Germany would have more to gain by negotiation than war' and though Hitler might resort to a show of force during the bargaining, it was unlikely that he would wish to go over the brink. Churchill and General Sikorski on 20 May discussed the likelihood of a German attack on Russia; such an eventuality at that time 'does not seem to enter into consideration', though General Sikorski submitted a formidable written appreciation of German concentrations in Poland. Almost at once additional information about new Luftwaffe wireless installations in the east and the actual deployment of Luftwaffe squadrons called the conclusion of 20 May into question, yet this kind of evidence did not dispose of the idea of a German 'demonstration'. But what Sir Stafford Cripps later called 'this period of lull' was now drawing to a close. On 22 May, Stalin received yet another warning from Berlin, from the Soviet deputy military attaché Khlopov, who signalled that a German attack on the USSR was scheduled for 15 June, though the Soviet officer added that 'it is possible that it may begin in the early days in June'. Golikov no doubt filed this under 'doubtful'.

The Soviet General Staff, bereft of 'hot' information and deprived of full authority over frontier defence, could nevertheless modify Soviet internal military dispositions. Lieutenant-General P.A. Kurochkin, commander of the Trans-Baikal Military District and engaged in late May inspecting the 16th Army, received on the twenty-sixth a cipher signal routed to the Chita head-quarters of the District, recalling 16th Army to European Russia. The divisions were to be withdrawn by night, armoured formations first, followed by the 152nd Rifle Division and then the remainder, with the staff bringing up the rear; four days later, the staff was told that it would move 'some considerable distance, for training'. By 3 June, it was on the move, in railway trucks with sealed doors and from which no one was allowed to detrain. Some three weeks later, the 186th Rifle Division, commanded by Major-General N.I. Biryukov, was ordered from the Urals Military District to a position on the old 1939 fortifications of the Soviet-Latvian border. Although increased military traffic had been observed on the Trans-Siberian Railway, and there had been move-ment since the late spring, the General Staff was cautious in its interference with the Far Eastern forces. In March Yeremenko had been ordered to split the 1st Special Red Banner into two, the 1st Red Banner Army and the 25th Army. Now he was ordered to relocate the staff of the 1st Red Banner Army, which was at Spassk, by 1 July.

A.A. Lobachev, commissar to 16th Army, arrived in Moscow on 10 June, where he reported to the Defence Commissariat, the General Staff and the Political Propaganda Administration. At the General Staff, where, as everywhere, there was intense activity, Zhukov's deputy Sokolovskii told him that 16th Army had been destined originally for the Trans-Caucasus, but in view of the situation would go to the Kiev Special Military District. The Defence Com-missariat now had information that the German deployment would be complete by the end of May or beginning of June; if the Germans should decide on war, then 'certain measures' would be taken, such as moving armies like the 16th from the interior up to the 'western lines'. A.I. Zaporozhets told Lobachev and other senior commissars that 'in the new situation' propaganda, particularly that 'unmasking' the 'reactionary nature of Fascism', must be intensified.

Not all were reassured. At a meeting of senior officers of the 4th Army on 10 June, attended by the commander (Major-General Korobkov), the aviation commander, Colonel Belov, Commissar Rozhkov and 14th Mechanized Corps commander, Major-General S.I. Oborin, the discussion became heated. General Korobkov began by stating what orders he had received from the District commander:

4th Army is instructed to proceed on 22 June to the Brest artillery test grounds for tactical exercises, at which there will be present a representative of the District command and the Defence Commissariat. For these exercises units of the 42nd Rifle and 22nd Tank Divi-sions will be moved from Brest. All senior officers will attend the exercises.

Rozhkov asked at once what significance the command attached to the concentration of German troops on the frontiers. Korobkov told him that 'neither
the District command nor the High Command in Moscow' thought that the
Germans intended to break the 1939 Pact; the object was to 'strengthen their
position while deciding political questions with us'. Were there, Rozkov then
asked, any orders about operational readiness? To proceed with the work on
the fortifications, to keep units located at some distance from their appointed
stations in a state of readiness: in telling Rozhkov that, Korobkov's remarks
were amplified by Belov who announced the arrival of new fighter planes on
15 June: the concreted runways needed by the Yak-1s and the Pe-2 light
bombers were almost ready and should be finished within a month. Korobkov
then proceeded to order the preparation of command posts outside the towns,
in the event of 'extraordinary circumstances' 47th Rifle Corps
deployed round Bobruisk-Gomel-Slutsk would reinforce the 4th Army.
General Oborin reported that his command posts were already dispersed, but
this did not affect the fact that more than half of his corps were untrained
recruits, that his artillery units had received field-guns and howitzers but no
ammunition for them, that his tanks and lorries had come from the former tank
brigades, enough to move about a quarter of the corps: the rest would have to
go on foot. When after these disquieting admissions, Rozhkov returned to
the theme of the German concentrations Korobkov turned on him:

And what do you want us to do? Institute mobilization and start concentrating our
troops on the frontier? That could equally well bring on a war. As you know very well
from the history of the First World War, mobilization by one state automatically leads
to mobilization on the part of the opposing state and to the outbreak of war.

Meanwhile, the troops in the Brest fortress slept fully clothed and their officers
spent the nights in the barracks with their men, a precaution which lasted from
10–15 June.

It was at this time that Kirponos tried again to stir Moscow into action. He
wrote to Stalin, informing him that the Germans were on the Bug, that a
German offensive in the near future was more than likely, that 300,000 people
should be evacuated from the frontier areas, and that the fixed defences should
be manned. He was told that any of this would be 'provocation'; the Germans
must not be given 'a pretext for the initiation of military action against us'.
Already on his own orders Kirponos had moved some sections and units into
more favourable positions at the frontier. The Red Army movement was
observed by the NKVD troops, whose commander reported it to the chief of
the Ukrainian NKVD frontier troops, whence it travelled to Beria. Kirponos was
instructed to countermand his orders at once. In mid June, Kirponos tried again,
this time by telephone, to get permission to bring his specialist units off the
training grounds and to man the defensive positions. He was refused and told:
'There will be no war.' The Kiev commander's gloomy view of the future was

shared by his operations officer, Colonel I.Kh. Bagramyan, who, while pointing to the groups of twenty or so German planes going about their daily reconnaissance tasks, never doubted that Hitler would attack. Worst of all, Kirponos and his staff were quite unable to give the unit and formation commanders any precise briefing or operational clarification of the situation.

They could, of course, read the newspapers which on 14 June were issued with a statement (handed also by Molotov to von Schulenburg) which denounced all 'rumours of war' as baseless and proclaimed the opinion 'of Soviet circles' that,

the rumours of the intention of Germany to break the Pact and launch an attack against the Soviet Union are completely without foundation, while the recent movements of German troops which have completed their operations in the Balkans, to the eastern and northern parts of Germany are connected, it must be supposed, with other motives which have nothing to do with Soviet-German relations.

'Nado polagat' 'it must be supposed', this was the phrase which triggered off, not the complacency which Soviet commentators subsequently condemned, but the confusion and bewilderment which did even more damage. A senior naval commissar, I.I. Azarov, had only recently in Moscow heard Rogov urge naval political staffs to intensify verbal instructions to ratings on 'the aggressive activity of German Fascism' and to instil a greater sense of urgency and preparedness; now, back with the Black Sea Fleet and on board the cruiser *Krasnyi Kavkaz*, he was asked by her commander Captain Gishchin to 'amplify' the newspaper statement to the crew. The squadron commissar Semin had already reported on the heated rows among the ratings about it – and Semin himself had no idea what it meant. Azarov, asked to explain a statement he failed to understand at all, plumped for a 'positive' line, urging the sailors not to let the newspaper statement 'demobilize' them. As for the Germans, for whom the statement was intended, they did not reply.

Stalin loosed off this statement at a time when even more information had come in to confirm German offensive designs. Sorge, at the end of May and the beginning of June, transmitted details of the German concentrations and gave the exact date of the German attack. On 6 June, Stalin was presented with intelligence data confirming the concentration on the borders of some four million German and Rumanian troops. Five days later, Stalin was told that the German ambassador in Moscow was instructed on 9 June to prepare to leave Moscow in seven days and to burn documents. Information from the Far East, information from Europe – all tallied exactly. From Switzerland, Soviet intelligence operators, of whom one was the Englishman Alexander Foote, transmitted prime data, messages which to Foote in early June had 'an ominous sound'. The cream of this information came from an agent identified as 'Lucy', an intelligence operator as astonishing in his virtuosity as Sorge; the very precision of the items caused 'the Centre', the Moscow espionage and intelligence administration, to suspect an *Abwehr* plant designed to lead the Soviet command to ultimate disaster, having first misled it with specially prepared information. In mid June, 'Lucy' supplied news of outstanding importance – the date (22 June) of the German attack, with details of the German order of battle and objectives, and a German estimate of possible Soviet responses. In view of Moscow's suspicions of 'Lucy', the Soviet agents in Switzerland hesitated before transmitting this; the information finally went off, and did something to stifle Moscow's doubts, though these were far from stilled. Very shortly, Moscow would be clamouring for all of 'Lucy's' items.

If Stalin was not convinced of the likelihood of war, his intelligence reports notwithstanding, the British were. In early June, the Joint Intelligence Committee revised its previous opinion which was now 'that matters are likely to come to a head during the second half of June'. Eden at the end of May had already talked to Ambassador Maiskii about the Soviet attitude and the significance attached to the German troop movements; Maiskii promised to 'request instructions'. On 10 June, Maiskii asked to see Eden and told him that Moscow instructed him 'to inform the British Government that there was no agreement either military or economic between Russia and Germany . . .'. To questions about the German concentrations, Maiskii referred once again to his statement that 'no military or economic agreement existed between Russia and Germany'. Of the questions on Russian policy in south-eastern Europe, Maiskii promised to 'telegraph his Government'. Sir Stafford Cripps had meanwhile been recalled and on the night of 12 June the question of Soviet-German relations had been lengthily debated by Churchill, Eden and Cripps. They had before them the JIC assessment, with its hints of danger; it was decided to summon Maiskii once again. During the morning of 13 June, Eden pointed out to Maiskii the possibility of 'an early military attack on Russia'. The British government was bearing in mind the possibility of assistance in this event: diversionary air attacks in the west, the dispatch of a military mission to Russia, economic aid. Ambassador Maiskii now admitted the presence of German concentrations and asked for any British information on 'the location and numbers', and suggested 'a more sympathetic reception in Moscow' to any British proposals 'if they could be preceded by general negotiations to improve relations'. 'Mr Eden said "I suppose you mean questions concerning the Baltic states and related problems" and Mr Maisky said "Yes".' A few days later (18 June), Sir Stafford Cripps talked at length with General Sikorski about the state of Soviet-German relations; the British ambassador thought war 'would start within a few days', and the British government would, in that event, assist Russia. General Sikorski, commenting on the Red Army and the impact of the purges, remarked that 'Stalin killed the soul of the Red Army'. Timoshenko was not 'a commander on Tukhachevskii's scale'. and the Red Army, though it would fight, 'will not be able to stand the impact'.

While Eden was talking to Maiskii, Colonel-General Voronov put almost the same questions to Marshal Kulik; the latter dismissed the whole thing with a complacent shrug, 'That's high policy, it's not our idea.' The defence commissar was not quite so easily satisfied; two days after Stalin received the reports of the NKVD and the frontier guards command that a German attack could be expected on the night of 21–2 June, Timoshenko on 19 June ordered the camouflaging of forward airfields, military units and installations. The special order pointed to the bad state of airfield camouflage and the congestion of the parked aircraft; in the armoured units, and in the artillery, tanks and guns were painted in a way which made them far too visible from ground and air level. Like the planes on the ground, tanks and armoured vehicles were bunched up, presenting splendid targets. Dumps and installations were also far too plainly visible. Kuznetsov in the north-west ordered on 18 June the formation in the 8th and 11th Armies of 'mobile anti-tank mining squads' and the creation of dumps of anti-tank mines and explosives. Demolition squads were to be in position by 21 June on the bridges located in the area from the frontier to a line Shauliya-Kaunas-river Niemen; in 11th Army area, on the Niemen bridges the 4th Bridging Regiment would be assigned to blow up the bridges on the direct orders of the army commander. At the same time, the AA defences were brought up to greater alert.

In the Kiev Special Military District, the commander of the 15th Rifle Corps, Colonel I.I. Fedyuninskii received on the evening of 18 June an urgent telephone call from the NKVD frontier troops; a German deserter had crossed the Soviet lines with 'very important information'. The German corporal, who had fled from German military justice, announced that on 22 June the German Army would take the offensive. Fedyuninskii telephoned Major-General M.I. Potapov, 5th Army commander, with this news; Potapov evidently thought it 'provocation', though a couple of days later, in a talk with Major-General Rokossovskii, 19th Mechanized Corps commander, Fedyuninskii heard the sound advice to 'stick near your unit these days'. The same undulations of mood and opinion prevailed almost everywhere. In the 80th Rifle Division (Major-General Prokhorov), the officers in mid June discussed with frontier guards reports of German movement and the sounds of tank-engines. This was the Western Ukraine on 16 June.

After 18 June Soviet forward units in the north-west reported that German troops were taking up their start-positions. From Brest on the western frontier came similar reports of German troops taking up their stations, all against a background of noise of tank-engines. Meanwhile, the routine of Soviet military life went on, returns, reports and instructions: there were the investigations of the 'anti-Soviet statements' made by disgruntled soldiers, or the stringent terms of *Order No. 0219* (18 June) warning Red Army personnel about carelessness with notebooks and documents, or the report from Depot No. 345 dated 19 June on the laxness of security. Far from routine, however, was Marshal Timoshenko's telegram to Yeremenko on 19 June ordering him to hand over his Far Eastern command without delay to his chief of staff General Shelakhov and to return forthwith to Moscow. The Soviet naval command had also begun to stir itself. For more than three and a half months senior Soviet naval officers had grown increasingly worried as German planes flew – always with impunity – over Soviet naval bases in the Baltic, photographing Soviet naval dispositions. Admiral Kuznetsov early in March had prepared orders for Soviet naval AA guns to open fire on these photo-reconnaissance intruders, but Stalin, with Beria sitting in on this chastisement of the Soviet naval commander-in-chief, countermanded the orders: on 1 April the Main Naval Soviet issued a new directive to replace that of 3 March: 'Fire will not be opened [on German aircraft], but Soviet fighters will be sent up to force down hostile airarcft on our aerodromes.' Five days later a German plane appeared over Libau, aerial cameras clicking. Soviet fighters went up: the German aircraft refused the 'invitation' to land, whereupon the Soviet interceptors fired twenty warning shots. Wisely the German crew turned for home and the salt went into the wound when the German embassy subsequently protested at wanton Soviet firing on a 'weather plane'.

The Soviet Baltic Fleet was hardly secure in its new-found Baltic coast bases. Tallinn provided no proper protection, being scarcely fitted out as a main naval base, though it housed two Soviet battleships. Libau was an even riskier proposition. Admiral Kuznetsov planned to re-deploy his main units, but this had to go before the Main Naval Soviet at a session which Andrei Zhdanov attended, only to insist that the matter be referred to 'higher quarters', to Stalin. In the event Stalin agreed to a re-deployment, giving Kuznetsov the requisite permission verbally. The battleships *Marat* and *Oktyabrskaya Revolyutsiya* would move back to Kronstadt – move they did, but with fearful slowness. In the Black Sea, Soviet naval units had their own encounters with 'unidentified aircraft' and mystery submarines: Admiral Oktyabrskii ordered increased readiness and all units to signal 'Contact actual' on the occasion of these surface, submarine or aerial encounters. The Soviet naval command began to keep a plot of German surface movements.

There was more to it, however, than merely sightings. From Berlin came the Vorontsov report, specifying the probable date and form of the German attack; this was no 'doubtful source' but what Admiral Kuznetsov calls 'an official and responsible source'. There is no argument about the immediacy of Kuznetsov's action in passing this to Stalin: what is in doubt is the interpretation he laid upon this information. Kuznetsov asserts that, for all its origin and though it conformed to what had been learned elsewhere, he found nothing 'conclusive' in Vorontsov's signal. Equally, Admiral Kuznetsov admits that at that time he believed what was said about the situation in 'higher quarters' – where war was discounted – and accordingly issued orders for Vorontsov to return to Moscow from Berlin to deliver a personal report. Apparently Vorontsov's accurate and informative signal had gone forward to

Stalin as 'doubtful', with Kuznetsov himself diminishing its fading authenticity in the process.

Kuznetsov saw Stalin sometime between 13–14 June to report on current intelligence appreciations, on the Black Sea Front training exercises and also on the virtual German embargo on the delivery of material for the cruiser *Lützow* (purchased earlier by the Russians). The matter of fleet readiness did not come up. Over the question of peace and war, Kuznetsov had come to the conclusion that Stalin realized that war was – one day – inescapable, and that he reckoned on war: the 1939 Pact gave him only a breathing-space, not a full reprieve. On the other hand, Stalin remained convinced that Great Britain and the United States were plotting to involve Germany in a war with the Soviet Union: information emanating from Great Britain and from British sources about a supposed 'German attack' could only be part of this process. Nevertheless, Kuznetsov had looked at the navy plot of German movements and wanted to discuss this with Stalin. At the end of May the Political Administration of the Soviet Navy had submitted to Malenkov the reports of Soviet merchant marine captains about heavy German troop movements by transport and the shifting of equipment from Stettin and Swinemunde to Finland, only to be greeted with sustained silence. On 4 June, at a meeting of the Main Military Soviet, Malenkov had lashed out at the officers of the Political Administration who wished to introduce a new political training programme – a programme conceived 'as if we were going to be at war tomorrow'. This was precisely the retort Kuznetsov got a fortnight later when he proposed new orders to increase the readiness of the Soviet Navy; even though Zhdanov backed up the naval command, as on previous occasions he did nothing and Malenkov proceeded to countermand these instructions to the fleet. Meanwhile Kuznetsov had talked to Vatutin, Deputy Chief of the General Staff and head of the Operations Section: Vatutin had studied the daily reports which the Naval Staff passed to the General Staff and promised to inform Kuznetsov immediately of any change in the situation.

On the evening of 19 June Admiral Tributs, Baltic Fleet commander, together with his staff, deliberated over the reports coming in from the guard ships and from the frontier units. The news was plainly disquieting. A telephone call to Moscow elicited permission from Admiral Kuznetsov to bring the Baltic Fleet up to 'Readiness No. 2' state, which meant fuelling the ships and putting their crews on alert. The trucks rolled out of the garages and the officers dispersed from the headquarters building to man the Flag Officer's command station on the coast. The situation with the Northern Fleet seemed less alarming but it too went over to higher readiness. With their exercises completed by 17 June, ships of the Black Sea Fleet had for the most part made for their main base at Sevastopol, where the fleet was maintained at 'Readiness No. 2' rather than routine running. Close to the Rumanian frontier, the light craft of the Danube Flotilla, motor patrol boats, monitors and minesweepers, supported by coastal defences and fifteen 1-16 fighter planes, under the command of Rear-Admiral N.O. Abramov, were kept close to their stations and in regular contact with the staff of the Red Army 14th Rifle Corps holding the land sectors.

The Navy at least had some guidance. The Red Army, apart from stray instances of individual foresight, had as yet none.

Code-word 'Dortmund': to German commands in the east, as outlined in the High Command advisory order of 14 June, this would signify that Operation 'Barbarossa' must proceed: 'Altona' indicated postponement or cancellation, but all preparations were to be complete by 15 June. For six months, 17,000 trains had rolled into the eastern concentration areas, unloading the troops in five huge echelons. Late in May, the infantry had moved closer to the Soviet frontiers, always at night, but only after mid June did the armour and motorized forces begin to take up their final positions. Infantry destined for the Rumanian *place d'armes* and drawn from what had been the Balkan theatre marched to their areas – more than three hundred miles. The final disposition of Luftwaffe units was decided by the end of May and shortly after the first week in June the squadrons began their concentration. At this time also, the *Oberkommando des Heeres* issued its final instruction on sabotage and 'diversionary' activities, and the 'activation' of the anti-Soviet groups, displaced nationals or dissident natives, in whom the Germans naturally took the greatest interest; bridges, post offices, section of railway lines, signals centres, railway stations and other 'sensitive points' were now marked down for attack. In the north-west, *Abwehr II* marked down forty-five objectives for special attack, either by *Regiment 800* or by *Widerstandsgruppen* of the 'national minorities'. *Regiment 800* would be concerned, in the first instance, with objectives lying within fifteen kilometres of the frontier, so as to paralyse the defence, and to destroy the enemy's will to fight (*Wehrwille*). All German Army Groups had, without over-estimating the Soviet forces facing them, prepared defensive schemes to guard against a surprise Soviet blow: in the south-west, to oppose a thrust into Rumania, Operation 'Hubertus', and in the centre, 'Akk Berta' directed against the possibility of Soviet airborne landings and surprise ground attacks. But the offensive planning went forward relentlessly; on 9 June, Colonel-General Halder visited Fourth Army and discussed the special measures for 'surprise attack' – artillery, smoke-screens, rapid movement and evacuation of civilians from the operational zone. Plans for the assault on the river Bug, when the German *Ostheer* on 'B-Day at Y-Hours' would take the field, were far advanced, and drafted on 13 June.

The situation report on Soviet strength for 13 June, compiled by *Fremde Heere Ost*, noted the increase of Soviet forces in European Russia by the movement of 5 rifle divisions, 2 armoured divisions and a mechanized brigade: total strength, 150 rifle divisions, 7 armoured divisions, 38 armoured brigades. In the Baltic, 4 rifle divisions had been moved up and 2 cavalry divisions withdrawn. In the centre, movement continued, men and equipment alike, though the summer training programme could account for much of this; movement from Rostov-on-Don to the south had been noted, but no mobilization – merely the drafting of workers for defence construction – was reported. In sum, the situation was largely unchanged, though as German officers examined the 'voluminous' air photos, it became apparent that the Red Army would be committed in some strength in the region of the frontier.

The time and place – 22 June at 03.30 hours* – became known on 15 June in the commands. The code-words were established, the final dispositions to proceed after 18 June; signals, sabotage, security requirements had the finishing touches put to them, while at night the armour moved closer to its start-positions. From time to time, Soviet frontier guards had caught the sound of tank-engines; by day, the German assault forces lay hid. Army Group Centre set out the list of targets, signals centres and communication posts, which it required *Luftflotte II* to destroy: Kobrin, Volkovysk, Bialystok, Lida, Slutsk, Baranowice, Minsk (and its air force signals centre), Gomel, Moghilev, Orsha and Smolensk.

Of the 3,800,000 men of the German *Feldheer* as a whole, almost 3,200,000 were turned against the Soviet Union: 148 divisions – including 19 Panzer divisions, 12 motorized infantry divisions, 9 line of communications (*Sicherheits-divisionen*) divisions, reinforced by the anti-aircraft, anti-tank, engineer, heavy artillery units of the *Heerestruppen*: 3,350 tanks, 7,184 pieces of artillery, 600,000 lorries and more than 600,000 horses: three *Luftflotten* with over 2,000 aircraft. The *Ostheer* was supplemented by the allied forces of Rumania and those of Finland joined in 'Waffen-brüderschaft' if not actual alliance; after 24 June, Hungarian, Slovak, Italian and Spanish troops swelled these ranks still further.

The preparations were complete. The Nazi-Soviet Pact, which Hitler spurned completely and to which Stalin clung so desperately, had almost lived out its loathsome life.

---

* Military-operational timings have been presented here in this form, as they stand in the original documents or orders. (There was a difference of one hour between Moscow time and German summer time.) All other times are set down in the more conventional fashion.

BOOK TWO

Halting the Blitzkrieg
22 June 1941—19 November 1942

3
The Sunday Blow: 22 June 1941

Not all Soviet soldiers invited their own destruction. From Minsk at 02.40 hours on the morning of Saturday, 21 June, Major-General V.E. Klimovskikh (Chief of Staff in the Western Special Military District), in one more effort to impress Moscow with the seriousness of the situation, sent this signal:

German aircraft with loaded bomb-racks violated the frontier 20 June. According to report of 3rd Army commander, wire barricades along the frontier on the Augustovo, Seina roads though in position during the day are removed towards evening. From the woods, sounds of engines.

All through Friday Klimovskikh had received information about German activity on the frontier; like the rest, this was given to Pavlov and sent on to Moscow, to the General Staff. General Klich, district artillery commander, and already worried enough about his untrained gunners and his immobilized guns, summed up the results so far: 'Always the same reply – "Don't panic. Take it easy. 'The boss' knows all about it".' Commissar Pimenov, head of the political propaganda section of 6th Rifle Division, had already been branded 'panic-monger'; he had written to Pavlov asking for permission to take up defensive positions and to evacuate the wives and children from the Brest fortress. The staff of the NKVD frontier troops in Bialystok had put the frontier posts on alert on 18 June and all were standing by at noon on 21 June. But the orders about no firing on German aircraft still stood; when this order was confirmed in May, all personnel had to sign their receipt and understanding of it. The commander of the 97th Detachment who did open fire on aircraft was himself very nearly shot for it. No further orders were forthcoming, though the commander of the Soviet frontier troops, Lieutenant-General G.G. Sokolov, was at that time in Bialystok. Another senior officer from Moscow in the area was Lieutenant-General D.M. Karbyshev, a considerable expert on military fortifications, who had since early June carried out an inspection of the western defences – but not the most forward defensive positions, from which he was barred. Some of his fellow engineer officers, present at the field exercises of Red Army engineers supervised by General Vasiliev, saw with their own eyes that things were not quite so peaceful as was thought in *Building No. 2* of the Defence Commissariat.

What happened on the frontier, however, and what was made to happen – and not to happen – in its most immediate vicinity had become and still remained the exclusive prerogative of Stalin. Responsive to this will, the General Staff had once again between 15–18 June circulated a directive to the frontier commands, forbidding any concentration of troops in the frontier areas and continuing the ban on action against German aircraft. Scattered the troops undoubtedly were, both by deployment and by training plans; many in the Western Special Military District were on field exercises, like the 28th Rifle Corps (responsible for the Brest fortress and its area) with 9 rifle, 3 artillery and all engineer battalions at work on defences, its anti-aircraft guns and their crews away at Minsk on practice shoots, and its signal battalions in camp. The corps commander had reported that 'not less than $1–1\frac{1}{2}$ days' would be needed to assemble the corps. Meanwhile, in the old, historic, crenellated fortress of Brest, the Germans could see Soviet soldiers carrying out their routine drills, complete with band. Elsewhere on the Soviet side, the frontier appeared quiet and without alarms.

The situation in the Baltic district was not much different. Denied permission to concentrate, Kuznetsov had managed a few precautionary measures; some of his artillery was on its way to its positions, but the lack of gun-towing equipment slowed everything down and even when some of the guns reached their sites, they still needed ammunition. An anti-aircraft alert to AA guns had gone out on 18 June, operative to 21 June, but the gun-sites were short of crews and trained officers; black-outs in Riga, Kaunas, Vilna, Dvinsk and Libau had been ordered after the evening of 19 June, but all this took time and organization. The bomber forces continued with their night-training programme from 20–22 June; in most of the bomber regiments, the machines were undergoing their post-flight checks round about dawn – their fuel expended and their crews exhausted. The activation and laying of minefields had come on 21 June to a sudden halt; Major-General V.F. Zotov, chief of the Baltic military engineers, had begun to call out the civilian population to dig trenches and positions in the frontier areas, but he called off his engineers when cows from a collective farm had detonated some of the mines – an order given to prevent 'the spread of panic'.

In Leningrad, Andrei Zhdanov, member of the Military Soviet and Secretary of the regional Party Committee, left on 19 June for the Black Sea resort of Sochi. The day after Zhdanov left for his summer holiday, the Leningrad command received instructions from the General Staff to mine the frontier areas; the Finns on the Karelian isthmus were in the process of 'activating themselves'. For more than a month, the General Staff had pressed for the completion of the fixed frontier defences to the north of Leningrad. But to the south, where in 1940 the Leningrad command had handed over the Pskov–Ostrov 'fortified district' to the Baltic district, nothing at all had been done to plan any defences. The only troops in this area, which was so soon to become a terrible danger-spot, was an armoured formation located near Struga. Otherwise, the military cupboard was bare. As for moving troops, permission was impossible to come by. On the morning of 21 June, Lieutenant-General V.A. Frolov, commander of 14th Army (Leningrad MD) asked to be allowed to start the movement of his rifle and armoured troops; the Defence Commissariat refused him, but in the afternoon, 'at his own risk' – which was considerable – Frolov began to move the 52nd Rifle Division to its position in the Murmansk area. 42nd Rifle Corps (Kandalaksha) was similarly alerted. No doubt the terrain, grim and demanding as it was for man and machine alike, and the subsequent confusion, helped Frolov to get away with what turned out to be a sensible insubordination.*

What Frolov had accomplished with part of his army Kirponos at Kiev, in spite of repeated efforts, had so far failed to manage for his whole command. The signs of impending German attack were taken very seriously; the military observed the German build-up and attack preparations, the frontier guards reported on the frontier violations for intelligence and sabotage purposes. In the ten days from 10–21 June, NKVD guards intercepted eight agents of the OUN,† the Ukrainian nationalist movement which had fallen increasingly under German auspices; in German-occupied Poland, the special regiment *Nachtigall*, officially German-officered but with Ukrainian 'officers' also, had been training under the Wehrmacht for many months. For the moment, the scattered frontier forces, alerted by the cipher-signal of 18 June about the 'mass' of German troops, were under orders to observe further German movement and to stand by. The Red Army, however, lacked any such preliminary instruction. Kirponons's covering formations remained dispersed, his mobile reserves remained in the interior and his general reserves – 31st, 36th and 37th Rifle Corps, 15th, 9th and 19th Mechanized Corps – located in the Zhitomir–Kiev area.

On the morning of 21 June, the naval patrols reported nothing of significance, although the movements of three German transports, moving from Rumanian ports, caused some mystification in the Black Sea fleet command. Black Sea Fleet warships were coming in to Sevastopol; their crews required some rest after the training exercises, and no sailings were planned for the 22nd. Only a few aircraft were up, and no night flying had been scheduled. In the Baltic, the officers stood to, though no order had as yet been issued.

At the Soviet embassy in Berlin, where 'only a small group of Soviet diplomats was obliged to remain behind', most made ready to enjoy the promise of a fine day on 21 June. Ambassador Dekanozov had received another report about a German attack on 22 June; while this fell upon the ambassador's disbelieving ears, the information was transmitted to Moscow, which, during the morning of the 21st instructed the embassy to arrange an interview with

---

* In fact, operations by Frolov's adversary 'Army Group Norway' did not begin until the end of June, but Frolov did derive some benefit from his preliminary precautions.

† OUN: *Organizatsiia Ukraïn'skykh Natsionalistiv* (Organization of Ukrainian Nationalists) was formally established in 1929. As a result of the factional struggles within the nationalist movement, it split into two 'wings': OUN-B (the Bandera group) and OUN-M (the Mel'nyk group). Early in 1940, the Germans had set up training units for Ukrainians, and OUN-B came to play a pronounced part in this. *Nachtigall* formed up in 1941, and OUN-B and particular German officers had discussions on the role of the Ukrainians in the event of war. For a detailed treatment of this question, see John A. Armstrong, *Ukrainian Nationalism* (New York and London 1963), Chapter IV.

Ribbentrop. The Soviet diplomat charged with this duty, V. Berezhkov, found that Ribbentrop was 'out of town' and everybody else was 'out'. In the early afternoon, Director Wörmann promised to pass on any message, but Berezhkov was instructed to communicate directly only with Ribbentrop. The 'communication' was 'a demand for an explanation from the German government of the concentration of German troops on the Soviet frontier'. Moscow telephoned several times to hurry delivery of the message, but Berezhkov learned only that 'Ribbentrop was out and no one knew when he would be back'. In a diplomatic sense, he never returned. It was left to Molotov to summon Ambassador von Schulenburg to his office at 9.30 pm, there to repeat this hitherto unanswered and miserably plaintive query:

> There were a number of indications that the German Government was dissatisfied with the Soviet Government. Rumours were even current that a war was impending between Germany and the Soviet Union. They found sustenance in the fact that there was no reaction whatsoever to the TASS report of 13 June; that it was not even published in Germany. The Soviet Government was unable to understand the reasons for Germany's dissatisfaction . . . He would appreciate it if I [von Schulenburg] could tell him what had brought about the present situation in German-Soviet relations.

Von Schulenburg, uninformed himself of the German attack plans, could give no answer. The final crisis, however, had begun.

In the Soviet military commands, there was nothing as yet, apart from private premonitions, to distinguish this Saturday evening, 21 June, from any other; it promised to be, as Colonel Sandalov (Chief of Staff to 4th Army) described it, 'quite ordinary'. Red Army officers, senior and junior alike, made their way to the numerous garrison shows and theatres; many, like the Red Army men also, were actually at home. In the Minsk Officers Club, a popular comedy *The Wedding at Malinovka* was playing to a full house, with Colonel-General Pavlov, his chief of staff Klimovskikh and the district deputy commander, Lieutenant-General V.I. Boldin, in the audience. These evening pleasures were briefly interrupted by Colonel Blokhin, head of intelligence in the Western Special Military District, who reported to Pavlov that 'the frontier was in a state of alarm'; German troops had been brought to full combat readiness and firing had been reported in some sectors. Pavlov, who passed this on to Boldin, dismissed it as 'some kind of rumour'. Boldin, however, could not help recounting the latest intelligence summary to himself: by the evening of 21 June, German troops had been fully concentrated on the East Prussian, Warsaw and Deblin axes, and the bulk of the forces were now packed into a thirty-kilometre zone in the frontier areas. In Olshanka, south of Suvalki, heavy and medium tanks, heavy artillery, AA guns and 'many aircraft' had been reported. The Germans were setting up positions on the Western Bug; at Byalaya Podlyaska, forty train-loads of bridging equipment and large quantities of ammunition had been unloaded.

At about the time when Pavlov was interrupted in his box at the play, near Sokal (Kiev district command) a German deserter, Alfred Liskow, subsequently confessing himself a communist and a worker from Munich, crossed the Soviet lines at about 9 pm. He was taken at once to the area officer, Major M.S. Bychkovskii, who heard him say that his commanding officer announced a German attack at 04.00 hours on 22 June; German guns had taken up their fire-positions, and tanks and infantry were at their start-lines. Bychkovskii at once informed the commander of the Ukrainian Frontier District, Major-General V.L. Khomenko, of this information and passed it to 5th Army commander, Potapov. Further down the line, it went to the commanders of the 87th Rifle Corps and the 41st Tank Division. The matter having passed out of Bychkovskii's hands, he nevertheless ordered the guard to be doubled, and a close watch to be kept. Somewhat later, on his own initiative – dangerous enough – he ordered preparations for blowing up the bridge into Sokal; he sent one of his officers into the Strumilov 'fortified district' to get more explosives, but this was far from easy, since most of the Red Army officers had gone to Lwow for their free day on Sunday.

At the other end of what with devastating speed was so soon to become a colossal battle-front, the staff of the 5th Rifle Division was interrogating a Lithuanian deserter, who, with but faintly disguised relish, informed them that the German Army would attack at 04.00 hours and planned to 'finish you off pretty quickly'. The Germans were acutely well informed about the Soviet dispositions; they knew that the bulk of the corps to which the 5th Division was attached had its location at Kozlovo–Rudo, which they would bomb at dawn. Colonel Ozerov, divisional commander, was not himself in any two minds about whether 'war' or 'provocation' was afoot: he pointed to the evidence of the past week, with 'whole armadas' of German planes criss-crossing the Soviet lines in the Baltic. Corps Commissar Dibrov, a senior political officer who was also the third 'political member' of the major command organ, the Military Soviet of the Baltic district, had already telephoned twice from Riga, intimating that rifle sections should be left in the forward positions, but that their ammunition was to be withdrawn. Major-General M.S. Shumilov, 16th Corps commander, raged at this 'incitement to hysteria', but, with a sensible disregard for Dibrov, went ahead and issued ammunition. All this took place a little before midnight; not much before, the frontier troops reported to the military that they had received orders to evacuate their families. Had the Red Army, they asked, any contingency plan like this? Ozerov contacted corps HQ, which relayed this reply by telegraph:

You exhibit unnecessary nervousness. The families of the frontier troops live on the actual frontier, necessary to remove them from zone of possible provocation. As for your families who live in Kaunas, as far as is known nothing threatens them. Their evacuation would produce needless alarm among civilian population.

For the moment, Ozerov had his answer. As for deserters, the sardonic Lithuanian hardly disposed of the entire significance of their information. Stalin, who took the final decisions, was told of the news of attack brought by 'a German deserter', possibly Liskow, but elsewhere identified as one Wilhelm Korpik, a German communist labourer from Berlin, who crossed the Soviet lines after hearing the orders read to his unit. For his 'dis-information', Stalin ordered him to be shot forthwith. Liskow's interrogation had continued through the night and into the small hours of 22 June: it was not complete when at dawn German guns opened fire.

As Molotov in Moscow summoned von Schulenburg to his office at 9.30 pm, Dekanozov, all day denied access to Ribbentrop, finally called on von Weizsäcker to deliver a protest about German over-flights; stiffly, the German diplomat terminated Dekanozov's attempts 'to prolong the conversation some-what' and Dekanozov did not refer to those 'few questions' which he later explained were meant for the Reich foreign minister only, and from whom alone could come 'the clarification' which Moscow so avidly sought. Moscow's urgent telephone calls throughout the day had so far gone for nothing. That afternoon, from his East Prussian headquarters in the *Wolfsschanze* at Rastenburg, Hitler wrote to Mussolini at the end of 'the hardest decision of my life', to terminate 'the hypocritical performance in the Kremlin'. Now, on the eve of the 'final decision' – to be made at 7 pm, that evening – Hitler felt himself once more 'spiritually free', since the partnership with the Soviet Union had appeared 'a break with my whole origin, my concepts and my former obligations'; 'these mental agonies' were over. In this letter, useful for its summary of Hitler's strategic ideas but nauseating in its fake and forced moralizing, the Führer referred to the latest situation map of Soviet forces, whose 'concentration . . . is tremendous'. The latest compilation put Red Army strength at 154 rifle divisions, 10 armoured divisions and 37 mechanized brigades in European Russia. The *Lagebericht Ost* for 21 June noted some Soviet re-deployment, the transportation of tanks along the Minsk-Smolensk stretch of railway in the previous week and troop movements from the Far East and from the Urals in particular. Strong concentrations of Soviet parachute troops had been noted in the Ukraine (in fact, the exercises of the 6th and 212th Parachute Brigades had been reconnoitred on 20 June by a high-flying aircraft 'with Rumanian markings . . . which made off in a westerly direction'). The general situation, however, remained substantially unchanged, with no major modification in Soviet strength, dispositions and apparent intentions.

What German officers had themselves seen and could still see, crouched and waiting as they were on the Soviet frontiers, with their armour, artillery, assault and bridging units at the ready, merely confirmed the *Lagebericht*. Guderian's personal reconnaissance on 17 June convinced him, as he scrutinized the un-occupied Soviet strong-points on the Bug, that the Russians suspected nothing. After midnight on 21 June, the Berlin-Moscow express, cleared and checked without any deviation from normal practice, passed over the rail bridge and on to Brest-Litovsk without a hitch.* To the north, nothing disturbed the tranquillity of the East Prussian frontier. Southwards, in Army Group South's attack area, 48th Motorized Corps commander reported at midnight that 'Sokal is not blacked out. The Russians are manning their posts which are fully illuminated. Apparently they suspect nothing.'

That the Russians lacked suspicions was by no means true. The Soviet naval command, regional and central, was definitely uneasy. In the Baltic, Soviet patrol boats had reported nothing of significance (except noticeably less German shipping), but on the evening of 21 June the Military Soviet of the Baltic Fleet did not leave staff headquarters. At 22.40 hours, Admiral Tributs summoned Panteleyev, his chief of staff, and announced that he had talked to Admiral Kuznetsov in Moscow; Panteleyev at once summoned the senior staff officers, and at three minutes to midnight, in accordance with Kuznetsov's instruction, the Baltic Fleet went over to 'Readiness state No. 1', a fully operational state. Promptly at midnight, the staff transferred itself to the advanced command post, where, sitting at a table drinking tea, Operations Officer Captain Pilipovskii and Mobilization Chief Colonel Illin quickly reviewed their preparations. The patrol line, with the sweeper *Krambol* in the lead, was strengthened, but as yet nothing had been reported. Panteleyev ordered the Libau base commander to move his submarines to Ust-Dvinsk, and the Hango base commander to shift his submarines and torpedo-boats to Palkisk. A number of warships currently undergoing trials were now placed under operational command and would be 'accepted' for the fleet as from 22 June; others, tested but unfitted, were rushed back to the Leningrad yards.

Kuznetsov sent the same signal on operational readiness to the Black Sea Fleet at three minutes to midnight. (It went out subsequently to the Northern Fleet, to the Pinsk and Danube Flotillas.) At the Sevastopol naval base, the immediate concern of the duty officer had been to see to the movements of a tug towing barges laden with refuse. After midnight, duty officer Rybalko handed over to a subordinate in order to take a short rest; however, he was roused shortly and summoned to a senior officer, Eliseyev, who had him read Kuznetsov's signal. The fleet commander, Vice-Admiral F.S. Oktyabrskii, was alerted and very soon the warning signals went out to ships and shore installations. The base and its warships began to 'black out'. Within the hour (at 01.55 hours on 22 June) the officers and ratings of the fleet tumbled to a 'general muster' as the sirens wailed over Sevastopol.

Even so, these were but single alerts; as yet not a single order had been issued to either the Red Army or the Navy. Of Stalin's own activity at this juncture,

---

* Even later, a goods train with grain trucks was passed on to the German side. Not until dawn did the Soviet transportation administration send out a telegram to all track chiefs to 'hold all transit and export trucks destined for Germany'. A statement of the tally of such traffic was to be submitted by 18.00 hours, 22 June.

there are indications that he had begun to grasp at part of the danger which loomed so terrifyingly over the Soviet Union. On Saturday, 21 June, Tyulenev, commander of the Moscow Military District, was summoned to the telephone out of which issued 'the muffled voice' of Stalin, who put a question without more ado: 'Comrade Tyulenev, what is the position concerning Moscow's anti-aircraft defences?' Tyulenev duly reported on the readiness state, whereupon he was told: 'Listen, the situation is uncertain and therefore you must bring the anti-aircraft defences of Moscow up to 75 per cent of their readiness state.' Tyulenev passed this order to Major-General Gromadin, the AA defence commander in Moscow, without delay. Later that same evening (Saturday) Tyulenev went to the Defence Commissariat where he met Marshal Timoshenko, who informed him that signs of a very tense situation on the frontier were growing and were fully 'confirmed'. In Moscow the German embassy appeared to be very much on the alert and officials were apparently on the move. So far Soviet General Staff reports indicated that it was 'all quiet' on the frontier itself but information from military district commanders, fully supported by intelligence reports, emphasized the possibility of a German attack. The gist of all this Marshal Timoshenko had conveyed to Stalin, who thus far was inclined to dismiss it as 'panicking to no purpose'.

Precisely what was passing through Stalin's mind still remains something of a mystery. He certainly wanted no rash or premature move and was bent on steering wide of anything which might be construed as 'provocation'. Nevertheless, late in the afternoon of 21 June he acted as if he sensed greater danger. It is by no means easy to fix the chronology of the late afternoon and early evening interlude of 21 June, but about 5 pm Stalin set about some precautionary moves of his own. He ordered the Moscow Party leaders A.S. Shcherbakov and V.P. Pronin to make their way to the Kremlin to see him in person: once there, Stalin instructed them to warn all Party *raikom* (district) secretaries not to leave their posts and under no circumstances to leave their particular towns. '*Vozmozhno napadenie Nemtsev*', 'The Germans might attack' was the cryptic formula he used to cover all these instructions. But for the military there was as yet no order or instruction, and time was slipping away if any effective disposition was to be made. It was not the imminence of war but the phantasy of 'provocation' which seemed to occupy Stalin. With the civilian leaders he could perhaps be a little more forthright, for they could do nothing in effect but stand and wait, while the soldiers had to be held on some leash lest they succumb to 'panic' and were unnerved to the point of opening fire. The senior soldiers, however, began to realize that they could not leave it much later and had apparently resolved to get permission 'at all costs' to alert Soviet troops. Last minute information from a German deserter seemed to offer the chance to press this upon Stalin.

Tyulenev, having duly checked with Timoshenko and the General Staff, who intimated that as far as they knew the Germans on the western frontiers did not enjoy 'over-all superiority', took his leave and made for his *dacha* on the outskirts of Moscow. But even as Tyulenev sped to his week-end home, German troops were beginning to move to their battle-stations, closing inexorably on the Soviet frontiers: under cover of the night German armour advanced to its start-lines, all shortly after midnight. At 01.00 hours on 22 June 1941 the separate Army commands in the east transmitted their call-signs indicating full and final readiness – '*Kyffhäuser*' from Fourth Army, '*Wotan*' from von Rundtstedt's command. Guderian was on his way to his command post, which he reached at 02.10 hours. The assault troops made their way steadily forward, investing the thick, green banks of the Bug. The officers had read or were reading to their men the Führer's personal order, 'To the Soldiers of the *Ostfront*'. One order they did not read – the 'Commissar Order' prescribing death for military commissars of the Red Army when captured. The other directive, that concerning the rules governing the conduct of German troops in the East, had already had a turbulent career, and in some commands was not even circulated. Already obeying their own laws were the specialists of *Regiment 800*, the 'Branden-burgers', many of them Russian-speaking, infiltrated – or dropped by parachute – behind the Soviet lines; once there, they proceeded to blow up or incapacitate power and signals facilities, activate German agents, secure bridges vital for German movement from demolition, and spread, by false messages and fake orders, alarm and confusion. Dressed in Red Army uniform, the *800* men were making for Brest fortress or for the bridges over the Bug; a number of men, smuggled in on Saturday in goods trains or hidden under loads of gravel in rail trucks, had been in the town of Brest for many hours. At 02.20 hours the Soviet 4th Army command, having finished the interrogation of yet one more German deserter who had crossed the Soviet lines west of Volchin, began to circulate this latest confirmation of a German attack due in less than two hours. The news never got out. The telephone lines had already been cut.

This interruption of Soviet signals traffic was of the utmost importance, coupled with the fact that very late – too late – the Defence Commissariat finally stirred from its dangerous torpor. Earlier in the evening Lieutenant-General M.A. Purkayev, Chief of Staff of the Kiev Special Military District, telephoned to report that a German NCO had deserted to the Soviet lines and informed Soviet frontier guards that an attack was imminent and was timed for the morning of 22 June. General Zhukov in turn reported this to Timo-shenko and to Stalin: the latter ordered Timoshenko, Zhukov and his deputy Vatutin to the Kremlin without delay. With creditable presence of mind Zhukov took a draft operational directive for Soviet commanders with him. This time Timoshenko, Zhukov and Vatutin determined to get that vital permission to transmit an alert. It was a Stalin 'plainly worried' who received the commanders: he suggested to the officers that the German generals had sent this deserter over to the Soviet side 'to provoke a conflict', but his visitors disagreed quite bluntly, 'We think the deserter is telling the truth.' Members of the Politburo joined the meeting, but none could answer Stalin's question:

'What are we to do about it?' At this point Marshal Timoshenko broke the
eerie internal silence and proposed sending out an alert order to the troops of
the border military districts. Zhukov read his draft order, which did not meet
with Stalin's full approval:

> It is too soon to issue such a directive – perhaps the question can still be settled peace-
> fully. We must issue a short directive stating that an attack may begin with provocative
> actions by the German forces. The troops of the border districts must not be incited by
> any provocation in order to avoid complications.

Looking now at the revised draft, Stalin agreed to this shorter text, made a few
alterations himself and handed it to Timoshenko to sign. Vutatin took the order
to the General Staff for immediate transmission, a process which was complete
by 00.30 hours on 22 June. But Zhukov knew already that it was too late, if
the Wehrmacht did go over to the offensive in a matter of hours. Nor did the
directive provide any real guidance to District commanders, save for indicating
a late and cautiously phrased sense of danger:

To Military Soviets Leningrad MD, Baltic MD, Western MD, Kiev MD, Odessa MD.

Copy People's Commissar for the Navy

1 During the course of 22-23.6.41 a surprise attack by the Germans on the fronts of the
   Leningrad, Baltic Special, Western Special, Kiev Special and Odessa Military Districts
   is possible.
2 The assignment of our forces – not to give way to provocative actions of any kind
   which might produce major complications. At the same time troops of the Leningrad,
   Baltic Special, Western Special, Kiev Special and Odessa Military Districts to be at full
   combat readiness, to meet a possible surprise blow by the Germans and their allies.
3 I thereby order:
   (a) during the night of 22.6.41 secretly to man the fire-points of the fortified districts
       (URS) on the state frontiers;
   (b) before dawn on 22.6.41 to disperse all aircraft including military planes among field
       aerodromes and thoroughly camouflage the machines;
   (c) all units to be brought to a state of combat readiness. Troops to be held in dispersed
       form and kept camouflaged;
   (d) air defence forces to be brought to combat readiness without drawing on reservist
       personnel. Preparation of all measures to black out cities and installations;
   (e) no other measures to be taken without special authorization.

21.6.41   TIMOSHENKO ZHUKOV

This warning order went out under the designation of '*O razvertvyvanii voisk s
sootvetstvii s planom prikritya mobilizatsii i strategicheskovo sosredotocheniya*',
'Deployment of forces in accordance with the plan for covering mobilization
and strategic concentration'; towards 12.30 am, Timoshenko and Zhukov told
Stalin that most reports now indicated that German units were definitely
moving up to the frontier. Stalin asked if the warning order had been sent out
and was told that this had indeed been done.

The district commands, depending in no small degree upon the competence and shrewdness of their chiefs, reacted with varying speeds to this order, though Military Soviets were authorized to transmit 'analogical orders' by 02.25 hours. Colonel-General Kuznetsov in the Baltic instructed his army commander in this fashion.

During the course of the night of 22.6.41 secretly to man the defences of the basic zones. In the forward zone to move in field sentries to guard the pill-boxes, but the sections assigned to occupy the forward zone to be held back. Cartridges and shells to be issued. In the case of provocative action by the Germans, fire *not* to be opened. In the event of flights by German aircraft over our territory, to make no demonstration and until such time as enemy aircraft undertake military operations, *no fire* to be opened on them. In the event of strong enemy forces undertaking offensive operations, to destroy them. To position anti-tank mines and minor obstacles without delay.

Not a line of any of this gave the formation commanders any real notion as to what they should do or just how they decided between 'war' and 'provocation'. With dawn as the deadline, some tasks were beyond fulfilment; in the Western and Kiev military districts, the fighters and some bombers were so far neatly lined up on the runways on airfields thoroughly pinpointed by the Germans. Not hundreds but thousands of machines were thus displayed in a style best fitted to ensure their destruction. Only Major-General M.V. Zakharov, commander in Odessa where the 9th Army was being formed, had ordered his aviation to disperse by dawn on 22 June to the field aerodromes; this he did on the evening of 21 June, at which time he instructed his corps commanders to move their troops from populated centres and to organize close contact between covering detachments and frontier troops. Elsewhere, with communications even now being sliced away or shattered, the chances of a rapid dispersal had already vanished.

It was at 03.00 hours that Pavlov, following his general 'instruction' from Timoshenko, sent out the code-word GROZA which permitted formations to go over to full combat readiness and for the fire-points in the 'fortified districts' to be fully manned. This order, vague as it was, lost what little utility it had since it failed to reach many formations. The 4th Army in Pavlov's command had been isolated for some time, but not before it had heard from the Brest fortress that the electric power had gone, that the water supply was damaged and telephone lines cut. The signals officer, Colonel Litvinenko, sent out repair squads and at 03.30 hours 4th Army was again in contact with Minsk and Brest. At that point precisely, Pavlov came on the line to say that a 'provocationist raid by Fascist bands on to Soviet territory' was likely; there was to be no response to this 'provocation', these 'bands' were to be made prisoner but *the frontier must not be crossed*. Major-General Korobkov asked for specific orders: Pavlov told him to bring his troops up to full readiness, move elements of the 42nd Rifle Division from the Brest fortress to take up defensive positions and

to disperse aviation regiments to the field aerodromes. Almost on the stroke of
04.00 hours Korobkov contacted the staff of the 42nd Rifle Division – just as
the German guns opened fire. At 05.30 hours 4th Army finally received its
copy of Timoshenko's first warning order. There was no mention of the bridges
over the Bug; 4th Army guarded the six bridges over the river – two rail
bridges, four road bridges, and only the railway bridge at Brest was mined.
The others were not prepared for demolition and so far no order had come
through about blowing up the railway bridge.

One hour after Timoshenko's order to Red Army district commanders,
Admiral Kuznetsov sent a signal of almost identical language to senior Soviet
naval officers. Admiral Tributs in the Baltic found himself baffled in trying to
resolve the contradiction in 'not responding to provocation' and 'responding
to a surprise attack by the Germans or their allies with all available forces'. His
ships were manned, and at the highest state of readiness, No. 1, had been put
under the articles of war by their captains. They were, however, short of fuel,
in nearly every case by as much as 50 per cent of their operational requirements.
The commander of the Hango base, Major-General Kabanov had, without
declaring any 'official' alert status, during the evening of 21 June moved two
regiments up to the land frontier with Finland, deployed his forces and also put
into operation Admiral Tributs' personal 'recommendation' to him that the
6,000 women and children should be evacuated by fast passenger ship. The
light forces under Drozd cruised in the Gulf of Riga; submarines and torpedo
boats were on the move, and so were a number of Soviet merchant ships, like
the Latvian steamer *Gaisma*. At 03.20 hours, off Gotland, the *Gaisma* was
shelled by four German torpedo-boats; after the shells came torpedoes, which
broke the ship in half; an hour later (04.15 hours) her captain sent this last
signal 'Torpedoed, *Gaisma* sinking. Good-bye.'

At the moment when the *Gaisma* came under fire, the Black Sea Fleet had
manned its ships in Sevastopol and had reported the approach of unidentified
aircraft towards the blacked-out city. It had been difficult to signal to the light-
houses to extinguish their lamps; with communications once again widely cut,
Major-General Morgunov, garrison commander, suggested sending motor-
cyclists up from the nearest gun-batteries to have the lights extinguished. The
Upper Inkermann Light, however, could not be contacted and blazed out into
the night as the German bombers and minelayers flew in to the attack. At
03.17 hours Vice-Admiral Oktyabrskii contacted Zhukov at the Defence
Commissariat in Moscow, reported the approach of a large force of unidentified aircraft and requested instructions: on being asked by Zhukov what
he intended to do, the Admiral replied briskly that the only course was to open
fire. After a hurried consultation with Timoshenko, Zhukov told the Fleet
commander to 'act' and report to the Naval Commissar. At 03.13 hours
Soviet searchlights had been switched on and within minutes as the German
aircraft loaded with magnetic mines made their approaches at no great height,

AA guns opened fire from ship and shore batteries. The Fleet fire control officer, Colonel Zhilin, was evidently very sceptical about the order to open fire, which came through the duty officer: he insisted on recording in the war diary that he was not responsible for this particular order. Almost at once the parachute mines came floating down. Hearing no explosions but seeing the parachutes, the intelligence officer Colonel Hamgaladze assumed that an airborne attack on the naval base was imminent and ordered the duty officer Colonel Rayev to 'take measures' to defend the headquarters. Rayev replied that he had no men: the only recourse was to organize a company of sailors from a training squad. Many men, sailors and civilians alike, thought that all this was simply another exercise designed to increase 'vigilance', but the Black Sea Fleet had actually gone to war. Oktyabrskii reported to Moscow at about 4 am that the German air attack had been beaten off. The Fleet aviation commander Rusakov was summoned to Oktyabrskii and at 04.13 hours Soviet fighters were patrolling the naval base.

Admiral Golovko in command of the Northern Fleet also had troubles of his own with his orders. Two days previously, on 19 June, the Main Naval Staff had instructed him to prepare his submarines for sea. Golovko had as a consequence consulted Admiral Isakov about the nature of the operational tasks assigned to the submarine forces in the event of war. Golovko had plans of his own for using his larger submarines,* the 'pikes', against German communications, and even using the 'babies', the smaller craft in this role. Now, in the early hours of 22 June, he had no clear orders at all; the operational-readiness alert had been radioed to him, followed after twenty minutes by Kuznetsov's directive which puzzled Golovko as much as it baffled Tributs, followed by a third signal at 03.00 hours ordering the Northern Fleet to dispatch at 07.00 hours two submarines (the Naval Staff did not specify the type), the minelayers *Groznyi* and *Sokrushitelnyi* and a flight of MBR-2 bombers to guard the mouth of the White Sea. The Northern Fleet was alerted but bereft of actual orders which had any bearing on those 'unidentified' planes and ships whose movements very properly concerned Golovko. His command had not yet really gone to war.

These scuffles and clashes round the vast periphery waxed and waned. But on the enormous land front, where the German Army lay massed on its selected axes, the final moments had begun to tick away to zero-hour: 03.30 hours. To eliminate the possibility of the Russians having time to recover themselves between the air and artillery blows, German bombers operating against the Belorussian airfields had made high-altitude approaches under the cover of night, betraying no mass movement of aircraft over the Soviet frontiers; they were already sweeping down with open bomb-doors to obliterate at the first light Soviet fighters – massed on their sixty-six aerodromes – with one savage,

* Golovko had 15 submarines (medium and small), 20 light surface units and a few minesweepers in June 1941: there were 115 aircraft (80 fighters).

surprising and terribly wounding blow. In a wider arc, the bombers of the *Luftflotten* spread out and with the approach of dawn Soviet cities, towns and a cluster of select targets were under sustained attack: Kovno, Rovno, Odessa, Sevastopol, Minsk, the Baltic bases, rippling across Russia in great flashes of fire and destruction.

Reports of the German air attacks came tumbling into Moscow. At the Defence Commissariat Voronov, the Air Defence (PVO) commander, was passing all the information his command possessed on German air movement to Timoshenko. Voronov, a colonel-general of artillery, had only been in his present post for a week, for on 14 June Colonel-General G.M. Shtern was suddenly relieved of his command as head of the PVO. Voronov took over and now sat with Timoshenko, who without making any comment on the reports asked the PVO commander to use the signal pad in front of him and present his information 'in written form'. Lev Mekhlis, whose role as Stalin's watchdog usually boded ill for the military, scrutinized Voronov as he wrote and then suggested that he sign the document when he had finished. The net result was that Voronov was instructed to return to his own command post, though he went without operational orders of any kind and without an express instruction to activate Soviet AA defences. At about 3.45 am, however, Timoshenko ordered Zhukov to telephone Stalin and tell him about the wave of German bombing raids. Stalin's response, according to Zhukov, was to order a session of the Politburo: he made no reply to Zhukov's request for Soviet retaliation in the face of the German raids. Tyulenev, who earlier had gone to his *dacha*, was now brought hurtling back to Moscow and to the Kremlin: pausing on his way to consult Zhukov, he learned of the widespread German bombing and of Stalin's reaction to it. Once in the Kremlin, Tyulenev was met by the commandant upon whose heels came Marshal Voroshilov. Voroshilov straightway asked Tyulenev: 'Where has the Supreme Commander's command centre been set up?' Tyulenev was taken completely aback. No such centre existed; all he could suggest was that the Supreme Commander – whoever he might be – could make use of the Moscow Military District or Moscow Air Defence Command HQS, both of which were at least guarded.

Admiral Kuznetsov, the naval commander-in-chief, also found himself similarly bemused. It had been about 11 pm (21 June) when Marshal Timoshenko ordered him to report at once and in person: 'very important information' had just come in to the Defence Commissariat. Within the past hour or so Kuznetsov had come upon some quite important information of his own; the Soviet attaché Vorontsov, whom Admiral Kuznetsov had ordered back from Berlin to make a personal report on the spot in Moscow, had appeared and had reported at once to Kuznetsov as he had been ordered to do. This time there was everything that was 'conclusive' about Captain Vorontsov's report: for almost an hour the Soviet attaché retailed what was happening on the German side and repeated that a German attack would come at any hour. There could be ńo mistaking Vorontsov's emphatic statement: 'It's war.' A freak of the summer weather seemed to uńderline Vorontsov's words, for suddenly the thunder rolled, the wind spun the dust in the streets and driving rain scattered the Muscovites taking their casual, cheerful strolls on a Saturday evening in June.

When Kuznetsov left for the Defence Commissariat, the rain had stopped and the pavements had dried. The Defence Commissariat was the building next to his own, no great distance. Once inside, Admiral Kuznetsov found Timoshenko and Zhukov seated and writing: the Admiral saw the lengthy, three-page telegram which General Zhukov was on the point of dispatching to the Military District commanders. Kuznetsov asked Zhukov if 'resort to weapons' was authorized 'in the event of attack'. Zhukov replied somewhat tersely that it was, at which Kuznetsov sent Alafuzov, head of the Naval Staff, racing to send out signals authorizing 'No. 1 Readiness' state. That was the night Kuznetsov recalls, when Soviet admirals ran helter-skelter down the street, signal-pad in hand. Twenty minutes later Kuznetsov sent out his directive:

In the course of 22 and 23 June there is the possibility of a German surprise attack. The German attack may begin with provocations. Our task is not to respond to any provocations which may bring complications. Simultaneously fleets and flotillas will come to full combat readiness, to meet surprise attacks by the Germans or their allies. I order: transition to Readiness No. 1 to be carefully camouflaged. Reconnaissance in foreign territorial waters categorically forbidden. No other measures without special authorization.

KUZNETSOV

One by one the fleet commanders reported to Moscow: by 02.40 hours, 22 June, Kuznetsov recorded all fleets, ships and stations at full readiness. Half an hour later it was growing light in Moscow. For a moment Kuznetsov stretched out on a settee, only to be roused by the telephone – Oktyabrskii reporting the air attacks on Sevastopol. Kuznetsov checked the time: 03.15 hours. On trying to raise Stalin by telephone, Kuznetsov could only reach the Kremlin duty officer, who did not know Stalin's whereabouts. Kuznetsov telephoned Timoshenko to report 'a state of war' and tried Stalin again, whereupon the duty officer put him through to Malenkov, who greeted the Admiral's news with utter disbelief: 'Do you know what you are reporting?' Kuznetsov replied that he did and took full responsibility for it, at which Malenkov put the telephone down. (A little later a Kremlin officer contacted Sevastopol naval HQ separately.)

Hurt immediately by the German bombers, the Red Army had been struck some swift and secret blows even before the German artillery opened fire. At Koden, where the bridge across the Bug was vital for the rapid deployment of German armour, in the sector of the Soviet 4th Army, Soviet frontier guards were summoned from their positions by their German counterparts with shouts of 'important business'. The German assault parties quickly machine-gunned the Russians as they made their appearance and seized the bridge, which was not mined. Across the railway bridge at Brest, also spanning the Bug, German assault infantry and combat engineers cut down the Soviet sentry, machine-gunned the Soviet detail in its guard post and, after a rapid inspection, tore out the demolition charge from the central pier.

At 03.15 hours, the German guns on the front facing the Bug opened fire. From that moment, the giant arc of the Soviet land frontier rippled with flame and rocked with thunder as German batteries hammered the Soviet defences: German assault troops, rubber dinghies for the crossings, submersible tanks, bridging equipment, and the first clashes with the Soviet frontier guards who fought it out with their rifles and machine-guns. To the north, there was appreciably less artillery preparation; with the mist and half-light to aid the attackers, German infantry and armour slid out of their concealment and moved on the Soviet defences. Southwards, with the day beginning, von Rundstedt's armies used their guns on the Soviet defences, and then raced for their river crossing on the lower Bug and San.

With the *Ostheer* hurled irrevocably against the Soviet Union, in one enormous wave of attacks and assaults, in Berlin the Soviet ambassador faced Ribbentrop at 4 am to hear a German explanation. In his brownish ministerial uniform, and seated at a large table in a huge room in the foreign ministry, Ribbentrop launched at once into the reasons for the Reich taking 'military counter-measures'. Ribbentrop thereupon handed Dekanozov a memorandum with its 'detailed statement'; Dekanozov interposed to say that he had earlier asked for an interview with the Reich foreign minister in order to 'put a few questions that, in his opinion, required clarification'. This Ribbentrop brushed aside, and proceeded to catalogue the implications of the 'hostile policy' pursued by the Soviet Union. Hearing Ribbentrop out, Dekanozov expressed his regret and took his leave – perfunctorily, according to the German eyewitness, with a parting shot about this 'act of insolent, unprovoked aggression' according to the Soviet witness. In the Soviet embassy, the telephones had been disconnected. The embassy staff tuned in to Moscow radio, when the morning news (6 am Moscow time) was due; to the astonishment of these listeners, the news, preceded by a physical fitness interlude and an item for children, contained only non-Soviet war news and reports of progress in Soviet agriculture and industry. Cut off from Moscow, the Soviet officials tried to send news of the interview with Ribbentrop by telegram; slipping out of the embassy in a small yellow Opel-Olympia car, a Soviet diplomat succeeded in reaching a post office, in handing in a telegram for Moscow and in having it receipted. Not surprisingly, the telegram never reached Moscow.

At 5.30 am (Moscow time) von Schulenburg, who had asked for an interview with Molotov, delivered what amounted to the German declaration of war. For Molotov, who had heard of the widespread German bombing raids and who sought some·explanation, there was nothing to do but to read the final passage of the German statement:

> To sum up, the Government of the Reich declares, therefore, that the Soviet Government, contrary to the obligations it assumed
> 1 has not only continued, but even intensified its attempts to undermine Germany and Europe;
> 2 has adopted an increasingly anti-German policy;
> 3 has concentrated all its forces in readiness at the German border. Thereby the Soviet Government has broken its treaties with Germany and is about to attack Germany from the rear, in its struggle for life. The Führer has therefore ordered the Wehrmacht to oppose this threat with all the means at its disposal.
> End of declaration.

'The German Government has declared war on us.' This was the stark and terrifying report Molotov brought back to Stalin's office in the Kremlin. Who could now cling to any thought that the bombardment by land and air, followed by unmistakable offensive action on the ground by the Wehrmacht in full fighting array, was simply a 'provocation'? Stalin's notion that this was 'provocation' rather than full-scale, all-out war was possibly based on his assumption that a 'surprise attack' was really out of the question, that Hitler aimed at forcing the Soviet Union into being the first to breach the Nazi–Soviet Pact and that thereafter, branded as 'aggressors', the Russians would be an easy political picking. 'Border incidents' could only be designed to trap Stalin into playing Hitler's game, hence the tight clamp on the Red Army and the refusal to countenance effective operational orders. At the news of a state of war, Stalin 'sank down into his chair and lost himself in thought'. There was much for him to think on. The Pact was also Stalin's own creation, the foundation of his policy and, while it endured, the measure of his success. His fundamental miscalculation was perhaps in believing that Hitler needed it as much as he did. As for his opinion of the German Army, the subservience – and ignorance – of his advisers may have helped to implant the image of a Hitler held to ransom by his war-hungry generals. All this Stalin could reckon on in the calm of his quarters in the Kremlin. Timoshenko could take no steps without his approval. Both were almost wholly unaware of the havoc on the frontiers, where all the commanders could do was to wait amidst the destruction and chaos, or to signal higher staffs and then still be told: 'Wait'.

The most immediate of many crises was at the centre, in Pavlov's command. In Minsk, amidst communications which worked only fitfully, Pavlov heard the commanders of the 3rd, 10th and 4th Armies report German penetrations of the frontiers at Sopotskin, up to Augustovo, continued German bombing, and the fracture of the signals lines: two radio stations on which army commanders might have relied had also been put out of action. Shortly after 4 am, Timoshenko telephoned and Pavlov reported the situation; and all the while, the information seeped into Pavlov's HQ – bombing, sabotage, shelling, German attacks along the frontier. Colonel Blokhin produced another report: Pavlov's command was being assaulted by 13 German infantry divisions, 5 tank divisions, 2 motorized divisions and airborne units, supported by 40 artillery and 5 aviation regiments. Now the German bombers hammered Bialystok, Grodno, Lida, Volkovysk, Brest and Kobrin. The staff of 4th Army was located at Kobrin: Korobkov had already put the Brest and Vysoki garrisons on the alert, but the Brest fortress was already fully engaged:

The buildings and stores in the fortress, the military installations and also the railway station at Brest were swept by shelling, and at the same time fire broke out as a result of the continuation of the intensive bombardment. All communications were cut at once.

What the 28th Rifle Corps (Major-General Popov) recorded was similar to the entry in 4th Army's war diary:

... like thunder from a clear sky, throughout the depth of the frontier zone, unexpectedly, the roar of a barrage. The surprise Fascist artillery-fire burst on those points where the rifle and engineer units building fortifications were spending the night, on sections located on the Brest training ground and on the frontier guards' posts. The most intensive artillery fire was directed against the military cantonments of Brest and especially on the Brest fortress. The latter was literally covered all over with uninterrupted artillery and mortar fire.

4th Army command tried hard to get to Brest to direct the operations; failing this, the danger loomed of losing contact with mechanized and aviation formations, with the flank divisions of 4th Army, and with Minsk itself. But Korobkov first needed permission to move, and he was, for the moment, stuck fast in Kobrin. At 05.30 hours, just as 4th Army received a copy of Timoshenko's midnight order about the possibility of a 'surprise blow', German dive-bombers blew the Kobrin HQ to pieces; the staff moved some three miles away, to Bukhovich. Before communications went completely dead, Korobkov received a telegram from Minsk, timed 05.25 hours: 'In view of the large-scale military operations proceeding from the Germans I order you: mobilize your troops and proceed as with combat operations [po-boevemu].' Through Kobrin, lately evacuated by Fourth Army staff, and battered by German dive-bombers, walked those engineer officers who had just the day before been inspecting the district exercises. They were searching for the senior officers who were due to attend the exercises, and who might have orders of some kind. In the town, ripped by bombing, the populace listened amazed to the Moscow news broadcast relayed over the loud-speakers, with its breezy keep-fit exercises followed by news of socialist triumphs in Soviet factories (the same items heard by the stupefied listeners in the Berlin embassy). The engineer officers had also seen a shot-up Soviet aerodrome, with crews salvaging what they could from the burning wrecks. What they did not know was that the Luftwaffe had carried out an aerial massacre, strafing and bombing the neatly parked aircraft on the ground: in just a few hours (to noon, 22 June), the Western district lost 528 planes on the ground and 210 in the air. The Soviet Air Force lost in all 1,200 machines (many of them newly delivered) by the same noon. At 04.30 hours, twenty-eight Soviet fighters took off to intercept the German bombers and fighters: they were to fight and to ram them, but the German bombers cruised as yet largely unmolested.

In Minsk, Timoshenko telephoned from Moscow a fourth time, and Boldin, Pavlov's deputy, gave him a report. Timoshenko then instructed Boldin – 'I am telling you this and I wish you to pass it to Pavlov' – that no operations against the Germans were to be undertaken without Moscow's express permission: 'Comrade Stalin will not permit artillery fire to be returned against the Germans.' All that was permitted was reconnaissance for no more than sixty kilometres into German territory. Boldin apparently argued, pointing to the threat already developing to their communications, and the need to activate the mechanized forces and in particular the AA defences, but to no avail. Boldin scarcely thought that this was a German provocation; on the other hand, Korobkov of the 4th Army confessed to his chief of staff that he was not entirely convinced. At last Timoshenko gave permission for the 'red packets', the cover plans, to be opened; but even then, in the 3rd and 4th Armies, the staffs were able to decipher only a part of their orders, and 10th Army, already in a tight spot, had some heavy fighting on its hands, in which 'cover plans' meant nothing. German bombers had hit fuel dumps and signal points with persistent accuracy in 10th Army area, bleeding and unnerving the formation from the very first moments. Within a few hours, it began to break to pieces, uncovering Bialystok. The Soviet 3rd Army (Lieutenant-General Kuznetsov), on Pavlov's right flank, and covering the junction with the Baltic district, found itself attacked at its front and in its right flank; in the first hour, 3rd Army communications were cut and stayed out of action, there being no radio sets in use. Pavlov had only one signal from Kuznetsov; the rest was silence.

After 5 am fierce fighting began to develop in the area of the Brest fortress; the fire from Russian guns, small and medium, denied the Germans effective use of the railway bridges – the Brest bridge came under fire from the fortress, the bridge at Semyaticha was covered by the machine-guns of the 'fortified district'. The Russians, at first disorganized, suffered heavy losses; seven battalions of the 6th and 42nd Rifle Divisions (28th Rifle Corps), though far from fully manned, began to fight back. The Political Section of 6th Rifle Division reported that it was not possible to concentrate properly: men 'arrived in dribs and drabs, half-dressed. . .'. Worst of all, the German bombardment had put much of the Soviet artillery out of action. And the seven battalions were, in fact, mere shadows of their establishment; the combat report of the Political Section of 42nd Rifle Divison underlines that:

of the troops quartered in the Brest Fortress were two battalions of the 44th and 45th Rifle Regiments, part of which had no weapons; that complement, and also the independent reconnaissance battalion with its 7 armoured cars and a motor-cycle company, proceeded to Zhabinki and took up defensive positions; 393rd Independent AA Battalion brought up three guns but no shells.

The defence could not now be put into operation. Scratch units, augmented by sections falling back on the fortress, took up the defence which, long after the battle rolled eastwards, continued from the shattered turrets and ruined emplacements, and in the final agonizing phase from lone rifles in underground rooms or tunnels, from under the tombs of debris. This resistance, which initially denied the Germans access to the Bug and Muchavets rivers, became a ghastly but epic illustration of how Russian infantrymen could fight in traditionally ferocious style.

In the north-west, German bombers did a thorough job on signals and communications centres, on naval bases, and the Soviet aerodromes in particular; from Riga to Kronstadt, on Shauliya, Vilna and Kaunas the bombs rained on the carefully selected targets. Soviet aircraft had been on a one-hour alert, but were held on their airfields after the first wave of German bombers passed. As for Soviet bombers, they had no authorization to cross their own frontiers. Along the frontier, many of the defence positions were unmanned; the 11th Army (which covered the junction of the Baltic Special and the West Special Military Districts) had eleven battalions of the 5th, 33rd and 188th Rifle Divisions covering the approaches to Vilna, a fifty-mile sector. To the north, the 8th Army covered the Shauliya–Riga approaches. In the air attacks, both armies lost not only an appreciable amount of equipment, but also had their communications severed. With German attacks in full swing against its sectors, 11th Army had as yet received no orders; towards 6 am the 5th Rifle Division (11th Army) did receive orders from corps headquarters – *not* to engage in operations, since this was merely a 'provocation'. From the high ground, the officers of this division could see German units on the move and, with binoculars, pick out small details. Divisional commander Ozerov, practically pleading with Corps for orders, was admonished: 'We advise you not to engage in combat operations, otherwise you will answer for the consequences.' The German troops, boring into the Soviet positions and overwhelming the frontier guards, were meanwhile opening passages for the motorized and armoured formations poised to pour in.

From the naval base at Libau, the base commander reported just before 5 am: 'Bombs falling on military installations and in the region of the aerodrome; no serious damage.' Straight upon this came the report of the Chief of Staff of the Kronstadt base that magnetic mines – sixteen at least – had been dropped but the fairway was still clear. Into the Baltic Fleet headquarters a 'cascade' of reports rushed in; the intelligence officer, Colonel Frumkin, reported that the German radio had broadcast *en clair* the information that the whole of the southern Baltic had been mined. This, the Soviet officers assumed, was to inhibit Soviet submarine operations. In Leningrad itself, the Chief of Staff of the district, General Nikishev, summoned the commanders of the various armies at 5 am, and authorized the implementation of the 'mobilization plan'. From the safes the officers drew the 'red packets' – and the engineers, among others, got a rude shock. The 'engineering war plan' consisted of only one instruction: to form two engineering and one bridging regiments into independent battalions and to distribute them as reinforcements to the district armies. This was ludicrously irrelevant. A little later, the intelligence staff reported its latest news: a Ju-88 had been shot down over the Karelian isthmus, and interrogation of the two survivors showed that this had been a photo-reconnaissance mission from East Prussia to cover the southern part of the Leningrad district. The object was to search for Soviet movement to the south of Leningrad and the Karelian isthmus.

On the southern flank, in Army Group South's attack area, the same pattern of heavy bombing attacks, unexpected and punishing artillery fire and the assault on the Soviet frontier positions unfolded in all its fury. Ranging over the Soviet airfields, German bombers inflicted more serious losses: by noon on 22 June, these amounted to 277 machines. On the frontier airfield at Stanislav 36 machines were destroyed on the ground, and 21 on the forward field at Cernauti, although General Zakharov's aircraft in the Odessa district, thanks to timely dispersal, escaped this aerial blast with minute loss: three fighters. From the Soviet frontier as far as Odessa and Sevastopol, the German bombers went in search of their targets. In Lwow – the city where the non-Russian population had whispered 'the Germans are coming to get you' to the Russians – the 'uninterrupted bombing created panic' among the civilians; German-trained 'diversionists', in addition to blowing up fuel and ammunition dumps, added to the havoc as much as possible, not least by signalling the bombers and guiding them to special targets. The city commandant of Lwow was obliged to call out his military patrols and to augment them with the few tanks at his disposal, in order to restore order.

As the bombers passed over the frontier, Soviet guards, already alerted by the noise of the engines, saw bursts of white rockets from the German lines and responses from the aircraft. This, and other information, the frontier troops passed back to the staffs of the nearest military units; in the Rava-Russki 'fortified district', Colonel Yeremin, chief of staff, 41st Rifle Division, had a running commentary on 'unusual German movement' on the other side of the frontier. Precisely at 04.15 hours (Moscow time), the German guns opened fire on the frontier posts and positions, targets already accurately pinpointed. Army Group South had three river barriers to brave from the outset: the Western Bug, the San and the Prut. Nor was the German command unaware of the strong Soviet defences and the deep echeloning of Kirponos's armies in the northern part of the front. At the same time, there were gaps in these defences, which Army Group South exploited by committing the German Sixth Army and von Kleist's Panzer Group 1 at the junction of the Rava-Russki and Strumilov 'fortified districts', against the left flank units of the Soviet 5th Army and part of the right flank of the Soviet 6th Army.

Supported by their artillery fire, the German assault boats were launched into the Bug, which was on average some seventy metres wide in these southern parts, and made for the Soviet bank. Soviet frontier troops, with their rifles, light machine-guns and grenades, put up what resistance they could. Where possible, the unfortunate families of the frontier guards crowded into a block-house or took shelter in basements; at Sokal, Captain Bershadskii's detachment fought to defend the wooden bridge over the river, though his wife and eleven-year-old son lay dead in the shattered buildings of the frontier post. In the Krystynopol area, German assault troops seized the bridge, while units of the Soviet 124th Rifle Division rushed up from five miles away to support the frontier troops. At Vygadandka, the railway bridge over the Bug was guarded by the 128th NKVD Railway Regiment, with a strength of twenty men; here, a German motor-cycle assault troop tried to rush the bridge. Within an hour, the frontier on the Western Bug was the scene of scores of furious engagements; the frontier guards, lacking heavy weapons and short of ammunition, called for support from the Red Army.

Von Stülpnagel's Seventeenth Army, operating on the Tomashuv-Przemysl sector and aiming at Lwow, struck straight at the junction between two 'fortified districts', those of Rava-Russki and Przemysl; the former was defended by the 41st Rifle Division, 3rd Cavalry Division, 97th Rifle Division and a second echelon formation, 159th Rifle Division (6th Rifle Corps), and the latter by the 99th Rifle Division, with the 72nd Rifle and 173rd Rifle Divisions (8th Rifle Corps: 26th Army) in support. As the German guns fired off their opening barrages, these formations were moved from their camps and barracks and sent racing to the frontier. The alert system here functioned, in the opinion of the chief of staff of the 41st Rifle Division, 'without fuss'. The lightly armed frontier troops meanwhile kept the Red Army informed of the local developments on their sectors, as well as sending out immediate requests for reinforcements.

This relative efficiency, which cost the Germans dear and which contrasted so sharply with the chaos of the western and north-western fronts, had been achieved in the face of considerable odds. The particular competence of the individual district commanders and their staffs clearly played a considerable part in determining the outcome on the frontiers: Pavlov at the centre, dis-believing from the outset in the imminence of a massive German attack, clearly lost his nerve, while Kuznetsov in the Baltic command acted in a confused and half-hearted manner, disorganizing much of his own command. Colonel-General Kirponos at Kiev, in many respects a truly tragic figure, did not lose his nerve and he had behind him a tough chief of staff, Purkayev, whose nerves were equally good. Paradoxically enough, the previous permission to move troops, an order dated 12 June 1941, only served to increase the confusion. At the beginning of June, 793,000 reservists were called up for training, which enabled commanders to bring divisional strength up to an average of 12,000 men, but weapons had to be found for them. Movement of internal formations was permitted – that is, far from the actual frontier line –

but of seventy-seven divisions set in motion, only nine had reached their appointed positions: the rest were stuck on trains to the east. Kirponos had duly set his internal formations on the move further to the west: at 22.00 hours on 18 June rifle divisions in the Kiev Military District started off, but their movement was restricted to night marches, which covered only twenty miles at a time. Nor had the divisions taken on any reserve units. Meanwhile on 18 June also the three frontier military districts learned of their possible designation as 'Fronts' – North-Western, Western and South-Western – and were advised to man their key command centres at Panevezius, Obuz-Lesna and Tarnopol respectively by 22-3 June. On 21 June Kirponos had duly opened up his command post at Tarnopol. His stubbornness, persistence and foresight paid off in a few hours, for the German armies had to grind their way through his defences.

Initial reverses and confusions, however, could not be wholly avoided. The first bombings wrought considerable havoc among military and civilians alike. As the officers of the 41st Rifle Division took up their operational command post at Height 305 in the Rava-Russki 'fortified district', they watched a long column of dishevelled women and weeping children, many the families of divisional personnel, leaving the exposed villages for Rava-Russki itself. As for the frontier guards, their families died with them or vanished as the battle swept over them. The German Seventeenth Army had also to reckon on the difficulties of forcing the river San, whose bare banks provided the attackers with neither cover nor concealment. To the north-east of Przemysl, however, German assault troops seized the railway bridge over the San with a swift blow, but, as the Soviet rifle divisions had manned the Przemysl 'fortified district' by 06.00 hours, and the frontier guards fought on, this was merely the prelude to long and bloody Soviet resistance.

Timoshenko had meanwhile alerted two more rifle corps in the Kiev district, those commanded by the generals Zlobin and Chistyakov. Shortly after the German attack, these corps commanders reported to Kiev that they lacked the necessary equipment for full operations; they were told that the district had no adequate reserves itself, but that a request for more weapons had gone out to Moscow. The 'centre', Moscow, was already being inundated with pleas of this kind, to which the several administrations of the General Staff returned ominously unresponsive answers. From the Leningrad command, now committed to an urgent and emergency programme of frontier mining, had come a request for more mines and for engineering equipment, since the dumps could supply only a tenth of the armies' needs. The 'centre' abruptly dashed any hope of outside help: 'To cover your requirements from the centre or from the centre's own dispositions is out of the question. There are more important commands than yours. Organize the exploitation of local resources.' 'Local resources' were already plainly and terribly inadequate.

With communications shattered or fitful, with the disordered situation beyond many local comprehensions, the 'centre' had scarcely any idea of what was happening on the frontiers. By 6 am nothing less than a gigantic battle stretching from East Prussia to the Ukraine had been joined. In little more than two hours, the situation, particularly in the centre, had developed dangerously. Of all the *coups de main* which the Germans had planned against the vital rail and road bridges, not one had failed to succeed. Now, south of Brest, German armour crossed over captured and newly built pontoon bridges; to the north of it, a German engineer battalion laboured to finish the first pontoon bridge in the 4th Army's area, near Drohiczyn. And yet, with fuel and ammunition dumps blown to pieces, towns and bases bombed, raked airfields littered with burning planes, tank and vehicle parks in flames, with German troops advancing by columns upon and across the frontiers, the Soviet Union was still not at war and the Red Army lacked any precise orders to deal with the attacks.

After that first stunned realization in Stalin's office that this must be the catastrophe of war and not some 'provocation' which might be managed by consultation and diplomatic exchange, Zhukov broke in on Stalin's gloom to propose orders to the military designed to bring full Soviet strength to bear and thus 'hold up' any further German advance: Timoshenko interjected to insist on 'annihilation', not just 'holding up'. Stalin agreed to a second directive being issued, *Directive No. 2*, which went out at 07.15 hours, 22 June. Signed by Zhukov as Chief of the General Staff, the directive stipulated 'active offensive operations', a phrase which rang with terrible hollowness as hastily mobilized Red Army units were fighting off increasingly powerful German thrusts: that judiciousness about limiting any air attacks could certainly be followed to the letter, since Soviet fighters and bombers were being steadily pounded or shot to pieces as they lay stranded on the ground:

Directive No. 2

22 June 1941 at 04.00 hours in the morning German aircraft without any cause whatsoever carried out flights over aerodromes and towns along the length of the frontier and proceeded to bomb them. Simultaneously in a number of places German troops opened fire with artillery and penetrated the frontier.

In connection with the unprecedented attack by Germany on the Soviet Union, I issue these orders:

1　Troops in full strength and with all the means at their disposal will attack the enemy and destroy him in those places where he has violated the Soviet frontier.

　　In the absence of special authorization, ground troops will not cross the frontier line.

2　Reconnaissance and attack aircraft will locate the concentration areas of enemy aircraft and the deployment of his ground forces. Bomber and ground-attack aircraft will destroy with powerful blows the aircraft on enemy aerodromes and will bomb the main concentrations of his ground forces. Aviation strikes will be mounted to a depth of 100–150 kilometres in German territory.

　　Königsberg and Memel will be bombed.

　　No flights over Finland and Rumania to take place without special authorization.

None of this mentioned a state of war or envisaged general mobilization. None of it bore any relation to what had happened in the last three hours on what were now pulsing battle-fronts. By 8 am Timoshenko's directive had been received by all staffs, most of whom were convinced that a massive war had begun, but who still disposed of orders covering possible 'provocation'. Bemused as they were about the stipulation over Finland, the Leningrad command had no doubts that the Finns would join in the German attack, and possibly very soon. In the far north. Admiral Golovko was notified by the Main Naval Staff (*Glavmorshtab*) that war operations had begun, but Moscow refused to elaborate on this; when asked about the deployment of the Northern Fleet submarines, 'the centre' categorically ordered Golovko to send his large submarines to the mouth of the White Sea – this on the personal instructions of Stalin. Though he argued at this pointless contradiction of previous operational plans, Golovko had no course but to agree. At the other end of the Soviet Union, in the Soviet Far East, where the time difference made it already high noon, Timoshenko ordered a full-scale alert and troops to be brought to full readiness without delay, anticipating at this moment a blow (which never came) from the Japanese.

From the 'centre', confused and ill-informed as it was, unrealistic orders went out across a communications net which had already been seriously impaired. Frontier units were desperately trying to assemble often under heavy enemy attack. For many, this was still a 'provocation', for no announcement of war or general mobilization had been made, nor did one come for several hours. Even at this stage, calamitous as it was rapidly becoming, Stalin thought that he could still stop the war.

Only at noon did the Soviet government, through the limping phrases and the halting tone of Molotov, announce to the Russian people in a radio broadcast that the Soviet Union was now at war with Germany. The fiction of a 'provocation' could no longer be sustained, however much the wish might be father to the thought. Stalin, who had stubbornly refused to face the truth, or who thought that truth must be what he promulgated, had no option but to admit 'a state of war'. But those eight hours which had passed since the onset of the German attack were spent in part at least (to judge from German monitoring of Soviet radio traffic) in a final, frantic search by Stalin for a way of escape: Soviet radio messages rained down on the *Auswärtiges Amt* in Berlin and in one grotesque squirm Stalin had even turned to the Japanese for 'mediation' in resolving this Soviet-German 'crisis'. None of this, however, could call back the German bombers or the Panzer columns and their hard-faced, battle-tested crews which were slashing away in murderous style at the Soviet frontier areas. The war which could not be wished away by deceptive phrases or by lunatic concealments had finally and officially come to stay.

At this point Stalin removed himself from any public gaze and the Russian people heard not a sound from him until 3 July. There have been foolish and unfounded assertions that Stalin 'hid himself': not much credence can be given to accounts such as those of Ivan Maiskii, who was many thousands of miles from the scene at the Soviet embassy in London. Colonel-General (later Marshal) Voronov, who was there on the spot within the confines of the Kremlin, reports not Stalin's 'disappearance' into some world of drunken oblivion and wringing his hands over the loss of Lenin's heritage, but rather his erratic appearance at command meetings and his extreme nervousness when he did appear at this time. During these first hours there was at least the great blanket of ignorance, for communications had been largely severed. The Fronts were scarcely under the control of the high command, because no effective high command organization existed: the Main Military Soviet was not a command organ and there was neither 'supreme command' nor a 'supreme commander'. Not many hours before Voroshilov had rushed off to a non-existent command centre. The Defence Commissariat had prepared a draft decree which named Stalin as Commander-in-Chief, but he demurred and laid it aside for consideration by the Politburo: the result was that there were two Commanders-in-Chief, Timoshenko by right and Stalin by sheer weight of authority and intimidation. It was in this fashion that he acted towards one o'clock on 22 June. He had made up his mind that Soviet commanders were simply 'not up to it' – 'our front commanders . . . have evidently become somewhat confused' – and informed Zhukov that the Politburo had decided to send out very senior officers to assist the Front commanders: Colonel-General O.I. Gorodovikov to the North-Western Front, Zhukov to the South-Western Front, all in the capacity of 'predstaviteli Glavnogo Komandovaniya', 'representatives of the High Command'. Tyulenev in Moscow was ordered to assemble a staff and take command of the newly activated Southern Front (based on the Odessa Military District). There is something curious about this arrangement, for it appears that on 21 June the Politburo had already taken some decisions about Front commands – Marshal Budenny to take over the High Command Reserve armies moving to the Dnieper, Zhukov to be responsible for the South-Western and Southern Fronts, Meretskov the Northern Front. In extraordinary fashion the raising of the Southern Front (from the Odessa Military District) was vested with the Moscow Military District, which would have to dispatch an operational-command group to Vinnitsa. The next day Stalin quickly made his own dispositions, though he did not depart too drastically from this earlier decision.

It was clear, nevertheless, that 'the centre' – Moscow – had little idea about the extent of the chaos and the confusion on the frontiers. Within these commands the signals network, a crude affair from the start, was being sliced to pieces by bombing and by sabotage. In the absence of hard facts, Moscow took what amounted to a rosy view of the situation, to the extent that formations pressed to the point of desperation and destruction were refused permission to go over to the defensive. They must fulfil *Directive No. 2*: attack and counter-attack, all in the maelstrom of whirling German tanks and paralysing German bombing. The Russian dead began to pile up, strewn on the roads or flung about in their weapon pits and lying across their silent guns. The men in field-grey, perfectly practised as they were in the business of killing with almost surgical precision, lancing, cutting, and amputating with their military instruments, set about blinding and maiming the Red Army.

While sundry senior officers left for the Front commands, the Red Army struggled to mobilize. The front-line formations, already engulfed in battle, had to stand and fight however they had been scratched together: the interior and some reserve forces assembled as best they might, like the 100th Order of Lenin Rifle Division* under Major-General Russiyanov stationed near Minsk, which by 15.00 hours on 22 June had manned some of its regiments but required 'a few days' in which to complete its mobilization. A signal to that effect was sent off to Moscow in the evening. With men reporting either to the 'mobilization points' or to units themselves, confusion on a vast scale was hardly avoidable: when German bombers cut loose on the large cities near the front, the military administration, its buildings and communications smashed, came near to chaos. Elsewhere, deeper in the interiors of the Fronts, armoured and rifle divisions formed up; in many, after the noon broadcast, the political officers addressed the men, who (as in the 80th Rifle Division of the South-Western Front) unloaded their small suitcases, waterproofs and greatcoats from unit lorries and set off marching westwards. All too often, as they tramped or entrained to the west, they knew nothing of what awaited them, or even if they suspected it, they evinced a confidence which propaganda rather than rigorous training had induced. Too many Red Army men and their junior officers paid a catastrophically high price for this heedlessness in the early days of the war.

While the rest of Russia slowly recoiled from the shock, the lacerated frontier commands had to face up to a situation which hour by hour was becoming alarming, and in parts even perilous. By noon in the north-west and in the centre German armoured and mobile forces, the initial barriers behind them, were set to spring forward, while the Red Army, hurt and hammered by the Luftwaffe, scrambled to fight amidst its burning headquarters, blazing fuel and ammunition dumps, severed communications, broken or stranded tank columns and bomb-dazed infantry units. Sent out from Minsk to make contact with the 10th Army, Lieutenant-General Boldin saw a state of affairs on the Bialystok highway which appalled him – chaos, destruction, disintegration; overhead, German bombers careened at will. For many hours the Soviet frontier guards, bereft of heavy weapons, had fought stubbornly and well, but in fierce engagements many had been obliterated by German fire-power; the first line, shrunken

---

* One of the senior formations of the Red Army, raised on 1 November 1923, with its cadre taken from the 45th Red Banner Rifle Division: the new formation became the 100th, and later in 1941 the 1st Guards Rifle Division.

and slack with losses, was caving in, and only in the south-west under Kirponos was there anything like co-ordinated movement between the frontier screens and Red Army formations.

In the north-west, what had begun badly continued to deteriorate. From his operational command post at Suboch (south-east of Shauliya), the North-Western Front commander, Colonel-General F.I. Kuznetsov, hustled his forces to the frontier; at 09.30 hours he ordered 3rd Mechanized Corps and 12th Mechanized Corps (Major-General N.M. Shestopalov) to take up their counter-attack positions, though both would operate under 8th Army command. Berzarin's 27th Army, which had one division (67th) deployed between Windau and Libau on the coast and a brigade (3rd Independent) located on the islands of Osel and Dago, was also alerted. Strung out along the frontier from Libau to Grodno, Kuznetsov had eight rifle divisions from two armies (the 8th and 11th): 10th, 90th, 125th, 5th, 33rd, 188th, 126th and the 128th. Major-General P.P. Bogabgun's 125th Rifle Division covered the Tauroggen-Shauliya axis. Army Group North hit it with a massive armoured fist, three tank and two infantry divisions, plus the second echelon motorized forces of Panzer Group 4. By noon the 125th, trying to stem this armoured tide with three guns to the kilometre, began to fall back from Tauroggen. The German columns then swung against Rasienai, where Kuznetsov was concentrating his own armour for the morrow, and where Major-General Bogdanov's 48th Rifle Division, already battered by air attack, swung into action off the march. By the evening, the Soviet formations had fallen back to the river Dubissa; north-west of Kaunas, at 19.00 hours, 8th Panzer Division's forward elements (from von Manstein's 56th Panzer Corps) reached the Dubissa and seized the vital Airogola road viaduct across it. Without this crossing, German tanks might have been trapped in what was a giant natural tank ditch. A dash to Dvinsk would have been wholly ruled out. Now, as armour, motorized forces and the speedy infantry of 290th Division raced across, that spurt was on.

North-west of Kaunas, armour was over the Dubissa. South-west of Vilno more armour from Panzer Group 3 (Army Group Centre), which had ripped through the Soviet 11th Army, moved across the Niemen at Alitus and Merech. The bridges at Alitus remained intact; the commander of the 4th Bridging Regiment, specially detailed to blow up the Alitus bridges, received no orders to do so. He had no option but to stand idly by. The 5th Tank Division (detached from 3rd Mechanized Corps) fought as best it might to impede the German crossing; heavy bombing ground the regiments to pieces. Most serious was the breakdown in communications; thus, the Military Soviet of the North-Western Front, Kuznetsov, Dibrov and Klenov (Chief of Staff), drew up its counter-attack plans on the evening of the twenty-second in fearful ignorance of what had actually happened. Kuznetsov decided to prevent German breakthroughs to Shauliya, Kaunas and Vilno; the rifle formations of 8th and 11th Armies would be assigned to this, while the 12th and 3rd Mechanized Corps would attack the German concentrations which had broken through to the Dubissa, and which were operating on the Tilsit-Shauliya axis.

Kuznetsov assumed that the main German blow had developed along the Tilsit-Shauliya highway; in smashing this, he would decide the fate of the defensive battles in the frontier zone. The armour which he planned to use to accomplish this would then be switched back to 11th Army to deal with the threats to Kaunas and Vilno, 12th Mechanized Corps would counter-attack from Shauliya in a south-westerly direction, the 3rd, concentrating south of Rasienai, would strike north-westwards; both would come under the operational direction of 8th Army for these attacks planned for 12.00 hours on 23 June. Manstein, however, had already sprung this ponderous trap; the Rasienai tank-battle, when it came, took place far to his rear.

While Kuznetsov planned to block or to chop off the German spear-heads, he either did not know or failed to grasp that the bottom of his Front was in some danger of falling out. Army Group Centre's success against Kuznetsov's 11th Army, which had brought it across the Niemen bridges, simultaneously threatened Pavlov's right flank 3rd Army (of what was now the Western Front) with a deep outflanking movement. The junction of the North-Western with the Western Front had already begun to sway ominously. Lieutenant-General V.I. Kuznetsov's 3rd Army, with its telephone lines gone and its radio communications knocked out, was at once in a serious situation;* General Kuznetsov maintained what contact he could by runners, but his troops were short of ammunition and lacked any proper reserves. To its front, 3rd Army had been struck by Ninth Army (Army Group Centre); the Soviet 56th Rifle Division, covering Grodno, was assaulted by no less than three German divisions of 8th Corps. From 11th Army, Kuznetsov of the 3rd had no news of any kind; nor had he any from his left-hand neighbour, Golubev of the 10th Army. He was fighting blind; for the moment, all that Kuznetsov could do was to order Major-General D.K. Mostovenko's 11th Mechanized Corps into action from the Grodno area.

Almost from the outset the silence from Major-General K.D. Golubev's 10th Army had alarmed Pavlov, who proposed, somewhat rashly, to go to Bialystok himself. Marshal Timoshenko expressly forbade this, and authorized Boldin's journey, which turned into a nightmarish foray by plane, car and foot. At Bialystok railway station, which the bombers had found a plum target, Boldin organized working parties to bury the dead, clear the wounded and shift trains on to spare track. Towards 7 pm, in a little wood some six miles south-west of Bialystok, Boldin finally came upon 10th Army 'Headquarters' – two tents, wooden tables, stools, a telephone and a radio truck. Golubev painted a gloomy picture; in a few short hours, his rifle formations had suffered very heavy losses, and his armour was thin, Major-General Akhlyustin's 13th Mechanized Corps

* German radio intercept of a Soviet transmission: 'Stab 3. Armee zerschlagen, sendet Zerstörer.' Halder, *Kriegstagebuch*, 22.6.1941.

disposed of too few tanks, and those were old T-26s, with guns fit only 'for shooting sparrows'; Major-General M.G. Khatskilevich's 6th Mechanized Corps was deployed now on the eastern bank of the river Narev, in the Krushchevo-Surach area a few miles south-west of Bialystok. Golubev hoped to check the German 42nd Corps this way, but burst out; 'What are we going to fight with?' 10th Army aviation and AA guns had been destroyed; the fuel dumps had been bombed and the fuel tanks at Bialystok station destroyed. The armoured divisions were immobilized. The cavalry, as Major-General I.S. Nikitin, 6th Cavalry Corps commander reported, had been wiped out; his 6th Cavalry Division could not defend itself against aircraft.

With contact finally restored, Boldin talked with Pavlov in Minsk. The Front commander ordered Boldin to assemble a 'shock group' from 13th Mechanized Corps; the force would counter-attack on the Grodno-Bialystok line, and prevent a penetration to Volkovysk, after which it would revert to the command of 3rd Army. Boldin had the coming night in which to prepare. To arguments that neither the 10th nor the 3rd Army could muster this strength Pavlov turned a deaf ear. (Much later, Boldin learned that Pavlov continued to issue a stream of orders to this non-existent 'shock group'; none ever reached it, though the whole undertaking, Boldin hints, must have looked good in Moscow, which received copies of these 'signals'.) As for his 'force', Boldin had no idea where 11th Mechanized Corps was; 3rd Army remained ominously silent. The liaison officer sent out to establish contact never returned. The 'cavalry-mechanized shock group', which Pavlov wheeled and marched in some phantasy of command, did not and could not exist. Military wraith that it was, it received its brutal extinction at dawn, when German bombers caught the 3th Cavalry Division on the march, and in a slaughter of horses and men blew it to pieces.

On the left flank, Korobkov's 4th Army was pressed equally hard. The defenders of Brest were now immured in their fortress. Guderian's tanks and von Kluge's Fourth Army pressed on. Bombed out of Kobrin, 4th Army HQ moved to Zapruda, where at 16.00 hours Pavlov's chief of staff, Klimovskikh, directed fresh instructions by telegraph; Korobkov, using Major-General Oborin's 14th Mechanized Corps, was to attack to clear the enemy from Brest and reach the frontier. Since 10th Army could not be contacted for support, Korobkov should call on Akhlyustin's 13th Mechanized Corps. Sandalov, chief of staff to 4th Army, protested vigorously; Shlykov, operations officer, asked Korobkov to seek permission to take up defensive positions. Korobkov reacted violently, pointing out that this was merely an invitation 'to be labelled cowards and relieved of command'. In fact, permission to go over to the defensive was expressly withheld. Shortly afterwards Colonel Pern, liaison officer from 10th Army, appeared at Zapruda, followed by General I.N. Khabarov, 'Front representative' from Minsk; the latter had nothing to hand over but written confirmation of the morning order about 'Fascist bands', though his news about the moving up of 47th Rifle Corps was heartening. In the evening, Korobkov and his staff officers moved off to Zhabinka to prepare the counter-attack which Pavlov had not only ordered but insisted upon. Not a man thought it had the slightest chance of success.

Von Rundstedt's Army Group South, its left flank offensive launched against Kirponos's South-Western Front with the Sixth and Seventeenth Armies, collided with much more solid resistance. At Chelm, south-east of Lublin, German combat engineers had bridged the Bug; near Krystonopol, German troops had another crossing. By noon, although the Red Army managed to check enemy infantry attacks, tanks and motorized forces moved through the first breaches; the first echelons of the Soviet 5th and 6th Armies had managed, however, more or less successfully to man their pill-boxes and fire-points. Fedyuninskii's 15th Rifle Corps (Potapov's 5th Army) held the line from Vlodava to Vladimir-Volynsk; late in the day, with the divisions suffering losses, the left flank began to buckle in on Vladimir-Volynsk. For the moment, but not for long, the right flank (adjoining the Western Front) held, though there was no firm contact with Korobkov's 4th Army. The most ominous German pressure, however, came at the junction of the two Soviet armies, aimed at the gap between the Vladimir-Volynsk and Strumilov 'fortified districts'. Both 5th and 6th Army commanders, Potapov and Muzychenko, committed their armoured forces without delay – Major-General S.M. Kondrusev's 22nd Mechanized Corps (5th Army) and Major-General A.A. Vlasov's 4th Mechanized Corps (6th Army). At Przemysl, where von Stülpnagel's Seventeenth Army had cut into the Soviet defences, by 18.00 hours the major part of the town had fallen, but Colonel Dementyev's 99th Rifle Division launched a counter-attack one hour later. For the moment, the Germans had failed to lift the lid to the approach to Lwow. On the Lutsk-Kiev axis, however, in spite of the hard fighting of the 5th and 6th Armies, German troops had pushed some 15–17 miles into the Soviet defences. The threat of a deep penetration – and with it, the outflanking of the main Soviet forces from the north – was clearly developing. Kirponos recognized this, and resolved to attack the flanks of von Kleist's Panzer Group 1 with every available armoured formation – 8th, 9th, 15th, 19th and 22nd Mechanized Corps. While one great tank-battle loomed up in the north-west, a second projected itself in the south.

Sixteen hours after the opening of Operation 'Barbarossa' the German Army in the east had virtually unhinged two Soviet Fronts, the North-Western and the Western. At their junction the Soviet 11th Army had been battered to pieces; the left flank of the 8th Army (North-Western Front) and the right flank of 3rd Army (Western Front) had been similarly laid bare, like flesh stripped from the bone which lay glistening and exposed. North of Kaunas German armour was over the river Dubissa and south of the city German tanks were astride the Niemen. On the left flank of the Western Front the Soviet 4th Army was in no position to offer any effective defence: this precarious grip on its life threatened in turn the flank of 10th Army at the very centre of the Western Front and thence the right flank of the 5th Army on the South-Western Front, itself already menaced by a German thrust between 5th and 6th Armies. The covering armies in the Soviet frontier areas were being skewered apart.

Of the nature and extent of this catastrophe 'the centre' seemed to know little or nothing. The Defence Commissariat and the General Staff were painstakingly trying to piece together some of the details. Nevertheless, towards the end of this ghastly day, at 21.15 hours on 22 June 1941 Timoshenko issued the last of the blundering directives, *Directive No. 3*, which prescribed nothing less than all three Soviet Fronts *taking the offensive*. The object was to hurl the German Army back in one massive attack, ending it all with a single blow. The North-Western and Western Fronts, each employing their rifle divisions plus two mechanized corps, were to mount co-ordinated operations from Kaunas and Grodno, thus carrying the war on to enemy territory and by the evening of 24 June – having encircled and destroyed the enemy – would occupy the Suwalki area. Front operations would be supported by the long-range bomber force (ADD). The South-Western Front was ordered to use 5th and 6th Armies supported by 'several' mechanized corps to destroy with 'concentric blows' those enemy forces operating on the Vladimir–Volynsk/Krystonopol front and by the evening of 24 June the Soviet force would invest the area of Lublin, having also 'secured itself' from the direction of Cracow and simultaneously defending the state frontier with Hungary. On the flanks of the Soviet–German front Red Army troops were restricted to 'defensive assignments', covering the state frontier and preventing enemy penetrations.

The Front commanders, struggling desperately to maintain the cohesion of their forces, had no option but to prepare the massive offensive operations, envisaged to a depth of some 50–75 miles, which *Directive No. 3* demanded. All three looked to their mechanized corps for salvation. Kuznetsov in the north-west proceeded with his plans to strike at the flank of Panzer Group 4 from north-west of Kaunas; Pavlov, having first sent his 'shock group' into what he imagined was the attack, planned to employ his mechanized forces south of Grodno and near Brest; Kirponos, aware that he had yet to concentrate the bulk of his armour, decided to employ the formations immediately at hand (15th and 8th Mechanized Corps) to strike at the German spear-heads. The impediments to any kind of success, however, were enormous. Aircraft which might have covered the units during their concentration had long ago been shot to pieces on the ground; the artillery, like much of the infantry, was stuck for lack of transport; where transport existed, like many of the tanks it stood stalled for lack of fuel; where there was fuel, there was little or no ammunition. And even where all these requirements were met, there was no time.

The night came at last. For Lieutenant-General Boldin, as for so many in the beleaguered or hard-pressed Soviet divisions, it was 'lit by hundreds of flashes –

from raging fires, from the tracer of the machine-gun units, from shells and bombs exploding near by'. Under the cover of darkness officers struggled to put their units into some kind of order. The scanty supplies of food and ammunition salvaged from the burning dumps were distributed. Boldin knew now beyond all doubt that Pavlov's orders could not be accomplished; he hoped, nonetheless,

SOVIET MECHANIZED CORPS IN THE FRONTIER BATTLES: 22–27.6.41

Counter-attack area	Formation	Length of approach march	Duration of march	Date committed
SW of	12 Mech. Corps	80 km	22.23.6	23.6
Shauliya	3 Mech. Corps	100 km	night of 23.6	23.6
NW of	11 Mech. Corps	50 km	23.6	23.6
Grodno	6 Mech. Corps	70 km	night of 23.6	23.6
Lutsk–	8 Mech. Corps	about 500 km	22–26.6	26.6
Dubno–Brody	9 Mech. Corps	200 km	22–26.6	26.6
	19 Mech. Corps	200 km	22–26.6	26.6
	15 Mech. Corps	80 km	22–23.6	23.6
	22 Mech. Corps	100 km	22–24.6	24.6

Results

Date	Area	Formation	Breadth of Front (km)	Period of preparation	Gains
22.6	Grodno	11 Mech. Corps	15	1–1½ hours	7 km advance
23–25.6	Shauliya	12 Mech. Corps	35	None	5–8 km advance heavy losses
23.6	Grodno	6 Mech. Corps	—	One night	Insignificant forward movement
23.6	NE Brest	14 Mech. Corps	20	A few hours	Insignificant forward movement
27.6	Dubno area	8 Mech. Corps	22	Re-deployed on the move	40 km advance heavy losses

that Khatskilevich's 6th Mechanized Corps and the 36th Cavalry Division might hold off the enemy. By night 10th Army units were to take up the defensive positions behind the Narev which 6th Mechanized had been holding; the tanks and motorized infantry would concentrate by dawn in the thick woods northeast of Bialystok. Pulled in from Slonim to Sokulka, 29th Mechanized Division would cover the concentration of the 6th Corps, which Boldin intended to commit in attack towards Grodno, to the south of which he presumed 11th Mechanized Corps, under Mostovenko, was already fighting. Golubev himself had been very slow in deploying the 6th Mechanized Corps; he split up the tanks and used the infantry to hold the Narva crossing. And so Protaturchev's 4th Tank Division (6th Mechanized Corps) came to be chasing its own tail for too long. Even so, Khatskilevich's corps, unlike the 13th, had a strong complement of T-34 and KV tanks, though it was short on fuel and ammunition; its divisions were undermanned, but Boldin, struggling to make up for the time lost by Golubev, could hardly wait. In the end, wholly ignorant of the whereabouts of 11th Mechanized Corps and disastrously robbed of 36th Cavalry Division, Boldin proceeded to attack.

The night which brought momentary respite to parts of the frontier commands also brought the first operational digest (*svodka*) from the Soviet General Staff, compiled at 22.00 hours on 22 June. Of the urgency of the situation it contained not the slightest trace. Blatant with complacency and swelled with ignorance, it read:

Regular troops of the German Army during the course of 22 June conducted operations against frontier defence units of the USSR, attaining insignificant success in a number of sectors. During the second half of the day, with the arrival of forward elements of the field forces of the Red Army, the attacks by German troops along most of the length of our frontiers were beaten off and losses inflicted on the enemy.

In the course of the next few hours the '*predstaviteli Glavnovo Komandovaniya*', sent out on their separate missions from Moscow, were to see for themselves just what this 'insignificant success' amounted to. Even the brash and bumptious Kulik was aghast at what he found at the battle-front. General Zhukov, however, had few illusions: now with the South-Western Front, having fed on the tea and sandwiches the aircrew scraped up for him during his flight to Kiev, he learned from Vatunin (now placed in charge of the General Staff) on the evening of 22 June that the General Staff lacked 'accurate information' about either Soviet or German strengths and movements, that no information was to hand about losses and that there was no contact with Kuznetsov or Pavlov in the Baltic and Western theatres. In spite of this, Stalin was sticking grimly to *Directive No. 3* and ordered that Zhukov's signature be added to the document even in his absence. From Kiev Zhukov asked Vatutin just what *Directive No. 3* prescribed and on being told that it envisaged a 'counter-offensive to rout the enemy in all major directions' and then an advance into enemy territory, he burst out with the remark that the Soviet command had absolutely no idea of where and in what strength the German Army was attacking. Vatutin also pointed out ruefully that he would wait until the morning to issue an operational directive, but now the matter had been 'decided' and for the moment there was no choice but to go along with it. It was midnight when the directive arrived at South-Western Front HQ, whereupon Purkayev objected in the strongest terms, but the order had to be carried out: at least Kirponos and his staff had Zhukov with his skill and experience at their back, which accounted for the effectiveness of the armoured counter-strokes delivered in the south-western theatre and which hurt the Germans. But elsewhere the outcome of *Directive No. 3* was uniformly disastrous. On 23 June the gap prised open between the Soviet North-Western and Western Front had already widened to almost eighty miles: the Soviet armies covering the frontier were on the verge of being broken and dispersed, leaving them wholly incapable of checking the German advance.

4

The Disaster on the Frontiers:
June–July 1941

The Soviet Union went to war without a commander-in-chief: the post of *Glavkom* (commander-in-chief) had been abolished seventeen long years before during the 'military reforms' of the 1920s and never revived. The military re-organization of 1934 established the Defence Commissariat, the post of Defence Commissar and the Military Soviet (*Voennyi Soviet*), all of which finally super-seded the old Civil War command forms and the Revolutionary Military Council (*Revvoensoviet*) in particular. In 1938 the Red Army acquired a Main Military Soviet (*Glavnyi Voennyi Soviet RKKA*) and the Navy a naval equivalent presided over by Andrei Zhdanov. A Defence Committee (*Komitet Oborony*) also existed but its functions were vague and certainly did not include any com-mand role. The highest military office in the Soviet state was that of People's Commissar for Defence, but there was no specific commander-in-chief; none of the 'reforms' had established either the machinery of supreme command or a personalized post.

On the second day of the war, Monday, 23 June, 'the Soviet government' (which Stalin, at least in name) and the Central Committee hurriedly authorized the establishment of an improvised high command; the Monday decree, signed by *Sovnarkom* of which Stalin was chairman, created a curious hybrid with its 'High command headquarters', *Stavka Glavnovo Komandovaniya*: the *Stavka* (the equivalent of GHQ) recalled at once the military organization of the pre-1917 state, while the 'high command' (*Glavnoe Komandovanie*) signified Marshal Timoshenko's presidency of a 'collective organ' of operational military control. But Timoshenko was not appointed (and never became) 'commander-in-chief' of the Soviet armed forces. That position, in a somewhat more magnified style, Stalin reserved for himself, advancing towards it in two rapid strides in July and August. With Timoshenko's departure at the end of June to take command of the shattered Western Front, his 'presidency' of the collective command organ came to an end, so that in little more than a few days, the 'high command' organization underwent rapid and drastic modifications.

The *Stavka* was at once an institution and a location. As an institution, it included *ex officio* Marshals of the Soviet Union, the Chief of the General Staff, the head of the naval forces and air force, and, as time went on, heads of arms and services. The reorganization of the *Stavka* came quite quickly with the re-organization of the Defence Commissariat and the General Staff. In the first days of the war, operational control was maintained by the Operations Department of the General Staff (for the Red Army) run by Lieutenant-General German Kapitonovich Malandin. When Timoshenko left for the Western Front, he took Malandin with him, and Major-General Chetverikov took over Operations at the General Staff. Admiral Kuznetsov's naval forces operated in much the same way, through the operations section of the Main Naval Staff. The 'strategic' direction, on which the staffs based their activity, came from the *Stavka*, the 'collective' directorate. The morning and evening appreciations of the General Staff provided, at least in theory, the basis on which the *Stavka* could formulate its 'strategic' provisions and directives. The rapid breakdown in communications between the Front and its formations, and between the Front command and the 'centre' speedily put paid to that form of decision-making. Until 22 June, both the Defence Commissariat and the district commands had formed units of administrative rather than operational competence; thereafter, an immediate and enormous strain fell on the Operations Sections of higher echelons (which their limited facilities could not sustain), while Administrations such as Air Defence (PVO) assumed operational functions. The complete lack of any kind of 'rear services' (logistics) organization meant inevitably that operational and military-administrative requirements collided at once; what was essentially an 'operational-administrative' net became hopelessly overcrowded, jammed and choked with multiple traffic from widely divergent types of decisions, all further strained by the extreme centralization of the system as a whole. The *Stavka* also became a command centre within the Kremlin buildings, a 'war-room' which came to have its own staff and signals centre, and which rapidly became an instrument of extreme centralization. On 23 June, I.T. Peresypkin was put in charge of the supervision of military signals traffic; he was assigned three inde-pendent repair battalions and several service companies to secure the lines between the front commands, the *Stavka* and the Defence Commissariat (NKO). Major-General Gapich operated communications with the Front staffs through Lieutenant-General P.M. Kurochkin (North-Western Front), Major-General A.T. Grigoriev (Western Front), Major-General D. M. Dobykin (South-Western Front), and I.F. Korolev on the Southern Front when on 24 June this became operationally effective.

Administrative decree served to put the country on an immediate wartime footing following the Sunday declaration of war; an emergency decree of the Supreme Soviet (dated 22 June) prescribed the legal and administrative terms of the subordination of organs of 'state and regional defence' to the Military Soviets of Fronts or armies, or if no Military Soviet existed, then to the local military commander. This accorded with Article 49 of the Constitution and was pro-mulgated as a wartime code: *O voennom polozhenii*. The ammunition production plan, which had been approved on 6 June but which lay as yet inoperative, was adopted at once on 23 June, although it soon proved to be woefully inadequate. With rather greater prescience, an industrial evacuation group was formed (*Soviet po evakuatsii*) under the chairmanship of N.M. Shvernik, with A.N. Kosygin and M.G. Pervukhin as his deputies; that was a decision formally endorsed by the Central Committee, and announced on 24 June. The rubber-stamping went on for more than a week, a preliminary administrative mobiliza-tion which left much incomplete; national mobilization in the most fundamental sense did not begin until the second week-end, when a directive, countersigned by government and Party, finally made its appearance on 29 June. The reminder of things undone was brutal:

> In spite of the grave threat which our country faces, certain Party, local Soviet, trade union and *Komsomol* organizations and their leaders do not recognize the meaning of this threat and do not understand that the war had radically changed the situation, that our motherland is in terrible danger and that we must swiftly and decisively put all our work on a war footing.

After 'fighting to the last drop of blood' for each town and hamlet, the with-drawal of the Red Amy must be accompanied by,

> the removal of all rolling stock, leaving the enemy not a single locomotive, not a truck, not a kilogramme of bread, not a litre of fuel. Collective farmers must drive away their cattle . . . all property of value any, including ferrous metals, bread and fuel which cannot be taken away must, without any exceptions, be destroyed.

This was the first 'scorched earth' instruction, to which was added an order to establish in occupied areas partisan detachments and sabotage squads. By design and by necessity, this directive bore an uncommonly close resemblance to the famous, historically sanctified decree 'The Socialist motherland is in danger' issued by Lenin in February 1918.

That was not the only echo of the Civil War. Right on the heels of the Party directive came the announcement of the creation of the State Defence Com-mittee (*Gosudarstvennyi Komitet Oborony*: GKO), operational from 30 June and under the chairmanship of Joseph Stalin. At first sight, the GKO seemed to derive from the Soviet of Workers and Peasants Defence (*Soviet Rabochei i Krestyanskoi Oborony*) which dated back to the conflagrations of the Civil War. In fact, there was little but general association between the two bodies; the GKO from the out-set remained small in size (with a basic membership of eight) but with a massive, consuming competence, empowered to issue decrees (with the force of law), superior to all state, Party, local Soviet, *Komsomol* and military organs, responsible for the direction of the economy and military production, designed to supervise 'the structure' of the Soviet armed forces, and charged finally with matters relating to 'state security and public orders'. Quite soon, it spawned pleni-potentiaries and threw off 'local defence committees'; even sooner, the GKO and the *Stavka* were closely fused by giving GKO members the right to sit with the *Stavka* as part of it. Under this withering blast of super-centralization, it was inevitable that the few wisps of authority which Stalin had left to higher state bodies were speedily dispersed. But above all, the 'GKO-*Stavka* system', the unification of military and political direction which a decade ago Shaposhnikov had recommended in his writings on wartime leadership, produced in established Stalinist style that blurring of competences which may have promoted 'the cult of the individual' but which riddled the command organs with inefficiency, procrastination, internal competition and external indecision.

The decree on the GKO did bring Stalin's name – hitherto conspicuously absent – back into public circulation. For a week, it had been all the anonymity of 'the Soviet government', the 'Central Committee' and '*Sovnarkom*', the clamour of organization, and the rattle of Party exhortations, though none like the grim phrases of 29 June. Abroad, no Soviet mission received any instructions during the first days of the war and none dared take any independent initiative it might contemplate. Stalin, committed irrevocably to war in spite of himself, 'locked himself in his quarters' for three days at least after the first, catastrophic week-end. When he emerged, he was, according to an officer who saw him at first hand, 'low in spirit and nervy'; any task that he required done, had to be done in an impossibly short time. Stalin appeared to have no grasp of the scale of operations and the vastness of the war into which he had been hurled. The destruction of the enemy he demanded in the shortest possible time, unaware of what he was asking for and prompted to pursue this by vastly exaggerated preliminary reports of German losses. Not that Stalin put in more than rare appearances at the *Stavka* in these early days; the main military administration was, for all practical purposes, seriously disorganized and the General Staff, with its specialists dispatched to the Front commands, functioned with tantalizingly persistent slowness. The evening situation reports presented by the General Staff for the information of the heads of arms and services scarcely corresponded in these early days to the map deployments at the front. The *Stavka* discussions ground into an operational-administrative bog; while trying to formulate strategic-operational assignments, Stalin and his officers busied themselves with minutiae which devoured valuable time – the type of rifle to be issued to infantry units (standard or cavalry models), or whether bayonets were needed, and if so, should they be triple-edged?

Denuding the *Stavka* from its first moments, the Marshals of the Soviet Union, together with General Zhukov of the General Staff, had left Moscow during or after the first week-end for the battle-fronts. The bumptious Marshal Kulik, this time in pilot's flying kit, arrived by aircraft at the command post (not far from Bialystok) of an astonished Lieutenant-General Boldin; by then (24 June), 10th Army, shorn of communications, running low on ammunition and out of fuel, was fighting against enemy encirclement. Kulik, to whom Boldin reported, had lost his pre-war brashness; what he found appeared to come as a grievous shock to him. Of advice, help or orders, he had none, except to tell Boldin to 'get on with it'. At noon, Kulik left by plane and at his departure corps commander Nikitin observed aptly if sourly: 'Strange visit.' The Marshals Shaposhnikov and Voroshilov, who, like Kulik, had come to observe and to report, found themselves bolstering the dangerously sagging Western Front, control of which slipped from the grasp of Colonel-General Pavlov with terrifying speed. Timoshenko, who momentarily ran the war from a suddenly thinned *Stavka*, was under no illusions as to the extent of the catastrophe, at least in terms of the German penetrations. He made it all starkly plain to Lieutenant-General Yeremenko, who had been lifted from his train trundling back from the Soviet Far East at Novosibirsk and put on a fast bomber flying to Moscow; at the Defence Commissariat on 28 June, Yeremenko saw disaster laid out on the maps and listened to Timoshenko bitterly criticizing the frontier district commanders, in particular Pavlov. It had been decided to relieve Pavlov of his command and Yeremenko was to take his place, an appointment to which Stalin agreed.

For the last of the Marshals, Budenny, Timoshenko had a special assignment. Less than three days after he issued *Directive No. 3*, which put great if mistaken trust in the power of the covering armies to restore the situation, Timoshenko acknowledged that the counter-attacks had failed, that these armies had been broken or smashed to a degree which rendered them incapable of impeding German forward movement. In his directive of 25 June, Timoshenko ordered four armies of the *Stavka* Reserve – the 22nd, 19th, 20th and 21st – to form a 'reserve army group' which would come under Budenny's command. The group was to take up defensive positions on a line running from Sushchevo-Nevel-Vitebsk-Mogilev-Zhlobin-Gomel-Chernigov-the river Desna on to the Dnieper as far as Kremenchug. At the approaches to this line the *Stavka* hoped to stem the German advance, for which reason the 'reserve army group' was instructed to be ready to mount a counter-offensive; two days later, Timoshenko ordered Budenny to move his staff from Bryansk towards Smolensk, assigned the 16th Army from the High Command Reserve (*Rezerva Glavnovo Komand-ovaniya:* RGK) to the Smolensk-Yartsevo-Dukhovshchina area, and ordered two more reserve armies (24th and 28th), to take up defensive positions, with a depth of 10–15 miles and some 100–150 miles to the east of the first line. The North-Western Front commander was ordered to take up a defensive position, manned by his second echelon (27th Army) and surviving elements of the covering armies, running from the Western Dvina to Kraslava. Pavlov, now on the eve of his replacement, was instructed to use 13th Army and second echelon mechanized corps to hold Minsk and the Slutsk 'fortified district'. Timoshenko had one single intention; to pile up barriers to block the German advance at the centre, which had to be stopped at any price. The speed of the German progress, however, and the disasters which unfolded on the flanks, north- and south-west, burst these plans asunder, and embroiled the Red Army in a giant swirl of catastrophe, tearing out huge chunks of fronts and severing military, economic and political nerve centres from the Soviet body politic.

The 'peaceful' sectors of the entire front, first the southern and then the northern extremities, now began to crackle into life, as German–Rumanian and then Finnish forces took the offensive. General Tyulenev, who had left Moscow on 22 June, arrived in the south two days later; his headquarters, focus of the officially activated Southern Front, was at Vinnitsa, which he found bereft of telephones, telegraphs and radio equipment. To find the minimum necessary to set up a communications net, he had to raid 'local resources'; the Front forces were only just being assembled. The 9th Army had been more or less an administration, while the 18th Army, assigned to Lieutenant-General A.K. Smirnov, was formed from two rifle corps taken from the 12th Army of the South-Western Front. Tyulenev still had a few days left in which to bring his command into some kind of shape, before the German-Rumanian offensive against the Prut which broke at the very beginning of July. From Timoshenko on 25 June Tyulenev received a directive stipulating defensive action to hold back any enemy thrust; from Kirponos, with whom he finally made contact, Tyulenev learned what he already knew, that the situation on the South-Western Front was deteriorating, but that Kirponos still hoped to check the German thrusts. Though these activations at the extremities did not mean any radical tilt in the strategic balance, they added, in the south in particular, serious complications; on Friday, 27 June, Hungary, stirred by the 'Soviet bombing raid' on its frontier areas, declared war on the Soviet Union. The tally of Soviet enemies mounted.

On the eleventh day of the war, Thursday, 3 July, Stalin finally brought himself back to the public scene; his speech, an 'elaboration' of the Central Committee directive of 29 June, opened sensationally: 'Comrades, citizens, brothers and sisters, fighting men of our Army and Navy. I am speaking to you, my friends!' (The list of territorial losses which Stalin catalogued even while minimizing them by geographical generality was sombre: Soviet Lithuania, Latvia, western Belorussia, and parts of the western Ukraine.) Like Molotov earlier, Stalin defended the Nazi-Soviet Pact: 'Had not a serious mistake been made? Of course not. No peace-loving state could have rejected such a pact with another country, even if rogues like Hitler and Ribbentrop were at its head.' After this passage of self-exculpation, Stalin went on to repeat the instructions of the June directive: intensive effort, 'scorched-earth' in times of retreat, the formation of partisan units and sabotage groups to harry the Germans in the areas which they had occupied. The horizon was not entirely black; in this war 'of Soviet people against German-Fascist forces', the signs of outside help from Churchill and from the American government were positive indeed. The people, with their partisans and *opolcheniye* (militia formations) were going to war; so was the state, with its GKO, which Stalin emphasized was the instrument of state power. Of the Party, Stalin said little; this was a 'patriotic war',

and his words were addressed to the Russians. Whatever initial fright he had
succumbed to, Stalin had recovered enough and more to demonstrate his nerve
and will to the nation at large. The GKO was now manned: Stalin (chairman),
Molotov (deputy to Stalin), Voroshilov, Malenkov and Beria, the first five
which grew ultimately to eight. Stalin now took the *Stavka* in hand; with
Timoshenko dispatched to command the Western Front, Stalin first took his
office of Defence Commissar, one step on his way to Supreme Commander. In
his speech, Stalin had denounced 'cowards, deserters, panic-mongers'. Front,
army and divisional commanders, who soon enough felt the weight of this new
Stalinist direction, learned also what drastic measures lay hidden for those
whom Stalin branded 'coward'. To these unfortunates, deprived of any defence,
Stalin meted out death and demotion; in ferocious and vicious punishments
they were scythed down by Beria, entrenched in the GKO as master of a swollen
NKVD now that the earlier sub-divisions of security functions (NKGB and NKVD)
had been revoked. This was how Stalin, the grey-faced man of the Kremlin
Stavka, embarked on his war-making, as overlord of the battle-fronts, overseer
of the drastic mobilizations, scrutineer of details, manipulator of vast bodies of
men; he was vindictive against failure, impatient for success, unyielding so often
to reality even at the cost of armies smashed and fronts consumed, unlearned as
yet in how to fight, how to halt and how to destroy the *Ostheer*.

Colonel-General F.I. Kuznetsov, North-Western Front commander, from the
outset staked his all on the counter-attacks, especially those of his armoured
forces, to win control of the frontier battle and to seal off the German penetrations. The situation in 11th Army area, however, had rapidly passed the point of
restoration. Lieutenant-General V.I. Morozov, 11th Army commander, was
much dispirited at his failure to contact North-Western Front HQ; he ordered
the units falling back on the old fortress town of Kaunas on the Niemen to
move on, to Ionava, some seventeen miles to the north-east, where the 'relatively
fresh' 23rd Rifle Division of Major-General V.F. Pavlov was concentrating.
Morozov then proceeded to attack the town which he had virtually given up
so prematurely. The attack was broken: Pavlov of the 23rd was killed, while
16th Rifle Corps (including 5th Rifle Division) pulled back eastwards – and into
'deep operational encirclement'. Morozo's attempt to correct his earlier
mistake had failed; when, on 25 June, he finally made contact by telephone
with Colonel-General Kuznetsov, the latter refused to hear him out about the
state of affairs on the left flank and actually denounced him as 'a German spy'.
Nevertheless, 11th Army was being crushed to pieces.

   To the north Kuznetsov intended to use the 12th and 3rd Mechanized Corps
in flank attacks on Panzer Group 4 which had broken through to the Dubissa.
Kuznetsov had ordered the tank commanders to 'operate in small columns to
avoid the attentions of enemy aircraft'. This tactic, which merely whittled away
Soviet strength, had little or no effect; 12th Mechanized, moving south-west of

Shauliya, was pounded by German bombers and could not reach its start-line on 23 June. Of the 12th's 690 tanks (many the old, 'sparrow-shooting' type), those of Colonel I.D. Chernyakhovskii's 28th Tank Division, although stalled for five hours on 23 June for lack of fuel, did engage the 1st Panzer Division. The Soviet 2nd Tank Division (3rd Mechanized Corps) moved at night towards its operational area, the Tilsit-Shauliya highway; this blow came from the south-east and was aimed at the 6th Panzer Division, whose units the Russians caught on the march. The Soviet war diary reads: '2 Tk. Div. 3 MC fought tank action in region of Skaudvila, destroying 100th Mot. Regt., up to 40 tanks, 40 guns, in the evening entered Rasienai area without fuel.' The 2nd Tank Division lay immobilized for much of 24 June for want of fuel. During these whirling tank-battles, which spanned the three days from 23–6 June, some 250 Soviet tanks went into action, many of them the older, flimsier machines but supported by 'armoured giants', the formidably massive KV-1s and KV-2s: 1st Panzer Division engaged in 'a fantastic exchange of fire', with German anti-tank shells 'simply bouncing off' the monster Russian tanks. 1st Panzer went over to the defensive, assailed as it was by these giants; the German command had not only a crisis but an unwholesome surprise on its hands. On 26 June, however, as 1st and 6th Panzer Divisions cut through the Russian units and linked up, the 3rd Mechanized Corps was blown to pieces by German guns positioned on the high ground; the 12th Mechanized Corps pulled out of the trap with the remnants of the 2nd Tank Division, by now spent in fuel and ammunition. The first sustained crisis had come and gone; Manstein, with this battle in his rear and meeting no 'organized resistance', pressed on, racing for the Dvina bridges. By the evening of 25 June, North-Western Front forces were in a sore plight; the 8th and 11th were being forced back in disparate directions, the 8th on Riga, the 11th behind Vilno to Sventsyani and to Disna. A breach of some proportions gaped in the Soviet front; from Ukmerg to Daugvapils (Dvinsk) there was nothing but a huge hole. Soviet communications had broken down (even though the radio sets worked, the failures in the land lines were enough to justify 'signals failure'); Lieutenant-General (Signals) T.P. Kargopolov, reporting on the North-Western Front signals situation, wrote somewhat despondently:

Certain officers of these [NW] staffs . . . continued to regard the telephone as the basic means of communication. In the event of the land lines being cut, they were faced with a lack of signals with subordinate units, although the radio links still worked. In such cases, in suggesting the use of radio to transmit vital information, this so often brought the reply: 'What sort of signals is that, radio?'

The retreating armies, their communications in disorder, also choked in their own traffic jams since all movement control had gone.

The destruction visited on Kuznetsov's Baltic forces caused the Leningrad command (Northern Front) grave misgivings and faced it with the need to look to the south-west. The Northern Front ran from the Barents Sea to the Gulf of

Finland and on to Pskov; in the north, at Murmansk, lay the 14th Army, to the north-east the 23rd Army covering the frontier with four rifle divisions (123rd, 43rd, 115th and 142nd) and 7th Army north of lake Ladoga with four rifle divisions (54th, 71st, 168th and 237th), a howitzer regiment, four frontier detachments and an aviation division (55th Mixed). These remained to be 'activated', though of eventual German and Finnish operations to the north the Soviet command had no doubts. On the morning of 23 June, Lieutenant-General M.M. Popov, Northern Front commander, returned from Murmansk and decided forthwith to take some precaution in the south-west. He instructed his deputy commander, Lieutenant-General K.P. Pyadyshev to 'investigate' the possibilities of a defensive position to cover the Pskov-Leningrad approach. Pyadyshev suggested the Kingisepp-Luga-lake Ilmen 'line', although where the troops would come from to man this position was another matter entirely. Moscow could offer no help in building the positions; the telegraphic reply to the Leningrad engineering administration's request repeated the previous formula: 'Local resources'. The failure of the North-Western Front counter-strokes and the German thrust to the Western Dvina meanwhile made some decision in Leningrad quite imperative; on 25 June, an enlarged session of the Northern Front Military Soviet – commander Popov, commissar Klementeyev, chief of staff Nikishev, Party officials A.A. Kuznetsov and T.F. Shtykov – convened. Pyadyshev's proposal about the 'Luga line' was accepted and he was nominated provisional commander. As for troops, Pyadyshev proposed moving two or three rifle divisions from 23rd Army – a point which Popov did not dispute but about which he wished to consult Marshal Timoshenko. The Party officials promised labour from Leningrad to work on the positions, and four days later (29 June) the Military Soviet set up a special administration, Rear Lines Construction (*Upravlenie stroitelstva tylovykh rubezhei*: USTOR) under Major-General P.A. Zaitsev, Popov's assistant commander for 'fortified districts'. Previously, the Leningrad command had considered the Vyborg sector as the most dire threat to Leningrad; now, from the south-west, where there were only 'women with shovels and a hundred sappers', a new and acute menace was developing.

The retirement of the Baltic district armies stripped the Baltic Fleet's advanced naval bases of their landward protection. On 26 June, Admiral N.G. Kuznetsov ordered the withdrawal of naval units from Libau, Windau and the Riga bases; Libau was already blockaded from landward, though an attempt to rush the base on 25 June failed. Soviet marines and the 67th Rifle Division, as if to show that all on the North-Western Front was not hopeless, fought tenaciously, even pressing their attackers back; units of the 291st East Prussian Division had to blast the defenders with howitzers and mortars before the base fell on 29 June. Three days earlier, streaking between the Soviet 8th and 11th Armies, Manstein reached Daugvapils (Dvinsk), seized the road bridge across the Western Dvina, flattened mere tokens of Soviet resistance and seized a bridgehead on the right bank of the broad western Dvina; 8th Panzer Division was across, followed the next day by a surprise success by 3rd Motorized Infantry Division a little to the north of Daugvapils itself. All this laid Timoshenko's planning in ruins. On 25 June, he had ordered Colonel-General Kuznetsov to organize a 'stubborn defence' of the Western Dvina, by deploying 8th Army (10th and 11th Rifle Corps, 11th Rifle and 202nd Motorized Rifle Divisions) on the right bank of the river from Riga to Livani; this covered the northern sector of the river, while the 16th Rifle Corps of 11th Army would defend the other sector from Livani-Kraslava (which included Daugvapils itself). Lieutenant-General Sobennikov, 8th Army commander, also preparing a counter-stroke near Riga, ordered his formations to take up their defensive positions by the evening of 28 June. South of Livani, the 5th Airborne Corps would support 16th Corps (11th Army); to co-ordinate these formations Colonel-General Kuznetsov decided to use Major-General Berzarin of 27th Army. Berzarin was to pull his troops off the islands and out of Riga, load them aboard supply trucks, ferry them back to Pskov and then bring them forward towards Daugvapils; on the evening of 28 June, he would assume general command. At the same time, the *Stavka* released Major-General D.D. Lelyushenko's 21st Mechanized Corps from the Moscow Military District to operate with 27th Army; Lelyushenko had exactly 98 tanks and 129 guns. The 22nd Army (Western Front) was also ordered to move north-west to close with the 27th.

It was all much too late. Lieutenant-General S.D. Akimov, deputy commander North-Western Front, commanded 5th Airborne Corps in the absence of Berzarin; he failed to dislodge the German spear-heads from their right-bank positions – not surprisingly, since he had only six guns to his corps, and no tanks. But with reinforcements moving in from Pskov, Moscow and Minsk, the Soviet attacks bit somewhat deeper; at 05.00 hours, 28 June, Lelyushenko attacked on Kuznetsov's orders in an attempt to destroy the German bridgehead. Manstein, halted on the Dvina, found the position at times 'quite critical'. Soviet bombers made desperate attacks on the bridges, with heavy loss and no result. A day later, 29 June, two formations of the *Stavka* reserve, 24th and 41st Rifle Corps, were under orders to move up to bolster 27th Army, but Kuznetsov and his chief of staff, having misread or misunderstood Timoshenko's orders, ordered them to pull back to the Pskov, Ostrov and Sebezh 'fortified districts'. Not that Timoshenko's 29 June directive was a model of unambiguity; he required continued operations on the Western Dvina and *simultaneous* concentration of 'powerful reserves' in the old, Pskov-Ostrov fortified lines. Now Kuznetsov changed his mind, prompted largely by his intelligence which reported German strength in the Daugvapils bridgehead at 'about one infantry division, supported by tanks'. Kuznetsov's counter-attack, planned for 29 June, coincided with the renewal of Manstein's advance; Kuznetsov timed his attack for 10.00 hours. Manstein, joined now by main forces, jumped off at 05.00, five hours' head-start on the drive for Leningrad.

At Riga on the afternoon of 29 June three German tanks and an infantry section crossed the railway bridge – not blown up – over the Dvina at Riga. Elements of the 10th and 125th Rifle Divisions, Workers' Guards (local militia) and an armoured train succeeded by the evening in eliminating the German bridgehead, but on 30 June Soviet troops withdrew from that part of Riga on the right bank of the Dvina which they still held and by 1 July were in retreat to Estonia. Further south on the Dvina, at Krustpils, where another German bridgehead was located, 8th Army was ordered to reduce it, as 27th Army was also ordered to eliminate the German foothold at Daugvapils. The 8th and 27th Soviet Armies were, however, both struck and hurled aside by the new German offensive, and the Soviet rifle divisions battered anew. Lelyushenko's 21st Mechanized Corps had seven tanks left, seventy-four guns and little more than four thousand men. Striking along the Daugvapils-Ostrov highway, the German offensive threatened to split the 8th and 27th Armies.

Timoshenko's 29 June directive to the North-Western Front, which Kuznetsov had mangled, stipulated that in the event of a withdrawal from the Western Dvina, the next river line, the Velikaya, was to be held and every effort made to get Soviet troops installed there. Round Pskov, Ostrov, Porkhov, the *Stavka* proposed to concentrate a powerful reserve, including Major-General M.L. Chernyavskii's 1st Mechanized Corps moved in from the Northern Front (Leningrad); one tank division (the 3rd) of 1st Mechanized Corps deployed in the woods some ten miles north-east of Pskov by 2 July, while 41st Rifle Corps (111th, 118th, 235th Rifle Divisions) was shifted to Pskov, 22nd Rifle Corps (180th, 182nd Rifle Divisions) to Porkhov and 24th Rifle Corps (181st, 183rd Rifle Divisions) to the Ostrov area. While these reserves piled up, the remnants of the 12th Mechanized Corps – thirty-five tanks – under the temporary command of Colonel P.P. Poluboyarov (Chief of Armoured Forces Administration, North-Western Front) tried to stop 41st Panzer Corps from breaking the 8th and 27th Armies apart. They failed.

At the very beginning of July, the *Stavka* was persuaded that to prevent a German breakthrough to Leningrad and to defend the major forward naval base of Tallinn, the North-Western Front was far too feeble. Losses had been excruciatingly heavy. The whole Front had 1,442 guns and mortars; rifle divisions which had not been from the start at full strength were down to a third of their men, and several – the 33rd, 127th, 181st, 183rd, 188th and the 202nd Motorized Rifle Division – had each no more than 2,000 effectives. On 3 July, Front HQ (Pskov) lost contact with its armies, and radio communication failed partially. Colonel-General Kuznetsov was removed as Front commander; Timoshenko took this decision at the end of June (as the removal of Colonel-General Pavlov was decided) and Sobennikov, 8th Army commander, took over the Front, effective from 4 July. Lieutenant-General F.S. Ivanov took over 8th Army. Sobennikov received a new 'third member', Corps Commissar V.N.

Bogatkin and a new chief of staff, Lieutenant-General N.F. Vatutin, at that time Deputy Chief of the General Staff. Corps Commissar Dibrov and Colonel-General Kuznetsov were both assigned to the Western Front and the responsibility for the crumbling of the Front was heaped on the former chief of staff, Lieutenant-General P.S. Klenov.

What the Lenigrad command had envisaged a week ago now came to pass, when the *Stavka* specifically assigned the 'south-western face' to the Northern Front; Popov was to man the Narva-Luga-Staraya-Russa-Borovich line, concentrating in the first instance on the defences along the river Luga. Here, to a depth of some 5–6 miles, barriers and obstacles were to be erected, firm in all parts but for passages for the retreating troops of the North-Western Front to move through. On 6 July, the 'Luga operational group' (*Luzhskaya operativnaya gruppa*: LOG), centred on Luga only some sixty miles from Leningrad and commanded by General Pyadyshev, came into official existence. It had already been the object of General Popov's close scrutiny in his investigation of 'south-western defence lines' for the city. On 25 June he had approved the 'Luga line', though without committing himself about which troops would actually man it. The Leningrad military engineers first marked out the Luga position to run from the Gulf of Narva to Tolmachevo, and then on to lake Ilmen. Pyadyshev himself selected Luga as the defensive hub, with a north-easterly sector to cover the road and rail links from Leningrad to Pskov and Novgorod. That left a gap, void of any defences, between Luga and Krasnogvardeisk (Gatchina), over which Popov could only shake his head. Behind the 'Luga line' came a second, designated the 'outer circle', running from Petergrof-Krasnogvardeisk-Kolpino, with a last line running within the city along the railway line from Avtovo to Rybatskoe on the river Neva. All construction work on major projects within Leningrad itself came to a halt on 27 June and the workers and equipment were transferred to building defensive positions; early in July, 30,000 civilians laboured night and day on the Luga 'line', spread out on a broad front, one half digging anti-tank ditches, the others building fire-points from concrete blocks: General Zaitsev saw this for himself (3–4 July):

Half were digging ditches and anti-tank slopes. The other half worked on hundreds of circular fire-points built of concrete blocks, wood, stone, in the zone of fixed obstacles. Everything was in short supply – trucks, tools, men, foremen. But everyone wanted the army to have its defence lines as quickly as possible. They worked day and night, they slept on the breastworks of the trenches and ditches, and they argued about the depth and width of the ditches, about the best place to put the barbed wire – in front of or behind the ditch, or they wanted to know why we built lots of fire-points and so few trenches.

On 4 July, into the central position, Colonel Mashoshin arrived with the 177th Rifle Division, the first of the defending units to arrive. Divisional officers argued with the labourers; ditches were not finished, fire-points in the wrong position. Mashoshin, however, worried most about his fourteen-mile front, with no neighbour as yet to his right or to his left. The Northern Front Military Soviet considered the report on the state of the Luga defences and next day (5 July) 15,000 more Leningraders, men, women and youths, went out to dig more ditches.

The Northern Front command struggled to man the entire Luga line, which extended for more than a hundred miles. At Kingisepp (to the north), 191st Rifle Division took up its position; Colonel S.V. Roginskii (staff officer of North-Western Front HQ) installed his 111th Rifle Division near Luga, the approach to which was covered by the 177th Rifle Division. The regiments of the Leningrad Infantry School, the Kirov cadets, had been mobilized, like the artillery schools; southwards, the 1st Mountain Troops Brigade, assigned to the extreme left flank at Shimsk was only forming up and could not be in position until 10 July. Colonel G.F. Odintsov took command of the 'special artillery group' (Luga), with its complement of officer-cadets, while Major-General (Aviation) A.A. Novikov, who had done much to pull the battered bomber and fighter squadrons together, took command of a composite air force (including Baltic Fleet naval planes and fighters from the Leningrad air defence command) to provide air cover at Luga. Just, but only just in time Soviet troops scrambled behind this barrier hastily raised to prevent Leningrad from being rushed.

Popov's Northern Front, now heavily involved to the south-west, could scarcely take the strain; at the beginning of July, to defend Leningrad to the north and north-east, Popov had eight divisions (six on the northerly frontiers, two as reserve for 23rd and 7th Armies), and one mechanized corps (10th, with the 21st and 24th Tank Divisions) as Front reserve. General Tikhomirov, chief of the Operations Section in Leningrad, was already receiving report on 1 July about the 'activation' of German-Finnish forces; including the 14th Army far to the north, Popov had thirteen divisions but a vast front to cover against an estimated nineteen German-Finnish divisions and three brigades. Popov had hoped to 'shave off' three rifle divisions from the Karelian commands to divert to the south-west; in this he was momentarily disappointed (though he could use part of his Front reserve). A little later, however, Marshal Voroshilov did remove the divisions in a manner which turned out to be a costly piece of bungling. Moscow, unaccommodating to Popov, returned its repetitive formula: 'utilize local resources', but this time not machines but men. At the end of June, Leningrad turned to forming the 'militia' divisions (*Divizii narodnovo opolcheniya*: DNO).

On 30 June, a preliminary organization for the 'Leningrad National Militia Army' (*Leningradskoi armii narodnovo opolcheniya*: LANO) was formed, with a Military Soviet, staff and political sections to supervise the recruitment and training of the militia divisions. At its second meeting on 4 July, the militia army Military Soviet decided to speed matters up, to cut the original plan of forming fifteen divisions and to prepare instead three DNO formations for the Luga defence line by 7 July. The men – students, workers, professional people, sometimes whole families – volunteered readily enough, and formed up within city districts or particular factories; the regiments took their designations from them. Early in July, DNO-1, DNO-2 and DNO-3, simply kitted up but without heavy weapons, with a tiny cadre of regular troops but in general barely trained, and wished on their way as gallant men (which they were) by friends and relatives, moved off for the Luga battle-lines. This dispatch to inevitable destruction of men scarcely trained, committed against and butchered by crack, battle-tested German divisions, blotted out by tank and dive-bomber attacks and shredded by artillery, shaped gruesomely into enormous tragedy. Four divisions were ultimately wiped out. The Red Army command, to its credit, tried as hard as possible not to squander men who were there because of 'political' decisions, and 'administrative' patriotism.

Tikhomirov of the Operations Section complained that the command lacked accurate intelligence data about the German forces assaulting the North-Western Front; what came from Moscow was 'much too general'. General Novikov reported that between 700–1,000 German aircraft were operating, the bombers confidently dispensing with fighter cover. To the south-west, the river Velikaya line had fallen rapidly and the rail and road bridges remained intact; although south of Ostrov the 111th Rifle and 3rd Tank Division counter-attacked in disorganized fashion, the long-established Ostrov 'fortified district' fell undefended. The 111th all but broke up, its regiments out of touch with divisional staff – only Colonel Roginskii (who took over from Colonel I.M. Ivanov) managed to shepherd the remnants of the division to Luga. At Pskov, north-east of Ostrov and also on the Velikaya, Sobennikov specifically ordered the 50th Motorized Engineer Regiment (1st Mechanized Corps) to organize the dynamiting of eight bridges: at 06.00 hours, 8 July, 8th Panzer Division moved to the Velikaya and one by one (except for the rail link) the bridges went up, even though this stranded Soviet units. At 16.00 hours, with German tanks upon it, the rail bridge itself was blown up. Pskov finally fell on the evening of 9 July; 11th Army commander was therefore ordered to move to Dno and to bring his three corp., 41st and 22nd Rifle, 1st Mechanized, back under 'unified command'.

To the north, on the Gulf of Finland, the Soviet 8th Army had been savagely mauled but still hung on; its two corps (10th and 11th Rifle) had little ammunition and fewer supplies. The divisions were in tatters; 10th Rifle Division (10th Corps) had 2,577 men and one anti-tank gun, 125th Rifle Division (11th Corps) 3,145 men and twenty-two guns or mortars. There were no reserves. These mangled units were now to prevent the rushing of the Narva neck towards Leningrad and the development of a threat to Tallinn; for that reason, at the beginning of July, they struggled to hold the Piana-Tartu line (from the Gulf of Riga to the Chudov lake).

At dawn on the morning of 10 July, hearing of the fall of Pskov, General

Popov expected an early appearance of German tanks on the 'Luga line', on which Soviet troops were falling back (and in danger of wandering into the newly laid minefields). The 118th Rifle Division had pulled back along the Pskov-Gdov road, leaving the Pskov-Luga highway uncovered. German bombers and tanks caught 90th Rifle Division on its forced march to the Strugi Krasnye-Ludoni sector to plug this gap. When, however, 41st Panzer Corps tried to rush Luga and its defences, the thrust was deflected; 1st and 6th Panzer Divisions swung north-west and on to Sabsk to work round and through the Soviet defences.

The crumpling of the North-Western Front on the Velikaya and the German sweep to Luga were grave set-backs; 8th Army was being rammed inexorably towards the Gulf of Finland. On 12 July, the battle of the 'Luga line' had begun. Dreadfully thinned the Soviet armies might have been but they had not yet been destroyed; with bridges blown up in time and positions manned, there was even a certain briskness in Soviet performance. General Popov had stretched himself admirably. But now, under Stalin's great July reorganization, the north-west received a new military overlord, GKO member, Stalin's military crony for nearly a quarter of a century, Marshal of the Soviet Union Voroshilov.

On 25 June, the day on which he first put his reserve armies on the move, Timoshenko also ordered Colonel-General Pavlov, Western Front commander, to withdraw his armies from the Bialystok salient and pull back to a line running from Lida-Slonim-Pinsk: with these formations, plus 13th Army, Pavlov was to hold the Minsk and Slutsk 'fortified districts'. Marshal Timoshenko thus hoped to draw an uncomfortably large number of Soviet divisions out of a vast German encirclement which was in the making and at the same time bar the way to a further German thrust at the centre with the Reserve Army Group under Budenny's command. Taken only ninety-six hours after the beginning of the war that decision came, nevertheless, very late – if not too late.

Colonel-General Pavlov was all but overwhelmed, as Panzer Group 3 on its northerly encircling sweep to Minsk through Vilno-Molodechno sliced through Soviet units and from the south-west Guderian's Panzer Group 2 swung towards Minsk through Baranovichi. To hold off these claws, Pavlov issued on 25 June withdrawal orders to his four cover armies: 13th Army would take the line Iliya–Molodechno–Listopad–Geranon, 3rd Army Geranon–Lida, 10th Army Slonim-Byten, and 4th Army Byten-Pinsk. The withdrawal was to begin on the night of 25–26 June, with armour in the van and cavalry, anti-tank guns and engineers bringing up the rear. Pavlov's withdrawal plan, however, was doomed to the same nightmarish failure which his first counter-offensive designs had met.

On the right flank of the Western Front, at the junction with the North-Western Front, the gap torn by Panzer Group 3 widened in less than thirty-six hours to some sixty miles and grew by the hour as 11th Army (North Western Front) fell back in disorder to the north-east and 3rd Army (Western Front) was pushed back to the south-east: this prised open the way to Minsk. Kuznetsov of 3rd Army had already committed Mostovenko's 11th Mechanized Corps (290 tanks including 24 T-34s, 3 KVs) to a counter-attack near Grodno, but only the 29th Tank Division was on the spot; the 33rd Tank Division was twenty Luftwaffe-dominated miles away and corps staff and the 204th Motorized Rifle Division even further – at Volkovysk, forty miles away. By 23 June, in spite of furious resistance, 56th, 85th and 27th Rifle Divisions (3rd Army) were pushed out of Grodno and behind the Niemen; the breach between the two Soviet Fronts (Western and North-Western) widened to nearly eighty miles. Boldin, prop-ping up Golubev at 10th Army, faced a grave situation as the flank armies (3rd and 4th) were smashed in; Khatskilevich, commander of the once powerful 6th Mechanized Corps (with over 1,000 tanks, many of them T-34s and KVs), repor-ted that ammunition and fuel were running desperately low. Boldin had sent a letter to Pavlov at Minsk, using one of the planes flying out of the heavily in-vested 10th Army area and pleading for an air-drop of fuel and ammunition. This, and a subsequent attempt to get help, failed. All the more astonishing therefore was the arrival of Marshal Kulik, who knew nothing of the desperate straits of the 10th and its equally desperate needs; he came quite empty-handed. On 26 June, with its main stocks of ammunition spent, 10th Army was no longer an organized fighting force and its units melted into the thick woods south of Minsk.

Korobkov's 4th Army on the left flank, pushed back from the Ysaelda to the Shchara river, faced a 'critical situation' on 24 June, when shortly after dawn Korobkov and his staff learned of the German penetration to Slonim and the threat to Baranovichi. Denuding the Slutsk–Bobruish sector of cover, Korobkov moved the 55th Rifle Division from Slutsk and the 121st from Bobruish; impor-tant as that axis was, it was still less vital than that of Slonim–Baranovichi, which covered Minsk. While the 55th deployed near Slonim, Colonel Konnov at-tacked a German column on the Ruzhana–Slonim road: Guderian himself, who was supervising the Slonim–Baranovichi assault at close range, ran into this attack and also into Korobkov's reinforcements for Slonim which had moved up in lorries. A quick turn of speed saved Guderian. During the night of 24–5 June, when for a few moments 4th Army established contact with Pavlov, Korobkov was ordered to defend the Shchara line and to incorporate all divisions in the Slonim area into 4th Army. That same night, 4th Army held its first session of the Military Soviet: discipline had degenerated seriously, with subordinate units failing to carry out orders, so that 'punitive measures' were now required.

Korobkov maintained contact with his units by liaison officers. On the morn-ing of 25 June Colonel Krivosheyev, army liaison officer, reported to Korobkov that near Baranovichi he had come upon three armoured cars with Colonel-General Pavlov in the middle one. Pavlov said that he intended to send General Nikitin's mechanized corps to support the rifle divisions near Slonim; mean-while, Korobkov was to be informed that reserve armies were concentrating on the Dnieper and that the Western Front had to cover this concentration. The task of 4th Army was to hold the Shchara, to man the Slutsk 'fortified district' and the Sluch river line. Korobkov proposed to use V.S. Popov's 28th Rifle Corps to defend Slutsk, but on being alerted to this, the commander of Slutsk 'fortified district' reminded Korobkov that all the weapons in the Slutsk defences had long since been sent to Brest and the equipment dismantled. The 'fortified district' was a hollow shell, guarded by a battalion, with not a weapon in the pill-boxes and pits. (At least the weapons sent to Brest were being put to good use; the fortress, now far to the rear, kept up its steady fire in spite of drastic attempts to reduce the garrison.) Korobkov was thus at a stroke deprived of what he himself called his 'solid, iron-clad cover' at Slutsk, while in the centre of his area, from Bereza to Baranovichi, he was facing catastrophe – and so therefore was Minsk.

With his instructions to Korobkov to hold the Shchara, Pavlov might have thought that he had averted disaster in the south-west. Now he had to deal with a threat to Minsk from the north-west, as Colonel-General Hoth's Panzer Group 3 swept down on Molodechno. Major-General P.M. Filatov's 13th Army, a new formation which had only taken shape in May, was, as Pavlov's second echelon, responsible for the defence of the Minsk 'fortified district'; its numerical designation, synonymous with bad luck, seemed to be a portent of the disasters to come. On 20 June, 13th Army staff was ordered by Pavlov to move to Novogrudok; on the move, it was re-routed to Molodechno, where it arrived at 18.00 hours, 23 June, without any equipment at all – even the officers had no personal weapons. At Molodechno, the staff was issued with three rifles and nineteen revolvers; without weapons, the staff was also without troops. 13th Army was 'collected' from the remnants of 6th and 148th Rifle Divisions and the Vilno Infantry School, units then in full retreat. A day later, 24 June, at 21.00 hours, Pavlov assigned 13th Army the 21st Rifle Corps (37, 17, 24 Rifle Divisions) and ordered a left-flank counter-stroke with 17th Rifle Division, to 'co-ordinate' with General Boldin's units attacking near Grodno-Merech. This was sheer phantasy. General Filatov meanwhile gathered up the remnants of the 5th Tank Division and Armoured Train No. 5 standing at Molodechno station. Having made some disposition to cover Molodechno, during the night of 25 June Filatov and his staff were again on the move, only to be caught, shot up and dispersed by a German tank column. With half of his staff killed – defenceless as they were – Filatov and the survivors arrived at Zhdanovich, about seven miles north-west of Minsk. Major-General B.B. Borisov's 21st Rifle Corps had already tried to carry out the 'offensive design' to 'co-ordinate' with General Boldin but at 13.00 hours, 26 June, General Borisov discerned that he was alone – to the right no Soviet units, to the left no contact with General Boldin's force (which had never ever existed). General Borisov went on the defensive, with a corps woefully short of fuel and ammunition.

Once in Zhdanovichi, Filatov subordinated the 44th and 2nd Rifle Corps (originally part of his pre-war force) to his command; Pavlov had meanwhile directed the 100th and 161st Rifle Divisions to the north of Minsk, to operate with Major-General A.N. Yermarkov's 2nd Rifle Corps. While awaiting orders in Minsk, 100th Rifle Division had suffered some preliminary losses; 44th Rifle Corps had all the divisional artillery, and most of the 100th's transport had been quietly diverted to other units. At 19.00 hours, 25 June, 2nd Rifle Corps staff reported an enemy tank column moving unhindered fifty kilometres north-west of Minsk. During the night, 100th Rifle Division, without a piece of artillery, was ordered to take up a blocking position; the divisional battle-line proved to be, as if some compensation for the loss of its guns, the formation's pre-war training ground. To fight off the tanks, the divisional commander raided a local glass factory, the *Belarus*, for bottles to make 'Molotov cocktails'; stripped of its guns, the division could do no better and on 26 June, the battle for Minsk was joined. In the morning Pavlov evacuated himself and his staff to Moghilev; Colonel Sandalov of 4th Army afoot in Minsk in search of the Front commander, found only a shattered town, with 'a flood of vehicles in the streets' making their way to the bridges over the Svisloch river or towards other exits. To the fires already burning German bombers added more, and the barrage to the north-west was plainly audible.

The inner encirclement of Pavlov's armies meanwhile proceeded as part of the massive 'double battle of Bialystok–Minsk'. By the evening of 25 June, 3rd and 10th Armies, withdrawing on Minsk, had only a narrow corridor between Skidel and Volkovysk – less than thirty miles – left to them. If there were any lorries left, there were no roads to drive on: staffs had no information where or in what condition units and formations could be found: dumps containing the equivalent of two thousand railway-truck loads of ammunition were blown up or lost to the enemy: with what ammunition they had left, those units still fought with fierce determination to break through the inner German ring, and these break-out attempts intensified towards the very end of June. By 28 June, 3rd Army was fully split up and cut off: very shortly, the left flank units of 10th Army near Volkovysk were sealed off, and the tally of trapped divisions mounted. Colonel-General Pavlov had totally and terribly lost control of the situation.

Timoshenko, although lacking precise details, was aware that a disaster of some magnitude had enveloped both the Western and North-Western Fronts: something, anything had to be done to check the German rush on 'the Moscow axis'. On the evening of 26 June, Timoshenko assembled the officers of the Red Army Engineers Administration and authorized them to operate, with 'broad powers', in destroying bridges and systems in the path of the German advance. Lieutenant-General Malandin at the General Staff could supply only 'general information' about the course of operations; nevertheless, a rough calculation could be made about the number of mines need to 'cover' the line to be taken up by Budenny's 'reserve army group'. Unfortunately, no one knew how many mines were actually available. One aspect, the tension apart, about Timoshenko's short address struck the engineer officers as odd; he made no mention, not even ritualistically, of Stalin. Timoshenko, having dispatched the Marshals Voroshilov and Shaposhnikov to Western Front headquarters, now issued new orders to Marshal Budenny in an effort to establish a 'stable line', resting on the lower Western Dvina and the Dnieper – running from Kraslava–Disna–Polotsk–Vitebsk–Orsha–the Dnieper – on to Loev. Budenny was given precise instructions on deployment: 22nd Army to the middle reaches of the Western Dvina, 21st Army westwards to the lower reaches of the Berezina. Behind these forces, two reserve armies (24th and 28th) would man an additional line running from Nelidovo–Belyi–Dorogobuzh–Yelnya–Zhukovka (north-west of Bryansk)–Sinerzerki (south of Bryansk); the defence of the approaches to Smolensk–Vyazma and Rogachev (east of Bobruisk)–Medyn (north-west of Kaluga) was impressed upon Budenny as being of the greatest importance, and embodied in the *Stavka* directive which he received on 27 June. The frantic rush to block the way to Moscow with anything and everything was on; out from Moscow sped the three special 'destruction detachments' (one detained on its urgent way by zealous NKVD sentries alarmed by 'Russian officers' with a lorry-load of explosives near bridges) to Budenny's new lines.

The line at Minsk had meanwhile cracked. Guderian from the south-west and Hoth from the north-west finally closed on the capital of Soviet Belorussia; the trap sprang shut on 28 June. The escape route eastwards for 3rd, 10th and now 13th Army was now barred. In all, the elements of four armies were sealed off – to disintegrate, to be pounded to pieces or to make a bloody and desperate attempt to break out – in this giant encirclement. Forced back on Minsk, 13th Army had by the morning of 28 June lost contact with its 64th and 108th Rifle Divisions: 100th and 161st had suffered heavy losses. Pavlov, however, still hoped to hold Minsk. By courier on 28 June he transmitted this order – or explanation – to 13th Army commander:

People's Commissar (*Narkom*) and Military Soviet of Western Front confirm to 13th Army that the Minsk fortified district must be held even though this might mean fighting in encirclement. But that [encirclement] should not happen, since units of 3rd Army are collecting in the area of Stolba and will be moved on Minsk, Ratomka: 6th Mechanized will be routed through Stolbtsa, Pukhovich for a final blow at the enemy's rear.

This, in all its appalling phantasmagoria, had more of Pavlov's spectral units and phantom attack formations on the move: 3rd Army was being strangled in a noose pulled tight by German infantry divisions: 6th Mechanized Corps, Pavlov's pride, had disintegrated, its tanks stalled, burned out or with empty magazines: Khatskilevich, corps commander, lay dead and all life flickered out of the corps when the remnants of one of Khatskilevich's finest divisions, 4th Tank, rallied by Colonel Yashin, fought a final, savage action west of Minsk. Boldin, with a battered column from 10th Army, ignorant of where the battle-lines lay, moved by compass and struck east: 'Group Boldin', without ammunition and laden with wounded, finally existed. Elsewhere in the fiery ring, dispirited collapse and late rallies marked multiple local disasters among the dissected Soviet divisions.

North and south of Minsk German spear-heads raced for the Berezina. On his very left wing Pavlov had uncovered Slutsk by draining off units to Korobkov's 4th Army for the abortive 'counter-offensive' near Slonim (25–6 June); here, 4th Army's right flank was amputated, and its left went limp at Slutsk which fell on 27 June. In the afternoon of 27 June, 4th Army staff retired to Bobruisk, and in the evening Soviet units also fell back on the eastern bank of the Berezina. Major-General S.I. Poverkin's 47th Rifle Corps, with some artillery, units which had been sent to Baranovichi, the Bobruisk Motor-Tractor School and a road repair battalion, held Bobruisk. That same evening Pavlov ordered 4th Army to hold the Berezina 'as long as possible'. At noon the next day Bobruisk fell. Korobkov sent Colonel Sandalov to report to Pavlov at his headquarters at Moghilev. Sandalov found Pavlov a much-changed man, his face sunken, his body hunched. Sandalov asked for reinforcement at Bobruisk: Pavlov rounded on him for 'giving up the town so easily'. The Front commander proposed to give 4th Army a mechanized corps (Nikitin) and an airborne force (Zhadov): these could strike at the rear of the German forces moving to the Berezina, while 4th Army had to get Bobruisk back in Russian hands. Orders went out to Major-General A.S. Zhadov of 4th Airborne Corps to use his 7th and 8th Brigades in the Berezina operations. Pavlov also alerted Major-General B.R. Terpilovskii of the Lepel garrison (many miles north-east of Minsk) to activate his garrison.

Colonel Sandalov was not the only visitor at the Moghilev HQ. Marshal Shaposhnikov was there, awaiting the arrival of Marshal Voroshilov and there was one officer yet to come – Pavlov's replacement, Lieutenant-General A.I. Yeremenko. Early on the morning of 29 June Yeremenko arrived at Western Front headquarters, situated in a wood not far from Moghilev: the Front commander was having his breakfast. Yeremenko pushed Timoshenko's dismissal order in front of Pavlov, who asked: 'Where do I go now?' To Moscow, Yeremenko told him. Pavlov tried to make some explanation to Yeremenko – the tardy arrival of his orders, the dispersal of his troops on the training grounds, the peacetime routine . . . At the close of this rather odious interview, brief and strained as it was, the Front staff assembled; as these officers gathered, Yeremenko presented himself to the Marshals Shaposhnikov and Voroshilov, who evidently spared little in their criticism of the previous Front command. Voroshilov made his point plain: 'Pavlov led his forces badly.' Shaposhnikov rather more to the point, showed Yeremenko where to commit his reserves. Voroshilov concerned himself more with organizing sabotage groups and partisan detachments, seventy-four of which had been formed in Moghilev, and on 29 June, Voroshilov briefed the commanders of the sabotage groups who were sent out against German aerodromes and rear services.

Marshal Shaposhnikov attended the extraordinary session of the Western Front Military Soviet which officially informed the staff of the change of command somewhat later in the day. Lieutenant-General Malandin had arrived, and P.K. Ponomarenko, First Secretary of the Belorussian Communist Party (who had been working with Voroshilov on the partisan plans) attended. Yeremenko found 'scant' intelligence data about the enemy and disorganization in the administration of Soviet operations. The first task was to reinforce Borisov (north-east of Minsk) and Bobruisk, to hold the Berezina. As much as he needed time, Yeremenko needed men – good ones, and he mentioned Colonel Kreizer's 1st Moscow Motorized Rifle Division as one of the formations he wanted moved up in a hurry. Even as he went through the Front reports with Malandin, Yeremenko was not fully aware of the wreckage on the Western Front and in committing himself to the fight for the Berezina, he picked a battle already part lost. Yeremenko, however, had no option: his specific instruction from Marshal Timoshenko was – 'halt the German offensive'.

The 1st Moscow Division was being rushed to the front, but under conditions which were largely characteristic for the whole formation of the 'reserve group'. Colonel Kreizer's crack division belonged to the 7th Mechanized Corps commanded by Major-General V.I. Vinogradov: 7th Corps had a full complement of 1,000 tanks and 500 guns. On 20 June, the Corps staff, carrying out a reconnaissance in the Kaluga–Tula area, was ordered back to Moscow: on 21 June the Corps went on full alert. The war was two days old when 7th Corps was assigned to the *Stavka* reserve and ordered to Gzhatsk. The motorized infantry drove there along the Moscow–Minsk road, the tanks and corps staff went by rail. Kreizer's units led the road movement. Before reaching Gzhatsk, a General Staff signals officer intercepted the column to route it to Vyazma. The division passed through Vyazma, was there re-assigned to Yartsevo and from there to Smolensk. During the night of 26 June 7th Corps staff arrived at Smolensk railway station, to be met by 20th Army commander, Lieutenant-General F.N. Remizov. Remizov brought information that Kreizer's division was to take up defensive positions west of Orsha. The remainder of 7th Corps would man the line Vitebsk–Rudnya–Bogushevsk–Orsha. To the right of Polotsk (in the direction of Vitebsk) there was a rifle division under Colonel Gagen. To the left of Orsha there was nothing. Of the situation at the front Remizov had little to say, for there was little he knew; communications with Front HQ kept breaking down and there was none between separate armies. Major-General V.S. Bodrov, 20th Army artillery commander, consulted by his opposite number of 7th Corps about ammunition supplies, confessed to not knowing where the dumps were. Nor did Colonel N.P. Lyubimov, chief of staff to 20th Army, and neither, apparently, seemed to be making much effort to find them. This is how the reserve formations moved behind and into the 'lines' which the *Stavka* drew across its maps: they were jerked, half-formed often, from one location to another, with roads jammed, commanders ignorant of the over-all situation, rear services non-existent, and committed to 'doorstep' defence.

Yeremenko, after a day (30 June) of studying the Western Front's forces and becoming more aware of the extent of the destruction, determined to stop committing the units in 'bits and pieces'. On 30 June, in a somewhat unrealistic start, he and Malandin ordered 13th Army to 'unify' all its elements and those operating near Minsk (2nd, 44th, 21st Rifle, 20th Mechanized Corps and 8th Anti-Tank Brigade) to attack Rakov; this was quickly amended to a withdrawal order and a defence assignment on the eastern bank of the Berezina. The next day (1 July) Yeremenko issued his first Front directive:

Directive No. 14
Staff Western Front
17.45 hours   *1.7.41 Moghilev*

1 The enemy has taken Minsk and, in trying to reach the Dnieper, has directed his main forces towards Moghilev and Zhlobin.
    Basic enemy force estimated at 1,000–1,500 tanks east of Minsk and up to 100 tanks which have broken through the Berezina in the area of Bobruisk.

2 To right and left flanks are open.
    Tasks of Front armies not to permit the enemy to reach the Dnieper and until 7.7 to hold the line of the Berezina on the front Borisov, Bobruisk, Parichi, securing themselves against outflanking by tanks to the right north of Borisov.
    Tanks which have broken through in the Bobruisk area are to be destroyed.

3 13th Army . . . on the night of 3.7 to fall back and stubbornly defend the line of the river Berezina on the front Khokholnitsa, Borisov, Brodets, with 50 RD in reserve at Pogodishcha and 7 Anti-Tank Brigade at Pogost.

4 4th Army . . . during night of 3.7 to fall back on the line of the river Berezina and stubbornly defend the front Brodets, Bobruisk, paying special attention to anti-tank defence in the direction Svisloch, Moghilev, using holding detachments, allowing no breakthrough on the line Sloboda, N. Gorodok, Ozertsa.

5 To commander 17th Mech. Corps to move corps by 3.7 to Kolby, Slobodka, Suma, to bring order into units. 4.7 to be ready to operate in direction of Bobruisk to capture latter in co-operation with 204 Para. Bde. and 34 RD.

6 To commander air force
  1 To cover withdrawal and concentration of troops to line of the Berezina.
  2 To be ready to secure operations of 7th Mech. Corps and 155 RD in the direction of Bobruisk from the air . . .
  3 Repeater sorties to destroy the enemy on Bobruisk aerodrome and enemy tank columns east and south of Bobruisk at Smolevich and at Borisov.

7 Command post 13th Army 4.7 at Gerin, 4th Army at Rogachev.

8 Command post Front Staff woods 12 kilometres north-east Moghilev.

Directive No. 14, in spite of its great air of purposefulness, did not differ so very much from what Colonel-General Pavlov himself had discerned and worked to achieve on 28 June. Both Pavlov and Yeremenko were committed to the impossible.

Yeremenko also used the kinetic energy of the new broom to 'hot up' Soviet air operations, though the Front command had only 120 patched-up machines to deploy: on 1 July Yeremenko squeezed out an extra 30, giving him a grand squadron strength of 52 fighters. These he employed, in part, in sweeps over Bobruisk. Soviet combat aviation had taken terrible punishment, though it fought back as best it could. Soviet ground troops continuously bewailed the lack of air cover and the dearth of AA guns: the Political Section, 2nd Rifle Corps made a typical report: 'Beginning with 27 June to 30 June our aviation did not show up once at the front in the area of Minsk; in these conditions enemy aircraft operated with impunity.' For his military bricks, however, Yeremenko had precious little straw; in the first week in July, Western Front tank strength for the first echelon divisions stood at little more than 145. Major-General A.G. Nikitin's 20th Mechanized Corps, which bore something of a charmed life, had nevertheless lost all its 'mechanization': his 38th Tank Division had 3,000 men and 3 howitzers, 26th Tank 3,800 men and 5 guns. General Zhadov's para-troopers (4th Airborne Corps) had 1,100 men in 7th Brigade and 1,000 in the 8th. Yeremenko's concern about speeding up Kreizer's tanks and the rifle divisions rolling up behind him was understandable enough.

In spite of his brave directive, Yeremenko was outpaced by the Panzer divisions on the Berezina. At Borisov a 'dangerous situation' had arisen by 2 July; from south-west of Minsk, 18th Panzer Division had streaked along the motor road to Borisov, hurled the Soviet defence on the Berezina's western bank aside and stormed over the undestroyed bridge. Corps Commissar I.Z. Susaikov and the officer-cadets of the Borisov Tank School were unable to dislodge the German bridgehead. Yeremenko had given personal instructions for the demolition of the vital bridge; but in the subsequent investigation, 'technical reasons' were advanced for the failure to destroy the bridge. Yeremenko himself cites 'negligence , though reluctance to strand their fellows might have weighed not a little with the demolition crew. Yeremenko hustled Kreizer's motorized division, with its goodly complement of T-34 and KV tanks, from Orsha to the Borisov bridgehead. Faulty tactics, not inferior equipment or lack of fighting spirit, caused Kreizer's counter-stroke to falter and finally fail, though not before the sleek T-34s and monster KV-2s brought consternation to the German gunners and tank-crews. Yeremenko, up at the Borisov fighting himself, reported on 4 July:

13th Army during the day continued to fight to defend the Berezina crossings. 50th Rifle Division, brought over to the eastern bank of the Berezina, went over to the defensive on a front Kholkholitsa, Studenka. 1st Motorized Rifle Division and composite detachment of Borisov garrison continued to engage enemy motor-mechanized units which had crossed in the area of Borisov and Chernyavka . . . The division suffered heavy losses. One regiment (1st Motorized) defending north of Borisov suffered heavy losses from air attack . . . Enemy used only armour-piercing shell, which did not penetrate KV armour, but tore the tracks to pieces. Division on the defensive.

But Yeremenko was no longer Front commander. The Berzina 'line', in spite of all his strivings, had shrivelled almost as soon as it had formed. He had lost the race to and on the Berezina. The *Stavka* dare not lose that to the Western Dvina and the Dnieper, although by 4 July Panzer Group 3 and Panzer Group 2 (united now into Fourth Panzer Army) had reached the Western Dvina (at Tsacniki–Ulla and Disna–Polotsk) and the Dnieper (at Rogachev) in their respective operations. Guderian with Panzer Group 2 was to swing south of Smolensk to Yenlya, Hoth with Panzer Group 3 would smash through the Vitebsk–Nevel line and move to the north of the city, and after Smolensk – Moscow. Faced with a dire emergency, Stalin, now stirred out of his June torpor, handed over the Western Front to Marshal Timoshenko; the order (2 July) installed Yeremenko and Budenny as his deputies. To build up a force to man the Western Dvina and Dnieper, the *Stavka* had already (1 July) incorporated Budenny's 'reserve army group' into the Western Front, and these slabs of armies were now being moved into position to the north and south, just as Timoshenko arrived at his head-quarters at Gnezdovo near Smolensk on 4 July. The German command thought the establishment of '*eine geschlossene Abwehrfront*', a firm defensive front, beyond the capabilities of the Red Army: Yeremenko himself, while recognizing that no 'stable front' existed, thought that he had at least formed 'a front of some kind' but it was up to Timoshenko to form the 'stable' Dvina–Dnieper front. German aerial reconnaissance and radio intelligence had already noted the presence of fresh Soviet armies and new commands – between Orsha and Vitebsk, north at Nevel and right to the south, at Gomel.

The wreckage of the Western Front now lay strewn over more than 200 miles. The Soviet formations and units trapped west of Minsk (where the Germans claimed the capture of 287,704 prisoners and 2,585 tanks) thrashed about as they broke up or broke out: on 9 July, German 'mopping up' operations came to an end. The dun-coloured columns of Soviet prisoners moved back to the rear, the majority later to die like animals as they were beaten, shot or starved. German security units searched for those who should be killed at once: 'Commissars, Communists, Jews – forward!' Inside and outside the ring, Soviet military commissars had tried to rally the men, often with pistols in their hand; Commissar Kochetkov was one, haranguing his encircled unit, when a political officer shot one 'panic-monger' down: 'A dog – and a dog's death.' But successful break-out had its terrors, this time at the hands of the NKVD; once behind the Soviet lines, men from units lost or encircled ran foul of intense, if exaggerated NKVD suspicions. Others, like Colonel Nichiporovich (who was arrested in 1938 as an 'enemy of the people'), used their shattered units as a basis for organizing partisan regiments in the enemy rear; a number of which, like Nichiporovich's, became formidable bodies and provided the first basis of effective partisan operations.

For all of this, the GKO determined to exact fearsome punishments.

Colonel-General Pavlov, with Klimovskikh and Grigoriev, as well as Klich were forthwith arrested. Colonel Starinov, who had brought Pavlov a load of explosive and mines, watched the colonel-general being arrested. Artillery commander Klich protested: the NKVD and the Military Tribunal officers cut him short or snubbed him, repeating the formula that 'Comrade Stalin knows all about it and is very concerned'. The 'punitive right hand of Stalin' had fallen, to salvage his own authority. Now, 'no one was sure of his tomorrow' and all 'remembered 1937 too well'. The Red Army, pounded by its external enemies, had now to face its 'internal' foes, not least Beria and Mekhlis. Front, corps, army, divisional and unit commanders were in their turn lined up before execution squads.

While the Western Front trembled with internal crisis, Hoth and Guderian rocked it with powerful blows. Timoshenko had 7 armies, 24 divisions in his first echelon, less than 200 tanks and 389 patched up planes. Lieutenant-General F.A. Yershakov's 22nd Army held the Western Dvina from Drissa to Vitebsk where Lieutenant-General I.S. Koniev's 19th Army (moved from Belaya, Tserkva on the South-Western Front) was forming up: in the vital strip of land between the Western Dvina and the Dnieper, Lieutenant-General P.A. Kurochkin's 20th Army had moved up from Moghilev: from Orsha to Rogachev on the Dnieper was held by Lieutenant-General P.M. Filatov's 13th Army, and the left flank of the Front, from Togachev to Rechnitsa (south-east of Gomel), by Lieutenant-General V.F. Gerasimenko's 21st Army. The Soviet 4th Army was falling back continuously from the Berezina into the area of 13th and 21st Armies. Timoshenko thus had four armies in position, one in retreat and two – the 19th and 16th – on the move.

Lukin's 16th Army, moved in May from the Trans-Baikal to the Kiev district (South-Western Front) even though still waiting for its divisions to roll in from the east, was ordered on 26 June to move to the Western Front and concentrate in the Orsha–Smolensk area. Alekseyenko's 5th Tank Corps (an element of 16th Army) had arrived from the east, only to have Lukin re-load it into rail trucks at Shepetovka and route it north. But so far only a third of 16th Army had turned up; as Lukin waited at Shepetovka, he suddenly found himself in command of an improvised combat group fighting off an attack. To lose Shepetovka meant losing the South-Western Front's vital ammunition dump. The 16th's rifle divisions, given the 'green light' wherever possible, were finally routed through Kiev and Bryansk, where Koniev's 19th Army was also in transit. These old neighbours of the Trans-Baikal did not meet as the trains pulled out at ten-minute intervals and raced for Smolensk. At Pochinok, some thirty miles south of Smolensk, 16th Army detrained during the night of 1–2 July; part of the time it was bombed. Smolensk itself had been heavily bombed; 16th Army officers going into Smolensk in the morning met civilians, who had slept in the outlying fields to escape the air attacks, going in to work. The Party officials were harassed and gloomy. Front HQ at Gnezdovo had just heard that Timoshenko was the new commander; Marshal Budenny had in fact already left Smolensk on his way to the Ukraine. No one, not even Malandin, knew where the 16th was to deploy. (The concentration area turned out to be Zhukovka, a suburban collective farm, while 16th Army staff, switched south then north on its way from Novosibirsk, had ended up near Orsha.) Koniev with the 19th had even less luck; he came under fire while detraining, and had to fight back with what regiments he could muster.

Timoshenko had to decide at once how he might fend off the Dvina and Dnieper thrusts. He selected a flank blow against 39th Panzer Corps (Panzer Group 3): the object was to eliminate the most serious of present threats, that facing the whole right flank of the Western Front, where the Soviet 22nd Army on the Western Dvina was in sore straits. Timoshenko's general Front directive, authorized by the *Stavka*, stipulated 'durable' defence of the Polotsk 'fortified district', the Western Dvina, Senno, Orsha and the Dnieper itself, preventing an enemy breakthrough to the north and to the east. The marshal deployed his three serviceable armies to cover these points and lines: 22nd Army (Polotsk, the Dvina and Beshenkovich), 20th Army (from Beshenkovich to Shklov, south of Orsha), and 21st Army (to hold Moghilev, Bykhov and Loev). At the same time (4 July) Kurochkin's 20th Army received attack orders: Timoshenko ordered Kurochkin to strike at enemy forces 'driving from Lepel in the direction of Vitebsk'. Two mechanized corps, 5th and 7th, would attack from north of Orsha and advance on Senno, also taking the 39th Panzer Corps in the flank. The commanders were ordered, 'while holding the Western Dvina and Dnieper firmly, from the morning of 6.7.41 to go over to a decisive offensive to destroy the Lepel enemy concentration'. Before the attack went in, Timoshenko held a hurried conference north of Orsha with Yeremenko, Kurochkin and Major-General A.V. Borzikov, Western Front director of tank forces. What worried Yeremenko was the prospect of committing the mechanized corps so deep – about sixty miles – in isolation from other troops and without air cover. The *Stavka*, however, had decided.

The Soviet attack went in on 6 July, as Panzer Group 3 fought for its bridgeheads on the northern bank of the Western Dvina. The two corps, 5th and 7th, had each three hundred and four hundred tanks, but no air cover, few AA guns, and barely enough fuel and ammunition. By 10.00 hours 6 July Soviet tanks were in action, skilfully handled even though committed – and here Yeremenko was right – without support, without co-ordination and 'in driblets'. Alekseyenko's 5th Corps (late of 16th Army), with its three divisions, did well at the outset, advancing on Senno. Vinogradov's 7th had two divisions (Kreizer's division had been snatched earlier for the Borisov fighting) though no infantry and few AA guns. The Soviet corps now ran into 17th and 18th Panzer Divisions, protecting their flanks. Soviet officers observing 7th Corps' 14th Tank Division saw more burned or smashed tanks piling up on the battlefield – a scene repeated across the whole area. Then came the German dive-bombers but to defend itself 7th Corps had merely a handful of 37-mm AA guns. For seventy-two hours, as the Russians regrouped and attacked again, the tank battles waxed and waned. Vinogradov's divisional commanders and staff begged him to break off the action, to avoid useless losses. He refused. A week later, what was left of 7th Corps was sent to Bryansk to re-form, after fighting with the 5th on the Western Dvina.

Tanks not unnaturally dominated the minds of Soviet commanders. Yeremenko on 7 July wrote to Stalin, urging him to consider giving rifle divisions 1–2 tank companies, or at least a tank battalion to the rifle corps. Timoshenko had immediately on 6 July issued a special directive on anti-tank defence; he followed this up on 9 July with another, to the effect that 'properly organized defence' had defeated and would defeat German 'Panzer and motorized troops'. Out of sheer necessity and the impact of enormous losses, the *Stavka* and the GKO had already started work to reorganize the Red Army; the first directive emerged on 15 July. Armoured forces, force structure, tactics, the badly needed 'rear organization', these and a mass of related items came under closer scrutiny. All, however, searched for cures for the Red Army's *tankoboyazn*, 'tank fright'.

Timoshenko's directives could not stem the dangers on his right flank. The 22nd Army, where Yeremenko was sent after his meeting with the Front commander, was unable to hold its sector of the Western Dvina; on 7 July, 20th Panzer Division was installed on the northern bank of the Dvina at Ulla, yet of this German offensive 22nd Army staff heard nothing from its own formations, although communications were intact. Only at midnight did 62nd Rifle Corps signal that its 166th Regiment had been attacked by '200 planes', and the regiment had fled. This massed German bombing night attack against a regiment proved to be a 'panic-monger's' agitated fancy. But north, at Sebezh, the 'fortified district' had fallen and 22nd and 27th Armies (North-Western Front) were now separated. The very grim reality unfolded with disconcerting speed. As 7th and 12th Panzer Divisions struck from the south-west at the junction of 22nd and 20th Armies, Yeremenko moved up Koniev's 19th Army to Vitebsk. Koniev moved on 8 July: aware of Soviet intentions, 20th Panzer Division on the northern bank of the Dvina raced straight into Koniev's units as yet forming up. In fierce street-fighting, General Koniev did not give up easily, committing his half-formed regiments, devoid of artillery support, to holding Vitebsk. By the evening of 9 July the situation in Vitebsk was grave; the entire rear of the Western Front was threatened. With no reserves – 5th and 7th Mechanized had been smashed up already – the prospect of 'catastrophe' struck Yeremenko, who was at that moment reporting to the Marshals Timoshenko and Shaposhnikov on the crisis in 22nd Army. Yeremenko was sent hot-foot to Koniev's embattled 19th Army. That same day (10 July), as Panzer Group 3 stove in the Dvina line, Guderian with Panzer Group 2 took the offensive on the Dnieper. Koniev's furious counter-attack at Vitebsk with one division (220th Motorized) was part of a desperate Soviet effort to restore the situation at the centre and on the left flank.

Timoshenko, with his right wing caving in, continued to mass and deploy divisions, thirty-one rifle, six tank and four motorized so far, 'more than half' the forces ultimately destined for the Western Front. On the Dnieper, strong defences went up at Orsha, Shklov, Moghilev and Rogachev. Here 13th Army (whose commander General Filatov was killed by air attack on 8 July and replaced by Lieutenant-General F.N. Remizov) and 21st Army stood fast on Timoshenko's orders. At the same time, Shaposhnikov, who had seen for himself the dimensions of potential disaster, recommended to Stalin the formation of a new 'Reserve Armies Front', under Lieutenant-General I.A. Bogdanov, with six *Stavka* Reserve armies: 29th, 30th, 24th, 28th, 31st and 32nd. Stalin was also selecting a defence line for Moscow. But on 10–11 July Guderian was astride the Dnieper and the battle for Smolensk was joined, from north and south. Stalin ordered massive and immediate counter-attack.

Alone of the first Soviet Fronts engaged, the South-Western under Kirponos faced only one Panzer Group (as opposed to two in Army Group Centre), but Army Group South had to grind its way through solid Soviet defences manned by troops skilfully led and determined to fight. Von Rundstedt's left wing, with von Stülpnagel's Seventeenth Army and von Reichenau's Sixth Army, had to crack the Soviet frontier defences, then drive to the south-east: thereafter, with von Kleist's armour in the van, they were to swing southwards and trap Kirponos's armies. The stubby right hook to this left one, von Schobert's Eleventh Army on the Soviet Rumanian frontier, had yet to open its offensive. For more than a week, Army Group South had to batter its way in from the north.

By the morning of 23 June, German penetration at the junction of the Soviet 5th and 6th Armies was an accomplished and menacing fact. To stave off further threats, and in fulfilment of Timoshenko's *Directive No. 3*, Kirponos determined to use all the armour attached to 5th, 6th and 26th Armies in one heavy counter-blow. The first task was to concentrate this formidable force, while the formations in the frontier areas were committed without delay – Vlasov's 4th Mechanized (Lwow), Rokossovskii's 9th Mechanized and Major-General N.V. Feklenko's 19th Mechanized Corps north-east of Rovno. West of Brody, at Toporuv, in 6th Army's area, was Major-General I.I. Karpezo's 15th Mechanized Corps, while Major-General D.I. Ryabyshev's 8th Mechanized, ordered to Brody, moved its units up, scattered as they were over some 200 miles. The formation commanders had to make do with what they had: Rokossovskii's 9th had only one combat-ready tank division (the 35th – the remainder had training machines), just as the 19th disposed of only one division (43rd Tank) in fighting shape. Karpezo's 15th disposed of 133 brand-new T-34s and KVs in addition to its light tanks, but lacked lorries to move its motorized rifle division (the 212th) and tractors for its artillery; Ryabyshev's 8th was even more powerful, with 170 T-34s and KVs out of its 600 tanks. These excellent new machines, however, were not concentrated to make particular formations compact and effective 'tank fists', but spattered over a multitude of units. Major-General S.M. Kondrusev's 22nd Mechanized Corps (5th Army) also had a complement of new tanks in its 41st Tank Division. These formations were now about to be hurled into the third of the great tank battles which had loomed up in the first week of the war: Kirponos assembled six mechanized corps – 4th, 8th, 22nd, 9th, 19th and 15th (the latter three from the Front reserve) – to assault the flanks of Panzer Group 1 from north and south and to destroy von Kleist west of Lutsk-Dubno. To stiffen the covering forces, Kirponos speeded up the Front infantry reserves – 31st, 36th and 37th Rifle Corps – to the battle-line and ordered them to take up defensive positions from Stobykhva to the rivers Stokhod and Styr, thence to Kremenls-Pochayev.

The German Sixth Army and von Kleist's armour jabbed at the Soviet defences on Kirponos's right; on 23 June, they took Berestechko, thereby slicing the 5th from the 6th Soviet Armies, and drove for Dubno. The next day the breach between the two Soviet armies had widened to some thirty miles. Further south, von Stülpnagel's infantry found the weak spot between the Rava-Russki and Przemysl 'fortified districts' and smashed into the junction between the Soviet 6th and 26th Armies, so that a twenty-mile breach was opened between them by 24 June, when Nemirov, north-west of Lwow, fell. To seal up the first breach, Kirponos ordered 15th and 8th Mechanized Corps to attack 48th Panzer Corps' right flank. Ryabyshev's 8th was still on the move and did not finally concentrate until 26 June; Karpezo's 15th, positioned on a seventy-kilometre front, floundered in bogs and on poor roads, so that only forward elements of his 10th Tank Division were committed near Radekhov on 23 June. The 37th Tank Division had been ordered to Adama, to deal with what turned out to be non-existent enemy armour. But the next day, 48th Panzer Corps turned on its attackers. Lieutenant-General Muzychenko, 6th Army commander meanwhile ordered Vlasov's 4th Mechanized to counter-attack at Nemirov on 24 June, a blow pre-empted by a new German thrust, which by the end of the week rolled upon Lwow itself.

The Military Soviet of the South-Western Front – commander Kirponos, chief of staff Purkayev and commissar Khrushchev – decided on 24 June to mount a massive armoured counter-attack. Two mechanized corps, 4th and 22nd, were left to operate in the areas of their own infantry formations (6th and 5th Army respectively); the remaining four, 8th, 15th, 9th and 19th, would operate at the crisis points, Lutsk-Rovno-Dubno-Brody, to eliminate the German penetrations with a concentric blow. The attack order of 25 June assigned the 'main blow' to the 8th and 15th Mechanized Corps; Potapov's 5th Army would take command of 9th and 19th Mechanized Corps, and Potapov himself would co-ordinate his operations with the 8th and 15th. Potapov would attack along the Lutsk–Brody railway line: concentrated in the woods north of Rovno, 9th Mechanized was to attack south from Klevany, and the 19th would strike from its wooded cover from Rovno to Dubno. The Front command itself took control of the southern corps (8th and 15th), organizing them into a 'Front mobile group': the 8th was to advance on Berestechko from Brody, the 15th from Toropuv to Radekhov. All corps would attack at 09.00 hours, 26 June.

Karpezo's 15th Mechanized had already taken much punishment on and since 23 June; it was now committed in difficult terrain (with five river lines) and forced to fight across bog and swamp. On the morning of 26 June, Karpezo had only one division ready for operations. To the right of this division, 8th Mechanized, having speeded its tanks all the way from Uman, some 150–200 miles away, formed up near Brody; 12th Tank Division (8th Mechanized), had only 60 tanks transhipped and the 34th Tank Division, 150. To strengthen the 15th, Vlasov lost a tank division (the 8th) from 4th Mechanized Corps; he lost another for ever when its commander took it into a swamp. The Soviet tanks and motorized infantry scrambled into battle, a giant four-day collision in which several hundred Soviet and German tanks fought out this fiercest of the first armoured engagements. Karpezo crashed ahead to Radekhov, striking at 48th Panzer Corps' southern flank; Colonel-General Halder groaned in his war diary about these Soviet blows which slowed and hurt Panzer Group 1. During the night of 26–7 June, Kiponos ordered Ryabyshev's 8th to fight its way to Verba and Dubno, with the 15th attacking towards Berestechko. Karpezo himself had meanwhile been battered like his tank units by the Luftwaffe; his deputy Colonel Yermolayev took command when Karpezo was knocked out of action. Ryabyshev, with his units still scattered, decided to form a 'mobile group' from the 34th Tank Division, a tank regiment and a motor-cycle regiment, under the command of Brigade Commissar N.K. Popiel. This striking force, suddenly launched, burst into the rear of the 11th and 16th Panzer Divisions, and drove for Dubno.

General Potapov, in spite of orders to unify the command of 5th Army, 9th and 19th Mechanized Corps, evidently failed to do so; nor did he co-ordinate with Karpezo and Rybayshev (though these formations were much scattered). The 9th Mechanized Corps, striking south of Klevany, hit the 13th and 14th Panzer Divisions (3rd Panzer Corps), while the 19th Mechanized Corps struck the left flank of 11th Panzer Division. On 27 June, from north and south Soviet tank units pressed forward to Dubno; 19th Mechanized and elements of 36th Rifle Corps drove for Dubno from the north-east, while Ryabyshev's 'mobile group' came from the south-west. The Soviet units did not, however, make contact. Feklenko's 19th Mechanized was forced back; Luftwaffe reconnaissance nailed the 8th's 'mobile group', and 16th Panzer Division held this force and the 12th Tank and 7th Motorized Rifle Divisions (also of 8th Mechanized) from joining up at Dubno. Ryabyshev's 8th was now split into two groups; by the evening of 29 June hopes of joining up at Dubno dimmed to virtual extinction. Kirponos ordered 19th Mechanized and 36th Rifle Corps to make one more attempt to link up with Ryabyshev's embattled tanks at Dubno. In spite of furious

Soviet attacks, 16th Panzer Division, finally reinforced with infantry, held the Soviet prongs apart. Popiel's 'mobile group' (34th Tank Division) was encircled, its exit to the south-west and to the body of 8th Mechanized blocked off. On 2 July, Popiel decided to break out eastwards (and finally made it to the Soviet lines in August).

Earlier in the week (26 June), Kirponos had ordered 6th and 26th Armies to disengage from the Przemysl and Rava-Russkii 'fortified districts' and fall back on Lwow, the defence of which was entrusted to Major-General Vlasov and his 4th Mechanized Corps. Lwow, capital of Galicia, fell on 29–30 June in a night-mare of chaos and carnage; to the fierceness of the fighting was added the horror of the 'Lwow massacre', in which the NKVD massacred its Ukrainian political prisoners or herded them eastwards in prisoner columns, shooting them down as they lagged or faltered. In their own confusions, Soviet troops and refugees broke for the east; Vlasov had to cut his way with the shattered 4th out of repeated encirclement. The Ukrainian nationalist 'diversionist' groups continued to create considerable havoc in the Soviet rear, although the NKVD struck back savagely; now, regiment *Nachtigall* and OUN-B enjoyed the triumph of entry into Lwow, even if it was behind German guns.

Northwards, Kirponos tried once again to hold von Kleist. Potapov, with 5th Army (27th Rifle, 22nd and 9th Mechanized Corps) was ordered on 29 June to attack southwards from the woods of Klevany and strike Panzer Group 1 once more in the flank. That same day Kirponos also issued a special directive on eliminating operational shortcomings – security of flanks, proper organization of intelligence, use of radio, infantry-artillery co-ordination. But orders, how-ever emphatic, could not compensate for acute shortage of equipment or lack of spares: 15th Mechanized had only two radio units (instead of eight), 22nd Mechanized lost 119 tanks in eight days (22 June–1 July) of which 58 were blown up by their crews for lack of spares or often minor repair facilities. Vlasov's tanks had to be abandoned too often for similar reasons. 11th Panzer Division had meanwhile forced its way to Ostrog and threatened Shepetovka, a major Soviet supply base and transportation point. Lukin, 16th Army commander, was waiting here for his troops, already under orders to proceed to the Western Front; unable to use the civilian telephone network, which had broken down, Lukin finally got in touch with Kirponos's deputy, Lieutenant-General Yakovlev, by using the railway telephones. Yakovlev told him to hold Shepetovka, or 'the Front will have no ammunition'. Lukin set to work. The supply dump chiefs, refusing to issue ammunition without a requisition order, were forced to disgorge: 250 lorries, standing idle 'at the disposition 'of the district military commissariat, shifted ammunition, while civilians were loaded on to trains. 'Group Lukin' – elements of 213rd, 109th Rifle Divisions, 19th Mechanized Corps – came into existence, controlled by railway telephone. Officer losses were heavy – all company commanders, two-thirds of the battalion commanders and five regimental commanders: sergeants took over companies and stiffened battalions. Lukin fought with 'motorized detachments' until he handed over to Major-General Dobroserdov's 7th Rifle Corps rushed up from Dnepropetrovsk.

Kirponos reckoned that mauling Panzer Group 1 on his right had prevented a breakthrough behind and into his centre and left; his forces were pulled out of the Lwow salient. On 30 June, with the authorization of the *Stavka*, the South-Western Front and the right wing of the Southern Front pulled back to the line Simonovich-Belokorovich-Novograd/Volynsk-Shepetovka-Proskurov-Kamenets Podolsk. This line, almost on the old Soviet-Polish frontier, lopped more than 200 miles off Kirponos's frontage; he was falling back on the old fortifications (part of the 'Stalin line') and issued a general order to take up defensive positions along a line Korosten-Novograd/Volynsk-Shepetovka-Starokonstantinov-Proskurov by 9 July. Kirponos had done that 'good job' upon which Colonel-General Halder commented so ruefully. The blitzkrieg had to grind forward but the Soviet lines did not crumble. German and Soviet formations alike bled with heavy losses. Panzer Group 1 had crunched into a furious tank battle. And behind new lines Kirponos formed up again, covered his rear, moved up reinforcements.

In the south, Tyulenev's 'quiet sector' suddenly roared into life on 1 July, as German-Rumanian forces took the offensive on the Prut. Tyulenev, with Zaporozhets as his commissar and Major-General G.D. Shishenin as chief of staff, had twenty-four divisions at his disposal (without the 9th Special Rifle Corps stationed in the Crimea): Major-General M.V. Zakharov commanded 9th Army on the left flank and Lieutenant-General A.K. Smirnov the 18th on the right, linking with the left flank (12th Army) of South-Western Front. To support them, Tyulenev had three mechanized corps (2nd, 16th and 18th) forming up. Zakharov's 9th covered the Beltsa, Kishinev and Odessa approaches, Smirnov's 18th was deployed northwards.

Von Schobert's blow with the Eleventh Army had been slowed by the delays imposed on the Sixth and Seventeenth Armies, on the northern wing. When it came, it fell at the junction of the Soviet 9th and 18th Armies – and caught Tyulenev not fully on guard. The German assault north of Jassy crashed into Major-General R.Ya. Malinovskii's 48th Rifle Corps covering Beltsa. North and south of Jassy the Germans won bridgeheads on the eastern bank of the Prut; Tyulenev on 3 July ordered 18th Army to pull its right flank on to Khotin-Lipkany (behind Cernauti). Zakharov was ordered to liquidate the bridgehead at Stefanesti, and counter-attack at Beltsa; 48th Rifle Corps (Malinovskii), 2nd Mechanized Corps (Major-General Yu.V. Novoselskii) and Major-General P.A. Belov's 2nd Cavalry Corps were all finally embroiled in these operations north-east of Kishinev. Smirnov meanwhile reported to Tyulenev that pulling back his right wing was impossible without bridging equipment: he had the Seret, Prut and Dniester to cross. Tyulenev ordered the 19th Bridging Regiment to Khotin to build a pontoon bridge over the Dniester and 60th Mountain Division to defend it. Lorries, guns, carts and men began to pile up beside this slender lifeline to the east. The Luftwaffe bombed it repeatedly and on 4 July, under German artillery and mortar fire, the bridge was blown to pieces; on the southern bank Soviet troops and their equipment lay stranded. A reserve bridge was hastily positioned by 21st Bridging Battalion under heavy German fire, an arduous job which nevertheless saved more of 18th Army.

By the end of the first week in July, Tyulenev was battling with the German bridgehead over the Dniester at Moghilev-Podolsk (18th Army area), organizing 48th Rifle, 2nd Mechanized and 2nd Cavalry Corps (9th Army) into a 'shock group' to counter-attack north-east of Kishinev and forming a new subordinate command, Coastal Group (*Primorskaya gruppa*) out of the 25th Chapayev, 51st and 150th Rifle Divisions to cover the eastern bank of the Prut, the northern bank of the Danube and the Black Sea coast. As his commitments increased, Tyulenev's forces diminished. He had already lost the 7th Rifle Corps, rushed to Shepetovka. The *Stavka* now decided to transfer the 16th Mechanized Corps plus the 116th, 196th and 227th Rifle Divisions to Kirponos (who had already lost Lukin's 16th and Koniev's 19th Army to the Western Front). The transfer merely weakened both the Southern and South-Western Fronts: Tyulenev thereby lost his reserves, and Kirponos gained nothing in actual strength deployed.

While Tyulenev committed his 'shock group' at the junction of the Eleventh German and the Fourth Rumanian Armies, Kirponos tried to shore up a situation along the Zhitomir-Kiev axis which deteriorated day by day. The northern wing of Army Group South stabbed the Soviet lines repeatedly to find weak spots. At Starokonstantinov 16th Panzer Division fought it out with the Soviet 6th Army, finally calling on the Luftwaffe to air-drop ammunition and to blast Soviet tank concentrations.

11th Panzer Division took Berdichev on 7 July. Potapov's 5th Army was smashed apart from the 6th, and the breach between them provided the narrow front against which von Kleist exerted continued pressure. The *Stavka* had already instructed Kirponos to pull the 5th Army back to the Korosten 'fortified district', north-west of Kiev; 13th Panzer Division had broken into the Novograd-Volynsk 'fortified district' and drove on for Zhitomir which fell on 10 July. One day later, with 25th and 14th Panzer Divisions in its wake, 13th Panzer forward elements reached the river Irpen, less than ten miles from Kiev. Muzychenko's 6th Army held on grimly at Berdichev-Ostropol, and further south the 26th and 12th Armies held a line from Ostropol to Bar. Kirponos had, at all costs, to close the forty-mile gap between the 5th and 6th Armies; his right wing had been pierced to a depth of 60–75 miles, and the battle brought to the gates of Kiev. Potapov with the 5th was cut off in the north-west from the Front.

Before von Kleist's tanks had got to the Zhitomir highway, Kirponos had tried to put in an armoured counter-attack; he had ordered 15th Mechanized

Corps from the north (Korosten) to cut off and to destroy Panzer Group 1's spear-heads. Kondrusev's 22nd Mechanized Corps, however, was a spent force, with less than twenty tanks and fourteen guns. The *Stavka* nevertheless persisted with orders for a powerful counter-blow, which Kirponos was even now putting in. The right wing of the South-Western Front also came in for the close and personal attentions of the very top echelon of the Soviet command. General Zhukov lent his aid at Kirponos's HQ; Marshal Budenny, the Civil War stalwart who had fought with his 1st Cavalry Army across the Ukraine in 1919, had arrived from Smolensk to assume over-all command of the South-Western and Southern Fronts. From these various talents came the flank blows at the Sixth German Army and Panzer Group 1 which brought the German command anxious moments and German divisions heavy losses.

Potapov's 5th Army (15th, 31st Rifle, 9th, 19th and 22nd Mechanized Corps) would strike northwards from Berdichev and Lyubar. Muzychenko's force was stiffened with 'Operational Group Berdichev', commanded by Major-General A.D. Sokolov of 16th Mechanized Corps (still mostly on the move from the south); 15th Mechanized Corps was no longer a corps in any effective sense, so that three 'composite detachments' were organized from its remnants and put under the command of Major-General S.D. Ogurtsov, who was subordinated to Sokolov. To the north-west, Potapov was little better off; 9th Mechanized had sixty-four tanks left, 22nd Mechanized less than half of that, and the rifle regiments of 31st Corps, 193rd and 195th Rifle Divisions had no more than three hundred men. As he observed himself a little later: 'Potapov has three mechanized corps, they say, so he can fight!' Even so, he was stronger than Muzychenko. Both armies, 5th and 6th, ripped into the German flanks. Potapov cut the Zhitomir highway to the east. Muzychenko's battle groups, first 8th Tank Division of Vlasov's 4th Mechanized Corps and then 'Group Berdichev' fought ferocious actions with 11th Panzer Division in the area of Berdichev. Soviet artillery broke up German counter-strokes: Army Group South pushed in reinforcements and called up the Stukas. The day after the Soviet counter-attacks began, however, on 10 July, German armour had begun to swing south-east of Kiev, developing a drive to cut the Soviet 6th, 26th and 12th Armies from the Dnieper at their backs, and then to destroy them. Although at Berdichev the German advance was stalled, 9th Panzer Division swinging south-east of Zhitomir forced its way into Skvir. The Berdichev and Fastov-Skvir fighting raged for five full days, but German tanks were at 6th Army's rear finally. North-West, Potapov's infantry and tanks kept up their pressure on the Zhitomir highway for all of seven days.

On Friday, 11 July, with 13th Panzer at the Irpen, Kirponos assembled a meeting of his top commanders and political members: Purkayev (chief of staff), Parsegov (artillery commander), Ilin-Mitkevich (engineers), Astakhov (aviation), Khrushchev the 'political member' of the Front Military Soviet, and two arrivals from Kiev – M.A. Burmistenko, Secretary of the Ukrainian Party

Central Committee, and M.P. Mishin, secretary of the Party *obkom*. All assembled at Brovar, Kirponos's HQ some ten miles north-east of Kiev, a few small buildings and a house for the Front commander. Kirponos authorized Lieutenant-General M.A. Purkayev to present the latest situation report on the 'Zhitomir corridor', which separated the 5th and 6th Soviet Armies, and provided von Kleist with passage to Kiev. Enemy intentions were: to take Kiev, and the bridges over the Dnieper, thereafter breaking into the rear of the South-Western and the Southern Fronts. With this accomplished, 'broad perspectives' opened up before the German command. Soviet requirements were: to hold Kiev and to prevent a German breakthrough to the Dnieper south of the city. Purkayev suggested sending all troops recovered from encirclement – after equipping them – to the Kiev 'fortified district', the edge of which 13th Panzer had already reached; Soviet bombers should be used to break up the German columns moving on Kiev. At this, Purkayev took his seat. Kirponos asked Astakhov about the air operations: the aviation commander insisted that 13th Panzer had already been attacked from the air and forced into the woods. Kirponos now demanded intensified aerial reconnaissance, the complete interdiction of the Zhitomir highway, and heavier attacks on German aerodromes. Astakhov pleaded lack of planes, but Kirponos demanded results and Astakhov's personal report on them. The approaches to Kiev had already been stiffened with paratroops, NKVD motorized troops, the 1st Kiev Artillery School, a tank regiment and two anti-tank battalions. Parsegov pointed out that artillery and ammunition were in critically short supply; even before 22 June, the district (now the Front) was short of 3,000 guns and mortars as against its establishment. Armies now got one, and only one replenishment of shells; there were too few lorries to shift ammunition and the railway system was 'paralysed' in the operational zones. Kirponos asked his artillery commander what he was doing about this; Parsegov pointed out that he had urged the Main Artillery Administration (GAU) to speed up weapons and ammunition from 'the centre'. Khrushchev added that he was trying to get as much locally-produced ammunition (especially anti-tank grenades) as possible, and that he was pressing Moscow. Battlefield salvage was being organized. Ilin-Mitkevich reported on the activation of the Kiev UR (which the dead Yakir had first supervised in 1935), but he was woefully short of barbed wire and anti-tank mines.

Kirponos, listening to all this, stood at the wall map and announced his decisions. The counter-blows by 5th and 6th Army must continue (although their eventual lack of success was plainly foreshadowed): the 'Zhitomir corridor' had to be closed. While Potapov attacked Zhitomir and Radomysl, 6th and 26th Armies were to hold their lines (26th Army staff would move to Pereslavl-Khmelnitskii, and bring all forces moving to the Dnieper under its command). For the Kiev UR Kirponos assigned two brigades of the 2nd Parachute Corps, plus units of 147th and 206th Rifle Divisions (although, having just broken out of German encirclement, these units were thin on the ground). With the greatest forcefulness Kirponos impressed on his commanders that the Front had nothing left with which to stem the German drive on Kiev. He was waiting for two rifle divisions to form a new 27th Rifle Corps (from *Stavka* reserve) and the two-division 64th Rifle Corps from the North Caucasus, though what he had heard so far about the 64th Corps disturbed him: short of weapons, horse-drawn guns, disorganized staffs, no wireless sets. Reports of the 27th were just as discouraging; only one division had a commander, for a start. One final point was to plug the gap between the Kiev UR and 6th Army units at Fastov – a thirty-five-mile hole; Kirponos proposed to put in a 'composite detachment' (94th Frontier Troops Detachment, 6th and 16th Motorized Rifle Regiments), a minute force glaringly unequal to the job but all Kirponos had left to do it. After a brief discussion, the Military Soviet of the South-Western Front confirmed all decisions and dispersed, or tried to as the HQ came under a heavy bombing attack.

Kirponos had so far fought his way out of von Rundstedt's traps. The jolting Russian counter-blows continued: Purkayev informed Kirponos that only the 27th Corps would be ready for action, and that not until 15 July. Already it was agonizingly plain (12–13 July) that the 'Zhitomir corridor' could not be closed; for that, Kirponos needed a whole new army, and at this juncture he had not even a single division in reserve. Potapov's 5th was ordered to continue attacking and Kirponos hoped to strengthen Muzychenko's (6th Army) right wing in the Berdichev fighting. Colonel Bondarev (Chief of Intelligence, South-Western Front), however, brought Purkayev very grave news, his confirmation of Panzer Group 1's outflanking swing to the south-east, driving on Popelnaya-Belaya Tserkov; German armour had also outflanked 6th Army's right wing east of Kazatin. Kirponos had neither force nor plans to deal with this emergency and the most he could do was to fling in flimsy units to counter-attack. For the first time, Army Group South, deprived so far of any overpowering success, glimpsed the shape of a feasible encirclement.

'*Die Lage der Roten Armee beginnt kritisch zu werden*': this critical Soviet military plight, recorded by the German command in its *Feindnachrichtenblatt No. 14*, was appallingly plain to Stalin and the *Stavka*. Thursday, 10 July, when Stalin announced a new command configuration, of all these fiery days stamped itself into the war as one of far-reaching decision and circumstance: the battle for the 'approaches to Leningrad' had begun as Army Group North swept on the 'Luga line', the battle for Smolensk (the 'Moscow axis') had opened and Guderian was forcing the Dnieper, while Army Group South had stabbed through Kirponos's right wing, pushed to the edge of Kiev, and spun south-east to snare three Soviet armies. Under these immense pressures the simple structure of the first *Stavka* organization had cracked and fallen apart; the marshals were in any event in the field, as was Zhukov, Chief of the General Staff. The enormity of the battle-fronts and the speed of events were far beyond the capacity of the 'collective organ' which had been so hastily set up a fortnight ago. Stalin now interposed an extra 'high command' echelon between the *Stavka* and the Fronts; three 'high commands' (*Glavkom*) were set up for the three major 'axes' (*napravleniya*) – the North-Western (Northern, North-Western Fronts, Northern and Baltic Fleets), the Western (Western Front and Pinsk Flotilla) and the South-Western (South-Western, Southern Fronts and Black Sea Fleet). Voroshilov took the north-west, with Zhdanov as the 'political member' of his Military Soviet; Timoshenko took the centre (Western) with Bulganin as his 'political member', and Budenny the south-west with Khrushchev as 'political member'. As political boss in Leningrad, Zhdanov was already installed and a power to be reckoned with. Bulganin, an old *Chekist*, industrial manager and political operator, began his wartime rise to real power by volunteering at a session of the Central Committee for 'service at the front'; this offer Malenkov seized upon avidly, and Stalin took silent note of this estimable – and shrewd – display of apparent self-sacrifice. Krushchev was much more lowly, outranked and snubbed by the initiates to the magic ring of the GKO. The clashing political rivalries of peacetime became the snarling collisions and personal vendettas of war.

The '*Stavka* of the High Command' was now swept away and became instead that of the 'Supreme Commander', *Stavka Verhovnovo Komandovaniya*, under the presidency of Stalin. The post of 'Supreme Commander' stood as yet formally unoccupied, although as 'president' of the new *Stavka* Stalin was to all intents and purposes the '*Supremo*'. Three weeks later he did become, finally and formally, 'Supreme Commander of the Soviet Armed Forces'. Even now, Stalin was chairman of the GKO and 'president' of the *Stavka*; the renaming of the *Stavka* was done on the 'authority' of the GKO. The 'boss' had now recovered from his earlier frights, enough to demand the impossible, to punish an army largely in its present straits due to 'over-fulfilment' of his own pre-war instructions, and to press for that 'decisive' counter-blow. Stalin's first *Stavka* was manned by five officers: Voroshilov, Timoshenko, Shaposhnikov, Budenny and Zhukov. Almost at once, he introduced the interchangeability of GKO and *Stavka* personnel, as well as 'co-opting' new men to the *Stavka*. As Zhukov was sent to shore up critical sectors – from the Ukraine to Leningrad – his incumbency of the General Staff passed eventually to Shaposhnikov; Vatutin as deputy chief of the General Staff finally went to Leningrad, and his place was taken by Vasilevskii, Shaposhnikov's 'favourite pupil'. Major-General Chetverikov took over the Operations Section (General Staff), Golikov the Intelligence Administration and Lieutenant-General Trubetskoi remained as chief of the Transportation Section. Stalin ultimately accepted advice about reorganizing the Soviet air force and went about setting up a separate Air Force Command (*Komanduyushchi VVS Krasnoi Armii*), entrusted to Lieutenant-General (Aviation) P.F. Zhigarev, with his own Military Soviet; the problem was now to get some aircraft to replace the astronomical losses. Some of this helped to sort out the milling mess in the *Stavka*, clogged with administrative and operational burdens as it was, flooded with 'fantastic reports' of German losses, and hampered by irregular contact with the Fronts. Stalin, after several incomplete briefings, had turned on Shaposhnikov and demanded the punishment of those who failed to report promptly. Shaposhnikov, who had been 'covering up' in the tradition of the 'old' army, replied that he had in fact issued orders for timely submission of Front reports. One more step in sorting out the operational-administrative muddle involved Stalin in re-establishing the post of Chief of Artillery, which Kulik had not so long ago abolished; the job went – or reverted – to Colonel-General Voronov, who went to work to reorganize Red Army artillery.

The GKO now undertook the salvaging of the wreck of the Red Army. Divisional strength (averaging 10,000–12,000 before June 1941) had fallen to below 6,000: enormous stocks of fuel, ammunition and stores had been captured or destroyed: weapon shortages (AA guns, anti-tank guns, automatic weapons) created by unsound pre-war procurement had been compounded by wartime losses: ammunition (ordinary and specialized, such as armour-piercing shell) was in critically short supply: tanks and aircraft had been lost or abandoned by the literal thousand. Stalin used the shrunken state of the formations to rationalize the command procedure: he proposed 'small armies', abolishing corps altogether. The shortage of able officers meant concentrating competence at the top, at army level, a drastic simplification which made a virtue of necessity. The circular instruction, *No. 01* 15 July, from the *Stavka* gave the three new *Glavkom*, all Front and army commanders this notification:

War experience has shown that the existence of large and unwieldy armies with a large number of divisions and with intermediate corps administrations powerfully inhibits the organization of combat operations and the administration of troops in combat, especially in view of the youth and the inexperience of our staffs and command staff. The *Stavka* considers that the transition should be made, gradually and without prejudicing present operations, to a system of small armies with five and a maximum of six divisions, without corps administrations and with the direct subordination of the divisions to the army commander.

The *Stavka* urges Front commanders to take into account these considerations of the experience of the three-week war with German Fascism and to put them into practice under the direction of the *Glavkom*.

The mechanized corps would be disbanded; their tank divisions were to be independent unities but subordinated to infantry new commanders. Motorized rifle formations would revert to being ordinary rifle divisions; at the same time, a huge expansion of Red Army cavalry forces was authorized and set in motion, up to thirty corps. Voroshilov, pointing to the pre-war decision to 'motor-mechanize' cavalry divisions, gleefully exclaimed: 'Now we'll put that mistake right.' He had yet to learn, and in the learning sacrifice many good men, what kind of war the Red Army had to fight. Zhigarev's aviation also assumed a shrunken shape; strategic (long-range bombers: ADD) unities were abolished, tactical (front-support) aviation turned over to a two-regiment division, with thirty – formerly sixty – planes to a regiment.

The Red Army command had so far fielded or deployed in immediate reserve (including *Stavka* reserve armies) nearly two dozen armies, just double what German intelligence had reckoned on for Soviet forces in European Russia: by its own calculation, the *Ostheer* had so far encountered 12 Soviet armies, 25 corps (staffs), 164 rifle divisions, 11 mechanized corps and 29 armoured divisions (more than twice the amount of armour estimated in the pre-June tallies). Stalin himself reckoned on mobilizing a total of 350 divisions (as against his figure of 300 for maximum German strength); in late July, 240 Soviet divisions were at the front by Stalin's reckoning, with 20 in reserve – so far, two-thirds had been committed (making a total of 180) and mauled in varying degrees. This was the point when the German command (27 July) insisted that 'the mass of the operationally effective (*operationsfähig*) Russian Army has been destroyed'; the Soviet command was assumed to have at its disposal now only 20 divisions, 13 armoured divisions and 2–3 cavalry divisions. Of the 25 divisions being raised, some of these were of only one regiment strength; armoured units were operating at what amounted to battalion strength. All the Russians could hope to do now was 'wear down' (*Zermübung*) the German forces and this as far west as they could manage; yet 'the Russians' will to fight had not been broken', and Colonel-General Halder noted 'fanatic and dogged' (*fanatisch und verbissen*) Soviet resistance at Smolensk. The overweening optimism of very early July, the campaign 'won in a fortnight', had flattened somewhat: a staff study on the 'reorganization of the Army after the conclusion of Barbarossa' (*Umbau des Heeres nach Abschluss Barbarossa*) nevertheless went ahead, envisaging a subdued 'military heartland' from which probes would be made to the Urals. Brauchitsch's summary of 27 July assessed real Soviet strength in terms of total numbers and divisions fit for battle: before Army Group South 73 (30) rifle, 16 (6) armoured and 5 (2) cavalry divisions, before Army Group Centre 46 (32) rifle, 4 (3) armoured divisions (10 new divisions in the Moscow area), and facing Army Group North 30 (2) rifle, $4\frac{1}{2}$ ($3\frac{1}{2}$) armoured divisions. In Leningrad $5\frac{1}{2}$ rifle divisions were committed against the Finns and $11\frac{1}{2}$ rifle, $2\frac{1}{2}$ armoured divisions against the Germans.

The situation was demonstrably deteriorating as the *Stavka*'s reserves (from interior districts and the south-eastern frontier zones) dwindled and began to dry up. The North-Western and Northern Fronts were consuming their own fat too quickly; when disaster threatened at Smolensk, Timoshenko reported to the *Stavka*: 'We do not have any trained forces in adequate strength covering the Yartsevo–Vyazma–Moscow axis. The main deficiency – no tanks' (16 July). Budenny was no better off. Stalin hurried, through the GKO, the creation of a 'reserve armies administration' (*Glavnoe upravlenie formirovaniya i ukomplektovaniya voisk Krasnoi Armii: Glavuproform* KA) linked with a revival of the Civil

War 'universal military training' (*Vsevobuch*) programme. All this, however, took time and at the moment the losses piled up inhumanly and disastrously. Stalin continued to hold his hand over moving his Far Eastern forces in any strength; Sorge had not yet provided conclusive evidence of Japanese intentions, although he had reported the likelihood of the 'southern advance' (against the Americans and the British).

The GKO sessions touched on tactics, weapons, organization, Soviet strengths and weaknesses: a great inquest was held on the failure of Soviet anti-tank fighting. New instructions went out to the commanders. The debate on weapons was prolonged and was to continue; at least one decision was taken, to try out the secret *Katyusha* rocket-launcher – which passed its test near Smolensk with spectacular results – and another to mass produce it. It was in July that the GKO made a start on the massive labour of centralizing the Red Army's rear services: supplies (food, ammunition, weapons), transport and medical services were finally concentrated in the hands of a Chief of Red Army Rear Services, a post which Lieutenant-General Khrulev took up in August (and with it, a permanent place on the *Stavka*). These were much-needed rationalizations. But what Stalin demanded was not merely rationalization but coercion, the restoration of discipline through drastic punitive moves. This task devolved in large part upon Lev Mekhlis, Army Commissar 1st Grade, who seized every occasion to goad and to humiliate the officer corps. He now had opportunity enough to suit his malevolence. The 'political propaganda administration' was reorganizing into the Main Political Administration/Red Army (*Glavnoe politicheskoe upravlenie* RKKA: *Glav*PURKKA) under Mekhlis. Zaporozhets, the former chief, was on the Southern Front with Tyulenev. The political sections, which Stalin had mistakenly abolished in 1940, were forthwith restored. 'Unitary command', which Timoshenko had won for the officer corps in 1940, was now abolished; 'dual command', with the military commissar put into a position of direct control and supervision, was re-imposed (16 July). Mekhlis laid down his own requirements for political departments and military commissars in the field in *Directive No. 81* (15 July): the commissars became guardians of discipline, the bulwark against panic, cowardice and treachery. Commissar control, which inevitably complicated command procedures, was always and was now a sign that Stalin had lost confidence in his officer corps. To the humiliations of defeat the Soviet officer had to add the indignities of surveillance by Mekhlis's watchdogs. And, as Stalin loosed his killers on the Red Army, the same officer had to fear for his life.

On 27 July, in the name of the GKO, an order condemning nine senior Soviet officers to sentence by military tribunal was read out to all officers and men: Colonel-General Pavlov, his chief of staff Klimovskikh, Western Front signals commander Grigoriev, 4th Army commander Korobkov, commanders and commissars of the 60th and 30th Rifle Divisions were all publicly incriminated. General Pyadyshev, who had done much to organize the 'Luga line' was not publicly arraigned; he was shot speedily, secretly and inexplicably by the NKVD.

Mekhlis took a personal part in branding General Kachalov as a 'traitor', although he was killed in action conducting a gallant defence. There were those who committed suicide, and those like 6th Cavalry Corps commander Nikitin, or military engineer Karbyshev who were taken prisoner and who ended up in German concentration camps. For 'panic-mongering', 'dereliction of duty', 'cowardice', 'abandoning weapons', the harshest penalties were meted out; General Oborin, 14th Mechanized Corps commander was tried by military tribunal, as was General Klich. By 19 July, the Western 'axis' high command and Front command had been completely reorganized: with Timoshenko as *Glavkom*, Marshal Shaposhnikov became his chief of staff and Bulganin the 'political member', Yeremenko the Front commander, Lieutenant-General V.D. Sokolovskii his chief of staff and Malandin chief of operations staff (Western Front). Commanders found themselves under open and dire threat. Biryuzov, commander of the 132nd Rifle Division, was told, like so many others: 'In the event of non-fulfilment of assignments, we will convene a military tribunal!' In the case of General V.D. Tsvetayev, whom 7th Army commander had decided to arrest and to arraign for losing contact with his troops, the Front commander, General Frolov, decided in this instance that the punishment was not justified. Leniency, however, was not a commodity in common supply.

Rank-and-file Red Army men were subject to fierce new disciplinary bonds. In his order of 20 July, Stalin commanded that all units 'should be purged of unreliable elements', and that officers and men coming out of German encirclement should be rigorously investigated by the NKVD 'Special Sections' (*Osobyi Otdel:* oo) to root out 'German spies'. The 'Special Sections' provided the NKVD with detailed information on morale and combat performance within Red Army units and formations; in addition, NKVD troops formed 'holding detachments', *zagraditelnye otryadyi*, whose function it was to keep Red Army troops in the line. The 'Special Sections' attached to General Lukin's army near Smolensk provided their chief, Colonel Korolev, with some grim reading: drunkenness, panic, incompetence, self-inflicted wounds. On 25 July, NKVD troops rounded up 1,000 'deserters': before the assembled regiment, seven men were shot and five more without trial – three deserters, two 'traitors to the Fatherland' – and then a further twenty-three (deserters, self-mutilators, deserters to the Germans) were shot by orders of the military tribunal. 'Panic-mongering', 'desertion', 'abandoning weapons and battle-stations' (which often meant merely getting lost) cost many more their lives. At the same time, Mekhlis and Beria allowed a larger trickle of officers back from the labour camps where pre-war NKVD 'investigations' had sent them; an officer working with a labour gang on the Murmansk railway found himself whisked back to command a tank battalion, a case by no means exceptional. What Stalin did take objection to was Beria's request for 50,000 rifles to arm more NKVD units; Stalin, cutting short Beria's explanation in Georgian, gave him grudgingly 25,000 and then cut it to 10,000. Private armies, like private empires, were limited.

In his letter to Winston Churchill of 19 July (seven days after the conclusion of the Anglo-Soviet diplomatic agreement), Stalin admitted that the situation of the Soviet forces was at this time 'tense'; however, it might have been much worse had the Soviet forces not been able to meet the 'unexpected' German onslaught on the new Kishinev–Lwow–Brest–Kaunas–Viborg line. By way of alleviation, Stalin proposed the establishment of a double 'second front', one in northern France, the other, in the Arctic, as a joint Anglo-Soviet military and naval venture. Stalin was presumably arguing, in his passages about the 'favourable line' he had earlier obtained, that he had made the best of a bad job, and one which ought not to prejudice Allied aid to the Soviet Union. Ten days later, in talking to Harry Hopkins in Moscow, Stalin retracted all he had said about the 'favourable line': the line upon which they now stood, precariously enough, was the best, Odessa–Kiev–Smolensk–Leningrad. In all, Stalin exhibited a certain optimism. By mid October, bad weather should halt operations; the front should be stabilized no later than 1 October, and in those crucially important intervening weeks the German advance should not reach 'more than a hundred kilometres' east of the present line. The Red Army could and would defend Leningrad, Moscow and Kiev, key regions where three-quarters of Soviet arms production was concentrated: any major German breakthrough to the east of these centres would be 'crippling'. Stalin, however, thought that the line could be held; the Red Army would hold on here during the winter and then in the spring of 1942 counter-attack.

The beautiful simplicity of all this was, to the great peril of the Soviet Union, terribly scarred by the giant German encirclement operations in the Ukraine and the isolation of Leningrad: with its armoured wings peeling off to the north and to the south, Army Group Centre itself would go over to the defensive. The struggle between Hitler and his generals over the implications and consequences of this decision raged within the German command after the end of July and dragged through blood-drenched weeks when Timoshenko sucked nine German divisions into a savage battle of attrition in the 'Yelnaya bend', the Soviet barrier fifty miles to the east of Smolensk and high ground vital for the development of any blow directed against Moscow. On the Soviet side there was also some flurry but it was settled swiftly: Stalin simply dismissed General Zhukov as Chief of the General Staff and replaced him with Shaposhnikov, in whose company he went on to commit blunders whose magnitude had much to do with accelerating those 'crippling' German successes which he professed to fear.

General Zhukov reported to Stalin on 29 July, ready to make a full report on the situation though the meeting did not convene until Mekhlis was summoned to attend. Laying his maps on the table, Zhukov began to survey the whole operational scene, beginning with the north-western theatre and moving down to the south-west, adding data on Soviet losses and the formation of reserve armies, referring finally to German deployments and the probable course of their operations. Mekhlis interrupted to ask where Zhukov got his information about German operations; Zhukov replied that he knew nothing of the actual German plans but by looking at present deployment it was possible to suggest 'certain things', above all what the Germans planned to do with their armour. 'Continue with the report,' Stalin advised Zhukov, who then rapped out his main conclusions:

on the strategic axis of Moscow the Germans are unable to mount a major offensive operation in the near future owing to their heavy losses and they lack appreciable reserves to secure the right and left wings of Army Group Centre.

on the Leningrad axis it is impossible for the Germans to begin an operation to capture Leningrad and link up with the Finns without additional forces.

in the Ukraine the main fighting will reach its peak somewhere in the area of Dniepro-petrovsk-Kremenchug which has been penetrated by the main armoured forces of Army Group South.

the most dangerous and the weakest sector of our (Soviet) line is the Central Front, since the armies covering Unecha and Gomel are weak and badly equipped – the Germans can use this present weak spot to strike into the flank and rear of the South-Western Front.

'What do you suggest?', Stalin asked. Zhukov had a ready answer – strengthen the Central Front with not less than three armies, give it more artillery, pull one army from the Western Front, the other from the South-Western Front and a third from *Stavka* reserve, send in an experienced and energetic commander like Vatutin. But will this not weaken the defences along the approaches to Moscow, Stalin countered: not at all, replied Zhukov, for in 12–15 days we can pull in from the Far East at least eight fully equipped divisions, including an armoured division, a force which would actually strengthen the 'Moscow axis'. So we then give the Far East over to the Japanese, Stalin retorted. Zhukov did not reply to this but went on to insist that the South-Western Front must be pulled behind the Dnieper and five reinforced divisions deployed at the junction of the Central and South-Western Fronts. 'And what about Kiev in that case?' was Stalin's next rejoinder.

When Zhukov suggested good military reasons for giving up Kiev, Stalin exploded – and so in turn did Zhukov, incensed at being accused of talking 'rubbish'. If the Chief of the General was only able to 'talk nonsense', then there was nothing left for him to do and on the spot he asked Stalin to relieve him of his present post for an appointment at the front. 'Don't get heated', Stalin broke in on Zhukov's outburst, adding that 'since you mentioned it, we will get by without you.' After Zhukov's final justification of himself and his work as Chief of the General Staff, Stalin closed the interview and informed Zhukov that the matter 'would be discussed'. Gathering up his maps, Zhukov left. Forty minutes later Stalin called him back, having 'discussed the matter'; Zhukov would be released from his post as Chief of the General Staff and replaced by Shaposhnikov. The latter's health was not good, Stalin admitted, but that did not matter too much since 'we will help him'. Over the question of his new appointment, Zhukov bridled again: 'I can command a division, corps, army or a front.' 'Calm down, calm down', repeated Stalin, adding that since Zhukov had talked about a Soviet counter-blow at Yelnaya, he had better make himself useful there and take command of the Reserve Front. Shaposhnikov would soon arrive at the General Staff, Zhukov could hand over but Stalin reminded him that he would still remain a member of the *Stavka*. At last the business was done. Zhukov asked for permission to leave whereupon Stalin suggested that he sit down and drink a little tea since there were some things 'to be talked over'. Though the tea duly arrived, the talk flagged and Zhukov finally left, much dispirited.

Stalin had his way. Zhukov handed over to Shaposhnikov at the General Staff and then moved on to Gzhatsk, where the headquarters of the Reserve Front was located. As for the 'rubbish' that Zhukov talked, it proved all too soon to have been the soundest military logic. Stalin could not say that he had not been warned and even warned in time.

5

Towards the Edge of Destruction

'Little by little', in the words of Admiral Kuznetsov (Soviet naval commander-in-chief), Stalin worked his way to the top of the military command and into the immediate direction of military operations. Soon after his 3 July broadcast he began to put in an appearance at Timoshenko's office in the Defence Commissariat, where in mid July Kuznetsov himself was summoned to answer some of Stalin's questions: in front of a table spread with maps but without charts, Stalin asked Kuznetsov about the feasibility of moving artillery from the Baltic islands to the mainland. Only the defence of Tallin and the islands of Osel and Dago interested him, nothing else. Not long after this Stalin was able to address his commanders as their Supreme Commander, for on Friday, 8 August, the Supreme Soviet 'appointed' Stalin *Verkhovnyi Glavnokomanduyushchii*, the Supreme Commander of the Soviet Armed Forces, all legally tied up.

This was the signal for another great reshuffle at the top. Stalin himself now held all the key posts, chairman of the State Defence Committee (GKO), Defence Commissar (with sixteen deputies) and his latest appointment, Supreme Commander: by a decision of the GKO, the General Staff was reorganized as the 'General Staff of the Armed Forces', combining the staffs of arms and services. As Supreme Commander Stalin duly 'authorized' this on 10 August. The *Stavka* also came in for its share of these upgradings, emerging as the *Stavka* of the Supreme Command (*Stavka Verkhovnovo Glavnokomandovaniya*) with an added weight of membership including men who served on the GKO.

Marshal Shaposhnikov, an ailing and ageing former imperial officer, took over the enlarged General Staff once Zhukov departed; at once he installed Major-General Vasilevskii as Chief of the Operations Administration and very quickly recommended him as Deputy Chief (General Staff). Vasilevskii's talents have never been in question but two schools of thought prevail about Shaposhnikov's own competence; those, like Vasilevskii who worked with him, are unstinting in their praise of his insight and ability, whereas Front and formation commanders who had to apply some of his more questionable decisions are less charitable; to judge by one set of results, Shaposhnikov does not emerge at all favourably from the ghastly mess in the south-west. He was throughout this critical period the man at Stalin's elbow, proffering professional advice, but not for him Zhukov's professsional candour and rigour. The strategic summary

exuding studied calm and calculated optimism which Stalin presented to Harry
Hopkins, President Roosevelt's personal representative at the Moscow meetings
held at the end of July, was more in Shaposhnikov's line.

What Stalin asked of Hopkins was aluminium for aircraft, steel for tanks,
light AA guns (in fact, 20,000 AA guns of all types), heavy machine-guns and
rifles, at least a million or more of the latter. With anti-aircraft guns to cover his
bases and lines of communication, and with aluminium to build more planes,
Stalin announced that 'we can fight for three or four years'. As for present
Russian production, this amounted to 1,800 aircraft and 1,000 tanks per month,
but Stalin insisted that the outcome of the war in the east would finally depend
on what strength, in men and material, could be fielded in the spring (1942)
campaign, when he anticipated that Germany could out-produce Russia in
what he called the 'all-important' winter race over tank output. Meanwhile, he
envisaged a front-line 'probably not more than 100 kilometres' east of its
present siting, with Leningrad, Moscow and Kiev still in Soviet hands; about the
location of Soviet war plants Stalin gave 'no detailed reply' but admitted more
or less indirectly that three-quarters were to be found in the Leningrad-Moscow-
Kiev complexes. German penetration here would destroy the corresponding
degree of Soviet industrial capacity. Cagey and oblique in his statements, Stalin
showed as little as possible of his hand and obliged others to comply; when
Hopkins talked to General Yakovlev, Colonel-General Voronov's deputy in
the newly activated post of Chief of Artillery, Yakovlev could not modify –
even though he knew the real front-line requirements – Stalin's priorities and
could make no supplementary proposition about anti-tank guns and tanks for
which the field armies were shouting so desperately. Faced with Stalin's list,
Yakovlev fell back upon the remark that 'the most important items had been
covered'; Yakovlev 'could think of nothing else', suppressing no doubt all
thoughts of tanks, ammunition, radio equipment, anti-tank guns, medium-
calibre guns, and transport. Whether Stalin had really settled upon the significance of a 'long war', as opposed to a hard winter and a smashing spring
counter-blow, looks doubtful; in either case and in any event, Stalin had to hold
the line he specified, and this above all else required the correct determination of
German intentions. It was miscalculation here which produced in August-
September 1941 a sustained crisis in the command and a terrible catastrophe in
the field.

When Stalin talked in the sepulchral stillness of his Kremlin quarters with
Hopkins, Smolensk had been a fortnight in German hands; three Soviet armies
(20th, 16th and 19th) were in semi-encirclement and the enemy trap, which
Stalin ordered prised apart and Smolensk retaken at all costs, was closing in a
great ring of fire. The day on which Smolensk fell, 16 July, Timoshenko
sent his pessimistic signal to Stalin, announcing the dearth of tanks and the
absence of trained reserves; from the Reserve Front and from the elements of
shattered armies the *Stavka* formed five so-called 'Army Groups' (sixteen rifle,

four tank divisions in all, each identified by the name of its commander – 'Group Rokossovskii', 'Group Khomenko', 'Group Kachalov', 'Group Kalinin' and 'Group Maslennikov') which were ordered to mount, along the lake Dvina-Roslavl sector, flank attacks from Belyi, Yartsevo and Roslavl 'in the general direction of Smolensk', to encircle the German armoured formations and then to link up west of Smolensk with the main body of the Western Front. On 18 July Stalin ordered the manning of the 'Mozhaisk line' with three armies (32nd, 33rd and 34th), which would come under the command of the chief of the Moscow Military District, Lieutenant-General P.A. Artmeyev; a week later, the *Stavka* ordered 13th and 21st Armies (Western Front) to form the critically important Central Front under Colonel-General F.I. Kuznetsov, the man lately behind the disasters in the north-west. On 19 July, however, 10th Panzer Division reached Yelnaya and the next day ss Division *Das Reich* took up positions to the left of it, the vital bridgehead for advance upon Moscow and simultaneously a great easterly bulge in the German line, which by late July sloped southwards to Kiev and ran northwards, past the bloody indentation of Smolensk itself, along an arc drawn on Leningrad.

The complex of operations conducted by Timoshenko's 'Western axis' in July-August drew in Fronts other than the Western and armies operating far beyond the radial point of Smolensk; these massive upheavals, the full scope of the 'Smolensk battles', drew no less than six Soviet armies into the Smolensk and Yelnaya whirlpools, as Timoshenko slashed and jabbed at the German flanks. North of Smolensk itself, at the centre of the conflagration, Kurochkin's 20th and Lukin's 16th Army, fully encircled by Hoth, in early August had begun their fierce break-out across the Dnieper: Kurochkin's divisions were down to between one thousand and two thousand men, his tank force ground to sixty-five, and his exhausted ammunition was fleetingly stocked by air-drops from ten bombers, which was all the Front command could spare. In the German rear, at Moghilev, the poor 13th Army fought it out until it was battered to pieces. From Velikie Luki in the north to Gomel in the south Soviet divisions lunged wherever they could. Almost a dozen Soviet armies – 13th, 21st, 19th, 20th, 16th, 22nd, 29th, 30th, 24th, 28th and the 3rd – were flung into these fiery mazes of attack and defence.

It was upon this complex of carnage that both Hitler and Stalin were concentrating, both to commit themselves at this juncture to decisions of far-reaching consequence and fundamental import. These were decisions which were to end by seriously discomfiting the field commanders, Soviet and German alike.

When Marshal Voroshilov arrived in Leningrad as the new *Glavkom* North-West, he had on paper at least thirty divisions available for the defence of the region; in fact, only five of these divisions were fully manned and the rest had only one-third of their men and equipment, so that the German command (at least by its 27 July reckoning) overestimated effective Soviet strength by about

a half or more. At the moment when Army Group North bumped into the first
of the 'Luga line' defences, Voroshilov embarked on an attempt to rationalize
the tangled command in his area; on 13 July, he detached that military wraith,
the stubborn and apparently indestructible 8th Army, with 41st Rifle Corps (11th
Army) from the North-Western Front and assigned them to the Northern
Front, with orders not to permit an enemy breakthrough into Leningrad.

This made sense, since these formations were now fighting on the Northern
Front's doorstep; Popov at once ordered the 41st Corps to the Luga defences.
The other battered troops of the North-Western Front, pressed back in a south-
easterly direction, were ordered to hold the German thrusts at Novgorod,
Staraya Russa and Velikie Luki. This decision was confirmed on 14 July by the
Stavka, which added an instruction about reinforcing the Soviet 8th Army
operating in Estonia, in order to prevent a German rush on the coast of the Gulf
of Finland as well as draw off enemy forces from the Luga and Staraya Russa
sectors. The 'Luga operational group' (LOG), with its regular Red Army and
DNO divisions, had some three hundred kilometres of front to man; 41st Rifle
Corps moved to the east of Luga itself to regroup and reorganize, so that what
strength it possessed was not immediately felt.

The German drive on Leningrad from the south-west, checked at Luga,
swung in mid July to the north-west and applied pressure against the Kingisepp
sector of the 'Luga line', planning a breakthrough to Leningrad through
Ivanovskoe and the Koporskoe plateau, although originally the main weight of
the German attack was to have been on the right wing, in the direction of
Novgorod. Hoepner put infantry divisions along the main road to Luga and
brought his three motorized formations across the swamp and bog, bisected by
just one road, to the assault on the lower Luga (the Kingisepp sector). Surprised,
Popov had to fling in against the German bridgeheads at Ivanovskoe and Sabsk
the first troops to hand, the 2nd DNO and the two companies of the Leningrad
Red Banner Infantry School. At the cost of savage fighting, bit by bit the
German bridgeheads were enlarged, to serve for the final thrust at Leningrad
now a mere seventy miles away. To close the gap between the Gulf of Finland
and lake Peipus, Popov rushed in a battalion of marines, a regiment of the 16th
Rifle Division and a regiment of the 4th DNO, hastily assembled into the 'Narva
operational group' (NOG).

To block the German drive on Novgorod, which was Manstein's objective,
Voroshilov ordered 11th Army to attack 56th Panzer Corps, reinforcing 11th
Army with 21st Tank Division (1st Mechanized Corps), the 70th and 237th
Rifle Divisions; as Manstein pushed past Soltsy, over yet more marsh and swamp
the 11th Soviet army attacked in a four-day battle (14–18 July), operating in
two groups, 'Northern' and 'Southern'. Manstein finally mastered this crisis, and
took this opportunity to urge the unification of the two Panzer corps (41st and
56th) and the exploitation of the lower Luga bridgeheads; in spite of this
proposal, however, he was ordered to break through at Luga itself.

R.T.S.—G

Meanwhile on the left wing of the Soviet North-Western Front rifle divisions were being moved up to block the advance of the German Sixteenth Army on Staraya Russa-Kholm. By late July German units had reached the line Narva-Luga-Mshaga, upon which they regrouped and waited; while the German High Command argued, the *Stavka* showered instructions upon Voroshilov and demanded from him, as *Glavkom*, and from the Northern and North-Western front commanders drastic measures to ready the defence on the Luga and Mshaga river lines. On 23 July, on the orders of the *Stavka* and the instructions of the *Glavkom*, Popov split the 'Luga line' into three separate commands: the Kingisepp (Major-General V.V. Semashko), the Luga (Major-General A.N. Astanin) and the Eastern (Major-General F.N. Starikov). General Pyadyshev, the former commander, had by now been certainly arrested, if not actually shot.

Voroshilov, who had last swung a sabre in the Civil War with the 1st Cavalry Army, had gone up to the front line at Ivanovskoe on the Luga to rally the militia troops and Red Army officer cadets; Front commander Popov himself leapt into a tank to conduct a battlefield reconnaissance, to ease the militia men's attack, aggravated as he was at Voroshilov's criticism of the 2nd DNO. Besides berating the front-line commanders, Voroshilov tore into the military engineers for their tardiness in readying the defence lines; his directive of 29 July listed a whole row of deficiencies in the 'Luga line', while six days earlier he had issued special instructions to the North-West Front command on preparing the Krasnogvardeisk 'fortified district', divided forthwith into three sectors – Krasnoselsk, Central and Slutsk-Kolpino – and the whole organization put under the direction of Major-General P.A. Zaitsev, chief of engineers Northern Front. The larger undertaking of building defence works round the Leningrad area (and including the 'Luga line' also) was assigned to a new mixed military-civilian group, the Special Defence Works Commission headed by the Secretary of the Leningrad Communist Party *gorkom*, A.A. Kuznetsov, and staffed by the president of the city Soviet, P.S. Popkov, the chief of the *oblast* Soviet, N.V. Solovev, the commander of the Leningrad district, Lieutenant-General T.I. Shevaldin, two Academicians, N.N. Semenov and V.G. Galerkin, plus the director of the Kirov Factory, I.M. Zaltsman. Empowered to draft up to half - million workers for digging trenches and building pill-boxes, the Commission disposed also of the lorries and trucks or such mechanical equipment as there was, with authority to arrange the arming of the emplacements with locally pro-duced weapons. Any technical questions came under the aegis of a military *troika* subordinated to the Northern Front command and composed of General Zaitsev, Major-General (Artillery) V.P. Sidorov and Engineer Colonel Bychev-skii.

Almost at once, however, Voroshilov took violent exception to the concen-tration on defence lines so near the city; in that erstwhile ladies finishing school in Leningrad, the *Smolnyi*, once Bolshevik headquarters in 1917 and now the military and political command centre for the north-west, Voroshilov rounded on Zaitsev, Kuznetsov, Popkov and Bychevskii – 'Where', he demanded, 'do you propose to defend the city? In Krasnogvardeisk, in Petergof? . . . And why are more people working at Krasnogvardeisk and Kolpino than at Luga?' Voroshilov wanted the labour force shifted to Luga and Novgorod, and so they were duly shifted: in all, some 30,000–35,000 women and youths worked round the clock on the defences, often bombed and strafed by German planes, while another 30,000 civilians were specially drafted to build the Kolpino positions. The right wing of the 'Luga line' was slowly stiffened, while the 1st Tank Division was moved into the Krasnogvardeisk positions; Pshennikov's 8th Army had meanwhile been split into two separate parts, with the 10th Rifle Corps pushed into the naval base of Tallinn and the 11th pulling back into the Narva neck. Bychevskii's engineer map was increasingly dotted with red points indicating trenches, pill-boxes and tank-traps; Popov, Front commander, was nevertheless seriously concerned that a German breakthrough on the right of the 'Luga line' and the final entrapment of the 8th Army would bring German units into the rear of the Soviet coastal defences. He therefore ordered more defence lines from Kipen to Petergof (east of Oranienbaum), on the coast.

During all this frantic activity as the German units stood halted in their bridge-heads, Voroshilov also acquired considerable, even astonishing reinforcement. The *Stavka* by the beginning of August dispatched nine rifle and two cavalry divisions to the North-Western Front and on 6 August, from the Reserve Front, the 34th Army, five rifle, two cavalry divisions, four artillery regiments and two armoured trains, was detached for operations in the north-west; with the troops went strict instructions not to use the army in 'little pieces' but in its entirety as a counter-attack force. The General Staff on 7 August ordered the 48th Army to form up, based on a militia division (1st DNO), three rifle divisions (70th, 128th, 237th), a brigade (1st Mountain Troops) and a tank division (21st); the 48th was also assigned to the North-Western Front. Voroshilov had at the same time tried to build up a 'High Command reserve' of four rifle divisions and a tank division (the 1st), the latter brought down from Karelia, and stationed near Batetskaya, midway between Luga and Novgorod. The idea was to strike flank blows at German units breaking through at Luga or Novgorod, admirable enough in theory but the infantry and armour had already been used prematurely, and Voroshilov's reserve had actually vanished, because the 'robbing Peter to pay Paul' technique would not work.

Voroshilov had earlier done what Popov shrank from: he had taken divisions away from the Karelian front (7th and 23rd Armies) engaged in holding the Finnish offensive which opened north of Leningrad on 31 July. The 48th Army was built up from these 'stolen' divisions; the four divisions Voroshilov had taken he had finally to put back. Nikishev, chief of staff to the Northern Front, was appalled, for the 'Luga line' still lacked adequate forces and yet the northern sector, facing the Finns, had been seriously weakened. Voroshilov had to split up his 'reserve'; the 272nd Rifle Division went to Petrozavodsk, the 265th to 23rd

Army where the Finns had broken through in the direction of Keksholm, the 268th was assigned to 8th Army to keep it alive, and the 281st Rifle Division alone actually went into the 'Luga line' at Kingisepp. The 1st Tank Division had already been smashed up in the fighting at Kandalaksha.

The crisis came to a head on the evening of 11 August, three days after the German break-out from the Luga bridgeheads, which had begun at 09.00 hours on 8 August, in heavy rain which deprived the German assault for the moment of air support; the objective was the open ground to the south of the Narva–Kingisepp–Leningrad railway, beyond which the assault force, strengthened with 8th Panzer and 36th Motorized Infantry Division, would turn east for Leningrad itself. Popov, aware from prisoner interrogation of the presence of 36th Motorized Infantry Division in the Luga bridgeheads, knew the lull was over; however, his attempts to eliminate the German bridgeheads with militia divisions failed. With the threatened encirclement of the left wing of 23rd Army up north in Karelia, Popov was obliged to rush the last available reserves northwards. Manstein had attacked on 10 August in a bid to take Luga itself, battering through the deeply echeloned Soviet defences, while the German Sixteenth Army had already been committed in a bid to seize Staraya Russa far on the German right flank.

Nikishev let the operations map speak for itself: in the Karelian isthmus two divisions were trapped near Keksholm and cut off from the Vyborg group of 23rd Army, 168th Rifle Division was pinned in Sortavala on lake Ladoga, while Finnish troops moved down the eastern side of Ladoga: in Estonia the 8th Army was now sliced in two, while on the 'outer approaches' to Leningrad there were numerous penetrations. The Northern Front report to the General Staff (13 August) stressed the multiplicity of perils:

Objective of main enemy forces:
1 Seizure of Leningrad, operating on the axes:
  (a) Narva–Kingisepp–Leningrad
  (b) Luga–Leningrad
  (c) Keksholm–Leningrad

To count on effective resistance to the enemy merely with newly formed and badly equipped militia units and re-formed units assigned to the North-Western Front after they have pulled out of Lithuania and Latvia is completely unjustified.

Major-General Nikishev accompanied this formal report by a letter to Marshal Shaposhnikov, pleading for reserves – of which divisional, army and Front commands had absolutely none; each German thrust had to be dealt with by 'scratch sections and units', while Nikishev reckoned that 12 divisions, 400 planes and 250 tanks were needed to fill what he called this 'three-cornered hat'. He admitted to his officers that he expected nothing, not even a reply. He was mistaken: three days later he received a signal from the General Staff, 'In connection with prevailing tactical situation, groups of North-Western Front forces comprising 1st DNO, 237th and 70th Rifle Division will be temporarily attached to Northern

Front and not detached therefrom without *Stavka* authorization'. The *Stavka* had merely given back Nikishev his own formations; but these troops had already been used by Voroshilov, a force which in Nikishev's own words 'a whole German corps is dragging about all over the place', in the wake of Voroshilov's counter-stroke at Staraya Russa.

Three armies – 48th, 34th and 11th – were earmarked by the *Stavka* for operations against the German right flank, in particular 16th Army, in the Soltsy–Staraya Russa–Dno area, due to begin on 12 August; driving into the 'corridor' between Army Group North and Centre, 34th Army would attack towards Morino, 48th Army from north of Shimsk to Utorgosh and 11th Army's left flank from south of Staraya Russa. It was this attack which crashed into 10th Corps (German Sixteenth Army), threatening to push it backwards into lake Ilmen; with 10th Corps broken, Voroshilov could strike for lake Peipus and cut the rearward German communications. Manstein, who had finally moved north to join the Panzer attack on the left wing, was just at the moment of his arrival there brought swiftly south to deal with the Staraya Russa crisis; on 19 August, 3rd Motorized Infantry Division and ss Division *Totenkopf* – the former diverted from its dash north to join 'the drive on Leningrad' – slammed into the flank and rear of the Soviet 34th Army, as 10th Corps fought it frontally.

At the other end of lake Ilmen, Lieutenant-General Akimov's 48th Army had lost control of the situation before Novgorod, that ancient and hitherto un-conquered city of old Russia which advance German units entered on 16 August; striking north-east, cavalry, self-propelled guns and infantry of the German 21st Division seized Chudovo off the march four days later, cutting the 'October (Moscow–Leningrad) Railway line' and racing on to the river Volkhov.

Kachanov's 34th Army and Morozov's 11th Army had been flung back to the river Lovat; the 48th Army had been able to contribute nothing to the Staraya Russa counter-stroke, embroiled as it was with the German thrust at Novgorod, and now it lay smashed – a mere 6,235 men, with 5,043 rifles and 31 guns, the sole force covering Leningrad from the south and south-west, hanging on to the 25-mile line from Lyuban to Gruzino (on the Volkhov). By 24 August, when Reinhardt's 41st Panzer Corps moving meanwhile from the west over the Luga had reached the outskirts of Krasnogvardeisk, Lyuban and the Lyuban–Chudovo section of the October railway had fallen, and a German thrust north-east threatened to sever Leningrad's last land link with the rest of Russia.

Voroshilov was overwhelmed, although he was no longer sole master in his house. On 20 August, the Military Soviet of the North-Western Front had decided to set up a special body, the Military Soviet for the Defence of Lenin-grad (*Voennyi Soviet oborony Leningrada*), with Kuznetsov, Popkov, A.I. Subbotin and L.M. Antyufeyev as members; this Defence Soviet began to work at once, instructing Colonel Antonov to present by 16.00 hours on 21 August a defence plan for the city, co-ordinated with the Northern Front operational plan. While

Leningrad prepared for street-fighting and urban action against parachute troops, Stalin hauled both Voroshilov and Zhdanov over the coals for their initiative in setting up the Defence Soviet; in a rebuke delivered over the direct telephone line on 21 August, Stalin growled about the creation of the Defence Soviet without permission and ordered Voroshilov and Zhdanov to 'review' its personnel forthwith. Stalin rejected out of hand Voroshilov's explanation that the Defence Soviet was merely an 'auxiliary organ', set up to deal with the situation as it had actually developed. Stalin ordered Voroshilov and Zhdanov to join this Soviet, and Voroshilov to become its chairman. This meant only duplication of effort, with Voroshilov as *Glavkom* tangled up in questions which others should have dealt with, while two bodies, the Defence Soviet and the Military Soviet of the North-Western High Command, simply got in each other's way, their functions being all too similar. Stalin, however, had successfully axed down the Defence Soviet: in six days it was disbanded, and on 30 August its functions formally handed over to the Leningrad Front.

At a meeting of the Communist Party *aktiv* in Leningrad on 20 August, Voroshilov and Zhdanov explained the grave position at the front. The danger of the situation could scarcely be disguised, with German units near Krasnogvardeisk, twenty-five miles away, and an assault from the south-east taking shape at Lyuban. Stalin had also considered the operational map, received reports of the 'initiative' of his subordinates and listened to pleas for help. With the city trembling on the brink of disaster, Stalin ordered a GKO mission to Leningrad, a top-level command group with all the sweeping powers of the GKO behind it; the mission, headed by Malenkov and Molotov, was ordered north on 21 August with the formal assignment of 'organizing the city's defences'. Colonel-General Voronov asked Zhigarev for a fast bomber with fighter escort to transport the GKO officers to Leningrad; they duly arrived at Cherepovets and chugged into Mga by train. Andrei Kosygin was in charge of the group of engineers sent in with the GKO mission. Voronov was himself astounded at the 'peaceful atmosphere' which prevailed, suited more to the battle 'being rather at the walls of Berlin, than Leningrad'. With complete and utter ruthlessness, the GKO plenipotentiaries got down to work. The *Stavka* had already formally split the Northern Front into two, the Leningrad Front under Popov and the Karelian Front under Lieutenant-General V.A. Frolov. In a private battle, Nikishev was dismissed as Chief of Staff (and with him his Operations Officer Tikhomirov) for having run foul of Voroshilov, who found him 'awkward'; Colonel Gorodetskii late of 23rd Army, became the new chief of staff, though he only lasted about a fortnight.

The question of immediate reinforcement had still to be resolved, and in this Stalin took a personal hand. On 26 August, Popov and his officers talked by telephone with the *Stavka*, more particularly with Stalin: in view of the German pressure at Lyuban, Stalin authorized Popov to take from the Leningrad plants four days' tank production for his own Front, and promised four air regiments and ten reinforcement battalions. Stalin's orders were simple: to pull 48th Army into shape, mine the Moscow–Leningrad highway and the whole area north of Lyuban and use any aircraft for immediate support of front-line operations. Popov himself also 'took measures', bringing the 168th Rifle Division by ship from the northerly shore of lake Ladoga, pulling the 4th DNO from Krasnogvardeisk, and using them as stop-gap forces to the south and south-east.

At the end of August, the GKO mission abolished the 'North-Western High Command', just as it wiped out the Defence Soviet; the elimination of Voroshilov's command position was glossed over as 'unification' of the High Command (*Glavkom*) with the Leningrad Front command, but the Military Soviet of the Leningrad Front was and thereafter remained under the direct control of the GKO, an arrangement unique to Leningrad. In spite of all his heroics and bluster, Voroshilov was clearly not up to the command requirements of modern, mobile war; for one week only (5–12 September), he remained in command of the Leningrad Front, when he was abruptly and speedily replaced by General Zhukov. Major-General Sobennikov's tenure at the North-Western Front was also terminated at the end of August, for the Front was directly subordinated to the *Stavka*; only in October did the Front receive a new commander, General Kurochkin. The real power in Leningrad rested with the Military Soviet, although administrative measures and local decisions were put into effect by 'civilian' bodies; Zhdanov, although not a member of the GKO, acted more or less as its instrument, while the GKO had actual plenipotentiaries, like D.G. Pavlov, in charge of supply and provisioning, industrial production, or evacuation (of civilians and machines). Above all, the Party cemented its control, and at the very top Stalin made his presence as ever immediately felt. It was an organizational form which had to carry the city through the imminence of this vast crisis, and later the nightmarish conditions of prolonged siege.

While the GKO mission cleared the decks in Leningrad, the 'Luga line', rendered useless as a main barrier with the German breakthrough to the southeast, was finally battered to pieces; the 41st Rifle Corps had German units in its rear, and General Astanin was authorized to try a break-out, not least because the Luga troops were desperately needed for the Krasnogvardeisk positions. In small groups, low in ammunition and lacking fuel, Soviet troops fell back in three main groups, forced off the only road which was now in German hands; at night, German searchlights sought out the retreating columns. Falling back also through Narva and Kingisepp was the 11th Corps of the Soviet 8th Army, moving on the northern flank of 41st Panzer Corps; 10th Corps (8th Army) was on 14 August subordinated by Voroshilov to the Military Soviet of the Baltic Fleet and committed to the defence of the naval base at Tallinn, which was evacuated on 28 August when the Baltic Fleet was drawn back to Kronstadt. To avoid its being completely sliced up, the remnant of the 8th Army was pulled back north-east of Kingisepp; on 25 August, 8th Army commander reported 100 per cent losses in regimental and battalion commanders and staffs, although reinforcement of a kind was supplied by including the 'Koporoe operational group' (units formerly belonging to the Kingisepp sector of the 'Luga line') within 8th Army. Early in September, this force established itself in a pocket (the Oranienbaum bridgehead) on the Baltic Coast to the west of Leningrad, remaining henceforth a permanent pressure on the German flank. The 8th Army – quite miraculously – had survived, even if it was totally locked up.

Not much else, however, had escaped the wrecking of Leningrad's 'outer defences', where Marshal Voroshilov had been so keen to fight. Out of the Krasnogvardeisk 'fortified district' Popov sought to form two armies; on 31 August the *Stavka* agreed to his proposal, establishing the 55th Army (Major-General I.G. Lazarev) from the Slutsk-Kolpino units (168th, 70th, 90th, 237th Rifle Divisions, 4th DNO) and the 42nd Army (Lieutenant-General F.S. Ivanov) from the 2nd and 3rd DNO and the 291st Rifle Division. The 48th Army, by the evening of 30 August pressed back to the railway line in the Mga-Kirishi sector, was ordered to re-form by 6 September, taking in the 311th and 128th Rifle Divisions and utilizing equipment made in Leningrad factories. At the beginning of September, Major-General Shcherbakov's four left-flank divisions of 8th Army were being packed into their Baltic bridgehead, two divisions of 42nd Army, supported by the guns of the Baltic Fleet, held a line from the Gulf of Finland to Pustoshka, four divisions of 55th Army held from Pustoshka to the river Neva, while the Leningrad Front command reserve consisted of two rifle divisions and a naval brigade. On 4 September, German long-range (240-mm) guns opened fire on the city from sites north of Tosno, a prelude to the final assault on the city in which Reinhardt's 41st Panzer Corps would play the major role.

The *Stavka* on 1 September severely reprimanded Popov and his officers for badly organized and insufficiently stubborn defence, and demanded 'more positive' measures. Popov had more or less improvised two armies which were now putting up an organized fight, but once more a crisis with 48th Army brought dire results. The 23rd Army operating north-west of Leningrad on the Karelian isthmus against the Finns was in desperate need of reinforcement; Popov dispatched the 265th Rifle Division from his reserve and the 291st from Krasnogvardeisk, leaving him with no more men to spare and none for 48th Army, which received only a small contingent of NKVD troops formed into a 'division' from the survivors of frontier guards. Inside the city, the principle of 'sector defence' was adopted, in which each *rayon* (district) set up its 'defence staff' from the secretary of the *rayon* Party organization, the chairman of the *rayon ispolkom* (executive committee), the local NKVD officers and *Vsevobuch* officers. Large factories, like the huge tank plants at Kolpino, organized auxiliary *troikas*, three-man committees (director, Party secretary, Trade Union chairman) to speed the formation of workers' units; from Kolpino factories the KV tanks, unpainted and manned by worker-soldiers, rolled straight into the battle-lines.

Just why it had proved impossible to form a 'powerful shock group' to wrest the 'initiative from the enemy and go over to active operations' the Military Soviet of the Leningrad Front in its early September report – Voroshilov's military swan song, as it turned out – tried to explain:

Unfortunately those divisions [four DNO, three Guards DNO, one NKVD rifle divisions and four rifle divisions sent by the Stavka] which were nevertheless completely untrained and badly equipped with automatic weapons had out of sheer necessity to be thrown in at the most threatened sectors. This was the situation in the second half of July as a result of simultaneous enemy blows at Petrozavodsk, Olonets and Ivanovskoe.

In the middle of August this repeated itself on a large scale, when the enemy, simultaneously with the breakthrough of our front at Novgorod split the 8th Army in two in Estonia and attacked towards Krasnogvardeisk and on the Karelian isthmus. The very same thing happened again at the end of August and at the beginning of September when the enemy attacked simultaneously in three directions: Mga, Krasnogvardeisk and Karelia.

Only local attacks could be mounted. Fuel and power supplies were diminishing; the decision by the Leningrad Military Soviet to evacuate over one million inhabitants meant nothing now that the exits from the city had been blocked, for the capture of Mga meant Leningrad could be supplied only by air and water. The GKO had ordered on 30 August the organization of supplies across lake Ladoga (and the setting up of AA defences to cover the lake traffic from bomber attack), while a small air-lift shuttled in and out of the city, governed by weather, operational efficiency and German interdiction. On 8 September, Schlusselburg fell as a thoroughly emaciated 48th Army struggled on but could not yet be effectively reinforced, and Leningrad was deprived of its last land link with the rest of the Soviet Union.

For the fast approaching and apparently final battle for Leningrad, Stalin, already hammering upon the defenders through the GKO, sent General Zhukov to take command, as German artillery and aerial bombardment intensified as part of the process of battering down resistance. On the morning of 13 September Zhukov took off from Vnukovo aerodrome in Moscow for Leningrad, taking with him in the Il-2 the generals Fedyuninskii and Khozin: German assault units had taken Krasnoe Selo and Pushkin, had broken into the rear of the Krasnogvardeisk positions, occupied part of Petergof and reached the Gulf of Finland at Strelna; to the east, with an attack from Tosno, Mga and Schlusselburg were fast in German hands, and German units moved eastwards to the river Volkhov, where south of the river Svir they might meet Finnish troops advancing southwards between the Ladoga and Onega lakes.

Zhukov fell on the Leningrad command like a thunderbolt. On his arrival, Voroshilov relinquished his command: both signed the intelligence and operational maps, and Zhukov reported to Vasilevskii at the *Stavka* by telegraph on his arrival and on his assumption of command. Voroshilov, silent at this encounter, made a short farewell speech to the various arms commanders; that same night with his staff he flew out of the city back to Moscow, over the battle-lines which reached deep into the suburbs and across the 700 kilometres of anti-tank ditches, the 5,000 pill-boxes and fire-points, the twenty-five kilometres of barricades upon which he had set so many thousands of Leningraders to labour. Zhukov took control at a critical moment, as the German assault developed its momentum after its renewal on 8–9 September; in 42nd Army sector a dangerous situation built up as German assault regiments broke in north of Krasnoe Selo, aiming for Uritsk. Zhukov used his remaining reserve, 10th Rifle Division, at once, in support of 42nd Army; his general operational order was at least unambiguous:

1 To smother the enemy with artillery and mortar fire and air support, permitting no penetration of the defences;
2 To form by 18.9 five rifle brigades, two rifle divisions and to concentrate them for the immediate defence of Leningrad, where four defence lines will be set up;
3 8th Army will attack the enemy in the flank and rear;
4 [8th Army] will co-ordinate its operation with 54th Army, whose objective is the liberation of Mga and Schlusselburg areas.

(54th Army was in fact the old 48th, now outside the Leningrad perimeter, and command of which was assigned to another of Stalin's stalwarts, Marshal Kulik.)

In his operations room, Zhukov, in a rough but apparently effective demonstration, swept all the 'co-ordinating maps' off the table and concentrated on the single wall map of the city defence. Those who mentioned 'co-ordination' were bawled at. To 42nd Army went orders to fire off a two-day supply of ammunition in an artillery *kontrpodgotovka*; 55th Army was told to defend the area Pushkin-Krasnogvardeisk-Kolpino with all stubbornness. Zhukov on his second day started upon gathering a reserve, deepening the defences, activating 8th Army, using every artillery battery (including the Fleet) in Leningrad, and sent Fedyuninskii to look over 42nd Army; Fedyuninskii, so recently a corps commander in the Ukraine, found General Ivanov of 42nd Army sitting with his head in his hands, unable even to point out the location of his troops. From Major-General Larionov, chief of staff, Fedyuninskii found that 42nd was holding 'literally by a miracle', while Ivanov at once asked to move his command post back from the line; Fedyuninskii refused outright. Reporting back to Zhukov, Fedyuninskii learned that 42nd Army command post had now been moved further behind the line, into a school basement opposite the Kirov plant; Zhukov's reaction was prompt and in the direction of Fedyuninskii – 'Take over 42nd Army – and quick.' Zhdanov and Kizetsov signed the order hurriedly in pencil and Fedyuninskii returned to the 42nd – to find the Military Soviet of the army in uproar.

The essence of Zhukov's 'plan' was to build 42nd Army into a defensive slab, able to resist the main German assault, and to use the 8th Army 'Oranienbaum bridgehead divisions' to attack the German flank; by 16 September Zhukov had given 42nd Army not only a new commander but also a second echelon (21st

NKVD division, the 6th DNO and two brigades formed from Baltic Fleet sailors and anti-aircraft gunners), and stationed it on the outer circle of the Leningrad 'fortified line', from which it could not move without Zhukov's express permission. Grand though 'second echelon' sounded, 42nd Army War Diary showed into what shreds this whole force had been ripped. The battered 55th Army, defending Pushkin, had also indulged in an unauthorized withdrawal. And now in the 8th Army, for which Zhukov had important plans, discipline had deteriorated – but equally important, ammunition had almost run out. The planned counter-attack of 14 September did not take place, because 8th Army commander, Major-General V.I. Shcherbakov, reported that it simply could not be done. After a second refusal, Zhukov tossed out both the commander, Shcherbakov, and the commissar, I.F. Chukhnov. Stalin himself was incensed over a reported unit desertion in the Slutsk-Kolpino sector, and issued a savage order about the 'merciless destruction' of 'helpers' of the Germans; *Order No. 0098* subsequently informed the Leningrad garrison about the executions and reduction to the ranks carried out as a consequence.

The appointment of Zhukov had signified an undesirably late but certainly unalterable decision to fight to hold the city at whatever cost; what could not be held would be blown up. The Leningrad Military Soviet passed on Moscow's instructions about demolitions; Zhukov's chief of staff, Lieutenant-General M.S. Khozin (who had commanded the Leningrad district in 1938), ordered bridge demolitions to be made ready by 17 September, the day on which the Military Soviet placed at the disposal of the '*rayon* triumvirates' – directed by the Party First Secretaries of the Moskovskii, Kirov, Voldarsk and Leninsk sectors – forty tons of high explosive for securing the demolition of industrial plants. The fortification of the city itself, with barricaded streets, reinforced cellars, upper storeys converted into firing points, proceeded during the very height of the September crisis, but German armour pierced the main defence 'belt' despite Zhukov's mobilization of men and guns, and his insistence upon 'uninterrupted counter-attack'. A last position in 42nd Army sector had been prepared to the rear of Pulkovo. Beyond it lay the inner city. If by 09.00 hours on 17 September Colonel Antonov's 6th Militia Division was not on station here, Zhukov would stand those responsible 'against the wall of the Smolny and shoot them there as traitors'. Even Zhdanov was a little taken aback at this.

Pushkin had fallen on 16 September, and fierce fighting raged for Slutsk and Kolpino; the Alexandrovka tramcar terminus of the Leningrad tram service was captured, complete with tram and passengers en route, but though Slutsk was penetrated and Greater Kuzmino also, Kolpino held out against a furious assault. On 19 September, the Fifty-fifth Army's suburban front stabilized at Pulkovo-Kuzmino-Purtolovo. Meanwhile to the east, in response to a *Stavka* order, the 'Neva operational group' from inside the ring and Kulik's 54th Army from without, aiming for the rail junction of Mga and the supply base of Sinyavino battled for a fortnight (10–26 September) to de-blockade Leningrad.

The attempt failed and, Kulik himself went down with the disaster to the 54th; Khozin took command, while Kulik was later court-martialled, stripped of his marshal's appointment and reduced to major-general.

To the north of Leningrad, since the Germans had failed to break across the Neva, the Finns in spite of intense German prodding showed no inclination to press the assault to Leningrad; on 1 September, the Soviet 23rd Army moved back to the 1939 frontier, stabilizing the line northwards; 12,000 men of the 'Vyborg group' were brought off from Koivisto back to Leningrad, while the 7th Army had for its part fallen back by 10 September to the river Svir, where the line was also ultimately stabilized.

Army Group North had already learned on 12 September of Hitler's decision not to press the storming of Leningrad but rather to envelop it; Stalin, through the agency of the Soviet espionage organization *Rote Kapelle* which had penetrated the German command, also knew of this decision, though the Leningrad command (which appears to have remained ignorant of this intelligence) continued to fight as if an overwhelming assault upon the inner city threatened. The close envelopment, at the range of medium artillery, did not materialize, even as second-best; Zhukov's counter-attacks further weakened and slowed the German assault forces, which were themselves on the eve of being diminished by the withdrawal of Panzer and motorized divisions. The impossibility of drawing the net, the *Einschliessungslinie*, any tighter was admitted by Halder on 18 September.

On the night of 19–20 September, Zhukov's intelligence officer, Brigade Commander P.P. Evstigneyev, was sifting and evaluating an increasing number of reports about the movement of German armour away from Leningrad; that same night the Front engineers had just received a very drastic order, marked 'Immediate', which called for demolition charges to be laid and primed in the city's railway junctions. This top-secret order had been passed from Moscow, like that on organizing the demolition of the major plants and factories in the city, explosive for which had already been distributed. There was, however, growing evidence of German re-deployment; was there any real proof of any slackening in the German attacks? Zhukov was not prepared to accept Evstigneyev's assessment; he shouted that the reports were merely 'provocations' fed in by agents, yet partisans from Pskov and near Krasnogvardeisk both confirmed in detail the German movement and the loading of armour on to flat-cars. At this juncture the German Eighteenth Army had broken through to the Gulf of Finland, thereby threatening the Baltic Fleet's main base; Ju-87 dive-bombers and ships of the Baltic Fleet, whose guns had been trained on and fired at landward targets, were now fighting out what Admiral Tributs called 'their duel', in which the Soviet battleship *Marat*, the cruiser *Kirov* and smaller surface units were crippled by air attack. The city was ablaze with battle; the hospitals were admitting 4,000 civilian casualties a day, and a daily tally of 200 fires was recorded.

Yet on 23 September the German attack on Pulkovo was mounted with only twenty tanks. This and other front-line signs indicated a very real slackening. With the engineers poised over their charges, the gunners and infantrymen crouched in their 'last stand positions', with the city preparing to go to what looked so terrifyingly like its imminent death, this salvation looked unreal. Panzer Group 4, however, was definitely being drained away from Leningrad, just as Evstigneyev's agents reported, in order to take part in Operation Typhoon (*Taifun*) against Moscow.

On 24 September von Leeb, Army Group North commander was reporting that his situation had 'worsened considerably' (*erheblich verscharft*): Finnish pressure in Karelia had 'quite stopped' and he was feeling the hurt of the losses inflicted on his divisions by the 'heavy fighting' of the past days. Zhukov could count on a stabilization of the line by 25 September, but Leningrad was completely cut off, except for the lake Ladoga route. Rations had already been cut on 2 September, the second reduction, and this time the cut was very serious in its implications. The only real relief would have to be managed by some breach of the land blockade, for which Soviet troops had struggled furiously in September; although the 'Neva operational group' managed, at the cost of deadly losses, to establish and to hold a bridgehead on the opposite (southern) bank of the Neva west of Schlusselburg, smashing in the Mga–Syinavino salient, thus freeing the southern shore of lake Ladoga and gaining the use of the Leningrad–Vologda railway proved wholly impossible. What Army Group North had been unable to effect by a quick kill it proposed now to accomplish by the slower and perhaps even more agonizing method of starving the city out.

In the latter part of July the fighting on the Eastern Front had ceased to be ambiguously and unquestionably favourable to the Wehrmacht, although the imbalance was not of such a magnitude as to justify all of Stalin's optimism expressed in his talk with Harry Hopkins. Yet in spite of all its staggering losses, even more staggering, not least to German intelligence registering the presence of fresh Soviet divisions, was the fact that the Red Army had not been obliterated west of the Dnieper–Dvina line; equally unpalatable was the fact that the conclusion of the first phase of 'Barbarossa' had not brought the principal objectives, Leningrad, Moscow and the Donets basin, within effective German reach. Along the German lines of communication and deep in the rear Soviet units continued to fight desperately, while the first signs of a co-ordinated partisan activity could be detected in several areas; the slow, unsure but not entirely unsuccessful Soviet attempts at breaking eastwards through gaps or weak spots in German encirclements made the closer co-operation of German Panzer and infantry formations (with a diminution of the distance involved) a pressing necessity. Blocking the German advance frontally was Timoshenko's force covering Moscow, while Soviet armies and 'operational groups' exerted fierce pressure on exposed German flanks: a situation evolved by the slower advance of Army Group North and South in relation to Army Group Centre. Between Army Group North and Centre, in the 'interval' formed by the marshland of Staraya Russa and Velikie Luki, Soviet divisions had assaulted both German flanks; southwards, between Army Group Centre and South, Potapov's 5th Army had been drawn back to Korosten on the edge of the Pripet Marshes, where it presented an obvious threat to Army Group Centre's extended right flank as well as weighing upon the left wing of Army Group South. These Soviet wedges jammed into the German flanks and front intervals caught an immense share of Hitler's gaze, while his attention was fully seized by the economic goals – the grain, metals and oil – which lay in southern Russia.

Of overriding importance was the need to settle upon the future commitment of Army Group Centre's Panzer forces in the light of Hitler's reservations about the implementation of the original 'Barbarossa' directive; they could swing north (against Leningrad), south (to speed up von Rundstedt) or remain with von Bock for a full-strength drive against Moscow. It was for the latter that the military declared themselves, to strike in full strength and at full speed against Moscow, accepting the calculated risk on the flanks; an operational plan to this end was therefore drawn up and submitted. Hitler evolved a variant of his own, which with vital re-adjustments of time and space changed the issue from that of 'Moscow or the Ukraine' to 'Moscow *and* the Ukraine'. His *Instruction* of 21 August levelled the opposition of the high command, making 'the seizure of the Crimea' (and the Donets) of prime operational importance, while in the north Leningrad was to be 'isolated' and a junction with the Finns effected; only the hermetic sealing off of Leningrad, the junction with the Finns and the destruction of the Soviet 5th Army would provide those 'prerequisites' for a successful outcome of an assault on Timoshenko at the centre. It was a design not lacking in a subtlety of its own, but the precautional overtones, explicit in the present renunciation of an immediate and rapid blow at the centre, spelt admission that the blitzkrieg had been bludgeoned to a pause by Timoshenko and by Kirponos, each in his own way.

Amidst all this scurry of conferences and consultations within the German command, the fury of the Soviet counter-attacks began to wane at the end of July. Voroshilov's flank blow at Manstein had been parried by 18 July, although under instructions from the *Stavka* he was preparing his major blow at Staraya Russa with 48th, 11th and 34th Armies (the latter moved from the Reserve Front for this very purpose). On the right wing of the Western Front, a German division on 20 July had broken into the rear of 22nd Army and taken Velikie Luki; in very fierce counter-attacks the body of 22nd Army operated with its other elements east of Nevel to hold up a deep German envelopment from the north and a threat to the left wing of the North-Western Front. By the end of July, 22nd Army supported by its neighbour 29th Army was struggling to dig in and hold the line running from the upper reaches of the river Lovat–Velikie Luki–lake Dvina; this barrier continued to hold throughout the month of

August. In the German rear, at Moghilev on the Dnieper, Lieutenant-General Gerasimenko's 13th Army with its two rifle corps (61st and 45th) fought on doggedly; surrounded by four German divisions, on the morning of 26 July the Soviet garrisons blew up the wooden bridge connecting the western and eastern parts of the town and immured themselves within their positions. Four days earlier the Soviet General Staff had asked Timoshenko for 'definite information' on the Moghilev defenders: Major-General Romanov, 172nd Rifle Division commander, finally reported from the town, asking for ammunition, a small amount of which was air-dropped. Major-General Bakunin's 61st Corps was 'in full encirclement', though a break-out attempt was timed for dawn, 27 July, with three columns moving on Mstislav–Roslavl; meanwhile elements of 45th Corps had managed to fight their way out eastwards and cross the river Sozh, on whose far bank a whole assortment of units gathered, including a remnant of 13th Mechanized Corps, the rear echelon of 4th Army and part of 13th Army.

Neighbour to 13th Army on the very left of the Western Front was 21st Army, with three rifle corps (63rd, 66th and 67th) and Krivoshein's 25th Mechanized Corps; two armoured trains (No. 51 and No. 52) with 2,000 riflemen were even so now cut off to the west and contact with them had ceased. To hold a line from south of Moghilev (Novy Bykhov) to Loev, 21st Army had eight rifle divisions; in command, 21st Army had a virtual procession of senior officers, first Gerasimenko, then Marshal Budenny himself, followed by Lieutenant-General Yefremov, Colonel-General F.I. Kuznetsov and Major-General V.N. Gordov. In mid July, 21st Army counter-attacked between Rogachev and Zhlobin in the direction of Bobruisk, and a week later a 'cavalry group' (three divisions) swinging south-west of Bobruisk raided the German Second Army's lines of communication. The *Stavka* decided on 24 July to combine the 21st and 13th Armies on 24 July into the Central Front under Colonel-General F.I. Kuznetsov, the gloomy ex-commander from the Baltic, still hampered by his leg wounds; for air support, the *Stavka* scraped up 136 planes (seventy-five of them patched and repaired) and assigned Major-General (Aviation) G.A. Vorozheikin as tactical air commander. Colonel Sandalov, one of the coolest heads from the sorely-tried 4th Army, took over as Front chief of staff. Establishing the Central Front amounted to splitting the Western Front; Kuznetsov was ordered to secure the junction between the Western and South-Western Fronts, and at the same time to continue his 'active operations' to support Timoshenko battling north and south of Smolensk. Small and disorganized as it was, the Central Front formed the main Soviet barrier to the North Ukraine, and was built out of the 'Gomel concentration' of Soviet units – a 'lid' which needed to be kept fastened down at all costs. It was Stalin himself who unbarred it.

At the very centre, two Soviet armies, 16th and 20th, had to be pulled out of encirclement north of Smolensk; to provide some support in depth for the shattered first echelon of the Western Front, on 20 July the *Stavka* ordered General Zhukov's Reserve Front to move westwards. This brought four armies, 29th,

30th, 24th and 28th, which had been forming up on the Ostahskov–Rzhev–
Yelnaya line, into action to support the 16th and 20th; 29th Army would attack
south of Toropets, 30th south-west of Belyi, 24th at Yartsevo (in conjunction
with the 16th), 28th from south-east of Roslavl. Operating as 'Army Groups'
finally, identified by their commander's name, these formations crashed against
the Yelnaya salient during the days when Hitler was contemplating his second-
stage objectives. By 8 August, Guderian had broken up Kachalov's 28th Army
with its 'assault groups'; on 4 August, 28th Army had signalled its desperate
plight to Western Front HQ,

> 28th Army fighting superior enemy forces, encircled in area Yermolino, Samodidino,
> Lyslovka, Shkuratovka, Ozeryavino. Formations making their way in a south-easterly
> direction, one group through Roslavl, other to the east. Assignment to break through to
> river Oster. Formations suffering massive losses, unfit for combat. Request air support
> particularly fighters.
>> Yegorov (Chief of Staff) Prilonko.

Such remnants as survived from 28th Army were sent to the Reserve Front;
General Kachalov himself died fighting in a tank near the village of Starinka.
In the subsequent inquiry conducted by Mekhlis, the officers of the Military
Soviet who defended their commander were brutally silenced by Mekhlis him-
self who called them 'political juveniles, who do not understand that Kachalov
had with premeditation gone over to the Germans . . .'.

Guderian had cleared the way to Bryansk; he now proceeded to clear his right
flank by swinging 24th Panzer Corps south-west from Roslavl to Krichev, a
second encirclement which was concluded on 14 August, followed by yet one
more plunge, this time southwards, against the 'Gomel concentration'. In one
week, Guderian's armour and mobile forces had sliced through the Gomel–
Bryansk–Moscow rail link, and reached advanced positions at Starodub and
Pochep. It was during this mid August crisis on the left wing of the Western
Front, with Guderian's armour wheeling and slicing through Soviet forces on
his flank, that Stalin blundered outright. At the beginning of August, Timoshenko
had ordered Yeremenko to report to his headquarters at Kasna, some ten miles
north of Bryansk; Yeremenko had been supervising the withdrawal of 16th and
20th Armies, but on his arrival at Kasna he was told by Timoshenko to proceed
to the *Stavka* in Moscow, where he arrived on 12 August, reporting that night to
Stalin and Shaposhnikov. Yeremenko went into the *Stavka* war-room with
Colonel-General F.I. Kuznetsov who was under similar summons. With Stalin
were the GKO members Malenkov, Molotov, and Beria, and Shaposhnikov of the
General Staff; Shaposhnikov led off with a 'short outline' of the situation at the
front, concluding that in the immediate future the enemy would strike in the
south at the Crimea, in the central sector of the front from Moghilev–Gomel at
Bryansk and thereafter at Orel and Moscow.

Here Stalin took over, showing Yeremenko and Kuznetsov the situation on his own maps, repeating some of what Shaposhnikov had said, but emphasizing that the German drives had to be halted on both the Bryansk and the Crimean axes. For that reason, it was proposed to establish the Bryansk Front and an Independent Army to cover the Crimea. Where, Stalin asked, did Yeremenko wish to be posted? Yeremenko made some remarks about serving where he was needed, at which Stalin turned on him for a precise answer; Yeremenko, having asked to be sent to the 'most difficult sector' was told that both – Bryansk and the Crimea – were 'difficult'. Finally Yeremenko blurted out that he knew something about armoured war and should be sent where enemy armour would attack. This remark pleased Stalin. Kuznetsov, similarly grilled, replied that he was a soldier and would fight wherever he was sent. 'So, so, a soldier,' mocked Stalin, 'but what is your own opinion?' Kuznetsov clung to his martial dignities and merely repeated himself, whereupon Stalin swung on Yeremenko and announced his decision:

You, Comrade Yeremenko, are appointed commander of the Bryansk Front. To-morrow you will go there and organize the Front at top speed. Guderian's tank group is operating on the Bryansk axis, and there will be some heavy fighting. So you will have your wish. You will meet the mechanized forces of your 'old friend' Guderian, whose methods should be known to you from the Western Front.

Yeremenko was also to go at once to Mekhlis at the Main Political Administration and select his officers for the Military Soviet of the new Front. Kuznetsov was told that he would go to the Crimea and both appointment orders were signed on the spot. Stalin turned once more to Yeremenko with a final remark: 'We are laying a major responsibility on the Bryansk Front – your main target – to cover the Moscow strategic area from the south-west and not to permit Guderian's tank group to break through the Bryansk Front to Moscow.' At this, and scrutinizing Yeremenko, Stalin seemed to wait for a reply; Yeremenko added, 'I understand the assignment and will see that it is carried out.'

Stalin's incisiveness was certainly prompted by his receipt of intelligence that the German plan was to strike at Moscow through Bryansk area; Guderian's present thrusts seemed to confirm this. Such high-level information as Stalin's intelligence service had obtained did correspond to the actualities of German military planning, but confined as it was to the first half of August, it did not include Hitler's subsequent 'prerequisites' for the success of the Moscow operation. Stalin's estimate and presentation of German intentions was basically correct, but it was only provisionally valid. In its instructions to Timoshenko, the *Stavka* interpreted German movement on the flanks as the consequence of the failure to succeed by frontal assault; for this reason, Timoshenko was ordered to concentrate on the Velikie Luki and Gomel salients, and his attack orders of 25 August (which involved the Western, Bryansk and Reserve Fronts) envisaged intensified counter-attack, one object of which was to relieve pressure on the Central Front, the 'Gomel group'. Meanwhile Voroshilov had already set in motion his Staraya Russa operations, in which the 'interval' between Army Group North and Centre was utilized, not least by 34th Army.

The commander of the Reserve Front, General Zhukov, was nevertheless disturbed, and drew his own conclusions from this mighty threshing on the flanks. On 18 August, he submitted his own report to Stalin and the *Stavka*:

> The enemy, persuaded of the concentration of powerful concentrations of our forces on the road to Moscow, having on his flanks the Central Front and the Velikie Luki grouping of our forces, has temporarily given up the blow at Moscow and, turning to active defence against the Western and the Reserve Fronts, has thrown all his mobile shock and tank units against the Central, South-Western and Southern Fronts.
>
> Possible enemy intentions: to destroy the Central Front, and, breaking into the area Chernigov-Konotop-Priluki, with a blow from the rear thereby to destroy the South-Western Front.

Zhukov therefore suggested a rapid and effective concentration in Bryansk in order to strike a flank blow at this German assault. Zhukov got a reply within twenty-four hours (19 August):

> Your considerations concerning possible German movement in the direction of Chernigov-Konotop-Priluki I consider to be correct. Such German movement would signify the outflanking of our Kiev concentration from the eastern bank of the Dnieper and the encirclement of our 3rd and 21st Armies. Having foreseen such an undesired eventuality, and in order to prevent its taking place the Bryansk Front with Yeremenko in command has been set up. Other measures are being taken, about which I will inform you specially. We are hoping to stop the Germans.
>
> Stalin. Shaposhnikov.

The Gomel–Starodub thrust had not escaped the attention of Marshal Budenny, who was concerned for his flank and thus for his nearest neighbour, the Central Front. On 16 August, he had signalled the *Stavka* about the danger to Potapov's 5th Army north-west of Kiev in the event of further German southerly movement. This, and Zhukov's intervention, brought a flood of orders within hours.

As he replied to Zhukov, Stalin ordered South-Western Front Forces (with the exception of 37th Army at Kiev) to be pulled back to the Dnieper, to hold the river line from Loev to Perevochna, and thus to cover the Chernigov–Konotop–Kharkov approach; the bridgeheads south of Kiev were to be evacuated to reinforce the defences on the left bank of the Dnieper and also to provide a reserve. Potapov with the 5th disengaged very skilfully but Artemeyev with 27th Corps a little to the south made a mess of the operation. The next day (20 August) Stalin assigned Yeremenko a new task – the destruction of Guderian's Panzer Group 2; Major-General Yefremov in command of Central Front was instructed to pull back the 3rd and 21st Armies to secure the front (Bryansk–Central) junction. Meanwhile 3rd and 4th Panzer Divisions ground south past Starodub to the river Desna, where just north of Novgorod–Severskii 3rd Panzer captured intact the 750-yard bridge on 25 August; this drive was covered to the east by 17th Panzer also driving south through Pochep.

Immediately before Stalin had contacted Yeremenko by telegraph; the Supreme Commander was obviously bemused by the movement of German armoured and mobile forces, and desperate to halt Guderian:

Stalin: I have some questions to put to you:

    1 Does it not follow to disband the Central Front, unite 3rd Army with 21st Army and subordinate them to you?

[Question 2 misnumbered to 3]

    3 We can send you in some days, tomorrow, in a very short time, the day after tomorrow, two tank brigades with a few KV tanks and two–three tank battalions How badly do you need these?

    4 If you promise to beat that villain Guderian, we can send you a few more aviation regiments and some RS [RS: 'Katyusha' rocket-launchers] battalions. Your reply?

Yeremenko:

    1 My opinion about disbanding Central Front as follows: in connection with the fact that I wish to beat Guderian and really beat him, it is necessary strongly to secure that approach from the south, but that means solid co-operation from the Bryansk area. I therefore request you to subordinate 21st Army united with 3rd Army to me.

    3 I thank you very much for reinforcing me with tanks and aircraft. I ask you only to speed their dispatch, we need them very, very badly. As for the villain Guderian we are trying at all costs to beat him, to fulfil the task assigned by you, which is to beat him.

The Central Front was disbanded forthwith. Yet as Stalin put his questions to Yeremenko, Shaposhnikov gave him another set of orders; Shaposhnikov insisted that Guderian was striking at the northern (right) wing of the Bryansk Front, against 217th and 279th Rifle Divisions of 50th Army, with a possible blow 'against Zhizdra and the outflanking of Bryansk from the north'. Shaposhnikov ordered Yeremenko forthwith to reinforce this sector for an assault expected 'tomorrow or the day after' (25–6 August). This meant shifting 50th Army in the very opposite direction to where it was needed – away from Pochep and up to Zhizdra; Yeremenko thus lost his main striking force but still had 'to beat Guderian', for which purpose Stalin and Shaposhnikov, with almost ludicrous faith, appeared to think the Bryansk force adequate. Yeremenko had on paper two armies, 50th and 13th, with eight rifle divisions each, three cavalry divisions and one tank division but many of these formations were badly whittled down by battle losses. The two new armies he was getting – 21st and 3rd – were in any case dispersed or spent, although the *Stavka* promised a reinforcement of 27,000 men for 21st Army.

Marshal Budenny also had a vital interest in the Central Front, seeking to keep the 'lid' on his own front battened down. On 25 August he had himself suggested to the *Stavka* that the Central Front be reinforced with Potapov's 5th Army, or that the two armies of the Central Front be subordinated to the South-Western Front so that it could then secure its junction with the Bryansk Front.

Budenny's suggestions, which would have set up a unified command north-east of Kiev, were turned down. What Budenny did get was the 40th Army (formed out of the 37th and 26th Armies), put under the command of Major-General K.P. Podlas and assembled by 25 August out of the 135th and 293rd Rifle Divisions, 2nd Parachute Corps, 10th Tank Division and 5th Anti-Tank Brigade all, either new units or units already badly worn down by battle. This was to underpin the Bryansk-South-Western Front junction.

Soviet aerial reconnaissance on 25 August put the southerly German movement into plain relief, yet with German units over the Desna, and with only the flimsy 40th Army deployed, it was essential to anticipate the direction of fresh blows. Using the tanks and aircraft sent by Stalin, who had dipped into his special 'Supreme Command reserve', Yeremenko had already launched his first counter-attacks, which only brought 13th Army into further disrepair. Stalin on 2 September sent Yeremenko and the special aviation commander at Bryansk, no less than the deputy commander of the Soviet Air Force, Major-General I.F. Petrov, a furious signal:

To Yeremenko and Petrov:
    The *Stavka* is much displeased with your work. In spite of the efforts of aviation and ground units, Pochep and Starodub remain in enemy hands. This means that you are just nibbling at the enemy, but you can't shift him. Guderian and the whole of his group must be smashed into smithereens [*vdrebezgi*]. Until this happens, all your statements about success are worthless. I await your reports on the destruction of Guderian's group.

This was an unpromising start to Yeremenko's concentric blow against Starodub; Stalin was clearly aggrieved at the lack of results with the air strikes, which had 464 aircraft behind them – 230 bombers, 179 fighters, 55 ground-attack planes (the combined air strength of the Reserve, Central and Bryansk Fronts, the 1st Reserve Aviation Group, and units of the Long-Range Bomber Force, ADD).

Yeremenko now received his full instructions; on 30 August the *Stavka* had transmitted orders for a double operation by the Bryansk Front, to cover the period up to 15 September. The first attack was to be made in the Roslavl direction, in co-operation with the 43rd Army of Zhukov's Reserve Front, for which Yeremenko was to allocate at least four divisions of his 50th Army. The second operation was aimed south-westwards, directed against 24th Panzer Corps in Pochep-Staroduv-Novgorod Severskii region, to be mounted with not less than ten divisions supported by armour. Yeremenko had argued for just one powerful blow; in this he was overruled by the *Stavka*. The responsibility for destroying Guderian was laid squarely on the Bryansk Front, nevertheless, and Yeremenko had the elements of four armies with which to do it – 50th, 13th, 3rd and 21st. (He was on the point of dismissing from his command Major-General K.D. Golubev, the commander of the 13th, for gross inefficiency; the *Stavka* had agreed to appoint Major-General A.M. Gorodnyanskii in his place.)

For eight fierce days Yeremenko fought Guderian's armour at the Desna; early in September, 3rd Panzer ripped 3rd and 21st Armies apart, and pressed 21st Army back on to the Desna, where it was cut off from the main force of the Bryansk Front. On 2 September, the *Stavka* ordered Marshal Budenny to secure the defence of Chernigov, but Budenny had nothing, having been earlier denied 31st Army, with which to close the hole between Shostka on the Desna and Chernigov. Meanwhile 3rd Panzer, followed rapidly by 4th Panzer Division to the east, raced for the river Seim, crossed by 7 September and raced faster for Konotop. Guderian was in Budenny's rear. For all its reinforcement, the Bryansk wall had fallen in; the Bryansk and South-Western Fronts had been torn apart, and the breach stretched now for more than twenty miles. For all his assurances to Stalin, Yeremenko had not destroyed 'the villain Guderian'.

On the 'South-Western axis', where Marshal Budenny was in control with Kirponos and Tyulenev as his front commanders, it had been throughout August the situation at the junction between the South-Western and Southern Fronts which first gave rise to acute anxiety. Potapov's 5th Army continued to lie on the German Sixth Army's northern flank; General Vlasov's 37th Army held the Kiev 'fortified district' against German assault, which had however swung south-eastwards. Two Soviet armies, the 6th and 26th, were split apart; Kirponos could keep contact with his left only by radio, and could in no wise supply them from his bases. Since 6th and 12th Armies were cut off in what was practically Southern Front territory, late on the evening of 25 July the *Stavka* subordinated these formations to the Southern Front Command. Kirponos's 26th Army was struggling to defend the Rzhishchev and Kanevsk crossings over the Dnieper south-west of Kiev; to hold the Cherkassy bridgehead on the Dnieper, Kirponos ordered the 38th Army to form up, using the staff and administration of 8th Mechanized Corps and keeping Lieutenant-General Ryabyshev as commander. Ryabyshev took over such units as were then in the Cherkassy area.

Panzer Group 1 under Kleist, striking south and south-west from Belaya Tserkov, had by the beginning of August trapped two Soviet armies, 6th and 12th, with elements of the 18th, in the Uman 'pocket'. Budenny ordered 26th Army to attack in the Boguslav–Zvenigorodka direction, in an effort to relieve the pressure on Uman; it was a brave attempt to promote a break-out, but it failed. Tyulenev was beside himself with rage; on 25 July, 6th and 12th Armies, even then in semi-encirclement, had been unified under the command of Major-General P.G. Ponedelin (12th Army), and ordered to pull back to escape von Kleist. Reporting to the *Stavka* and to Marshal Budenny on 4 August, Tyulenev denounced Ponedelin bitterly:

Group Ponedelin continues to remain in its present positions, on account of a completely incomprehensible slowness in carrying out repeated orders to pull units back behind the river Sinyukh.

We are in contact with Ponedelin by radio, and by aircraft and even on 2 August a staff officer from Ponedelin arrived at Front HQ by lorry. 3 August a plane took off from him, sent by us to meet aircraft carrying ammunition and fuel to Ponedelin. The pilot reported that in spite of the complete concordance of recognition signals and the landing sites for transport aircraft, to fly on to make the landings was impossible because of the hurricane of fire opened up by Ponedelin's forces against our own aircraft. One of them was shot down.

Tyulenev's 18th Army, fighting on the right flank to assist a break-out, was itself now half-encircled, being forced therefore to fall back on the Southern Bug. Tyulenev at this juncture had to face the fact that the whole of his right wing between the Dniester and the Southern Bug was being smashed in. The question facing the Military Soviet of the Southern Front was: where to now? This was the substance of Tyulenev's report to Budenny and the *Stavka* on 6 August:

The availability of Southern Front forces due to losses and wear as a consequence of uninterrupted six days of operations makes it quite out of the question for those lines – particularly at the junction with the South-Western Front at Kirov-Znamensk and Kremenchug – to be firmly held by our forces.

This consideration on the part of the Military Soviet of the Front does not meet with the approval of the General Staff, but the Front forces under the blows of superior enemy forces on the right flank have fallen back and are falling back and are fighting in unfavourable conditions.

Comrade Stalin's order in conversation with the commander of the South-Western Front for a basic defence line running from Kherson-river Ingulets-Krivoi Rog-Kremenchug – thence along the Dnieper seems in the prevailing conditions to be the only reasonable measure.

The line Znamenka-Kirovo-Nikolayev, suggested by the *Glavkom* South-west, can serve as a forward position in relation to the establishment of a basic defence line. For this, in order to exploit this line as a forward one, it is very urgent to hold and defend its battle-worthy units in the Smela-Kirovo sector; both of these points are at present under direct enemy threat.

Tyulenev then relayed his present positions, reported on the formation of a 'reserve army' under Lieutenant-General Chibisov from the *Stavka* reinforcement of nine rifle and three cavalry divisions, and asked 'what help the central operational organs' could give.

For a fortnight, Tyulenev received no reply; in that time, 9th Army had to fall back eastwards to Nikolayev, and the Coastal 'group' to the south on Odessa. On 14 August, Tyulenev called a meeting of his commanders, the generals Smirnov, Malinovskii, Belov (cavalry commander) and their staffs; three days later, the 2nd Cavalry Corps, 18th and 9th Armies moved across the river Ingulets and were ordered to the eastern bank of the Dnieper. Chibisov's 'reserve army' was at Dniepropetrovsk, eight rifle and three cavalry divisions, two tank brigades – with not an anti-tank gun or machine-gun between them; Chibisov was now to move west to bear upon the German attack against Nikolayevsk.

The Soviet naval base of Odessa, attacked from its landward side, had now to fight for its life: the Military Soviet of the Black Sea Fleet received on 27 July categorical orders to the effect that, 'the situation on the land front notwithstanding, Odessa is not to be surrendered'. Rear-Admiral G.V. Zhukov, Odessa base commander, was in turn given immediate instructions to set up a land-based defence, to halt the evacuation of troops and to send on to Sevastopol only those units not needed for the base defence. Militia units were hurriedly formed and hastily armed. Admiral Oktyabrskii had already stamped on general evacuation plans: 'Cut out the talk, suppress any panic, build up the defences, fight and don't surrender.' The garrison orders of the 'Odessa defensive zone' (OOR) went into immediate effect: 'From 19.00 hours 8 August Odessa and its environs are placed on a siege footing.' Until October the 'Odessa defence zone' hung on as grimly as it had been ordered to do, a joint Red Army-Soviet Navy operation which reflected much credit on both, and which was a hint of things to come in the great siege of Sevastopol. Stalin, at the session where Yeremenko was assigned to Bryansk, had just entrusted to Colonel-General Kuznetsov the defence of the Crimea to the east and the blocking of the German advance upon it.

In mid August, however, as the great lateral fissures appeared in the Soviet fronts to the north, Budenny's attention, fixed till now on defending on the Dnieper and securing the Southern–South-Western Front junction, swung sharply to his right wing as German armour struck down to Starodub. Both extremities of the 'South-Western axis' were seriously menaced. Zhukov had already uttered his warning about the possible destruction of the South-Western Front to Stalin and the *Stavka* on 18 August, one more pressure to follow Budenny's signal to the *Stavka* of 16 August requesting permission to adjust his right wing deployment:

The withdrawal of the right flank is prompted even more by the fact that our neighbour the Central Front, according to the information to hand, is fighting at the approaches [to] the Bryansk-Uchena line. The quicker we establish reserves for the right flank of the South-Western Front, the more stable will be our position . . .

If the *Stavka* of the Supreme Commander will permit the withdrawal of our Fifth Army and 27th Rifle Corps of South-Western Front to the river Dnieper, that will make possible the bringing into reserve 2–3 rifle divisions and lead to the reorganization of seven tank and motorized divisions. This will give the possibility of having in reserve a couple more rifle divisions.

S. Budenny
N. Khrushchev

16 August

The *Stavka* on this occasion responded positively and gave Budenny permission on 19 August, although four days later units of the German Sixth Army did cross the Dnieper in 27th Corps area at Okuninov and struck on for Oster, north-west of Kiev. That serious reverse had a drastic and unwholesomely surprising counterpart a week later on the left flank when on 31 August Major-

General Feklenko (who had just taken over 38th Army from Ryabyshev) reported a successful German assault crossing of the Dnieper south-east of Kremenchug. As he himself had predicted, Budenny was nailed down mercilessly on his flanks, with threats to his rear from north and south. To protect the north he proposed (25 August) giving 5th Army to the Central Front (or alternatively giving him 21st Army); he had in mind a plan to unify 21st, 26th and 38th Armies in the latter event. He had only the flimsy 40th Army to hold the 'lid' on his front, and this formation was already committed to holding off Guderian between the Desna and the Seim, northwards from Konotop to Bakhmach.

With a sharper sense of impending doom than that prevailing in the *Stavka*, Front and field commanders hammered upon Moscow for aid and comfort. On 4 September Budenny submitted a special, personal report to 'the Supreme Commander', underlining the grave threat to his flanks and asking for immediate reinforcement, or, if this was beyond the resources of the *Stavka*, for authorization to create his own reserve by taking two divisions from the Kiev garrison and two divisions from 26th Army. Shaposhnikov duly replied the very same day, informing Budenny that 'the Supreme Commander' would not permit any such internal regrouping. Kirponos had meanwhile ordered a special command group, Parsegov (artillery), Volskii (armour) and Lozovskii-Shevchenko (aviation), to 38th Army, where the German bridgehead at Kremenchug presented a serious threat; the command group found the 38th bereft of tanks and short of ammunition and without any air cover, but a counter-blow was planned for 8 September. The army which Budenny had earlier asked for, the 21st, was on 6 September finally subordinated to his command, since it was (and had been for some time) operating between two of the South-Western Front formations; 21st Army had been ten days under Yeremenko, to whom the *Stavka* 'threw' the gap between the Bryansk and South-Western Fronts, although Stalin and Shaposhnikov knew now that Yeremenko could not close it.

The intensity of the crisis grew apace between 7–10 September. On Budenny's right flank, 5th Army was threatened with being split in two (by the German Second Army coming from the east and the Sixth Army with its northerly out-flanking of Kiev); Kirponos could not extricate his exposed 5th Army for the *Stavka* refused permission, still hoping for results from the Bryansk Front blows. But 'only a miracle' (in the words of Kirponos's operations officer, Colonel Bagramyan) could save 5th Army; on 7 September the Military Soviet South-Western Front sent a special signal to the *Stavka* insisting on the urgency of withdrawal. To the south, elements of Panzer Group 1 were present in the Kremenchug bridgehead. Shaposhnikov decided to consult Budenny about the 5th Army's position also on 7 September; Budenny backed Kirponos to the hilt. Two days later, 9 September, Shaposhnikov signalled Kirponos: 'The Supreme Commander has authorized the withdrawal of 5th Army and right flank 37th Army to the river Desna.' But it was much too late. Potapov's 5th Army was trapped.

On the morning of 10 September, 38th Army's counter-attacks against the Kremenchug bridgehead were pushed in once more, with Colonel A.A. Grechko's 34th Cavalry Division enjoying some success. But on that same morning Podlas of 40th Army reported the exhaustion of available reserves; when Guderian attacked again, there would be nothing to stop him. Guderian crashed in Konotop and raced for Romny, in the deep rear of Budenny, while from the south Panzer Group I was now loosed across the Dnieper at Kremen-chug, from which 16th Panzer Division drove furiously for Lubny and towards Guderian's Panzer Group 2, the outer armoured wings of a mighty encircle-ment. Kirponos could not bring even one regiment to bear against Guderian in his furious drive for Romny; with 40th Army split and broken, only the twenty tanks of Major-General Semenchenko's 10th Tank Division were left. Potapov had fallen back on the Desna, only to find German units in full possession there. Kirponos appealed to Budenny for help; Budenny, his reserves fully spent, could offer none. All that Budenny could do was to press for an evacuation of the Kiev salient. Kirponos was evidently under no illusions about that. Discussing it with his staff, Kirponos pointed out that Shaposhnikov would 'put the question, academic-style, to Comrade Stalin: "What do you propose, Comrade Stalin, permit them to withdraw?"' Stalin and the *Stavka*, Kirponos argued, were still convinced that Yeremenko could bring down Guderian.

Kirponos was right. Budenny found this for himself on the night of Septem-ber 10, when he complained to Shaposhnikov that the 2nd Cavalry Corps had been assigned to Yeremenko, who never received these troops, to close the gap which had now grown to a full thirty miles: this deprived the Southern Front of its 'only instrument' in the Dniepropetrovsk–Kharkov area. And why give it to Yeremenko, anyway, which was the case of the 21st Army all over again? Budenny continued: 'I beg you to turn your attention to Yeremenko's opera-tions, which were to destroy that enemy grouping, but in fact nothing has been achieved in that particular direction.' Shaposhnikov now swung Stalin on Budenny, reminding him that, 'The responsibility for that operation the Sup-reme Commander assigned to Yeremenko. I request you, no delay, route Cav. Corps to Putivl.' Budenny was not yet finished, however: 'Very well . . . I will issue the order at once about the Cav. Corps. I ask you to pass my opinion to the Supreme Commander and in particular my opinion about the operations of the Bryansk Front.' The next day Budenny sent Stalin a signal requesting permis-sion to withdraw from the Kiev salient. After refuting Shaposhnikov, Budenny went on:

For my part I suggest, that at the present moment an enemy intention to outflank and to encircle the South-Western Front from the direction of Novgorod-Severskii and Kremenchug is perfectly apparent. To circumvent this a powerful concentration of troops must be established. In its present state the South-Western Front cannot do this.

If the *Stavka* for its part cannot concentrate at this time such a powerful concentration, then withdrawal for the South-Western Front appears to be absolutely ripe.

Delay with the withdrawal of the South-Western Front will lead to losses in men and a huge quantity of equipment.

This produced two results: Stalin telephoned Kirponos at once and categorically forbade him to pull any troops back, and Stalin relieved Budenny of his command. That same night Shaposhnikov, too, telephoned Kirponos (he had also telephoned on the 10th, to reassure Kirponos that he would give Stalin the full picture 'at the first favourable moment'); Shaposhnikov repeated his assurances about Yeremenko, adding,

. . . it is essential that you liquidate in the next three days the enemy's forward elements at Romny, for which, I think, you can quickly shift two divisions with anti-tank guns to Lokhvitsa to meet up with enemy motor-mechanized units. And, finally, most essential – smash him up with aircraft. I have already ordered Yeremenko to employ the mass of the Supreme Command Reserve aircraft against 3rd and 4th Panzer Divisions operating in the Bakhmach, Romny area. The terrain here is open and the enemy is easily vulnerable to our planes.

It was much as Kirponos suspected; Shaposhnikov was afraid to disclose the true state of affairs to Stalin.

On 11 September also, Kirponos and Budenny talked by telephone about the situation at Romny, and to discuss the fate of five armies: 40th, 21st, 5th, 37th, 26th. The only way to supply them now was by air. 'Such a mass of troops cannot be supplied by air: order at once the most stringent economy in ammunition and supplies.' That, with the hope that they would soon have permission to pull back, was all Budenny could suggest. He was, however, no longer *Glavkom* South-West; on 12 September Stalin appointed Marshal Timoshenko to this post, and abolished Timoshenko's *Glavkom* 'West' completely. Timoshenko fell in with Kirponos's plans to halt 38th Army offensive operations and to use 2nd Cavalry Corps in the north, but on evacuating the Kiev garrisons he referred this to Stalin. Tupikov, chief of staff to Kirponos, tried once again to convince Shaposhnikov that the situation was grave almost beyond repair; on his own initiative he sent a telegram on 14 September to the General Staff, ending with, 'This is the beginning as you know of catastrophe – a matter of a couple of days.' Whether Shaposhnikov ever showed this to Stalin remains in doubt, but he replied first to brand Tupikov a 'panic-monger' and second to repeat 'You will execute at once the orders of Comrade Stalin, issued to you on 11.9.' That day, at 18.20 hours, Panzer Group 1 (Kleist) and 2 (Guderian) linked up more than 100 miles to the east of Kiev, in the Lokhvitsa-Lubny area; five Soviet armies were now skewered by these armoured spikes. Shaposhnikov's telegram to Tupikov had forbidden 'glancing backwards'; now there was nowhere to glance as a result of *Stavka* stubbornness.

The white Very lights, which always signified German presence, and which had been exchanged between Guderian's 3rd Panzer on meeting Kleist's 16th Panzer east of Kiev, were themselves the mere tokens of encirclement. But the outer armoured ring thickened: the inner infantry ring tightened. Colonel Bagramyan had been sent by Kirponos to Timoshenko's HQ to report on the situation; Marshal Timoshenko talked at length with Bagramyan, hinting that he might be consulting Stalin later during the day, and giving him finally the verbal authorization of the Military Soviet of the South-Western *Glavkom* for a withdrawal by Kirponos to the rear line at the Psel. Timoshenko was quite blunt: 'Each fresh day of delay only increases the scale of the catastrophe.' But Bagramyan had no written order to confirm this decision; all he had was Timoshenko's order to be flown out from Poltava, back to Kirponos, who immediately asked for confirmation. Burmistenko advised Kirponos to radio Stalin about Timoshenko's authorization; on the sixteenth Kirponos sent off his signal:

Glavkom Timoshenko through the person of the deputy chief of staff of the front issued verbal instruction: basic assignment – withdrawal of Front armies to river Psel, and destruction of enemy mobile formations in Romny-Lubny area. To leave behind minimum forces to cover Dnieper and Kiev.

Written directives of *Glavkom* especially make no mention of withdrawal to river Psel and authorize withdrawal from Kiev garrison of only a part of the forces. There is a contradiction. Which order to fulfil? I consider that pulling troops back to the Psel is correct, which means immediate and complete withdrawal from Kiev and the river Dnieper. Urgently request your instructions.

KIRPONOS

At 23.40 hours, 17 September, Shaposhnikov sent a *Stavka* signal to Kirponos: 'The Supreme Commander authorized withdrawal from Kiev.' But nothing was said about falling back to the rear. Burmistenko, looking at this 'non-logical decision' in the early hours of 18 September, remarked that 'he says "a" without wishing to say "b" '; he advised Kirponos to follow Timoshenko's instructions.

Within twenty-four hours, Kiev fell. In the early hours of September 18 Kirponos had issued orders from his Front HQ at Verkhoyarovka (six miles north-west of Piryatin) for a Front break-out: no signal could be sent to Vlasov's 37th Army in Kiev, for contact had been lost. Timoshenko's staff had left by now for Kharkov, though Major-General Sergeyev, one of Timoshenko's special adjutants, was left behind to report on the situation. He later flew over Kirponos's HQ, but sighted only 'large columns of German tanks to the north and south'. The whole of Stalin's Ukrainian command now began to topple in enormous ruins; in groups large and small Soviet units tried to break east. At dawn on 20 September, some seven miles south-west of Lokhvitsa, Kirponos's command column, a thousand strong, with his own staff and that of 5th Army, was ambushed and encircled; in the evening, already wounded in the leg, Kirponos was hit by mine splinters in the head and chest. He died in less than two minutes.* Potapov and his officers were taken prisoner. Bagramyan had elsewhere broken out with about fifty men. Vlasov from Kiev fought his way back east: General Kostenko of 26th Army, V.I. Kuznetsov of 21st Army, generals Lopatin, Moskalenko and Korzun also made it. The Germans claimed 655,000 prisoners: the Russians assert that the entire strength of South-Western Front in late August was 677,085 men, and that 150,541 men had escaped or fought out of the trap. Losses in Soviet divisions had been demonstrably very heavy; in early September, 21st Army had only 8 per cent of its men left in the rifle divisions. But by any reckoning the wound to the Red Army was deep and dangerous.

At the end of September, Stalin abolished the *Glavkom* South-West; Timoshenko was put in command of the South-Western Front, with its remnants of the 40th, 21st and 38th Armies plus units of the 6th Army from the Southern Front, from which Tyulenev had been taken wounded and Ryabyshev put in his place. Of the three *Glavkom*, only one had survived, Timoshenko; Voroshilov had been removed for incompetence, Budenny for insubordination. On the scene of his former triumphs, where the 1st Cavalry Army had once fought its way to supremacy in the Civil War in the Ukraine, Budenny could look now only upon an unparalleled disaster; his fellow cavalrymen of the 1st Cavalry were now if not dead, then disgraced or captured – like Potapov, or Kulik or Voroshilov. Also at the end of September, to strengthen the defence of the Crimea, Stalin ordered the evacuation of Odessa; a special commission reported to the Odessa command to prevent a repetition of the mistakes of the Tallinn evacuation. Earlier in the month, the Odessa base command had 'contravened' Stalin's directive by pulling back the main defence line – and Shaposhnikov was quick to point out the violation – but the defenders had had to be withdrawn from under heavy shelling; Admiral Zhukov and his officers had reported to the *Stavka*:

> Odessa under intensive bombardment by enemy batteries. For last nine days OOR has had flow of wounded to the hospitals – 12,000. Local resources of manpower exhausted. To fulfil assignment – splitting enemy and holding town and port installations beyond artillery range – requires dispatch of well-equipped division.

To this succession of signals (6–10 September), Shaposhnikov replied with his usual aplomb, mentioning 'local resources': the Odessa command should 'organize 2–3 powerful air strikes with Black Sea Fleet planes, also warship guns and coastal defence batteries, to operate against enemy positions. Stubborn though the defence of Odessa was, Admiral Oktyabrskii realized that the

---

* *Voenno-istoricheskii Zhurnal* (9, 1964, pp. 61–9) takes issue with authors – R.G. Umanskii, L. Volynskii and V.D. Uspenskii – over the assertion that Kirponos, having been wounded, killed himself. Colonel V.S. Zhadovskii's eyewitness account of the death of Kirponos is printed in the *Voenno-istoricheskii Zhurnal* (the other witness, Kirponos's personal adjutant Major Gnennyi, was killed in action in 1942), and a section from the report of the Exhumation Commission (1943) on its findings with Kirponos's body, traced through Zhadovskii's and Gnennyi's first reports.

defence of the Crimea, from whose bases Odessa was supported, came first; on 29 September, after a meeting of the Black Sea Military Soviet, Oktyabrskii approached Stalin with a suggestion to evacuate Odessa and bring the troops to the Crimea, thereby strengthening 51st Army. Stalin agreed. On the night of 1 October, the deputy commander of the Soviet Navy, Vice-Admiral G.I. Levchenko, and the Black Sea Fleet Operations Officer, Captain O.S. Zhukovskii, arrived in Odessa. Evacuation came as a real shock to the base command; since August, when talk of evacuation had been squashed, no evacuation plans had been discussed. Rogov, chief of the Naval Political Administration, sent off at once (1 October) a signal about avoiding the Tallinn errors – day movement of transports, no anti-submarine defence, no air cover for convoys, no loading space for equipment, panic on ships due to poor distribution of officers and commissars. The Odessa evacuation was planned from the start as a calculated risk, loading and movement details being worked out by a Technical Commission (under Odessa's chief of staff Major-General Shishenin); the final plan envisaged lifting off the Coastal Army as one echelon (not two, as first proposed) in one night (15–16 October, instead of the original idea of a twenty-day evacuation period). At noon on 15 October, the 'Odessa defence zone' staff transferred to sea and boarded the cruiser *Chervonaya Ukraina*: at 02.00 hours, 16 October, Soviet rearguards took up their positions in the port and in the town. The Coastal Army which Petrov now commanded after General Safronov suffered a heart-attack, had already received its *Combat Directive No. 0034* and the 'Order of Embarkation', detailing times and locations to all rifle units. Any important objectives still left working Red Army engineers proceeded to blow up, toppling the cranes into the harbour and dynamiting the port installations; at 03.00 hours engineers destroyed the coastal batteries and AA defences, after which the survivors among the rearguards were picked up by the last ships. Petrov, who had joined his staff on the cruiser, made a final signal: 'Troops moving according to plan. Great obstruction at approaches to port. Front line calm. PETROV.' The thirty or so transports were gone and with them the last of the 35,000 troops lifted off all in one night, to join the 86,000 men moved earlier in the siege; over 400 guns, 20,000 tons of ammunition and more than 1,000 lorries were shipped out in a total of 192 sailings. At 05.10 hours on 16 October the last transport set course for Sevastopol.

The Soviet commanders had managed this evacuation, itself a small Dunkirk, with great skill and cool nerves, saving a large body of men and rescuing many of their machines to fight another day. It was a major feat which shone out amidst the confusion and chaos which ruled elsewhere.

The calm which Stalin had displayed a few weeks before in talking to Harry Hopkins was shattered by the lurch into disaster in the Ukraine, and his agitation showed plainly in his September messages to Winston Churchill. The pressure for a 'Second Front', from which Stalin never desisted, had been applied straight away in August 1941, and directly in London by Ambassador Ivan Maiskii. In his personal message of 3 September, Stalin proposed opening a second front 'this year somewhere in the Balkans or in France, one that would divert 30–40 German divisions from the Eastern Front'. That first measure of aid must go hand in hand with supplying the Soviet Union 'with 30,000 tons of aluminium by the beginning of October and a minimum *monthly* aid of 400 planes and 500 tanks (small or medium)'. This gloomy signal had ominous overtones, painted in by Stalin with the phrase: 'Without these *two* kinds of aid the Soviet Union will either be defeated or weakened to the extent that it will lose for a long time the ability to help its Allies by active operations at the front against Hitlerism.' Ten days later, having pondered the British prime minister's reply about the total impossibility of a Second Front in Stalin's sense, Stalin in his personal message of 13 September now suggested as a measure of 'active military aid' that the British 'land 25–30 divisions at Archangel or ship them to the southern areas of the USSR via Iran for military co-operation with Soviet troops on Soviet soil in the same way as was done during the last war in France'. The instigator of this plan was Marshal Timoshenko, and sensible though '25–30 divisions' sounded in military terms, it left out of calculation the problem of ships – ships for troops, for tanks, for aluminium, for machine tools and raw materials. This was, nevertheless, a very serious proposal on the part of Stalin, one which he continued to press as a realistic solution; a few weeks earlier also, in talking to Harry Hopkins, Stalin had mentioned the possibility of American troops on any sector of the Russian Front *under complete American command*, though he cannot have seriously reckoned upon this eventuality and Hopkins disabused him at once of any earnest hope. The next practical step rested with the supply conference due to convene very quickly in Moscow, and which did so in the midst of disaster at the front.

The slaughter in the south, brought to completion with dreadful efficiency as German infantry and armour of the inner and outer encircling wings cut the Soviet formations within their grip to pieces, was merely a preliminary to – a 'prerequisite' of, in Hitler's formulation – a massed assault upon the Soviet armies defending Moscow. For Stalin and the *Stavka*, meanwhile, the complex of operations connected with Smolensk had drawn to a close on 16 September when the Reserve Front was ordered to go over to the defensive. On 25 August, Stalin had approved the attack orders which had gone to the Western, Reserve and Bryansk Fronts: Western Command Front was ordered to continue with its assault operations north-east of Smolensk, to co-operate with Reserve Front forces and by 8 September to reach the line Velizh–Demidov–Smolensk, while Zhukov's Reserve Front – still committed to readying the Ostashkov–Olenino–river Dnieper (west of Vyazma)–Spas–Demyansk–Kirov defence line – was with its left flank twin armies to recapture Yelnaya and then exploit its success in the Pochinok–Roslavl direction. Yeremenko's Bryansk Front was to attack on 2 September, with the object of destroying German forces in the Pochep–Surazh area.

These counter-blows had a double object: first to tilt the balance on Timo-shenko's 'Western axis' as a whole and second, to disrupt the German offensive against the Central Front. Yelnaya, in a surge of very savage fighting, fell to the Russians on 6 September, a psychological boost of no mean proportion, though what there was of the town had been pounded into rubble and ruin. Further south, the Bryansk Front counter-blows were virtually unhinged from the start. By mid September, as the crisis reached its peak in the south, the Soviet centre was given a respite from its offensive labours; with Timoshenko's departure for the south-west, the Front command was reorganized. Koniev took over the Western Front; after Zhukov's departure for Leningrad, Budenny took over his command at the Reserve Front (until 8 October). Stalin also continued his prac-tice of calling upon NKVD generals to take field commands, for instance, Artemeyev of the Moscow district; all, with the exception of Khomenko, who had commanded the Ukrainian frontier guards and who had controlled 'Group Khomenko' at Smolensk, proved to be more or less military incompetents. All this was part, however, of an intensification of Stalin's control, exercised in another way by hauling his generals before a 'session' of the *Stavka*-GKO, where Beria had a seat, or else leaving them to the tender mercies of Mekhlis.

At the end of September, the Soviet western concentration comprised three fronts: Colonel-General Koniev's Western, with six armies (22nd, 29th, 30th, 19th, 16th and 20th) running from lake Seliger to Yelnaya, Budenny's Reserve Front with two armies (24th and 43rd) running from Yelnaya to Frolovka, and four armies (31st, 49th, 32nd and 33rd) drawn back as the Supreme Com-mander's Western reserve, while Yeremenko's Bryansk Front was held by three armies (50th, 3rd and 13th). All these Front armies were deployed in a single operational echelon, which called for extensive defensive positions, and produced a great shortage of units. Koniev had concentrated his reserves to the north of the Smolensk-Moscow highway: Yeremenko held his at Bryansk. On the eve of the renewed German offensive, these three fronts had a total strength of 800,000 men, 770 tanks and 364 planes. They had between them almost half the entire Red Army strength in men and guns on the entire Soviet-German Front, and one-third of the tanks and planes. Of the three Fronts, Koniev's was the strongest, with six infantry armies and 483 tanks (of which, however, only 45 were KVs or T-34s). Koniev had also one singular reinforcement; fighting his way steadily eastwards, Lieutenant-General Boldin had successfully brought 1,654 armed men and officers back to the Soviet lines in a 45-day break-out march. In mid August he had run up to Koniev's lines, and was brought in to the Soviet positions through a special 'corridor'; now Koniev gave him com-mand of a 'Front staff operational group'. In all, these were very valuable, indeed irreplaceable, eggs in a dangerously fragile basket.

The signs of a fresh German offensive against the 'Moscow defensive con-centration' were not lacking, though the reaction of the *Stavka* was very sluggish, a dangerous symptom when the new German offensive, timed for

2 October, was code-named 'Typhoon' (*Taifun*). The German plans called for a breakthrough on the Soviet Western Front in the Smolensk sector north and south of the Smolensk-Moscow highway, through which gap Panzer Group 3 and 4 would sweep on to form the northern and southern arms of a pincer movement designed to close near Vyazma. Guderian's Panzer Group 2 would strike at Yeremenko, and once in his rear, wheel on Bryansk. The main forces of the Western, Reserve and Bryansk Fronts were to be encircled and destroyed, followed by a general pursuit (and after the seizure of Kalinin, by co-operation with the right wing of Army Group North to cut off the easterly escape route for the Soviet North-Western Front). Thereafter came Moscow, the supreme prize of this 'battle of annihilation'. The assault forces were formidable indeed: three infantry armies (Ninth, Fourth and Second), three Panzer Groups (Hoth, *3*: Guderian, *2*: and Hoepner, *4*, brought down from Leningrad), with their 14 Panzer divisions and 9 motorized divisions, and strong air support and anti-aircraft defence. To halt them the three Soviet Fronts had 80 rifle divisions, 2 motorized infantry and 1 tank division, 9 cavalry divisions and 13 tank brigades. The average 'maximum strength' of a Soviet division did not exceed 7,000 men, and it fell usually as low as 5,000. There were also 12 militia divisions (DNO), but terribly deficient in arms, equipment and training.

Only on 27 September did the *Stavka* issue a general directive; it called for a full mobilization by each Front of its engineer resources to build a system of trenches and defence lines, the emplacing of wire and obstacles, as well as mine-fields at the approaches to these lines. Front commanders were ordered 'by stages' to build up their Front and army reserves, and to move their weakest divisions into the immediate rear for reinforcement. The Front commanders devised, within this general instruction, their own requirements: Koniev ordered a transition from 'mobile defence' to 'stubborn defence' of those positions already held and fortified in the course of recent operations. Western Front reserves were deployed north of the Smolensk-Moscow highway. Yeremenko's Front directive of 28 September advised that a German attack on Bryansk and Sevsk or Lgov was most probable; in the light of this, Yeremenko proposed some regrouping. Time, however, had quite run out. On 30 September, Guderian had already begun his attack on the Bryansk Front, and at 05.30 hours, 2 October, under cover of artillery bombardment, air attack and smoke-screens, Army Group Centre joined battle for Moscow.

Guderian struck east from Glukhov; 24th Panzer Corps smashed into Yermakov's 'operational group' which by 13.00 hours, 1 October, had been sliced away from 13th Army. Yeremenko's left wing had been split open with astonishing speed and 24th Panzer drove from Sevsk on Orel, while 47th Panzer Corps turned north-east for Karachev – and Bryansk. On his right wing, Yeremenko's 50th Army was in a dangerous situation as the German Second Army pierced the defences of 43rd Army (Reserve Front), and split these two armies asunder. On the night of 2 October, Stalin telephoned Yeremenko and demanded a restoration of the position but all Yeremenko could do during the course of the next day was to commit isolated tank brigades to a counter-attack which caused Guderian no major concern.

At the same time as he ordered Yeremenko to halt Guderian, Stalin authorized a reinforcement for the Bryansk Front, subordinating the administration of 49th Army from his 'Western reserve', plus the 194th Rifle Division, to Bryansk: in addition, Stalin ordered the air-lifting to the Orel area of the 1st Guards Rifle Corps (5th and 6th Guards Rifle Divisions, 4th and 11th Independent Tank Brigades, 6th Reserve Aviation Group with two fighter regiments, one ground-attack regiment, a light bomber Pe-2 regiment and one *Katyusha* regiment), all under the command of Major-General D.D. Lelyushenko. This force was meant to secure an exit for the Bryansk Front and to hold the Germans at Orel, for which purpose it was further strengthened with the 5th Parachute Corps, the Tula Military School and the 36th Motor-cycle Regiment. Too late to save Orel, 1st Guards Corps nevertheless did a good job, and none better than Colonel Katukov's 4th Tank Brigade which by 4 October was in position at Mtsensk, with a goodly complement of T-34s, which Katukov knew how to use on the road to Tula.

With his right caving in, Yeremenko's left was punctured to collapse on 3 October, when German armour raced into Orel, passing the trams in the street. Yeremenko had reported the crisis on his left to the Orel district command on 30 September; the district commander Lieutenant-General A.A. Tyurin was not at his HQ, but his chief of staff reported that there were four artillery regiments in the town, not enough to hold but sufficient to check a German thrust. The Orel staff hoped at the least to have time to evacuate men and machines, to destroy factories and dynamite the rail installations. In this they were abruptly deceived. Orel was swept into the German grasp at one fell swoop, a prize of considerable magnitude as an important administrative centre and a vital road-rail junction.

On the night of 2 October, Yeremenko had also talked to Shaposhnikov, suggesting that a more 'mobile' defence might be adopted; to any suggestion of this or of withdrawal Shaposhnikov returned a flat refusal, insisting that 'stubborn defence of manned defence lines' was and remained the *Stavka*'s response, the 'pernicious linear defence' which Stalin later castigated as if it had been the witless practice of others but not himself. Yeremenko had left his command post to supervise the counter-attack which Stalin had ordered; on his return he tried once more to interest Shaposhnikov in his 'ideas', and the latter promised 'to bring this to the attention of Stalin'. During the night of 5–6 October Yeremenko waited anxiously for a call from Stalin, at a time when the Bryansk Front was literally cut to pieces: its communication centres were in enemy hands, its escape routes to the east sealed. The Bryansk Front lived by railway lines, and these were now chopped and severed by German movement. On the morning of 6 October, at 09.00 hours, Yeremenko was instructed from

R.T.S.—H

Moscow merely to report the Front situation over the telephone. Stalin remained silent. Five hours later, Yeremenko's duty officer at Front HQ – two
houses, one for the Military Soviet, one for the Political Administration –
reported German tanks only 200 yards away. There was a rush to cut communications and gather operational documents for transfer to the reserve
command post. Yeremenko, with the help of three tanks and a squad of infantry
only just got out. (The *Stavka* was told he had been killed.) That same day,
Bryansk itself – of no less importance than Orel as traffic junction – with its
bridge over the Desna fell to another speedy German stroke.

With three armies (3rd, 13th and 50th) of the Bryansk Front encircled or in
the gravest danger of it, at Vyazma a disaster of even greater proportions involving five armies (19th, 16th, 20th, 24th and 32nd) as well as Boldin's
'operational group' was building up at the same frenzied pace. On Koniev's
Western Front twelve German divisions on the morning of 2 October had
shattered the junction of the 30th and 19th Armies, bursting open a gap of some
twenty miles which led through Vadino to Vyazma, north of the Smolensk-
Moscow highway. While Panzer Group 3 was wreaking this havoc, Panzer
Group 4 tore into Budenny's 24th and 43rd Armies on the Reserve Front,
whose task it was to secure the junction between the Western and Bryansk
Fronts; by the evening of 4 October, Koniev's five armies were in dire straits,
Boldin's counter-attack had failed and Budenny was about to report to the
Stavka that the entire situation along the Warsaw highway (Spas-Demensk-
Yukhnov-Kirov), was wholly out of control, the Reserve Front bereft of any
forces to hold the Germans, and the situation on his right critical, leaving
Koniev's flank exposed. Only with the greatest tardiness did the *Stavka* respond;
on 5 October Stalin authorized bringing the 31st and 32nd Armies of the
Reserve Front under Koniev's command as from 23.00 hours, while Koniev
was instructed to fall back on the Rzhev-Vyazma line. Budenny was during the
night of 6 October to move what troops he had back to the Vedreniki-Mosalsk
line.

The reason for Stalin's belated response through the *Stavka* lay in the lack of
information available on the course of the operations; the news of Guderian's
breakthrough against Yeremenko on September had occasioned no undue
alarm. The only reaction in the Moscow Military District to General Staff
intelligence summaries on the regrouping of German forces on the 'Moscow
axis' had been to speed some trench digging and set up regular fighter patrols
along the Rzhev-Vyazma-Kirov line. Artemeyev had gone to Tula on 2
October in some haste, where he heard more disturbing news of the Bryansk
Front; his report may have hastened Stalin's decision about moving up
Lelyushenko's corps. No downright alarming news came through to Moscow
staff on 3–4 October but on 5 October, at 11.00 hours, Colonel Sbytov, Moscow
district fighter commander, relayed a pilot's report who had spotted moving on
Yukhnov a massive armoured and motorized column some twelve miles long –

and German. The General Staff duty officer still reported no 'alarming' news; Shaposhnikov himself informed General Telegin that 'there was no basis for disquiet'. A second reconnaissance plane went out, and confirmed the first sightings. Marshal Shaposhnikov, consulted once more, made the same reply. As a third reconnaissance plane took off, the Moscow garrison was brought to a preliminary alert.

The third reconnaissance report left no room whatsoever for doubt; Marshal Shaposhnikov, telephoned a third time, became thoroughly testy but on hearing the full reconnaissance report broke off the conversation. Four minutes later Stalin telephoned the Moscow district staff, asking Telegin if he had telephoned Shaposhnikov, whether the information was reliable, and what measures had been taken. Stalin's response was terse: 'Good. Mobilize everything you have, but the enemy must be held if not stopped for 5-7 days, during which we can move up *Stavka* reserves. You, the Military Soviet of the [Moscow] district are responsible for that.' Shortly afterwards Beria of the NKVD telephoned the District staff to ask about the source of the information on the Yukhnov breakthrough. The sequel was rapid and not pleasant. Beria ordered the interrogation of Colonel Sbytov as a 'panic-monger' and Abakumov threatened to put the colonel in front of a field tribunal for disseminating 'provocationist' intelligence about German movements.* But no amount of NKVD intimidation could dispose of the brute fact that the Soviet armies at Vyazma-Bryansk had been blasted to pieces.

Stalin summoned an immediate and emergency session of the State Defence Committee (GKO); faced with the virtual dissolution of three fronts and thus the force covering Moscow, the GKO meeting decided upon the 'Mozhaisk line' as the rallying point for the Western Front, and where Voroshilov as GKO plenipotentiary was sent with all speed. The *Stavka* was directed to organize a defence force, and on 6 October issued a directive ordering the Mozhaisk position to be brought to full readiness; 6 rifle divisions, 6 tank brigades and some 10 artillery and machine-gun regiments were hurried there from the *Stavka* reserve. By the following day, as many reserve formations as possible were on the move and Stalin ultimately gathered up 14 rifle divisions, 16 newly formed tank brigades, more than 40 artillery regiments and about 10 flame-thrower companies to man this defensive zone. The other fronts had to yield priority to Moscow. From the south-west the 2nd Cavalry Corps under Belov, about which Budenny and Shaposhnikov had wrangled a month ago, was ordered to Moscow, and from the interior, central Asia and the Urals, formations

---

* According to Colonel (now General) Sbytov himself, at 19.00 hours, 5 October, he was presented with a copy of his interrogation to sign: the interrogation had been so recorded as to obscure the fact of the German breakthrough, so that the colonel wrote on the document in his own hand: 'Latest reconnaissance confirmed that Fascist tanks are in the area of Yukhov and should take the town by the evening of 5 October.' Sbytov had earlier explained to the NKVD that the fighter planes did not carry cameras and therefore he could not produce reconnaissance-camera photographs but the pilots, flying at 300 metres, were reliable.

were moved west, among the first to arrive being General Panfilov's 316th Rifle Division from Kazakhstan which was moved straight on to Volokolamsk.

So far, Stalin had drawn with the uttermost caution and most sparingly on his Far Eastern concentrations; initial re-deployments had brought formations like the 26th Zlatoust Rifle Division, one of the senior divisions of the Red Army, from lake Khasan to the coastal railheads. With Sorge's signal to Stalin in early October about the final and irrevocable Japanese decision to move 'southwards' against the Americans and the British rather than the Russians, the brakes in the Far East could be released, but the movement took time and Stalin needed men on the spot to man the Moscow line in the place of his dozen armies which had been so thoroughly decimated.

On 9 October, at a joint session of the *Stavka* and the Moscow district Staff, an emergency mobilization was set in motion; the 'Mozhaisk defence line' which had been selected by the GKO on 5 October as the place to make a stand, was transformed into the 'Moscow reserve front' under Artemeyev. Panfilov with his 316th Division was made commander of the Volokolamsk sector; Colonel Bogdanov, who had first fought at Brest with his tanks and who was now commander of Moscow district armour, went to the Mozhaisk sector, and Colonel Naumov with his 312th Rifle Division was sent to Maloyaroslavets. So far three rifle divisions were on the way to this line, although of 110 miles of front, only 70 could be covered; there was no depth and the flanks were exposed. Training school regiments, and militia units were hurried along, but these scarcely sufficed. On 12 October, Kaluga had fallen and two days later Kalinin (ninety miles north-west of Moscow and leading into the rear of the Soviet North-Western Front) also fell, in spite of the furious resistance of units formed out of Moscow AA gun-crews, motor-cycle companies, machine-gun squads and more militia. On 10 October, the Reserve Front was formally liquidated and incorporated into the Western, and the whole command assigned to General Zhukov, who had been rushed down from Leningrad.

The total force which Zhukov had at his disposal when he took command was 90,000 men, the remnants of the Western and Reserve Fronts: 16th Army under Rokossovskii (which was reconstituted) took over at Volokolamsk, General L.A. Govorov finally took 5th Army (raised from the 1st Guards Rifle Corps) at Mozhaisk, General K.D. Golubev went to Maloyaroslavets with the 43rd, and General I.G. Zakharin near Kaluga with the 49th. These armies had to man a 150-mile front. The 33rd Army was at that time being formed from reserve units at Naro–Fominsk and, under Lieutenant-General M.G. Yefremov, was subordinated to Zhukov's command. The civilian population was mobilized by the GKO; a quarter of a million (75 per cent women) Muscovites were drafted to dig trenches and anti-tank ditches, and the 'Moscow defence zone' (*Moskovskaya zona oborony*: MZO) was brought into existence. This ran parallel to the second line of the Mozhaisk defences, extending in the north to the Moscow Canal and to the south to Serpukhov on the river Oka, with its main defensive line running in a semi-circle round Moscow in a radius of some ten miles. The main defence line was divided into sectors (north-west, west and south-west) and the sectors divided into combat zones. Here tank-traps, wire and timbered obstacles, buried tanks and fire-points were constructed as fast as possible – a rudimentary defence, but all that was possible. The defence line was divided into two main parts, 'main' and 'urban', the latter running along the city's circular railway; inside that circle, Moscow was divided into three sectors to the front and three lines to the rear designated 'circular railway line', 'urban ring A' and 'urban ring B'.

Upon the Vyazma–Bryansk battlefields, where the first snow had fallen, turning earth roads to mud as it quickly thawed, the nightmarish scenes of armies being torn apart were spread over wide areas, with scores of Soviet units fighting to make their escape. At the centre, Lukin with the 19th Army begged at least one division from the 16th, which was itself being ground to pieces; Commissar Lobachev could only tell Lukin: 'We are generals without troops.' Lukin was taken prisoner. Rokossovskii with a staff column from 16th Army fought his way out eastwards. Yeremenko on 12 October was severely wounded by bomb splinters and flown out; seven divisions of Major-General M.P. Petrov's 50th Army (217th, 290th, 279th, 278th, 258th, 260th and 154th divisions), in groups of three thousand men, fought their way north-west to Belev on the river Oka, but General Petrov himself died of gangrene in a wood-cutter's hut deep in the Bryansk forests. The Germans claimed officially 665,000 Soviet prisoners; the Russians dispute this, but if only 90,000 men could be gathered on the Mozhaisk line, then Soviet losses had been desperate.

Critical though the situation was at the centre, it was dangerous on the flanks; at Kalinin, Stalin had to prevent a German breakthrough into the Soviet rear. General Vatutin, chief of staff of the North-West Front was ordered to take command of two rifle and two cavalry divisions, with a tank brigade to form an 'operational group' for the defence of the Kalinin reaches, while three rifle divisions and a tank brigade were taken from Zhukov's right wing to form the 'Kalinin Group', where Koniev took command on 12 October. If Zhukov lost men, he had his front shortened appreciably; the Kalinin Front was formally established by *Stavka* directive on 17 October, and allocated three armies – 22nd, 29th and 30th – from Zhukov's right, plus Vatutin's 'group'. Panzer Group 3 had to be held here, else it would burst into the rear of the Mozhaisk line or the North-Western Front.

At the centre, a fraction more than sixty miles from Moscow, on the hills of Borodino Lelyushenko with elements of 5th Army – two regiments (17th and 113th) of 32nd Rifle Division, two tank brigades (18th and 19th), all that had so far arrived – attempted to halt 10th Panzer and ss *Das Reich* Motorized Infantry Divisions striking along the motor road to Mozhaisk. On 10 October Lelyushenko had talked to Shaposhnikov who told him to form the 5th as rapidly as possible, and to cover the Mozhaisk fortified line – 'though it's far from ready', so Lelyushenko could scarcely count on its support. At least Shaposhnikov had warned him. Borodino had been one of Napoleon's bloodiest battlefields; its reputation for carnage was confirmed when Lelyushenko's Siberian riflemen, moved in with the 32nd from the Far East, fought savagely with the élite troops of the ss. Lelyushenko was wounded: Govorov, the unsmiling artillery general took over. The reserves, thin as they had been, were now all spent: there was no more Govorov could do. On the morning of 18 October German units advanced from the west upon Mozhaisk, turned into blazing ruins by German bombers; this was also the day when German tanks burst into Maloyaroslavets exposing Naro–Fominsk, and to compound disaster Tarusa north-west of Kaluga was taken, thus visibly increasing the immediate threat from the south.

At this point, Moscow's nerve snapped. Just before midnight on 15 October Molotov had warned the British and American ambassadors to prepare for evacuation, together with the Soviet government, to Kuibyshev. The real crisis, however, spilled on to the streets and into plants and offices; a spontaneous, popular flight added itself to the hurried and limited official evacuation, accompanied by a breakdown in public and Party disciplines. There was a rush to the railway stations: officials used their cars to get east: offices and factories were disabled by desertions. Behind Mozhaisk itself, Zhukov had ordered anti-tank squads to take up positions on the approaches to Moscow: at the same time, eight demolition units equipped with lorries for rapid movement mined 56 bridges and laid 584 tons of explosives, and the railway troops were told to mine their tracks and junctions. Factories were prepared for demolition. Sixteen bridges deep within the city were mined, and crews at other mined objectives issued orders to blow up their charges 'at the first sight of the enemy'.

That Artemeyev was an NKVD general was highly relevant in this situation. The secretary of the Moscow Party Committee, Shcherbakov, broadcast on the seventeenth over Moscow radio, stating that Stalin was in the capital, that he would stay there and that Moscow would be defended 'to the last drop of blood'. On the evening of 19 October, Artemeyev and his officers were summoned along with others to an extraordinary session of the GKO. Artemeyev's report on the conditions in the city made it obvious that martial law must be enforced and it was forthwith imposed. Responsibility for the immediate approaches to the city and for the city itself was assigned to Artemeyev: to Zhukov went command of the area up to 120 kilometres west of the Soviet capital. In effect, Moscow was delivered into the hands of the Soviet military and a hard core of the NKVD. For the defender of Moscow Stalin fastened on Zhukov, who had Bulganin as his 'military member' – a relationship which was far from easy, though Koniev (who commanded the Western Front from 12 September to 10 October) is at pains to convey the impression that he and Bulganin, working through the GKO 'special commission' made up of Voroshilov, Malenkov, Molotov and Vasilevskii which had arrived at Front HQ in Krasnovidovo, were the prime movers in 'nominating' Zhukov for the post of Western Front commander. Early on the morning of 10 October Zhukov himself arrived at Western Front HQ and found the GKO commission already at work; from their presence Zhukov deduced that Stalin was 'extremely worried about the very precarious situation'. In Zhukov's view, the commands of the Western, Bryansk and Reserve Fronts had been guilty of 'serious miscalculations': for six weeks these forces had been stationed in defensive positions and 'they had had enough time to prepare for the enemy attack'. But lack of proper preparation, failure to determine the strength and directions of the German attack, the lack of anti-tank defence in any depth and the absence of any attempt to use air and artillery strikes against German forces about to jump off increased the chances of disaster: once the Soviet defences in the area of Vyazma had been penetrated, the Front command failed to organize the withdrawal of five armies, 16th, 19th, 20th, 24th and the 32nd, which promptly fell into complete encirclement.

Inevitably, Koniev took a different view. The fact that the Germans held the strategic initiative along the entire length of the Soviet-German front placed the Soviet command at a heavy disadvantage: German superiority in tanks and aircraft exacted a fearful toll, resulting in the 'incessant withering bombing of our troops by enemy aircraft' which could not be prevented owing to the lack of anti-aircraft guns: superior German mobility facilitated 'extensive manoeuvring' which the Soviet forces could not inhibit, again due to the lack of adequate air and anti-tank forces: the Western Front was inadequately supplied with weapons and ammunition: finally, the breakthrough towards from the north could have been localized by regrouping, but once the German troops got to Spas-Demensk they were free to break into the rear of the Soviet armies, with the Reserve Front unable to deploy any forces in that critical direction.

When Zhukov telephoned Stalin on 10 October, he received the news that he was the new Western Front commander. If Koniev had hoped to placate Stalin with his report submitted on 10 October, he had obviously failed. Zhukov gathered that Stalin intended to replace the entire command of the Western Front, whereupon he apparently intervened to suggest that Koniev be kept as deputy commander and entrusted with 'the leadership of the units in the Kalinin sector', troops which were 'too far removed from headquarters and in need of additional supervision'. 'Organize the Western Front quickly and take the necessary measures', were Stalin's final words to Zhukov. The decision to defend Moscow was taken, whatever Stalin's qualms: there is little to show that it could have been otherwise. There was, for all the mass convulsion of fear and panic, a resolute minority who intended to hold on to the end. Stalin's own elder son Yakob, a senior lieutenant with the 14th Howitzer Regiment who had been captured on the Western Front in July 1941, had told his German interrogators this much and his prediction proved to be right. For all the careless and incompetent commanders, a small but very capable command group was emerging: Zhukov the strategist, field commanders in the style of Rokossovskii, Koniev, Vatutin, specialists such as Voronov and Govorov, energetic armoured commanders in the persons of Katukov, Rotmistrov and Bogdanov, Novikov with the air force, men who knew their job and learned more each day Yet by squeezing them between the GKO and the NKVD, Stalin made sure that they remained submissive to his will and to his alone.

With the Soviet military machine so desperately and terribly strained, though not yet actually smashed, the conditions for the defence of the Soviet capital were all too disastrously plain: the reserves had vanished. When Vlasov, survivor of Kiev, arrived in Moscow at the beginning of November and was asked by Stalin what he thought might ensure the successful defence of Moscow, Vlasov replied that reserves might tip the scales: Stalin simply snorted that 'any idiot could defend the city with reserves' and, in assigning Vlasov command of an army, doled out his largesse in tanks – fifteen all told. Malenkov, acting as military book-keeper, confirmed the tally of the available stock, fifteen machines, and glumly read it off to Stalin. What Stalin and his *Stavka* had earlier disposed of, whole trains of armies which were trundled into the line one after another, had been washed away in this tidal wave of defeat. The tally of almost three million prisoners of war in German hands and of the Red Army's strength falling to its lowest point in the whole war was lamentable proof of a persistent and ignorant profligacy with these once enormous armies and an almost soulless indifference to their fate.

6

The Rear, the Deep Rear and Behind the German Lines

By mid October, as German armies gouged their way through the Soviet defences on the flanks and at the centre, the Soviet rear, with its industries and grain belts became speedily and terrifyingly exposed. Much had already been engulfed by the German advance. The areas so immediately threatened included no less than 45 per cent of the total population, some eighty-eight million souls; one-third of Soviet production was managed here, and as the month advanced the Soviet Union was stripped of more than half (62·5 per cent) of its pre-war coal output, more than two-thirds of its pig-iron, steel and rolled metals (71 per cent, 68 per cent and 67 per cent respectively) and 60 per cent of its aluminium. Ammunition production fell sharply as 303 plants in European Russia were put out of action due to evacuation or enemy seizure. Almost half the land under grain crops (47 per cent) was in enemy hands, and again almost half (41 per cent) of the railway network was in German-occupied areas. For the Wehrmacht, it was a race to cut the Red Army to pieces in the field and simultaneously to stop up those remaining wells of industrial power which provided the substance of Soviet resistance, while the Russians, gripped almost fatally in this brutal and terrible encounter, had to salvage some armies and keep, at all costs, a bare but vital minimum of production flowing into the front lines.

The burdens imposed upon the Soviet administrative machine were massive, committed as it was to a huge mobilization which at times was engulfed by the easterly movement of the battle-lines. There had been only scant pre-war contingency planning; there were no actual plans for any strategic industrial withdrawal into the eastern hinterlands, where the building of new plants and the construction of vital railroads had proceeded very slowly: the weight of pre-war investment had fallen always on the 'central region' into which the Germans were now bursting so speedily. There were a few but not many 'shadow factories' for tanks and aircraft in Eastern Siberia and the Urals, but a full-scale survey of easterly fuel resources and mineral deposits was undertaken only when the war had begun; this survey went into high gear with Academician Komarov's 'Commission for the mobilization of Urals resources for defence purposes'. In the western regions, those actually under or exposed to attack, a wartime regime had been formally and legally introduced by the June decrees, with Front and Army Military Soviets forming the first extraordinary agency and combining military with political administrative control: the 'third member', the political member of the Military Soviet represented the Party and the administrative machines within the command. The Military Soviet had powers of requisitioning and local mobilization, assuming also in the first weeks of the war local responsibility for organizing partisan detachments. The central power was quickly embodied in the GKO, which after June embarked ruthlessly on tightening local responses to central requirements. The multiple 'Defence Committees' (*gorodskoi komitet oborony*) sprang up at every threatened urban point: Leningrad, Sevastopol, Tula, Moscow (with its several Defence Committees), Rostov, Kalinin. In towns under actual attack, a state of siege (*osadnoe polozhenie*) was proclaimed, while the *gorodskoi komitet oborony*, combining Red Army, NKVD and Party personnel, could within its general direction from the GKO in Moscow make use of the local citizenry for defence purposes, organize special defensive measures, raise a militia (*opolchenie*), take over plant and machinery for defence work and issue orders for specialized production: special food rationing or supply measures (like controlling the water supply in Odessa) were fully within the competence of these urban defence committees.

Leningrad's Defence Committee, being under the direct control of the central GKO, was a unique political-administrative animal: the reason for that, in view of the great crack-up in the Leningrad command, was not hard to seek. Tula, on the approaches to Moscow, was more typical in its organization; the *oblast* Party organization had already taken a hand in adopting special defence measures, and on 22 October the Tula Defence Committee (*Tulskii gorodskii komitet oborony*) was officially established with V.G. Zhavoronkov, the first secretary of the Party *obkom* organization as its chief. The highest Party echelon took control, and drew up plans to defend the town – mobilizing the 'Tula workers regiment', keeping up weapon and ammunition production but evacuating industrial plant, and mobilizing civilians from seventeen to fifty years of age to build defence lines. The garrison commander of Tula, Colonel Ivanov, signed this labour mobilization order. In addition to the workers' regiment, Tula, like every other town and city, raised its own 'tank-destroyer battalions', armed with anti-tank grenades and petrol bottles; the Tula branch of the Red Cross concentrated its nurses and orderlies; small, picked groups were designated for partisan and sabotage work in the event of the town falling to the Germans, and underground cadres were established in thirty *rayons* of the whole district. In the mud of melting snow and the heavy rain which thickened the morass, Major-General A.N. Yermakov's 50th Army took up its defensive positions around Tula in late October, where the 'Tula combat sector' had been originally manned by the Tula Military-technical School, a workers militia regiment and the 14th Reserve Rifle Brigade.

The Tula Defence Committee was not large but highly representative:

Zhavoronkov headed it, with his co-workers drawn from the *Oblast* Executive Committee, N.I. Chmutov, the Obkom propaganda secretary, A.V. Kalinovskii, the chief of the *oblast* NKVD administration, V.N. Sukhodolskii and the president of the town Soviet, Lyubimov. The army commander attended Defence Committee sessions; Zhavoronkov, his deputy Chmutov and Sukhodolskii attended the Military Soviet meetings of 50th Army. Here, as elsewhere, the formal organization meant much less than the talents of an energetic minority in political and administrative control; in the case of Tula, they proved to be more than adequate in a very serious situation. But in general, the rigid subordination of the periphery to the centre, and the overlapping of responsibilities proved to be a dangerous weakness.

The Red Army itself had suffered badly from the same overlapping when operations and logistics were not even separated in principle. At the end of July, Stalin had agreed to the establishment of a formal rear services organization, assigning Lieutenant-General Khrulev to the post of Chief of Rear Services (*Nachalnik tyla Krasnoi Armii*): the duties and competence of the new 'deputy commanders for rear services' at Army and Front level were laid down in Order No. 252 for 31 July 1941. Khrulev himself became one more of Stalin's sixteen Deputy Defence Commissars, with a permanent place on the *Stavka* and close contact with the GKO. The new 'deputy commanders' were charged with organizing the 'timely and unbroken' supply of food and clothing, the distribution of mobile bakeries and workshops and also with keeping accurate lists of losses and requirements; rear service deputy commanders at army and Front level were to work out supply requirements and plans to meet them, consulting with army and Front commanders for the 'material security' of operations, as well as organizing battlefield salvage of Russian and enemy equipment. The same deputy commanders were charged with organizing local supply, foodstuffs or forage, and with regulating the 'military rear' services and securing local transportation. All this was a task of immense proportions: the shortage of lorries complicated supply as much as it impeded operations. Armoured formations in particular suffered from the lack of spare parts and the paucity of repair facilities: 22nd Mechanized Corps in June had lost 50 per cent of its tanks due to lack of repair facilities. The mobile repair base (*podvizhnaya remontnaya baza:* PRB) and the 'salvage collection points' (SPAM) were innovations introduced at the end of 1941, with salvage sections attached to tank brigades and regiments; they were, however, too weak in manpower and machines to do all that was incessantly required of them. The ChTZ-60 tractors were the main salvage equipment to hand, but one bullet in the radiator or fuel tanks put them out of action, requiring the salvagers to be salvaged.

Shortages were everywhere crucial, made worse as falling production coincided with appalling battlefield losses. On the Soviet-German front, Red Army strength was falling frighteningly to its lowest ever ebb, 2,300,000 men, from the 4,700,000 who were or could be fielded in June 1941. The Soviet claims for German losses were wild and fantastic: 2,000,000 men (killed and wounded), 8,000 tanks, over 7,200 planes, all for the first two months, made no doubt to offset the minimized but still doleful tally of Soviet losses, when in October the Russians admitted the loss of 5,000 planes. The whole massive swarm of Soviet tanks which had existed in June 1941, was now more or less obliterated: those left were brigaded very abruptly, but the few divisions left and the current brigades were more often than not mere paper units. The 54th Army on 1 October had one tank division (21st) attached to it but the 21st had not a single tank to its name. A fortnight later, two tank brigades were moved up as reinforcement (16th and 122nd), with fifty-two tanks between them (twenty being KV or T-34). Of the fifty or so tank divisions which had previously existed (even though their full tally came as a shock to the German command), most were now unfit for action. Red Army artillery compressed into dangerous straits, suffering calamitous losses in guns and gun-crews, so many of whom, as Colonel-General Halder noted with a surprised respect, were killed at their guns: a high total of guns destroyed or captured, but so few gunners by comparison taken prisoner. Voronov had to persuade Stalin of the need for drastic reorganization of Red Army artillery; before the new equipment came to the front from the factories (many of which were rolling to the east with waggon-loads of evacuated equipment) the rifle divisions would have to be stripped of half of their artillery (one regiment), the guns assembled into a High Command Artillery Reserve and used where the threat was greatest. To save ammunition and to compensate for lack of training among new crews, direct fire – sticking the guns up front – would be the main technique. To fill the gaps in the guns, a crash programme to produce mortars went into operation; to supplement the artillery, mortars mounted on lorries would have to serve as mobile fire support.

Much as Stalin selected from the thousand-strong command group he had promoted in 1940 the wartime generals who had shown some skill, so from the mass of the Red Army, through the device of 'Guards' designation, he picked out formations which had shown themselves effective and efficient in combat; under Defence Commissariat *Order No. 308* for 18 September, the first 'Guards Divisions' of the Red Army, the 100th, 127th and 153rd and 161st Rifle Divisions, were created, following a precedent set by Voroshilov in Leningrad when he set up 'Guards Workers Divisions', mainly as a fillip to morale. The Guards formations were a conscious attempt to filter quality from quantity; to the Guards went what was available (and best) in equipment and supplies, and the Soviet command learned in time to use these quality troops as such. Colonel Katukov's 4th Tank Brigade, which had ambushed and actually mauled Guderian's armour south of Mtsensk, became the 1st Guards Tank Brigade of the Red Army, in fact its premier tank unit (which grew ultimately into a tank army).

But in the very grimmest days of October-November, Guards units were few on the ground. Somehow the Red Army had to be slewed round, decimated as it was, and brought to battle even to its last shreds. Units which had almost no equipment were inevitably pounded to pieces: mass infantry attacks with riflemen advancing in ranks twelve deep or riding in trucks abreast with the tanks on to the German firing line had piled up enormous casualties: infantry officers to the fore of these endless attacks had fallen in their thousands: untrained militia, scooped off the streets and skimmed from the factories, clung to improvised and shaky defences. The 'no treason' orders sown by Stalin produced a crop of 'illegal repression' – discipline through the revolver – in Soviet units: in his order of 4 October, Stalin tried to put a brake on this 'repression', listing 'violations' of what was in any event and by any standard a harsh code. Officers, already fearful for their own fate, drew their weapons too readily on sub-ordinates and used them: the adjutant of the 529th Rifle Regiment battered a junior officer in the face with his pistol for moving too slowly, the military commissar of the 28th Tank Regiment handled a sergeant savagely for smoking. The army's political baggage train grew more unwieldy with the weight of commissars and political inspectorates: deep in its wake came the NKVD.

The army, with its reinforcement racing in from the Far East or trundling to Moscow from north and south, was like much of European Russia – on wheels, clacking over railway tracks: like Russia also, it fought as yet in an improvised fashion, with all the shortcomings and impediments which that imposed. Moscow, which had partly emptied itself in the October panic, was being more systematically evacuated: almost a million had been evacuated by the end of July, but between 16–31 October 200 trains hurried more civilians eastwards. The traffic on the Moscow–Ryazan line was immense. Evacuating whole factories required trucks by the thousand; 7,500 were used to ship three large enterprises to the hinterland, and a plant turning out infantry weapons needed twelve trains to itself. In all, 80,000 trucks were used to pull out the 498 factories and industrial installations from the capital; only 21,000 of Moscow's 75,000 metal-cutting lathes were left, and 14,000 of those were turned over to weapon or ammunition production. Not only the industrial but also the governmental machine was set in physical motion; the very highly centralized state machine was scattered behind the Volga, and in November General Khrulev issued the formal order detailing the new location of governmental agencies. A subordinate but vital centre of administration was located in Kuibyshev, while the various commissariats were separately scattered in their evacuation sites.★

The State Defence Committee (GKO) had in effect become 'the government', whose status symbol remained nevertheless the Party; as an administrative agent, the Party worked indifferently and actually collapsed in its lower echelons. Its strength lay at the top. The GKO ruled by decree, direct intervention and 'plenipotentiary'; if it could not always co-ordinate then at least it managed

★ Order No. 022 is reproduced on pages 228–30.

SECRET ORDER No. 022
5 November 1941
Moscow

Chief of the Rear Services (Nachalnik tyla)

Dispersal of People's Commissariats and the administration of the People's Commissariat for Defence

(1) Provisional re-location of Commissariats and Administrations

Place	Designation of Commissariat, Committee and Administration
Kuibyshev	Defence Commissariat *Gosplan* (State planning) Foreign Affairs Commissariat Internal Affairs Commissariat Transport Commissariat
Astrakhan	Merchant Marine Commissariat Fishing Fleets Commissariat

Saratov	Aircraft Industry Commissariat
	Supply (Provisions) Commissariat
	Main Administration,
	    Naphtha distribution
	    Central Commercial Bank
	Administration,
	    State Food Reserves

Engels	State Arbitration,
	    Council of People's Commissars
	    (*Sovnarkom*)

Sysran	Trade Bank Osoaviakhim
Penza	Machine Building Commissariat
Ulyanovsk	Navy Commissariat Internal Waterways Commissariat Traffic Commissariat
Kazan	Rubber Industry Commissraiat Food Industries Commissariat Health Commissariat Finance Commissariat State Bank

Kazan	Committee for Higher Education Institutions
	Main Administration,
	Civil Air Traffic
Gorkii	Electrical Industry Commissariat
	Shipbuilding Commissariat
Kirov	Wood Industry Commissariat
	Main Administration,
	Distribution Wood Products
	Main Administration,
	Wood Spirit
Molotov	Armaments Commissariat
	Coal Mining Commissariat
	Chemical Industry Commissariat
	Paper Industry Commissariat
Sverdlovsk	Ferrous Metals Industry Commissariat
	Non-Ferrous Metals Industry Commissariat
	Heavy Industry Commissariat
	Main Administration,
	Military Construction
	Building Materials Commissariat
	Main Administration,
	Labour Reserves
Chelyabinsk	Industrial Bank
	Building Trade Commissariat
	Electricity Works Commissariat
	Munitions Commissariat
	Tank Production Commissariat
	Medium Machine Building Commissariat
Ufa	Naphtha Extraction Commissariat
	Information Commissariat
	State Control Commissariat
Novosibirsk	Trade Commissariat
	Tsentrosoyuz
	Committee for Film Industry
Orsk	Meat and Dairy Products Commissariat
Omsk	Agriculture Commissariat
	Agricultural Bank
Tomsk	Committee for Applied Arts
	Committee for Physical Training and Sport
	Central Statistical Administration of *Gosplan*

Krasnoyarsk	Main Administration,
	Sevmorput (Northern White Sea traffic)
	Machine Tools Commissariat
Chkalov	Collective Farm Commissariat (*Sovkhoz*)
	Justice Commissariat
	State procuracy
	Supreme Court
	Main Administration,
	Rail and Road Traffic

(2) Military administrations (Defence Commissariat in Kuibysher, together with central military administration)

Place	Designation
Ulyanovsk	Red Army Training Administration
Sverdlovsk	Military Schools Administration
Ulyanovsk	Inspectorate of Infantry
	Military Surveying Administration, Red Army
	Editorial Staff, *Voennaya Mysl*
	Military-Scientific Section, General Staff
Chkalov	Main Administration for Universal
	Military Training
Bugurusian	Veterinary Administration, Red Army
Sverdlovsk	Quartering Administration,
	Main Supply Administration,
	Red Army
	Fire Services Inspectorate
	Main Supply Administration
	Main Administration,
	Military Engineers

(SIGNED)
Lieutenant-General Khrulev   Brigade Commissar Bayukov

to get results, by dint of drastic and brutal emergency mobilization, or peremptory and mandatory order. The inefficiencies inherent in the Stalinist system of super-centralization were inevitably carried into wartime organization, the chief distinguishing feature of which was the further concentration of power at the top; the GKO itself was a visible and powerful manifestation of this in its own right. The decision-making process remained massively centralized and persistently cumbersome. Although Moscow demanded incessantly the exploitation of 'local resources', the centre's own instructions on the use of these frequently prevented it. The very lowest echelons of the Party and administrative machine proved to be inflexible to the point of inertia; the 'initiative' which senior officials demanded (and which the situation required) conflicted with the need to show proper zeal in the execution of duties, zeal which too often congealed into bureaucratism. The chain of command thus tended to snap at its lower links.

There were, however, few constraints, either moral or political, which the authorities felt in implementing their emergency mobilizations. Too much was often heaped on the populace: civilians were to man the militia, yet keep production going; train in reserve formations, run the administration, yet fulfil a host of para-military duties. The women, the youth and the aged had by their extreme exertions to plug great gaps left by failure to plan or failure to forecast. 'Popular response' thus became one of the highest priorities of the regime; its counterpart was a direct, and often dramatic relationship between the populace and 'the authorities', when the latter failed to do their job. The Moscow panic was a prime example of this; the contract of obedience was broken when 'the authorities' failed to provide minimum assurance of security. The fierceness of certain local patriotisms, however, made the general picture of popular response extremely uneven; pride of place and person contributed more than once to efficient, dogged defence – like Tula – which had a flexibility suited to the needs of the moment.

The transformation to a 'patriotic war' was accompanied by a pronounced campaign to identify 'Party' with 'motherland'; all the political shibboleth was dumped as the Party tried to combine with signs of a genuine, slow-burning national Russian mood of resistance, stimulated not only by internal propaganda but by growing evidence of what the 'New Order', with all its maniac killings and brutal exploitation, meant for Russia. Despair, anger and disgust were felt by Russians at the failure of 'the authorities' to deal with the German attack: there were senior officers who raged at the stupidity, even the criminality of an apparently disorganized leadership: civilian leaders shouted at the impossibility of doing everything on shrinking resources: there was a populace which was either overly coerced or rudely abandoned. But almost every occasion of effective leadership produced a vigorous and rapid result, and shrewd Germans discerned the potential shape of things to come.

The very lack of sophistication of Soviet society also contributed to its survival, its excessive communalism preventing total breakdown, its interlocked administrative nets bringing confusion but also the chance of an eventual response to instructions, its capacity for absorbing immense damage yet living on improvised norms and disordered patterns, above all – for all the years of Stalinist 'repression' and NKVD coercion – its basic moral resilience which 'patriotic war' intensified. In a senseless and self-defeating addiction to the *Untermensch* idea, the 'subhuman' Slav, German propaganda, viciously implemented by the SS and given bestial shape in the mass-murder rampages of the *Einsatzgruppen*, saw Russians only as a 'conglomeration of animals'. The weight of German success could not fail to strengthen the more extremist view of Russian inferiority; the German command, although by no means reassured on looking at its own casualty figures, could choose to ignore any contrary signs. The commander of the Soviet 6th Army, captured and interrogated, pointed out the true situation: with the fate of Russia in the balance, the Russians would fight – loss of territory meant nothing and the shortcomings of the regime became irrevelant. So it proved, for all the ghastly loss and nightmarish sacrifice.

The Supply Conference, which met in Moscow at the end of September, was almost a step forward in Anglo-Soviet amity; at the sessions under the chairmanship of Molotov, the Beaverbrook-Harriman mission appeared to reach agreement with a minimum of discussion on war supplies for the Soviet Union and the monthly requirements of equipment (aircraft, tanks, lorries and guns), and raw materials (tin, lead, cobalt, copper, zinc and aluminium, armour plate, industrial diamonds, down to cocoa beans); of the Soviet requirement of 1,100 tanks per month, it was decided to supply 500 (from British and American sources), of the 300 light bombers, 100 (from the USA); 1,000 tons of American armour plate would be forthcoming to meet the first part of the Soviet requirement of 10,000 tons. The first of many convoys laden with tanks and fighters had set sail for Murmansk, but the conference, like the ships, could not solve the almost catastrophic weapon and ammunition supply situation at one stroke. The great frontier dumps of ammunition and stores had long been lost; every Front was gravely short of 37-mm, 76-mm anti-aircraft and divisional gun artillery, hand-grenades and carbine cartridges. The output of tanks and aircraft was falling and factories were dropping out of production; fuel and power resources were also dangerously curtailed by the German advance.

The first Economic Mobilization Plan (for the third quarter of 1941) took a week to work out after the beginning of the war. This, like the ammunition production plan which was hastily approved on 23 June, was swept aside by the mobilization for the fourth quarter of 1941 and for 1942, which a special commission under N.A. Voznesenskii (head of the State Planning Commission: *Gosplan*) worked out early in August. On 16 August the plan was approved. Voznesenskii's plans covered not only evacuation but also the exploitation of Western Siberia and the Urals, Kazakhstan and Central Asia. Here, great 'evacuation bases' were to be set up, and plants evacuated eastwards were to be merged with local factories. The Evacuation Soviet, operating under GKO orders just as *Gosplan* now did, had early in July begun work on shifting major armaments plants to the east: the armour plate mills of Mariupol were to be shifted to Magnitogorsk, and more than a score of small arms factories moved from the 'central region' to the east. Kharkov's tank-engine plant would go to Chelyabinsk in the Urals, and technicians as well as plant from the Kirov Factory in Leningrad were scheduled for evacuation.

Plant conversion had not gone very well. The agricultural equipment factories, specified in what 'shadow planning' there was, could not turn out ammunition as they were supposed to because they lacked the necessary machine-tools. The Lugansk Locomotive Works, which was to produce shell-cases, received instructions to produce something quite different, which brought chaos. By November, the loss of over three hundred factories to the enemy deprived the Red Army of what had been a monthly production of eight and a half million shell-cases, nearly three million mines and two million aerial bombs. The loss of chemical plants slowed up the output of explosives, a grave crisis when the Red Army had almost exhausted its pre-war stocks of ammunition: the imbalance between gun production and ammunition output grew wider week by week. The Main Artillery Administration, which had a number of filling factories under construction, had estimated that it could mobilize its production without undue difficulty. The Administration was never more wrong. Ammunition output began to fall in August and dropped steeply by the end of the year: in August five million rounds were produced, four in September and October and an excess of three in November–December. In the July–December period, industry supplied twenty-six million rounds of ammunition, which was just half of its required output. Aircraft production toppled wildly from 1,807 in July, 2,329 in September to the catastrophic 627 in November; in the whole of 1941 the Soviet Union turned out 15,874 aircraft altogether (of which 12,516 were combat planes). The new machines had not yet gone into real quantity production: 1,542 Il-2 ground-attack fighters were turned out in 1941 and 207 Yak-7 fighters, and by the beginning of 1942 Soviet air strength was made up of only one-third modern machines. For the second half of 1941, only a little more than half of the planned output of tanks was managed, the total production for 1941 being 6,542 machines (2,996 of them T-34).

In August–October, Russian war industry was as much as 80 per cent 'on wheels', *na kolesakh*; from the Eastern Ukraine the steel mills of *Zaporozhstal* and the Dniepropetrovsk tube-rolling plant were loaded on to rail trucks and sent to the Urals, where they arrived in the first week in September and began production by the end of the year. Each People's Commissariat and administrative agency set up its 'evacuation bureau' and special commissioners to supervise both evacuation and last-minute on-site production. On 9 October, in collaboration with the People's Commissariat for Electric Power Stations the GKO began planning the evacuation of the Donbas power installations although it was intended to keep the power stations running to the last possible moment before shipping the generators to the Southern Urals. On 29 September the Novo-Kramatorsk heavy machine works received its orders to strip the plant for evacuation, including the only 10,000-ton press in the USSR; in five days the heavy equipment was stripped down ready for loading, in spite of damage and interruption caused by German bombing. When, on the afternoon of 21 October, 2,500 technicians assembled to be taken out by train, German troops were seven miles away and there was not a train in sight: the engineers then marched in columns for twenty miles to the nearest station left working.

On 4 October, Stalin had ordered Zhdanov and Kuznetsov to hurry on with arrangements to pull more industry and technicians out of Leningrad (a hazardous and complicated operation when Leningrad was sealed off); Stalin wanted the heavy tank works brought out, although ninety-two plants in Leningrad had already been part-evacuated by August. Technicians and equipment had to be brought out in stages, and then moved on a vast journey to Chelyabinsk and Sverdlovsk in the Urals, where sections of the Kirov and Izhora plants were finally installed. Up to the end of August, 282 trains had left Leningrad loaded up for the rear, but by the beginning of September the occupation of Mga shut down the rail nets. The only way out for heavy traffic was through Schlusselburg, and thence by barge across lake Ladoga, where railway troops under Lieutenant-General (Technical) V.A. Golovko were in charge of movement. Golovko had special barges, built fitted for carrying locomotives and trucks and operated on a shuttle across the lake, making as many as ten trips a day. Golovko got 150 locomotives, 4,000 waggons and 100 tanker-trucks out that way. By mid September, when Leningrad was closed to the outside world, there were still 2,177 trucks jammed on lines and sidings, 277 loaded with Defence Commissariat equipment. The Donbas evacuation was similarly cut short. The Commissariat for Heavy Industry had asked for 13,383 railway trucks to ship the steel installations out of the Stalino *oblast* but only 3,460 could be rounded up, and Tevosyan had to report to Stalin that the evacuation had been cut short by German penetrations. What could not be moved had to be blown up or disabled, the most spectacular act being the dynamiting of the Dnieper dam, the pride of Russia's earlier Five Year Plans.

The tidal wave of evacuation orders rolled on the Soviet railways administration under Kaganovich. The dismantling went on often under air attack, and the railway lines were frequently severed by bombing; in Belorussia, the main lines were cut forty-nine times in July and August. The first improvised evacuations had been little short of disastrous: reporting on the operations of the Brest-Litovsk line, its director pointed out that evacuation had begun under enemy fire 'with a complete absence of communications with the military command, and with wholly contradictory instructions from the Party and Soviet organizations in the Varanovichi and Minsk *oblast*, who looked on evacuation orders as a sign of panic, or violations of state discipline'. The railway had also to evacuate itself; by 10 July, 2,318 trucks loaded with railway equipment were being pulled back from the front lines (where railway self-evacuation was under the orders of the Military Soviet of the particular Front), but there had been heavy losses of locomotives and trucks in the frontier zones. By the end of June, seventy-four trains (3,224 trucks) were pulling civilians back to the rear, and in July 300,000 trucks were used in evacuation. Locomotives had to be run flat out with minimum servicing: this was maintained by 'GKO columns' which squeezed out every ounce of mileage. What the railways achieved was nevertheless enormous: in the first three months of the war they had moved two and a half million troops up to the front lines, and shifted 1,360 heavy plants (1,523 plants altogether), 455 to the Urals, 210 to Western Siberia, 200 to the Volga and more than 250 to Kazakhstan and central Asia, in addition to moving 150,000 railway men themselves and substantial numbers of locomotives and rolling-stock. The evacuation had used 1,500,000 trucks, and by mid November 914,380 waggons had shifted 38,514 loads for the aviation industry, 20,046 for ammunition plants, 18,823 for weapons factories, 27,426 for steel plants, 15,440 for the tank industry, and 16,077 for heavy industry.

In late October, the GKO decided on moving food supplies and even light industries from Kursk, Voronezh, and the North Caucasus, another responsibility loaded on to Mikoyan's Evacuation Soviet and Kosygin's evacuation inspectors. By December, the Evacuation Soviet had turned its attention from uprooting factories to unstopping vast bottle-necks in railway transit traffic. The Traffic-Transit Committee (*Komitet po razgruzke*) directed by Voznesenskii, Khrulev, Mikoyan and Kosygin took over from the Evacuation Soviet, which was more or less wound up at the end of 1941.

The re-location of the central government, with Commissariats of Aircraft, Tank, Armaments, Ammunition industries and the administration of heavy industry located after October in Kuibyshev, brought an additional strain. Voznesenskii, the master-mind of Soviet war industry, was instructed to submit weekly reports to Moscow on the armaments industry, while the Central Committee administrative agencies also in Kuibyshev were ordered to send out orders to regional party committees in the eastern hinterland to facilitate the reception and installation of evacuated industry. Getting the plants to the east was one problem: getting them into production was yet another. Large combines had become split up and had to be integrated anew with existing eastern plants. In Saratov, machinery began operating as the walls of a new factory went up around it; fourteen days after the last train-load of machines were unloaded, the first MiG fighter rolled out. On 8 December, the Kharkov Tank Works turned out its first twenty-five T-34 tanks, just short of ten weeks after the last engineers left Kharkov, trudging along the rail tracks.

What was little short of a second industrial revolution in the Soviet Union created immense demands for fuel, raw materials and construction of plant.

Only a third of the country's blast furnaces were working: steel production had dropped by two-thirds, and the coal-mines of the Donbas and the Moscow basin were lost to the Russians. There were critical shortages in aluminium, copper, tin, nickel, non-ferrous metals, all of which the Russians had asked for in their 'shopping list' presented to the October Supply Conference. New fuel deposits and raw material reserves, manganese ore and molybdenum, had to be opened up in the Urals, Kazakhstan, in the Kuzbas and the Karaganda. Production and exploitation of resources had to be speeded at any cost through all the rigours of a Siberian winter. The production targets under the current mobilization-output plan which the GKO had adopted (running from 1941–2) were massive: by January 1942, the Urals and Siberian plants were to reckon on an annual supply of 100,000 tons of pig-iron, 770,000 tons of steel and 326,000 tons of rolled metal. On 14 November, the GKO accepted the estimate of aircraft output for 1942 as 2,200–2,500 aircraft, and 22,000 medium and heavy tanks. All this had to be done (doubling the pre-war aircraft output and almost quadrupling tank production) with a labour force which had fallen, through enemy occupation or the impact of evacuation, from twenty-seven million at the beginning of the war to nineteen million; this labour also had to be fed by the 'differentiated ration system' and housed, however primitively.

The Commissariats, driven along relentlessly by the GKO, faced a giant task: D.F. Ustinov was now in charge of the Commissariat for Armament (Weapons), an assignment which brought him into close contact with Voronov of the Artillery administration, while Malenkov himself took charge of erasing bottle-necks in the aircraft industry and speeding the output of new fighters and bombers. This last was a 'trouble-shooting assignment' which Malenkov extended to the tank industry, where he and Molotov exercised a general supervision. The production of mortars was assigned to a special Commissariat organized in November; on 12 July the GKO had rescinded Kulik's previous lunatic decision to cut back the production of 76-mm field guns, and by the end of the month manufacture had been resumed, with some 4,000 being turned out by December. Output could also be speeded by technical improvement: the time needed to assemble the body of a tank was cut in the *Uralmash* tank factories from 110 hours to 30–40, and the main tank factories, the Gorkii Automobile Plant, *Uralmash* and the Chelyabinsk Tractor Works (which now contained sections of the Kharkov Diesel Factory and the Kirov workshops), were able to draw on skilled workers and accumulated experience to reduce work-hours required for many processes.

To hold Moscow, commanders and administrators had to lay hands on every and any item conceivable: Moscow converted its remaining factories to ammunition production after a GKO decision on 26 October. The Moscow Automobile Works turned out Shpagin's machine-pistols, planning a daily output of 1,500: with such machines as they had left factories produced grenades, infantry weapons and ammunition. The GKO also called on Leningrad to help out with the situation facing the Soviet capital. In addition to the Ladoga barges, an air-lift, flown by the 'Special Northern Aviation Group' had been flying out technicians and equipment from the Kirov Plant for transit to the Urals; between October–December, 11,600 Kirov and 6,000 Izhora workers were flown out on Stalin's orders, while 1,100 scientists and research workers from the Academy of Sciences were also flown out and routed to Kazan. Much more staggering was the air-lifting into the Moscow defence zone of more than a thousand guns and considerable quantities of ammunition, which Leningrad was to need desperately itself in a furious de-blockading attempt. Lenigrad meanwhile improvised more of its own armament; mortars were mounted on the chassis of a ZIS-5 or GAZ-AA lorry, screened with a little armoured plate and used to fire off mobile mortar-barrages, or naval guns were assembled into railway-truck mounted batteries. In spite of the evacuation of plant, Leningrad still managed to turn out more than three million shells by the end of 1941, some of which Moscow siphoned off.

For all the superhuman effort of the evacuation (which even a minimum of forward planning would have made less critical), much remained and was overrun. Until the giant plants in 'the east' started up or worked full blast, the resources to be eked out shrank day by day: a trickle of planes, a few hundred tanks, less and less ammunition. Practically everything now depended on the proper concentration of what was available going to the right place at exactly the right time. That, and digging deep into the Soviet rear for reserve formations, was the only possible option, which tested not only the capability but above all the nerve of the Soviet leadership.

Locked up in the Soviet Far East Stalin had more than three-quarters of a million excellent troops, organized into more than a score of well-trained divisions with very strong tank and air support. This was a rear, nevertheless, which could itself become a highly dangerous Front, facing as it did the formidable strength of the Imperial Japanese Kwantung Army, with whom the Red Army had already fought one savage round at the Khalkin-Gol two years ago in Outer Mongolia. For ten years, the strength of the Far Eastern forces had been steadily built up, and had reached some 30 divisions, 3 cavalry brigades, 16 tank brigades and over 2,000 tanks and aircraft; all forces east of lake Baikal were considered first line formations for operations involving the Japanese, while a second line force was maintained to the west of Baikal, consisting of the Siberian district garrisons and the Urals troops, to act as reinforcement for either the Far Eastern or European theatres. Soviet tank strength in the east had lain by the nature of the terrain in the Trans-Baikal, leading as it did into the great plain of Mongolia: in the Ussuri and the Amur areas, infantry predominated, but an independent tank brigade was assigned to operate along each operational road to Manchuria, and the infantry formations had 'infantry support' tanks assigned to them.

The Soviet Far Eastern formations had to cover a 2,000-mile frontier, and a major dilemma faced the Soviet command in considering its deployment, complicated still further by geographical and transportation peculiarities; which segment of the giant horseshoe shape should be totally invested and held? The eastern segment (containing Vladivostok, the coast bases and the terminal of the Trans-Siberian railway) was clearly vital, but cramped and vulnerable; nevertheless, its loss would be an unparalleled disaster, and Soviet strength in the eastern Ussuri sector was always maintained at a high level (some twelve divisions). Its perimeter was massively fortified, and its internal garrisoning strict. The Amur region was also closed in by fortification while the Trans-Baikal relied upon its mobile forces as a deterrent. As early as March 1941, troops had been on the move westwards, but they followed in strict order from the Urals 'central reserve', to the edge of the Trans-Baikal: in May, Lukin's 16th Army was ordered west to the Ukraine, where a large number of Khalkin-Gol veterans, Feklenko, Fedyuninskii, Potapov being among the more distinguished, were concentrated. But the main forces were intact and were brought to operational readiness on 22 June 1941 to face a possible Japanese attack, which so far had not come: knowledge of which way Japan would jump – for the 'northern solution' (against the Soviet Union) or the 'southern solution' (against the British and Americans) – was of critical importance to Stalin, and he had the means in Richard Sorge to acquire it.

Two days after the beginning of the war on the western frontiers of the Soviet Union, the Army and Navy Sections of the Japanese Imperial General Headquarters set out Japanese objectives in their paper 'Outline of Japan's National Policy to meet changes in the International Situation', which proposed a southern advance and *independent* settlement of the 'northern' question. A war-plan, *Hachi-Go* Plan, first formulated in 1937 and revised in 1940, for operations against the Soviet Union did exist: 'Guide to Operational Planning against the USSR for Financial Year 1941' had gone into effect as from 1 April 1941. Foreign Minister Matsuoka pressed during the June debates on policy for Japan to enter the war against Stalin before the outcome was 'clear' but the military reserved its position, and at the Imperial Conference on 2 July, General Sugiyama argued against immediate Japanese intervention. Nevertheless, to promote an 'eventual' solution of the 'northern problem', the Japanese command proceeded to reinforce the Kwantung Army under the guise of a 'Special Exercise', *Kan-Toku-En*: twelve cadre divisions were increased to fourteen, aircraft strength increased to 600, auxiliary units were expanded and ground strength doubled, from 350,000 to 700,000. The Korea Army and the Northern Army (southern Sakhalin and Hokkaido) were also reinforced. By the end of September, Japanese forces facing the Soviet frontiers had reached their peak.

Although Sorge maintained a traffic of sorts with Moscow over Japanese intentions, it was not until the end of September that he was able to assemble the items of information gleaned in August about the July Imperial conference into a positive message that there would be no Japanese attack on the Soviet frontiers before the spring of 1942. This was information which Stalin both received and acted upon, to draw off divisions from the Far Eastern command and rush them to the defence of Moscow; the first, like the 32nd Rifle Division at Borodino, was flung into action as it was hustled through Moscow to the battle-line, even though only two regiments had been assembled. That they were immensely tough troops German units soon discovered to their cost.

Stalin set about moving what was eventually to amount to half the divisional strength of the Far Eastern command (including the formation transferred in the late spring of 1941); between eight and ten rifle divisions were moved in October and November, together with 1,000 tanks and 1,000 aircraft. Not that this left gaps in the Far Eastern ranks: by immediate mobilization, eight rifle divisions, one cavalry division and three tank brigades were established by the end of 1941, and the number of men under arms levelled out again at just over three-quarters of a million, although many of them were recruits undergoing training. Even if the previous Soviet superiority over the Kwantung Army had been wiped out, the over-all equality of strength was sufficient for effective defensive operations and therefore adequate for Soviet purposes. The district which lost most heavily and most immediately was the Trans-Baikal (which had already lost an army headquarters); the withdrawals elsewhere were rather more restrained, and accompanied by another reorganization of the Khabarovsk-Vladivostok defences and command (which covered the Ussuri region). Three commands, 25th Army at Voroshilov, 1st Red Banner in the centre and 35th Army to the north at Iman, had been set up to improve the operational facilities of this 'front', where, as on every other stretch of the Far Eastern frontiers, the border defences were expanded and manned on a wartime footing. A new air division was also organized to fill the gap left by planes sent westwards.

At the same time as he reached into his Far Eastern hoard of men and tanks, Stalin sent a high-powered command contingent to the Urals to supervise the training of reserve and recruit formations. General Tyulenev, who had arrived in a Moscow hospital after being wounded on the Southern Front, was visibly disappointed at being given a 'rear assignment' after he had written to Stalin and asked for a posting; Stalin in the course of a personal interview disabused him of any misgivings on that score. 'The situation at the front depends entirely on how quickly and how effectively we can prepare our reserves'; in stressing that, Stalin demanded of Tyulenev, who was to be accompanied by Lieutenant-General (Artillery) A.K. Sivkov and Lieutenant-General P.S. Rybalko, that the new divisions be trained in close combat, in particular anti-tank tactics, and that the officers should be told how to handle operations. This was a State Defence Committee (GKO) assignment, for which Marshal Voroshilov was held ultimately responsible; (both Voroshilov and Budenny had been removed from operational commands and assigned to training).

The minimum of these fresh divisions were sent to the front: only when the situation became altogether desperate did Stalin allow fresh regiments to dribble through his fingers, which otherwise remained clamped tight around his 'Supreme Command Reserve'. Into his own ledger of survival, a notebook containing details of every unit and piece of equipment passing into or through Moscow, Stalin with that ubiquitous blue pencil checked off the allocations of regiments, tanks and guns, minutely controlling each with all the rigour at his command. Skilful as the withdrawal from the Far East was, equally skilful was the concealment of these divisions from the German command (and from the Soviet field command also, who had to stand amidst wholly decimated ranks before Stalin would yield to frantic and despairing requests).

When the German 'general offensive' began to roll again upon Moscow, with the roads and fields hardened by the frosts which eased movement through October's inland lakes of mud, the Soviet commanders had some 890 tanks (just under 800 of them the outmoded T-26 type) to fight off the German assaults: to strengthen the Western Front, a process of almost continual re-grouping was set in motion, although even this often lagged behind events. The subordination of the 30th and 50th Armies to the flanks of the Western Front was very tardily effected in November: the 50th Army on Zhukov's left had six rifle divisions, where the average strength wavered between 600 and 2,000 men to a division (and two artillery batteries to a division); only one formation, 413th Rifle Division, was anywhere near full strength, with 12,000 men and 100 guns and mortars. The 58th Tank Division which in mid-November was hastily pulled out of 16th Army and sent as 'reinforcement' to 30th Army had 350 men, fifteen light tanks and five guns all told. It was little wonder that Zhukov's staff had the front hospitals combed for volunteers, walking wounded or men recovered sufficiently to man 'independent battalions' armed with anti-tank weapons to stiffen the attacks on German Panzer units. Between 9 and 12 November Zhukov had received four cavalry divisions (20th, 44th, 17th and 24th), which amounted to 12,000 men for this entire force sent to Rokossovskii's 16th Army. Not without reason did the German command come to conclude that the Russians were almost at 'their last gasp' (*um die letzte Krafteanstrengung*).

Not long after his purge of the military command in 1937, Stalin had put a stop to the experimentation and limited contingency planning connected with possible partisan operations on Soviet territory. The supply dumps were emptied and the secret 'rear bases' allowed to lie forgotten and untended. This aspect of Soviet war-planning, like so much else, suffered from the dominant theme of 'carrying the war on to enemy territory' and winning it there: the relevance of partisan operations was therefore almost automatically ruled out, while at the same time Stalin was scarcely likely to encourage 'guerrilla' initiative, with its inevitably decentralized emphasis, during a period of high political tension. Both from the point of view of morale – the maintenance of the thesis of the 'inviolability' of Soviet territory and the 'invincibility' of the Soviet state – and from the dictates of maximized internal security, the regime could scarcely promote the organized dissidence which was implicit in organization for guerrilla war. Contingency planning at the highest level (for which there is some evidence of very limited activity) was of necessity kept a state secret; it is unlikely, however, that even this was conceived on the scale of such territorial loss as the Soviet Union had suffered by October–November 1941. The Soviet state and command had behind it the partisan experience of the Civil War, though no 'theory' of rear insurgency had been developed, and historical experience had been crusted over with ideological plasterings; if anything, the Civil War guerrillas had proved to be as much a political embarrassment – the very word *partizanshchina* suggested this – as a military asset. The essential and indispensable individualism of the partisan, ranging all the way from a self-indulgent banditry to persistent political or military subordination, was also a real memory which died hard, for on more than one occasion the Red Army had been obliged to turn on its erstwhile insurgent-peasant allies, 'anarchists' like Makhno or the stubborn ataman Grigori'ev, and shoot them down ruthlessly.

The first attempts at partisan organization and activity in the 'Great Patriotic War' were directly in line with the other measures of mass mobilization, such as the militia divisions, for holding up the German advance in any and every conceivable way, adding one more counterweight to the enemy's advantages. In this form, the partisan operations conformed more or less to the *malaya voina*, the 'little war' operations discussed at some length by Soviet commanders in the 1920s. The *Sovnarkom* and Central Committee directive of 29 June contained one paragraph, not then made public, on the tasks of 'partisan detachments (*otryadi*) and sabotage groups (*diversionnye gruppy*)' organized for 'action with units of the enemy army, for kindling partisan war everywhere and anywhere, for blowing up bridges, roads, telephone and telegraph lines, destroying dumps and the like.' A little more than a fortnight later, the Central Committee issued a more detailed specification under the instruction of 18 July, 'On the organization of the struggle in the rear of the German troops': this laid down the main outlines of 'partisan war', and placed the responsibility for activating resistance behind the lines directly upon the republic, *oblast* and *rayon* Party and Soviet (administrative) organs. These bodies were also responsible for preparing for future resistance in areas already threatened with being overrun; there, underground Party organizations and *Komsomol* cells should be set up without delay. In addition to the specially created commission to handle partisan warfare and sabotage at the highest Central Committee level, the preliminary work of organizing would be handled also by the special departments within the Political Administrations of Fronts or the Political Sections at Army level. The first secretaries of the Party organizations would select 'experienced fighters . . . personally known to the leaders of the Party organization and experienced in the work of organizing' to build up the partisan cadres: the arms, ammunition, supplies and money which this work would require must be organized in advance, communications between partisan groups or sabotage units organized which would call for radio sets, codes, couriers and liaison men. The secret, underground cells were to be kept in general ignorance of each other, with only single persons providing the necessary inter-cell contacts.

The 10th Sections of Front and Army Political Administrations were specially charged with handling preparations for partisan war and sabotage operations: towards the end of July, the North-Western and South-Western Front administrations had both sent out very detailed instructions on organization and tactical principles suited to partisans. On 13 July 1941 the Political Adminis- tration of the North-West Front had already submitted its first report to Mekhlis at the Political Administration on the organization of partisan units, which were about 50 to 80 men strong, and divided into smaller units each of 10 men; 22 units had so far been set up in the Velikie Luki, Luga and Bologoye areas (including one special unit, commanded by a Party official and with an officer of the NKVD frontier troops as chief of staff, armed with 300 rifles and 14 machine-guns), together with 'mopping-up units' used to tackle German parachutists dropped in the Soviet rear and then employed as partisan cadres as the district was overrun. On the ground itself, partisan detachment commander Dudin reported in late September on the organization and early activities of one of these squads:

> 30 June 1941 I was ordered by the *rayon* committee of the VKP (b) to form a company of a destruction battalion in the district covered by the Zapolsk, Zaoisensk, Bolshe-Lzinsk and Zaplius village soviets.
>
> Time to 5 July taken up with forming the section, drill and tactical training.
>
> 6 July mass withdrawal of construction battalions and Red Army units from Pskov to Luga. I collected from units pulling back 123 rifles, 2 Degtyarev light machine guns and ammunition, with which the company was armed . . .
>
> 9 July 1941 after heavy fighting Plius area was evacuated by the Red Army.
>
> From that time [we] went over to the position of a partisan detachment (*otryad*), taking refuge with the population in the woods.
>
> From 9.7 to 24.8.1941 my detachment carried out 25 large and small diversions in the enemy rear. We destroyed more than 20 lorries, killed more than 120 Fascists, not count- ing those accounted for by the Red Army on the basis of information we gave. At the present time there are only 12 men left with me in the detachment.

To the west, at Gdov, other detachments tried to form up, often in the fashion of Pushkov's:

> We decided to form two partisan detachments from our destruction battalion. But things happened so quickly, that from 15 to 16 [July] Gdov was captured, the road was cut. We stayed in the Polnov district. I decided this way: once we were staying we should get on with the business. We decided to move in with the partisan detachments into the collective farms and look about, to see how things should be got going, to help organizing the work of partisan detachments . . . In the district 4 detachments were set up. The strength of the detachments – from 20 to 35 men. The biggest detachment was in Semirenko.

The detachments were pressed for weapons:

All have rifles, there are still rounds of ammunition, but very few grenades. We got grenades from retreating Red Army men, but there are very few. We couldn't get hold of any machine-guns. [In the detachments] there are single Degtyarev machine-guns, but not in every detachment. Fillipov's detachment has no machine-gun at all. No bottles [Molotov cocktails]. We couldn't get any pistols at all. Pistols – very small weapons, but absolutely essential for reconnaissance.

In the Velikie Luki district, other detachments fared better:

The detachment [Kuninshoe district] has established a good supply base. Detachment has a fair armament: Russian and German rifles, 2 Lewis guns, 1 heavy machine-gun, grenades and so forth. At present preparing a group of 8 men to burst into the Krebtovsk village Soviet, which has been taken by the Germans.

Further north, in Karelia, fifteen partisan detachments had been organized, and to direct them the Karelian Central Committee had set up a special three-man commission, a *troika*, which in August met Voroshilov in Leningrad to draw up a plan of operations and establish a 'partisan staff' to direct these undertakings: Kuprianov, first secretary of the Karelian Central Committee, itemized tasks very similar to those underlined in the 29 June directive, 'blowing up bridges, railway tracks, destroying enemy telephone-telegraph communications, blowing up enemy ammunition dumps'.

Budenny's south-western command issued similar directives and instructions, although the Ukrainian Communist Party leadership had apparently been the first to promulgate quite detailed instructions on partisan planning as early as 27 June, two days before the first directive from 'the centre'. Perhaps it was no coincidence that the first real experiments with partisan operations had taken place in the Ukraine in the 1930s; presumably the files had been preserved. On 20 June an 'operational group' of Party and government officials, Zlenko, Drozhzhin, Spivak, Strokach, was assembled under the 'direct control' of M.S. Khrushchev, Burmistenko and Korotchenko, the top political echelon. Spivak had already (27 June) received instructions from Khrushchev to organize partisan detachments in Kamenets-Podolsk: Lwow, Tarnopol, Stanislaw, Cernauti, Volynsk and Rovno *obkoms* were instructed to set up similar 'operations groups', while rear areas set about establishing shadow organizations and secret cells, in one great ripple across the Ukraine. Some 140 detachments, nearly 2,000 men, were assembled under the first orders and slipped through the German lines into enemy-occupied territory: in Kiev, two large partisan units, each of more than 1,000 men, were organized and placed under the command of NKVD (Frontier Troops) officers. Khrushchev, who appeared to take a very personal interest in these activities, suggested that factories should start local production of weapons and equipment specially needed by or suited to partisan units.

In Belorussia, where the partisan movement was to enjoy greater success than in the Ukraine in spite of the latter's energetic start, the session of the Belorussian Central Committee and republic *Sovnarkom* met in Moghilev on 30 June to discuss its plans and possibilities, producing *Directive No. 1* 'On the transition to underground work by the Party organizations in enemy-occupied territory'; this meeting decided to start operations by sending through the lines not single underground workers, but 'small organizational groups', each of which could and would become the nucleus of a partisan unit. Squads like this had already been formed or were forming up: seventy-eight were assembled in Moghilev by early July, more than 2,300 men. There were volunteers by the score and more, all of whom were rigorously screened – date of Party membership, pre-war employment, relationships with persons held by 'Soviet repressive organs' (the NKVD). The NKVD also interviewed these partisan-candidates, who had to be in possession of a 'clean sheet'. Even if politically acceptable, the majority of the candidates were innocent of all experience or training in 'conspirational work'. On the evening of 1 July the *podpolshchiki*, the underground workers and partisans, assembled to hear P.K. Ponomarenko, first secretary of the Belorussian Communist Party, as well as the Marshals Voroshilov and Shaposhnikov, talking on the scope and nature of their assignments. Ponomarenko advised his agents to link up with communists in the occupied regions, establish a 'Party centre' in each district and agitate among the civilian population, whose aid should be sought in collecting arms dumped after the fighting had ceased: 'Blow up bridges . . . destroy single trucks with enemy officers and soldiers.' Shaposhnikov stressed the importance of using 'any opportunity to slow up the movement of enemy reserves to the front. Blow up enemy trains full of troops, equipment or weapons, blow up his bases and dumps.' Voroshilov for his part dwelt more on Civil War experiences as a guide to present actions.

What Ponomarenko presented in his outline corresponded (with regional scaling down) to the first ideas on partisan organization – small partisan units evenly distributed throughout occupied territory along the lines of the administrative structure: one *rayon*, one partisan unit (with its sub-units). The very artificiality of the many-'special groups' infiltrated through the lines nevertheless contributed to their isolation and eventual neutralization: manned by Party and NKVD men, or filled with strange men from strange cities, the infiltrated units were unable to build up and maintain proper contact with the local population. Pressure was applied precisely at those points where the Soviet administrative system had proved weakest – in the lowest echelons, and in its most vulnerable sector, the countryside. German counter-guerrilla activity found, as Soviet partisans themselves admit, ready sources of information and support: there was the extreme danger posed to partisan units in the Bryansk forest by a group of collaborationists, one a woodsman who not only knew the woods but also the partisan locations, another a deserter from a 'destruction battalion' who went over to the Germans. The improvised local units, hard pressed for weapons, ammunition and supplies, were ground to pieces or simply broke up; more successful organization actually brought on its own disasters, for large-scale units, tied down territorially, were easier to hunt down and destroy. The small units thus perished and the 'brigades' made large targets.

The wide variations in terrain, the general lack of weapons and the particular shortage of special equipment, the administrative breakdown brought on by German advance and occupation, the habit of 'passive observation' if not downright collaboration on the part of local populations, the 'lack of a single centre for the direction of the partisan movement' (in the words of a report from the North-Western Front Political Administration) contributed to smothering this first wave of guerrilla war. On 19 August Mekhlis intervened with a directive from the Main Political Administration of the Red Army (*Glav*PURKKA) on 'Work among the population of the occupied areas' and the Party-political direction of the partisan movement, with 'partisan units often broken up or lacking concrete assignments'. Red Army units, cut off in the rear and 'waging also partisan war' in the same way 'did not receive the necessary leadership, and did not always co-ordinate their operations with partisan detachments'. The Front political administrations stepped up their 'Party-political work', prodded by Mekhlis: on 29 August, *Glav*PURKKA sent out a telegram to all Fronts ordering an intensification of indoctrination, through leaflets and pamphlets to be distributed to partisan units and civilians in the occupied areas. The Fronts also received a copy of the 'Instruction on the Organization of Partisan Detachments' issued in 1919 in the struggle against Denikin – dug out of the Red Army archives and re-issued.

The rapid changes in the situation at the front and the obvious weaknesses in organization brought about constant modification and intervention; on the Leningrad Front, the 'Partisan staff' drew up for 29 September its 'Plan for organizing communications and command among the partisan detachments of the Leningrad *oblast*' which the Front command approved. The breakdown in communications, the weakness of the command, the actual disintegration of partisan units made a rapid overhaul imperative. Detachments without 'fixed local bases', located near the blockade line were to operate against enemy HQs, sabotage siege gun batteries, fuel and ammunition dumps, cut communications and mount night raids on barracks and aerodromes. Long-range detachments, operating from their own 'supply bases' would attack German garrisons, disrupt the German administrative machine and seek out collaborators. The grim and often brutal business of driving a wedge between the German occupiers and the occupied Russians had begun.

By the autumn of 1941, the Soviet leadership in the Party, security and military administrations had perhaps a clearer idea and more realistic notions of the situation obtaining in the occupied rear areas: in August, when the Political Administration was obviously trying to get some grip on the 'partisan situation', the first training centres were set up with Red Army and NKVD instructors, to give instruction in demolition techniques and simultaneous parachute training. Although here and in the Military Soviets the Red Army was drawn into partisan work very quickly, the NKVD appeared to predominate at all levels from the top to the detachments themselves; many of the NKVD were, nevertheless, officers of the frontier troops seconded to this new employment, a group distinct from the 'Special Section' (OO) or internal security men close to Beria. The Party resorted to widespread employment of its 'cadres administrations' to staff or direct partisan units, and, as P.Z. Kalinin points out, the Party and NKVD worked closely in screening recruits; the men from the cadres sections had the necessary knowledge to facilitate this co-operation. The central apparatus of the Party, the *Komsomol* organization, the NKVD and the Red Army were all involved in setting up the movement; as a result, there was inevitable confusion, even competition and little of that 'unified direction' for which local operators cried out so frequently. The Leningrad command had already set up a prototype 'partisan staff'; the 10th Sections of Front and Army political administrations devoted much of their attention to problems of organization and agitation (propaganda), and partisan units operating under immediate military control (as they did at the approaches to Moscow) could carry out limited reconnaissance and intelligence assignments. Otherwise, the military results were at first meagre and scattered; detachments broke up by losses or desertion, or the flight of leaders. Many disintegrated through lack of 'supply bases', or else the 'underground' failed them. One of the organizers of the Minsk 'underground', I.P. Kazinets, who finally took it into his own hands to organize a 'central Party underground' pointed to these disadvantages:

Having a solid mass of comrades capable of operations, we have several times tried to set up a Party group, which could carry on mass agitation work among the population of Minsk. The work goes ahead in bits and pieces, but to this day firm leadership is lacking.

The 'solid mass' to which Kazinets was referring came from the Red Army men marooned in the rear, who subsequently formed the basis for a thoroughly reinvigorated and reorganized partisan movement.

The German encirclement battles had left many thousands of men stranded in their wake, especially in Belorussia where dense forest provided concealment, if little else and for these broken or dismembered units, the battle for sheer survival continued. Not infrequently, partisan units were used by front commands to bring bodies of troops out of encirclement; 21st Army in October used this technique to bring 800 men out of encirclement in the Poltava *oblast*, and the Western Front reclaimed General V.I. Kuznetsov of the 3rd Army, with 600 men. There were units which retained enough cohesion and discipline to fight on as a military force: Colonel Nichiporovich, commander of what had been the 208th Motorized Rifle Division, formed a powerful *otryad*, 'Detachment No. 208' which continued to operate against German lines of communication in Belorussia. The first detachments set up by local Party and

NKVD organs found frequent reinforcements in refugee Red Army men. Kazinets' Minsk organization, which had had not time in which to organize any 'underground' structure, had an infusion of the ill-fated garrison of 13th Army to swell and stimulate operations. The Party 'underground' did on occasions organize Red Army men into partisan units, or else Party personnel were sent to detachments formed from the *okruzhentsy* (the 'encircled'), like the official of the Vitebsk *obkom* Party organization dispatched to Danukalov's improvised 'Red Army-partisan' squads.

Although Soviet intelligence agents proper operated in strict seclusion from the partisans, the earliest systematic use of partisans for field reconnaissance occurred in the fighting at the Moscow approaches in October-November: intelligence and sabotage assignments were issued by Panfilov (316th Rifle Division), Beloborodov (9th Guards Rifle Division), Pronin (144th Rifle Division), while the staff of the Western Front used partisans in reconnaissance in the Mozhaisk area. In the Moscow area's 'pre-frontal zones', a rather more deliberate partisan preparation had taken place as supply bases were set up with medical supplies, ammunition and even clothing 'depots'. Dovator's cavalry corps, raiding in the German rear, appears to have operated a 'systematic' contact with partisan groups, which had a number of radio sets; a particular assignment from the Western Front staff was the determination of the co-ordinates of enemy targets (airfields and ammunition dumps). For attacks on German units or garrisons, 'special detachments' of the Red Army worked with partisan units behind the lines, and then jointly tried to fight their way back. These lunges into the German rear bore of necessity an improvised and hasty stamp; the patterns of co-ordination had yet to establish themselves in what was rapidly becoming a whole new dimension of brutal and terrible slaughter, with the German forces turning to all the unlimited punitiveness of anti-partisan war, *Bandenkrieg*, and the partisans out of self-protection and self-interest, committed inescapably to their own nightmarish rigour.

The population was slowly but inexorably squeezed between German and Soviet-partisan pressures. Through the partisans, however thin they might be as yet on the ground, the long finger of Soviet authority poked back into their lives. After October 1941 a deliberate effort to 're-establish' Soviet presence and with it a form of authority appears to have been made. Intensifying propaganda among the occupied population was a first but highly difficult preliminary; underground leaders found 'verbal propaganda' of little use, and complained that 'only rarely and with great difficulty' did Soviet leaflets or news-sheets reach the populace, and air-drops put leaflets too near the front line, 'where there are few people and from which it is impossible to take them into the rear because of searches *en route*'. In the area between the Leningrad and Kalinin *oblasts*, a partisan *krai* (zone) had been set up, and here, as in other spots, the partisans brought back 'the government'; Partisan Brigade No. 2, operating south of Dno, reported on the change in the mood of the populace:

R.T.S.—I

The most characteristic feature in the relations between the population and the occupying forces [appears to be] that now after 2 months of occupation, all, and that includes the most reactionary category of the workers, turn an unfriendly and united face to the Fascists, based on the facts of life.

Everything has gone to show that to stand aside from the struggle between the Soviet people and German Fascism is impossible.

Bringing back 'authority' was now not only possible but necessary:

The command of the brigade considered very rightly that without close contact with the population, without a fight to re-establish the collective farms, to establish Soviets and the laws of the Soviet state, it was impossible to create for the partisan movement a powerful economic and political basis, it was impossible to win the sympathy and support of the population.

This suggests very plainly that sympathy and support had been earlier forfeits. 'Government' came back through an *orgtroika*, the 'three-man group' with its Party, state and NKVD representative (the latter an officer of the Frontier Troops): the *orgtroika* was to re-establish the organs of state power in the village, resume the normal activity of the collective farms and exterminate German agents or traitors. The *orgtroika* came under the command of the brigade.

These were as yet mere straws in a fierce and destructive wind, under which the Stalinist state and the Russian people bowed and bent. The two 'rears' were torn with dislocation and ravaged by loss. The dams of resistance which Stalin tried to build so frenziedly were terrifyingly thin, and the resumption of the German offensive in November against Moscow, as evacuation trains rolled east passing troop trains moving west with Far Eastern and reserve divisions, as partisan traffic through the lines thickened, and when equipment could just trickle from the factories, bid fair at first to batter everything in, at the centre and on the flanks.

7

The Moscow Counter-Stroke:
November–December 1941

'If they [the Germans] want a war of extermination, they shall have one.
This challenge Stalin threw down in his speech of 6 November, a speech
delivered on the eve of the anniversary of the October Revolution: delegates
from the Party, from the city administration and the Red Army filled the
marble cavern of the Mayakovskii underground station to hear it. With
emphatic exaggeration Stalin announced that the German Army had suffered
more than four million casualties in its war on Russia, yet the blitzkrieg had
failed, failed because 'the Hess mission' did not bring in Britain and the USA
as either partners or even neutrals in Germany's eastern venture, failed because
the Soviet Union had not disintegrated, and failed above all because the Red
Army was still unbroken in the field. It was true, Stalin admitted, that certain
German technical superiorities still had a telling effect, but the Red Army
would go on to become 'the terror of the German Army': it was true that as
yet there was no Second Front, but this too would come 'unquestionably' and
'within a very short time'.

The next morning, with German troops less than fifty miles away, Stalin
held the traditional military parade in Red Square; squads of Soviet riflemen
and columns of old, out-gunned T-26 tanks, with a few of the new, formidable
T-34s, paraded in the winter light and crunched across the snow, moving off
at once to the battle-lines. Although Stalin wanted the parade, he was not
prepared to take any undue risks; at the beginning of November he summoned
General Zhukov to the *Stavka*, outlined the plans for holding the anniversary
parade and asked for Zhukov's estimate of German intentions. Zhukov replied
that the enemy was in no condition to launch a major attack in the next few
days: German troops were busy reinforcing and regrouping, having recently
suffered heavy losses, but this did not rule out German air attacks, so that one
necessary precaution must be to reinforce the Moscow air defences and move
up fighter aircraft from neighbouring fronts. The parade duly went forward,
but in contrast to his speech the night before, this time Stalin spoke out more
brutally and brusquely, dismissing fears that 'the Germans could not be beaten'
as the panic of a bunch of frightened little intellectuals – a gratuitous sneer, if

ever there was one. In 1918, Stalin observed, the Red Army was in a worse position that it was today when 'we have no serious shortage of food, weapons or equipment . . . ', yet the Soviet forces went on to win in those far-off grim days and they would win once more, inspired as they were by 'the great figures of our heroic ancestors' – Nevskii, Dmitri Donskoi, Suvorov, Kutuzov – and fighting now as in 1918 'under great Lenin's victorious banner'. That same day in Kuibyshev Marshal Voroshilov reviewed the anniversary parade, Marshal Timoshenko in Voronezh took the salute at another, but neither had the drama or the impact of this sombre Moscow march. For all his comparison with 1918, Stalin could not disguise the grimness of the present situation; his account of German losses and the hope hovering on the horizon of the 'Second Front' was but scant encouragement. His words were meant first to steady and then to stimulate Russian nerve, his phrases were at once defiant and gloomy, but he hammered on the consciousness of Russian achievement and historical self-respect. He gave notice that the *Untermensch* intended to fight back.

By late October, with the Donbas overrun, Kharkov captured (24 October) and the Crimea threatened, German assault divisions had breached Moscow's first outer defence line, running from Kalinin some 90 miles north-west of the Soviet capital to Kaluga 100 miles to the south-west, and were jabbing into the second, curling from the southern shore of the Moscow Lake at Nove Zovidovskii, through Klin and Solnechnogorsk to Istra and thence to Zvenigorod on the river Moskva: following the line of the river Nara, the latter wound on to Serpukhov and Tula, its southern bastion, just a fraction more than 100 miles from the Kremlin. Where it bulged inwards at the centre, Moscow was only 43–7 miles away. Behind these outer lines lay the three belts of inner urban defences under the immediate control of the Moscow garrison, the VMZO. Heaving itself forward out of a sea of clinging mud, the German attack on 9th Army front was held up at Kalinin, where Panzer Group 3 (re-designated Third Panzer Army) was under fierce attack by the Soviet 30th and 31st Armies: driving straight on from the west, the German Fourth Army ran into fresh Soviet formations (49th, 43rd and 33rd Armies) and on its southern wing could push no further than the Nara-Serpukhov area: Guderian's force (now Second Panzer Army) had crashed into Tula at the end of October, but the town, the 'little Moscow' of the south, did not fall to a *coup de main*. The Chief of the Reich Press Office might announce loftily on 9 October that 'Russia is finished', and the German command might pinpoint objectives, like Rybinsk and Vologda, far to the east of Moscow (to cut Soviet escape routes), but the front-line divisions, infantry and armoured alike, were more immediately aware of their heavy losses, the stiffening Soviet resistance – more broad-tracked T-34s to sail the October mud seas, more fresh units from the deep rear, more sharp and savage local offensives. But for all the losses and increasing hardship, the Wehrmacht intended still to press forward: Stalin and his *Stavka* were determined to hold. That determination the *Stavka* scorched into the minds of Soviet commanders. On 28 October, Volokolamsk, held by Rokossovskii's 16th Army with its three ragged divisions, finally fell after heavy fighting, a highly unpalatable piece of news which Rokossovskii deputed his artillery commander Kazakov to break to Zhukov. Two days later, on the orders of the *Stavka*, a Western Front HQ staff commission arrived at 16th Army HQ, there to inter-rogate commanders, check operational orders and confiscate operational maps. The *Stavka* would not tolerate troops 'giving up town after town' at the very approaches to Moscow, but at this censure of his 16th, Rokossovskii felt, rightly, that an injustice had been done.

There were compelling reasons why units should stand and be pounded to pieces: Zhukov had no option but to fight for a breathing-space. The dozen militia divisions raised in Moscow were ultimately taken into Red Army strength proper: the Far Eastern units were carefully filtered into the front. With frantic haste, three new reserve armies, 10th, 26th and 57th, were being raised at the end of October, and six more, 28th, 39th, 58th, 59th, 60th and 61st, were ordered by the *Stavka* to start manning the great arc running from lake Onega-Yaroslavl-Gorkii-Saratov-Stalingrad-Astrakhan. (German intelligence subsequently discovered from prisoner-of-war interrogation that an 'easterly defence line' to the rear of Moscow was under construction. Zhukov had been forced to man his outer line with scattered and hurriedly regrouped formations; after 1 November, Stalin embarked on more systematic reinforcement, dis-patching 100,000 men, 300 tanks and 2,000 guns to Zhukov. On 24 October, the GKO set up a special railway command in Moscow (*Voenno-ekspluatsionnoe upravlenie*) to handle reinforcement traffic; work had already begun on a new circular railway to link up the feeder lines, and more than 300,000 railway waggons were concentrated in the Moscow marshalling yards to shift men and supplies. Of the 8,000 or so lorries available, Zhukov had only 2,000 subordinated to his front command, far too few to cover his needs so that once again the rail-ways had to take the strain. Stalin was defending the capital and the most important traffic junction in the whole of the Soviet Union.

Both sides, clamped in the seamless mud as they were, reinforced as best they might. On the morning that Stalin reviewed his columns in Red Square, winter had already come with its snapping frosts: on the night of 6–7 November, the roads hardened and the fields were sheeted with a surface upon which armoured fighting vehicles could once more move. The German commanders debated the pros and cons of a futher offensive at the Orsha conference, which convened on 13 November. Army Group North, stripped of its armoured striking forces, was effectively on the defensive: Army Group South, already on the Don in the south-east lay advanced more than 200 miles to the east of Army Group Centre, whose commander von Bock pressed nevertheless for a resump-tion of the drive on Moscow. Everything considered, only one decision was really possible.

The German plan envisaged one more envelopment and the closing of the 'pincers'; Guderian would drive north-east to Kolomna, with deep flank cover provided by the Second Army linking up with the left wing of Army Group South, halted near Belgorod: the Fourth Army with Panzer Group 4 on its northern wing would attack at the centre, and the Ninth Army with Third Panzer Army in the north was to strike for the Volga Canal to the east and then swing down on Moscow. The northern wing would attack on 15 November, the southern on the seventeenth: the Fourth Army, its assault not specifically timed, would wait for Russian movement to left and right flanks and then strike at the denuded centre. For reserves, Army Group Centre had all of two divisions, and the immediate prospect of losing strong forces for much needed flank cover.

Zhukov, assessing the situation from his Front HQ at Perkhushkovo had also come to his conclusions. On 8 November, Western Front HQ discussed German deployment and plans – and the Soviet position. The outlines of German order of battle were generally established, except for 11th Panzer and 137th Infantry Divisions (Volokolamsk and Serpukhov sectors respectively), which observed very strict radio traffic discipline; Front intelligence reckoned that the heaviest German concentration was in the Volokolamsk area (seven Panzer, three motorized and three infantry divisions) and at Tula (four Panzer, three motorized and five infantry divisions plus two brigades). Rokossovskii, reporting to his own HQ that night, repeated Zhukov's estimate of German intentions:

The measures taken by the German command seem to add up to preparations for an offensive against the wings of the Western Front to outflank Moscow; on the right wing – in the direction of Klin and Dmitrova, and on the left – to Tula and Kolomna. It follows we can expect a frontal blow in the Naro-Fominsk area.

Zhukov therefore proposed to do what he could, by way of spoiling attacks, to hinder German deployment and regrouping. Rokossovskii selected Skirmanovo for 16th Army's local attack, to keep control of the Volokolamsk highway.

Zhukov was understandably concerned about his right and left flanks. At the beginning of November, the Bryansk Front was formally liquidated, and on the 10th the *Stavka* decided to transfer elements of 50th Army to Tula, and the remnants of 3rd and 13th Armies to the South-Western Front. But as Kreizer's Third Army pulled right back on Yefremov, uncovering the Western and South-Western Front junction, Zhukov in his report of 14 November to the *Stavka* warned that his left would have to be shored up near Tula. Looking north, only one division, the weak 107th Motorized Rifle Division (30th Army), secured the Western-Kalinin Front junction, where two Panzer divisions and one motorized division were poised, concentrations which Koniev had also reported to the *Stavka* on 11 November. In spite of these promptings, the *Stavka* was alarmingly sluggish in its response, waiting far too long to bring 30th and 50th Armies under Zhukov's Front control.

The limited attacks ordered by Zhukov had already been set in motion, to improve the tactical situation of 16th, 5th, 33rd, 43rd and 49th Armies. In 49th Army area, at Serpukhov, Zhukov planned to use General Belov's 'cavalry-mechanized group' (2nd Cavalry Corps, 415th and 112th Tank Division, two tank brigades and 15th Guards Mortar Regiment equipped with *Katyushas*) to break through what was thought to be a weakly held sector and surround the German 13th Corps. On 10 November, Zhukov ordered Belov to accompany him to Moscow, to discuss the details of the attack with Stalin.

Passing through the Borovitskie Gate of the Kremlin in the late afternoon, Zhukov and Belov picked their way past a bomb crater and entered an underground chamber down steps which led into a long corridor, heavily guarded and with doors off it to the right, 'like a railway sleeping car'. Zhukov put Belov into a 'cubicle' and went on himself. With the appearance of one of Stalin's secretaries, Belov was taken to the end of the corridor, through an open door into a brightly lit room; there was a huge writing table with a few telephones in the far left corner, and Stalin standing in the centre. Zhukov presented Belov to Stalin. Belov had last seen Stalin in 1933: 'He had changed a great deal since that time; before me [Belov] stood a smallish man with a tired sunken face . . . in eight years he appeared to have aged twenty.' But what astonished Belov was Zhukov's behaviour: 'He spoke brusquely, in a very authoritative way. The effect suggested that the senior officer here was Zhukov. And Stalin took it all for granted. At no time did any trace of annoyance cross his face.'

Stalin approved the plan, and the idea of having Rokossovskii's 16th Army attack on the upper sector to hinder any German movement of reserves. Belov was closely questioned about weapons for his corps and explained that he needed automatic weapons, using the rifles only for snipers. Stalin promised him 500 automatic weapons, and two batteries of the latest 76-mm guns, a godsend since his available artillery badly needed repair. The session over, Belov stepped out again into the Moscow night.

At this time also Stalin was concerned with the situation which had developed on the Soviet 'flanks' at large, in Leningrad and the north-eastern theatre of operations, in the Crimea, in the Donbas and the whole of the south-east. Immediately after the height of the first crisis outside Moscow, he had ordered Voronov to Leningrad; with Voronov went a bundle of plans and orders for a 'de-blockading operation', in which the 'Neva operational group' and 55th Army were to fight westwards to meet the 54th Army driving from the east, both forces to link up at Sinyavino. This would clear German forces from the southern shore of lake Ladoga and create a 'land passage' between Leningrad and Soviet-held territory. The *Stavka* plan scarcely raised any wild hopes in the Leningrad command, which Fedyuninskii had assumed on Zhukov's departure. For what was undoubtedly a strenuous and difficult operation, no less than eight rifle divisions, 100 tanks, all available heavy artillery and *Katyusha* battalions, supported by Front and Baltic Fleet aviation, were to be employed;

in fact, the de-blockading force, due to begin operations on 20 October, lined up 63,000 men, 475 guns and 97 tanks (including 59 heavy KV tanks) against 54,000 German troops holding fortified positions in depth and screened by marsh and bog. For all the odds, nevertheless, many a spirit in the beleaguered city rose at the thought of the 'rescue army', the 54th, but Marshal Kulik, 54th commander, by his bungling and incompetence very soon torpedoed any optimism.

The de-blockading drive had been anticipated, however, four days earlier on 16 October by Army Group North jumping off in an easterly drive for Tikhvin and the north at Lodeinoye Polye on the river Svir (running between the lakes Ladoga and Onega), there to link up with the Finnish Karelian Army, a German-Finnish link-up which would have bottled up Leningrad for good and all. On the inbent arc running south between lakes Ladoga and Ilmen, three Soviet armies (north to south, 54th, 4th and 52nd), plus the 'Novgorod Army Group' at the southern extremity, were stretched all too thinly. The 54th was already committed to the de-blockading action. Almost at once, the 4th and 52nd Armies were split apart and German troops drove along three axes, towards Kirishi in the north, to Budogoshch and thence on Tikhvin at the centre, and to Malaya Vyshera in the south-east. Kulik had been finally removed from the 54th, replaced by General Khozin who in turn was replaced by Fedyuninskii (as a junior commander, Fedyuninskii asked to be relieved of the Leningrad Front command and finally went to the 54th). To bolster up Lieutenant-General V.F. Yakovlev's 4th Army, the *Stavka*, now pouring every available man into Moscow, ordered the Leningrad command to help out here as well, but this meant weakening the de-blockading force; four divisions were transhipped across a stormy lake Lagoda and one also moved up from North-Western Front reserve.

Halted momentarily, Army Group North regrouped and on 8 November burst into Tikhvin itself, cutting the last rail link with lake Ladoga and threatening the rear of the Soviet 7th Army holding the Ladoga-Onega interval and the Svir river line. The junction between the 54th and 4th Armies had also been split wide open, causing Fedyuninskii (with the 54th since 24 October) the gravest anxieties: the threat to Volkhov, with its aluminium plant and generating stations, was growing. To seal up the breach, Fedyuninskii signalled the *Stavka* for permission to take over right flank units of 4th Army operating in his area: 'If this is done today, the situation can be restored. If it is done tomorrow, that will be too late: Volkhov will fall.' On the evening of 11 November, the *Stavka* telegraphed:

Stavka of Supreme Commander orders troops of 4 Army operating in Volkhov area on eastern and western banks of river Volkhov including 285, 310, 311, 292 rifle divisions, 6 naval brigade, 3 Guards rifle division, two battalions 281 rifle division, 883 corps artillery regiment, 16 tank brigade, from 06.00 hours 12.11.41 subordinated to command comrade Fedyuninskii and incorporated in strength 54 Army.

Fedyuninskii was now merely getting back some of the troops earlier dispatched from the 54th to 4th Army. Even so, should he blow up the industrial installations and the railway bridge? On the morning of 12 November, a *Stavka* signal authorized the placing of charges but demolition only on Fedyuninskii's personal order. Fedyuninskii decided to hold on.

Stalin had meanwhile ordered Meretskov of the 7th Army, in the course of a telephone conversation on the morning of 7 November, to take over 4th Army, leaving Gorolenko in charge of the 7th. As for more men, two divisions (191st and 44th) had already been air-lifted into Sitomliya and Tikhvin, but the *Stavka* had nothing more to spare. Meretskov therefore moved in a tank brigade and an infantry regiment, counter-attacked and actually broke into the northern outskirts of Tikhvin, though not for a week was the Soviet line properly stabilized north-east and east of Tikhvin. Meretskov did nevertheless re-establish communications with the Leningrad Front, to the north and with 52nd Army, holding off the German Sixteenth Army, to the south. Finns and Germans were still held at arm's length from a junction on the Svir.

In a warmer climate, far from the bogs and snowy marshes of the Tikhvin-Volkhov sectors, Army Group South, the bulk of the Ukraine in its grip at the end of September when Stalin ordered the South-Western and Southern Fronts over to a strict defence, continued to roll south-east and east. On the northern wing, the Sixth Army took Kharkov on 24 October and proceeded to secure the junction of Army Group South and Centre; by late October, in spite of desperate measures including the mobilization of more than 100,000 miners, the 'Soviet Ruhr', the Donbas, had been overrun. All attempts to build up a defence west of Kharkov, including Shaposhnikov's belated mass-mining instructions, had failed; the *Stavka* therefore ordered Timoshenko to pull back to the line Kastornoye-river Oskol-Krasnyi Liman-Gorlovka-river Mius, a shortening of the front to enable Timoshenko to bring ten rifle divisions and two cavalry corps into reserve. The North-Caucasus Front command received orders to 'activate' 5th Independent Army, put it under Lieutenant-General F.N. Remezov and start deploying it near Rostov-on-Don.

The Southern Front (commanded by Cherevichenko after Tyulenev was wounded) met with near disaster early in October. The German Eleventh Army (which Manstein came south from Leningrad to command when von Schobert's plane blew up in crash-landing on a Soviet minefield) headed for the Crimea in an attempt to rush the Soviet defences. Cherevichenko ordered 12th, 18th and 9th Armies of Southern Front to hold the line Pavlograd-Bolshoi Tokmak-Melitopol-lake Molochnoe (on the Sea of Azov) by 5 October, but from the bridgeheads at Dniepropetrovsk and Zaporozhye Kleist's Panzer Group 1 (re-designated First Panzer Army) burst into the flanks and rear of the Southern Front, and on 7 October linked up with the Eleventh Army north of Osipenko, pinning down the 18th and 9th Armies, squeezing them into the sea. The day before these jaws snapped shut, Lieutenant-General Smirnov, 18th Army commander, was killed in action; the remnants of 18th Army fell back on Stalino, what was left of the 9th fought its way back towards Taganrog, and 12th Army moved to the north-east also to Stalino which fell in a fortnight.

Tied frontally, the Southern Front threat to Manstein's Eleventh Army never quite materialized, but it prevented an immediate dash into the Crimea and the seizure of Sevastopol. Petrov's Coastal Army, shipped from Odessa, was only just arriving. The *Stavka* on 22 October put Vice-Admiral Levchenko in command of the Crimea forces, and ordered Lieutenant-General P.I. Batov to take over Kuznetsov's 51st Independent Army. Kuznetsov had continued to stick blindly to the 'old (pre-war) plan', a sea-borne assault, leaving the Perekop and Sivash approaches too thinly held. Manstein pushed past these defences: Kuznetsov was, for a second time, sacked. Early in November, when Sevastopol was invested, the *Stavka* put Vice-Admiral Oktyabrskii in general command, confirmed Petrov as Coastal Army commander. Major-General Morgunov (soon replaced by Rear-Admiral Zhukov) as coastal defence commander, and Major-General Ostryakov for aircraft; all told, when the investment began (other Soviet forces having been swept off the Crimea) Sevastopol mustered 52,000 men, 170 guns and about 100 planes. For all the previous blunders and present improvisations, an epic defence had begun within Sevastopol's perimeter and deep inside its forts and gun-batteries. Manstein's Eleventh Army had to tear away the defenders, who hung on, not for days or weeks but for month after agonizing month, for 250 fire-drenched days.

On 9 November, Timoshenko submitted to the *Stavka* proposals to attack German concentrations in the Rostov area. Stalin and Shaposhnikov gave their general approval, but turned down flat any suggestion of troop movements to strengthen the Southern Front forces which might be involved. Timoshenko therefore produced an operational plan in which he organized his main assault force, Lopatin's 37th Army, by regrouping the South-Western Front; his intention was to strike for Kleist's rear, with 18th and 9th Armies mounting supporting blows in the company of Major-General Khorun's independent cavalry corps. The offensive was timed for 17 November, and envisaged employing (with 56th Independent Army) a total of 22 rifle and nine cavalry divisions, plus five tank brigades.

There was every reason for Stalin to urge Timoshenko to stop Kleist. To hold the passage-way of the Don was of vital importance, for this was the road which led to the great Soviet oilfields of the south-east, to the Caucasus and on to Persia, where Soviet and British troops had been installed since August to secure the overland supply route along which war materials shipped to the Persian Gulf rolled into Russia. With the ground hardened once more by the frosts, Timoshenko and Kleist had each selected 17 November for their operations, Kleist with his right wing to hammer upon this doorway of the Don, Timoshenko to hold him off.

As this encounter, significant enough as it soon proved to be, fanned itself into fierce fighting, the final German thrust had begun to roll upon Moscow, its streets and squares barricaded, its approaches pitted with anti-tank ditches and dotted with fire-points. One by one, the divisions of Army Group Centre slid into this massive battle between 15–19 November at their appointed time and place. The Western Front had some warning; that an assault was imminent Zhukov learned from a prisoner taken from the German 183rd Infantry Division, and alerts went out on 14 November to all army commanders. Colonel Beloborodov with his Siberians of the 78th Rifle Division attached to 16th Army received his warning signal on the fifteenth to man all positions for the assault expected on the sixteenth. Zhukov's six armies – 16th, 5th, 33rd, 43rd, 49th and 50th (the last only lately subordinated to his command) – now faced the full test to destruction.

On the raw and misty morning of 15 November, with the sun dim and red, Soviet units were cramped into their defensive positions in the snow-covered fields and woods (snow as yet light and thinly spread) or were locked in the spoiling attacks which Zhukov had ordered a week ago. That morning, in the first phase of the 'final' offensive against Moscow, German forces in the north-west surged against Lelyushenko's 30th Army in the Kalinin area: Panzer Group 3 was to drive north-east of Lotoshino on Klin, 4 Panzer north of Ruza on Istra. On the fifteenth, 27 Corps (German Ninth Army) on the German left fell on the Soviet 5th Rifle Division, 21st Tank Brigade and 20th Reserve Regiment (30th Army) and struck out for the Volga; south of the Sea of Moscow, German units crossed the river Lama in strength on the afternoon of sixteenth, the day when 3 Panzer attacked Rokossovskii's 16th Army, which had been fighting its offensive action aimed at Volokolamsk. Shaposhnikov in mid-morning (16 November) telephoned Rokossovskii to warn him about the plight of his neighbour (30th Army), ordered him to break off his assault and pull his units out of the monastery of Teryava-Sloboda – or he would be encircled. Faced with the unhinging of 30th and 16th Armies, the *Stavka* finally pulled itself together and on 17 November subordinated 30th Army to Zhukov, who ordered Lelyushenko to cover Klin. Rokossovskii's situation was dangerous in the extreme: one flank had been attacking while the other was being crushed in. Losses were excruciatingly heavy. After a day's furious fighting, 17th Cavalry Divison had 800 men left; three divisions were no longer in touch with Army HQ. The whole of Zhukov's right wing was fighting desperately to hold off a threatened encirclement which would have exposed the entire approach to Moscow. To pin down the Soviet 5th Army and to inhibit any movement between the 5th and 16th, on 19–20 November German units assaulted the right flank of 5th Army and drove for Zvenigorod. Having no reserves at this juncture, Zhukov ordered the 108th Rifle Division from 33rd Army and a tank brigade (145th) to close on Zvenigorod to bolster up the 5th. To hold Klin, where 30th and 16th Armies had been ripped apart, Zhukov assigned Major-

General F.D. Zakharov (deputy commander 16th Army) to take over an 'operational group' (two divisions, two brigades), to plug the gap between Lelyushenko and Rokossovskii. To help Lelyushenko, Zhukov had moved a division from 16th Army to the 30th – one division (58th Tank) with 350 men, fifteen light tanks and five guns.

The shreds of these Soviet formations hung on like grim death, where many died inconspicuous and wretched, others in a great glow of fame, like Panfilov's 316th anti-tank men, ground to pieces fighting German tanks on the Volokol-amsk highway. Rokossovskii kept good close order, and the German tank 'fists' began to break now into long probing steel fingers, poking into the Soviet defences. On 21 November, Zhukov signalled to Rokossovskii by telegraph: 'Klin and Solnechnogorsk – vital. Rokossovskii to proceed in person to Solnechnogorsk: Lobachev [commissar 16th Army] to Klin. Secure defence of both towns.' Solnechnogorsk was already cut off, though still in Soviet hands. Rokossovskii therefore took himself to Klin, and reported to Sokolovskii, Zhukov's chief of staff: 'Operations in immediate area of Klin, in its suburbs. Only exit is to the east, to Rogachev, but to the south, Solnechnogorsk, com-munications cut.' From a white-faced woman telegraphist in the post office he was using as HQ Rokossovskii received his orders to hold on to the last, just as a shell struck the building. On 24 November both Klin and Solnechnogorsk fell after heavy fighting. Rokossovskii's regiments were down to 150–200 men: Colonel-General Halder was also noting in his war diary that German regiments were now led by an *Oberleutnant*, battalions by junior officers – German commanders reported their troops 'sorely tried' (*stark beansprucht*), clawed to the ground. But these ragged, freezing men pushed on into the Soviet defences. With the news of the fall of Klin, Zhukov merely said: 'It gets worse from hour to hour.' At Istra, now a key point in the defences on the Volokolamsk-Moscow highway, Beloborodov's Siberians of 78th Division were waiting, along the river (Istra) and at the high dam of the Istra reservoir. Peshki, where Rokossovskii had reported to General Kurkin, Zhukov's assistant commander, fell on 25 November and German units pressed up against the Moskva-Volga Canal, the last major obstacle before Moscow was completely outflanked from the north. At Yakhroma, 25th Panzer Regiment had taken the bridge over the canal and was dug in on the eastern bank. At his new command post south of Kryukovo, Rokossovskii was given one further order:

Kryukovo is the final point of withdrawal: there can be no further falling back. There is nowhere else to fall back. All and any measures must be taken quickly to win a breathing space, to stop the retirement. Each further step backward by you is a breach in Moscow's defences. All commanders, from juniors to seniors, to be in their places, on the battlefield.

On the morning of 28 November, German units were circling Moscow to the north and not more than twenty miles from the Kremlin.

Zhukov's three centre armies, 5th, 33rd and 43rd, were so far holding quite firmly: but to speed the disintegration of Rokossovskii's 16th Army, Govorov's 5th Army had been attacked on the morning of 19 November, and two days later the right flank of 33rd Army was assaulted in an effort to open the Naro-Fominsk Kubinka road, leading into 5th Army's rear. For the moment Zhukov could siphon off one or two units to help out elsewhere on the flanks, but no one was under any illusions about the main blow which must come from 4th Army. More immediate were the threats from the south, Zhukov's left flank, where on the 18th Guderian had taken the offensive to seize Novomoskovsk, Venev, Kashira and the crossings of the river Oka, to sweep behind Moscow from the south-east and meet the northern German 'pincers' at Noginsk. Already on the 18th, Guderian's 3rd Panzer Division had crossed the river Upa south-east of Tula and within a week Tula itself had been encircled from this direction. Stalin assigned to Boldin the command of 50th Army holding Tula: Boldin had already managed two successful break-outs, first from the frontier and then from Vyazma-Bryansk. Marshal Shaposhnikov briefed him very carefully on his responsibilities before he left for Tula on 22 November. The weight of Guderian's attack struck two divisions of 50th Army's left flank, the 413th and 299th, the latter not more than 800 men strong, while the reserve, 108th Tank Division, had 2,000 men, and thirty old and flimsy T-26 tanks. By the 20th, all that remained of the left flank amounted to the strength of only one regiment. The 293rd Rifle Division, recently arrived from the Far East, was detached from 3rd Army (South-Western Front) and moved under 50th Army command. When on the night of 23 November Boldin attended the Tula Military Soviet and Defence Committee session, although Zhavoronkov reported the internal situation under control and adequate stocks of ammunition, the town was being lashed by German fire to the west and north-west, while to the north-east, well to the rear of Tula at Venev, heavy fighting was raging. Venev itself was held by a regiment (173rd), two tank brigades (11th and 32nd) with a grand strength of thirty tanks between them, and a militia battalion. Zhukov, fearing for Kashira, had already ordered 50th Army to hold Venev and the 'Venev operational group' to be set up from 50th Army left flank units. As Major-General Tereshkov took over his Venev command, on 25 November, Major Smirnov, using his AA guns with their barrels fully depressed, was engaging the lead tanks of 17th Panzer Division approaching the southern limits of Kashira. At Tula, Boldin had also pressed AA guns into service against tanks, but only in the face of violent protests from Major-General Ovchinnikov, who considered that weapons should be used 'only according to their specification' and who complained to Shaposhnikov, who merely reminded Boldin that these private fights should be settled on the spot.

Venev fell on 25 November and Soviet units fell back north-east. Kashira was under attack. Zhukov had already on the 24th ordered Major-General Belov's 2nd Cavalry Corps, which had been engaged up till the 23rd on its Serpukhov counter-stroke, to move to the Chernevo-Zaraisk area and Belov to come under Boldin's command. This forced march along roads thick with ice and swept with German bombs was a nightmare for Belov's corps: at every point he was hustled along by orders urging greater speed to fill the gap at Kashira, with its important electric power station, its rail bridge over the river Oka, its major rail junction and above all the gaping hole from Kashira to Kolomna where there was not a single Soviet formation. If Kashira fell, the road to Moscow was open. Mordves and Kashira had been heavily bombed, and as General Belov observed. 'Where they [the Germans] bomb, they attack.' Belov, after talking to Boldin who had come up from Venev, set up his HQ in the Kashira post-office, thought he had no contact with his own units as yet. He could, nevertheless, telephone the outside world, and he contacted Zhukov's HQ, from which he received one order: 'Restore the situation at any cost.' Belov was dumbfounded: what 'situation'? Was he to retake Venev, push back Guderian, recapture Mordves? Sokolovskii's telegrams began to clear up the 'situation'; Belov's telegraphic talk with Zhukov established that Belov was 'subordinated to the Front Staff' and that Belov was personally responsible for the defence of Kashira.

One by one, Belov's squadrons closed on Kashira; up to 15.00 hours on 26 November Belov knew German units could take Kashira off the march, but they halted at the village of Pyatnitsa, less than four miles away. Belov's cavalry and tank support closed up tighter all the while, and the 'situation' looked distinctly better. Having already reported to Zhukov, Belov was almost immediately interrogated by Stalin, who telephoned the Kashira *gorkom* (Party town committee): Stalin promised Belov two tank battalions at once and asked where they should be sent. Since the Oka bridge at Kashira would not take heavy tanks, Belov asked for them to be routed through Kolomna on to Zaraisk. And there were, Stalin added, two rifle brigades, 'light brigades of a new type manned by picked men for manoeuvre operations', plus a Guards designation for Belov's corps. Here were bonuses and honours in a heap.

Belov 'shared' some forces with Zakharkin, commander of the 49th Army to his left; split between Belov and Zakharkin was Colonel Getman's 112th Tank Division, which 49th Army was using to cover Serpukhov through Ivanova. Belov proposed to use his 'share' for a counter-attack, planned for 27 November at 09.00 hours. Zhukov had turned down flat Belov's request for a 24-hour delay to move cavalry. Belov had now been reinforced with a *Katyusha* regiment, 9th Tank Brigade and two independent tank battalions (35th and 127th), a rifle division (173rd, Zhukov's Front reserve), Moscow AA gunners, a special engineer regiment, a junior lieutenant training school, the sergeants' training courses from 49th Army and militia units from Kashira itself. On Wednesday, 27 November, Belov's operations opened at 09.00 hours with a thiry-minute artillery barrage and a rocket salvo from the 15th Guards *Katyusha* Regiment. Reporting to Stalin as he did twice or more a day, Zhukov signalled:

Belov began operations from the morning [27.11]. Moving forward. Enemy covering units operating against Belov. According to situation 16.00 hours 27.11 enemy has fallen back 3–4 kilometres. Prisoners taken. Tank battalions and tank brigade not committed today. Held up on way owing to bridges. Moving through the night and will be committed as from morning. 112 Tank Brigade in position and operating 16 km south-west of Kashira.

The day on which he reported to Stalin about the Kashira operations, 27 November, was for Zhukov and for his whole Front the deep pit of the crisis. The battle sectors to north and south, into which German units bit piece by piece, were now deep with snow and riveted with ice, with the temperature low enough to bring savage and killing cold to ill-clad German soldiers spiked by the freezing winds and icy fogs. Over the town that had fallen Soviet bombers flew missions of deliberate destruction, to blast away any shelter from the cold. The machines, like the men, froze up, with lubricants congealed and useless. The fighting went on in ferocious spurts and lunges. At Istra, Beloborodov's Siberian troops fought hand-to-hand with the ss infantry of *Das Reich* Division, the young Aryans who died icy and bare-footed in their boots. Istra fell and on the 28th Beloborodov's men drew back. Sokolovskii went on scraping up reserves, taking from each rifle division of 5th, 33rd, 43rd and 49th Armies one rifle section and moving them in lorries to Rokossovskii's sorely pressed 16th Army; this helped to fill out three rifle divisions. From the Moscow Defence Zone garrison Major-General A.I. Lizyukov formed and commanded 'a group' (subsequently 20th Army) from the 28th and 43rd Rifle Brigades and a company of KV tanks. Govorov of 5th Army was ordered to Front HQ to set up a 'mobile reserve' to secure the junction with 16th Army; Govorov assembled a tank brigade (22nd), and three motor-cycle battalions, 800 men and twenty-one tanks all told.

There were, nevertheless, formidable reserves concentrating even as Zhukov's armies had to cannibalize themselves in this drastic fashion. Lieutenant-General F.I. Kuznetsov's 1st Shock Army with seven independent rifle brigades (29th, 47th, 50th, 55th, 56th, 44th and 71st) and 11–12 ski battalions had been concentrating since 25 November in the Zagorsk-Dmitrov-Yakhroma area. Lizyukov's 'group' was on the verge of becoming a full field army (20th). Down in the south on Zhukov's left, Lieutenant-General F.I. Golikov's 10th Army was being shunted into the Ryazan-Kanino-Shilovo area by train, though German bombing of the rail tracks held up its concentration. To Zhukov's repeated requests to loose a counter-blow Stalin manifestly turned a deaf ear; only when it looked as if the eastern bank of the Moskva-Volga Canal would cave in did Stalin unleash Kuznetsov's troops, on 29 November, a day as fiercely critical as the 27th to some minds. On the 29th also, Zhukov was also able to reinforce his 16th and 30th Armies with fresh divisions, one division (354th) and five brigades to Rokossovskii, two more divisions (379th and 271st) to 30th Army, formations neither fully equipped nor even properly trained but desperately needed to plug the gap which Zakharov and his 'operational group' had tried manfully to fill.

While the Front and field commanders took the immense strain in this fashion, 'the military', men like Belov at Kashira, of necessity virtually took over the denuded or trembling administrative echelons in their areas, very much as Belov 'took over' the *gorkom*, the town Party committee, of Kashira. This pattern was repeated many times over during the very deepest crisis of the Soviet state from November 1941 to April 1942. For all its humiliations, loss of prestige and terrible battering, the military at this desperate and bloody stage was the only instrument capable of 'doing the job', and of seeing it through on its own terms; in that very real sense, the army did begin to 'take over' the state, if only because no one else wanted the assignment. The criss-cross of subordinations and institutional affiliations brought many furious clashes, in which Political Administration and Party missions travelled out of Moscow to 'investigate'. The big urban Defence Committees, like that in Tula, had settled down to some kind of stability, but the bulk of the immediate administrative and executive work had to be done at *gorkom* level, where the army or corps commander pitched straight in, improvising, commandeering, supervising. Corps commander Belov, thrust almost unwittingly into a situation like this, had to make some quick decisions when faced by the several functionaries of the *gorkom* in the Kashira area. Could Kashira be held? Belov could give no guarantee. Should the civilians be evacuated? Belov certainly thought so. Should the electric power station be shut down or what? Let it run to the last moment, Belov advised. 'And now I have some questions for you, comrades' was how Belov put his own list of requirements, ranging from horseshoes to towing trucks for heaving tanks and lorries over the iced-up approaches to the Oka bridge.

There was, therefore, every reason for Stalin to keep watch through his several agencies upon his soldiers, who were shoring up his state.

While decimated Soviet and German units grappled with each other not only at the approaches but in the very suburbs of Moscow, on the distant Soviet flanks, at Tikhvin in the north and Rostov in the south, there had been events of great import in the making, each working their own influence on the apparently doom-laden final week of November. While Moscow awaited its fate, Leningrad in late November began (physically at least) to die; bread rations in the beleagured city had been cut five times during September-November, and bread rations for troops had been reduced thrice, the ration for front-line troops being cut by almost half (44·4 per cent) and for rear units by almost two-thirds. The huge and terrible famine had begun and with it all the medieval horrors of siege. Water supplies and canals froze: transport stopped: for lack of fuel factories fell idle; power stations came to a stop. More than 1,000 tons of high-calory foods were flown in but so much more was needed; the sugar and fats ration, temporarily increased in September, would have come in very useful now. Cotton-seed oil cake was used for human consumption; to replace valuable vegetable oils used for baking, an 'emulsion' of sunflower oil, soap stock, corn flour, second-grade wheat flour and water was compounded and used. Vile meat jellies were made from sheep-gut. No more than seven men – two hand-picked men who recorded deliveries of food by air and water and five who knew the actual state of the stocks on hand – were aware of the real state of affairs.

With the winter came the ice, and ice to lake Ladoga, making as yet thin but solid connection between Leningrad and a Soviet shore. By 17 November, the ice on the lake was 100 millimetres thick (half that needed for a loaded one-ton truck); three days later the ice was 180 millimetres thick and on 22 November a column of sixty lorries under the command of Major Parchunov following the tracks of the horses and sledges, which had tried the 'crossing' already, began moving over the *Ladozhskaya ledovaya doroga*, the Ladoga 'ice road' which was in all truth to become the *Doroga zhizni*, the 'Life line'. The first lorry, an M-1, had done a trip on 20 November from Konkorev to Kobona and in it had travelled Major-General Lagunov, Chief of Rear Services (Leningrad Front). It was feasible but dangerous, risky but rewarding: only 800 tons of flour were moved in by truck and sledge by the end of the month, yet these staved off disaster for a few more days.

With Tikhvin in German hands, the section of the Tikhvin-Volkhov railway line which could have been used to ship supplies up to lake Ladoga, and then over the 'ice road' into the city, was denied to the Russians. Stalin ordered Meretskov, who had taken over the disorganized forces in the Tikhvin area, to get this line back, a task which Meretskov approached cautiously but method-ically. Time was important; the first de-blockading attempt had come to bloody grief since the German troops had been able to dig in and fortify their sectors at Mga-Sinyavino. The plans for this operation, or series of inter-linked operations, called for the expulsion of all German forces east of the river Volkhov and for a Soviet bridgehead on the western bank of the river, for which purposes three Soviet armies, 54th (Leningrad Front), 4th and 52nd would be used, with some units from the North-Western Front.

Meretskov's own 4th Army would carry out the main attack on the German units of 39th Panzer Corps in the Tikhvin area; Meretskov divided his command into three groups, Northern, Eastern and Southern, to split up the German forces and to cut their escape routes south-west of Tikhvin. After this encircle-ment, the main forces of 4th Army were to strike for Budogoshch-Gruzino, with one force detached in the north-west to operate with 54th Army to seal off German units at Volkhov. The main weight of 54th Army's attack would be directed towards Voibokalo-Kirishi; in the event of 4th Army enjoying complete success in its drive for Gruzino, then the whole of the German force (designated *Group Beckmann*) would be encircled. The southern blow at the

German flanks would be carried out by 52nd Army and units of the Novgorod Army Group (North-Western Front) to crack the strong point of Malaya Vyshera and to cut German communications in the Gruzino area. Only Fedyuninskii's 54th Army was subordinated to a regular Front command (Leningrad); the 4th under Meretskov and the 52nd under Lieutenant-General N.K. Klykov were directly subordinated to the *Stavka*, since the Tikhvin 'area' had not been constituted a Front. Rolling up German troops to the east of the river Volhkov was important in itself in easing the supply situation for Leningrad, but it was in the eyes of Stalin and the *Stavka* an absolute precondition for the de-blockading of Leningrad as a whole. These ambitions, however, ran far too far ahead of present resources and capabilities.

Klykov with the 52nd opened these 'Tikhvin attacks' at dawn on 12 November, as the 4th Army was fighting desperately to hold Tikhvin itself. The first attacks petered out as weak groups of Soviet troops with ineffective artillery support got tangled up in the German fixed defences. On the night of 18 November, Klykov infiltrated two shock groups into the German rear and attacked frontally at dawn; this time the German garrison at Malaya Vyshera was encircled and heavy fighting swept the outskirts of the town, swirling in and out of each street and house. Leaving tommy-gunners to simulate a garrison defence, German troops in small groups moved back west through a twenty-kilometre corridor, though the final storming of the town left it strewn with dead men and smashed trucks. As the 52nd fought its way into the strong-point of Malaya Vyshera, Meretskov on the nineteenth attacked in the Tikhvin area itself. It was up to Klykov to get a move on and to inhibit German reinforcement towards Tikhvin, but in fact the German command were able to move up almost all of 61st Infantry Division against Meretskov. The *Stavka* weighed in with categorical orders to Klykov to speed things up, while Meretskov's 4th Army attacks were also hung up on the German defences round Tikhvin. Fedyuninskii had yet to open his offensive, for which reinforcements had come from Leningrad itself via the 'ice road'. Although it was living through ghastly days which were to become yet ghastlier, and though food and fuel ran excruciatingly short, Leningrad pulsed on, sending men and equipment to the battlefronts; when Voronov, detached once more to Leningrad for command and advisory duties (especially the organization of counter-battery fire), reported on weapon and ammunition production to the GKO, the latter flatly refused to believe the figures at first (though it had helped itself to Leningrad arms output to supply Moscow).

As Meretskov hammered his way into Tikhvin, at the very opposite end of the entire Soviet-German battle front Timoshenko had a striking success, this time at Rostov. It grew out of the plan Timoshenko had already submitted to Stalin on 9 November. At that stage, the *Stavka* had ruled out any external reinforcement, so that Timoshenko regrouped his Southern Front forces. To the north, the Soviet 12th and 18th Armies were to block a German drive on

Voroshilovgrad: the Southern Front (stiffened with South-Western Front troops) was to attack south-westwards against the flank and rear of Kleist's First Panzer Army and to co-operate with Remezov's 56th Independent Army in destroying Kleist's tank force. The main striking force was Lopatin's 37th Army, forming up in the Krasnodon area and built up from reserve units of Southern and South-Western Fronts, and Timoshenko had altogether twenty-two rifle, nine cavalry divisions, and five tank brigades available for his offensive – a numerical superiority in divisions offset by Soviet inferiority in tanks (and by undermanned Soviet divisions).

Russians and Germans moved simultaneously on 17 November in attack and counter-attack. Left flank divisions of 18th Army failed to register any success: 37th Army had to battle with increasing German resistance, and Southern Front formations, denied air cover during four days of non-flying weather, were slow in getting off the mark. Mackensen's 3rd Panzer Corps, covering the exposed flank of 14th Panzer Division with 60th Motorized against which Remezov flung himself, burst into the northern suburbs of Rostov by 19 November and by the following day Rostov had fallen, its major bridge over the Don intact. The Southern Front, had so far exercised little influence in support of the Soviet 56th Army, but the situation reversed itself dramatically. Mackensen's southerly sweep into Rostov had opened a gap between First Panzer and the German Seventeenth Army, a gap which Timoshenko and Colonel-General Cherevichenko (Southern Front commander) seized upon to break into the rear of 3rd Panzer Corps. The Soviet objective was now the liberation of Rostov and to strike for Taganrog later: 37th and 9th Armies would burst into the rear of 3rd Panzer while 56th Independent Army would hit Rostov itself from the southern bank of the Don, where Remezov had split his forces into three 'operational groups' Western, Central and Eastern.

While Mackensen moved 13th and 14th Panzer Divisions to the Tuslov sector to hold off Lopatin's 37th Army from breaking into his rear, Remezov with the 56th and Kharitonov with the 9th crashed into his southern and eastern flanks. The German southern flank lay on the bank of the Don itself on the southern outskirts of Rostov, where five miles of front were held by ss *Leibstandarte* units with more than 1,000 yards of solid frozen water in front of them. Massed in close order and with fixed bayonets, Remezov's riflemen crashed into these units, when the final Soviet attack opened straight through the German mines on the ice and into the *Leibstandarte* machine-guns. Night crossings established a Soviet bridgehead, from which units broke into the town, on the morning of the 28th two more companies fought their way over the ice and reinforced the bridgehead, while two militia battalions took the cement factory with the streets leading to it and on 29 November, Central Group (56th Army), the Novocherkassk units of 9th Army and the Rostov *opolchenie* battalion cleared Rostov, battered by the fighting and burning from German demolitions. Between them the generals Kharitonov and Remezov (now incorporated into the Southern Front from the Trans-Caucasus command) deserved Stalin's congratulations, which he signalled that same day.

The Wehrmacht, 161 days after opening hostilities against the Soviet Union, had suffered its first major reverse, which had far-reaching consequences on the German command, as Hitler refused to allow Rundstedt to pull back. Runstedt resigned, Reichenau (the Sixth Army commander) took his place, only to do what Runstedt had proposed: withdraw behind the river Mius. Such units as were disengaged were rushed down from Kharkov to stabilize the German positions. While they were thus embroiled in the south, they could not be moved to Moscow.

Between 05.00 and 09.00 hours on 1 December, preceded by surprise artillery barrage and air attack, and at the centre of the Soviet defence covering Moscow in the area of 33rd Army, Field-Marshal von Kluge threw 20th Corps into one final, furious and dangerous bid to seize the shortest route to the Soviet capital, along the Minsk-Moscow highway. After breaking through 33rd Army defences in the Naro-Fominsk area, and breaking into the rear of 5th Army, German troops would be astride the highway. By noon the Soviet defences were pierced to a depth of two miles: German units swung on Akulovo, four miles from the highway, although the mining of the Naro-Fominsk-Kubinka road held up German tanks. The danger of 5th Army being split from 33rd and the whole threat to the Soviet rear if German formations got to the highway was nevertheless agonizingly plain. Zhukov was well aware of what the operations at Kubinka implied, and put several emergency measures into effect at once. Every available reserve was sent to the 5th–33rd Army breach, to be launched not later than 3 December as a 'composite group' in a counter-attack; Lieutenant-General M.G. Yefremov, 33rd Army commander, took over personal control of this 'composite group' made up of a rifle brigade, a couple of tank battalions, ski troops and a *Katyusha* unit. Govorov, 5th Army commander, hurried to 32nd Rifle Division (the Siberians who had fought at Borodino) to supervise this key link formation. Since Western Front HQ was not so very far away at Perkhushkovo, Zhukov and his staff kept a close personal watch on things. To make doubly sure, Zhukov issued personal orders for the left flank units of 33rd Army, south-east of Naro-Fominsk, to be reinforced with units rushed in from 43rd Army.

In a deep and terrible freeze-up, with German soldiers screaming in the snow that they could not go on, Yefremov attacked on 2 December in the Yushkovo-Burtsevo area, in whose villages the Soviet T-34s hunted and were themselves hunted by German SP guns. By the evening of 4 December, with German units falling back or being trapped by raiding Soviet groups, the situation was practically restored to what it had been four days ago; the 32nd Rifle Division was in complete possession of Akulovo, 1st Guards Motorized Rifle Division was pushing the Germans back across the Nara. The last German bid for

Moscow had failed. Already at the end of November, Zhukov and his staff considered that they had 'won' in the north-west, the German advance slowed to one measured in single metres, German reserves exhausted; on the right flank, Guderian was still bumping up against Kashira. Von Kluge's thrust had been a deadly one, perfectly aimed, but it had been finally parried. All round the perimeter at their several distances from the heart of Moscow lay the German indentations: in the north-west 7th Panzer Division astride the canal at Yahroma, forty miles away, at Krasnaya Polyana 2nd Panzer a mere fifteen miles (with one detachment having poked right into Khimki), thence the somewhat thicker bulge at the centre and the Kashira block due south.

Less than a week earlier, on 30 November, Zhukov had presented to Stalin and the *Stavka* his plans for the Soviet counter-stroke at Moscow. The situation itself dictated the main outlines of Zhukov's plans, which called for the destruction of the two powerful German armoured wedges jammed into the Soviet positions and south of the capital. The first stages envisaged the destruction of German units on Zhukov's right flank by blows at Klin-Solnechnogorsk and in the direction of Istra: on his left, Zhukov proposed striking at Guderian's flank and rear through Uzlovaya and Bogoroditsk, to a depth of forty-five miles or so. On his right, Zhukov planned for penetrations up to twenty-five miles, both sets of operations to be 'surprise blows' pursued without pause to prevent any German regrouping. The right would attack with four armies (30th, 1st Shock, 20th and 16th), the left with 10th Army, Belov's 1st Guards Cavalry Corps (reinforced with rifle and tank units) and 50th Army, to attack Guderian from three sides. At the point of the greatest danger, the north-west, Zhukov proposed to use four armies, two from *Stavka* Reserve (1st Shock and 20th) and two recently reinforced, 16th and 30th. These assault formations were confined to a single echelon: the reserves amounted to one rifle division, one tank brigade and a few artillery regiments. The formations at the centre (5th, 33rd, 43rd, and 49th) during this first stage were to contain the German units facing them and to inhibit any transfer of forces to the wings, in short, the original plan reversed; after the first stage, the centre formations were to go over to a general offensive to accomplish the 'general destruction' of the whole German force. The requisite operational directives were issued to the right flank armies of Zhukov's Front on 3 December; the centre armies, owing to von Kluge's thrust for the Minsk-Moscow highway were after 2 December already launched on their attacks, but were ordered to go over to general offensive operations after 4–5 December. On the left, 10th Army would attack on 6 December, followed by Belov and Boldin. Attack armies would operate from their present positions, bursting into gaps in the German line on sectors un-favourable for defence. Into such gaps all available men and machines were to be poured to obtain a 'swift and decisive transformation' in the operational scene.

At the same time, however, a much vaster design was being contemplated by

Stalin, Shaposhnikov and Vasilevskii, the outlines of which began to emerge in the allocation of missions to other Fronts, the Kalinin under Koniev and the right wing of the South-Western Front (which abutted on to Zhukov's command). Lieutenant-General Vasilevskii, Shaposhnikov's deputy at the General Staff, pressed for the full utilization of Koniev's forces, a point he made strenuously to Koniev himself on 1 December:

> To frustrate the German offensive on Moscow and at the same time to save not only Moscow but to make a start on the effective destruction [ser'eznyi razgrom] of the enemy is possible only through offensive operations with a decisive aim. If we don't do this in the next few days, it will be too late. The Kalinin Front is holding what is clearly a favourable operational situation, and it is up to you to collect literally everything you can lay your hands on to strike at the enemy.

'In the next few days': this had provoked a great deal of argument. Stalin had proved obdurate in the face of all of Zhukov's persuasions for an earlier attack, but news that German siege guns were being moved up to Krasnaya Polyana to shell the capital underlined the need for speedy action. Stalin had already moved the 1st Shock Army to block any easterly movement from the Moskva–Volga Canal and ordered the elimination of the German bridgehead at Yakhroma. In addition to the three field armies lurking behind Zhukov's front, Stalin had authorized the movement of eight rifle divisions, seven cavalry divisions, four rifle brigades, six tank brigades and ten independent tank battalions plus a parachute corps into the defensive actions at the end of November and the beginning of December.

Behind the armies moved up to the December battle-lines were others designed to thicken the Moscow defence still further. In the MZO area, the Moscow Defence Zone, the 60th and 24th Armies concentrated from 29 November–2 December, 60th to hold the line running from Tarasovka-Nakhabino-Perkuskovo, the 24th on the line Davidkovo (in the south-west) to the Moskva river in the north-east. Behind Moscow itself the 26th Army held the triangle Noginsk-Voskresensk-Orekhovo-Zuevo to cover Kolomna, while south of Ryazan the 61st Army formed up in the area Ryashk-Ranenburg-Michurinsk to hold the approaches running from Epifani and Yefremov. The 61st was drawn up in the area of the right wing of South-Western Front, which, like the Kalinin Front, was drawn into the whole offensive design, both Fronts forming the upper and lower reaches of the giant 'horseshoe' (with Moscow at its centre). The directive issued to the right flank armies of South-Western Front laid out the main aims of this offensive operation:

> With the aim of regularizing the situation on the right wing of the South-Western Front, to create the conditions for a breakthrough into the rear of Guderian's mobile forces and to effect its destruction with the forces of the Western Front at the approaches to Moscow, the right wing of the South-Western Front will go over to the offensive on the morning of 6.12, its most immediate task being the destruction of the Livny-Yelets enemy forces.

That directive was dated 4 December, and had been preceded three days earlier by a *Stavka* directive to the Kalinin Front under Koniev:

[Front command] will concentrate in the next 2–3 days a shock group of not less than 5–6 rifle divisions, to mount a blow on the front (inclusive) Kalinin, (inclusive) Sudi-miraka in the direction of Milkulino Gorodishche and Turginovo. Assignment: to break into the rear of the enemy concentration in the Klin area and to effect the destruction of the latter by the troops of the Western Front.

Koniev, in the light of his instructions and recommendations from the *Stavka*, issued orders to 29th, 31st, 22nd Armies. On the right wing of the South-Western Front, the main blow was to be mounted by the 'operational group under Front subordination', commanded by the deputy commander of the South-Western Front, Lieutenant-General Kostenko, and aimed at Livny, with a supporting blow from 13th Army. With permission from the *Stavka* and Timoshenko, Kostenko modified his attack plans in the light of the German dispositions.

The battle for men, as opposed to that for machines (a conflict which he had envisaged in October) Stalin appeared to have won: on 1 December 1941, there were 219 Soviet rifle divisions on the entire front (as opposed to 213 in October). In addition to the two armies already committed at the Front (1st Shock and 20th), the *Stavka* had nine new armies (including the 10th, assigned to Zhukov on 1 December, the 26th, 28th, 39th, 57th, 58th, 59th, 60th and 61st, a grand total of fifty-nine rifle divisions and seventeen cavalry divisions, deployed or concentrating on a great arc running from Vyterga-Kostroma-Gorkii-Saratov-Stalingrad-Astrakhan. Machines and equipment were not in such abundance (and even the great surge in totals of formations was misleading: 10th Army with its ten divisions was only 80,000 men strong, the reinforced divisions of 3rd Army amounted to 2,190 men and in 13th Army 2,850 men, while the eleven divisions of the right wing of South-Western Front totalled no more than 60,000 men). The refurbished divisions of the Red Army just about equalled the decimated formations of Army Group Centre. The large tank formations which Zhukov needed to make the breakthroughs he envisaged were almost wholly lacking; three tank and three motorized rifle divisions attached to the Western Front had almost no armour. Formations like the 112th Tank Division had 86 light tanks, 108th Tank had 15, 58th Tank Division had one medium tank and 30 old T-26 machines. The artillery situation was no better: from the 46 artillery regiments of Supreme Command Reserve (RVG) brought up to support the assaults there were only 612 guns. Ammunition was available only for the assault formations. Lorries, tractors, radio sets, horseshoes, infantry weapons – items large and small – were everywhere in short supply.

Organization, however, cost nothing and Zhukov made particular stipulations about the operational administration he expected; staffs would operate in two echelons, the first made up of the operational, cipher, intelligence, vvs (air), artillery, signals and services, the second comprising the remainder of the staff organization and physically separated from the first by some six to seven miles. Timoshenko on the South-Western Front proposed to supervise operations through 'sub-staffs' detached from his Front administration. For all Fronts, the basic planning document came to the 'decision-map' (*Karta reshenie*); on the basis of his 'map', Zhukov issued split directives to his armies, in order to keep operational timings and objectives as secret as possible, issuing first the left flank and then the right flank objectives and timings. The full operation was 'charted' and logged on the main 'decision-map', and Zhukov's staff demanded the same precisions, in miniature, from subordinate staffs. The master map was kept under strict guard.

Of all the shortages, that of time itself was of fundamental importance. There were only hours in which to assemble large formations, as the margins narrowed critically at the beginning of December. There was not enough time to train all the forces engaged, nor to carry out the special preparations which were obviously necessary. The newly arrived 10th Army, its concentration already delayed, was a case in point; 10th Army had no heavy artillery, and no tanks, with over-all shortages of infantry weapons, signals equipment, engineering equipment and lorries. All armies had to rely on their divisional artillery which had been drastically reduced in the recent heavy defensive fighting; those with even half left were lucky. Zhukov's command had nine engineer and five bridging battalions subordinated to it, but with so little time to spare, many more were needed to wheel and hoist many of the attack divisions into a favourable position. Kuznetsov's 1st Shock Army had to build three bridges of 10-tons, 20-tons and 60-tons capacity over the Moskva-Volga Canal to get really rolling.

For all their imperfections at least the reserves were there, bunched up behind Zhukov's Front, concentrating on Timoshenko's right and moving into Koniev's area. The German command for its part believed early in December that the Red Army had been fought to its last battalion: on 2 December Colonel-General Halder noted the Russian defence had reached its climax (*Höhepunkt*), and after this there was nothing, *Keine neuen Kräfte mehr verfügbar*: 'No fresh forces available.' The situation at Tikhivin was as yet by no means clear, but Russian troop movements from Vologda and across lake Ladoga looked as if a major attack was in the offing, what Halder called *Vorbereitung eines Grossangriffs*, even an attempt to de-blockade Leningrad. At the moment Army Group North did not share these forebodings. In the south, the Sixth Army was sending reinforcements from Kharkov to the Mius sector, but they were moving very slowly. *Fremde Heere Ost* under Colonel Kinzel had prepared its estimate of Russian capabilities and present strength, a forward-looking document which peered as far as May 1942 (but which never glimpsed the possibilities of 5–6 December 1941); the Red Army would be able to reinforce with some thirty-five brigades and twenty armoured formations by the spring of 1942, but the report, *Die Kriegswehrmacht der UdSSR* (*Stand*, Dezember 1941) envisaged no present Soviet offensive capability. The reports of Luftwaffe pilots who had seen the movement of 1st Shock Army and other formations north-west of Moscow were discounted or ignored. This was, like the Marne, a battle to the last battalion and in the opinion of the German command, these were already in the field. What tormented the German commanders was that for more than 700 miles of front there was no effective reserve, while the drive for Moscow was petering out in a series of individual tactical engagements, any strategic significance being blotted out by losses, exhaustion and undiminished Soviet resistance.

The *Feindlage*, the estimate of Soviet intentions and strength attached as an appendix to Brauchitsch's report on the tasks of the *Ostheer* 1941–2 (*Weisung für die Aufgaben des Ostheers in Winter 1941/42*: General Staff, Operations Section, Nr. 1693/41) was dated for 1 December. It put Soviet field strength at 200 rifle formations, 35 cavalry divisions and 40 armoured brigades: with formations held in the far north, in the Caucasus and in the Far East (63 rifle formations) and with the 'Polish Legion' forming up north-east of Astrakhan, the Red Army had 265 divisions to hand, 40 cavalry and 50 tank units, though 'it was known' that reserve formations were being assembled in the Volga area and in Siberia. Present formations were much reduced in strength and fire-power; in European Russia, there were some 900 aircraft available to support them. No new major formations had been encountered of late; fresh troops had been scraped up from quiet sectors and committed at dangerous points, so that the obvious conclusion remained: '*at present there are no large reserve formations on any significant scale.*' Soviet forces in the Far East had already supplied twenty-four rifle divisions, one cavalry division and ten tank formations; no more could be expected to reach the European front within the foreseeable future. 'Conditionally', the Red Army might turn to positional warfare, though with units withdrawn for training and reinforcement, Soviet attacks 'could be reckoned on'. When that report was actually submitted, the Japanese had attacked at Pearl Harbor (thus disengaging Stalin's Far Eastern frontiers), the 'large reserve formations' had materialized, and three Soviet Fronts, the Kalinin, Western and South-Western, had launched themselves with fifteen armies plus Belov's 1st Guards Cavalry Corps and General Kostenko's 'operational Group' on the stretched and straining *Ostheer*.

Army General Zhukov, forty-five years of age, with his offensive triumph on the Kahlkin-Gol now two years behind him but the defensive achievements of Leningrad, and now Moscow so fresh, had devised a good plan, one which relied on speed and surprise to counterbalance the lack of fully trained troops, the paucity of equipment and the absence of any appreciable strength in mobile formations. For air support, Zhukov was relying on the 6th Aviation Corps, normally part of the Moscow PVO (Air Defence) system, and Major-General Golovanov's long-range bombers, part of the strategic bomber force (ADD), not disbanded as a separate entity but retained under High Command control. The timing of the Soviet counter-stroke was also of crucial importance and hence a highly delicate matter. To wait, but not to wait too long, this was the essence of Stalin's decision-making. If the Red Army lacked any major superiority, as it did, in spite of the reserves, then a favourable force level *vis-à-vis* the Wehrmacht must be reached, bearing in mind also the state of German reserves. To wait too long might mean a massive German wedge immovably stuck within Moscow's immediate defences. There were important economic factors, bearing on the fate of this central industrial region, and there were secrets known only perhaps to Stalin himself, information from Sorge on a definite Japanese movement 'southwards', the great raid on Pearl Harbor. Perhaps also the main key was not the complexity of Stalin's calculations but their simplicity: what Stalin was reckoning on his strategic abacus was the 'main chance', a tremendous finishing blow delivered when the Far Eastern coast was definitely clear and the European one open through German over-commitment and exhaustion. There was clearly, as subsequent events showed, a great divergence between the 'military' objectives and the greater 'war-winning' designs being hatched by Stalin and his entourage.

But calculation there had to be in view of the figures: on 1 December, when the final outlines of the counter-offensive plans took tangible form, the Red Army had 4,196,000 men in its field armies, 32,194 guns and mortars, 1,984 tanks and 3,688 combat planes, against 36,000 German guns, 1,453 German tanks and 2,465 German aircraft. That was the general calculation, to be offset against a reckoning involving the 'Western axis' (*Zapadnoe napravlenie*), in particular with its 718,800 Red Army men, 7,985 Soviet guns and 720 tanks as against 801,000 German troops, 14,000 guns and 1,000 tanks and 615 aircraft. What Stalin and the *Stavka* had tabulated before them, in terms of the strength and equipment of the Soviet forces of three Fronts committed to offensive operations as from 5–6 December, was this:

Koniev	*Kalinin Front* (22nd, 29th and 31st Armies), 250 kilometre frontage: 15 rifle, 1 cavalry division, 1 motorized rifle brigade, 2 tank battalions: strength 100,000 men, 980 guns, 67 tanks: *air strength*: 13 dive-bombers, 18 Shturmoviks, 52 fighters.
Zhukov	*Western Front* (30th, 1st Shock, 20th, 16th, 5th, 33rd, 43rd, 49th, 50th, 10 Armies and Belov's mobile group), 600-kilometre frontage: 48 rifle divisions (plus three being formed in the rear), 3 motorized rifle, three tank (two without tanks) divisions, 15 cavalry divisions (12 of the new 3,400-man strength, paper establishment not realized), 18 rifle, 15 tank brigades and 1 parachute corps: 558,800 men, 4,348 guns, 624 tanks, 199 planes under Front command.
	Of the 624 tanks, 439 were the old 'pea-shooting' type, (T-26).

Zhukov   *Right flank strength:*
14 rifle, 1 motorized rifle, 1 tank, 9 cavalry divisions, 15 rifle and 8 tank brigades: 216,400 men, 1,673 guns, 285 tanks (133 T-34s and KVs).

Left flank strength: (excluding 10th Army)
7 rifle, 5 cavalry, 2 tank divisions, 2 tank brigades: 115,000 men, 747 guns and 137 tanks.

Reinforcements to right and left flank from 1–6 December: 216,400 men raised to 222,400 and 115,000 men raised to 210,800.

Centre strength:
16 rifle, 2 motorized rifle divisions, 5 tank, 1 rifle brigade: 125,000 men, 1,238 guns and 194 tanks.

Timoshenko *South Western Front* (right wing)
(3rd, 13th Armies, Kostenko's special operational group) 11 rifle, 1 motorized rifle, 6 cavalry divisions, 1 rifle, 2 tank brigades, 1 motor-cycle regiment;
60,000 men, 388 guns and about 30 tanks, 79 aircraft.

The margins were, on this inspection, fearfully narrow. Few, however, were to know, for the attack orders issued on 5 December to divisional commanders made no mention of assignments to neighbours or of any wide design. It was Zhukov's intention to fall not only with swiftness but also with the utmost secrecy upon the German armies crouched round Moscow.

At 03.00 hours on the morning of Friday, 5 December, in temperatures −25–30° C. and with snow lying more than a metre thick, the Soviet counter-offensive opened. Major-General V.A. Yushkevich's 31st Army (Kalinin Front) attacked south of Kalinin across the ice of the river Volga: eight hours later, at 11.00 hours that same morning, Maslennikov's 29th Army attacked to the north, and by 14.00 hours Soviet rifle units were over the ice and fighting for bridge-heads on the southern bank of the Volga. While the battle for Kalinin was only just beginning, Zhukov's right wing formations attacked on Saturday, when Lelyushenko's 30th Army attacked in the direction of Klin and Rogachevo and Kuznetsov's 1st Shock Army fought its way into Yakhroma, aiming for Fedorovka and the southern limits of Klin, where it was to link up with the 30th. Simultaneously the 20th Army, entrusted to one of Stalin's favourite commanders, Lieutenant-General Andrei Vlasov, also took the offensive, in which it was joined on the seventh by Rokossovskii's 16th Army, both armies being assigned to the liquidation of German forces in the Krasnaya Polyana area; then they were to re-group and attack Solnechnogorsk. The battle of the Klin bulge with the attempt to destroy Panzer Groups 3 and 4 was fully engaged by 7 December, when at noon Soviet units from Lelyushenko's formation suddenly burst out to the north-east of Klin, right on top of 56th Panzer Corps HQ.

Klin, much more a townlet than a town assumed a significance out of all proportion to its size, for it was the lynch-pin of Panzer Group 3 and the hinge of the entire left wing of Army Group Centre. The following noon (8 December), the danger of Panzer Group 3 being cut off grew visibly, with Lelyushenko sweeping past Klin to the north, severing the Moscow–Kalinin highway, pressing down on Klin itself from Yamuga: only one road lay open to the west and the river Lama line. Zhukov's problem was to speed up Kuznetsov's 1st Shock Army operating in the interval between Klin and Solnechnogorsk: on 7 December Zhukov had issued categorical orders to Kuznetsov to move faster, to break down the German line from which units could be moved to reinforce Klin. Only on 8 December did Kuznetsov's right flank units begin to develop their north-westerly drive for Klin, and a day later centre units captured Fedorovka, due west. The slowness of the Red Army advance prompted Zhukov to examine its operational performance, and the result was the Front Directive of 9 December, which demanded an end to frontal attacks, to 'negative operational measures which play into the enemy's hands', enabling him to disengage with small loss, to retire to new lines and to fight on: Soviet troops must outflank and attack the German rear, infiltrating the German positions, for which special combat groups of tanks, infantry men and cavalry should be formed to operate against the German lines of communication. (Lelyushenko, with *Order No. 97* of 10 December set up his *podvizhnaya gruppa*, a mobile group under Colonel Chanchibadze with tanks, motorized riflemen, ski troops and cavalry to press on to Teryeva-Sloboda to cut the German escape route westwards.) At the same time Zhukov sent a special command signal to Kuznetsov, insisting that by the morning of 10 December he must be astride the motorway on the sector between Klin and Solnechnogorsk, which 20th Army was already outflanking from the north, and where heavy fighting was developing. Rokossovskii, with his *Order No. 054*, was on the point of splitting his command into two groups, Major-General Remizov's right flank units to co-operate with the 20th Army and Major-General Beloborodov's left flank forces to attack Istra. Beloborodov was back at Istra, where not so long ago he had fought a fearful engagement with ss *Das Reich*, and was about to fight another. Govorov's 5th Army, topped up with some reinforcement, its 'shock group' re-assembled from three rifle divisions and tank units, was on the morning of 11 December to go over to the offensive in the general direction of Ruza-Kolyubakovo: right flank units of the 5th would operate with 16th Army's left flank against Istra, while the 2nd Guards Cavalry Corps was to be introduced into the German rear. The whole of Zhukov's right wing was now fully engaged, committed to a race with time to prevent a German withdrawal to a line running from Volokolamsk-Ruza, a race in which Zhukov urged all possible speed on his commanders to prevent the Panzer formations slipping out of his grasp.

To the north-west, in a maze of burning towns, Soviet infiltrations and break-throughs, feverish German movement on switch lines shored up threatened sectors and junctions: meanwhile, on the left flank Zhukov's three armies and Belov's corps were fighting to encircle Guderian. After 5 December, Guderian, with his attack stalled, was engaged in pulling his units back to the Don-Shat-Upa river line, a movement into which the Soviet units crashed full-tilt when their offensive opened on 6–7 December. Golikov's 10th Army, its formations only just formed up and going into action straight off the march, attacked in the direction of Mikhailov-Novomoskovsk on 6 December, and by the evening of 7 December was fighting its way into Mikhailov, while Guderian's 10th Motorized Division fought a hard but costly delaying action. South of Kashira, 17th Panzer fought to hold up more Soviet attacks, but by the evening of 6 December Belov's 2nd Guards Cavalry Division and 9th Tank Brigade had cut the road from Mordves to Venev, slicing away the only path to the rear for the German units. In the fierce blizzards of night and day, in waist-high snow and paralysing cold the German motorized units fell back, stabbed by raiding Soviet ski-teams and in turn striking back in savage lunges with rifle companies in armoured carriers screened by self-propelled guns. Belov and his assault units passed the dead horses, smashed lorries and guns on the roads and in the ravines. At Tula, Regiment *Grossdeutschland* contained one Soviet break-out to the south-east, which would have sliced into the German withdrawal line. Tula, although in Soviet hands, had been practically encircled: Zhukov, in asking Boldin why he was not at Laptevo as ordered, reminded him that this was his third time in encirclement and asked sarcastically if he was not overdoing it a bit. But a small 'corridor' had been kept open to the north, and the first Soviet blows widened it to almost twenty miles. Tula's own offensive began with this south-easterly thrust:

1322 Rifle Regiment at 18.00 hours [5 December], concentrated in eastern section of woods one kilometre west of Kolodeznaya, attacked Kolodeznaya and at 02.00 hours on 6 December captured it, destroying 5th battalion Regiment *Velikaya Germaniya* [*Grossdeutschland*].

With Belov pushing down from the north and Golikov advancing on a fifty-mile front from the west, Zhukov by the evening of 7 December (although Tula was by no means out of danger) anticipated speeding up the destruction of Guderian's Panzer forces in the Tula-Novomoskovsk-Plavsk area. For that reason, Zhukov ordered Boldin to commit 50th Army, with every possible unit he could scrape up, in thrusts south and south-east of Tula to cut Guderian's escape route westwards. On the afternoon of 8 December, Boldin's 50th duly attacked, though making little headway against the German 296th Infantry Division and 3rd Panzer. Zhukov thereupon instructed Boldin to mount two attacks to bring him out just south of Shchekino (due south of Tula), to enmesh Guderian southwards; but the attacks which began on 11 December brought no visible change in the situation by the twelfth. The 50th, which was a badly battered army, was running out of ammunition, was short of tanks and guns and running into fierce German resistance. Belov enjoyed greater success, moving south of Venev on 10 December, and getting to Novomoskovsk on 11 December, where fighting raged all night for the town: at this juncture Zhukov swung Belov's formations south-west towards Shchekino, in one more attempt to nail up Guderian's units. Golikov's 10th was now striking three of Guderian's divisions in the flank, divisions falling back south-westwards and fighting their way out of the trap east and south of Tula. On 9 December Sokolovskii talked at length with Golikov, pointing out the need to change the axis of the advance to close the trap and first to cut the German communications at Uzlovaya. Belov and Golikov were to join forces in slamming the door shut on the German units falling back out of the Tula trap.

Guderian had hoped to hang his right wing on the Upper Don-Shat river line, which was at least fortified, but this hope was literally blown to pieces with the offensive mounted by the right wing of the South-Western Front, when Major-General A.M. Gorodyanskii's 13th Army, and Major-General Moskalenko's operational group (55th Cavalry Division, 150th Tank Brigade and 307th Rifle Division) smashed in the front of the German Second Army on both sides of Yelets to Guderian's south. Moskalenko took Yelets on the morning of 9 December. Kreizer's 3rd Army to the north, exploiting the 13th Army's successes further south, jumped off on 8 December for Yefremov: the Third and Thirteenth Armies co-operated in reducing the Yefremov-Yelets area, while the German 34 Corps was crushed in the Yelets-Livny region. Timoshenko now prepared to commit the 61st Army under Lieutenant-General M.M. Popov between 10th Army (Western Front) and 3rd Army (South-Western Front).

Zhukov decided to bring Belov and Golikov south-westwards to Plavsk (on the river Plava), and ordered Zakharkin's 49th Army to strike down north-west of Tula at Aleksin. With his right flank flopping in the empty air, Guderian was himself obliged to pull back to the Plava fifty miles to the west, a movement which unhinged Guderian's Panzer Group from the German Fourth Army to the north, leaving a gap of some twenty miles staring out between Kaluga and Belev. The Soviet success at Yelets had opened up the possibility of a drive on Orel. Vast new possibilities altogether were beginning to gleam through this winter murk, though Zhukov had first to force a decision at Klin, over which another rain of the Front commander's categorical military imperatives fell on the assault formations of the right wing. Klin, under heavy Soviet fire, was defended by German combat groups, screening the road out to the west with armoured shields hastily pushed into position. The temperature had for a brief period shot up from its Arctic levels, bringing rain on Zhukov's left and soft, slithery roads on his right; German wounded and Panzer Group heavy equipment now moved behind the battle group screens in one great withdrawal movement out of the Klin bulge, a withdrawal which ultimately slithered into panic and headlong flight. Zhukov peremptorily ordered Lelyushenko's 30th Army and Kuznetsov's 1st Shock into Klin, which had to be encircled by 13 December. In a general directive to the Western Front armies, a new advance line was set out, and the main body of the Front was to be brought forward by the evening of 16 December. During the night of 15 December, Lelyushenko's and Kuznetsov's men finally broke into the centre of Klin; Panzer Group 3's front had been finally smashed in, while to the north-west 31st Army under Yushkevich and 29th (now under Major-General V.I. Shvetsov) finally recaptured Kalinin on 16 December. On noon of that day, the *Stavka* ordered Zhukov to hand over 30th Army to Koniev's Kalinin Front; the taking of Kalinin had made it possible for Koniev to start striking south-westwards, and 30th Army was earmarked for a thrust into the rear of the German Ninth Army, the whole of whose eastern wing had now to be pulled back since the German front on the Volga was shattered.

Not until 13 December did the Soviet press indulge in a triumphant roll of drums with the *Sovinformburo* communiqué on the German repulse at the gates of Moscow and with a flourish of portraits of the Soviet commanders who had made outstanding contributions in both defence and attack, Zhukov, Rokossovskii, Belov, Boldin, Kuznetsov, Govorov, Lelyushenko and Vlasov. There was also the success of the recapture of Tikhvin (9 December) to celebrate. The results of the counter-offensive by mid December were vastly encouraging, and the sights and scenes of the savage mauling which had been inflicted on the German troops intoxicated the Soviet troops, padded and furred against the cold. But the Panzer Groups which Zhukov had marked down for destruction had so far emerged from all the traps which Zhukov tried to spring shut as fast as he could. With Kalinin and Yelets in Soviet hands, and with the unhinging of the German centre, a strategic operation on an immense scale – reminiscent of the gigantic German encirclement operations at Bialystok-Minsk, Kiev, Vyazma-Bryansk – was already printing itself across the Soviet decision-maps. One gap had been torn open in the south; in the north, the German frontal structure was beginning to totter. Now as never before, even in the days of nightmarish defeat, was there an immense premium on the correct decision and on the most scrupulous use of military resources. While Zhukov and Timoshenko wrestled with the critical factors of their counter-blows, Stalin and Shaposhnikov in that same vital mid December period turned the *Stavka* into a stamping ground where an even larger offensive design was pressed out in Stalin's interviews with one commander after another, summoned to conference.

Embroiled with Army Group Centre, Stalin turned almost at once to Army Group North. The day after Tikhvin was freed, Meretskov and the Leningrad command were summoned peremptorily to the *Stavka* there to face Stalin with his military and political entourage. Meretskov and his chief of staff General Stelmakh, found themselves in distinguished company, with Andrei Zhdanov, General Khozin and two other generals, Sokolov (26th Army) and Galanin (59th Army). Stalin seated his officers round a table covered with maps of the north-west, while Shaposhnikov discussed the general situation; the unification of the armies operating to the east of the river Volkhov would now be best served by setting up the Volkhov Front, whose main task would be to co-operate with the Leningrad command in de-blockading the city and destroying the German forces investing it. Meretskov was appointed commander of the Volkhov Front forthwith, Stelmakh his chief of staff and Zaporozhets commissar. Meretskov was given two new armies, 26th (later designated the 2nd Shock Army) and the 59th – hence the presence of Sokolov and Galanin. Shaposhnikov repeated that the Volkhov Front had a decisive part to play in the de-blockading operation and in the destruction of the main forces of Army Group North; Meretskov's troops were to clear the enemy from the whole area east of the Volkhov, force the river off the march and wipe out the German divisions holding the western bank. Striking north-west, Meretskov would then operate with the Leningrad command in encircling the Germans, while 52nd Army was to aim for Luga and Soltsy to eliminate the German group at Novgorod. The Leningrad Front would use 54th Army under Fedyuninskii to destroy the German troops in the Ladoga area enforcing the land blockade, while at the very opposite point of its operations the Volkhov Front would be assisted by the 11th Army of the North-Western Front in the Novgorod-Luga attacks. To Meretskov, it looked as if a great deal depended on the timely arrival of the 59th and 26th (2nd Shock) Armies (still rolling along in railway trucks east of Yaroslavl). Shaposhnikov repeated once more that the situation in Leningrad was extremely grave, an assertion which Zhdanov and Khozin reinforced with vehemence, arguing that delay would be fatal to the fortunes of Leningrad now sinking fast through famine and bombardment. The Volkhov Front must attack with the minimum of delay with the forces at its disposal. The General Staff reported that the two new armies would be in position between 22–5 December. Stalin promised Meretskov that when his troops were over the Volkhov he would be given one more army and 18–20 ski battalions from the reserves. With that Meretskov had to be content, and on 17 December the *Stavka* operational directive duly appeared, when Meretskov was back in his HQ planning the new offensive in the company of Zhuravlev as his aviation commander, Kurkin for armour, Taranovich for artillery and Colonel Vasilenko for Front intelligence.

The 'consultation' with Meretskov and the confrontation with Zhadnov was, however, merely the first stage in outlining a much more gigantic operation, in which Kurochkin's North-Western Front was vitally implicated and which was planned more or less simultaneously with the Volkhov-Leningrad operations.

The day after Meretskov received his *Stavka* directive (17 December), Kurochkin was staring down at his, apparently thunderstruck at its contents. The strategic objective lay tremendously deep in the German rear – Smolensk. Stalin was bent on nothing less than 'exploding' the whole of Army Group Centre, by striking through the junction between Army Groups North and Centre, then driving deep into the rear of the latter. The *Stavka* directive laid this out in all its starkness: Kurochkin's two left wing armies were,

in co-operation with the troops of the Kalinin Front to cut the enemy escape route, and to give him no opportunity to hold previously prepared defence lines on the line lake Otolovo, Andreapol, the western bank of the Western Dvina, Yartsevo. The next blow will be on Rudnya to cut off Smolensk from the west.

The secondary attack (with right flank units of the Soviet 11th Army) was 'to outflank Staraya Russa, mount its next blow at Dno and Soltsy, and in co-operation with the troops of the Volkhov Front cut the enemy line of retreat in the direction of Novgorod and Luga'. Kurochkin's centre (34th Army) would 'hold the enemy on the Demyansk axis', the left flank operations being specifically in support of the Volkhov Front, whose operational objective was here defined as to achieve 'the destruction of enemy forces defending the river Volkhov, then to encircle them and in co-operation with the troops of the Leningrad Front to take them prisoner or to annihilate them'.

General Kurochkin was faced with a difficult situation. The logistical base of his Front was far too narrow to facilitate such a massive undertaking (flank offensives in multiple directions) yet in preparing his attack plans he was very strictly controlled by Stalin and Shaposhnikov, who would brook no discussion of the main plan. The terrain was bog and marsh, intersected by lakes (frozen, but not easy for movement): the main railway line (Moscow-Kalinin-Vyshnii-Volochek-Bolodorog) was badly damaged, and the single road running from Yaroslavl-Rybinsk-Boloroye was also the main artery for the Kalinin Front and for the left wing of the Volkhov Front, not only overloaded but also severely damaged by German bombing. The nearest railhead was more than fifty miles from the start-lines, and lack of lorries, lack of roads on which to run them or lack of fuel with which to keep them moving gravely restricted Kurochkin's opportunities. Stocks of fuel, food and ammunition were desperately low, and the chance of acquiring more looked dismal. With 11th and 34th Armies, there was nothing for it but to string them out in a straight line in one echelon; neither formation had any reserves. Staring out at Kurochkin was also the Demyansk problem, held by five powerful German divisions and evidently supposed to be 'contained' by the five ragged divisions of the 34th, with one regiment of anti-tank guns between them all. As subsequent events were to show, Kurochkin's prescience about Demyansk was certainly not misplaced, and his misgivings were fully justified. His army commanders proved to be a tough bunch: Morozov with the 11th, Berzarin with the 34th, and for the two Shock

Armies, two shock-minded commanders, Purkayev with 3rd Shock and Yeremenko (who, as a Colonel-General, outranked the Front commander) with the 4th Shock. The 4th Shock Army was the old 27th Army (Berzarin's former command), as yet far from concentrated but intended to comprise eight rifle divisions, three rifle brigades, four artillery regiments, three tank battalions, mortar units and ten ski battalions; at this point for all practical purposes, 4th Shock was one division, the 249th, a picked force full of former frontier guards under an officer from the frontier troops, Colonel G.F. Tarasov. The division covered the concentration of the whole army. Kurochkin's Front after mid December was hard at work preparing the offensive operations, but there were many ominous signs. Kurochkin himself had significant reservations about the whole *Stavka* plan. Yeremenko, who was very soon briefed personally by Stalin, pinned his star to the 4th Shock, which was to spear Army Group Centre to death. Yeremenko (who had had Kurochkin under his command at Smolensk) soon came to have grave doubts about his Front commander, whose 'stinginess' enraged him. The supply situation, aggravated by catastrophically bad communications, quickly grew worse, to a point where the Chief of Rear Services (North-Western Front) and his commissar were put in front of a Military Tribunal. The infantry in the assault groups forming up had not had a proper meal between them, because there was no food. One formation after another ate up its meagre supplies.

Stalin, nevertheless, continued to sharpen this northern prong, the outer encircling hook which was to reach down into the vitals of Army Group Centre from the north-west, jabbed in at the junction between the two German Army groups. The planning was complete shortly after mid December, the Volkhov and North-Western Front directives following speedily upon each other's heels, emanating from Stalin standing round his maps. In the middle of December, when the first phase of the Moscow counter-stroke was concluded (with both German pincers north and south of Moscow broken off), with reports of German demoralization and defeat flowing in, as the hinges securing the flanks of Army Group Centre were under immense strain, Stalin took personal control of the counter-offensive and handled the planning of its next phase. As the *Stavka* directives rolled on to the Fronts, Stalin's massive plan became clearer – the destruction of Army Group Centre, the annihilation of Army Group North, and a great lunge into the Ukraine. Of two solutions, one 'limited' and involving the crippling of Army Group Centre only, the other expansive in the extreme and envisaging rolling up the Wehrmacht, Stalin now judged the moment ripe to promote the second. In his Kremlin war-room, with only the maps to speak, with the commander summoned to take orders, as the gaps torn in the German front showed up so dramatically, the project, studied in all the quietude and organized calm with which Stalin impregnated his tight environment, must have seemed dazzling. The scents of 1812 and *la Grande Armée* were in the air.

Stalin ordered Koniev, Zhukov and Timoshenko to broaden their offensive operations: Koniev and Timoshenko were fully to activate their right flank formations, while Zhukov was to pursue on the flanks and to open his attack at the centre, where his armies had so far been conducting a holding action. Lelyushenko's 30th Army had already passed (as from 12.00 hours, 16 December) from Zhukov to Koniev. Zhukov had already issued orders for his whole Front to advance to the line Ledniki-Kuchino-Mikhalevo-Borodino-Maloyaroslavet-Likhvin-Odoyevo-Livny by the evening of 21 December. Zhukov's front had been shortened, but he had lost the 30th Army in the process, when Lelyushenko's force would have been invaluable in gaining the Lotoschino-Shakovskaya line. By the 20th, the main forces of Zhukov's right wing were on the three river lines, the Lama, Ruza and Moskva, all of which proved impossible to seize off the march, for here was a German line held tenaciously; to the rear, Soviet units finally cracked open German formations pinned in this welter of fighting – 78th Infantry Division, 46th Panzer Corps, 11th Panzer Division, 7th Corps, a great litter of abandoned and shattered equipment, snow-drifted bodies of men and animals. On 19 December two Soviet mobile groups, general Remizov (20th Army) and general Katukov (16th Army), had out-flanked Volokolamsk from the north and south-east; they took this important junction on the morning of 20 December, the day on which Major-General L.M. Dovator, the brilliant Jewish commander of the 2nd Guards Cavalry Corps, which Zhukov had unleashed into the German rear across the Zvenigorod-Istra sector, was killed in action. Zhukov was not disposed to think that the Lama-Ruza 'line' was the limit of the German withdrawal, and therefore issued on 20 December a further set of orders prescribing a new advance line running from Zubtsov to Ghzatsk, which was to be reached by 27 December, fifty miles west of the Lama-Ruza positions; a mobile group from 20th Army, operating with 16th Army was to take Ghzatsk by the evening of the twenty-seventh. The advance line for the evening of 22 December was fixed at Kuchino-Mikhalevo-Borodino-Korovino as the objective for the right flank formations.

In pursuit of his main plan to tie down the Fourth Army at the centre, and under orders from Stalin, Zhukov now committed his own centre armies on 18 December, the left flank of Govorov's 5th Army, Yefremov's 33rd Army, Golubev's 43rd Army, Zakharkin's 49th right flank and centre. The orders had been prescribed on 13 December, the attacks originally planned for the fifteenth, but delayed for three days, although the objectives were again confirmed on the sixteenth. Both the 33rd and 43rd Armies, attacking on the eighteenth, became snagged in the German defences on the river Nara in the are of Naro-Fominsk, though to prevent German movement towards the Lama or to Kaluga the Soviet attacks were pressed home again and again. Zhukov intervened directly on 20 December over the operations of 33rd and 43rd Armies, ordering this time that the two armies reach the Simbukohovo-Borovsk-Balabanovo-Voroba line by the evening of 22 December. Meanwhile, the flank formations of 5th and 49th Armies had achieved nothing but small 'local successes' in their assault on the German tactical defence zone.

Zhukov's attention, however, like that of the German command, was riveted on the Kaluga-Belev sector. On Zhukov's left, where Guderian's Panzer army had been torn away from the German Fourth Army, Zhukov wanted Kaluga tight in his grasp: Kaluga led to Vyazma and then the Moscow-Smolensk motorway, straight into the rear of the Fourth Army. Boldin of the 50th was assigned to the Kaluga operation; Shaposhnikov himself telephoned Boldin to give him this news and to impress on him the importance of taking Kaluga. A little while later Zhukov contacted Boldin and gave him the Front orders. Boldin put his deputy, Major-General V.S. Popov, in command of a 'mobile group' (154th Rifle, 112th Tank Division, reinforced on 18 December by 31st Cavalry Division, a Tula militia regiment and 131st Independent Tank Battalion). Popov's orders were simple: to penetrate into the gap between the German 43rd Corps and Guderian's Panzer units, and to cover the forty-five miles to Kaluga (thirty of them deep in the German positions) at top speed, to approach Kaluga from the south and seize it. The next job was to bring 49th and 50th Armies up behind Popov, pushing 43rd Corps north-west and Guderian south-west, towards Orel. By the evening of 20 December, Popov's group was in sight of Kaluga to the south-east: Belov's cavalry and Golikov's 10th Army were fighting westwards to Odoyevo-Livny, the 10th being across the river Plava. The first consummations of Zhukov's counter-offensive were now in sight and his revised orders went out on 20 December to his left flank formations, which were to swing north-west while the right flank, breaking out from the Lama-Ruza line, was to swing south-east (and the Kalinin Front in co-operation with the Western would strike into Panzer Group 3 communications in the Rzhev area).

On the morning of 21 December, Popov's riflemen tried to storm Kaluga. Zakharkin's 49th was still well back. First into Kaluga was the 31st Cavalry Division which ran straight into the furious resistance of the German 137th Infantry Division. To support Popov, Boldin ordered his left flank 217th and 413th Rifle Division to race for Kaluga, where Popov was encircled. It was a fight for every house and each yard of each street. The Soviet troops were to take the town at all costs and give no quarter. On 24 December, Boldin received this signal from Zhukov:

24 December *Stavka* received information that German garrisons in Kaluga have categorical orders to defend the town to the last and not to give it up. *Verhovnoe Glavno-komandovanie* [Supreme Command: Stalin] underlines the necessity for special vigilance from our side. It is necessary to use special energy to beat the enemy in Kaluga, to break him into little pieces, to make no concessions at all and to give the enemy no quarter. Quite the contrary, everything must be done to destroy the enemy in Kaluga.

Perhaps Stalin had in mind the incident of the white flag at Klin, when the

Russians prevailed upon the Germans to surrender. To get Kaluga Boldin had to take it apart in a week of fighting at close quarters.

In Belov's cavalry corps, meanwhile, man and beast alike flayed by the cold and run ragged in the great sweep from Kashira to south-east of Tula, were beginning to tire. On 19 December, Belov's Guards received reinforcements and took a moment's rest, a brief but welcome calm which was abruptly shattered by new orders for the 2nd Guards Corps:

To commander Cavalry-Mechanized Group Major-General Comrade Belov.

The Military Soviet [Western Front] has a special assignment for you: to break at high speed into the area of Yukhnov and to destroy the rear and staff of the 4th German Army. To secure flanks and rear of the group, necessary to seize and to hold Sukhinichi, Meshchovsk, Mosalsk.

Military Soviet of the Front will place at your disposal additionally three cavalry divisions (from 10th Army), one–two rifle divisions, reinforced with up to 50 tanks. In working out operational plan, bear in mind that Kaluga at the moment of [your] group's jump-off will have been captured.

Golikov's 10th Army, operating south of Belov, was subsequently given assignments to support this operation.

With a 100-mile forced march ahead of him, with food and ammunition not exactly abundant, with forage for his cavalry in short supply, with three German divisions, 112th, 167th and 296th, apparently directly ahead of him, there was every reason for Belov to prolong the 'holiday' for his Corps just a fraction longer, while the operational plan was worked out. This plan envisaged taking the road junction of Odoyevo, then forcing the Oka in the Likhvin-Belev sector and reducing German resistance in Kozelsk. Only then could Belov strike up to Yukhnov towards the end of December. These details were radioed to Zhukov's HQ. And closer inspection of the reinforcements gave cause for concern – men without weapons, horses without saddles. Captured German weapons were distributed. But Belov had received a goodly contingent of NCOs, 'young, tough lads', reasonably trained and desperately needed to replenish the ferocious losses in NCOs. What grieved Belov was the stupidity of not allowing wounded men back to their own units; his men more than once risked being caught as deserters to get back to 'their' unit. After repeated requests, Belov managed to have a 'reserve regiment', stationed at Kovrova, set up to take back his veterans. In the midst of refurbishing his corps and planning the Yukhnov strike, Belov had a rude shock, another Front signal: 'Tomorrow, 21 December, in honour of the birthday of Comrade Stalin the corps must take Odoyevo.' Belov had no option but to obey, though it meant tipping his hand. He compromised by detaching a special force to do this, while preparing the main body for Yuknov, where he could slash away at vital German communications. As Belov jumped off, Zhukov ordered Golikov's 10th Army to make for Kozelsk and to set up mobile ski- and sledge-units in order to take Sukhinichi off the march in one fast swoop.

Stalin's personal orders about the full activation of the flanks brought Koniev's Kalinin Front an independent strategic role after mid December. When in mid December Shvetsov and Yushkevich had fought their way into Kalinin itself, the eastern wing of the German Ninth Army had to be pulled back. Whereas earlier it had been planned to destroy the Ninth Army by striking from the south-west at its right flank and centre, a joint Kalinin-Western Front operation, now this entire task devolved on Koniev, for which he had been given the 30th Army from Zhukov's right. Koniev assumed that on the Kalinin sector itself the Ninth Army would fall back south-westwards on Staritsa, while on the rest of its front running from Ostashkova to Volyntseva, German troops would hold their positions. To smash in the German right wing, and to break in even further to the flank of Panzer Group 3, Koniev decided to use his brand-new 39th Army and to drive on Rzhev. The new offensive was timed by the *Stavka* for 22 December at the latest; the same directive adjusted the lateral boundaries of Koniev's and Zhukov's commands (to run from Kotlyaki to Zubstov, both points inclusive for the Kalinin Front) as well as recommending new assignments for 31st and 30th Armies. Koniev's own orders, based on this instruction, assigned an advance line running from the river Volga-Sukhodol-Burgovo-Tolstikovo-Zubtsov to be reached by the evening of 28 December, the main attack being against Rzhev from the north and north-east, thereby encircling the main body of the German Ninth Army and cutting its escape route to the west and south-west. Five Front armies, 22nd, 39th, 29th, 31st and 30th – would be committed, with Maslennikov's 39th co-operating with 31st and 30th Armies in the destruction of the German forces in the Rzhev-Staritsa area. The offensive was timed for the morning of 22 December, even though the 39th had not finished concentrating and could put only two divisions (220th and 183rd) into the first phase of the attack. The intermingling of the flanks of the Kalinin and Western Front, however, caused the *Stavka* to think again and to reset the lateral boundaries, running it now from Kotlyaki to Sychevka, the effect of which was to alter appreciably the depth of Koniev's proposed offensive and to suggest that it might be better to dig straight into the rear of the two Panzer Groups (3 and 4) facing Zhukov's right than to plan for the Rzhev-Zubtsov encirclement. In this highly complex situation, the consequences of Stalin's abrupt transfer of Lelyushenko's 30th Army to Koniev were becoming very plain, though a solution scarcely recommended itself. Zhukov's right and Koniev's left had by the evening of 25 December moved up to the Kotlyaki-Ostashevo line, where all formations ran into the resistance offered by German units on Lama-Ruza river line; the northern flank units of Koniev's Front were pressing down on the Ninth Army on the Volga bend, where this great over-hanging cliff of Soviet armies seemed likely to fall right on Army Group Centre's very northern flank, which screens of machine-gunners, *Panzerjäger* units, Luftwaffe AA troops using their guns depressed to fire at ground targets, fighting in numbing cold in the murk and snow flurries, were desperately trying to prop up. As long as the Panzer Groups held on the Lama-Ruza line, the Ninth Army also had to hold its positions. At Torzhok, meanwhile, most of Maslennikov's 39th Army had now formed up and on 26 December this formation, with its full complement, six divisions (220th, 183rd, 361st, 373rd, 355th), jumped off on its drive to Rzhev. Koniev had expressly reminded Maslennikov that the 'main blow was to be on the right flank to bring the main body of the formation out to the west of Rzhev'. Shortly afterwards, Koniev had to order Maslennikov to speed things up, though the 39th was considerably hampered by having to commit its units to the offensive in bits and pieces. Nevertheless, Maslennikov began to grind his way to Rzhev, spilling into the Volga bend and smothering the German defence sector by sector. What was to become the giant crisis of Rzhev was already in the making.

Koniev disposed of 30 rifle, 5 cavalry divisions, and 2 tank brigades, a third of the infantry strength of Red Army troops operating on the 'western axis' – totalling in all 93 rifle, 23 cavalry divisions, 30 rifle brigades (including two parachute brigades) and 16 tank brigades. For his 180-mile front, running from Chekchino-Volokolamsk-Ruza-river Nara-Kaluga-river Oka and to the east of Belev, Zhukov had 45 rifle and 11 cavalry divisions. To the south of Zhukov, Stalin had interposed the Bryansk Front, reconstituted on 18 December and made operational on 24 December, put under the command of Cherevichenko and assigned the 61st, 3rd and 13th Armies, plus Kostenko's operational group, a force numbering 18 rifle, 7 cavalry divisions, 2 tank, 1 rifle and 1 motorized rifle brigade, committed to a drive on Orel-Bolkhov. These were formidable forces, but the counter-offensive had already cost the Red Army dear. Divisions were down in many cases to between 3,000 and 4,000 brigades to less than 1,000, tank brigades reduced to one T-34 tank apiece. Ammunition was short, transport grossly deficient.

The Western Front staff appreciation of the situation on 25 December, when the second stage of the Moscow counter-offensive was closing, pinpointed the Kozelsk-Sukinichi gap as the gravest weakness in the German positions; in fact the 'line' had been broken, and only scattered units of the German 84th Infantry Regiment, and independent ss regiment, four companies of railway troops, a company of field gendarmerie, a regiment of ss *Gross Deutschland*, and elements of the 296th Infantry Division were milling about in it. The greatest density of German troops was on Zhukov's right wing and centre, from Lotoshino to Naro-Fominsk. The *Stavka* appreciation was that the greatest concentration of German forces was, as at the beginning of the counter-offensive, on the flanks of the Western Front, where Western-Kalinin (and now Bryansk) Front flanks conjoined. The main weight of Red Army troops had been committed on a front running from Parshino-Volokolamsk-Ruza-Belev. From 25 December, the *Stavka* adjusted the offensive axes of the Kalinin and Western Front: while Koniev's first thrust had been in a south-westerly direction with the 39th Army (towards Rzhev-Vyazma), this was now changed to one due south, while the right wing of Zhukov's front shifted its axis from the west to south-west. This was implicit in the shifting of the Front lateral boundaries. Zhukov's right continued to press on the Lama–Ruza line, while his left on the Kaluga–Belev sector went for the right flank of the German Fourth Army, aiming for Kozelsk–Vyazma (with 10th Army driving almost due west on Kirov). The Red Army was fighting now to break into Army Group Centre's 'redoubt', the Rzhev–Lotoshino–Naro-Forminsk–Maloyaroslavets–Vyazma 'line', the loss of which on the reckoning of the Soviet command spelled utter disaster for the entire German force. Nor, for that matter, did the German command see it in any appreciable different light, the main discord being over what should be done to save the situation – pull right out of harm's way, or stand fast and hold the line. In the end, Hitler's 'Stand fast' orders prevailed, though to many it seemed that this merely condemned Army Group Centre to destruction.

The ultimate kill was what Stalin was now aiming for, all the more convinced that to physical defeat must be added the effects of moral collapse within the German Army in the east. It was under the overriding influence of these impressions that Stalin embarked on putting the final touches to what was soon to become a general Red Army counter-offensive, to be unleashed early in the New Year. The Volkhov and North-Western Front operations were already well advanced in their preparatory stages, the *Stavka* directives delivered into the hands of the Front commanders, and their operational plans were now under Stalin's scrutiny. The most sensitive part of Stalin's personal control of Soviet operations was the assignment of particular objectives to individual armies (which in one case, shifting Lelyushenko's 30th Army, had already brought confusion in its wake). Much more fundamental, however, was the question of utilizing the present resources of the Red Army which for all the arrows and dots of rifle divisions on the battle maps were not so abundant. The cost of the counter-offensive continued to show in commanders' reports. Rokossovskii submitted at the end of December that his battalions were down to 'less than a dozen men' in strength; on the Bryansk Front, which was stalled south of Belev in its drive for the river Oka, 3rd Army reported that its five rifle divisions had only 16,028 men between them and 138 guns, while five rifle divisions of 13th Army amounted to 11,833 men all told, with 82 guns left. This was not promising for the operational assignments prescribed for the Bryansk Front, which on 24 December included moving into the Orel–Kursk area (in co-operation with the right wing of the South-Western Front) – by 5 January 1942. Koniev's Front alone had divisions up at the 10,000-man mark, but he had only four of these, and that comparative wealth in men was counterbalanced by a drastic poverty in mobile formations; the only real military magnate was Colonel-General Yeremenko, whose 4th Shock Army, 382nd, 358th, 334th, 360th Rifle Divisions had divisions up to strength under the revised establishment. The 112th Tank Division (Western Front) which had at one time been shared out between Zakharkin and Belov, was almost expended to the point of having a single T-34 tank and fifteen T-26s left. Stalin at this critical juncture, between late December and early January, when the fate of Army Group Centre seemed to hang in the balance as its lines were apparently being torn apart one by one, had three reserve armies at his disposal, the 24th, 26th and 60th, the Moscow defence zone garrisons, all fresh reserve armies standing at the ready: If they were to crack open the German central 'redoubt', they must go to the right wing of Koniev's front and to Zhukov's left, to bear from north and south in one great destructive swoop on the Vyazma concentrations, to break the back of Army Group Centre. Ambitious though that plan was (yet not unrealistic), it did not compare with Stalin's immense undertakings which reached out for nothing less than instant victory.

Not all, however, enjoyed this haughty confidence in the future. The 'far-reaching conclusions' which Stalin drew from the Soviet victory at Moscow were apparently not wholly endorsed by Marshal Shaposhnikov, or at least he did not display any great ebullience when on 22 December General Batov, commander of the 51st Army which had earlier been brushed out of the Crimea, was summoned to his presence. Batov assumed that he had been ordered to Moscow in connection with the forthcoming Kerch landing-operations, a major amphibious assault which 51st Army was preparing. Batov (successor to Colonel-General F.I. Kuznetsov who was at this moment deputy commander of the Western Front) had handed over his command to General Lvov. General Batov found Shaposhnikov gloomy and preoccupied, brooding over the difficulties of the offensive in which tanks, lorries, and equipment in general were lacking to facilitate rapid Soviet manoeuvre. 'We still need', said the marshal, 'to assimilate the experience of modern war', adding that though the Germans had been thrown back from the capital, 'neither here, nor today, will the outcome of the war be decided'; on the contrary, in Shaposhnikov's view, 'the crisis is yet far off'. And so it proved to be.

Shaposhnikov was almost perfunctory in his remarks to Batov about the Crimean collapse. Instead, he took Batov in the small hours, at 3 am, to a session of the *Stavka*, where Stalin told him that there were 'no complaints against him' over his handling of the 51st; a hard lesson had been learned in the Crimea (where the defenders had been strung out), but now Batov was to proceed forthwith to the Bryansk Front to take command of the 3rd Army. The brief interview over, an astonished Batov did as he was bid, and moved off for his new command, 'no simple matter' in those days even for an army commander, who had to improvise his transport; once installed, he made the acquaintance of Front commander Cherevichenko, a colonel-general, one of the victors of Rostov, who nevertheless frightened Batov with his antiquated Civil War Cavalryman's approach to his assignments, all for the 'dashing attack'. Batov landed in his new post as the planning for the great southern offensive was being completed, a time in Batov's opinion when the prevailing influence was similar to that 'which in 1940 led us in Finland to a frontal storming of the Mannerheim line'. The army which Batov had just left, for good, as it turned out, was being prepared for the landings on the Kerch peninsula, 'a deadly threat' to Manstein's Eleventh Army which was trying in late December to batter its way into Sevastopol, the sole offensive operation which Hitler authorized in the welter of withdrawal and confusion attending German armies elsewhere. The Kerch landings were no mere diversion, but a major effort to reconquer the Crimea, for which Stalin soon established the Crimean Front.

While the final orders were being relayed and the last preparations made for the Kerch-Feodosiya landings, Marshal Timoshenko, commander of the South-Western Axis (the only surviving major strategic command of the three earlier *Napravleniya*) had approached Stalin with his plan for a 'broad offensive' by the Bryansk, South-Western and Southern Fronts, to take place in January-February 1942 and consisting of two major operations. The first would be carried out by the Bryansk Front and General Kostenko's 'operational group', an outflanking operation aimed against the German troops in the Moscow area and designed to bring the Bryansk Front forces to the Bryansk-Sevsk line, and Kostenko's men up to the town of Suma. The second offensive strike would be mounted by the left wing of the South-Western and the Southern Fronts, to free the Donbas and bring Soviet troops up to the river Dnieper, with northern cover for this being provided by South-Western Front forces also moving into the Kharkov area. Timoshenko's price was steep – half a million field reinforcements at once, plus 10 rifle divisions, 15 tank brigades, 24 artillery and 25 aviation regiments. Half a million men on tap Stalin did not have, and 15 tank brigades actually possessing tanks was like asking for the moon. Little wonder that Shaposhnikov, ailing as he was with his work-day reduced on strict medical orders to four hours, was worried: there was a strong case both for the Leningrad operations, where the situation was truly desperate, and for the spearing operations at Army Group Centre, but to take on three German Army Groups in full battle with margins by no means expansive was another matter. Timoshenko's grand plan was scaled down somewhat, though its scope was still impressively wide: Cherevichenko's Bryansk Front (3rd, 13th, 61st Armies) with the right wing of South-Western Front (40th and 21st Armies) was to strike westwards and seize the Orel-Kursk area, while the South-Western Front, over which Lieutenant-General F.Ya. Kostenko was given full command, would prepare to attack with the 38th and 6th Armies in the Chuguev-Balakleya-Izyum area and seize Kharkov and Krasnograd, thereby covering Southern Front offensive operations from the north-west. When Cherevichenko had gone to the Bryansk Front, Lieutenant-General R. Ya. Malinovskii took over the Southern Front (with Lieutenant-General A.I. Antonov as his chief of staff); Malinovskii's armies (57th, 37th and 9th) were to attack in the direction of Pavlograd, and seize crossings over the Dnieper at Dniepropetrovsk and Zaporozhe. Ryaby-shev's 57th Army would drive through Barvenkovo on Pavlograd, Lopatin's 37th through Krasnoarmeisk on Bolshoi Tokmak, and to exploit these gains Malinovskii could call on the 1st and 5th Cavalry Corps and 9th Army, all of which had been drawn into Timoshenko's strategic reserve. With his hands on the major traffic centres of Dniepropetrovsk and Zaporozhe, Timoshenko would be able to strangle Army Group South forces east of the Dnieper and in the Crimea, and he would be astride the only useful crossing area for the Dnieper. Even though scaled down in terms of force levels, Timoshenko was preparing nothing short of a paralysing blow designed to seal the fate of Army Group South, while two Soviet armies, 51st and 44th, were already embarked on the enterprise of eliminating Manstein's Eleventh Army in the Crimea by first leaping on the two German divisions (reckoned to be not more than 25,000 men) by amphibious assault on the northern, eastern and southern shores of the peninsula, an operation dependent on the ships of the Black Sea Fleet and timed for 26 December.

The Kerch operation was planned while the fighting for Sevastopol reached a new and furious climax, Manstein having committed the Eleventh Army to the final storming of the Soviet fortress, which had been battered by bombing and by bombardment from giant siege guns; the main German blow was directed against Sector No. 4 of the Sevastopol defensive zone, from Duvankoi along the valley of the river Belbeck, which was the shortest route to Severnaya Bay and to the town and port facilities themselves. A second thrust from the south-east of Nozhnii Chorgun would take Manstein's troops up to Inkerman, along the line of the river Chernaya. By 4 December, the Sevastopol command reported to Stalin that its defences were now in order, with the scattered and shattered units which had been swept into the Sevastopol perimeter reorganized, re-armed and brought up to strength. While Sevastopol was under the fire of German 360-mm guns, monsters specially brought up to crack open the forts and defences, units of the Black Sea Fleet moved in reinforcements for the garrison, principally the 388th Rifle Division which arrived just in time to face the German attack opening at 08.00 hours (17 December) with a powerful artillery preparation, followed by the *Stukas*. All the Russian defenders could see was a horizon blackened with smoke.

After forty-eight hours, the Soviet defenders hanging on grimly to every inch of ground and holding each pill-box to the last marine, were in dangerous straits, with men and ammunition almost exhausted. Stalin at once subordinated the Sevastopol defensive zone to the Trans-Caucasus Front under Kozlov, who was ordered to send in either a rifle division or two brigades, not less than 3,000 reinforcements, air cover and ammunition. Vice-Admiral Oktyabrskii, Black Sea Fleet commander, was ordered on 20 December from Novorossiisk to Sevastopol, though this meant taking him away from direct supervision of the Kerch landing preparations. Oktyabrskii himself commanded the naval units, the cruisers *Krasnyi Kavkaz*, *Krasnyi Krim*, the flotilla-leader *Kharkov* and escort ships, which ran into the besieged base with the 79th Independent Marine Brigade, followed on 21–2 December with the 345th Rifle Division shipped in from Tuapse and the fast flotilla-leader *Tashkent* loaded with ammunition, just as a savage battle was reaching its climax on the Mackenzie Heights, steeped in the struggles of the first Crimean War; groups of German infantrymen broke through Colonel Kudyurov's 40th Cavalry Division to a point only two kilometres from Severnaya Bay in the north-east. This is where Oktyabrskii threw in the newly arrived Soviet marines.

As German troops on the peninsula were gripped by the winter cold, Soviet ships were harried by the winter gales, a significant factor in the proposed landings at Kerch, where two Soviet armies (51st and 44th) were to be used in a major amphibious assault, jabbing right into the rear of Manstein's army now pressed up against Sevastopol. The landings had been planned originally for 21 December, but the crisis at Sevastopol caused immediate postponement, for the forces rushed to Sevastopol had been earmarked as assault units for Kerch. The landings were put back five days, and only on the night of 25 December did ships of the Azov Flotilla, the Kerch naval base and Assault Group 'B' load up with equipment and assault parties, all in a Force 8 gale and with reports that ice was adrift in the Sea of Azov. The landing force had been divided into two groups, 'A' (the bulk of Major-General Pervushin's 44th Army and Captain Basistii's ships, in all 23,000 men, 34 tanks and 133 guns), and 'B' (3,000 men from the 44th), committed against Feodosiya, and 51st Army under Major-General Lvov (a landing force of 13,000 men) against Kerch. The main weight of the attack was directed against Feodosiya, for which the troops embarked on the night of 28 December at Novorossiisk, a confused affair in which warships were overloaded or delayed by units pulling in late, but by 23.00 hours the armada was on its way.

On the morning of 26 December under cover of a smoke-screen 51st Army units on the Azov Flotilla ships tried to move ashore, this time in a Force 5 gale. Cutters and barges spilled men into the sea, while German guns and aircraft harried the landings. Without any special equipment, in ferocious weather and with frequent breakdowns in command and organization, more than 3,000 men were finally put ashore; at 03.50 hours, 29 December, the Feodosiya landings began, and two days later 40,519 men, 236 guns, 43 tanks, 330 lorries and other heavy equipment had been landed. In temperatures of − 20° C. Soviet troops had waded neck-high through icy water to the shore, where without supplies they clung grimly to bridgeheads in which the immobile wounded inexorably died as stiffened blocks of ice. Although the 44th was contained, the 51st Army fell on Feodosiya, just as Manstein was about to try his final break into Sevastopol, from where German troops had to be diverted to seal off the Soviet penetrations on the Kerch peninsula. In the event, the German forces at Kerch-Feodosiya were not sealed up in a Soviet bag, but the pressure on Sevastopol had been relieved, the Kerch peninsula was once again in Soviet hands and the 'Crimean Front' under Kozlov had come into being.

For all the sights and sounds of victory, as the Red Army hacked away at the German troops, there were disquieting signs that commanders could scarcely fail to notice: Batov, although he sensed the intoxications produced by the first successes, was gloomy about the implications of what he saw about him – flinging the Red Army 'unscientifically' and almost unprofessionally at the still very formidable German formations. Gorbatov, recently promoted to major-general, had spent long enough in one of Stalin's penal camps labour to know the value of discretion but was appalled at the standards of the command and the quality of its decisions, and this when many a first-rate senior commander was being worked to death in the slave camps of Kolyma. A great deal of subsequent accusation was levelled at Rumyantscv, head of the Cadres (Personnel) Administration of the Red Army, an officer often without the remotest notion of the capabilities (or lack of them) of the officers he was posting to field commands. Biryuzov, who had shown himself to be very capable, Rumyantsev proposed to post to the rear. Stalin picked his own men for special jobs, a system which did not always work: there were the non-military generals in key commands, men like Maslennikov of 39th Army, a former NKVD Deputy People's Commissar, who approached operational questions from a 'purely administrative point of view'. Then there were Stalin's super-commissars, Mekhlis, Bulganin and even Malenkov, who without any military training waded into the thick of decisions, laying about them in the name of Stalin. Zhukov had managed to divest himself of Bulganin, who was now destined for the north-west, where he proceeded to wreak a fair amount of havoc: Mekhlis was at this moment hounding Meretskov to speed his Leningrad attack.

The mistakes were not all Stalin's; the Red Army soldier on the whole placed substantial confidence in Stalin. Nor was all the over-confidence confined to him, and no amount of it could excuse the tactical inadequacies and incompetences which enraged so many subordinate officers. Zhukov himself and in person lashed out time and time again at costly and uninspired 'frontal attack' methods, time-wasting ventures which robbed his offensive of its non-stop momentum, though most serious was the over-all lack of mobile formations, which Zhukov was now trying to compensate for by earmarking and preparing parachute troops (independent airborne units, air-lifted rifle regiments and the 4th Parachute Corps) for rapid strike operations in the German rear. There were, nevertheless, specific operations carefully and skilfully handled: the Kerch landings, for all the miscalculation and confusion, had proved an astute, astonishing and in parts brilliant improvisation. The forthcoming strategic operations had been planned at breakneck speed: in that sense, they were an improvised strategic solution (in fact, almost overly obvious), the initial effect of surprise was wearing off and the German command and its troops were pulling themselves together, measuring the distance between them and catastrophe. The Red Army for all the fantastic straining of its resources enjoyed no decisive superiority on any particular front or conjunction of fronts, the offensive was running on a logistical shoe-string, casualties had already been heavy, and equipment was in drastically short supply. With this, Stalin proposed to smother the *Ostheer* in one great swoop. The decisions were taken and the *Stavka* directives either issued or on their way to the Front commands. Little wonder that Shaposhnikov sat tense and worried.

After the first successes against the Germans, whose demoralization and dis-organization he believed to be greater than was in fact the case, Stalin turned also to defining his war aims, at least in a territorial sense. He was evidently anxious to stake out his claims, possibly in anticipation of being soon quite near the lines he had begun to mark out. The wrangle of what a post-war settlement involved had already been indicated by Stalin's exchanges with the Poles, the 'London Poles', with whom an inter-allied agreement had been additionally concluded in August 1941; from being prisoners and waifs in the Soviet Union, the captive Poles were now co-belligerents, though they continued to go short of food, to go freezing and unsheltered in appalling weather and, as soldiers, to go short of arms. The Polish authorities were increasingly disturbed by the failure to account for a substantial number of Polish officer-prisoners who had been in camps run by the NKVD. Vyshinskii, as was his way, had already handled Polish Ambassador Kot very roughly in an October exchange over the fate of the Poles in the USSR: General Sikorski and Prime Minister Churchill later in October discussed the fate of Polish troops in Russia, and decided upon the solution of moving them out 'within reach of the British strategy – southwards, to the Middle East'. General Sikorski was evidently of the opinion that 'in spite of the lack of trust and sympathy between the two partners', Britain would ultimately be forced to yield to Stalin's pressure to put British troops on the Soviet battle-front; the British were therefore looking for a 'Soviet compensa-tion'. After multiple interventions (Polish and British), a Polish army on Soviet soil, limited to 30,000 men, was authorized by telegram, dated 6 November, addressed to Lieutenant-General Anders (Polish Army) from General Panfilov, designating himself 'Plenipotentiary of the Red Army High Command for the formation of the Polish Army' – address, Moscow, No. 6 Gogelevskii Bulevard.

Stalin discussed the Polish Army question with Ambassador Kot on 14 November; the case for a larger army (possibly 150,000 men) Stalin threw out, arguing that 'the Protocol' did not envisage it and that the Russians could not equip them. If the Poles could get equipment, they could have more divisions. General Anders had a week earlier confronted two Soviet liasion officers about the Polish troops held in the Red Army and its labour battalions, and Polish prisoners still held in labour camps: above all, 5,000 Polish officers were missing. Ambassador Kot now brought up these points with Stalin, who had already shown some fury over one of Panfilov's orders; on the question of

Polish prisoners, Stalin connected himself with the NKVD. What he heard when the NKVD telephoned a little later to answer his enquiry Stalin did not communicate. Throughout the talk he behaved with the utmost courtesy. The real confrontation came on 3 December, when General Sikorski, Ambassador Kot and General Anders faced Stalin and Molotov, a day when German troops were still striking at Moscow's defences and the battle-line snaked into the city suburbs. General Sikorski handled Stalin carefully but forcefully: Anders and Stalin met head-on in a splintering crash, though Stalin began to lose his temper with General Sikorski over moving Polish troops 'south'. At this point Stalin interjected angrily: 'I am a person of experience and of age. I know that if you go to Persia you will never return here. I see that England has much to do and needs Polish soldiers.' After becoming increasingly truculent over the question of the Polish Army, Stalin lashed out furiously at the Polish generals, 'It amounts to this, that a Russian can only oppress a Pole, but is unable to do anything good for him.' There, through Stalin, spoke three hundred years of history. 'Then, be off! However, we can manage without you. . . . We will manage ourselves. We will conquer Poland and then we will give her back to you.' As for the British, Stalin warned the Poles, '*tomorrow* Japan will attack' and the Poles would perhaps die in Singapore. (Twice Stalin in this talk insisted on the imminence of Japanese attack.) A little later Stalin had Panfilov in and dressed him down very abruptly, for failing to carry out Stalin's previous orders to deliver supplies to the Poles, orders handled administratively by General Khrulev. At this, the heat of the conversation subsided, though Stalin jabbed away at the English – for Stalin the best airmen were Slavs, 'a young race which has not yet worn out. . . . The Germans are strong but the Slavs will crush them.'

At a dinner the next night, Stalin was more amiable, even to General Anders. When the talk came round to frontiers, Stalin advised his guests, 'We should settle our common frontiers between ourselves and before the Peace Conference . . . we should stop talking on this subject. Don't worry, we will not harm you.' With General Sikorski Stalin patched up a peace, promising him a declaration signed by himself, 'It will be the first time that a declaration has been signed by Stalin and not by Molotov.' At Molotov's description of what Hitler's reaction would be, General Sikorski remarked that, to judge by the details of the description, Molotov must 'know him [Hitler] intimately'.

For all the reversion to formal courtesies, these had been bitter and biting talks, in which (as General Sikorski later reported to Churchill) Stalin suspected an 'Anglo-American intrigue' over the proposed transfer of Polish troops. At the same time, Stalin had established himself in a highly advantageous position *vis-à-vis* the 'common frontier' question. Soviet-Polish relations were due for a surface improvement and for a brief moment they got it, while Stalin unleashed his second bolt, this time upon Eden who met him in Moscow in mid December. On this occasion, Stalin produced an entire blueprint for carving up Europe. Eden, who journeyed to Russia on the cruiser *Kent* in the company of

Ivan Maiskii, Soviet ambassador in London, had previously prepared a memorandum for Stalin to clear the air about any 'Anglo-American ganging up' to
make peace without apparently considering Russian interests: Britain and Russia
would pledge themselves to fight until final victory over Germany was attained,
and the peacemaking, based on the Atlantic Charter, would be governed by
Stalin's own principles enunciated on 6 November that the Soviet Union was
not in the war for territorial gain or the subjugation of others. Early in November
Anglo-Soviet relations took a gloomy turn when Stalin demanded a British
declaration of war on Finland, Rumania and Hungary, and a clarification of
war aims and post-war plans on the part of the British and the Russians. The
Foreign Office even then emphasized Stalin's fear of an 'Anglo-American
peace' at Russia's expense, and hazarded a guess that Stalin's 'war aims' might
include access to the Persian Gulf, revision of the Montreux Convention, and
Soviet bases in Norway, Finland and the Baltic States. Maiskii tried to smooth
away the impression left by Stalin's abrasive terseness, what he had himself
described to the Poles as his 'roughness' – ya grubyi, 'I am rough.'

Before the beginning of the Eden-Stalin talks, which opened on the afternoon
of 16 December, Stalin took Maiskii aside and showed him two draft documents
which he pulled out of his pocket. The first was for an extension of the Anglo-
Soviet wartime treaty, to make it binding in time of peace, the second an outline
of the territorial reconstruction of post-war Europe; Yugoslavia, Austria,
Czechoslovakia and Greece were to be restored to their pre-war frontiers,
(and Bavaria might also become an independent state). Prussia would lose the
Rhineland, and East Prussia would go to Poland, while the Lithuanian Republic
of the USSR would acquire Tilsit and German territory to the north of the
Niemen. If France did not emerge from the war as a great power, then Britain
might hold Boulogne and Dunkirk as bases, with forces in Belgium and the
Netherlands if necessary; the Soviet Union would not oppose British bases in
Norway and Sweden, while it wanted its pre-June, 1941 frontiers in Finland
and the Baltic states, a frontier line with Poland possibly related to the 'Curzon
line', the annexation of the Northern Bukovina and Bessarabia, from Rumania,
Petsamo from Finland.

There were shades of Stalin's confrontation with the Poles in this plan which
made Europe into a chopping block. Stalin had not agreed with General
Sikorski that the French 'are already finished', but he had proposed a frontier
settlement to General Sikorski without the mediation of either Great Britain
or the United States, the lines to be settled 'as soon as the Polish Army enters
into action'. The first session between Stalin and Eden had been devoted to a
general discussion; at the opening of the second, Stalin suddenly produced his
'protocols' from his pocket and asked Eden if he would mind 'adding a small
protocol' to the Anglo-Soviet statement on the principles of post-war reconstruction. Maiskii was stupefied, for what had been 'lines for discussion' suddenly
became concrete and formal territorial propositions, in particular the recogni-

tion of the Soviet 1941 frontiers. Eden pointed out that he could not sign this 'protocol' without consulting London, whereupon Stalin turned on the 'roughness'; at the third session, held at midnight on 17–18 December. Stalin and Molotov went into the attack, reminding the British minister that without a settlement of the Soviet frontier question (and especially the inclusion of the Baltic states within the Soviet Union proper), then there would be no agreement of any kind. The continuation of the argument merely sealed the deadlock; Maiskii for his part was left utterly baffled why, with immense military operations ahead and vast areas to recover, Stalin should choose to 'rub his ally the wrong way' over an issue of no 'immediate practical significance'. Stalin, however, had expressed himself in terms of high confidence over the military situation to Eden – the defeat of Germany in a year, and that of Japan in six months, a war in which the Soviet Union could not immediately join, but 'the situation might change by the spring [1942]'.

Eden had already explained that the Japanese attack in the Far East now precluded the dispatch of British ground and air forces to the Russian front (earlier in November, the sending of the British 18th and 50th Divisions, with 8–10 RAF squadrons had been secretly contemplated to bolster up the defence of the Caucasus, an intention not communicated to the Russians). Nevertheless, General Nye was vigorously pursuing the idea of a joint Anglo-Soviet seaborne assault on Petsamo (and possibly Kirkenes), a scheme which had been mooted earlier and which the Russians now favoured – 'something tangible', regarding British acceptance as 'tantamount to a fulfilment of the Military Agreement'. About Soviet participation in the Far Eastern war, Stalin pointed out that to replace the Soviet divisions withdrawn westwards would take about four months: in the spring when Soviet Far Eastern forces were up to full strength, then the subject could be discussed once more. Perhaps Japan might decide the issue, by making war against the Soviet Union or by some hostile move, but otherwise it would be difficult to persuade the Russian people of the utility of a war in the east. The broad hint proffered by Eden about making available Soviet submarines in the Far East Stalin chose to ignore and rushed away from the subject by pointing out that the British and Americans could build all the submarines they needed in six months.

In this way, Stalin maintained the consonance of his political and military strategies. He had effectively pre-empted an 'Anglo-American peace', cunningly linked the Far East with a British 'presence' in his own operations, and staked out his territorial demands, labelling them 'not negotiable'. Maiskii might have thought all this irrelevant to the situation on the ground, but he had not seen the array of *Stavka* directives waiting to go out to the Soviet front commanders; when he plucked up courage to ask Stalin why he had said in November that the Germans would be defeated in a year, Stalin shrugged and said that something had to be done to raise Russian spirits – hence his forecast of twelve months. At that, Stalin walked out of the room. That might have well been true in November, but as Maiskii remarked to Stalin himself, the Soviet leader was 'not a man to waste his words on the wind'. To Eden, Stalin had specified the period of two months during which the Soviet operations could proceed at full speed and before which Stalin did not anticipate the Germans moving up new formations. (A little later, Sir Stafford Cripps in a talk with General Sikorski severely criticized the Foreign Office for having failed in July to agree 'general principles' with the Russians over post-war frontiers. A weak Russia would have then accepted conditions, but not now, and the lack of any 'positive agreement' actually strengthened Stalin's position: success and inflexibility went side by side with Stalin. As for the Soviet-Polish frontier, Sir Stafford Cripps anticipated 'rather far-reaching demands'.)

Those demands were duly made. In the event, when the British war cabinet was obliged 'to choose giving way to the Russians or to the Americans' (early in 1942), it decided 'to satisfy the Russians'. With his diplomatic groundwork securely laid, and his military onslaught about to unroll, the one linked with the other, Stalin had apparently justified his retort to his Polish guests: 'I am a person of experience and of age.' But in his military role, he was to blunder to the point of seriously disjointing much of his grand strategy.

8

Stalin's First Strategic Offensive: January–March 1942

On the evening of 5 January 1942, the *Stavka* assembled for a fateful meeting: on the agenda was the scope, form and timing of the Red Army's offensive operations, the transition to a general counter-offensive which, with the Wehrmacht now reeling and shocked, could be of immense significance for the course of the war both on the Eastern Front and farther afield. It was an enlarged session of the *Stavka* which gathered now, to include the members of the State Defence Committee (principally Malenkov and Beria), the General Staff represented by Marshal Shaposhnikov and his deputy Vasilevskii, and not least N.A. Voznesenskii, the brain behind the Soviet military-economic effort. The session opened formally with Shaposhnikov presenting an appreciation of the battle-front situation: what the *Stavka* envisaged was now a transition to a general counter-offensive, the main object of which would be the destruction of the enemy forces in the region of Leningrad, west of Moscow and in the south. The main blow would be launched against Army Group Centre, whose destruction was to be encompassed by the left flank of the North-Western Front, the Kalinin, Western and Bryansk Fronts, mounting concentric attacks to encircle and destroy the main body of the German forces in the Rzhev-Vyazma-Smolensk area. The Leningrad Front, the right flank of the North-Western Front and the Baltic Fleet would operate to relieve Leningrad and destroy Army Group North; the South-Western and Southern Fronts were to strike down Army Group South and liberate the Donbas, the Caucasus Front, the Crimea. All this Stalin very shortly summed up in one phrase: 'The Germans are in disarray as a result of their defeat at Moscow, they are badly fitted out for the winter. This is the most favourable moment for the transition to a general offensive.' The plan of offensive operations was cast on a grandiose scale. Nor was its size, incommensurate with present Soviet resources, its only fault. General Zhukov found it strategically topsy-turvy. Instead of homing on the destruction of Army Group Centre and thereby exploiting the successes of the Western Front inwardly, the *Stavka* proposed to expand outwardly to every Soviet front. When Stalin asked for observations on the plan, Zhukov made precisely this point:

On the Western axis, where there is the most favourable set of conditions and [where] the enemy has not yet succeeded in re-establishing the combat efficiency of his units, we must continue offensive operations, but for successful offensive operations it is essential to reinforce our forces with men, equipment and to build up reserves, above all tank units, without which we can have no basis for anticipating particular success. As for offensive operations by our forces at Leningrad and on the South-Western axis, then it must be pointed out that our troops face formidable enemy defences. Without powerful artillery for support they will not be able to break through the enemy positions, they will be ground down and will suffer heavy, not to say unjustifiable losses. I am all for reinforcing the Western Front and mounting the most powerful offensive operations there.

Zhukov's arguments found immediate support from Voznesenskii, who emphasized that the necessary supplies for simultaneous offensive operations on all fronts simply could not be forthcoming. Stalin was quite unconvinced. He announced that he had talked to Marshal Timoshenko, who was in favour of attacking: 'We must grind the Germans down with all speed, so that they cannot attack in the spring.' Malenkov and Beria supported Stalin. Voznesenskii's objection was itself ground underfoot with the remark that he always brought up difficulties which would have to be overcome. Stalin invited any further observations. There were none, whereupon Stalin declared the session and the matter closed. General Zhukov left the *Stavka* meeting, convinced that the decision had already been taken long before the meeting convened, which indeed it had, and that Stalin had more or less set up this *Stavka* session to 'ginger up' (*podtolknut*) the soldiers. Marshal Shaposhnikov, with whom Zhukov talked briefly, confirmed this impression immediately by telling Zhukov that he had argued back for nothing: the directives had gone to Front commanders some time ago, Stalin had decided the matter well before the *Stavka* met and offensive operations were to begin almost at once. It was also clear to General Zhukov from Marshal Shaposhnikov's manner and mien that it was not the General Staff which had fathered this general offensive.

The results of the *Stavka* meeting were not long in showing themselves. In less than forty-eight hours Zhukov had the new operational directive in his hand:

To Commander Western Front
To Commander Kalinin Front: 7 January 1942   20.40 hrs.

The *Stavka* of the Supreme Commander orders the reinforced Western and Kalinin Fronts to aim at the encirclement of the Mozhaisk-Ghatsk-Vyazma concentration of enemy forces, in pursuit of which:

   1 Commander Kalinin Front, having split off part of his forces for the destruction of enemy forces at Rzhev, with a Front shock force consisting of two armies made up of 14–15 rifle divisions, cavalry corps and large tank forces to mount an attack in the general direction of Sychevka-Vyazma, with the aim of cutting the railway and the highway running from Gzhatsk-Smolensk to the west of Vyazma, thus depriving the enemy of his basic line of communications. In the further pursuit of operations together with troops of

the Western Front to encircle, then to take prisoner or to annihilate the entire enemy Mozhaisk–Gzhatsk concentration.

2 Without waiting for the movement of the cavalry corps and the final concentration of the whole force of the shock group in the area of Rzhev, using the existing forces of 39 Army as the basic strength of the shock group, to develop with all speed offensive operations in the direction of Sychevka–Vyazma, and with the remaining forces to establish a second echelon behind the main shock group, so calculating as to be in the area of Sychevka and capturing Sychevka not later than 12 January 1942.

3 Commander of Western Front, having destroyed no later than 11 January the Yukhnov–Mossalsk enemy concentration, to mount the main attack with a shock group made up of Belov's group and 50 Army against Vyazma and thence complete the encirclement of the Mozhaisk–Gzhatsk–Vyazma concentration of enemy forces in co-operation with the troops of the Kalinin Front shock group.

4 Simultaneously troops of 20 Army to break the enemy front and to mount an attack on Shakhovskaya–Gzhatsk, part of the forces of this army to turn into the rear of the Lotoshino enemy group and together with 30 Army of Kalinin Front to encircle and annihilate it.

5 Confirm receipt.

Stavka Verkhovnovo Glavnokomandovaniya
No. 151141

J. STALIN
A. VASILEVSKII

Like Zhukov, other Front commanders now had fresh and inordinately ambitious plans laid before them.

And so it was that towards the end of the first week in January 1942, in response to Stalin's categorical order and undiminished insistence that offensive operations must continue without delay and without waiting for the final assembly of assault formations, the Red Army went over to the general offensive. Soviet troops were to engage simultaneously the three German Army Groups, North, Centre and South, under orders from Hitler since late December to 'stand fast', to offer 'fanatical resistance' and to hold 'at all costs' territory won previously. As Hitler brutally rammed down the brake on withdrawals, the German formations and units shuddered to a halt, holding a 'front line' so often bereft of any depth and whose steel-hard frozen ground had to be blasted away with explosives to provide rudimentary defensive positions where decimated battalions of less than 100 men now crouched and round which artillery batteries reduced to a couple of guns were set up. The air temperature fell to below − 20° C. and these ragged, desperate defenders were seared with a cold reaching − 30–40° C. Snowfalls of exceptional heaviness obliterated the roads and piled into chest-high freezing ramparts. On their roads Soviet soldiers struggled to shift food and ammunition, both of which were in dangerously short supply; the Western Front dumps contained one day's supply of food but no reserves of fuel, and in several armies of the Western and Kalinin Fronts there was not one round of ammunition for the regimental and anti-tank artillery. Yeremenko's shock troops had already consumed their meagre food supplies, and the Front staff was 'liberating' Yeremenko's carefully hoarded reserves to feed the famished riflemen of other divisions, though Yeremenko hoped to scrape up enough to give his men a meal on the evening of the first day of the offensive.

Stalin's over-all design comprised the armies of the Leningrad, Volkhov and right wing formations of North-Western Front, in co-operation with the Baltic Fleet, falling on the main forces of Army Group North and de-blockading Leningrad, the Kalinin and Western Fronts (in association with the North-Western and Bryansk Fronts to north and south) encircling and destroying Army Group Centre, while the Southern and South-Western Fronts would destroy Army Group South and liberate the Donbas. The Caucasus (Crimean Front), in co-operation with the Black Sea Fleet, would recapture the Crimea. Timoshenko's South-Western Front 40th and 21st Armies had already jumped off, aiming at Kursk and Oboyan. Meretskov was being hounded to speed his preparations for the Volkhov Front offensive, which had been formally ordered by the *Stavka* directive of 24 December, and which Mekhlis now came north to see realized without more delay, though only one division of the first echelons of the 59th and 2nd Shock Armies had arrived (in spite of the General Staff's assurance they would arrive by 25 December). Meretskov managed to get a delay until 7 January, but even then only half of the 2nd Shock and 59th Armies had turned up. Meretskov turned on the heat at this point, for his guns had no sights and he had only a quarter of his ammunition and food; Colonel-General Voronov arrived from Moscow with gun-sights, field telephones and ammunition. The first attacks had taken place on time, as the *Stavka* ordered, but they had fizzled out. Meretskov needed more time, and argued it out with Stalin and Vasilevskii by telegraph:

Stalin, Vasilevskii on the line. According to all information, you will not be ready to take offensive by eleventh. If this the case, necessary to postpone one day or two days, in order to attack and break through enemy defences. There is a Russian proverb: too much haste, and people will laugh. This happened to you, you hastened with the offensive, not preparing it and now people are laughing.

Meretskov could scarcely relish the joke because this was a major rebuke, but one difficulty piled on another. Mekhlis aggravated the situation by behaving as the thorough-going 'go-getter', yet no amount of Mekhlis' meddling could get round the fact that the 2nd Shock and 59th Armies were ill-equipped and untrained, and that Lieutenant-General Sokolov, 2nd Shock commander, a former Deputy People's Commissar of the NKVD, was absolutely incompetent. At the Military Soviet conference of 6 January, Sokolov for all his dash and 'aplomb' had not the remotest idea where his units were or what they were supposed to do. Meretskov had to ask Stalin to replace him, and on 10 January Sokolov was recalled to Moscow and the 2nd Shock handed over to Lieutenant-General Klykov (52nd Army commander).

As Meretskov pleaded with Stalin for more time, the North-Western, Kalinin, Western and Bryansk Front commanders were putting the final touches to their own plans to Stalin's general directive dated 7 January, which formally set out the plan to drive on Vyazma from the north, south and east with Kalinin and Western Front forces, while the left wing of the North-Western Front would strike south-westwards to cut the German escape route to the west. Stalin's directive prescribed:

Kalinin Front to employ part of its forces to destroy enemy forces at Rzhev and to capture Rzhev. In addition, Kalinin Front will attack in the direction of Sychevka-Vyazma with two armies, a cavalry corps and a large tank force, cut the Minsk–Moscow road and rail links west of Vyazma and deprive the enemy of his vital communications.

Western Front will not later than 11 January accomplish the destruction of German-Fascist forces in the area of Yukhnov and Mosalsk, and thereafter with a thrust by 50th Army and 1st Guards Cavalry Corps in the direction of Vyazma will co-operate with the forces of the Kalinin Front in completing the encirclement of the Mozhaisk-Gzhatsk-Vyazma enemy force. 20th Army will use its main force to break the enemy defences in the Volokolamsk area, and mount a cleaving blow in the direction of Shakhovskaya-Gzhatsk and with a part of its strength break into the rear of the Lotoshino enemy group, in order to accomplish the encirclement and destruction of this force in co-operation with 30th Army, Kalinin Front.

North-Western Front to set up a shock group on the left flank and to attack in the direction of Toropets-Velizh-Rudniya.

Bryansk Front to develop the offensive in the direction of Orel, outflank Bolkhov from the north-west, destroy enemy forces south of Belev and cover the Western Front assault forces from the south.

Within this requirement, the three Front commanders worked out their operational plans, in which their latitude was also liable to Stalinist veto or modifications.

Koniev's Front directive (8 January) ordered that when 39th Army had broken German defences west of Rzhev, this attack was to proceed in the Sychevka-Vyazma direction (with the specific assignment of reaching Sychevka by 11 January): 39th Army would co-operate with the 30th in destroying German forces at Sychevka itself: the exploitation of successes on the Vyazma axis was assigned to Gorin's 11th Cavalry Corps, which would erupt through the breaches made by 39th Army: 22nd Army would meanwhile cut the Rzhev-Velikie Luki railway line in the Nelidovo area, advance on Belyi and thus secure the Kalinin Front from the west. Zhukov's two directives (6 and 8 January) assigned objectives for his right, centre and left formations: the right (1st Shock, 20th and 16th Armies) would attack from Volokolamsk to Gzhatsk (thus co-operating with Koniev's left), the centre formations (5th and 33rd Armies) would outflank Mozhaisk from the south, and the left wing (43rd, 49th, 50th Armies and Belov's corps), after first dealing with enemy forces in the Kondorov-Yukhnov-Medyn area, would strike north-west for Vyazma to complete the encirclement of the Mozhaisk-Gzhatsk-Vyazma enemy forces (also to be accomplished in co-operation with Koniev). The 10th Army would cover these operations from the west and south-west: Vlasov's 20th Army would mount the main blow in the Volokolamsk-Gzhatsk attack: Belov's 50th Army was principally responsible for the Yukhnov-Vyazma drive. General Kurochkin of the North-Western Front issued his directive on 2 January (having received a specific *Stavka* order somewhat earlier): from Kurochkin's left, 3rd and 4th Shock Armies were to seize Ostashkov and Toropets, to co-operate with Koniev in eliminating the Ostashkov and Rzhev groups, to inhibit German utilization of prepared defences and to cut into the flank and rear of German forces west of Smolensk. The fate of these operations and of Army Group Centre was to be decided at Vyazma, which made the North-Western attack, directed to a point more than eighty miles west of Vyazma, operationally cogent only if the Kalinin and Western Fronts could rapidly reduce the Vyazma group of German forces. The Soviet offensive was to open in stages from 7 to 10 January and even later: the Kalinin Front opened its operations on 7–8 January to the south of the Rzhev-Velikie Luki railway line in the area of the Monchalovo station, North-Western Front would attack on 9 January, Zhukov's right on 10 January, and his centre and left a few days later.

To send the offensive thundering on its way, Stalin issued a series of instructions to all Front and Army Military Soviets, tactical injunctions which were based on a revival of the military ideas of the 1930s (plus an analysis of shortcomings during the recent operations): for the first time, Soviet artillerymen heard the term 'artillery offensive', while from the infantrymen Stalin demanded more 'shock groups' (though his high-speed offensive did not give the Front commanders adequate time in which to regroup and form these 'shock' units). Even with 'shock groups', the shortage of equipment caused them to be dispersed to stiffen other formations; even the weaker formations had to be split, like Boldin's 50th Army which was to act as 'shock group' with Belov and with the 49th and 43rd Armies. And the breakthrough troops suffered appalling casualties, but there was nothing like a second echelon to take over. To all this Stalin paid no heed: what he thought and wanted he made plain in his instruction of 10 January, circulated to all commanders who must now,

hunt [the Germans] westward without pause, force them to expend their reserves up to the spring, at a time when we will deploy fresh major reserves just when the Germans will have no effective reserves left, so that this will accomplish the total destruction of the Hitlerite forces in the year 1942.

Stalin also sprinkled the Soviet officer corps with promotions on the eve of and throughout the early days of the offensive: no extensive changes in command took place, and Stalin was content to arrange commands and assignments in his own special style. When Stalin talked to Colonel-General Yeremenko, who was destined for the 4th Shock Army (his first command after leaving hospital, where he found himself after being shot up on the Bryansk Front), he asked him: 'Are you touchy?', to which Yeremenko replied that he was not particularly so. Stalin enquired, because he was appointing him subordinate to Kurochkin, and quoted to Yeremenko his own experience of being subordinated – he, twice a People's Commissar, was subordinated to Sklyanskii (Trotsky's deputy during the Civil War). Not that the formal Front command organization was overly sacred to Stalin; when he required, he merely connected himself by direct wire or telephone to the formation commander he wished to advise or chastise, directing the hunting of the Germans westwards himself. These Stalinist thunderbolts, that he hurled into the ranks of the command, had two effects, either to force decisions or to confuse those already taken. For information, Stalin could rely on many sources – his own direct enquiry, the reports of the General Staff liaison officers, Front command reports, or his personal 'go-getters', Mekhlis, Bulganin and their like, who were the bane of the military's life. But as Stalin never visited the front (in spite of the many fictions that he did), and since commanders who were summoned to him had to face also his 'entourage' (who, according to Admiral Kuznetsov, advised officers 'not to make trouble'), the chances of Stalin being persuaded of reality – stiffening German resistance, decimated Soviet formations, over-extended fronts, dangerous multiplicities of objectives – vanished almost completely from the horizon of decision-making. In all this airless artificiality, caverned in the bunker in the Kremlin, the doctrine of Stalinist infallibility prevailed in war, just as it had come to prevail in peace, but on the battle-fronts it needed more than Stalin's verbal grapeshot to sweep away the great iron rocks of German resistance which stood out in a Soviet sea at Demyansk, Rzhev and Sukinichi.

Across almost one thousand miles of icy front the Red Army was now either engaged on major offensive operations or about to embark upon them. On 1 January, Marshal Timoshenko's South-Western Front had been launched into an attack with its 40th and 21st Armies in an effort to seize Kursk and Oboyan, the opening phase of what became seventy days of savage and continuous fighting as Timoshenko tried to burst in the walls surrounding Kharkov and Dnepropetrovsk and thus bring disaster down on Army Group South. On 7 January, two days after Timoshenko had ordered Maslov's 38th Army to join battle for Belgorod – when Maslov dawdled calamitously and threw away all advantages of surprise – the 61st Army of the Bryansk Front renewed its offensive (and was joined three days later by the 3rd and 13th Armies) for the Bolkhov-Orel-Kroma line; that same 7 January Lieutenant-General Kurochkin's North-Western Front, holding the 'passive' narrow sector between the lakes Ilmen and Seliger, opened its offensive when Morozov's 11th Army on the right of the front swept into the attack, without preliminary bombardment but with a terrifying flurry of armoured infantry-carrying sledges, heavy tanks and glider troops, to storm the key German depot of Staraya Russa. Morozov was to smash in the flank of the German Sixteenth Army and swing north-west where, in co-operation with the Volkhov Front armies, he was to drive into the German Eighteenth Army, thus bringing about the ruin of Army Group North, which was to be attacked by the Novgorod operational group, the Volkhov Front, the Leningrad Front and the 'Coastal group' (8th Army locked up in the Oranienbaum bridgehead). Between lake Ladoga and lake Ilmen, Fedyuninskii's 54th Army had begun its attack and Meretskov on the Volkhov Front tried to get his offensive going on the seventh, but this fizzled out. At Staraya Russa, Morozov slammed into the stubborn resistance of the German 18th Motorized Infantry Division, brought here to rest after the December fighting at Tikhvin, and though 11th Army ski battalions fanned out cutting off the ancient and battered city from the outside world, to the west a half-mile 'corridor' remained open, while Morozov tried to storm his way into the city from the east.

Kurochkin's other great drive, to the south-west, opened effectively when almost ten divisions and a dozen rifle brigades of the two shock armies, Purkayev's 3rd and Yeremenko's 4th, erupted between 04.00 and 10.30 hours across the ice of lake Seliger on 9 January. Purkayev's attack was supported by a couple of regiments from Berzarin's left flank formations. These were the shock troops who had scarcely a crust between them, and who would get bread only on the evening of the first day of the attack. Under Yeremenko's training schedule, they were no strangers to agonizing hardship: Yeremenko and his divisions spent four days buried in the snow of the forests, without fires and food, in a temperature racing down to − 40° C., carrying out a full training schedule all the while. When they captured the giant German dumps at Toropets, the troops could feed, but first they had to fight their way into them.

Yeremenko planned to drive straight into the junction of two German armies, the Sixteenth and the Ninth (and the junction of Army Group North and Centre) along the Peno-Andreapol-Toropets line with two divisions forming a 'fist' and one division on each flank: the junction with 22nd Army, Yeremenko's neighbour to the left, was secured by a rifle brigade. In chest-high snow, after a two-hour artillery bombardment and a few flights by the small force of LAGG-3 fighters for 'show', Yeremenko's shock troops plunged forward across the ice straight into the German machine-guns covering Peno. Peno was taken, Fegelein's ss Cavalry was swamped and Yeremenko had punched his first hole in the German line.

Pukayev's 3rd Shock made little progress at first, which prompted a rebuke from Kurochkin (and revised instructions to Yeremenko, which contributed to inflaming Yeremenko's ill-feeling about Kurochkin: in Yeremenko's view, Kurochkin either did not understand the scope of the operations or else was undercutting them). Aiming first at Kholm, Purkayev had got hung up in the German defences; to support the 3rd Shock, Yeremenko was ordered to mount a second operation (which Yeremenko claimed interfered with his prime undertaking), but after a few days both armies began to roll forward, though after a week this presented a fresh problem, because the 3rd and 4th Shock Armies were becoming separated by a gap of some magnitude as Purkayev approached Kholm and Yeremenko drove through Andreapol to a point north of Toropets, the Western Dvina and to Nelidove. After an attack from three sides, Andreapol was stormed on 16 January, Major-General Tarasov's crack 249th Rifle Division scooping up the German stores as it went along, and four days later the storming of Toropets began, where even vaster German stores were housed, and from which six tanks, hundreds of infantry weapons, 723 lorries, 450,000 shells, several million rounds of ammunition, a thousand drums of fuel and forty food dumps fell to Yeremenko's famished men.

But while Yeremenko worried about his assault, Kurochkin worried about his Front. Into the utterly frenzied Staraya Russa battle, Kurochkin poured the 1st and 2nd Guards Rifle Corps to swell the 11th Army: with the Front locked at Staraya Russa and at Kholm, this left the German forces at Demyansk with its bogs and forest in a pocket, with the road connecting it to Staraya Russa cut. By turning south from Staraya Russa and north from Kholm, the encirclement of the Demyansk force (the German 2nd Corps) would be complete, with Berzarin's 34th Army pressing in from the south. Six German divisions (almost 100,000 men) of the Sixteenth Army's 2nd Corps were locked up in the Valdai hills, a major encirclement which turned into the longest encirclement ever waged on the Soviet-German front; the problem of Demyansk had troubled general Kurochkin before his two-directional offensive began. Now it had come home to roost, though he thought first to hatch a victory. On 17 January, Kurochkin sent Stalin a written report, analysing the results of ten days of operations: he suggested that 11th Army should be reinforced with one rifle division and two brigades and moved from Staraya Russa to Kholm to seal off the Demyansk pocket, while the 1st and 2nd Guards Rifle Corps should strike westwards, both operations being carried out in two stages, for a speedy collapse could be expected within the German Sixteenth Army when it was beset by 'disintegration of morals, an army left without ammunition, or food supplies, its stability shaken to pieces'. The *Stavka* accepted in principle Kurochkin's plan to seal off the Demyansk group and cut its communications from the north, but the basic task of the North-Western Front was defined as moving 11th Army on Soltsy and into the rear of the German forces at Novgorod and swinging 1st and 2nd Guards Corps towards Pskov to cut the lines of communication of the 'Leningrad-Volkhov enemy concentrations'. This was to be carried out, not as a two-stage operation as Kurochkin suggested, but simultaneously even though German troops hung on tenaciously to Staraya Russa, to Demyansk and Kholm, where Purkayev found his way barred to Velikie Luki. The Demyansk pocket, against which several Soviet armies were now beginning to strain, might be encircled but it lived, supplied from the air by the white-painted, lumbering Ju-52s, the *Tante Jus* who unloaded food and ammunition through swathes of Soviet AA fire. Westwards at Kholm, which was finally surrounded, an improvised *Kampfgruppe* of some 5,000 men, 'Group Scherer', likewise lived from its air-dropped supplies, holding the barrier into the rear of Sixteenth Army. Meanwhile Yeremenko's 4th Shock, Tarasov's Siberians in the van, raced as best it might through snow and cold for Toropets, and when that encircling attack succeeded, the German line from Velikie Luki to Rzhev gaped open with a sixty-mile rent torn in it, the 'Vitebsk gap' through which Yeremenko could lunge at the rear of Army Group Centre; Purkayev's 3rd Shock Army, with part of its strength locked in a contest at close quarters for Kholm, where Soviet troops had burst into the eastern outskirts, made for Velikie Luki and forward units cut the Kholm-Toropets road.

Between 19–22 January, Stalin made decisions of fundamental and far-reaching importance, all intended to reinforce his intention of encompassing the destruction of the two German Army Groups, North and Centre. Kurochkin already knew that moving north-west and moving against the Demyansk pocket were to be executed as simultaneous manoeuvres. Just how this was to be done must have baffled him completely. On 19 January, he had his answer in Stalin's new dispositions: Kurochkin was to lose the 3rd and 4th Shock Armies, which would be subordinated to Koniev's Kalinin Front, while the 1st Shock Army would be shifted from Zhukov's Front up to Staraya Russa (and to be ready for action east of that fiery city by 6 February). In addition to the 1st Shock Army, Kurochkin would receive two rifle divisions and two rifle brigades to be deployed east of Staraya Russa, though these formations would *not* be directly subordinated to Kurochkin but assigned to the operational control of the commander of the 3rd Shock Army; the four divisions and brigades were to strike from Staraya Russa to Kholm, thereby cutting the German escape route from Demyansk, while the destruction of the German 2nd Corps would be accomplished by these fresh formations operating with the 34th Army. Once in Kholm, the divisions would link up with the main body of the 3rd Shock Army. Thus the elimination of the Demyansk pocket was to be a two-Front, two-stage operation.

Pavel Alekseyevich Kurochkin, a very professional soldier who had served both in Europe and in the Far East, stuck to his guns and argued back to Stalin and Shaposhnikov about depriving him of the 3rd Shock Army; Stalin had practically amputated Kurochkin's left wing. In a consultation by radio, Stalin turned down Kurochkin's request for a unified command over the 'Demyansk operations': part of Kurochkin's plan had been adopted, but the forces allotted for this operation were grossly inadequate. Again on 24 January, Kurochkin discussed with Stalin the question of the priorities of the operation – moving the North-Western Front armies westward and fastening up the Demyansk pocket; the *Stavka* worked out a new set of variants which indicated its view that in 'a comparatively short time' the Demyansk defenders would be split up and destroyed. This was not the only sign of optimism. The *Stavka* directive, issued at 21.15 hours on 19 January, embodying Stalin's orders about handing over the two Shock Armies to Koniev, and in which Stalin personally assigned the objectives to the various armies, clearly envisaged the capture not only of Rzhev but also of Smolensk:

(a) 39th Army and 11th Cavalry Corps (Kalinin Front) to attack 'decisively' towards Semlevo, west of Vyazma, and not later than 21 January close the ring, in co-operation with Western Front troops attacking from Mosalsk, and destroy the Gzhatsk-Vyazma German force;

(b) not later than 21 January to take Rzhev and Zubtsov with 29th and 31st Armies (Kalinin Front);

(c) 3rd Shock Army to attack from Kholm towards Velikie Luki and thence to Vitebsk, Orsha, cutting off Smolensk from the west, having secured possession of that town [Smolensk].

This was pumping diminishing manpower out in expanding circles, and inflating the strategic objectives of the Kalinin Front to include Rzhev, Sychevka, Vyazma, Toropets, Rudnya and Smolensk, at a point when men and machines were in desperately short supply. Yeremenko had started his operations short of 1,000 officers and 20,000 other ranks (as well as 2,000 horses); his divisions which had been 8,000 strong three weeks ago were now down to less than 2,000; the time was not far away when Colonel-General Koniev had only 35 tanks left to his whole Front, and divisional strengths were falling to 3,000 men, artillery regiments being left with only a dozen guns – all this to consummate the mammoth strategic assignment doled out by Stalin.

Rzhev was another of those breakwaters against which the Soviet offensive dashed in vain, producing a prolonged and costly struggle in this battle of the Volga bend. West of Rzhev, the Soviet divisions had hammered out a nine-mile gap, through which infantry, armoured and sledge columns moved southwards; 39th Army of Koniev's Kalinin Front swept west of Rzhev, which fell into the area of 29th Army. On 11 January, as 11th Cavalry Corps was passed through the gap torn by 39th Army and moved southwards towards the motor highway west of Vyazma, the *Stavka* ordered Koniev to take Rzhev on the eleventh – 'and under no circumstances later than the twelfth' – using two or three rifle divisions from 39th Army and the whole of the 29th; Rzhev pointed like a dagger at the flank of Koniev's assault force and had to be eliminated at all costs and with all speed. South at Sychevka Soviet units had already broken into the railway depots, where major German stores were located – Koniev had ordered 39th Army to swing in on Sychevka and also to attack Rzhev from the west; 29th Army might seize Rzhev by a rapid blow off the march. What the German troops had to fight for, jammed in as emergency units as they were, was the Vyazma-Sychevka-Rzhev railway line, for if this were completely cut, the German Ninth Army was doomed. Rzhev and Sychevka offered each desperate resistance: Koniev, facing the dagger of Rzhev, was for a whole week obliged to hold back 11th Cavalry Corps on the flank of 39th Army until the position was cleared up. Gorin's 11th Cavalry Corps, ordered to spear down southwards to Vyazma to link up with Belov's cavalry driving from the south-west, scarcely counted as a formidable force, its four divisions (18th, 24th, 82nd Cavalry and 2nd Guards Motorized Rifle) numbering less than 6,000 men with 5,000 horses, plus two 122-mm howitzers, 47 field guns, 35 mortars and 27 anti-tank weapons. While Gorin paused, 29th Army tried to carry out its Rzhev assignment; neither 39th nor 29th could break in and by the end of the second week in January, 29th Army needed to be pulled back to regroup, its regiments run ragged with only 50–100 men left in them. On 17 January, with the Rzhev-Sychevka perimeter still unbroken, Koniev issued a new set of orders to his army commanders:

22nd Army: to secure the right flank
29th Army: to fight for Rzhev with an assault group, north of the town to go over to the offensive
39th Army: continue its offensive on Vyazma, secure its positions at Sychevka and Osuga
11th Cavalry Corps: to attack towards Semelevo (west of Vyazma)
31st Army: to attack with its left flank towards Zubtsov
30th Army: to attack in the general direction of Pogoreloe-Gorodishche/Sychevka.

At this point, Stalin assigned Koniev 3rd and 4th Shock Armies, whereupon Koniev issued a new set of orders with his newly enlarged Front:

3rd Shock: to attack towards Velikie Luki
4th Shock: to attack towards Velizh
22nd Army: securing the flank and rear of 39th and 29th Armies to take Belyi
39th Army: to complete the destruction of the enemy at Sychevka and Osuga, allowing no break out north-west or west
29th Army: to capture Rzhev
31st Army: to attack in the direction of Zubtsov.

Stalin's re-disposition of forces and Koniev's re-assignment of objectives came almost at the moment when Panzer General Model, the new commander of the Ninth Army, decided to strike back and to thrust the Rzhev blade into the attacking Soviet formations; at 10.00 hours on 22 January two regiments of the German 6th Corps, supported by dive-bombers and tanks, went over to the offensive west of Rzhev while 23rd Corps, cut off at Solnenino, also punched its way out of the Soviet ring. On 23 January at 12.45 hours the two German Corps were in contact once more, a 'corridor' which cut the Kalinin Front into two parts, one (22nd, 30th, 31st, and parts of 29th Army) on the northern bank of the Volga and near the northern approaches to Rzhev, the other (39th Army, main forces of 29th, 11th Cavalry Corps) to the south-west and west of Rzhev, between Certolino and Sychevka.

   While Koniev ordered the elimination of this 'corridor' by 30th and 29th Armies, 39th Army attacked on 22 January in a bid to seize Osuga and Sychevka, but while the fighting raged in and out of the railway yards and depots, the railway stayed in German hands. After 20 January, Gorin's cavalry moved south again, and in six days reached the motor highway, though it proved too weak a force to try to overcome the German garrisons at Vyazma, so that Gorin turned to the defensive north-west of this great foundation stone of Army Group Centre. Yeremenko's 4th Shock Army moved on Velizh and Rudnya, crashing into the hurriedly assembled German divisions being rushed in from France, but slowing down as unit commanders stayed to fight pitched battles for separate German strong-points; the battle for Kresty cost the Germans 1,000 dead, but Yeremenko's units were worn down to the bone. Slowly but inexorably, and as Third Panzer Army moved in to take up the strain between the Ninth and Sixteenth Armies, the power was ebbing from this Soviet outer encirclement drive. The 3rd Shock Army, similarly worn by its efforts, dragged to a halt before Velikie Luki, and both flanks of the 4th Shock Army lay exposed, its right neighbour fifty miles away, its left at a distance of nearly sixty. On 27 January, Yeremenko transmitted a special report to Koniev on the state of fuel and ammunition in 4th Shock; the report also described the shortage of signalling equipment, which was by now acute as the formations fanned out over widening distances. Attempts to raise the neighbouring armies had failed, the flanks were open, and of German strength and disposition at Vitebsk-Rudnya-Smolensk intelligence knew next to nothing, due to lack of air reconnaissance. Tarasov's 249th Division was moving from Surazh on Vitebsk, but running into fresh German units: 360th Division was attacking Velizh and fought its way into the north-western part of the town, as 332nd Division encircled Demidev but could not attack because it had run out of artillery ammunition. Nor could his neighbours help, and in fact Yeremenko had to help them, as 3rd Shock struggled at Kholm and at Velikie Luki and 22nd Army tried to wrest Belyi from a strong German grip; to cover his flanks and secure lines of communication Yeremenko used 334th Rifle Division to provide cover at Nelidovo and Ilino. Two rifle divisions (155th and 158th), destined for the 4th Shock as reinforcement, were diverted en route to Vostrukhov's 22nd Army.

With ammunition in short supply, without proper stocks of fuel and food, lacking officers and trained men, from the outset 4th Shock Army had almost done the impossible. Tarasov's 249th (later 16th Guards) Division acted as the equivalent of many a Soviet army. Yeremenko's miniscule tank force (two battalions, 141st with 4 KVs, 6 T-34s and 20 T-60s, 117th with 12 MK-2 tanks, 9 MK-3s and 10 T-60s) played an occasional role, but from the Toropets dumps Yeremenko fitted out his divisions with motor-cycle combinations to speed up movement of liaison officers, and assembled radio stations out of captured equipment. Officers using light aircraft kept up the stream of orders to units far advanced on the line of march. For all these energetic initiatives and skilful direction, 4th Shock could not ward off the steady drain of casualties and the onset of severe battle-fatigue. The great outer pincer hung dangling in the air, waving over the Ninth Army at Velizh-Surazh-Demidov, but unable to bite any deeper and incapable of exercising any decisive influence on the crucial inner encirclement battle, which had already run into grave trouble at Rzhev, where Model now made ready to turn on the 39th and 29th Armies and lock these would-be encirclers up in a vicious, swinging German encirclement.

Zhukov's Western Front locked in continuous fighting had a triple part to play in the encirclement of Army Group Centre with its three main blows: the right wing would break the improvised German line west of Volokolamsk and, driving on Shakovska, would co-operate with 39th and 29th Armies of the Kalinin Front in bringing about the total destruction of the German Ninth and Third Panzer Armies. To Vlasov's 20th Army went the honour of spear-heading the main attack: the centre armies were to seize Mozhaisk, Gzhatsk, Borovsk and Veriya and then strike straight for Vyazma: the left wing, where the great gap had been torn between Kaluga and Velev, would capture Myatlevo, Kondrovo, Yukhnov, smash in the German defences south-west of Yukhnov along the motor highway and then operate with Zhukov's centre armies and the 11th Cavalry Corps of the Kalinin Front strike for Vyazma. With the encirclement of the Rzhev-Vyazma forces, the Red Army would have the German Ninth and Fourth Field Armies, Third and Fourth Panzer Armies in an iron grip. As Koniev's 39th and 29th Armies fought their way to Rzhev and Sychevka, but not actually into these spiky 'hedgehogs', Zhukov opened his offensive on his right wing, with Vlasov in the van, his first echelon made up of five rifle brigades, two rifle divisions and three tank brigades, his 'breakthrough echelon' organized into the 2nd Guards Cavalry Corps (now under Major-General Pliev after General Dovator's death) with three divisions, one tank brigade and five ski battalions. The attack was to be supported by six artillery regiments and two batteries of *Katyusha* rocket-launchers.

At 08.00 hours, Vlasov's guns opened fire, and at 10.30 hours infantry supported by tanks jumped off for their attack against the German 35th Infantry Division. Vlasov's left flank neighbour, 1st Shock Army, also opened its offensive. Zhukov refused to allow Vlasov to introduce his mobile force, 2nd Guards Cavalry, until he had punched a clear hole in the German defences, otherwise the cavalry would have no effect and merely be torn to pieces in the breakthrough fighting. Zhukov's right had to grind through a very determined German defence, and Rokossovskii's 16th Army now joined in the attempt to push down this German wall. Govorov's 5th Army meanwhile pressed on Mozhaisk, where German units were being squeezed from both sides: at this point Fourth Panzer began to pull back towards the Gzhatsk line, whereupon Zhukov shifted the axis of Vlasov's advance a little southwards, to Sereda and Gzhatsk. By mid January, these Soviet divisions were being ground down by the severe fighting, but when the *Stavka* made two rifle divisions available to Zhukov, 344th and 385th, the Front commander decided to commit them on his left wing, confident that he could maintain his right wing offensive at the necessary pressure. Stalin's decision of 19 January shattered that confidence very

Soviet infantry

(*Opposite top*) Frontier evacuation of women and children, Peremyshl, June 1941

(*Opposite*) Soviet infantry attack, Belorussia, June 1941

(*Above*) Front line, Leningrad, 1941

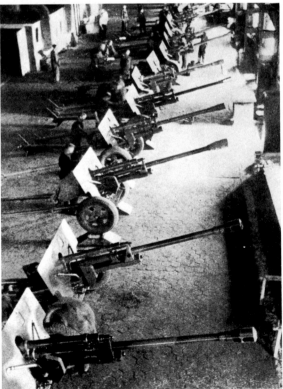

(*Above*) Leningrad militia,
September 1941

(*Left*) Soviet artillery production, 1941–2

Stalingrad, October–November 1941

(*Above and below*) Workers' militia units, Stalingrad, October–November 1942

(*Right and below*) Stalingrad,
October–November 1942

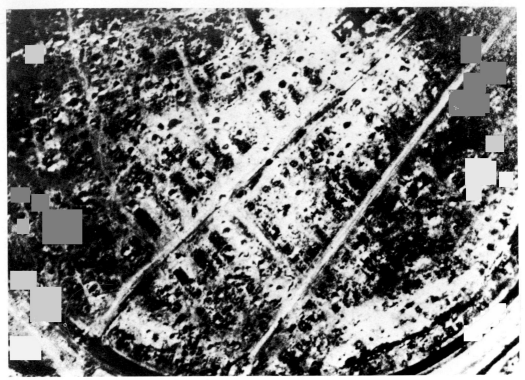

Mamayev Kurgan (aerial photograph), Stalingrad, November 1942

German surrender, Stalingrad, January 1943

rudely, when Zhukov lost the 1st Shock Army to the North-Western Front. Stalin had not only unhinged Kurochkin's left wing but he managed also at the same time to paralyse Zhukov's right, where the 'shock force' suddenly collapsed like a pricked balloon. Kurochkin had argued with Stalin, trying to sort something out of the wreckage of his left wing: Zhukov chose not to do this, although he tried to persuade Shaposhnikov and Vasilevskii at the General Staff that this was a disastrous decision, that Army Group Centre could be toppled into catastrophe if only the right forces were concentrated at the right place. Stalin had assured himself that Army Group Centre now lay 'at its last gasp', could no longer defend itself effectively and, like the Demyansk divisions, would be speedily swept away. What was swept away involved the chances of Vlasov's offensive, supported by 1st Shock and 16th Armies, attaining a decisive result; Zhukov's right wing armies were already bumping into the 'Führer Line', but any effective conclusion to the Kalinin-Western Front co-operation began to ebb away, even though only twenty-five miles, on a line running from Karamanovo-Sychevka, separated the prongs of this inner encirclement. Neither the 39th nor the 20th Army could make it.

Now another shock waited for Zhukov, concerned as he was with the paralysing of his right wing, the weakness at the centre, the crisis on his left and the fifty-mile gap between the Western and Bryansk Fronts, which uncovered Zhukov's flank and rear from the south. At this stage, Stalin decided to pull Rokossovskii out of Zhukov's line; at an evening meeting, Rokossovski, Vlasov and Govorov assembled at Zhukov's HQ at Akulovo to hear their new assignments, and Sokolovskii quickly reviewed the progress of the offensive the next morning. Govorov's 5th, Belov's 50th and Yefremov's 33rd Armies were making good progress; for Yefremov there was a chorus of praise, because he had whipped his Moscow *opolchentsy* into a good fighting force and maintained it with the most paternalistic discipline. Zakharkin of 49th Army Sokolovskii knew from the old days; his real strength was his chief of staff, Colonel Grishin, in Sokolovskii's view the best staff officer going. Rokossovskii disagreed and put forward his own chief, Malinin, as the very best, who had done much to keep the 16th going. When Zhukov came in, Rokossovskii learned that he was destined for the left wing, for Sukinichi, where the Germans were 'weak, with divisions pulled in from France', milling about all over the place. Rokossovskii doubted this from what he had himself seen of how German units grimly hung on in their major and minor 'hedgehogs'. In fact, Rokossovskii was on his way to a very sticky assignment, as he guessed himself; he was to split 10th Army with Golikov, half to Rokossovskii, half to Golikov. Like Rzhev, or Staraya Russa, Sukinichi had become another 'rock' against which the Soviet attack rolled and then recoiled, a point where a shattered front could be knitted up to stave off complete disaster. Staraya Russa had forced Stalin to seek reinforcement from another front; Sukinichi demanded the same measure, and both decisions pounded Zhukov's right flank on the head.

R.T.S.—L

While his right was driving in the Volokolamsk-Gzhatsk direction, Zhukov's centre, which had hitherto operated to hold German reserves from any movement to the wings (a successful but terribly costly method), struck out directly for Vyazma. Govorov, the unsmiling but highly capable commander of 5th Army (19th, 32nd, 50th, 108th, 144th, 329th, 336th Rifle Divisions, 82nd Motorized Rifle Division, 37th, 43rd, 60th Independent Rifle Brigades and 20th Tank Brigade) received orders to take Mozhaisk by 16 January; by mid January, his troops were rolling along towards Mozhaisk, and on 20 January Mozhaisk fell and Govorov's units moved along the motor highway, advancing now to a depth of some forty-five miles at a time when Vlasov's 20th Army was held back by lack of forces. But now the same blight struck Govorov, as his rifle divisions fell below 2,500 men in strength and 5th Army could not burst through the German defensive positions. Late in January, 5th Army was also running out of steam. Yefremov's 33rd Army took up the running, with its seven rifle divisions (93rd, 110th, 113th, 160th, 201st, 222nd, 338th) and the 1st Guards Motorized Rifle Division, a force committed to outflanking Mozhaisk from the south and taking Veriya by 15 January. To speed up his advance, Yefremov split his force for the attack on Veriya, two divisions to attack from the south, two from the east. Veriya fell on 19 January, by which time it was clear to Zhukov that Govorov could carry on unaided and that Yefremov could be given a fresh assignment; two days before the fall of Veriya, Zhukov ordered Yefremov to proceed to the liquidation of enemy forces at Veriya, to move by the morning of 19 January to the Dubna-Zamytskoe area and thereafter 'depending on the tactical situation' to strike directly for Vyazma or to outflank it from the south, while Belov's cavalry force also drove for Vyazma.

As 5th Army went for Gzhatsk and the 33rd for Vyazma, Zhukov's left wing rushed to exploit the Kaluga-Belev gap, which menaced the very existence of the German Fourth Army, separated as it was from Second Panzer Army to the south and in danger of being sliced away from Fourth Panzer Army to its north, holding from Yukhnov to Gzhatsk. The gash ripped out between the Fourth Army and Second Panzer now stretched for more than seventy miles. Zhukov's directive of 9 January (and its revision of 14 January) assigned to the left wing the task of destroying German forces in the Kondrove-Yukhnov-Medyn area, cutting the Vyazma-Bryansk railway line in the region of Kirov-Lyudinovo, and then striking for Vyazma to complete the encirclement of the Mozhaisk-Gzhatsk-Vyazma German forces. The three divisions of 43rd Army, after taking Maloyaroslavets, were ordered to capture Medyn, a key German strongpoint on the motor highway. Medyn fell on 14 January but the 43rd had to struggle hard to move ahead after that; outflanking the Yukhnov German forces proved beyond the capacities of the 43rd. Zakharkin's 49th (six divisions, four brigades, two tank brigades) renewed its advance on and after 9 January, but six days later ran into stiffened German resistance; on 19 January, Zakharkins'

49th took Kondorovo and pressed on for the motor highway, although the general movement of the 49th was slow.

The success of 49th Army helped to ease the path for Boldin's 50th, but Belovs' and Boldin's front had already been swung northwards by a decision taken at Zhukov's HQ. Belov's corps had already poked its way deep into the gap which exposed the Fourth Army flank and felt Yukhnov right within its grasp. To Belov's intense rage and disgust, his corps was suddenly disengaged from the battle at Yukhnov and sent sweeping to the west. The first inkling of what was afoot came on 2 January with a Front order, timed at 15.25 hours, which defined operational assignments:

There exists an extremely favourable operational situation for the encirclement of the 4th and 9th Armies of the enemy, in which case the main role will be played by Group Belov, operating through the Front staff in association with our Rzhev concentration.

The foundation of the success of your operation will consist of a rapid breakthrough into the Vyazma area and seizing the enemy escape route. Your movement from the area of Yukhnov into Vyazma must be organized according to the following plan:

(a) First stage – 2–3 days. Destruction of the German forces at Yukhnov and complementary destruction of the enemy by 43, 49, and 50 Armies by a blow from the rear. In this stage introduce as quickly as possible not less than two rifle divisions of 50 Army (217 and 413 RDs), one light cavalry division to be used in forced march to capture Chiplyaevo and Zanoznaya stations.

(b) Second stage. Leave in Yukhnov two rifle divisions of 50 Army with assignment of completing the liquidation of retreating enemy, yourself with combat group to seize Vyazma and all enemy exits by forced march, moving on Vyazma from southwestern flank.

Your operational plan to be presented not later than 4.1.42.

Zhukov.   Khokhlov.   Sokolovskii.

Belov, while admiring the breadth of the operation, could only ask: how? These new orders seemed to contradict those he had only just received. On 3 January, Belov in an order from Zhukov had been instructed to turn the main body of his forces to Mosalsk, to break up any German attempt to close the 'gap'; he was to speed into Meshchovsk and Mosalsk the two divisions he had on loan from 10th Army. For all his protests, Belov had to turn to Mosalsk first; Belov tried to persuade the Military Soviet of the Western Front that his best course of action was to outflank Yukhnov from the left, cut the motor highway, and turn in to Medyn, which, with 43rd, 49th and 50th Armies, would chop up a goodly portion of most, if not all of the Fourth Army. But Moslask it had to be, the point from which Front HQ considered it best to mount the Vyazma raid, an additional assignment from the outset which cost Belov seven days. Boldin was handed the task of taking Yukhnov specified in Zhukov's radio signal of 4 January:

Comrade Boldin
1 Belov is turning on Mosalsk. For the future, he will operate on a northerly axis.
2 Destruction of the enemy and closing of all escape routes through Yukhnov assigned to
50 A. Move up with all speed 217, 154 RD, 112 Tank D, 31 Cavalry D, and after breaking
enemy resistance in the Plossk area, seize town of Yukhnov without further delay.

ZHUKOV

The motor highway remained in German hands, and what the Chief of Staff
of the Fourth Army, General Blumentritt, feared most of all, the closing of the
Yukhnov-Maloyaroslavets road, the nightmare which Belov almost turned into
dreadful reality, failed to materialize. Belov's cavalry moved on seeking a point
for their breakthrough to the north, the weak spot being located by a ski
battalion during the night of 25 January; it was a gap through which Belov
passed three cavalry divisions on their way to Vyazma, a 'corridor' which he
held across the Moscow-Warsaw highway and which General Zakharov
promised him would be shored up properly with two rifle divisions and one
more division brought in from 50th Army. But almost at once German units
locked their flanks on Belov's 'corridor' and shut it tight, sealing Belov from the
main body of the Soviet forces. Much of his artillery and rear service organization was thus abruptly and disastrously snatched away from Belov, for these
could not break the German lock, and the Roslavl-Yukhnov road was barred
tight.

Gorin's 11th Cavalry was now bearing down on Vyazma from the north-west,
Belov from the south-west and Yefremov from the south-east with his own
combat group from 33rd Army. Hindered by deep snow and hampered by
German counter-attacks, 33rd Army was spread out over a distance of some
forty miles; to fight his way into Vyazma, Yefremov had split his forces into
one group of three divisions under the command and the main body assigned
to his chief of staff, Major-General A.K. Kondrateyev, an event which at first
did not unduly worry either the army nor Front command, but as Yefremov
closed on Vyazma Front HQ showed much more concern at this separation. At
this stage Zhukov called on his parachute troops to strike into the German rear
and hold these tenuous lines until all formations moved up.

The great airborne strike arm, which Tukhachevskii had demonstrated so
vividly at the 1936 manoeuvres, had fought so far largely as ground infantry,
but large-scale parachute operations were in the offing. One of the first plans
had been to drop paratroops along the line of advance of 43rd Army, to cut the
Medyn-Gzhatsk road and all roads leading north-west, to close the line of
retreat from Medyn to Yukhnov and to prevent any German withdrawal
through the rail junction of Myatlevo to Yukhnov. The Soviet command
proposed to drop a detachment of 220 paratroops to seize an airfield half a mile
from Myatlevo, fly in a rifle regiment, and put another detachment astride the
Medyn-Yukhnov road. More than a thousand men would be flown in after
the airfield was captured. On the night of 16 January the first detachments were

dropped (416 men instead of the 202 originally planned); they took the airfield by evening, but deep snow and heavy German resistance caused the subsequent phases to be abandoned. On 19 January these paratroop detachments linked up with 49th Army. In place of this operation which ended abruptly, Zhukov now proposed to drop paratroops in the Znamenka-Zhelanie area, midway between Vyazma and Yukhnov; during the night of 18 January, sixteen aircraft dropped 452 paratroopers under the command of Major Soldatov. At 17.50 hours on the same day, the *startovaya komanda* was dropped, followed by 200 more paratroops; during the next three days, more than 1,000 men were air-lifted or dropped in, bringing Soviet strength to 1,643 men with arms and ammunition, though German fighters jumped the Soviet transport planes bringing in the additional men.

Zhukov meanwhile proposed a major airborne operation using the full strength of Major-General A.F. Levashov's 4th Parachute Corps to assist with the Vyazma encirclement operation; Zhukov wanted the corps in action by 21 January, but first it had to be shifted from its base in Moscow to airfields at Kaluga – an unfortunate choice, because these were the fields well-known and accurately pinpointed by the Germans who had so recently used them, and Soviet air cover was weak. Thirty fighters were earmarked for covering the assembly points, 72 to cover the actual drops, but it was a much smaller force than this which got off the ground; none of the fighters was equipped for night operations, and of the 65 transport aircraft promised only 39 could be mustered, and only 19 fighters could be spared from front operations. From Moscow 4th Parachute moved to its assembly area by train, seriously delayed on its way by the unrepaired blown-up bridge over the Oka. Levashov learned of the final details of the plan only on 24 January and had thirty-six hours in which to make his preparations. On 26 January, he issued his own orders to the three brigades of the corps, which were to be dropped on the evening of 27 January, preceded by seven 'diversionary groups' of 20–30 men dropped to make contact with Soviet cavalry in the area and with 'Group Soldatov', the earlier arrivals at Zhelanie.

Exactly on time on the evening of 27 January, though not quite on target, 4th Corps made its first drops west of Vyazma from a considerable altitude in one great stick which scattered men over a fifteen-mile radius; 476 of the 638 men dropped managed to collect into their units, though the lead detachment of 8th Parachute Brigade sent in to set up a landing zone was dropped eight miles away from its target, Ozerechniya.

On the night of 28 January, German bombers went for the old familiar Kaluga airfields from which 4th Corps was operating, knocking out seven aircraft and blowing up a fuel dump; more aircraft were damaged. Under these conditions, only 8th Brigade got on to the ground in any strength, dropped over a period of six days and over a wide area, 2,232 men of whom only 1,320 managed to form up into units. Corps HQ remained ignorant of what was

happening on the ground, in spite of having sent out several reconnaissance
aircraft. On 29 January, Senior Lieutenant Aksenov, deputy intelligence officer
to Corps, flew out in a tiny U-2 biplane, located some 200 men and put them
under his immediate command. By now, German air activity over the dropping
zones ruled out further drops, and German interdiction over the base aerodromes
caused great confusion; 4th Corps was temporarily withdrawn to its base in
Moscow, while Colonel Onufriev's 8th Brigade remained to fight it out on the
ground, with Major Soldatov's group and with the Soviet cavalry closing on
Vyazma. Zhukov had another assignment for the corps, now secured on its
well defended Moscow aerodrome; the corps was to be dropped in full
strength into the area south-east of Vyazma, in an operation to be directed by the
commander of Red Army parachute troops, Major-General V.Ya. Glazunov.
Since Major-General Levashov had been killed in action, Major-General A.F.
Kazankin, chief of staff, took over 4th Corps for these future drops.

As Soviet infantry, cavalry and parachute commandos clustered round
Vyazma and gathered in the Ugra bend to the south-east, where a grinding,
tearing battle was about to open, Golikov's 10th Army on Zhukov's extreme
left, part of the cover which had once been wrapped round Belov, was dragged
into a major crisis as German counter-attacks smashed into the southern prong
of the Soviet offensive. At Sukinichi, the German garrison was completely
encircled; the garrison was a scratch force fighting furiously to hold the town,
a 'hedgehog' hurriedly manned which the German command decided to relieve
by driving into Golikov's formation, so that Second Panzer could once more
link up with the Fourth Army. Rzhev-Yukhnov-Sukinichi formed one arc of
German resistance which had at all costs to be broken down. Golikov in the
first week in January was attacking on a sixty-mile front running from Mosalsk
to Zhizdra, his divisions spread out and separated from each other by as much
as fifteen miles or more; Zhukov on 9 January instructed Golikov to capture
Kirov, cut the Vyazma-Bryansk railway line between Zapoznaya and Lyudinovo, thereafter to secure his formations for a thrust against Vyazma. Lyudinovo
fell on 9 January, Kirov on the eleventh, and Golikov's right flank aimed for
Chiplyaevo, his left for Zhizdra. But in 10th Army's rear General von Gilsa's
216th Infantry Division, rushed in from France at the end of 1941, held out at
Sukinichi, dependent on occasional air-drops to keep them going. Second
Panzer Army thereupon decided to drive from Zhizdra to Sukinichi, cutting a
narrow corridor straight through 10th Army.

The weakness at the junction of the Western and Bryansk Fronts concerned
Zhukov, and also attracted Stalin's attention. To correct this situation,
Lieutenant-General M.M. Popov's 61st Army (Bryansk Front) was subordinated
after 13 January to Zhukov's command, although the *Stavka* failed to alter the
previous operational assignments of the 61st, which was now supposed to seal
the breach between the two Fronts, while from Orel and Bryansk the German
Second Panzer Army moved up a small but agile striking force (208th Infantry

Division, 4th Panzer Division and 18th Panzer) to burst into Golikov's left flank, which unrolled at alarming speed. On 19 January, as the German counter-blow developed in the forest and snow-covered lake area at Lyudinovo, 10th Army's 322nd Rifle Division was cleared from the town in one great savage burst of street-fighting. From Golikov's staff Zhukov's Front HQ received highly alarming reports, stressing the dangers and difficulties of the situation, clearly to justify the present predicament of 10th Army. Moving up the Front reserves (12th Guards Rifle Division) took time and on 22 January this formation was still twenty-five miles from any useful operational area; a major decision to shore up Golikov involved moving Rokossovskii down to the south, but it was to be a full week before this had any effect at all. Already on 24 January the 338th Infantry Regiment had linked up with von Gilsa's garrison at Sukinichi, a forty-mile lifeline, narrow but usable, enough to start moving out the thousand wounded men huddled in the cellars of the smashed houses.

The Zhizdra-Sukinichi counter-blow by Second Panzer had rocked not only 10th Army but the whole of Zhukov's left wing; to fill in the gap between the Western and Bryansk Fronts, Zhukov decided to raise a fresh 16th Army on his left, taking five rifle divisions from Golikov (323rd, 328th, 324th, 322nd and 12th Guards) and leaving 10th Army three. The Second Panzer attack had had a limited aim, but Western Front HQ saw no guarantee that it could not happen a second time, and then with a more decisive aim; setting up a 'new' 16th Army was not a reinforcement merely a regrouping which in fact weakened the left wing elsewhere. Certainly Zhukov now had the 61st Army, but this could exercise little or no effect on the situation.

Colonel-General I.F. Kuznetsov, Zhukov's deputy commander, came down to Rokossovskii's HQ to supervise the Sukinichi operation, interfering quite unwholesomely in the planning, so much so that Rokossovskii protested to Zhukov. Zhukov allowed Rokossovskii to have his way, and the 10th/16th Armies prepared a Soviet counter-attack. In another furious round of fighting Sukinichi was finally taken on 29 January, though the commander of 24th Panzer Corps had decided already to pull out. When Rokossovskii signalled that Sukinichi had been taken and the town was being 'mopped up', Front HQ demanded to know just what 'mopping up' involved. To settle these agitations, Rokossovskii moved his HQ into Sukinichi.

At the beginning of February, though Army Group Centre faced a multitude of dangers, the mortal crisis seemed to be fading. In the south, the Soviet offensive prong had been jammed back; north of Vitebsk, Yeremenko was slowing down with his great northerly sweep: at Vyazma, its perimeter dotted with Soviet attackers, the vital junction was still in German hands: at Rzhev, Model was preparing to face another wave of Soviet attacks, but 39th and 29th Armies had already been cut off from their rear communications and supplies; Kholm held out in the rear of the 3rd Shock Army which was stalled in front of Velikie Luki, while through the winter fogs and blizzards the daily 'run' of 100 (and occasionally 150) German transport planes shuttled in and out of the Demyansk 'pocket'.

The Soviet thrusts were nevertheless deep and very dangerous, deep enough for Stalin to maintain his hopes that the *coup de grâce* could yet be delivered to the central German Army Group. On 1 February, Stalin formally re-established the *Glavnoe komandovaniye Zapadnovo napravleniya*, Timoshenko's earlier 'Western theatre' command which had been wound up in the early autumn of 1941, and which Stalin now assigned to General Zhukov, with Lieutenant-General F.I. Golikov as deputy commander of the Western Front (of which Zhukov still remained the full commander). Stalin demanded of Zhukov the completion of the destruction of the main body of Army Group Centre. General Zhukov was to 'co-ordinate' the operations of the Kalinin and Western Fronts, and his 'most immediate task' was the seizure of Vyazma together with the 'encirclement and capture of the German forces at Rzhev-Sychevka'. Soviet aviation commanders also received simultaneous orders to intensify their air-supply operations for Soviet formations deep in the German rear.

At Rzhev, the situation was dangerous: at Vyazma, where the first Soviet attacks had failed, Belov and Yefremov were similarly cut off from the main body of the Soviet forces, and a decisive shift in the Vyazma area could be achieved only by a successful conclusion to the operations of the 43rd, 49th and 50th Armies, destroying German forces at Yukhnov. But those attacks also were stalled. In the first week in February, although optimism still reigned in Stalin's *Stavka*, deep anxieties could no longer be suppressed over the Rzhev-Yukhnov developments. Zhukov now prepared to hurl in everything he had left.

On the Volkhov Front, Meretskov's first attacks came grinding to a halt almost as soon as they were started. While Meretskov put his forces in order to jump off on 13 January, Fedyuninskii at 54th Army (Leningrad Front) used the breathing-space to regroup his formations. Even before Meretskov's first attack, Soviet probing of the German front had gone on persistently enough for the German command to suspect a major blow; in the Soviet 52nd Army area, north of Novgorod, German monitors intercepted a Soviet signal advising that the offensive was postponed (which it was) and that present positions were to be held. When on the morning of 13 January Soviet guns opened fire, the German defenders scarcely thought that this was the harbinger of the great attack, but Meretskov, at the very limit of the deadline which the *Stavka* had extended for him, was attacking in full strength. Northwards, Fedyuninskii's 54th Army jumped off for its objectives at Pogoste and Tosno. To the left, below lake Ilmen, Morozov was already trying to charge into Staraya Russa and swing round into the German rear. In the area of the Soviet 4th Army, Fedyuninskii's neighbour, German units went into the attack and forced the 4th on to the defensive; 59th Army, neighbour to the 4th, also failed to stamp through the German defences. Only the 2nd Shock and 52nd Armies enjoyed any success, their ski units slipping over the Volkhov and assault units taking positions on the western bank of the frozen river, but the heaviest fighting was necessary to take the Russians the few miles to the Chudovo-Novgorod road.

The 2nd Shock Army ran straight into more of the German strong points which held to the bitter end: Mostki, Spasskaya Polist and Zemtitsy, fortified points on the Novgorod-Chudovo railway and highway. Further north, 4th and 59th Armies had almost expended themselves and were to all intents and purposes halted; on 17 January, Fedyuninskii's ammunition was almost exhausted and his offensive slowed up and stopped. Meretskov was harried from Moscow to speed things up with *Stavka* reminders that 'considering the gravity of the situation in Leningrad, all possible measures must be taken and a rapid advance must be ensured'. On 21 January 2nd Shock Army was enmeshed in the German defences, with German units fighting desperately to hold open their main supply line, the road; the Germans brought up reserves, artillery and aircraft, the Russians moved in more reinforcements and their artillery.

By mid January, the part of the Soviet plan which envisaged 54th and 4th Armies (Leningrad and Volkhov Fronts) encircling and destroying German forces, which had been attacking towards lake Ladoga and which blockaded Leningrad from the east and south-east, was practically a dead letter. In the forest and icy scrub in front of 54th Army, German gunfire brought Fedyuninskii to a halt; 4th Army was held on its twelve-mile front, 52nd Army attempting to advance on Novgorod and Soltsy enjoyed little success, and 2nd Shock was hung up. To increase the distribution of forces, the *Stavka* ordered the 'new' 8th Army to be raised from part of the 54th and handed over to Major-General Sukhomlin, Fedyuninskii's chief of staff, a post assumed by Major-General L.S. Berezinskii; the Leningrad Front Military Soviet not without some trepidation decided to send a regiment of heavy tanks over the 'ice road' to Fedyuninskii's troops. The tanks made it without sliding beneath the ice.

On the night of 24 January, however, 2nd Shock Army succeeded at last in blasting a passage through the German defensive field, and with infantry, armour, cavalry units and ski battalions Soviet troops began to race through the gap with orders to widen the breach, outflank the German defences and strike for Lyuban; 13th Cavalry Corps, commanded by Major-General N.I. Gusev, with 25th and 87th Cavalry divisions, plus a rifle division taken from 59th Army moved on. The gap through which the Soviet divisions now moved at high speed under German fire was, nevertheless, only half a mile wide, though the weight of the Soviet assault had been against a twelve-mile front. Meretskov decided to exploit the gap because he expected one new army promised by the *Stavka*; widening the breach and exploiting it in depth could be a simultaneous operation. But in the rear the German strong-points hung on strenuously. The new Soviet army did not turn up. Gusev's 13th Corps shot out north-westwards to Yegline, then swung north-east as German resistance materialized and swung

on Lyuban; as 2nd Shock Army came through the gap, Soviet formation,
began to be strung out in a long line, their flanks completely exposed. Controls
communications and supply began to impose an impossible strain, which
Meretskov repeatedly reported to the *Stavka* without avail until finally on
28 January General Khrulev himself, head of the Red Army Rear Services,
arrived at the Volkhov Front, and actually got supplies moving systematically.

After 2nd Shock went through, the task of widening the gap was assigned by
Meretskov to 52nd and 59th Armies; they were both to drive from opposite
ends down the Novgorod-Chudovo road. The communications of 2nd Shock
had at all costs to be secured, and repeated German attacks were directed at
closing the gap and sealing off 2nd Shock Army. Bit by bit the gap was chewed
apart, until after nearly three weeks 2nd Shock Army's communications with
the rear were secured against German machine-gun and artillery fire. But that
was all Soviet troops could do – and 'not a metre more', in Meretskov's own
words. To close the gaps in the flanks, Meretskov organized two 'operational
groups' one under General Privalov, the other under Major-General Alfereyev;
2nd Shock was advancing, but not where Meretskov wanted it to, and Stalin in
a spate of telegrams showed his great displeasure. It was Lyuban Stalin wanted,
and to make sure he got it he sent Marshal Voroshilov to the Volkhov Front
to look into the operations of the 2nd Shock Army. At the breach on the
Volkhov, German troops hung on day after day, while Soviet troops laid
down minefields and used flame-throwers to keep the gap intact.

The earlier plans to bring 11th Army of North-Western Front swinging
through the flank of Sixteenth Army and into the rear of Eighteenth Army
had been drastically modified in view of the blockage at Staraya Russa,
the Demyansk complication and the lopping off of Kurochkin's left wing. The
Stavka had entertained the idea of swinging 11th Army on Soltsy, and using
1st and 2nd Guards Rifle Corps to attack in the direction of Pskov to cut
German rear communications, and to deal with the Demyansk 'pocket'
simultaneously; but the Demyansk problem continued to escalate, so that
towards the end of January the two corps, 34th Army and elements of 3rd
Shock Army were heavily involved. In place of the first plan, the *Stavka* now
suggested that the 1st Shock Army should be introduced at Staraya Russa and
swung north-west, on or about 6–7 February by which time the Demyansk
'problem' should be fully wound up. But by the end of January, 1st Guards had
failed to finish its concentration; a General Staff liaison officer reported to
Marshal Shaposhnikov that the corps had been delayed in transit, and that its
operations should be postponed. Stalin would not delay; Major-General
Gryaznov's corps went into the attack as it was, half-ready and with little
intelligence of the German positions. Very soon (3 February) Stalin telephoned
for news, and had himself connected directly with Gryaznov, whom he now
instructed on how the offensive should be conducted. Defective intelligence
could be corrected by using the U-2 biplanes in all weathers (though the corps

had no U-2s available); Gryaznov should 'drive ahead in a powerful group', 'have groups all the time', and not 'split up regiments and battalions'. Major-General Lizyukov's 2nd Guards now went into action and did establish an external encircling front, a 'favourable condition' for committing 1st Shock Army in a westerly drive. V.I. Kuznetsov's 1st Shock, however, had already been raided by the Front command for reserves or for reinforcements for 11th Army; in moving up from the Western Front, 1st Shock had used up its fuel and food supplies. In spite of Kuznetsov's plea for a postponement, it too was flung in half-ready on 13 February, advanced to the river Polist and was thereafter snagged in the German defences.

On the Leningrad-Volkhov Fronts, Stalin ordered Fedyuninskii to prepare a fresh operation, assigning the 4th Guards Rifle Corps as reinforcement (one rifle division, four rifle and one tank brigade, three ski battalions and a *Katyusha* unit): objective – Lyuban. Earlier Meretskov and Voroshilov sat debating how to get 2nd Shock Army moving on Lyuban; it was decided to regroup, move up supplies, and send Taranovich (artillery commander) with Kurkin (armoured commander) up to Army HQ. To Meretskov's proposals to strengthen the 2nd Shock Army and 13th Corps the *Stavka* returned no basic objection, but the offensive must *not* be slowed down; on the contrary, on 26 February a *Stavka* directive categorically forbade any relaxation of the drive for Lyuban (2nd Shock) and Chudovo (59th Army), and ordered the Chudovo-Lyuban railway line to be taken by 1 March. The *Stavka* intimated that Fedyuninskii was now committed to an attack on Lyuban. The day of the directive (26 February) 2nd Shock had managed to penetrate the German front at Krasnaya Gorka, but the gap was sealed almost at once. Now the *Stavka* ordered all formations to form 'shock groups', one of four divisions in 2nd Shock, three divisions in 59th and two divisions in 4th Army; this, however, did not compensate for the lack of men, ammunition and air cover. Meretskoy decided to go to Krasnaya Gorka and see for himself with General Klykov, 2nd Shock commander; officers and men complained bitterly about the shortage of ammunition and the lack of air cover. The Military Soviet blamed the 'lack of agreement' between army and Front HQ; Meretskov for his part found disgraceful neglect of reinforcements, chaos in the records of killed and wounded, and Colonel Pakhomov (2nd Shock Chief of Operations) submitting 'lying reports'.

In a great rage, Stalin had the chief of staff (Major-General Vizzhalin) and Colonel Pakhomov removed forthwith, and Major-General Alfereyev was installed as deputy commander to Klykov; not to be thwarted in his aim of bringing down Army Group North, Stalin ordered a high-powered mission north early in March, sending Malenkov with Voroshilov who had been ordered back to the Volkhov. Bulganin was meanwhile with the North-Western Front, to the consternation of all intruding himself as a separate 'echelon' between the Front HQ and the *Stavka*. Lieutenant-General Novikov, the tough deputy commander of the Soviet air force, also came up to the Volkhov and in the same plane was Lieutenant-General A.A. Vlasov, who was made deputy commander of the Front. Just as Stalin had entrusted a 'mission' to Yeremenko, he now entrusted one to Vlasov, who had attended the GKO session which considered the Volkhov mess. In less than a fortnight Klykov fell ill, and Vlasov took over the 2nd Shock Army. Fedyuninskii's offensive had enjoyed some local success but had not broken the German defences: 2nd Shock, pinioned deep in the German rear in the frozen marsh and forest area between the Chudovo-Novgorod and the Leningrad-Novgorod roads, had advanced units eight miles south-west of Lyuban and about fifteen miles from 54th Army units. It was almost success, when the German counter-blow crashed down with full force and sealed the gap, cutting off the 2nd Shock Army. On 19 March, the German pincers met and cut clean through 2nd Shock's lifeline.

Meretskov, whom the *Stavka* had charged personally with reopening that line, could learn little definite about the German attack from 52nd and 59th Armies; with a formation hurriedly drawn from 54th Army, Meretskov now supervised the frenzied attempts to open the gap in a week of fighting at close quarters. It was finally done and Vlasov's army saved momentarily from strangulation.

Orders for the attack on Vyazma were issued by Zhukov on 4 February, when 11th Cavalry Corps was some six miles west of the town on the Moscow-Minsk highway, and Belov and Yefremov were closing in from the south and south-east. Both Yefremov and Belov were operationally encircled, their 'gaps' sealed behind them by German assault units; in both formations conditions grew more severe each day: Yefremov had finally 2,700 wounded men and 150 infected with typhus to cope with. Yefremov and Belov, being in close contact, decided to form a joint front and to congeal their flanks; to the amazement of Belov, permission to do this was refused by Western Front HQ – 'Junction links with infantry /33 Army not necessary.' Several days of heavy fighting brought no break-in to Vyazma, only serious losses and the dispersal of the Soviet attackers; Belov's 75th Division was doubly encircled and had to fight its way out to the main group, now pushed back some seven miles from Vyazma. Belov also helped the Soviet paratroops to fight their way out of encirclement, and 8th Parachute Brigade (with other units) was subordinated to 1st Guards Cavalry Corps. On the other side of Vyazma, 11th Corps went into the attack at Semlevo, but neither it nor the 114th Ski Battalion could make much headway against heavy German mortar fire; at night, the bombardment continued as German aircraft dropped flares and also bombed these garishly illuminated targets. Zhukov had also ordered Belov and 11th Cavalry to 'cut forthwith the Vyazma-Smolensk railway line, to stop enemy rail traffic'; this Belov proposed to accomplish by destroying the Dnieper bridge five miles west of Izdeshkova, and Zhukov also instructed Belov in co-operation with 11th Cavalry to attack Vyazma from the west. Belov also made contact with large partisan formations, one of which launched a substantial attack on Dorogobuzh; in Yeremenko's drive from the north-west, the Partisan Staff attached to the Military Soviet of the Kalinin Front managed a rudimentary co-ordination between Red Army and partisan forces, so that a 'corridor' to pass men, supplies, arms and ammunition behind the German lines was set working, using the 'Surazh gate' as entry. With the 3rd Shock Army, partisan units were armed with captured weapons, and in both 3rd and 4th Shock Armies these 'corridors' were jammed with traffic, not least food supplies which Partisan staffs ordered to be collected for the hard-pressed Soviet troops. Belov radioed to Front HQ for permission to recoup his manpower from these 'partisan' units (many men having served in the Red Army); Belov was authorized to mobilize former Red Army men and civilians up to forty-five years of age, an assignment handled by the 'special induction commission', run by the Political Administration officers with his corps. (In a month's work, the commission directed 2,436 men to 1st Cavalry.)

While all these actions crackled in the Vyazma area, and the Soviet formations threshed about trying to stamp down the German resistance (growing each day stronger, with more and more equipment on hand), at Rzhev Zhukov faced a major crisis. Panzer General Model had already succeeded in slicing away formations of the Soviet 39th and 29th Armies from their communications in this furious fighting in the Volga bend. During the first week in February, Model split 29th Army from the 39th, and though waves of Soviet attacks beat frantically against the Rzhev positions, the Rzhev 'pocket' held out; and like the 33rd Army of the Western Front, the 39th of the Kalinin was in semi-encirclement. The stalling of the Soviet offensive caused the first great stir of apprehension in the *Stavka*, which now issued orders to the Western and Kalinin Fronts to bring all the force available to them to bear; the *Stavka* instructions to the Western Front insisted on the destruction of the German forces in the Rzhev–Vyazma–Yukhnov area, so that by 5 March Soviet forma-tions would reach the line Olenino–river Dnieper–Yelnaya, continuing thence to the Desna up to Snopoti, twenty miles east of Roslavl, while the left wing of the Western Front would destroy German forces in the Bolkhov–Zhizdra–Bryansk area and liberate Bryansk itself. Stalin decided at this stage to reinforce both the Kalinin and Western Fronts. To Koniev went seven rifle divisions, one Guards rifle corps and four aviation regiments, to Zhukov 60,000 front-line reinforcements plus three rifle divisions, one Guards rifle corps, two parachute brigades, 200 tanks and 400 planes.

With these orders in view, Zhukov as commander of the 'Western theatre' instructed the 22nd, 30th and 39th Armies of the Kalinin Front to take the Olenino area, and the 43rd, 49th and 50th Armies of the Western Front to capture Yukhnov: the 'new' 16th and 61st Armies on the left wing would take Bryansk. When these assignments were complete, the main body of the Western and Kalinin Fronts would close in on Vyazma and Rzhev, thus finally eliminating Army Group Centre. At the same time, Zhukov sprang his major paratroop operation: the whole of 4th Parachute Corps (9th, 2nd, 14th Parachute Brigades and one battalion of the 8th) was to be dropped west of Yukhnov to break the enemy front from the rear, Boldin's 50th was given orders to attack in conjunction with the 4th Corps. On the night of 17 February, twenty transport aircraft, flying singly, took out the lead elements of the 14th Brigade. Nineteen planes turned back having failed to find the DZ, and only one plane dropped its paratroopers though not in the right spot, since a partisan-held area had been selected for the drop and bonfires were used to signal but the Germans too lit bonfires which put the pilots off their marks. Nevertheless by the morning of 20 February, 6,988 paratroopers had been dropped, time also for German units to assemble to surround the paratroop detachments, of which only half managed to form up, short of weapons, ammunition and heavy equipment. At the same time, the transport aircraft were urgently needed to supply Belov's cavalry and Yefremov's 33rd in the Vyazma area.

On 17 February, as Zhukov hurled in the paratroopers to finish off the Yukhnov battle and to bridge the isolation between 1st Guards Cavalry and 33rd Army inside the German perimeter, and 49th and 50th Armies outside it, Model succeeded in encircling 29th Army west of Rzhev; 39th Army pressed from the west and 30th Army from the north in an effort to squeeze Model away from the 29th, and one battalion of the 204th Parachute Brigade was dropped during the night of 17 February into the Mochalovo-Okorokovo area, wooded country where combat groups of 1st Panzer Division compressed the perimeter of the nine Soviet divisions trying to break southwards to join up with the 39th Army. Only 6,000 men were left of 29th Army when it began its break-out, and as these remnants pulled out to the south the German 'block' which separated 39th Army also from the main body of the Soviet forces thickened appreciably, so that the 39th was in a worse plight. Between Sychevka and the Volga bend, the German Ninth Army and Koniev's 29th and 39th Armies mauled each other terribly, but this northern German redoubt could not be reduced.

In the other great 'pocket' at Demyansk, a Soviet outer encirclement line established by the 11th Army and 2nd Guards Corps ran from lake Ilmen, east of Staraya Russa and southwards to Belebelka, between which point and Kholm lay a 25-mile gap covered by Soviet partisans and patrolled by Red Army aero-sled and ski units. The distance between the external and internal ring was some twenty miles, while in the 'pocket' itself German resistance showed no signs of slackening. Stalin on 25 February expressed his grave dissatisfaction at the slowness of the operations, 'due to the weak co-ordination of operations between the 3rd Shock Army of the Kalinin Front with units of the 1st Guards Rifle Corps and 34th Army of the North-Western Front and through the lack of a unified command for these forces . . .'. Kurochkin was ordered to tighten the encirclement and 'in not more than a period of four-five days' liquidate the 'pocket'. 'Group Ksnefontov' (two divisions and five brigades) was detached to Kurochkin from the Kalinin Front, which forthwith ceased to concern itself with supplying this force. Pronin of the North-Western Front sent a desperate signal to Kalinin Front HQ stressing the plight of this force – 'no fodder, food supplies sufficient for half a day, ammunition nearly exhausted'; the tank brigades were without fuel and ammunition. Early in March, the *Stavka* proposed that the encirclement ring should not be further compressed, but that the 'pocket' should be split and broken along its 190-mile perimeter, while one more 'decisive thrust' should be made against Staraya Russa, German possession of which had invalidated earlier Soviet plans and still gravely impeded the North-Western Front.

At Vyazma, the Western and Kalinin Fronts had not for all their strenuous exertions and deep penetrations succeeded in linking up effectively. Crisis after crisis swept over the German command, but a major disaster had so far been averted. At Rzhev, the Soviet pincer had been snapped right off; Govorov's 5th Army was now fighting its way slowly to Gzhatsk, while another great surge of fighting was building up south-east of Vyazma, where the position of Yefremov's 33rd Army had now become desperate. In Belov's corps, the *Prokuror* (the military prosecutor) sent Front HQ a despairing message, describing the woeful condition of the force, and requesting that 'to preserve what is left of the battle-worthy units' the corps should be pulled out. Belov knew nothing of this submission. Front HQ radioed back that pulling the Corps out would have a disastrous effect on 11th Cavalry and 33rd Army and would weaken the partisans: Stalin himself had ordered 'that every possible measure should be taken to hold on to Dorogobuzh'. Belov himself meanwhile tangled with Zhukov over 1st Guards Cavalry operations:

> For what reason have you, in defiance of the orders of the *Stavka* and the Front Military Soviet, moved away from Vyazma? Who gave you the right to pick your own assignments? You evidently forgot that for failing to fulfil orders you can be arrested and put in front of a military tribunal.

In answer to Zhukov's radio message, Belov in mid March sent a report on his present intentions:

> Detailed report am sending you by plane (pilot Yefremov). At present, wish to report: operationally main body of corps remaining at approaches to Vyazma, but tactically I altered the direction of operations, to outflank enemy strong-points and in fulfilment of your operational assignments. The formal right of tactical manoeuvre was given to me by Orders No. 1921, 1690, 1774, 86/op.

It was equally urgent, however, to rescue Yefremov. Western Front HQ sent Belov an immediate signal: 'Do not abandon Yefremov or else he is done for.' Zhukov had proposed to Yefremov that he break for the woods in the Vyazma-Yukhnov area, but 33rd commander turned this down in favour of a break-through to the main Soviet forces in the area of Zakharovo. This decision taken, Yefremov broke off further radio contact with Front HQ, where it could only be assumed that he did this to secure his movements. The only possible response was to order 43rd Army to fight forward to meet Yefremov. Belov received his orders to fight his way to Yefremov on 24 March, whereupon Belov set up a special composite force, strengthened with partisans, a force which could not at any cost break into Yefremov's area, and suddenly Belov had to look out for the 4th Parachute Corps, whose forward units had managed a weak link with 50th Army, though Boldin could not break in the German defensive front and connect in any strength with the paratroops. For a second time 50th's breakthrough attempt had failed.

The *Stavka* had already issued a revised directive to the Western and Kalinin Fronts on 20 March, in which the strategic objective was defined as reaching the Belyi-Dorogobuzh-Yelnaya-Krasnoe (twenty miles south-west of Smolensk) line by 20 April, and digging in there. By 27 March the Western Front was to establish contact with the Soviet forces operating in the German rear and destroy the German units in the Rylyaki-Milyatino-Vyazma area, while 5th Army was to take Gzhatsk by 1 April, after which it was to co-operate with 43rd, 49th, and 50th Armies in capturing Vyzama. The left wing formations, 16th and 61st Armies, would continue to aim for Bryansk. The Kalinin Front was to employ 39th and 30th Armies in another attempt against Rzhev, cutting the Olenino German forces from those in Rzhev by 28 March and co-operating with 22nd Army in destroying them; 29th and 31st Armies together with units of 30th Army would assault Rzhev itself, to be taken not later than 5 April. For operations against Belyi, a special strike force of five rifle divisions would operate under the command of Major-General V.Ya. Kolpakchi. For all these operations, the *Stavka* poured into the Fronts what reserves it had at its disposal, since this was to be the final throw against Army Group Centre, one last urgent heave to topple the Rzhev, Olenino and Vyazma German bastions and to link up with Soviet troops operating to the north-west and south-west of Vyazma in the German rear. This was to be the consummation of Stalin's grand design from which he would not desist despite the signs of growing exhaustion and over-extension within the Red Army, and from which he could not be distracted by the major debate within the Soviet command about future strategic commitments.

During all these vast eruptions at the centre and on the flanks of the central and northern German Army Groups, turbulences and tremors which rocked the foundations of the German armies from lake Ladoga to Orel, Timoshenko's southern fronts had in two months of terrible fighting ground and hacked their way into Army Group South, a penetration which Soviet troops battled ceaselessly to turn into a large-scale strategic break-out which would wipe out German forces in the Donbas and in the Kharkov area. The Bryansk Front offensive had opened on 7 January, when 61st Army (transferred within a week to the Western Front) attacked the German forces in the Bolkhov-Orel-Kroma area, a task in which it was joined by the 3rd and 13th Armies; operations ground forward only slowly, and finally stalled, a set-back which sparked off a burst of recrimination and furious feeling on the part of the formation commanders against Cherevichenko and his Front command. A week earlier, 40th and 21st Armies (South-Western Front) had attacked in the Kursk-Oboyan area, where heavy fighting blazed up at once on the Seima river line: 40th Army's left wing moved ahead for some twenty miles, but at the centre and on the right 40th was held by the German defenders, as 21st Army cut the Belgorod-Kursk road and joined battle for Oboyan itself. Timoshenko introduced 21st Army without delay, issuing orders that 21st Army in co-operation with 38th Army under Major-General Maslov was to take Belgorod during the night of 5 January. Maslov fumbled the preparations for his offensive and attacked only on the evening of 5 January itself, by which time the Germans were well aware of what the Russian objective was, and stood ready and waiting; 21st Army's own attacks sank into a sea of German counter-attacks, and after 10 January German units broke into the rear of 21st Army's assault group, while a second blow fell flush upon the junction of 21st and 40th Armies.

Held to the north, Timoshenko now struck further south where the flanks of the South-Western and Southern Fronts were mingled (38th, 6th, 57th and 37th Armies); for four days (18–22 January), 6th and 57th Armies pushed ahead for some twenty miles. but at Balakleya and Slavyansk two German infantry divisions held on in a desperate attempt to stop the Soviet breakthrough widening. The northern prong of Timoshenko's hook was being held and even bent back near Belgorod-Volchansk, as this southern bulge swelled and swayed but did not for the moment rupture and spill Soviet formations out on to the German flanks. The German defence rested solidly on heavily fortified townlets and villages, even single farms and groups of huts, in and out of which Russian and German troops hunted each other with merciless persistence. To penetrate the German positions in depth, Timoshenko's Front commanders disposed of three cavalry corps, 6th, 5th and 1st, which during 22–4 January were introduced to the breakthrough operations, 1st and 6th Corps to the Krasnyi-Liman-Slavyansk railway line, right flank units of 5th Corps operating with 57th Army to take Barenkovo.

At Balakleya, 6th Army in the whipping winds of deep winter crashed into attack after attack against this vital corner post of the German defences, the northern shoulder of the Izyum bend penetration which Timoshenko wanted broken at all costs, for this high ground commanding the road to the west was the way to a major break-out. The Russians fought from their snow forts, the Germans huddled in the warmth of huts and houses, so that while the high command fought for strategic objectives, the infantrymen grappled with each other for simple but essential warmth.

On 24 January Timoshenko reported the decision to the *Stavka* to continue

operations and to introduce 9th Army, to operate between 57th and 37th
Armies: 38th, 6th Army and 6th Cavalry Corps were to continue their attacks
to outflank Kharkov from the south and south-west, to liberate Kharkov and
penetrate the Krasnograd area, for which Timoshenko asked for reinforcements
– tanks, aircraft, four rifle divisions and immediate replacements for his present
formations. Two days later the *Stavka* affirmed that Timoshenko's immediate
task was to cut German communications in the Slavyansk-Chistyakovo area;
one force would take the western bank of the Dnieper, and a second (depending
on the prevailing situation) would drive south, taking either the area west of
Mariupol or west of Melitopol. This was how Timoshenko was to burst out of
his 'bulge', for which he got an allocation of *Stavka* reserves – 315 tanks and
four rifle brigades, a goodly gift in those days of universal stringency.

On both sides of Izyum, Timoshenko proceeded to fill out this bulge: on
26 January, 6th Army and 6th Cavalry Corps cut the Kharkov-Lozovaya road,
reached the Orel river line and on the twenty-seventh captured Lozovaya itself,
a rail junction of considerable significance, as well as the site of a German
concentration camp in which Red Army prisoners of war died in their terrible
ways, of cold, of starvation, of brutal maltreatment. Soviet divisions, with
armour and rocket-launcher batteries in support, now rolled against the walls
of the breakthrough area, 6th Army pressing hard to the north in the direction
of Kharkov, to sweep out and link up with the 38th Army, thus slicing off the
Balakleya salient. But the German wall held and the Kharkov prong was held
once more. To the south, at Slavyansk and Artemovska, Malinovskii decided
to crush German resistance with 9th Army and a cavalry corps by breaking into
the rear of the German units in this area – and with 9th Army advancing upon
them from the west and 37th Army from the east, the German forces in the
Donbas would be speared to destruction; 57th Army would strike south-west
and secure the right flank of the Southern Front, while 5th and 1st Cavalry
Corps received orders to go for the Krasnoarmeisk-Gavrilovka area (west of
Stalino), to be invested by 5 February.

Having shored up the northern shoulder of the bulge with units drawn from
Kharkov, the German command proceeded to stiffen the southern, where a
Soviet eruption appeared more imminent. Units of 3rd Panzer Corps moved up
to Kramatorsk and into the Krasnoarmeisk area, into which one iron finger of
57th Army began to poke, though taking Krasnoarmeisk proved impossible.
Nor was 12th Army able to make much progress in that direction: 9th Army
battled for long days in the nests of fortified huts and villages, in sweeping
blizzards and the searching cold, while 37th Army could not break down the
German resistance on the southern shoulder. Three Soviet armies (6th of
South-Western, 57th and 9th Armies of Southern Front) with cavalry corps in
support had nevertheless broken across the German front on the Northern
Donets and penetrated to a distance of some fifty miles, though for the moment
they were being tied into positions running on a line Balakleya-Lozovaya-

Slavyansk. The bridgeheads on the right bank of the Donets were huge and menacing, threatening the flanks of the German forces at Kharkov and in the Donbas. At Slavyansk, which consumed Soviet rifle regiments, German casualties were telling and severe after beating off almost 200 Soviet assaults. Malinovskii had hoped to use the 9th Army for his break-out operations, but it too, with the 57th, was drawn inexorably into dealing with the persistent German counter-attacks. At Balakleya, one Soviet unit did break through to the vital Balakleya-Yakovenkovo road, positions which the men held until blasted away by Stukas and where no one was left alive, burnt to death in the hayrick concealments they had used.

While this seventy-day struggle waxed and waned in the heaving salient which Timoshenko had carved out over the Donets, on the Kerch peninsula, the Soviet command contemplated a major operation to liberate the whole of the Crimea, a restitution of the Soviet position in the south-east which could not but have a certain effect on Turkey and also put Soviet bombers back in bases from which they could strike at the Rumanian oilfields. On 2 January, the *Stavka* confirmed the plan whereby the main Soviet force was to strike through Dzhanka-Perekop-Chongar, a secondary force to operate against Simferopol and amphibious assaults would be launched on Yalta, Perekop and Eupatoria, the Soviet intention being first to bottle up the Eleventh Army and then to destroy it. General Kozlov, commander of the Crimean Front (which was formally established on 28 January) accordingly received express instructions from Stalin to 'speed up the final concentration of troops and to go over to a general offensive without delay', an ambitious undertaking thrown into disorder when on 15 January Manstein took the the offensive. In one fierce round of fighting, Soviet troops were driven out of Feodosiya. During the aerial bombardment 44th Army HQ was hit, Major-General Pervushin sustained serious wounds and his staff officers were killed; 44th and 51st Armies fell back to Ak-Monai and towards the sea of Azov. Stalin's great offensive now needed drastic revision.

Kozlov's new orders stipulated a thrust in the direction of Karasubazar (thirty miles west of Feodosiya) and break-out from that area into the rear of Manstein's Eleventh Army investing Sevastopol; the Black Sea Fleet was to prepare a powerful amphibious assault on Sudaka (twenty miles south-west of Feodosiya) and also to support 44th Army operations by naval bombardment of short targets. The offensive was timed for 13 February, and the revised operational plan issued from the *Stavka* on 28 January. Reinforcements rolled into the Soviet formations on the Kerch peninsula, including detachments of new T-34 tanks. German aerial reconnaissance followed the Soviet build-up on the Caucasian airfields and in the Black Sea harbours, while round the Sevastopol perimeter the artillery exchanges suddenly jerked into increased activity. The Crimean Front nevertheless found itself unable to jump off by 13 February and the offensive was therefore postponed for a fortnight, re-timed for

27 February. To safeguard his investment in the Kerch-Crimean offensive, Stalin detached Lev Mekhlis from his supervisory duties on the Volkhov (where Marshal Voroshilov had been sent) and dispatched him to Kerch, where he proceeded to worry the life out of every commander by his incessant day-and-night queries. Mekhlis was taking no chances about ultimate success, and ordered the Inspector-General of Soviet Armoured Forces, General Volskii, into the Kerch area to supervise the operation of the recently arrived tank reinforcements. This was one of the advantages of a 'direct wire' to Moscow and of being a deputy defence commissar enjoying Stalin's confidence.

On 23 February, the Luftwaffe roaring over the Soviet lines dropped leaflets announcing that the Soviet offensive would come on 27 February. In the morning mists of 27 February, the Soviet attack duly developed. General Volskii had failed to persuade the Front command, and principally Mekhlis, to wait a little; 51st Army's infantry went into the attack in columns, supported by tanks, but rain softened the ground, German artillery opened fire, and the tanks finally slowed to a halt. During the first fortnight in March, as Mekhlis interfered continuously and as Volskii tried desperately to persuade commanders to use their tank forces properly, one Soviet attack followed another, building up to a threat which Manstein decided to check decisively, and for which he proposed to employ his latest reinforcement, 22nd Panzer Division. The German attack rolled straight into a Soviet assembly for fresh offensive operations, and 22nd Panzer ran into heavy trouble. But when on 26 March the Soviet attacks were renewed, they were diminished in strength and limited in scope; Manstein still held the narrow neck of land, through which the Soviet armies had to break to strike into the Crimea. When on the misty morning of 9 April, 44th Army and elements of 51st Army with six rifle divisions and more than 150 tanks attempted to crash into the Crimea once again, Manstein, this time with his 28th Light Division in position, was ready and waiting.

But even without a break-out, the threat posed by two Soviet armies in Kerch was very real, the 'main threat' to the Eleventh Army which had to be eliminated. Soviet troops now set about building considerable fortifications; as Manstein had seen several times, they could also be reinforced more or less at will. At what date Sevastopol might be reduced, it was impossible to predict as the fortress went on spilling out its fire. Meanwhile Mekhlis tightened his own grip on the Kerch command, putting Kozlov into a kind of 'tutelage' to himself, a state of affairs which ultimately proved fatal. While the Kerch command was making its final attempt to storm into the Crimea, Stalin installed Marshal Budenny as commander-in-chief in the 'North Caucasus theatre', and decided to subordinate the Crimean Front to Budenny's operational direction. None of this appeared to interfere with Mekhlis's own estimate of his personal abilities as a powerful and high-ranking commander and when Mekhlis failed, the whole Soviet edifice at Kerch came crashing down with him.

Towards the end of March, and on the eve of Stalin's last lunge at his strategic objectives, the multiple Soviet penetrations were deep enough and dangerous enough to trouble most of the German command. On the Volkhov, Vlasov and Meretskov had managed to unlock the 2nd Shock Army, which stood as yet undefeated amidst the frozen bog and marsh near Lyuban: at Demyansk, the German Second Corps was undefeated but encircled, like the German forces at Kholm. East of Smolensk and west of Vyazma, Belov's 1st Cavalry, Yefremov's 33rd, 4th Parachute Corps and strong Soviet partisan brigades were cutting and hacking at the German lines, while to the north 11th Cavalry and 39th Army occupied the long and dangerous prominence west of Sychevka. Purkayev's 3rd Shock Army lunged out towards Velikie Luki, Yeremenko's 4th hung down over Vitebsk, pincers stopped in mid-air but not without their sharpness. At Kharkov, Timoshenko kept up an immense pressure, while in his great bulge over the Donets the Soviet bridgehead was now sixty miles deep – and if Balakleya and Slavyansk caved in, the Soviet divisions of two Fronts would spill out from the massive Izyum bulge. Farther to the south, Manstein stood outside the gates of Sevastopol, and though he had checked a Soviet eruption into the Crimea from Kerch, he still had two Soviet armies pointed at his back. Not one of the German Army Groups had been ripped to pieces, though the ragged edges of their lines and the deep penetrations into their flanks attested to the enormity of the crisis through which they were slowly but now more surely passing.

On the Volkhov Front, which Malenkov had been so recently inspecting on behalf of Stalin, Meretskov's Front command drew up three alternative lines of action; to ask the *Stavka* for one more army, and until the mud brought by the thaw arrived, to proceed with the present assignment: to pull 2nd Shock back and try on another sector: to go over to a rigorous defensive, ride out the mud and then renew the offensive. With the *Stavka*'s agreement, Meretskov chose the first variant, though the struggle to hold open Vlasov's lifeline was intense at the end of March: more German reinforcements were on the move, but Meretskov pressed ahead with plans to develop 2nd Shock's Lyuban offensive. To strengthen Vlasov a new rifle corps, 6th Guards, was being formed from the 4th Guards Rifle Division, and when complete, 6th Guards would be stronger than the whole of the 2nd Shock Army put together. Then this force would crash on to Lyuban. For the moment, Vlasov was relatively safe, his supplies secured through the mile-wide corridor drilled through the German block placed over 2nd Shock's communication route on the Volkhov. But once the ground thawed, Vlasov was bottled up in a massive marsh which would deprive him of all mobility. Meanwhile the plans for Vlasov to fight his way out collapsed in one crumpled heap when the Volkhov Front, to Meretskov's utter astonishment and consternation, was disbanded. Meretskov was transferred to the Western Front as Zhukov's deputy and as commander of the 33rd Army, Yefremov having perished in his break-out. Only at the *Stavka* did Meretskov hear what had actually happened. His first news of the disbandment came when General Khozin, Leningrad Front commander, arrived cock-a-hoop at Volkhov HQ, Stalin's directive in his pocket, announcing that henceforth the Volkhov Front was an 'operational group' subordinated to his command. Khozin, as Meretskov subsequently discovered, had persuaded Stalin that if he had the Volkhov force directly under him, he could de-blockade Leningrad in a trice. The new 6th Guards Corps plus a rifle division were at Khozin's prompting assigned to the North-Western Front: Meretskov was aghast, and tried to point out to Khozin in what straits Vlasov now found himself. Khozin preferred not to see it this way. Once at the *Stavka*, Meretskov reported on this calamity at a session where Stalin and Malenkov sat in: Meretskov was blunt enough,

> Second Shock is completely played out: it can neither attack nor defend itself. Its communications are at the mercy of German thrusts. If nothing is done, catastrophe can't be staved off. To get out of this situation, I suggest that 6th Guards Rifle Corps is not removed from the Front but used to strengthen that army. If that can't be done, then Second Shock must be pulled out of the swamp and forest back to the Chudovo–Leningrad road and rail lines.

It was advice which Stalin and Malenkov ignored, and Vlasov's men were finally doomed to starve in the swamps.

South-east of Staraya Russa, at dawn on the morning of 27 March, German guns opened fire in the first phase of an operation to blast a passage between the Soviet outer and inner encirclements of Demyansk, from which the 2nd Corps would drill its way outwards; the German forces would meet half-way. Leading the German relief force, Seydlitz struck at the junction of the Soviet 11th and 1st Shock Armies, laying down a carpet of fire and cracking the Soviet resistance with repeated dive-bomber attacks. All this fell like a bolt from the blue on Kurochkin's Front, where on 29 March all forces on the outer encirclement ring came under the command of Lieutenant-General Vatutin, Kurochkin's deputy and re-assigned on the direct orders of the *Stavka*, which also sent up anti-tank and anti-aircraft guns to Kurochkin in a bid to hold off Seydlitz. In the brush and forest between Staraya Russa and Demyansk, cracking through one Soviet line after another, Seydlitz's men fought their way for thirty days to the river Lovat, to the fiery rendezvous of Ramushevo and the link-up with the 2nd Corps, just as the mud sealed the North-Western Front into immobility.

Near Vyazma, Zhukov prepared one final throw, by which 50th Army would attempt to break across the Yukhnov-Roslave road and link up with Belov, attacking from the rear of the German forces. Only a narrow corridor separated Belov from Boldin, but it was packed with strong German units ready to face a front-and-rear strike. Zhukov ordered Belov to reconnoitre Milyatino (due south of Vyazma): on 10 April, Belov sent Zhukov a radio report on his present position, enemy strengths and what action he contemplated:

Circumference of Corps front now in excess of 300 kilometres. Enemy strengths: on Milyatino–Yelnaya line intelligence estimates six divisions. Towards Yelnaya are fortifications leading to Roslavl and Smolensk. West of Dnieper undetermined forces holding defensive position. To north – Yartsevo, Semlevo, Volosta Pyatnitsa – approaches to railway line covered by odd units, among them 35th and 23rd Infantry Divisions.
Conclusion: Corps participates in encirclement of Vyazma-Yelnaya-Spas Demyansk enemy force and is in its turn in operational encirclement.

Strength of Corps and length of front oblige me to turn to defensive operations. Initiative visibly with enemy. No reserves. In such conditions suggest offensive plan:

1 To break encirclement ring to meet 50th Army in general direction of Milyatino.
2 To this end to concentrate in Vskhoda area assault force of 1st and 2nd Guards Cavalry Divisions, 4th Parachute Corps, partisan detachment Zhabo.

. . . .

6 With 50th Army units and possibly 10th Army to seize Warsaw motor road in Zaitsev heights sector, Yersha and also Milyatino. Thereafter to dig in on motor road on indicated sector.
7 After my link-up with Boldin in Milyatino area to bring all my Corps together with my echelons including artillery, tank brigade, 7th Guards Cavalry Divisions and drive in Corps either to Yartsevo for junction with Kalinin Front or for other assignment.
[No. 1596. BELOV. MILOSLAVSKII. VASHURIN.]

In his detailed points, Belov had proposed to leave Dorogobuzh in the hands of partisan detachment *Dedushka*, and also asked for air cover and tank support. With understandable impatience, 1st Guards Cavalry HQ sweated out the time before the reply came. Zhukov in general agreed, but Stalin forbade any weakening at Dorogobuzh. Nor was there any encouraging news of 50th Army operations. On his own responsibility, Belov proposed now to probe southwards, towards the 50th when out of the blue on 14 April Western Front HQ reported 50th Army attacking and in possession of the Zaitsevo height on the motor road, and only three miles from Milyatino. Belov therefore proposed on his own responsibility again to bring his 1st Guards divisions from Dorogobuzh and fight out to the 50th: Zhukov absolutely forbade this, leaving Belov to burst out with his weakened 2nd Guards and the remnants of 4th Parachute. Half a mile separated Belov from Boldin when the German Stukas caught them, blasting forward units of 50th Army off the Zaitsevo height and flaying Belov's gaunt division. 'No reserves': Belov had already told Zhukov's HQ, and his only hope lay immobilized in Dorogobuzh. Yefremov's small force was now being systematically and literally cut to pieces. Yefremov himself was severely wounded in the back when his party was caught in a German ambush. By 18 April, when Yefremov was dying, his much reduced force practically ceased to exist in its last desperate push to cover the mile or so to 43rd Army lines; at night, Yefremov's party came under heavy German fire and lay in the woods lit up by German flares. Yefremov, unable to help his men and unwilling to die a prisoner, whispered, 'Boys, this is the end for me, but you go on fighting.' At that, he shot himself in the temple.

The partisan brigades, however, continued to swarm, some under firm control and legitimate authority, others self-installed, and yet others taken into regular Red Army formations, to swell very thin ranks. In the case of one unit run by Kiselev, Western Front HQ became suspicious of officers who claimed to act under Front HQ orders. Golushkevich, Zhukov's operations officer, radioed Belov:

The *Glavkom* [Zhukov] orders:
1 Report all you know about these partisan commanders.
2 Kiselev is ordered to arrest all of them until the situation is clarified.

The investigation subsequently carried out by one of Belov's officers resulted in all the partisan commanders being bundled on to a plane and flown to the rear, to the *Bolshaya zemyla* (the unoccupied rear) for interrogation. Zhukov's orders and Belov's dilemma (for he had detached one of his own officers to these partisan units) well illustrate the problem of controlling these various brigades and squads, many with cover-names, *Uragan*, *Dedushka*, and some commanded by strange and dubious men. Out of sheer necessity, Belov (and commanders like him) had to set up an intermediate command group to control these extensive activities, and for simplicity a regular military organization was generally adopted: detachment *Dedushka* was turned into a partisan 'division', the 1st Smolensk Partisan Division which was shortly to have 7,342 men, two BT-7 tanks, fifty mortars, ten field guns and assorted equipment, a formation which at once attracted the attention of the *okbom* authorities, so that the military, the Party and the political organs of Belov's corps all had a hand in its activities. In Belov's 'area', in the Yelnaya-Dorogobuzh district of Smolensk *oblast*, quite a powerful and uniquely well organized partisan movement grew up; there was a certain logic in Stalin's order to hold Dorogobuzh and all 'rear' territory, for even as the offensive slowed to a halt, this did not mean the end of plans to crush Army Group Centre. (Belov received formal, radioed orders to this effect on 4 May.) At the same time, through the Surazh 'gate' north of Vitebsk and through the Kirov 'gap' south of Vyazma, equipment and Red Army officer-advisers passed through to more partisan units which were organized into regiments at least, with one or two 'partisan divisions' in the making. In cases of immediate proximity, the partisan units came under the operational control of Red Army divisions and under the supervision of the political administration of divisional staffs; orders and assignments were handled by the Military Soviets at Front HQs where a general co-ordination was effected. (So demanding had the problem of partisan direction become after the winter of 1942 that in May a 'Central Staff of the Partisan Movement', a central, Moscow-based organization, was set up to provide a whole new top-level command.) During this spring regeneration of the partisans, many hands stirred the pot – the Red Army, the Party, the NKVD and a host of shadowy figures, locally known and locally based, who raised their highly individual detachments. Red Army divisions raised 'sabotage squads' from their own ranks and those of the partisans – ten men from each hundred, operating against German communications and other selected targets. Against these units and the Red Army as a whole were operating small groups of defector-Russians, men gone over to the Germans (one of whom, Bogatov, a former Red Army major of 160th Rifle Division, was blamed by General Belov for the infiltration of Yefremov's staff group and betrayal of their position to German units hunting them down).

As the Soviet winter offensive gradually slowed down and shuddered to its several halts, throughout March, and especially in the latter half of the month Stalin, the *Stavka*, the General Staff, selected Front commanders and the commanders of arms and services were engaged in the tense and conflict-laden business of determining what was to be the Red Army's aim and posture in the coming summer campaigns – defensive or offensive. The manner of determining this crucial choice reflected most sharply on Stalin's method of command and was itself a vital test of Stalin's military leadership, in which he exercised not only strategic but also a great deal of operational direction. During the great winter blows of December-January, Stalin showed himself to be a prey to two fundamental weaknesses: underestimation of the enemy and inability (or unwillingness) to mass Soviet forces on decisive axes. The limitations of command Stalin overrode repeatedly and not always successfully by frequent resort to his radio-telephone. Where it suited him, he enacted 'deals' with commanders, like that with Khozin, which contradicted all strategic and operational sense. Of intelligence, he apparently chose to believe only what suited his temper and his own estimates, though he was locked away from the sights and scenes of the war in general and the fronts in particular, convinced that he alone knew best. In the midnight sessions at the Kremlin, Stalin sought to salvage his grand design from the present obstructions, debating, if one-sidedly, strategic possibilities at a time when Hitler and his commanders were locked in the same type of discussion.

Marshal Shaposhnikov and Vasilevskii at the General Staff, having reviewed the strength of the Red Army, the quantity of its equipment and the volume of its supplies came to the 'firm conclusion' (in Vasilevskii's own words) that a 'provisional strategic defensive' was the proper posture for the Red Army in the early summer of 1942: the absence of large bodies of trained reserves reinforced this appreciation. The objectives should be defensive operations within prepared positions, designed to wear out the enemy with well-organized counter-blows, and finally to generate a situation where the Red Army could go over to a 'decisive offensive', the enemy being weakened substantially by his own losses. The 'main attention' of the Soviet command in this phase of the strategic defensive should be directed to 'the central sector' (Moscow). The main objectives of policy as a whole should be to build up by May-June 1942, powerful and well-equipped reserves, trained and in possession of the necessary armour, ammunition, aircraft and those supplies which the command now knew had to be in hand to effect a major offensive. In the middle of March, Marshal Shaposhnikov and his deputy Vasilevskii presented to Stalin personally this strategic appreciation, together with the basic calculations on reserves and equipment. Stalin more or less agreed with this estimate.

Marshal Shaposhnikov, however, was not alone in making representation to Stalin, the Supreme Commander. Also in the middle of March, Marshal Timoshenko submitted through his 'South-Western theatre' Military Soviet (commissar N.S. Khrushchev and chief of staff General I.Kh. Bagramyan) proposals for a renewed offensive with the forces of three fronts, the Bryansk, South-Western and Southern, with the object of destroying Army Group South and reaching the line Gomel-Kiev-Cherkassy-Pervomaisk-Nikolayev. The *Stavka*, in reviewing this proposal, came to the conclusion that lack of men and equipment ruled out such a massive undertaking, which would have required an enormous reinforcement for the South-Western front in particular. Timoshenko thereupon undertook to review the scale of his offensive, and to cut down on the magnitude of the objectives: in fact, Timoshenko produced a 'theatre' operation rather than a 'strategic operation' (which would have required the participation of several Fronts, including at least one not subordinated to his 'theatre' responsibility). Stalin, Beria, Voroshilov and the arms commanders who were members of the *Stavka* now agreed to what was shaping up as the 'Kharkov operation' – bursting out of the Izyum bulge in the north-west and attacking from Volchansk in the north-east to seize Kharkov – and issued orders to Shaposhnikov to regard this operation as an 'internal undertaking' confined to Timoshenko's theatre command alone. But for all the diminution in the magnitude of the operation, it was an ambitious undertaking of considerable strategic significance: the loss of Kharkov, with its vast stores and facilities, would have been a serious blow at Army Group South and then Timoshenko could leap out for Dnepropetrovsk and Zaporozhe. Decided definitely at the end of March, Timoshenko's offensive was timed for May.

While still accepting the main premisses of the General Staff, Stalin proceeded to consider simultaneously a number of 'partially offensive operations', schemes which were laid before the *Stavka*, while the GKO retained all its overriding responsibility for getting the tanks, guns and planes off the production line and into the fighting line. The recovery of the Moscow district eased that problem a little: industrial evacuation to the east came to a halt and the factories of the Moscow central industrial region started up again at full blast. Stalin meanwhile chose his 'partial offensives' either to improve the position of Soviet armies or to prevent German concentrations building up; this was the logic behind such attacks, orders for which were embodied in the *Stavka* directives authorizing the Leningrad offensive, which Stalin in a roundabout way was 'fixing' with Khozin, the Demyansk attacks, the operations aimed west of Vyazma and in the direction of Smolensk, the Lgov-Kursk operations, Timoshenko's Kharkov offensive and finally a continuation of the Kerch offensive against the Crimea. With this list of impending operations, the picture of 'partial offensives' had changed: though none on the General Staff dare speak out too critically, there was a deal of misgiving over the fact that Stalin proposed 'to defend and to attack simultaneously'.

While the collective opinion of the *Stavka* and the General Staff coincided in placing the main German threat in the early summer of 1942 in the centre, in the direction of Moscow, this did not dispose of some powerful individual reservations about Stalin's immediate plans and dispositions. Marshal Shaposhnikov did not wholly disagree with Stalin: 'limited active strategic defence' would wear down the enemy in the early summer, after which Soviet forces could go over to the counter-offensive, with the necessary reserves to hand. For his part General Zhukov supported Shaposhnikov, but he too entertained doubts: Zhukov thought it necessary to destroy German forces in the Rzhev-Demyansk area, which amounted to a large and powerful German bridgehead, though the *Stavka* and the General Staff held to the view that the Orel-Tula and the Kursk-Voronezh axes were by far the most dangerous, since the Germans could outflank Moscow from the south-west (precisely the reason for massing reserve armies on the Bryansk Front). Though in general agreement with Stalin's strategic forecast, Zhukov was not enamoured of 'partial offensives' on such a scale, since this number of separate undertakings could only spoil the chances of building up adequate reserves for any forthcoming strategic offensive by Soviet troops.

Zhukov duly reported his views to Stalin, proposing a powerful westerly attack to destroy German forces in the Rzhev-Demyansk area: troops of the Western and Kalinin Fronts, supported by aircraft detached from the Air Defence Command of Moscow, plus units pulled out of neighbouring fronts and the North-Western Front should suffice to do this. Such an attack would throw German forces off balance and contribute to weakening any offensive they might undertake in the near future. Faced with this divergence of views, at the end of March Stalin summoned a session of the State Defence Committee with Voroshilov, Shaposhnikov, Timoshenko, Zhukov, Vasilevskii and Bagramyan in attendance. Marshal Shaposhnikov opened with a thorough report, which substantially bore out Stalin's view of the strategic situation, only to draw somewhat different conclusions: German superiority in men, and the lack of a 'Second Front', suggested limiting 'active defence' for the moment: the main strategic reserves should be concentrated on the central axis and a part in the Voronezh area, for it was here, in the opinion of the General Staff, that the main operations in the summer of 1942 would take place. In reviewing the proposed offensive operations suggested by the South-Western theatre commander Timoshenko, Marshal Shaposhnikov was about to describe some of the difficulties inherent in this operation when Stalin interrupted: 'Don't let us sit down in defence, with our hands folded, while the Germans attack first!

We must ourselves strike a series of blows to forestall them on a broad front and upset enemy preparations.' Stalin continued: 'Zhukov suggests developing an offensive in the western theatre, but remaining on the defensive on all other fronts. I think that's a half-measure.' Timoshenko got up to present his views on the offensive in the south-west; his men were ready and waiting, and his command must mount a pre-emptive blow to disrupt German preparations for striking at the South-Western and Southern Fronts – in fact, by attacking first, to repeat in reverse what happened at the beginning of the war. As for offensive operations in the western theatre, Marshal Timoshenko fully supported General Zhukov's proposals which should do much to divert German forces.

In a final thrust at the plans for several 'partial offensives', Zhukov repeated all his previous objections, but now Marshal Shaposhnikov, who also feared the outcome of this dispersal of forces, chose to remain silent. Stalin had not been shifted from his position of 'simultaneous attack and defence', for which the Red Army simply did not have the necessary resources. Though Marshal Shaposhnikov tried to dissuade Stalin, he has been criticized for not trying harder and, as Zhukov reports, he finally lapsed into silence. Perhaps Shaposhnikov knew too well that there was no point in trying any more, that Stalin was bent on attacking come what may and that he had gone about 'fixing' offensive operations, behind the *Stavka*'s back, with individual commanders. Nor was Stalin ever persuaded of the desirability of defence, apparently out of a deep conviction that the Red Army could not successfully fight a protracted defensive action.

Convinced that the main threat in the summer of 1942 would make its appearance at the centre of the Soviet-German front, in the direction of Moscow, Stalin ordered a maximum concentration on this sector and at its approaches, of which the most dangerous was finally considered to be the Tula-Orel axis (the southern flank of the Moscow defences), though a drive through Kursk was not excluded after which the German assault would strike north, thereby deeply outflanking Moscow from the south-east. That being the case, the Bryansk Front, now commanded by Colonel-General Golikov, had a crucial role to play, though the Bryansk Front command (apart from having its own guesses) was scarcely aware of it. Analysing the experience of the past operations, Golikov (who arrived at his new command early in April) and his chief of staff General M.I. Kazakov assumed that Orel-Tula (thence Moscow) was a dangerous axis and likely to become so again: in addition, there was the Kursk-Voronezh line, a new approach which the Front had at all costs to keep intact. By stretching the Bryansk Front boundary southwards, 40th Army with its five rifle divisions came under Golikov's command, but that added fifty more miles of frontage, lopped off from the South-Western Front. This gave Golikov twenty-three divisions (before the shift, he had eighteen divisions with three armies, 61st, 3rd and 13th), plus three tank brigades. What Golikov and Kazakov thought the most alarming eventuality was a German assault on both axes – Orel–Tula, Kursk–Voronezh; that would rip the Front in half, a fate Golikov and Kazakov hoped to avert by suggesting to the *Stavka* that a new front administration, covering Voronezh itself, should be formed from the flank formations of the Bryansk and South-Western Fronts, 40th and 21st Armies, reinforced by two armies now in reserve, 3rd and 6th. This proposal Stalin and the *Stavka* turned down outright, but Golikov and Kazakov were suddenly aware that something enormous was brewing when the reinforcements quickly rolled down on the Bryansk Front – four of the new tank corps, seven rifle divisions, eleven rifle and four tank brigades, and large numbers of independent artillery regiments. Just what was in the wind Golikov had to wait to find out until he was summoned after mid April to a full session of the *Stavka*. Meanwhile on his own responsibility Golikov had used some of his recent reinforcement to form a new army, the 48th, to which Biryuzov was posted as chief of staff, an assignment not much to his liking. Rumyantsev had selected General Samokhin as commander of the 48th, and at Yelets his staff waited for his arrival by plane from Moscow. Samokhin never turned up. Mistaking his way, Samokhin's pilot put the general down, together with the directives he was carrying about the planning of the Kharkov operations and the role of the Bryansk Front, on a German airfield west of Mtsensk. Samokhin and his directives disappeared.

Stalin had already begun to make his re-disposition of the command in Leningrad. Early in April, Govorov, the non-Party commander of the 5th Army, was posted to the city as the new commander of the Leningrad Front, while Khozin was earmarked for command of the Volkhov's 'operational group' which now took the place of Meretskov's Volkhov Front. Thus the six armies stretched out from lake Ladoga to Ilmen came under Leningrad's command, which was subdivided into two independent command groups, one in Leningrad, the other at Malaya Vishera, where Khozin installed himself. The three armies operating within the blockade lines, trapped in the city, came under Govorov, himself an artillery specialist who from the outset devoted much of his attention to organizing the 'artillery defence' of the city. This duplication of staffs did nothing to ease the position of the Leningrad Front, and to the men on the spot, Khozin apart, the decision to wind up the Volkhov Front seemed senseless.

The purely defensive preparations involved orders to build up strong positions in the rear of the Bryansk, South-Western and Southern Fronts on a line running from Voronezh, through Starobelsk to Rostov; the rings of anti-tank ditches and the dottings of fire-points were also planned for the towns of Voronezh, Rostov, Saratov and Stalingrad, for which the local defence committees assumed responsibility. Apart from Stalin's personal re-deployment of commanders assigned to his special missions, decisions taken in the name of the *Stavka* in early April produced the liquidation of Zhukov's 'Western theatre' command and the subordination of the Western and Kalinin Fronts to direct

Stavka control, the proposal to subordinate the Bryansk Front to *Stavka* control, and the establishment of a new theatre command, the 'North Caucasus theatre' (including the Sevastopol defenders, the Kerch armies and the Caucasus troops) under Marshal Budenny, Timoshenko being left with South-Western and Southern Fronts as the components of his 'South-Western theatre' command. Of the entire nine Fronts (and two independent armies), those at the centre covering the approaches to Moscow were forthwith pulled into a tight net of highly centralized control.

Although the General Staff and the *Stavka* (and the majority of Front commanders, according to Marshal Vasilevskii) in March-April argued that any major German offensive would be directed against Moscow and 'the central region', Soviet intelligence reports in this same period indicated a German intention to strike in the south. The General Staff estimate was based on the evidence of German strength, that the most powerful concentration still remained at 'the centre'. Stalin for his part had at his disposal perhaps the most effective intelligence apparatus of any, operating right at the heart of German decision-making, the fantastically well-informed 'Lucy', whom Stalin personally added to the strength of Soviet intelligence agents in July or August, 1941: instructions dictated by Stalin to this end were passed to Foote and Rado, and thereafter the information assembled by 'Lucy' and 'Werther' received the highest priority. Data on German strategic plans, dispositions and operational intentions on the Eastern Front came daily from 'Lucy', whose real identity 'the Centre' in Moscow never learned, but whose information (as Alexander Foote also learned subsequently when he was interrogated in Moscow about a possible 'fix') provided the basis for shaping Timoshenko's Kharkov offensive. The over-all result, however, was that in the late spring of 1942 Hitler's attention was directed to the flanks, the south in particular, and Stalin's to the centre, thereby sweeping aside all the intelligence data; a little later, Stalin expressed vehement dissatisfaction with the work of Soviet intelligence operators (apparently because they produced incontrovertible proof of Hitler's 'southern' designs). Another of Stalin's personal inputs into the 1942 strategic plan was the assumption that a Second Front was a foregone conclusion this year, whereupon German front-line and reserve units would be drained off the Eastern Front. Although his Red Army Day message (23 February) sounded a more guarded tone than his November 1941 speech (and alarmed the British Foreign Office by its lack of reference to 'Allied' forces), Stalin had not yet abandoned his idea of clearing as much Soviet territory as possible. His advanced outposts, like Dorogobuzh, he intended to hold. While guarding the centre, Moscow, against any repetition of the 'near-thing' of 1941, he intended to punch forward wherever he could. He might conceivably de-blockade Leningrad, liberate Kharkov and the Crimea. The latest *Stavka* directive to the Western Front command had prescribed the line Belyi-Dorogobuzh-Yelnaya and on to the south-west of Smolensk as the objective to be reached by 20 April, but the spring thaw bringing the *rasputitsa*, the soggy, clinging inland seas of mud, dragged defender and attacker into immobility. Belov, locked in the German rear, proposed to Zhukov that another gap be blown in the Yukhnov-Roslavl road, that his second echelon (now virtually another cavalry corps under General Pliev) be moved through, and that the Western and Kalinin Fronts link up at Yartsevo, but on 26 April Belov's HQ received a radio signal that 50th Army, essential to open and hold the gap, had gone over to the defensive. Belov then knew that the attempt against Army Group Centre was finally off.

During the winter months, thanks to superhuman exertions in ferocious conditions, the industrial plants in the deep Urals hinterland had turned out more than 4,500 tanks, some 3,000 aircraft, nearly 14,000 guns and over 50,000 mortars. For commanders used to having a score or so of tanks, the new armoured unities came as novel surprise, the tank corps which presaged the tank armies, formations fitted out with the new models – KV, T-34 and T-70 tanks. Of the four tank corps which arrived in April on the Bryansk Front (1st, 3rd, 4th and 16th Corps) each had 24 KV tanks, 88 T-34s, and 69 light tanks, while the tank brigades had half their complement in T-60 light tanks. Golikov had finally 1,500 tanks at his disposal. Timoshenko was building up to a strength of 1,200 tanks. Two tank corps were on their way to the Western Front to form a strike force. Responsible for this reorganization was Colonel-General of Tank Troops Yakov Nikolayevich Fedorenko, a permanent member of the *Stavka*, one-time sailor in the Imperial Russian Navy, an early volunteer in the Red Army and commander of an armoured train in the Civil War, now chief of the Armoured Forces Administration of the Red Army. As yet, the Red Army had nothing to compare with the German Army's *Sturmgeschütz*, the much feared assault guns, but ideas were in the air for a Soviet self-propelled gun, the *samokhodnaya ustanovka* (SU) which finally evolved rather as a turretless tank. Red Army armoured forces, nevertheless, were on their way back, about to suffer one more terrible baptism of fire though that circumstance was mercifully hidden from the enthusiastic but insufficiently trained corps commanders.

While the oozing, glutinous fronts pinioned the armies and their machines, both sides concentrated on their plans and pressed forward with their preparations, each in its own way searching for the 'decisive solution' in the coming campaigns. Hitler, aiming for the final destruction of the Red Army and the elimination of the vital sources of Soviet strength, '*die wichtigsten kriegswirt-schaftlichen Kraftquellen*', set down his objectives in *Weisung Nr. 41* dated 5 April, committing himself to the drive on the flanks, in particular in the south, '*Durchbruch in den Kaukasusraum*' towards the oil and grain, towards the easterly Soviet supply lines, towards winning Turkey to the German side and towards shutting Russia off from Iran. West of Stalingrad, between the Donets and the Don, two great German pincers driving from North and South would meet and squeeze out all Soviet resistance: thereafter, German forces would drive down into the Caucasus, striking between the Black Sea and the Caspian. That had been mooted originally as Operation 'Siegfried', but now, with all the heroes of history and mythology spurned, it emerged as Operation 'Blau' ('Case Blue'). Stalin's *Stavka* continued meanwhile to convert all strategic 'planning' wherever possible into more and more offensive action, in sum neither the offensive nor the defensive prevailing. The *Stavka* and the General Staff persisted in believing that Moscow was the basic German aim, and therefore the Western and Bryansk Fronts were slab-sided with armour, their rear deepened with major reserves. Of one thing apparently Stalin was immovably convinced: the German drive in the south was merely a feint, designed to drain off Soviet reserves from the vital Moscow axes. Even when he had in his own hands the operational orders specifying the movements for Operation 'Blau', Stalin dismissed the seriousness of these intentions and abused his intelligence operators for not having uncovered the 'real' German intentions.

9

High Summer and the Road to Stalingrad

On 1 April 1942, at a time when estimating Russian strength in the field and forecasting Russian intentions was of critical importance, *Oberstleutnant* Reinhardt Gehlen took over the German General Staff intelligence organization for the Eastern Front, *Fremde Heere Ost* ('Foreign Armies: East'), from Kinzel. In the sleek, soft-spoken lieutenant-colonel, the German command had found a master of the craft of intelligence, deception and penetration. Not that Gehlen was a beginner. He played an important part in the briefing for 'Barbarossa', exploiting his 'contacts' inside the Soviet Union, the agents planted in the Baltic states, the Ukraine and the Crimea, but it was after the opening of hostilities with the Soviet Union that Gehlen displayed his astonishing talents in handling Russian prisoners of war, working upon those willing to co-operate with the Germans with great deftness and finally infiltrating them behind the Soviet lines, not infrequently into significant positions. (To turn over Gehlen's files is to come upon a vast stock of information on the Soviet Union: the reports of the '*V-männer*', Gehlen's own agents, statistics of Soviet industry, detailed compilations of Soviet order of battle, careful and informative analysis of captured mail, the tortuous trails of the *Funkspiele*, the 'radio games' played with fake radio stations and decoy operators all to trap Soviet agents, and at each turn bulging dossiers of Soviet strength, reinforcement, movement and preparation.)

Success of a spectacular kind came early for Gehlen. In the spring of 1942, within the special 'collection camps' and interrogation centres set aside for Soviet prisoners of war who showed some willingness to collaborate, Gehlen found a certain Mishinskii, senior commissar and high Party official (from the Moscow organization) taken prisoner in the ghastly days of October 1941. Beguiled and bribed by Gehlen, the disconsolate Mishinskii was persuaded to work for Germany, briefed for an espionage mission and carefully infiltrated behind the Soviet lines, impressively loaded with 'information' and primed with his story of daring escape from the Germans. The 'escape' was a myth and the 'information' planted by Gehlen, but on the strength of both Mishinskii bought his way back to favour at home and to a job in headquarters in Moscow (an operation code-named Flamingo). It was from this highly placed source that

Gehlen soon received his 'high-level' reports about secret Soviet conferences in the summer of 1942. Meanwhile other prisoners passed through the Gehlen pipeline, finding their way to army units, staffs, Party organizations and industrial posts, a spreading net of informers and agents cast well behind the front-line.

Nor did Gehlen ignore the traditional methods of acquiring information about enemy intentions and capabilities. In March and April 1942 patient work with card-indexes and with the collation of every conceivable scrap of information yielded invaluable results. From internal Soviet sources (newspapers, reported conversations and intercepts of broadcasts) and external sources (such as the German military attaché in Ankara or the Japanese military attaché in Kuibyshev) a steady stream of items indicated an impending Russian blow in the South. *Stab Walli*, a highly specialist German intercept and evaluation agency, reported at the end of April a conversation between Central Committee member Nossenko and the editor of *Pravda* emphasizing Soviet intentions to wrench the initiative from the Germans and to go over to the offensive on or about 1 May, the day on which Stalin himself issued another optimistic 'May Day order' hinting that the war could be ended in 1942; all this data emanating from agents and intercepts was packed into a special *Fremde Heere Ost* file, '*Angriff-Charkow: Chi-Abwehrmeldung*'. On 10 April, in the first of his major presentations dealing with Soviet intentions, Gehlen argued that a *Gesamtangriff*, a general turn to the offensive, was out of the question, but that *Teilangriffen*, Stalin's 'partial offensives', might well be expected where the German line was weak or in the vicinity of vital objectives. The Soviet *Schwerpunkt* would be in the south, though at the moment it was impossible to state with certainty whether positional defence or spoiling attacks would materialize; Moscow would be very firmly buttressed and Soviet attempts to break the Leningrad blockade were a distinct possibility. Three weeks later, on 1 May, Gehlen enlarged on these preliminary submissions in an eleven-page report, repeating once again that the general Soviet posture was and would remain defensive, but that *Zermübungsangriffe*, 'wearing down attacks', were very likely, against Army Group Centre, against the northern wing of Army Group South and from the Izyum bulge, where, to judge by the movements of the Soviet 28th Army and the development of the Soviet 6th and 38th Armies, a 'Kharkov offensive' was very likely. Now it looked as if the Soviet command was organizing 'several *Schwerpunkte*', but from none of them was there any likelihood of a major breakthrough.

For the 'Kharkov offensive', which Gehlen practically spelled out, Marshal Timoshenko (who had been assigned to command the South-Western Front as well as the 'theatre' as a whole, with Lieutenant-General F.Ya. Kostenko as his deputy) had a combined force (South-Western and Southern Fronts) of 640,000 men, 1,200 tanks, 13,000 guns and mortars with 926 planes. Gorodnyanskii's 6th Army would strike for Kharkov from the south, while Major-

General Bobkin's 'Army group' also operating from within the Izyum bulge would go for Krasnograd and thus secure 6th Army from the south-west: the northern prong of the pincer would come from the Volchansk area, with a shock group headed by Lieutenant-General Ryabyshev's 28th Army, plus flank units of 21st and 38th Army, to drive on Kharkov from the north-east and finally link up with the southern prong emerging from the bulge. Malinovskii's Southern Front received the general assignment of securing the southern face of the Izyum bulge with Podlas's 57th Army and Kharitonov's 9th. For the Kharkov blow, Timoshenko assembled twenty-three rifle divisions, two cavalry and two tank corps; the offensive would open on the morning of 12 May. While Timoshenko hurried to finish the preparations, Golikov of the Bryansk Front had received on 20 April a *Stavka* directive prescribing two quite disconnected attacks with 48th and 40th Armies in the Kursk-Lgov area; attacking only on the right with limited forces seemed to Golikov and Zakharov to indicate that the *Stavka* was 'saving up' for defence against a German push in the Orel-Tula direction. But when Golokov arrived at the *Stavka* on 23 April, Stalin had fresh instructions for him: the Bryansk Front was to attack Orel, using 61st and 48th Armies in 'concentric blows' to outflank Orel from the north-west and south-west, using part of 3rd and 13th Armies also. The Bryansk Front must be ready to take the offensive by 10–12 May, the date allotted to Timoshenko. His operational planning finished by 5 May, Golikov found that stocks of fuel and ammunition were still too low, and he therefore sought a postponement until 16 May, to which the *Stavka* formally agreed but left Timoshenko's start-time unaltered at 12 May. Thus from the outset, two Fronts, the Bryansk and Southern, were operationally isolated from Timoshenko's offensive which nevertheless anticipated by six days the German plan, Operation 'Fridericus', to eliminate the bulge by driving in the shoulders from north and south.

On the morning of 12 May, preceded by an hour of artillery and air bombardment, Timoshenko's northern and southern prongs jabbed into Paulus's Sixth Army which for three days and nights rocked and lurched in a highly dangerous situation as waves of Soviet riflemen and slabs of Soviet armour crashed down on it. From Volchansk 28th Army advanced more than twelve miles and in the south Gorodnyanskii's 6th Army struck out more than fifteen miles from the bulge. The evening of 14 May was the moment for Timoshenko to loose his armour and mobile formations through 6th Army. The marshal held back for two reasons; he anticipated an even more favourable opportunity and he restrained 21st Tank Corps precisely because his intelligence staff reported, mistakenly, as it turned out, a strong concentration of German armour at Zmiev (north-west of Balakleya). While Gorodnyanskii and Bobkin were sweeping out to the south-west of Kharkov, Paulus by dint of desperate exertion managed to hold Ryabyshev's 28th to the north and only a dozen miles from Kharkov. With the whole front heaving, von Bock himself resorted to desperate measures: he decided to mount Operation Fridericus but with one prong only aimed straight to the south of the Izyum bulge, where Kleist's First Panzer and the Seventeenth Army would dig into Timoshenko's open flank. Kleist would go in at first light on 17 May (the day on which Timoshenko had finally resolved to commit 21st Tank Corps).

At 03.15 hours on 17 May the first German assault units began to bite into the southern sector of the bulge. By noon they were ten miles into the positions held by 9th Army, threatening the rear of 57th Army and the entire Soviet shock group battering its way north-west from the bulge. To stiffen 9th Army Malinovskii at once drew 5th Cavalry Corps, one rifle division and a tank brigade out of reserve: south of Izyum itself 38th Army went on to the defensive but the German armoured strike groups relentlessly severed Malinovskii's communications. That evening Timoshenko's Military Soviet sent off an urgent report to the *Stavka* pleading for reinforcements to hold the bulge. Stalin agreed to make the men available, but they would need three days to be on the scene. The German thrust had already speared its way to the Northern Donets and *Stuka* squadrons, ploughing up the Soviet rear, had cut Timoshenko off from the Soviet troops trying to hold in the south. Both in the *Stavka* and at Timoshenko's HQ arguments raged about halting the whole Soviet offensive on Kharkov with the rear in such deadly peril. The *Stavka* ordered Timoshenko to continue his Kharkov drive, though the northern hook was blocked and halted and the southern swung away into empty air. Vasilevskii at the General Staff insisted that without *Stavka* reserves in the vicinity the Kharkov offensive should and must be stopped until Timoshenko pulled back 21st and 23rd Tank Corps to fight defensive actions against Kleist.

Stalin himself talked to Timoshenko that night; he was assured that defensive measures were adequate and therefore overrode Vasilevskii's opinion. But in the morning the situation was graver still: on 18 May Kleist had torn a forty-mile gap in 9th Army's positions and laid bare the communications of Soviet forces in the bulge. The situation in this slashing battle within a battle was careering out of control. At his Yelets HQ Golikov had already on 16 May received a *Stavka* signal that his offensive assignments must be altered and the next day Lieutenant-General P.I. Bodin, special emissary of the *Stavka*, arrived at Bryansk Front HQ with news that Timoshenko's offensive was in serious straits. The 40th Army on Golikov's extreme left (at the junction with Timoshenko) was now to go into action supported by the entire Front fighter and bomber forces, to relieve the pressure on Timoshenko. But the 40th was far from ready, although Golikov went to 40th HQ to speed up preparations. By the time it was fit to go into action, the *Stavka* had no hope of restoring the situation at Kharkov.

Vasilevskii once again during the day (18 May) approached Stalin about breaking off the offensive at Kharkov, to which Stalin returned an obdurate refusal. In the evening, Nikita Khrushchev, Timoshenko's commissar, telephoned

Vasilevskii and asked him to intercede with Stalin again, who once again laid down his iron negative about breaking off the offensive. Only on the evening of 19 May did Timoshenko order a halt to the offensive, to which Stalin finally agreed; now 6th, 57th Armies and Bobkin's 'Army group' stood in grave danger of encirclement, while a new danger loomed from the north as Paulus struck down into the bulge from the shoulder at Balakleya. Like fiery wasps trapped in a bottle, the Soviet armies turned inwards and stabbed at the German pincers, which by 22–3 May were on the point of closing. Timoshenko had got the worst of all possible worlds, his offensive blunted and his defence broken; on 13 May, his intelligence staff got hold of a captured German document, giving an outline of German plans at Kharkov, but it took four days to get this information to Timoshenko, when the flood was actually upon him. Kostenko now took command of the 6th and 57th Armies trapped in the Izyum pocket. Formations were running low on fuel and ammunition, trying desperately to blast a hole in the German ring; by the light of flares, massed Russian infantry attacks swayed against the German gun positions, but whichever way they swung, these columns met intense German fire. With tanks in support, Russian infantry with arms linked charged savagely against the rim of the pocket seeking a way to the Izyum road. After a week of appalling slaughter was over, Kostenko, Bobkin, Podlas and Gorodnyanskii with thousands of their infantrymen lay dead in the damp heat of the battlefield. Gorodnyanskii, one of the staunchest men at Smolensk in 1941 and a general of whom his troops had said 'a bullet will never get him', shot himself. Isolated groups, like that led by General Batyunya from Moskalenko's 38th Army filtered eastwards, but more than 200,000 Red Army men marched west as prisoners of war, while German troops picked over a massive pile of booty. It was too late to rectify the mistake which Timoshenko spelled out in his final report to the *Stavka* on the collapse of the Kharkov offensive:

As subsequent events showed, it would have been more correct to have broken off further offensive operations by 6 Army, withdrawn 18.5 from the offensive and turned eastwards not only one tank corps, but in fact the entire body of 6 and 57 Armies. Such a decision would have established more favourable conditions for warding off the blow by the Barvenkovo concentration of enemy forces.

'Subsequent events' from 20–30 May were the appalling clusters of Russian dead at the edges of the German gun-pits sited on the ring within the punctured bulge.

The disasters at Kharkov, grievous as they were, formed but a portion of the calamity in the south, where at Kerch Mekhlis threw away twenty-one divisions of three armies (47th, 51st and 44th) in a nightmare of confusion and incompetence. On the morning of 8 May, Manstein's Eleventh Army moved off, wireless deception and conspicuous deployment having ensured that the attention of Kozlov and Mekhlis was drawn to the possibility of a German attack to the north, though Manstein aimed to strike into the southern bulge. The Parpach 'neck' across which Mekhlis had earlier tried to burst into the Crimea was fortified with obstacles and fire-points: further to the rear a second defence line lay at the 'Tartar Ditch', defences which covered Kerch itself. Kozlov simply strung his troops out in a long line, with reserves gathered more or less in clumps. When the German assault came, it completely overwhelmed the Crimean Front command whose operational 'control' consisted of interminable, rambling and aimless sessions of the Military Soviet from which issued a stream of useless orders. Once the German attack opened every formation was committed with the exception of one rifle and one cavalry division. In the midst of this woeful muddle Mekhlis tried to insure his position with Stalin by sending him a special signal on 8 May:

This is no time to make complaints, but I must submit a report so that the *Stavka* knows about the Front commander. On 7 May, that is on the eve of the enemy offensive, Kozlov summoned the Military Soviet to study plans for forthcoming operations to capture Oi-Asanom. I advised that this proposal should be set aside and that orders should be issued without delay to the armies concerning the expected enemy offensive. In the orders duly signed the Front commander indicated in more places than one that the enemy offensive was to be expected 10–15 May, and suggested working things out until 10 May and with all command staff, formation commanders and staffs studying a defence plan for the armies. This was done when the whole situation on the previous day pointed to the fact that on the following day the enemy would attack. At my insistence the erroneous parts of the operational appreciation were corrected. Kozlov also opposed moving reinforcements into the sector of 44th Army.

To this blatant attempt to wriggle out of the responsibilities of a 'Stavka representative', Stalin returned a sardonic reply:

You are adopting the strange position of a detached observer who accepts no responsibility for the affairs of the *Krimfront* [Crimean Front]. That is a very comfortable position, but is one which absolutely stinks. On the Crimean Front, you – you – are no detached onlooker but a responsible representative of the *Stavka*, responsible for all the successes and failures of the Front and obliged to correct errors by the command on the spot. You along with the command are responsible for the fact that the left flank of the Front is wretchedly weak. If 'the whole situation pointed to the fact that tomorrow the enemy will attack', and you did not take all possible measures to repulse him, limiting yourself to mere passive criticism, then the worse for you. This means that you still do not understand that you were sent to the Crimean Front not in the capacity of *Goskontrol* [Mekhlis's civilian appointment] but as a responsible representative of the *Stavka*.

You demand that I change Kozlov and send you some kind of Hindenburgs. But you are not to know that we have no reserve of Hindenburgs. Your task in the Crimea is not complicated and you should be able to deal with it. If you had not used ground-attack aircraft on subsidiary targets but against enemy tanks and infantry, the enemy would not have penetrated your front and the tanks would not have gone through. It is not necessary to be a Hindenburg in order to understand such a simple matter after sitting for two months on the Crimean Front.

This verbal lashing, the first document ever to lay down what was meant by the 'responsibility' of *Stavka* 'representatives', Mekhlis deserved in full and flowing measure, the man who set out to humiliate Red Army commanders himself finally brought low, though again it cost many Red Army men their lives.

Manstein *versus* Mekhlis was no match: disaster rolled with terrifying speed upon the Crimean Front. On the morning of 10 May the *Stavka* signalled Mekhlis to pull all Soviet forces back to the 'Tartar Ditch', but all control had by now gone; units streamed back in any order and on the evening of 14 May Manstein's troops were fighting in the outskirts of Kerch itself. For the next six days Kozlov tried to organize a beach-head evacuation of his men and equipment to the Taman peninsula. Over these remnants of the Crimean Front Manstein now laid a mass artillery barrage, blowing men, guns and tanks and lorries to pieces; with more gunfire the Germans drove off the Black Sea Fleet motor gunboats trying desperately to lift the troops off the beach where they were being battered to death. In this 'ghastly mess', which cost the Crimean Front 176,000 men, most of its 350 tanks and 3,500 guns, Budenny as North-Caucasus *Glavkom* struggled to exercise some control over the situation but this broke down in the great welter of chaos and confusion.

General Zhukov was standing by when Stalin listened to the reports of the disaster telephoned to him: 'You see, that's where going on the defensive gets you' was his comment to Zhukov, followed by his threat to mete out 'severe punishment to Mekhlis, Kulik and Kozlov, to prevent others "loafing about" '. At Budenny's HQ, where survivors of the Crimean Front command collected, the disaster was investigated in detail for the benefit of the *Stavka*. The Front intelligence officer, Kopalkin, had evidently emphasized the likelihood of a German attack on 5 May but Kozlov merely dawdled: the report of the Operations Staff (Crimean Front) indicated that Front and Army reserves were concentrated almost exclusively in the north, but only one division was assigned to defend the straggling 'Tartar Ditch'. The moment the German attack opened, Marshal Budenny had ordered a counter-attack with four divisions supported by armour, but there was no hope of carrying this out since the forward HQs, exposed and uncamouflaged, were obliterated by Luftwaffe dive-bombers when German planes everywhere commanded the skies. Some units of 51st Army tried to strike back only to become hopelessly tangled with Soviet troops pulling precipitately out of the line. Finally, Kerch itself, which the *Stavka* demanded must be held at all costs, fell all too speedily.

The repercussions of this calamity spread out in a great wave of demotions. Mekhlis, whom the younger officers hated, was reduced in rank to corps commissar, removed as a Deputy Defence Commissar (and finally kicked out as head of the Main Political Administration of the Red Army). Kozlov, with his commissar Shamanin, was demoted and dismissed; Major-General P.P. Vechny (Front Chief of Staff) was reduced in rank with two formation com-

manders, Lieutenant-General Chernyak (44th Army) and Major-General
Kolganov (47th Army). Major-General Nikolayenko, aviation commander,
also lost his command: Belov, deprived of even token air cover on the Western
Front in December 1941, had once radioed to him in a great rage when he was
aviation commander on Zhukov's left flank, 'Stop being neutral: come out
fighting.' The collapse of Soviet air operations over Kerch had a calamitous
effect on ground operations: the Luftwaffe roamed free, smashing up the few
control centres, tearing formations and units apart with repeated aerial strikes,
mangling the front without respite as it crumbled and finally huddled at the sea.

Now that the Izyum bulge had been crushed in, German formations came
up to their start-line for the summer offensive. Destroying Soviet armies on the
Kerch peninsula was a further prerequisite for the crushing blows Hitler
planned, and wiping out Mekhlis's men made the reduction of Sevastopol, the
huge armoured nut which Manstein set out to crack, a readier proposition.
Sevastopol, ringed with forts on its perimeter and its life sustained by tunnelling
deep below ground, had already thrown off one major German assault at the end
of 1941. Now, in the freshness of a May morning, 17 May, Vice-Admiral
Oktyabrskii, the defence commander, assembled the Black Sea Fleet Military
Soviet, formation commanders, civilian authorities and Party officials to report
on the disaster at Kerch to the east and to issue final instructions to defend the
base against the rain of fire and destruction which all knew must surely and
swiftly come. Although the Soviet Navy squads had shown themselves staunch,
even unruffled defenders, the political staff sent morale-stiffening 'agitational
groups' to every unit and section, each battery and installation. The garrison,
some 106,000 strong, was deployed throughout many hundreds of concrete or
armoured gun-positions, clustered in the monster heavy gun-batteries or at their
stations in the rings of trenches screened by barbed wire and minefields, together
with the rocket-launchers sited deep in the steep slopes within the cliffs to the
west. The outer defences were largely trenches, covering the second belt with
the giant underground forts and the principal batteries located between the
valley of the Belbek and Severnaya Bay (screening the north-east approaches)
and finally the maze of pill-boxes and firing-points protecting the city itself,
all miles of defensive works and innumerable strong points, many of them sited
where only storming could reduce them. Faced with this immobile but armoured
monster, Manstein knew that mere conventional pre-attack bombardment
would scarcely blow a whole in the defences. He proposed therefore to lay down
not less than five days of 'annihilation fire' and to pour in a stream of aerial
bombardment. To reduce the great Soviet forts Manstein began to range the
mighty German mortars, king of which was *Karl* hurling a two-ton projectile:
to bore down into the Soviet fortifications he moved up *Big Dora*, an artillery
piece the height of a three-storey house, its barrel ninety feet long, drawn to its
firing point by a small armada of sixty railway trucks. *Big Dora* had a range of
just under thirty miles.

At dawn on 7 June, as German gunfire intensified, Manstein's Eleventh Army supported by Rumanian troops opened the final assault on fortress Sevastopol, twenty-seven days of unrelieved bombardment and savage attack which raged on by the hour as each Soviet position had to be smothered in men and fire before opposition was literally blotted out. To the north and south the enormous Soviet forts, like *Fort Stalin* or the massive *Maksim Gorkii* emplacement no less than 300 yards long, had first to be blown out of the ground in which they were anchored with all their concrete and steel; even when cracked open, the forts fought on and their labyrinthine interiors had to be cleared of Soviet marines and riflemen fighting gas-masked in the smoke and choking stench. As in December, the main German blow came from the north and was directed at Severnaya Bay, with a second attack mounted from the south-east. After ten days the Sevastopol garrison was dangerously low on ammunition and running short of men, many of whom were now entombed in their defences or merely solitary riflemen ringed by the dead and dying; piercing the German blockade, Black Sea Fleet warships brought in more ammunition and 3,000 men of the 138th Brigade, but this link could scarcely be maintained much longer. Between 22–6 June, the flotilla leader *Tashkent* brought in the very last reinforcements, took off wounded and then made course for Novorossiisk. The link by surface ship snapped, and thereafter only Soviet submarines could move in: seventy-eight submarine sorties shifted 4,000 tons of ammunition, oil and medical supplies. But the sea of fire rolled relentlessly on Sevastopol: the last submarines snaked out of the ruined port area: over the city hung the smoke of destruction and the dust palls of bombardment: below ground, troops and workers mingled in the underground factories, hospitals and command posts, but time had almost run out.

During the night of 30 June, Oktyabrskii assembled the Military Soviet in the defence control centre to discuss the evacuation orders just received from the *Stavka*: Major-General Petrov had already called a conference the day before when German units finally broke through to the northern shore of Severnaya bay and now under cover of darkness launched battle groups in assault boats across the dark water towards the southern shore and the city itself. Petrov's divisional commanders reported that their strength had almost ebbed away, with formations ground down to less than 300 men each. The survivors were falling back all along the line, blowing up batteries as they went, though here and there isolated strong points held out fiercely: having fired their last rounds, the crew of Coastal Battery B-35 blew up themselves and their guns as German infantrymen closed in for the kill.

Stalin himself radioed personal categorical orders that top commanders, Party and administrative officials must be brought out by two submarines. Oktyabrskii and Petrov flew out unscathed at the very last moment. Elsewhere along the cliffs of Severnaya bay troops and civilians huddled by the water, waiting for small boats and light craft to take them off and through the German blockading screen at the mouth. Desperate groups blew themselves up in caves or fought it out to the last round. Other detachments tried to break east to the Soviet partisans or slipped through the German ring only to end huddled at Khersones point. Slowly and agonizingly the remnants of the Soviet garrison dwindled and died, like the soldiers and civilians who immured themselves deep in the 'Kerch catacombs', cavernous communal tombs from which resistance flickered on until it was snuffed out when German troops poured in choking toxic smoke. Only then, with the passage of months, did the Sevastopol defenders cease struggling, and all that was left was a terrible panoply of corpses, men and women starved or suffocated to death.

Faced with a serious crisis on the Volkhov with Vlasov's 2nd Shock Army, Stalin called Meretskov to Moscow on 8 June to attend a full session of the *Stavka* where Vlasov's fate was being decided. Stalin was blunt and to the point: 'We made a great mistake joining the Volkhov to the Leningrad Front. Although General Khozin is there on the Volkhov, he has handled things badly. He has not carried out the *Stavka*'s order about pulling the Second Shock Army back.' Stalin therefore proposed to re-form the Volkhov Front and send Meretskov up there with Vasilevskii: the relevant directives Meretskov would get from Marshal Shaposhnikov. Vlasov's army had been cut off a second time, and at the end of May the German ring was tightly drawn, trapping Vlasov in the swampland west of the Volkhov with nine divisions and half a dozen brigades, starved, disorganized and by now bled white. When Meretskov and Vasilevskii got to Malaya Vishera, Stelmakh could only present a hazy picture of the situation; Vlasov's rearguards were slowly falling back eastwards, but the 2nd Shock was desperate for ammunition and supplies. Two armies, 59th and 52nd, were trying to widen the corridor between themselves and Vlasov. On 10 June, Meretskov and Vasilevskii ordered fresh attacks to make a passage to the 2nd Shock, attacks which they saw broken to pieces by repeated *Stuka* strikes on the Soviet infantry. After a week of slogging battles, 29th Tank Brigade cut a 400-yard passage to Vlasov, opening on to the railway line at Myasnoi Bor down which the wounded were passed, and through which the remnants of 2nd Shock suddenly rushed in great disorder. German dive-bombers and guns closed the gap; from the west German formations compacted Vlasov even more tightly, bringing his whole area under artillery fire by 23 June, the very day when at 23.00 hours 2nd Shock was scheduled to make its last attempt to break out, with drivers, gunners and signallers (the signals centre by now smashed to pieces) jammed into infantry units. All heavy equipment was to be destroyed. In what was a last desperate push of men driven beyond all reason by dreadful hardship, two small holes were punched in the German line, and the survivors trickled out, but at 09.30 hours on 25 June it was (as Meretskov says) 'all over'. On the previous day Vlasov had ordered his men to break up into small parties and make their way where and how they might, to flee the swampy death-trap.

Meretskov lost all contact with Vlasov, who was finally found by German intelligence officers in a farmer's shed, harrowed by the immolation of his army and transformed from this point forward into an impassioned enemy of Stalin. Vlasov the general-prisoner became the organizer of the 'Russian Liberation Army', the ROA, recruiting its men from German prison camps and assembling under the banner of virulent anti-Bolshevism.

Though he ultimately appeared to be many things to many men, Vlasov was no mere dupe or puppet of the Germans: his interrogators were unanimous in emphasizing his intelligence and judgement (*Urteilsbildung*). His Soviet detractors branded him traitor, braggart and opportunist. There are hints that some were not sorry to see Vlasov with enough rope to hang himself; certainly Vlasov had run foul of Beria, who had his quarters searched and kept him under surveillance, a necessary precaution with a young, rising and popular general, and therefore his ordeal on the Volkhov caused no great heart-searching (though German intelligence interrogated a special group of parachutists who claimed they were sent in to get Vlasov out of the trap, but once down a sudden radio signal cancelled their mission). Vlasov's first 'document' – it has no special title – written at Vinnitsa and dated 3 August (1942), with a supporting signature from Colonel Bayerskii (formerly 41st Rifle Division commander) remains unique as an unadulterated expression of his own views: subsequent 'manifestos' had of necessity the air of concoction about them. Vlasov stressed the patriotism of the Russians (an observation which excited an exclamation mark from the German reader of the document) but also Stalin's determination to fight in a way which ruled out any popular rising or revolt; the Soviet Union would not fold up and crumple internally. The military and civilian mass must be transformed into an oppositional core against Stalin, so therefore a start should be made upon organizing a 'Russian army', which brought out another exclamation mark. (The idea of creating an indigenous anti-Stalin force, not merely in military terms, was Vlasov's basic idea and one for which he worked, whatever the stigma of treason, without flagging: this was his 'mission'.) There were other schemes for anti-Bolshevik 'oppositions' in the German files, but Vlasov had rank, prestige and reputation, all of them used to promote the *Wlassow-Aktion*, a sharp escalation in political warfare but one in which Vlasov felt himself betrayed and defrauded – '*ein billiger Propagandatrick*' – and more than once threatened suicide, or else demanded to be sent back to a prisoner-of-war camp. And in what German intelligence called the *Anti-Wlassow Aktion*, Stalin sent out his agents to kill Vlasov and to infiltrate his movement.

Tragic though the present outcome had been on the Volkhov, it was nothing compared to the torrent of disaster which began to sweep away Russian positions in the south, to which Kerch and Sevastopol had been merely bloody preliminaries. The German offensive was planned to develop in four stages: the Second Army and Fourth Panzer would break through Voronezh to the Don, the Sixth Army would break out west of Kharkov and destroy Soviet forces west of the Don, where Fourth Panzer would turn south: after encircling Stalingrad, the fourth and final phase was the drive for the Caucasus. This was Operation 'Blau', the execution of which fell largely to Army Group South and was timed to open on 28 June, when Army Group *Weichs* struck east of Kursk. This precipitated the summer crisis which entirely engulfed the Soviet command.

The aerial reconnaissance carried out by the Bryansk Front in mid June disclosed German concentrations in the region of Kolpina, Shchigra and Kursk, from which Golikov and Kazakov deduced the build-up of a new German strike force. This information (without precise order-of-battle details) was nevertheless passed to the General Staff; General Staff Intelligence responded to this very strangely, emphasizing in a telephone message that this was not the axis to watch but the northern wing of the Bryansk Front, since the German command was building up a force of not less than four Panzer divisions and ten infantry divisions in the Yukhnov area, to strike into the Western and Bryansk Fronts. Golikov therefore moved to his right flank, to supervise the preparations to parry a German attack on Tula.

Four days later the Front commands and the General Staff had a very rude awakening. On the morning of 19 June Major Reichel, Operations Officer of 23rd Panzer Division, crash-landed in a light plane at Nezhegol, just inside the Russian lines; contrary to Hitler's personal instructions about carrying orders in this fashion, Major Reichel had in his briefcase the operational orders for Stumme's 40th Panzer Corps and the outlines of the first phase of Operation 'Blau'. With Reichel missing, a German patrol went out and succeeded in finding the wrecked plane in a small valley, but of Major Reichel there was no sign – only two graves, yet only one body and that stripped of its uniform. In addition to the papers, Reichel carried a great deal more about Operation Blau in his head, so that the failure to find the major either dead or alive produced the gravest anxiety at Corps HQ and much higher. All the occupants of the plane had, in fact, been killed, but the Soviet infantrymen who came upon the wreck retrieved the briefcase with its 1:100,000 map and documents. The Reichel papers were sent at once to Front HQ, and that same day (19 June) Soviet HQ, South-Western Front, transmitted the contents of the captured papers to Bryansk Front HQ and sent the actual documents on to the General Staff in Moscow. Golikov at Bryansk now knew that 40th Panzer Corps (3rd, 23rd, Panzer Divisions, 29th Motorized Infantry, 100th and 376th Infantry Division) would attack from Volchansk to Novy Oskol, would take part in an offensive aimed at Voronezh and would commit its main force against Ostrogorzhsk. It was plain for all to see that the German blow was going to fall on the junction of the Bryansk and South-Western Fronts. The General Staff, its gaze riveted on Golikov's northern wing, had been disastrously wrong in its estimate of German intentions, and now to back up the information obtained from the Reichel papers Soviet reconnaissance planes were bringing in aerial photos of considerable German concentrations.

Golikov's officers still had no precise information on German order of battle, apart from knowing the number of formations committed to the first echelon; above all, there was nothing specific about German armoured strength. On 22 June, the date set in Reichel's papers for the German attack, Golikov reported by radio telephone to the *Stavka* that six or seven Panzer and motorized formations were definitely concentrating in the Kursk area and more reinforcements were moving up by rail; since Marshal Timoshenko had done nothing to strengthen 21st Army, Golikov sought express permission to appoint a special commander for the 'Voronezh zone'. Stalin and Shaposhnikov refused to agree to this, apparently suspecting a German trap. When the German attack failed to materialize, even Golikov's staff began to fear a 'plant' over the Reichel papers. Front HQ had already moved from the pleasantly hospitable town of Yelets to its battle-station at Arkhangelsk: Golikov checked defensive readiness with each army commander. But for all the tension of the night, the day broke peacefully, without a sign of attack.

During the next twenty-four hours, Golikov reported more German traffic in the direction of Kursk and movement from Orel to Kursk, but his orders remained unchanged and his actions limited to sending out Soviet planes to bomb German concentrations. At this point Golikov was ordered to report at once to the *Stavka* in Moscow, and here on 26 June he came up against Stalin. With the papers taken off Major Reichel lying before him, Stalin swept them aside and told Golikov in no uncertain terms that he did not believe a word of Operation 'Blau': more than that, Stalin proceeded to lash out at the whole incompetence of the intelligence staff who could come up with nothing better than this. As for Soviet intentions, it was absolutely vital, Stalin continued, that 'the enemy is given no chance to break our forces piece by piece, and so we ourselves have to strike blows at the enemy'. For this reason Golikov would prepare an operation to seize Orel in co-operation with the Western Front: Bryansk Front would launch its main attack with 48th Army supported by the 3rd and 13th Armies, while 61st Army was to outflank Orel from the north and west, all preparations to be complete by 5 July. The next day, back at his own Front HQ, Golikov reported this to his staff and on the morning of 27 June work began on planning the Orel operations which Stalin had ordered. The plan was basically the same as the one worked out during the spring, but this time the General Staff passed on certain points it wanted included. At 03.00 hours, 28 June the draft plan of the Orel offensive operation was ready.

Three hours later the alarm bells were ringing at Front HQ: persistent reports of intensive German activity rolled in from the entire length of the sector covered by 13th and 40th Armies. The dawn air reconnaissance planes brought in pictures of formidable German concentration at the junction of 13th and 40th Armies: German infantry battalions with tank support were already jabbing into the Soviet defences. Bryansk Front HQ made up its mind: Operation 'Blau' was definitely on and this was it. Precisely at 10.00 hours on this fine June

morning the *Stukas* hurtled down on the forward Soviet positions, and German
artillery battered the Soviet defences; the tanks and infantry came on afresh in
this first stage of the offensive on 'the Voronezh axis', while groups of twenty
to thirty German bombers with excellent fighter protection struck into the
Bryansk Front rear areas and deeper still, up to the river Don. By noon Golikov
was all too well aware that he was facing a major German offensive, but his
operations were severely hampered since Soviet reconnaissance planes, hunted
out of the battle zone by German fighters, could supply little or no information
on actual German movement and concentration. As for German strength, that
evening Golikov and Zakharov reckoned that not less than ten German
divisions were already committed including at least two or three Panzer
formations.

General Hauenschild's 24th Panzer Division crashed through two Soviet
divisions and raced for the river Kshen, where Golikov on the evening of 28
June moved up his armour, 16th and 1st Tank Corps. The *Stavka* now took
fright, ordering 4th and 24th Tank Corps up from Timoshenko's front, and
moving 17th Tank Corps from its own reserve up to Kastornoye. Golikov also
had Lizyukov's 5th Tank Army (2nd and 11th Tank Corps) on his Front.
Altogether, seven Soviet tank corps (1st, 16th, 17th, 4th, 24th, 2nd and 11th)
were converging for the Voronezh counter-attack, as the German offensive
rolled deeper into the gap being torn between 13th and 40th Armies; 24th
Panzer hurtled into 40th Army HQ, its trucks and wireless vans abandoned as the
staff was forced 'to hop it', in General Kazakov's phrase. Winding up at
Kastornoye, 40th command had lost contact with its divisions. During the night
of 30 June, Stalin spoke directly to Golikov:

> Two items are worrying us.
> First, the weak securing of your front on the river Kshen and north-east of Tim. We
> are concerned about this danger because the enemy can drive into the rear of 40th Army
> and surround our units. Secondly, we are uneasy about the weak securing of your Front
> near Livny. Here the enemy can drive into the rear of 13th Army. In this area Katukov
> (1st Tank Corps) will be operating, but Katukov has no second echelon worth talking
> about. Do you think both of these threats are real and how do you propose to deal with
> them?

Golikov replied that he thought the blow in the south, against 40th Army, the
worst: 13th was holding off the German infantry. Both 13th and 48th Army had
reserves. But Front HQ still had no firm contact with 4th and 24th Tank Corps,
and 17th Tank Corps was running out of fuel. Since he could not now count on
these formations, Golikov signalled for permission to pull back the left wing of
40th Army. The telegraph clicked back Stalin's refusal:

> [*Stalin*] 1 A straight, unprepared withdrawal by Parsegov's units (40th Army) to the
> Bystrik-Arkhangelsk line would be dangerous, since the line is not ready and the with-
> drawal would degenerate into sheer flight [*begstvo*].

2 The worst and the most inexcusable aspect of your work is losing contact with Parsegov's army and with Mishulin's (4th Tank Corps) and with Badanov (24th Tank Corps). Until you get your radio net working you will have no signals net at all and the whole of your Front will degenerate into a disorganized rabble [*sbrod*]. Why don't you link up with these tank corps through Fedorenko? Do you have a signals link with Fedorenko?

Stalin next dictated possible movements for the tank corps to bring them into action not on the German flanks but against their spear-heads. Golikov refused to submit his own plans to the *Stavka* and now set about passing Stalin's suggested dispositions to the corps which were controlled through a command centre at Kastornoye, a very weak link but the only radio channel he had available just then. Fedorenko, commander of the Red Army's armoured troops, had himself arrived in Kastornoye on 30 June and had immediately dispatched orders to Golikov about the movement of the tank corps. Meanwhile the *Stavka* continued to send Golikov orders for the tank operations; he was reminded that he had 'more than 1,000 tanks, the enemy less than 500' and that now 'everything depends on your skill in utilizing these forces and handling them reasonably (*po-chelovecheski*)'. With these armoured formations still milling about – Feklenko's 17th was 'manoeuvring', 24th Corps was still at Novy Oskol, 4th Corps had only advanced detachments in action – Golikov could scarcely hope to concentrate his tanks, for all their formidable number. At 02.00 hours, 1 July, Colonel-General Vasilevskii (after 26 June the new Chief of the General Staff now that Marshal Shaposhnikov was incapacitated by advancing illness) interrogated Golikov brutally by teleprinter about the fate of these tank corps:

The *Stavka* is dissatisfied that on your Front several of the tank corps have ceased to be tank formations and operate with infantry methods – examples: Katukov (1st Tank) instead of destroying enemy infantry spends a day surrounding two regiments and you evidently go along with this ... And where are these tanks? Do they have to operate like this? You are to get a tight grip on them at once, assign them specific tasks suited to tank corps and demand absolutely that these orders are carried out.

Golikov pointed out that Fedorenko had done no better, since he was handling the tank corps single-handed without a staff or signals centre and his orders, even his presence, complicated the work of his own HQ. Vasilevskii nevertheless told Golikov that Fedorenko was there to help and that Bryansk HQ should subordinate itself to Fedorenko with the tank operations. At 02.50 hours that same night, the Bryansk Front and the South-Western Front received permission to pull back their left and right wing formations respectively. On 30 June, German formations had smashed through 21st Army on Timoshenko's right and were going for Novy Oskol. Staff officers from 40th Army took off in small biplanes to try to locate their formations; several orders did reach Zhmachenko, deputy commander of the 40th, but the short July night gave little cover for disengagement.

On 2 July, Golikov was ordered to Voronezh, where two *Stavka* reserve armies, 6th and 60th, were put at his disposal: he deployed them north and south of the town, upon which 40th Army, 17th, 4th and 24th Tank Corps were falling back. By the evening of 3 July forward German elements were on the Don west of Voronezh into which Soviet troops and armour were being steadily packed. At this stage Stalin proceeded to pour in reinforcements to hold Voronezh and to seal up the forty-mile breach between the Bryansk and South-Western Fronts: Lizyukov's 5th Tank Army, at that time concentrated south of Yelets, was ordered to attack Army Group *Weichs* in the flank, and there were two more armies, tank brigades, artillery regiments and fighter squadrons on their way. The high command also engaged itself directly in the battle for Voronezh; Colonel-General Vasilevskii was ordered to Bryansk HQ, Fedorenko of the Armoured Forces was on the spot and Stalin fought at close range with a telephone receiver in his hands. The General Staff took upon itself the handling of 5th Tank Army: on the morning of 4 July, Vasilevskii was at Lizyukov's HQ, where a *Stavka* directive ordered preparations for an attack south-west of Voronezh. To the Bryansk command, it looked as if the High Command was going about 5th Tank's attack a little too gingerly: Lizyukov had more than 600 modern tanks, and he proposed to commit them in columns, when using his six brigades *en masse* would have been more effective. Lizyukov's lead units got into action, but the bulk of his tank army was slashed and pounded by the Luftwaffe: the attempt to blunt Hoth's Fourth Panzer spear-heads failed in spite of an over-all Soviet superiority in tanks, among them some 800 KVs and T-34s, though these encounters lasted five days in the heat and dust near the Don. The separate tank corps fought like rifle formations and were unwilling to break away from the actual rifle formations on the defensive. Stalin personally removed Feklenko from command of 17th Corps and ordered Major-General I.P. Korchagin, once a subaltern in the Imperial Russian Army who had taken service with the Red Army, to take over at once. But on 4 July, when Stalin hurled down his thunderbolts from Moscow, 17th Corps was practically wrecked.

As the fate of Voronezh was being decided, when on 3–4 July 48th Panzer Corps forced the Don, Vasilevskii told the Bryansk command 'in confidence' that a new front, the Voronezh Front, would soon be set up and that Golikov would assume control of it: a new commander would come to the Bryansk Front. Stalin had meanwhile telephoned Vasilevskii and ordered him to report to the *Stavka* not later than the morning of 5 July, just as German troops were beginning to fight their way into the western suburbs of Voronezh. Vasilevskii hurriedly assigned Lizyukov his counter-attack orders and left the control of the actual operations to Bryansk HQ staff. For all his recent obsession with the centre, Stalin was facing a grave situation in the south, where on a front of some 150 miles and to a depth of almost 80 the Bryansk and South-Western Fronts' defence lines had been pierced; with Paulus's Sixth Army at Ostrogorzhsk and now turning south, Timoshenko could no longer protect himself from this northerly blow which would cut into the rear of his own two Fronts (South-Western and Southern). With the full reality of Operation 'Blau' staring at them, Stalin, Vasilevskii and the permanent members of the *Stavka* raced to set up the Voronezh Front, which Lieutenant-General Vatutin was to command, while Stalin proposed that Rokossovskii (earlier wounded by a shell-splinter in the spine and only just returned to 16th Army) should take over the Bryansk Front from Golikov, who held a temporary command at Voronezh while his deputy, Lieutenant-General Chibisov, held the Bryansk Front post.

At the protracted nightly sessions of the *Stavka*, decisions of far-reaching importance were reached during the second week in July, when Stalin had to accept the significance of Operation 'Blau'; at the same time, Stalin continued his personal direction of the battle for Voronezh. And the 'hunt for culprits', the search for scapegoats went on without any let-up; quite unjustly Bagramyan was selected as scapegoat for the Kharkov disasters, blamed officially on 'poor staff work', so that as Timoshenko's chief of staff Bagramyan fell foul of Moscow's opinion. Quite soon, however, Timoshenko himself was to be relieved of his command (while Bagramyan went to 16th Army which Rokossovskii was on the point of leaving). Much to M.I. Kazakov's disgust, Golikov was now singled out for the disfavour over Voronezh, even though the fighting was far from finished. On 7 July, Stalin telephoned Golikov and put a direct question: 'Can you give a definite guarantee that Voronezh will be held?' Golikov very realistically pointed out that this was scarcely possible. Vatutin, present at the HQ as a 'General Staff representative', was summoned to the telephone and he proceeded to give a much more optimistic assessment. The root of Stalin's disquiet lay with a report, submitted through a separate channel, from the chief NKVD officer attached to the Bryansk/Voronezh Front, that Red Army troops had pulled out of Voronezh and only two regiments of NKVD men were holding the town. This was sheer nonsense, since 40th Army battled on in the university quarter and in the eastern suburbs, but it was enough apparently to set Stalin off on a rampage against the military command, conducted through the telephone. Lieutenant-General Antonyuk, 60th Army commander, in the midst of a session of his Military Soviet, was summoned to the telephone link with Moscow; he emerged from the small office white-faced and stunned and indicated that Chernyakhovskii, 18th Tank Corps commander, should take the line. Chernyakhovskii in his turn emerged as the new commander of 60th Army, repeating instructions that Korchagin was to take over his 18th Corps, while Colonel Polyuboyarov, Koniev's front armoured commander on the Kalinin Front, would arrive in twenty-four hours to assume command of 17th Tank Corps. As he made these changes, Stalin also appointed Vatutin Front commander at Voronezh and demoted Golikov to deputy commander.

The German northern wing had to be tied down at Voronezh (and Golikov had in fact done a reasonable job) to give Timoshenko a chance to pull his divisions back over the Oskol and the Donets, and finally over the Don; covered by rearguards, Timoshenko's troops had begun this withdrawal on a large scale and so far in an orderly fashion. In this, one German general saw the Russians asserting 'their old mastery' in rearguard fighting. For the first time in the war, the Red Army was visibly and definitely pulling out of a threatened encirclement and the *Stavka* issued orders for further withdrawal. At this present moment, although Vatutin's optimism was not wholly justified, Russian troops still controlled the north-south railway running through the easternmost part of Voronezh, when much depended on possession of those north-south road and rail links. These were the key to such strategic mobility as Stalin possessed, a mobility markedly inferior to that of the Germans and probably the basic factor in inducing a massive sense of caution in Stalin, who could not afford to be caught 'on the hop' between Leningrad, Moscow and the south-west. But German forces had turned unmistakably south-east, and Stalin had now to trundle his reserve armies out of the Moscow block to build up a new front in this direction. Timoshenko's South-Western Front, weakened as it had been by the May disasters, was collapsing under the blows rained on it by Paulus's Sixth Army. The Bryansk Front had now been split into two entities; with Timoshenko's HQ at Kalach (some ninety miles south-east of Voronezh), the *Stavka* decided to try binding the centre and left of South-Western Front to the Southern Front, but as Malinovskii's Southern Front was struck by Ruoff's Seventeenth Army and Kleist's First Panzer, this proved to be quite unworkable. On 12 July, with the South-Western Front practically ripped to pieces, its rear and that of the Southern Front threatened by the German south-easterly drive, *Stavka Directive No. 170495* formally set up the Stalingrad Front with Marshal Timoshenko in command, Nikita Khrushchev as commissar and Lieutenant-General P.I. Bodin as chief of staff. For troops, the Front was assigned three reserve armies, the 62nd under Major-General Kolpakchi, the 63rd under V.I. Kuznetsov and the 64th under V.N. Gordov, armies which were only slowly detraining or remained as yet on the move, their echelons stretching all the way back to Tula and the north, their infantry facing staggering forced marches to a 'front' whose location was practically unknown to the commanders.

The German breakthrough to the south-east brought an eruption in the Soviet command: whatever battles raged within the *Stavka*, Colonel-General Vasilevskii had clearly won one, that there must be no more 'stand-fast' disasters in the style of Kiev and Vyazma in 1941. There was, however, every reason to hang on grimly at Voronezh, not merely to hold German forces which might otherwise turn south, but also to cover the Tambov-Saratov area through which ran Moscow's communications with the east, and alternative oil supplies, since the Volga line had been under heavy German attack for some time. Although Stalin had apparently no very high opinion of his commanders, and even less of the bulk of the Red Army troops, he had no option but to accept withdrawal in the south-east. (Gehlen's special compilation of intelligence reports, *Wichtigste Abwehrmeldungen*, contains one secret report of a supposed *Stavka* session of 13 July, in which the withdrawal plan was propounded and accepted: suspect though that item is, since Stalin scarcely disclosed his plans in the presence of Chinese and American attachés, timely withdrawal orders were issued to Timoshenko and to Malinovskii.) At the same time, Stalin proposed to tie up German reserves at the centre and on the northern flank by ordering offensive operations by the Kalinin and Western Fronts in the Rzhev area (four armies to attack towards the end of July) and by a renewal of offensive operations in the Leningrad area, where for eight weeks artillery and armoured reinforcements had been moved in.

The Political Administration of the Red Army, *Glav*PURKKA, which had hitherto been in the hands of Mekhlis, did not ride this storm unscathed. The disasters at Kharkov and at Kerch set off a debate within the Central Committee about the present deficiencies in the 'mass-political work' conducted within the Red Army, and there was clearly something wrong. This conclusion was also of some assistance to Stalin, who was able to change his 'line' about the final defeat of Germany within the year without appearing to have changed his mind. In mid June, by a 'decision of the Central Committee', Mekhlis was relieved of his post as Chief of the Main Political Administration and replaced by the secretary of the Central Committee, the round, bespectacled and thoroughly Stalinist A.S. Shcherbakov. To keep *Glav*PURKKA under stricter control, the General Committee set up the 'Military-political Propaganda Soviet' (*Soviet voenno-politicheskoi propagandy*) of which Mekhlis became a member, together with Shcherbakov (chairman), Zhdanov, Manuilskii, Yaroslavskii, Rogov (of the Naval Political Administration), G.F. Aleksandrov and the deputy chief of *Glav*PURKKA F.F. Kuznetsov. Shcherbakov was charged now with reorganizing the whole of the propaganda work in the Soviet armed forces and with formulating a specific programme for this; his special Soviet held its first session on 16 June, examining propaganda work both among Soviet troops and among German forces (leaflets, broadcasts). This scrutiny of 'mass political work' went on for weeks: the examination of Western Front methods and 20th Army's Political Section work directed against German units (27 June), the report of the Press Bureau of *Glav*PURKKA (30 June), Party-political work on the Karelian and Kalinin Fronts (24 August), and a separate scrutiny of propaganda activity among German-occupied Soviet civilians. While this went on, the political members of Military Soviets, chiefs of political sections and commissars from Red Army formations (army, corps and division) met in Moscow to discuss their own failings; top commissars like K.F. Telegin, political member of the Moscow Military District, Makarov, head of the Western Front political administration and M.F. Drebednev of the Kalinin Front took part in these intensive discussions. Three days later Shcherbakov's report was ready and submitted to the Central Committee, proposing an 'Agitation and Propaganda

Administration', *Upravlenie agitatsii i propagandy*, to which were subordinated the hitherto independent agencies of the Press Section, Propaganda-Agitation Section, and the Cultural-Educational Section. I.V. Shikin, chief of the Leningrad Front Political Administration was selected to run this new group and became *ex officio* deputy head of *Glav*PURKKA. To support this new initiative, Shcherbakov organized an 'extra-establishment' group of 75 *agitatory* speakers skilled in 'mass work' and ordered Front political administrations to set up similar groups of 7–10 men (5 men at army level). A great flood of printed lectures, pamphlets, leaflets and special publications, *Bloknot agitatora Krasnoi Armii*, the patriotic writings of Soviet novelists published in the series *Iz frontovoi zhizni*, descended upon 'agitator soldiers' on every Front.

As the sense of growing disaster if not actual doom began to spread, stimulating enormous and persistent mass indoctrination of the shaken Red Army, the Soviet command towards the middle of July began to organize the second phase of its defence in the south. While neither Stalin nor his generals had yet mastered the essentials of mobile defence, at least the appalling 'hold at any cost' policy had been abandoned, and a substantial element of the Soviet forces had got back across the Don, though they were (as the commanders of the fresh and raw Stalingrad Front armies discovered) a dispirited lot. As for Army Group South, on 10 July it was regrouped, into Bock's Army Group B (Sixth German, Second Hungarian, Eighth Italian, Third Rumanian Armies) and List's Army Group A (Seventeenth Army and after 14 July Fourth and First Panzer Armies): under the terms of *Weisung Nr. 41*, Army Group B in its drive down the Don was to link up with Army Group A, advancing from Taganrog-Artemovsk across the lower Donets and the Don towards Stalingrad and the Volga. On 14 July, Groups A and B had made contact with each other in the Millerovo area, but the previous day Hitler had precipitately abandoned the idea of a rapid advance on Stalingrad. The Stalingrad attack was broken off, and First and Fourth Panzer Armies were committed with the Seventeenth Army to an attack on Rostov; Fourth Panzer was turned south from the great Don bend. On the lower Don, with Rostov as its focus, Hitler determined to fight another giant encirclement battle, to deliver the *coup de grâce* to the Russians – 'finished', in his view – between the Donets and the Don. Paulus's Sixth Army would therefore plunge on to Stalingrad alone, bereft now of 40th Panzer Corps which streaked off to the Rostov battle. The day on which Rostov fell (23 July), Hitler issued *Weisung Nr. 45* directing that Army Group A (Seventeenth German, Third Rumanian Armies) should take Batum, First and Fourth Panzer Armies were to strike for Maikop-Grozny and the oilfields, while Army Group B would capture Stalingrad and prepare the Don as a defensive line. Manstein's Eleventh Army, to the consternation of its command, was now wheeled to the very opposite end of the front, to Leningrad whose capture had already been scheduled under Operation 'Nordlicht'.

Although a huge encirclement at Rostov eluded Hitler, for Soviet forces did escape east and south, the Red Army had taken some further fearful punishment: the Donbas had fallen in its entirety to the Germans, German armies were in the great bend of the Don while the threat to the Caucasus was great and growing. Three reserve armies were being rushed into the Stalingrad Front, which had a nominal strength by 20 July of 38 divisions, 20 of which were below 2,500 men actually mustered: 14 divisions had a complement of between 300–1,000 men. Between them, 63rd and 62nd Armies had 160,000 men, up to 400 tanks and 2,200 guns and mortars. The 8th Air Army attached to the Front could put 454 planes (172 fighters) into the air. As the South-Western Front was slowly wound up, 38th Army added the remnants of ten divisions, 28th Army the remainder of six divisions and 21st Army also what was left of six divisions to the Stalingrad Front. The directive of 12 July envisaged a German thrust to slice the Soviet 'strategic front' in two halves, cutting the last remaining north-south railway line running from Stalingrad-Tikhoretsk, and closing the Volga to traffic. The two reserve armies, 64th and 62nd, were ordered to hold west of the Don and under no circumstances to allow a German breakthrough to the east; 63rd would hold the eastern bank, while 21st – once it was regrouped – took up a defensive position on the northern bank of the Don between 63rd and 62nd Armies, to secure their junction. The Southern Front received orders to hold the German south-easterly drive at Millerovo. Slowly the remnants of Soviet armoured forces crossed the Don, to the north and south of Kalach: 22nd and 23rd Tank Corps, with 3rd Guards Cavalry Corps moved into 63rd Army area, while 13th Tank Corps reformed north-east of Surovikono with 62nd Army. The Stalingrad Front ran for some 220 miles, with 63rd on the left bank of the Don from Pavlovsk to Serafimovich, with 21st holding twenty-five miles to Kletskaya, and where the front swept southwards, 62nd and 64th Armies (their advanced elements on the rivers Chir and Tsimla) holding from Kletskaya to Verkhne-Kurmoyarskaya. In Stalingrad itself, the military cupboard was terrifyingly bare: since three armies to the west (63rd, 62nd and 64th) had exactly four anti-arcraft guns between them, Stalingrad's own AA guns were moved in part to cover the Don crossings and the bridge over the Chir at Oblivskaya. For the aerial defence of the city eighty-five fighters were attached to the Air Defence Command (PVO), set up earlier as a command entity under *Order No. 0071* of 24 April.

Stalin had already telephoned the Party and administrative authorities headed by A.S. Chuyanov, chairman of the Stalingrad *Gorodskoi komitet oborony* (City Defence Committee, established in October 1941) on 19 July, putting Stalingrad on an immediate war footing: the following day, after a meeting of the *Obkom* (Party) committee, Chuyanov reported back to Stalin and the GKO about the measures they proposed to adopt. A certain amount had already been done, especially the attempts to improve AA defences, but to convert an industrial city of half a million people into a fortress was a different matter: in what was now a familiar cycle, the civilian population, at least 180,000 of them, marched out to build the rushed and rude defences, trenches, fire-points and tank-traps, laid out for mile after mile, while the GKO ordered in the 5th Pioneer Army and the 28th Military-Construction Administration. In May, *Narkomstroi* (People's Commissariat for Construction) had moved in some of its men and materials, and these were now worked to the hilt. Although militia (*opolchenie*) units existed, these now went over to full alert and manning; to deal with possible German parachute drops, eighty 'annihilation battalions' formed up with some 11,000 men in their ranks. The industrial evacuation, halted a while ago, now resumed, and stores and livestock were shipped in increasing quantities over to the eastern bank of the Volga. The city was turned inside out and the surrounding steppe dotted with parties of men and women labouring by the river; streets were blocked with improvised barricades.

For Stalin, defending the city which bore his own name and which drew Hitler like a magnet, this battle was fought for a second time; more than twenty years ago, when Stalingrad was Tsaritsyn, Stalin and Voroshilov had held it against White armies in the south (out of which had been fashioned the all-embracing myth that it was here that the Revolution had been saved from its counter-revolutionary enemies) and here also the collusion between Stalin-Voroshilov-Budenny and Timoshenko, joined in mutinous and stubborn resistance to War Commissar Trotsky, had been sealed into a Civil War 'Southern clique'. Just as the battle for Stalingrad was about to be joined, however, Stalin removed Timoshenko from command; on the evening of 21 July, Gordov, commander of 21st Army and latterly in charge of the 6th, was summoned to Moscow and returned the next day as commander of the Stalingrad Front. Instead of Bodin, who had been chief of the Operations Section of the General Staff, Major-General N.D. Nikishev, who had clashed so violently with Voroshilov at Leningrad, came in as chief of staff. To ensure the highest calibre of direction, Stalin instructed Colonel-General Vasilevskii to fly at once to the Stalingrad Front to 'assist the command and measure up the situation' where on the morning of 23 July German units had attacked and broken into the right flank of 62nd Army, outflanking it from the north, and thereby gaining the western bank of the Don near Kamensk. At the situation on Kolpakchi's right, Moscow took real and immediate alarm, ordering that it be restored and that the German force should be pushed right back from the Don bend to the Chir. But two of Kolpakchi's rifle divisions and a tank brigade were encircled, and 64th Army's position was none too secure: with crossings over the Don, fast German units could strike straight across the neck of land between the Don and the Volga, thirty-five miles or so of steppe, straight on to Stalingrad, and as Kolpakchi's 62nd was snarled up in a German noose, Vasili Chuikov's 64th Army, half-formed as it was, came under further heavy attacks on 25-6 July. The junction between 62nd and 64th Army was exposed. Chuikov rushed tanks, artillery and a force of marines across the rail bridge over the Don, to hold the line of the Chir where it ran into the Don, but when a shout went up that the German tanks were moving in, Chuikov's rear units took to their heels on the instant. 'A mass of men and vehicles rushed towards the Don', bombed and strafed by German planes. On the evening of 26 July, Colonel Novikov (64th Chief of Staff) ordered a retreat across the Don, though the bridge at Nizhne-Chirskaya had been blown to bits in the late afternoon. After a tussle with his own troops, Chuikov finally managed to anchor himself on the Don.

Somehow, and with only scratch troops at their disposal, Gordov and Vasilevskii had to rescue 62nd Army, and also 64th from their predicaments. Vasilevskii opted for a counter-attack using the 1st and 4th Tank Armies, an improvised solution which he had the greatest difficulty in getting Stalin to accept when he first put it to him on 24 July. Major-General Moskalenko took command of the 1st Tank Army (13th, 28th Tank Corps, 158th Tank Brigade, 131st Rifle Division) to attack from Kalach in the direction of Verkhne-Buzinovka and then to turn for Kletskaya: Major-General V.D. Kryuchenkin's 4th Tank Army (22nd, 23rd Tank Corps, 18th Rifle Division, 133rd Tank Brigade and artillery regiments) was to cross to the western bank of the Don from Kachalinskaya (right in the depth of the bend) during the night of 28 July, and that morning attack due west to Verkhne-Golubaya and thence link up with 1st Tank at Verkhne-Buzinovka. Major-General Danilov's 21st Army behind the Don between Serafimovich and Kletskaya, would attack at 03.00 hours 27 July, and break into the rear of the German units gripping 62nd Army. In Vasilevskii's opinion, there was no other way out, even though the tank armies were scarcely fit for the job; 1st Tank Army was merely 38th Army given a new designation, as was 4th Tank (formerly 28th Army). These were the remnants of the South-Western Front, still fearfully undermanned. German reconnaissance planes watched the Soviet forces forming up, and leisurely counted their tanks, as they plotted their positions.

For Vasilevskii's counter-blow, three Soviet tank corps and two brigades – 550 tanks, more than half KVs and T-34s – five rifle divisions and Khryukin's 8th Air Army were to be committed. Nor was Gordov a man to be trifled with; absolutely impatient of any subordinate's suggestion and not to be moved from his own decisions, he had a rigidity which added a visible unreality to the proposed attack. Nikishev's orders, certainly precise enough, nevertheless specified tasks for divisions and corps which the commanders of 62nd and 64th Armies simply could not find: 'Look for them between the Liska and the Don' was all the help they got from Front HQ.

At the end of July, as the Soviet tank formations waded separately and under heavy air attack into their counter-attack, the situation in the bend of the Don came to a furious boil. Moskalenko's 1st Tank Army engaged its 13th and 28th Tank Corps on time, but to the right 4th Tank Army was two days late: by 16.00 hours on 27 July, only seventeen of 22nd Tank Corps had crossed the Don, and both tank armies were hammered mercilessly by the Luftwaffe, which (by

Soviet reckoning) launched more than 1,000 sorties against Moskalenko alone. German air attacks smashed up HQs and signal centres making co-ordination impossible. Vasilevskii himself went up to observe Moskalenko's attack and to question the tank corps commanders: bit by bit, 13th Corps chewed its way across the steppe to the north-west, towards Colonel Zhuravlev's encircled 'operational group' on 62nd Army's right wing, west of Verkhne-Buzinovka. Zhuravlev began to fight his way to the Soviet tanks. Kryuchenkin's 4th Tank, with a little more armour over the Don, also struck at 14th Panzer Corps; 1st Tank Army, for all its repeated attempts, could not break through to the north with its main strength, while Kryuchenkin had not yet managed to get more than 100 tanks across the Don. Stalin meanwhile directed Gordov's attention to the crisis south of Kalach, and a *Stavka* directive instructed him to move 23 Tank Corps to stiffen 64th Army, to use two rifle divisions of the *Stavka* reserve and to push the German forces back from Chir and the Don: any German breakthrough here would destroy the southern face of the defence and bring German units right out into the rear of the Stalingrad Front. To thicken the southern defences, Gordov decided to move up Major-General F.I. Tolbukhin's 57th Army to this face of the defences.

With Paulus's Sixth Army locked in the battles of the Don bend, its force plainly insufficient to flatten Soviet resistance, the Soviet command nevertheless learned to its consternation of the development of a major new threat from the south-west, where Hitler had swung Fourth Panzer Army away from the drive into the Caucasus, ordering this formation to strike from its bridgeheads on the Don at Tsymlanskaya to drive north-east along the Tikhoretsk-Stalingrad railway line and into the Soviet flank behind Kalach. On 31 July, Fourth Panzer crashed into Kolomiits's flimsy 51st Army and pushed it aside in a drive for Kotelnikovo. Gordov, although given control of 51st Army, had to do some speedy regrouping: in 62nd Army, Kolpakchi was relieved of his command and replaced by Lopatin who had practically lost an army during the earlier retreats to the Don, while at 64th Army Shumilov, who had begun the war with his corps in Lithuania took over full command as Chuikov established and controlled a southerly 'operational group', an improvised force which finally backed on the river Aksai, there to bar the way against Fourth Panzer. Gordov had now to face a double threat, from the north-west (Kalach-Stalingrad) and the south-west (from the Aksai to Stalingrad), his whole front running for some 400 miles, a fact which gave rise for concern in Moscow where Stalin and the GKO sat considering the problems of the Stalingrad Front, and in particular how to counter the peril from the south.

Early in August Colonel-General Yeremenko, recovering from leg wounds received in the spring, was summoned to a session of the GKO, to one of those night-time conferences in the large, oblong-shaped room with its subdued lighting; Stalin told Yeremenko that the GKO had decided to split the Stalingrad Front into two, and that he was a candidate for one Front command. Both

Yeremenko and Vasilevskii were to report back after studying the information available at the General Staff. Here Yeremenko spent the whole of 2 August. That evening, together with Vasilevski, Major-General V.D. Ivanov of the General Staff and Lieutenant-General Golikov (nominated as 1st Guards Army commander, a force assembled from Moscow district paratroops) Yeremenko attended Stalin's nightly conference. Colonel-General Vasilevskii presented a brief report on what was involved in terms of forces in splitting the Front, while Ivanov outlined the provisional decision on the map. With the draft directive on the table in front of the officers, Yeremenko asked Stalin for permission to make some points, since the final decision had not been taken. To this Stalin agreed, and Yeremenko pointed out the need to adjust the Front boundary lines, so that Stalingrad itself lay within one Front area. This provoked an irritable outburst from Stalin who swung on Vasilevskii and ordered him to finalize the directive: 'Everything stays as we proposed. Stalingrad Front is split into two fronts: the boundary line between the fronts is to run along the line of the river Tsarits and then on to Kalach.' In between pacing the room, Stalin asked for the name for the new front, whereupon one voice suggested that the front to the north should retain the old name, Stalingrad, the one to the south should be called South-Eastern. Stalin agreed and the directive was signed on the spot; on candidates for Front commands, two names came up – Gordov and Yeremenko, the latter to take the South-Eastern Front. At 03.00 hours the session was finished, the directive signed and the instruction that the staffs of both Fronts would be located in Stalingrad itself incorporated: two commands, two Fronts, two staffs, two sets of forces to defend the same objective.

As Stalin formed his new Front, the situation in the Don bend deteriorated drastically: breaking through 62nd Army's right wing, German units reached the Don on a front of some nine miles in the Malogolubaya area, splitting the Soviet forces in two. Gordov now proposed to use 21st Army with 1st and 4th Tank Armies again in an attempt to nip off this German penetration. Lopatin had already tried to get Gordov to examine the danger to the flanks of 62nd Army, and asked for permission to pull back to the Don. Gordov refused to listen and pressed on with his counter-attack plans involving tank corps with only fifteen tanks apiece. To the south-east, Fourth Panzer had reached Abganerovo. Gordov's attack was ground to pieces almost as it began, and at dawn on 7 August the German Sixth Army went over to a massive attack against Lopatin; within forty-eight hours, as 24th and 16th Panzer divisions linked up, eight rifle divisions and five artillery regiments of the 62nd Army were fully encircled.

Yeremenko's Douglas transport set him down in the northern outskirts of Stalingrad on 4 August, the eve of disaster in the Don bend: he was met by Nikita Khrushchev, commissar to the Stalingrad Front, and driven to the basement Front HQ in the centre of the city. Here, in oven-heat for all its ventilation, Nikishev presented the Front operational summaries to Yeremenko, who thus got some of the picture though intelligence of the enemy seemed deficient. All but two of the army commanders, Danilov of 21st and Trufanov now in command of 51st Army, he knew of old: Lopatin had served with him in Belorussia and the Far East, V.I. Kuznetsov and Kryuchenkin were also pre-war acquaintances. But what alarmed Yeremenko and confirmed the criticisms Khrushchev had already made, were Gordov's general assumptions about the battle, which 'seemed to play into the enemy's hands'. Yeremenko had also to set up his own command, with its three armies (64th, 57th and 51st); his Front HQ would be in a school building in the southern suburbs of Stalingrad, the staff being assembled out of Moskalenko's 1st Tank Army command group, brought back from Kalach.

Just as his Front came to life, Yeremenko received an urgent query from Vasilevskii, Stalin's own questions put across the telegraph line:

Vasilevskii [9 August]
Comrade Stalin has instructed me to discuss and obtain your opinion on these questions:

First: Comrade Stalin thinks it useful and timely to unite problems concerning the defence of Stalingrad in one set of hands, for which reason the Stalingrad Front is subordi-nated to you, leaving you for the moment as commander of South-Eastern Front. Your deputy at South-Eastern Front nominated as Lieutenant-General Golikov. Major-General Moskalenko nominated as commander 1st Guards Army in place of comrade Golikov.

Second: Comrade Stalin also considers it important to nominate as commander of Stalingrad town garrison comrade Sarayev of the NKVD, to whom NKVD division in Stalingrad will be subordinated. What are your comments on these questions?

Yeremenko: I am replying. There is no being cleverer than comrade Stalin and I consider this particularly correct and timely.

Vasilevskii: What will be your observations on the candidatures of Golikov, Moskalenko and Sarayev?

Yeremenko: I consider all these nominations will pass. Excellent candidates.

Gordov, in the formal *Stavka* directive, became deputy commander of the Stalingrad Front, and the new command set-up became effective from 9 August. Stalin, however, was taking no chances and now ordered General Zhukov as well as Colonel-General Vasilevskii to fly to Stalingrad to report on the situation now that German units were moving up to the external defence line of Stalin-grad itself, '*Line O*', behind which lay '*Line K*' and further back '*Line S*', with '*Line G*' within the city itself. On 12 August, Vasilevskii conferred with Yeremenko about the defensive preparations required to deal with this even more dangerous situation: Yeremenko was of the opinion that the first stage of the German offensive – wiping out the Soviet bridgeheads on the western bank of the Don and west of Kalach – was now done. He anticipated a heavy German attack against 4th Tank Army and the forcing of the Don, at the same time as German formations struck from the south. The intelligence data at Yeremenko's disposal confirmed this: for Kalach-Stalingrad, up to 10–11 German divisions, to the south (Plodovitoe-Stalingrad) some 5–7 German divisions, indicating a concentric blow. In the wake of Vasilevskii came V.A. Malyshev, deputy chairman of the GKO with a group of senior officials, to look into local supply, railway transport and the movement of Volga river traffic.

At 04.30 hours, 15 August, the German Sixth Army went over to the offensive against the Soviet 4th Tank Army in the small loop of the Don. With the road to the Don strewn with smashed Soviet tanks, there was little left of 4th Tank: its three rifle divisions mustered less than 800 men, 22nd Tank Corps had a handful of tanks, 22nd Motorized Rifle Brigade had 200 men. Gordov himself was ordered to take personal command, though he could not improve the ammunition and fuel situation, stocks of which were now almost gone. Shumilov and Chuikov were more successful in holding off Fourth Panzer Army, but the critical situation built up to a climax on the right flank of 62nd Army. German units were across the Don on the Trekhostrovskaya-Gerasimov sector in 4th Tank Army area, and at Perepolnyi-Luchenskii on the right of Lopatin's 62nd; by assault boat and kapok rafts Paulus's assault divisions made the hazardous crossings of the Don, while Soviet aircraft made repeated attacks to destroy the pontoon bridges being built to move the armour. During the night of 23 August the bulk of 16th Panzer Division moved across into its start-position east of the Don, a bridgehead about three miles long and a mile deep, ready to move at 04.15 hours straight through 62nd Army to the Volga, thirty-five straight miles over the steppe, bare of cover, in one close-packed armoured fist, overhead *Stuka* aircraft. During the short summer night Russian guns fired continuously into the bridgehead and Russian bombers guided by the glare from blazing vehicles tried to knock out the bridge but without success. At 04.30 hours, 16th Panzer moved off.

That same day Richthofen's 8th Air Corps hit Stalingrad with a massed blow, smashing in the residential and administrative centres, setting fire to the oil storage tanks so that the destruction was hidden in dense palls of smoke; on the Volga, the docks burned to their timbered shells, while in the late afternoon the workers in the northern sector suddenly received rifles, ammunition and orders to stand to against a German onslaught sweeping in from the north. Hube's armoured vehicles and Panzer Grenadiers gunned down any opposition in their scything path. At 23.10 hours, 23 August, 79th Panzer Grenadier Regiment radioed from the Volga that they were located in Spartanovka (the northerly suburb of Stalingrad) and leaguered on the Volga. Stalingrad was passing through its own special crucifixion, the dead lying out in the streets and German troops standing to on the Volga on 23 August.

Stalin received the news of the German breakthrough with anger and curses aimed at his commanders. Vasilevskii managed only two short reports by radio, the other communication links being shattered: only on 24 August did he manage to make a proper report, while Stalin gave full vent to his anger, even though Vasilevskii pointed that the centre of the town was still in Soviet hands, that Malyshev and the Town Defence Committee were in complete control. At

21.00 hours on that grievous August evening, Yeremenko, Khrushchev, Chuyanov, Malyshev and Vasilevskii gathered in the basement HQ while Yeremenko sent his report to the Supreme Commander. Stalin had already radioed his unequivocal orders to Yeremenko:

The enemy has broken our front with insignificant force. You have quite enough men at your disposal to destroy enemy units which have broken through. Assemble the planes of both fronts and throw them in against the enemy. Mobilize an armoured train and use it on the circular railway round Stalingrad. Use plenty of smoke-screens to confuse the enemy. Jab into the breakthrough units by day and also by night. Use all your artillery and *Katyusha* resources. The most important thing is not to let panic take hold, do not be afraid of the enemy thrusts and keep your faith in our ultimate success.   J. STALIN.

At 23.00 hours Yeremenko assembled the material for the daily operations report to the *Stavka* which had to be submitted every midnight. It was in all truth a sombre document: it could only retail disaster, that on the left flank in the Vertyachii-Peskovaka area the Germans had pierced the Soviet defences, struck east and in the Latashanka sector installed themselves on the river Volga, thus cutting the front in two. German units had bitten into the northern suburbs of Stalingrad, where they had been halted but from which they brought the Tractor Plant under fire and cut the two railway lines linking Stalingrad with the north and the north-west. Rail and river communications along which flowed fuel and food were now under direct enemy pressure; the savage German bombing of the city had inflicted shocking damage and grievously impeded its military and industrial activities. To this personal report to Stalin, Vasilevskii, Chuyanov, Malyshev, Khrushchev and Yeremenko added their signatures with the greatest of misgivings. Chuyanov had already raised the question of evacuating civilians and industry from the shambles left by the German bombers. Yeremenko, unable to take any decision on his own authority, consulted Stalin by telephone, who returned a sharp and rasping answer:

I am not going to discuss this question at all. But it should be understood that if the evacuation of industry and the mining of factories starts, then that will be taken as a decision to surrender Stalingrad. For that reason, the GKO forbids any preparations for the demolition of industrial installations and any preparations for their evacuation.

With these words, which needed no explaining to the company assembled in the basement HQ, Stalin had committed himself, the Red Army and the Russians at large to one of the most terrible battles in the whole history of war.

The fall of Rostov (23–4 July) and the capture of the great bridge over the Don leading to the south, towards the Caucasus, was turned into a fiery sign of the great distress of the Soviet state. Now was the time for all men to do their duty to the utmost. Not that Rostov had surrendered lightly: NKVD units, crack, fanatical troops under rigid command, turned the city into a death-trap, the streets tangled with spectacular barricades, houses sealed up into firing-points.

For fifty hours German assault troops fought ferocious battles in each sector of Rostov, and none more fierce than against the NKVD machine-gunners sited on the Taganrog road leading to the bridge. By dawn on 25 July Soviet units had fallen back behind the Don, but there still remained the embankment over the swampland leading to Bataisk and one more major bridge, though in the evening that too was in German hands and Army Group A could spill out from its bridgeheads into the Caucasus down through the steppe and into the high mountains to the south, on to the great goal of the oilfields.

Out of the disasters on the Don Stalin decided to make a forbidding example, a final stiffening of the will to resist now that danger even greater than that of autumn 1941 had swept upon the Soviet Union. The fall of Rostov was represented, with deliberate inaccuracy, as abandoning positions without orders; in reality, Soviet withdrawals under orders had robbed Hitler of what he had hoped would be a super-encirclement on a scale to surpass anything in 1941. This time, however, Stalin did not resort to punitive executions (though the hint was there). Instead, together with an urgent intensification of mass agitation and a burst of deeply impassioned anti-German propaganda managed principally by Ilya Ehrenburg, Stalin projected a paternalistic if forbidding image of himself, embodied in *Order No. 227* of 28 July, read out to units assembled to hear it, '*Prikaz Verkhovnovo Komanduyushchevo*'. This had had a salutary effect: Stalin stated flatly that though Russia was vast, the space in which to retreat had shrunk and was shrinking still further. '*Ni shagu nazad!*': 'Not a step backward' was now no mere phrase, but a statement of stern and inescapable realities. It was the duty of each Red Army soldier to fight relentlessly to the last drop of blood and to hold each piece of ground to the bitter end. 'Panic-mongers', 'cowards' and 'traitors' must be rooted out: officers must look to their duty, military commissars to their obligations to inculcate the right fighting spirit in the troops. Stalin had timed his response to the shudder which ran through Russia in the summer of 1942, with defeat laid on defeat and the cracking of the great geographic shell which many thought still conferred immunity against the unbelievable, quite consummately. The upheaval in the main Political Administration continued and the emergency mobilization of Communist Party members into the armed forces went on apace: at this point, Stalin also directed his attention to revising not only the outlook but also the practice of the Red Army, in which Marshal Shaposhnikov was put in charge of remodelling the combat manuals of the Red Army.

This was the period of Stalin's special conferences; on 20 August specialists on partisan warfare were summoned to the Kremlin, some like Kovpak from their guerrilla formations deep in the German rear, to attend discussions on maintaining links with the occupied population, on the role of commissars in partisan units, on equipment and weapons, or the Kremlin sessions on revising tactical doctrine and improving the quality of Red Army staff work at all levels. Even more fundamentally, Stalin was beginning to grapple with the

major issue of reshaping the Red Army, at once pumping in communists and
expanding the work of the Political Administration while coming nearer all the
while to the issue of the officer being left as the master in his own house, 'unitary
command'. Something like a revolt of the younger generals was in the making,
a reaction against inefficient commissar control and incompetence within the
officer corps as a whole, Civil War relics trying to cope with the complexities
of modern operations. Even though a new command group had emerged in the
winter of 1941–2, it was still largely untested and rested on a very narrow base;
as for Mekhlis's disgrace, Stalin was evidently pleased to let this run its course as
one concession to the officers. But now, with the war a year old, commanders of
growing reputation, like Rokossovskii or the rising young general Chernyakhovskii, were able to assemble 'their' men into their staffs and commands: young
professionals, meeting in the new Front commands, fell on each other's necks
with relief though they remained dumbfounded at the general incompetence of
their seniors. In the armoured forces especially, the time was not yet come for
them to establish their competence and ability, and after the Bryansk disasters
the fate of the 'tank armies' hung in the balance. But normalization had to come
before specialization, and in the summer of 1942 the fight to re-establish the
officer was on, even though the circumstances were far from propitious. The
Red Army, however, was in danger of breaking up through over-rigidity.
From the Stalingrad Front Colonel-General Voronov wrote a special letter to
the Central Committee recommending a return to the old position: 'There is
only one path to follow – *edinonachalie* [unitary command]'. Voronov's was by
no means an isolated voice, but the abolition of dual command, imposed during
the great autumn crisis of 1941, met with stubborn resistance from the 'politicals',
who yielded ground only slowly. And even this was only the tip of the iceberg
of military resentment and disillusion, which saw not only dual command but
the whole crude and cumbersome system of 'military soviets', the *triplice* of
command, staff direction and political control, as being thoroughly unsuited to
a modern fighting machine. For the moment, however, the struggle centred on
winning 'unitary command' for the officer, to squeeze out the commissar and
assert some military predominance.

Stalin's highly centralized machine remained for all this little changed, and
its principal weakness was the gap between decisions taken at the centre and the
requirements of the fronts. In the *Stavka*, which had its 'full sessions' and the
ad hoc meetings which Stalin called, it was apparently always Stalin who had the
last word; he could also amplify his instructions through his chairmanship of
the State Defence Committee (GKO). With the displacement of Shaposhnikov
(whose retirement was formally a decision of the GKO), both Zhukov and
Vasilevskii moved up the contorted Stalinist command tree: Vasilevskii had
assumed control of the General Staff, while Zhukov began to act as Stalin's
deputy, a post not yet formalized except by ranking him as first Deputy Defence
Commissar. By implementing the device of 'Stavka representative' (*predstavitel'*

Stavki) on a wider scale, the *Stavka* – simultaneously a location, a command group and a Stalinist organ – began to decentralize itself somewhat: the Front commands had a legitimate complaint that *Stavka*-General Staff directives failed widely to meet the realities of the operational-tactical situation, and never more than in the early stages of the Stalingrad Front fighting, when lack of information about enemy strength and movements as well as incomplete data about Soviet forces caused Soviet formations to be committed piecemeal or straight off the march. The *Stavka* would not listen to the Front command, the Front command, notably Gordov, would not listen to subordinate army commanders, who in turn often failed simply to look about them. The super-centralization was, in theory, designed to produce maximum co-ordination of several Fronts and through the *Stavka* with its permanent members to fix the right priorities of manpower, types of arms, logistical support, mass movement, political preparation, support facilities and, wherever necessary, naval and air support. In fact, Stalin to date took the brunt of the Front co-ordination upon himself and interfered in the Front operational direction. On the Bryansk Front, he personally issued detailed orders for the tank counter-attacks. Of up-to-date Soviet disposition Stalin was obviously magnificently informed, and he culled what he needed from the mandatory midnight reports submitted by Front HQs to the *Stavka*-General Staff. The directives sent out by the *Stavka*, drafted by the Operations Section of the General Staff, carried the signatures of Stalin and Vasilevskii in most cases. Stalin had begun to listen to his generals more than before, though this did not save them from being sworn at and personally abused when things went wrong, as they did when German tanks broke through to the Volga. Then, as Vasilevskii admits, reporting to Stalin was an unbearable strain: for most commanders a summons to the *Stavka* had a very ominous ring, or else, telephone in hand, Stalin would relieve commanders of their duties on the spot, violence delivered direct from Moscow. On the other hand, ranging the battlefields by fronts and sectors, he could pick out spots which required help or reinforcement, where the slow-moving machinery could not respond quickly enough to emergencies, though this put a premium on his judgement.

In the summer of 1942, the high command organization reverted to its two-echelon structure: Supreme Commander-Front. The last intermediate echelon, the *Glavkom* of the North Caucasus theatre, was wound up much as Timoshenko's and Zhukov's *Glavkom* appointments were shut down as their strategic operations folded. A very decisive development, however, was the slow and difficult decentralization of the *Stavka* through its 'representatives', the *predstaviteli* who were only beginning to make their appearance and who clustered first in Stalingrad. These representatives subsequently built up their own 'working apparatuses', hand-picked officers from the General Staff and arms – the 'flying circuses' which buzzed about the Front HQs, much to the latter's disgust. The presence of Zhukov and Vasilevskii helped to bridge the gap between the centre and the front, even if it unnerved the local commander, and

Stalin had up-to-the-minute reports from his top men. Front commanders complained that they 'lacked guidance' from the General Staff, or were given no 'orientation' about operations, a very legitimate grievance but an inevitable state of affairs in view of the stringency, even the ambiguity of the all-powerful *Stavka* directive; it was a natural consequence of the rigid centralization of all phases of operations, from the planning to the actual execution. It also enabled 'the centre' to off-load the responsibility for failure upon the local commanders, citing 'non-fulfilment' of the directive. In this way, the odium of Kharkov had been heaped on Bagramyan, though the chief of staff was scarcely responsible for the faulty strategic appreciations and expectations. There always had to be scapegoats, wild and rampant injustice notwithstanding, as Stalin sieved his commanders through his hands.

After more than a year of unparalleled mangling in the field, the Red Army immersed as it was in yet another great slough of defeat and despair, nevertheless stood on the verge of becoming a more viable and modern machine, slowly absorbing the lessons of the war thus far, painfully assimilating the pointers about its equipment, training and leadership. The unique period between December 1941 and April 1942 when it became of necessity the virtual substance of the state had passed and now it was moving towards a certain autonomy, signified in the early autumn by the restitution of 'unitary command' and by its transformation into a thoroughly conventional force: progress was marked enough for certain senior officers to think that the conditions of 'a capitalist army' pertained and to start demanding total autonomy. The wind of change was indeed given a public airing in a play, *The Front* by Korneichuk, presented with Stalin's approval and prompting. Behind the scenes, the Party die-hards battled to hold off these concessions to the military, while, from the front-line itself, the military leadership counter-attacked.

At the root of this crisis lay the basic lesson which the war had displayed so cruelly for the Red Army, that it lacked power equivalent to its mass; steam-roller it may have looked, but it had no real steam. Putting in the power was the basis of real and rapid modernization, while Stalin planned for an increase in strength and a build-up in striking power. But even at this dangerous stage, there were positive signs; the Soviet commanders were beginning to learn the technique of mobile operations and had carried out one tolerably successful planned retreat on some scale. It did not, as Stalin evidently feared it might, lead to wholesale rout and panic, though Chuikov for one was appalled when he saw the condition and morale of units reeling back over the Don. The preliminary disintegration which the Germans had also observed now came to a halt and they attributed this in part to the shock effect of Stalin's 'Not a step back' order. At the same time, behind the ragged edges of the fronts, Soviet arms plants in the Ural fastnesses worked at fever-pitch to overcome the final effects of 'surprise attack' and to ensure the main supply of the Fronts: from 9,600 planes produced up to June (1942), the second half-yearly production figures climbed to 15,800, for tanks the output figure rose from 11,000 to 13,600 and for artillery (76-mm calibre and over) from 14,00 to 15,600, an astonishing triumph over appalling difficulties.

The brunt of the military reformism, however, fell now on Zhukov and Vasilevskii, the two men at Stalin's elbow, both young, well-schooled in modern war and extremely able. This was the military tide with which Stalin elected to swim (having almost drowned with the previous one), yet at the same time he sought ways to preserve within the nation his own, and therefore the Party's prestige. In the cause of Stalin's exculpation the reputations of Golikov, Bagramyan and others less prominent were readily and ruthlessly sacrificed, and that portion of the blame not heaped upon the army was unloaded on to the British and the Americans, the dilatory and obstructionist allies, indicted in another carefully timed and specially configurated campaign conducted both at home and abroad. Even the total incompetence of men like the bumptious Mekhlis or Kaganovich (removed in the spring for the mismanagement of the railway system) helped to reinforce Stalin's reputation at large, for these spectacular dismissals placated some and reassured even more. The struggle against Party interference in military affairs was long, silent and bitter; its outcome for the future development of the Soviet armed forces was of decisive importance. Inch by inch, the Red Army began to recover some of its pre-war ground and added to it present priorities, as for example with the re-establishment in April 1942 of a separate long-range bomber force, the ADD, *Aviatsiya dalnevo deistvya*, put under the command of Major-General Golovanov, one of Stalin's favourites and a former pilot of the 'prison plane', the big machine used in 1938 to fly in purge victims to Moscow. After a shaky start, the armoured forces were being pulled into shape and 'tank-mechanized corps' were formed in the rear. Although Shaposhnikov had been bundled off the operational scene, he was at least able to exercise some influence on the revision of tactical doctrines which called for a great deal of experience; the new staff manual *Nastavlenie po polevoi sluzhbe shtabov Krasnoi Armii* had already been introduced under his auspices, and thereafter he occupied himself with more and more of the new combat manuals, while the Zhukov-Vasilevskii axis took increasing control of operational destinies and the shaping of the future Red Army.

Zhukov was all professional soldier, schooled now in several Front commands and with the experience of one full theatre command (*Glavkom* West) behind him; some thought him at times too rigidly subservient to 'the centre', while others found his shattering impatience with front-line command shortcomings unbearable. Colonel-General Vasilevskii had also served in the best schools, beginning as a subaltern in the Imperial Russian Army and mobilized for the Red Army in 1919; as a staff officer in the 1920s, Vasilevskii worked with Triandafilov, and became a candidate member of the Party in May 1931, at which time he was assistant to a section chief in the Red Army Training Administration. Vasilevskii's career with the senior staff began in the early

1930s under Yegorov; many of the papers in *Voennyi Vestnik* signed by Aleksandrov, Mihailov or Vasiliev were actually written by Vasilevskii, who joined the General Staff after finishing the 1936 course at the General Staff Academy. Up to the outbreak of war, Vasilevskii was deputy chief of the Operations Section (General Staff) headed at that time by G.K. Malandin and in 1941 worked out the frontier defence plans for the north-western and western sectors (the second deputy Anisov worked out those for the south-west and the Near East). After August, he took over the Operations Section entirely and became Shaposhnikov's formal deputy. Rising from colonel to colonel-general in some four years, Vasilevskii was essentially heir to Shaposhnikov's position at the General Staff, an officer long associated with its best minds and himself no mean talent. By August, German officers noted the rally in Russian performance in the field, but the real transformation was taking place well behind the scenes. The new establishment for rifle divisions envisaged cutting manpower and augmenting the quantity of automatic weapons, mortars, anti-tank weapons and divisional artillery: the re-equipping of existing tank formations and the creation of new corps (the components of Tank Armies) was slowly bringing a whole new armoured strike force into being. The formation of Air Armies as Front components and the establishment of Air Corps as a *Stavka* Reserve, the reconstitution of the Long-Range Bomber Force (ADD) and the refurbishing of the airborne troops also brought the mass employment and the centralized direction of air power so very much nearer realization.

In early August, when the German Army Group A (with its Rumanian and Slovak components) had leapt the Don, broken into the Kuban and was racing for the Northern Caucasus, the sights and scenes of 1941 seemed to be repeating themselves in the grim backdrop of mass refugee movement and the overpowering precision of the German blitzkrieg. List's assault divisions after mid August had overrun most of the Kuban, and were now cutting into the Caucasus, driving on the west to the Black Sea coast and in the east racing for the great oil centres of Grozny and Baku, the campaign which had been projected in October 1941. When German units had reached the lower waters of the Don, from Verkhne-Kurmoyarskaya to the mouth of the river, this 120-mile front was held by the 51st Army of the North Caucasus Front, and the 37th, 12th and 18th Armies of the Southern Front, the whole Soviet force numbering some 112,000 men, with 121 tanks, 2,160 guns and mortars and 130 aircraft (4th Air Army). Marshal Budenny's North Caucasus Front, in addition to 51st Army, included 47th Army, 1st Rifle and 17th Cavalry Corps and the 5th Air Army, responsible for defending the eastern shore of the sea of Azov and the Black Sea coast down to Lazarevsk; to the south, General Tyulenev's Trans-Caucasus Front covered the remainder of the Black Sea coast to Batum and ran on to the Soviet-Turkish frontier. Part of Tyulenev's force was also deployed in Northern Iran and covered the Iranian-Turkish frontier.

On the basis of Hitler's *Weisung Nr. 45*, Field-Marshal List of Army Group A proposed to use Ruoff's reinforced Seventeenth Army south of Rostov in a drive on Krasnodar, while Kleist's First Panzer Army went for Maikop in an outer encircling sweep, covered on the eastern flank by Hoth's Fourth Panzer aiming for Voroshilovsk. Across the ultimate German line of advance lay the Caucasian mountain range running from the Black Sea to the Caspian, preceded by the steppe lands of the Kuban intersected by the numerous watercourses threading to the Caspian and the Black Sea, the old battle grounds where Russian armies had fought their frontier wars for the subjugation of the Caucasian tribesmen in the days of the tsar. Going over to the offensive on the morning of 25 July, within forty-eight hours the German units had broken into the Soviet defences to a depth of more than forty miles, though Soviet formations managed by timely withdrawal to slip out of the planned German encirclement south and south-east of Rostov, falling back behind their rear-guards holding small river lines and villages. On 28 July, Budenny received orders to combine the Southern and North Caucasian Fronts into one command (the designation North Caucasus being retained), and to split his forces into two, the 'Don group' under Malinovskii (51st, 37th and 12th Armies), and the 'Coastal group' under Cherevichenko with the 18th, 56th, 47th Armies, and two independent corps. Malinovskii's 'Don group' would cover Stavropol, Cherevichenko's group Krasnodar: Budenny's orders envisaged the destruction of the German forces which had crossed the Don, while Tyulenev received urgent instructions to start building defence lines at Terek, Urukh and also in the passes of the Caucasus mountain ranges, defensive positions which were to be fully manned.

The danger of a German breakthrough to the Caucasus was now over-whelming, and as Army Group A units reached the line Proletarskaya-Salsk-Belaya Glina and advanced on Voroshilovsk and Kropotkin in early August, the 'Don' and 'Coastal' groups were pulled back to the river Kuban, while frenzied work went on both to evacuate food stocks and equipment from the Kuban and to mobilize the Trans-Caucasian Front, which had become fully operational. Under the direction of the GKO, the industrial equipment in Armavira, Krasnodar and Maikop was loaded on to trucks, on to which however refugees also scrambled, fleeing as best they might to the Caspian. On 5 August Voroshilovsk fell, although Soviet troops still continued to evade encirclement between the Don and the Kuban, so that First Panzer Army now swung south-west and attacked in the direction of Armavir-Maikop-Tupass to cut off the Soviet line of retreat, with the aim of encircling and destroying what was left of Budenny's armies in the Novorossiisk-Krasnodar-Tuapse area in co-operation with Ruoff's Seventeenth Army: for operations against Grozny, List proposed to use 52nd Corps and 40th Panzer Corps. Forcing the Kuban on 6 August, German troops took Armavir, while the Seventeenth Army reached the river Chelbas.

Budenny assigned the defence of the Maikop-Tuapse line to the 12th and 18th Armies, supported by the 17th Cavalry Corps with its Kuban Cossack troops and reinforced by 32nd Guards Rifle Division pulled out of 47th Army. At Tyulenev's HQ the debate raged about the location of the basic defence line – the Terek or the Sulak; in the first week in August, Tyulenev reported to Colonel-General Vasilevskii that the Military Soviet had decided to base its defence on the Terek river line, with powerful bridgeheads in the areas of Kizlyar, Staroshchedrinskoe, Mozdok, Maklinskii and Prishibskaya. The *Stavka* in turn gave Tyulenev full authorization to put this plan into effect. By mid August, when the breakthrough of strong German armoured forces into Tuapse, Novorossiisk and Grozny appeared imminent, Tyulenev decided to move his forces forward to Mineralnye Vody to support Malinovskii's battered troops. With the Rostov-Baku railway line jammed with trucks evacuating factory equipment, movement was almost impossible and the situation rendered more chaotic by the torrent of refugees – the 'doleful trains' crammed with the aged, with women and children, rolling through Nalchik to Beslana, on to Makhatchkala and from Derbent to Baku. The GKO was vitally concerned that the Trans-Caucasus Front should not be isolated as its communications were severed one by one, and ordered local plants to go over to the production of ammunition, equipment and weapons; a central repair base was set up in Tyulenev's rear, and only heavy equipment (tanks and aircraft) were sent in from the central industrial regions.

Grave though the supply situation was, it paled into insignificance compared with the dangers inherent in the instability of the local populations, the mountaineer nationalities who belonged to the complex of special autonomous states and territories constructed in the south; here were rebel movements anti-Soviet enough to stir up discontents in the Soviet rear and to give the invading Germans an apparently enthusiastic reception, such as that accorded to them in the Karachai region. And both Germany and the Soviet Union had to reckon on the attitude of Turkey, whose interest in the Turkic peoples of the south-east was pronounced and persistent; both the Russians and the Germans competed for the allegiance of these mountaineer groups, among whom Berlin found the Moslems to be the most ardent supporters of the German cause, while conversely Moscow found them a danger requiring drastic measures, for which purpose Lavrenti Beria was ordered to the Trans-Caucasian Front by Stalin in late August 1942. Beria arrived with his 'boys', Kabulov, Mamulov, Piyashev and Tsanava, who set about organizing a parallel NKVD staff for the 'defence' of the North Caucasus and building up a strong force of special NKVD troops. Beria and his 'special assistants' tangled straight away with Malinovskii, whom Beria threatened to put under close arrest; in the place of the *Stavka* reinforcements which Tyulenev asked for, Beria ordered in more NKVD troops and let his lieutenants Kabulov and Rukhadze loose on the Trans-Caucasus Front Military Soviet. Beria's job was to suppress the incipient revolt in the Northern Caucasus and the Volga delta, hence his transfer of strong NKVD forces and his absolute refusal to hand any over to the control of the military – or only a few and then only on the personal instruction of J.V. Stalin. All these minority peoples – the Chechens, Ingushi, Crimean Tartars, the Karachai, the Balkars, the Kalmyks (and the Volga Germans) – finally paid a terrible price in mass murder and deportation, their 'autonomy' broken to pieces in a welter of exile and murderous forced labour, the enactment of a monstrous revenge.

In mid August, Army, Group A regrouped for the second stage of its offensive, aimed at Baku and Batum: First Panzer Army would strike from east of Voroshilovsk in the direction of Grozny-Makhatchkala-Baku, the Seventeenth Army would move on Novorossiisk from Krasnodar and roll down the Black Sea coast to Sukhumi-Batumi with 79 *Jäger* Corps moving into the Caucasian mountain passes from Cherkesska to strike into the Soviet rear through a battle zone of cliffs and glaciers towering up to more than 10,000 feet, where passes were left only lightly guarded. The *Stavka* had already issued orders to Tyulenev to cover the passes and to close off the approaches to the Caucasus from the north; at that moment, the attention of the staff of the Trans-Caucasus Front was fastened on the Black Sea coastline, where the main force of 46th Army – a force raised internally within Tyulenev's Front, commanded first by Major-General V.F. Sergatskov and then by Major-General K.N. Leselidze – was to be deployed. Tyulenev's staff, too, was not a stable organization: headed at first by Subbotin, he gave way to P.I. Bodin who in turn was replaced by A.I. Antonov (Malinovskii's Front chief of staff) but he lasted for only two weeks. The Front Operations Section was run by Major-General S.E. Rozhdestvenskii, the aviation finally commanded by Colonel-General (Aviation) Vershinin, the armour by Major-General (Tank Troops) Dementeyev, senior echelons which worked quite efficiently, but the interference of Beria threw the strategic direction of the Front out of gear.

Beria, a member of the GKO, was at Tyulenev's HQ as a '*Stavka* representative' and used every ounce of his authority as well as the weight of his murderous reputation. On 23 August, Beria issued orders for the establishment of the 'Caucasian Range Operational Group', to which the troops assigned to the passes were subordinated. When Beria put in his own men, this was tantamount to removing Tyulenev's HQ Staff and the staff of 46th Army from any control over these operations, in the middle of which Beria ordered the command of 46th Army to be changed. Once the German *Jäger* troops were launched on their spectacular operations in the Caucasian heights, Operation 'Edelweiss', high in the mist and driving winds, in the rarefied air where shell or mortar explosions could push down avalanches, Stalin realized what a blunder had been made, and sent fierce instructions that a completely revised plan for the defence of the passes should be worked out, while to the east and in order to cover Grozny, Maslennikov was ordered to set up a 'Northern Group' (Trans-Caucasus Front) from the 44th and 9th Armies (and to which the 37th Army of the North Caucasus Front was very shortly attached). Marshal Budenney, who was living out the last days of his own Front, was now instructed to block the German route to the Black Sea coast by using Kamkov's 18th Army and the Kuban Cossacks of 17th Cavalry Corps (Lieutenant General Kirichenko's formation which at the end of August was promoted to Guards status as 4th Guards Cavalry Corps). Major-General A.A. Grechko's 12th Army was to secure the junction between the 18th Army and Ryzhov's 56th Army (Budenny's battered second echelon which had been brought back to operations). For the defence of Novorossiisk, Kotov's 47th Army was pulled out of the Taman peninsula and deployed in the naval base.

On 18 August, Maslennikov's 'Northern Group' with its forward units on the river Kuma, was in action against Kleist's tanks, and began to fall back on the main defensive line, the river Terek; one week later, Mozdok was captured and the *Stavka* moved up 58th Army from Makhatchkala, while frantic work went on building up the deeply-echeloned defences protecting Baku to the north. The Terek itself was a strongly fortified line and a formidable river to cross, 300 yards of swirling water covered by Russian guns; on 30 August, a German detachment made it to the southern shore at Ishcherskaya and held a precarious bridgehead, but not until 2 September, when German forces crossed at Mozdok, were any substantial units astride the river, where Maslennikov had simply strung out his formations along the length of his front even though Tyulenev pointed out that his left flank was especially weak. Maslennikov stuck to his opinion that only at Mozdok could the Germans strike, for elsewhere the terrain would hold him; in fact, Maslennikov's left flank did slowly begin to cave in.

On the Black Sea coast, as German reinforcements moved from Kerch to the Taman peninsula, the position of Novorossiisk became critical towards the end of August; during the first week in September, heavy street-fighting was raging in the port and the Soviet marines at Taman were finally pulled off by boat, to be landed at Gelendzhik. Budenny's 'Novorossiisk defence zone' (47th Army, Gorshkov's Azov Flotilla, the Temryuk and Novorossiisk naval base garrisons) was being smashed in, and the end of the North Caucasus Front was in sight; very soon this became the 'Black Sea Group' of the Trans-Caucasus Front, Cherevichenko was relieved of his command and Petrov, who had defended Odessa and Sevastopol, took over. At Tuapse, Rear-Admiral Zhukov assumed command of the naval base, supported by four divisions from Petrov's Coastal Group; the base was hurriedly fortified, split into three sectors and brought up to immediate readiness, though Admiral Zhukov reported on 4 September to Admiral Oktyabrskii at Black Sea Fleet HQ (Poti) that moving the defence force forward to the landward lines could seriously weaken the whole coast defence. The Soviet command, local and central, realized that this southerly German drive must be halted at all costs, for unless this was done the Black Sea Fleet would be rolled up from its few bases, the German forces could then turn through Tbilisi to Baku and in the event of an absolute degeneration of the Soviet position Turkey could enter the war – now not many miles away – by attacking the Soviet 45th Army deployed along the Soviet-Turkish frontier, a further seventeen hostile divisions for the Red Army to grapple with. Novorossiisk finally was being hammered into submission, though Soviet possession of one shore of the bay denied the Germans use of the port on any useful scale. Now it was the turn of Tuapse, its defenders crouched on the narrow coastal plain awaiting the assault from the wooded heights of the foothills of the Caucasus, while the *Jäger* regiments made their dizzy way through the high passes on to the coastal plain and Sukhumi.

During these great upheavals in the south and south-west, with Soviet forces flung back to the Volga and the Terek, operations in the north-western and western theatres necessarily assumed lesser significance, though the Soviet objective was to inhibit any substantial movement of German forces southwards. From July to September, Kurochkin's North-Western Front made three attempts to clean out the Demyansk pocket, which caused additional calls to be made from the German side for reinforcement from the Eighteenth Army and for more of the Luftwaffe's transport plane resources: before Leningrad itself, Hitler had decided in August to proceed with Operation 'Nordlicht', the plan to seize the city and link up with the Finns, an offensive scheduled for 14 September and for which Manstein's Eleventh Army was drawn northwards from the southern front. From within the Leningrad Front itself, Govorov had already begun to make a series of attacks round the perimeter, while Meretskov on the Volkhov Front was ordered to prepare the 2nd Shock Army – an army brought back from the dead – to attack in the Mga-Sinyavino direction to break the blockading ring from outside, an offensive which became simultaneously a spoiling attack directed against the newly arrived Eleventh Army. The day Manstein's forces arrived, 27 August, Meretskov attacked. The plan which Manstein worked out for capturing Leningrad, a plan which aimed to avoid getting his army tangled in major house-to-house fighting, was never put to the test. The first of his divisions to arrive went into action to shore up the Eighteenth Army's broken front south of lake Ladoga: 2nd Shock Army attacking from the area of Gaitolovo aimed to meet the 'Neva operational group' (Leningrad Front) which with 115th Rifle Division and 4th Marine Brigade attacked at 16.00 hours, 26 September, across the Neva and attempted to strike for Sinyavino. When Manstein had finally tied off Meretskov's bulge, the Eleventh Army was in no fit condition to resume its course against Leningrad, with its depleted divisions and ammunition stocks severely thinned. The Eleventh Army, the victor of Sevastopol, finally limped away to Vitebsk.

During the first week in July, Zhukov's left flank had carried out a series of operations against Second Panzer Army, but the main attack was to be carried by the right wing of the Western and the left wing of the Kalinin Fronts in the Rzhev-Sychevka area, the scene of the fierce winter fighting. German plans envisaged the liquidation of the Soviet salients at Toropets-Kholm and to the south at Yukhnov-Sukinichi; in three weeks of heavy fighting, the Soviet 39th Army had been encircled once more in its position south-east of Belyi, though units did manage to break back to the main body of the Kalinin Front. West of Vyazma, German divisions throughout June pursued Soviet partisans, Red Army parachute troops and Belov's cavalrymen; the latter began to break south, while Belov was finally flown out of the German rear on Zhukov's orders. For his men returned to the Soviet lines from the six-month raid, Belov obtained one concession from Front HQ: seventy-two hours leave.

Koniev's August operations with 30th and 29th Armies did manage to clear the German bridgehead from the northern bank of the Volga, but did not result in the capture of Rzhev: Zhukov's 31st and 20th Armies were to push in the southern face of the German salient to cut off the German forces at Rzhev-Sychevka from the south, and did succeed in penetrating the Ninth Army's defensive front to a depth of some twenty miles, recapturing Pogoreloe Gorodishche and Karmanovo. For all the partial success, these operations achieved two objects, the attraction of German divisions to a threatened sector, and the instruction of the Soviet command in breakthrough operations in depth, in particular with their armoured forces. Moving tanks along poor roads and over feeble bridges meant stringing them out in long columns, so that the large mobile groups were broken into small ones forced to operate with infantry or motorized units. The tank-crews needed to improve their signalling procedures and their ability to hold their course during the attack; once the tanks had churned up the roads (and smashed down the bridges), they were practically impassable to artillery and lorries. For infantry support work, the rifle divisions really needed nothing short of a full tank battalion and in tough going a full brigade, and these units had to be able to keep going for twenty-four hours on their own, separated from brigade. It was experience dearly bought but it all went to the making of a better army, and these operations did contain German formations about to start for the south; by Soviet reckoning, twenty-five German divisions had to be moved into Army Groups North and Centre, of which nine were moved up from the critical southern battle-fronts. Colonel-General Halder in mid August recorded the strained situation, as on 16 August: '*Sehr gespannte Lage bei Rshew*', and more calls from von Kluge.

The attention of both sides, however, was drawn inexorably to the great vortex of fire and bombardment which was the battle for Stalingrad, the titanic battle building up on the Volga, into which more German divisions were being drawn only to be finally ground down in ceaseless fighting. After 23 August, when German tanks had lanced their way to the Volga, the city was under constant aerial attack and German ground troops pushed their way on and in; it was a situation which Stalin watched hour by hour from Moscow, leading the *Stavka* to bear right down on the tactical situation. Just before midnight on 24 August, Lopatin of 62nd Army sought permission to pull his units and equipment back to the middle defensive line, while Yeremenko submitted his plans for a counter-attack in the direction of Vertyachii. At 05.15 hours, 25 August, Stalin transmitted his own orders to Colonel-General Vasilevskii:

It is evident from Lopatin's report that the enemy is freely moving his units into the area of Kotluban to the east of the Don. This means that the enemy will pierce the last defence line. Consequently Lopatin should be pulled back to the final line, east of the Don, and also 64th Army, a withdrawal to be carried out secretly and in good order, so that it should not degenerate into flight. It is necessary to organize rear guards able to fight to the death to give the army units time to pull back.

On receipt of the attack plans, Stalin changed his mind, and at 15.00 hours 25 August transmitted a new set of orders:

Received latest report of Lopatin of 25 August, in which he informs of his decision to cut off enemy forces which have broken through from the Don, and if Lopatin can really put his decision into operation, I suggest that he be given help to do it. In that case our earlier directive about the withdrawal of 62nd and 64th Armies to the east can be considered non-operative.

But Lopatin's attack failed, and meanwhile Yeremenko waited for a supporting attack to come from the north, from the Stalingrad Front. In the city itself more than 1,000 workers armed with rifles were mobilized to reinforce Red Army units; the City Defence Committee also issued instructions to erect barricades and strong-points in each plant and factory, to turn them into miniature fortresses. As German units closed in, the battle rolled down on the internal defence line as Yeremenko fought to win time to bring in more reserves from across the Volga and also to complete the hasty preparations to fight inside the city.

Towards the end of August General Zhukov, then directing operations at Pogoreloe Gorodishche, received a telephone call from Poskrebyshev, the chief of Stalin's secretariat: Zhukov was told that on the evening of 26 August the State Defence Committee had appointed him Stalin's deputy commander and that now he was to await a telephone call from Stalin himself. To all of Zhukov's questions Poskrebyshev turned an unreceptive ear, merely saying that 'he [Stalin] will presumably tell you himself'. Stalin duly telephoned on the afternoon of 27 August, asked Zhukov how the situation stood on the Western Front and then ordered him to report at once to the *Stavka*, because things were looking very black in the south. Late that same evening Zhukov arrived at the Kremlin and was received by Stalin, who then told him formally about his appointment as Deputy Supreme Commander. At the moment Vasilevskii, Malenkov and Malyshev were in Stalingrad: Zhukov was to go, Malenkov would stay and Vasilevskii would fly back to Moscow. At this point in a terse and sombre meeting, in which Stalin could not hide his forebodings, he asked Zhukov how long he would need before flying out; Zhukov replied that he could be ready in twenty-four hours after studying the maps and reports, whereupon Stalin expressed his satisfaction, asked Zhukov if he were hungry, called for tea and then proceeded to give a brief summary of the position as of 20.00 hours on 27 August. The *Stavka* had decided to send 24th, 1st Guards and 66th Army to the Stalingrad Front: Moskalenko's 1st Guards would move into the Loznoe area and be ready on the morning of 2 September to strike at German units pressing on to the Volga and then link up with 62nd Army. Under cover of Moskalenko's attack, Kozlov's 24th Army and Malinovskii's 66th would go into action – 'or else we may lose Stalingrad', Stalin concluded.

On 29 August Zhukov arrived by plane at Kamyshin, where Vasilevskii met him; together they went to Stalingrad Front HQ at Malaya Ivanovka, where Zhukov listened to the reports of Nikishev (chief of Staff) and Rukhle (chief of operations), Gordov being in the forward positions. Zhukov was far from impressed with the grasp these two officers showed of the situation and neither seemed much convinced of the possibility of holding off the Germans. The meeting with Gordov and Moskalenko, however, proved to be more encouraging; both of these commanders had an accurate picture of German strength and disposition and the capabilities of their own troops. But that estimate of Soviet strength proved to be depressingly correct: the troops moving in to the north, the three armies the *Stavka* had dispatched, were badly fitted out, manned by older reservists, short of fuel and ammunition. To attack with all three armies, 1st Guards, 24th and 66th, on 2 September was out of the question: Zhukov reported this to Stalin without delay and suggested 6 September for the attack from the north to relieve the battered South-Eastern Front which was being driven back into Stalingrad itself. Stalin raised no objection. There was a slim chance that Moskalenko's 1st Guards might begin its operations on 2 September, but lack of fuel prevented a more rapid concentration. Moskalenko asked for a delay of twenty-four hours; to avoid 'useless losses' and a 'haphazard commitment of troops', as Zhukov phrased it in his report to the *Stavka*, Moskalenko's attack was delayed until 05.00 hours on 3 September. Though 1st Guards duly went in to the attack that morning, the offensive was stopped short after winning only a few thousand yards in the direction of Stalingrad.

On 3 September Stalin sent an urgent signal to Zhukov about the situation in Stalingrad:

The situation in Stalingrad is getting worse. The enemy is three *versts* [one verst = 3,500 feet] from Stalingrad. They can take Stalingrad today or tomorrow, unless the northern group of troops gives help urgently. Get the commanders of the troops to the north and north-west of Stalingrad to attack the enemy without delay and get to the relief of the Stalingraders. No delay can be tolerated. Delay at this moment is equivalent to a crime. Throw in all aircraft to help Stalingrad. In Stalingrad itself there is very little aviation left.

Report at once on receipt and on measures taken.

STALIN

Zhukov did report, pointing out that if the 'troops to the north' attacked now they would have to do so without artillery support because the ammunition could not be moved up until 4 September. Stalin was furious and rounded on

Zhukov over the telephone: 'Do you think that the enemy is going to wait until you bestir yourselves? Yeremenko has confirmed that the enemy can take Stalingrad with his first push unless you strike quickly from the north.' Zhukov replied that he did not wholly share this view; as for air attacks, he had given orders to launch all available aircraft against the Germans, but he still wanted permission to wait until 5 September to attack. Reluctantly Stalin agreed, but added:

If the enemy begins a general offensive against the city, you are to attack him at once and not to wait until all your troops are ready. This is your main task: to draw the Germans away from Stalingrad, and, if you succeed, to eliminate the German corridor splitting the Stalingrad and South-Eastern Fronts.

On 5 September, under Zhukov's own supervision, 1st Guards attacked again, only to be beaten back: worse still, air reconnaissance reported strong concentrations of German tanks, artillery and motorized infantry on the move from Gumrak, Orlovka and Bolshaya Rossoshka. At the end of the day Soviet troops had made up 4,000 yards at the most, while 24th Army had been pushed back to its start-line.

When Zhukov reported on the day's fighting, Stalin expressed his satisfaction, particularly about German movement from Gumrak: 'That's good. That is a great help to Stalingrad.' The attacks were to continue, in order to draw off as many German troops as possible from Stalingrad itself. Zhukov accordingly ordered Moskalenko to continue his attacks by day with 1st Guards: at night Golovanov's bombers from the Long-Range Bomber Force went after targets in the German rear. Golovanov himself worked with Zhukov at 1st Guards HQ. Rudenko's 16th Air Army, recently re-formed, was assigned to operate with the Stalingrad Front and on 6 September Zhukov received a *Stavka* signal that two more fighter regiments were moving up to Stalingrad, with two more fighter groups arriving within the next forty-eight hours. Lieutenant-General Novikov, commander of the Soviet Air Force and *Stavka* 'representative', now enjoyed special authority to concentrate all fighter aircraft of the Stalingrad and South-Eastern Fronts on any sector where they were needed, while Khryukin's and Stepanov's fighter regiments were in part subordinated to Novikov. The *Stavka* threw in all available aircraft: Zhukov authorized 'unlimited right to manoeuvre' for air units to concentrate on threatened sectors. The fighting to 'draw off' German troops to the north continued: Paulus did detach German units to the north-west, as the Soviet 62nd and 64th Armies during the first week in September started to man the final defence line. Both of these Soviet armies were by this time reduced almost to shreds: 112th Rifle Division had only 150 men left, 390th Division just under 300, 187th mustered only 180 men and all that remained of 99th Tank Brigade was 180 men, with sixty tanks making up 62nd Army's available armour. On 12 September Yeremenko's Front took up position along the urban defence line: Stalingrad was now divided into three sectors, Northern, Central and Southern, with some 40,000 men and about 100 tanks to hold the central sector.

For a week Zhukov hammered away in the north, but by 10 September it was plain that there could be no breakthrough to the South-Eastern Front: Gordov, Moskalenko, Malinovskii and Kozlov all shared this view. On 10 September Zhukov reported this opinion to Stalin:

With the forces which are available to the Stalingrad Front we are not able to break through the corridor and link up with the troops of the South-Eastern Front in the city. The German defensive front has been appreciably strengthened owing to the renewed movement of forces from the environs of Stalingrad itself. Further attacks with these forces and with this deployment would be pointless, and the troops would inevitably suffer heavy losses. We need reinforcements and time to regroup for a more concentrated frontal assault. Army attacks are not of a strength to shift the enemy.

Stalin suggested to Zhukov that he might best fly back to Moscow and make a personal report on the situation.

On 12 September Zhukov flew out en route for Moscow. Before leaving he and Malenkov, acting as the representatives of the State Defence Committee, compiled a report for Stalin on the past week's operations:

Moscow: Comrade Stalin

We have not broken off the offensive operations begun by 1, 24 and 66 Armies and we will persist with them. In these operations, as we duly reported to you, all available units and materials are being employed.

We have not succeeded in linking up with the defenders of Stalingrad, since we are weaker than the enemy in artillery and air strength. Our 1st Guards Army, which first undertook the offensive, did not have a single artillery regiment as reinforcement, nor a single anti-tank regiment nor an AA regiment.

The situation at Stalingrad obliged us to commit 24 and 66 Armies on 5.9, without waiting for them to concentrate properly and for their artillery to move up. The rifle divisions went into the attack straight from a 50-kilometre march.

Committing these armies to action in pieces and without support meant that we could not break the enemy defences and link up with the defenders of Stalingrad, though nevertheless our speedy blow caused the enemy to turn his main force away from Stalingrad against our concentrations, thus relieving the situation of the defenders of the city, which would have been taken by the enemy without these [Soviet] attacks. We gave ourselves no other mission, nothing that is not known to the *Stavka*.

We propose to mount a new operation on 17.9, and about this Comrade Vasilevskii will report to you. The form of that operation and its timing will depend on the movement of fresh divisions, bringing tank units up to strength, strengthening the artillery and moving up the ammunition.

Today, as on other days, our units mounting the attacks have made little progress and have suffered heavy losses from enemy artillery fire and aircraft, but we do not think it possible to bring our offensive to a halt, since this would free the enemy's hands and leave him free for operations against Stalingrad.

We consider it obligatory for us even in these grave circumstances to continue our offensive operations, to grind down the enemy, who no less than us, is taking losses, and simultaneously we will prepare a more organized and more powerful blow.

In the course of our operations we have established that six [German] divisions are operating in the first line against the northern group: three infantry, two motorized divisions and one tank division.

In the second echelon for operations against the northern group no less than two infantry divisions and from 150 to 200 tanks have been concentrated in reserve.

12.9.1942.   MALENKOV   ZHUKOV

At dawn on 13 September, after a strangely peaceful night with only single German bombers over the Soviet positions, massed *Stuka* squadrons supported by artillery and mortar fire bombarded the south-central sector of the Stalingrad defences: at 08.00 hours German assault units went into the attack against the central sector itself, an attack pressed home with murderous determination in an effort to break right into Stalingrad itself. The city had become one great funnel of destruction and annihilation along the bank of the Volga: Stalingrad straggled along the high western bank of the river for almost thirty miles, running all the way from the small river of Sukhaya Mechetka in the north to Krasnoarmeisk in the south, yet nowhere did its depth exceed 4,000 yards and in places this shrank to under 1,500. The wooden buildings had long ago burned out under air attack; most of the more solid blocks were shattered by bombs or shells, or gutted by fire. In the northern part of the city lay the three huge factories, the Tractor Plant, the *Barrikady* Plant and the *Krasnyi Oktyabr* factory, to the south the large electric power station and more factories. By 9 September almost 7,000 workers were drafted into fighting squads to defend their factories and the male population at large formed an immediate reinforcement pool for Red Army units, particularly 62nd and 64th Armies. With its telephones, sewage system, water supplies and electric power all either knocked out or severely damaged, the city mobilized with frantic speed to hold off the impending assault on the inner defence line. With blazing buildings at their back, women and children in small groups made their way to the river bank, waiting in dug-outs or hidden under any available cover until the small boats sent to evacuate them slipped in by night or between the German flights. Larger craft never made the eastern bank; German guns firing over open sights caught river steamers and blew them out of the water. In one, the *Borodino*, several hundred wounded perished, and more than a thousand civilians drowned when the steamer *Iosif Stalin* met a similar fate.

Through the middle of the city ran the river Tsaritsa, its steep banks virtually bisecting Stalingrad; also at the outer centre lay *Mamayev Kurgan*, an ancient burial mound mapped as Height 102, commanding a view of the whole central and northern suburbs and looking out over the eastern bank of the Volga. It was here, as troops of the 62nd Army fell back on 'Line G', that Lopatin set up his command post. Lopatin, tired and dispirited, was relieved of his command: after consulting Stalin, who did not take lightly to others meddling in his

prerogative over command appointments, Yeremenko and Khrushchev decided
to assign Vassili Chuikov as commander of the 62nd. Before Chuikov took up
his post, to which he was formally appointed on 10 September, Krylov,
Lopatin's chief of staff and an officer who had served as Petrov's chief of staff at
Odessa and again at Sevastopol, was in temporary command.

Chuikov, personally guaranteed to Stalin by Yeremenko, had already in his
short service on the Soviet-German front shown himself to be tough and
reliable. Coming fresh to the war in the spring of 1942 from service as Soviet
military attaché in Chungking, he was not filled with that bile of defeat which
soured so many commanders. He possessed, moreover, great tactical flair and
soon demonstrated that he had an almost unbreakable nerve. Leaving his post
as deputy commander of 64th Army, Chuikov arrived at 62nd HQ on the
Mamayev Kurgan just before the huge German assault broke over his troops who
were holding the central sector. The 62nd Army had been well nigh bombed or
shelled to bits: divisions which normally mustered between 8,000–10,000 men
were down to 100–200 riflemen armed with only rifles and a few machine-guns,
tank brigades had less than a dozen tanks, and even a tank corps, forming up
under Major-General Popov, had less than fifty tanks, most of them repaired
and the majority useful only as fixed firing-positions. The Stalingrad 'fortifications' Chuikov had seen for himself, flimsy barricades which burst at the touch
of a lorry bumper; on 13 September Major-General Knyazev reported on the
state of defence, pointing out that only 25 per cent of the defence works had
been finished by workers mobilized to do the job, anti-tank defences were
incomplete and the ditches supposed to be dug in front of fixed barricades
simply were not there. The anti-tank defences would have to be finished,
buildings must be fitted out for defence by riflemen, buildings on the flanks of
barricades needed fortifying and mines should be laid in front of barricades.
But before any of this could be done German assault troops had literally hurled
themselves on 62nd Army.

12 September proved to be the day of great conferences. Zhukov reported
to Stalin in Moscow: Paulus paid a visit to the Führer's HQ at Vinnitsa. At the
Kremlin General Zhukov met Vasilevskii, who had also been summoned by
Stalin. Vasilevskii began by presenting to Stalin the latest information on the
movement of fresh German units into Stalingrad from Kotelnikovo, on the
course of the fighting at Novorossiisk and on operations in the direction of
Grozny. Stalin then demanded to hear from Zhukov about Stalingrad.
Zhukov repeated briefly what he had already said by telephone, that the three
northern armies, 1st Guards, 24th and 66th, were good fighting armies but they
lacked reinforcements, howitzers, tanks, all the things necessary to support the
infantry. The terrain on this sector of the Stalingrad Front scarcely favoured
Soviet troops, for here the enemy had good cover from Soviet fire in the ravines
and gulleys, as well as commanding the heights which gave him excellent
artillery observation from which to range his heavy guns at Kuzmichi and

Akatovka. Under these conditions the three Soviet armies could not possibly effect a·breakthrough.

What, then, does the Stalingrad Front need to break through the German 'corridor' and link up with the South-Eastern Front, Stalin asked. Zhukov replied: at least one fully reinforced field army, a tank corps, three tank brigades and no less than 400 howitzers, plus nothing short of one fully concentrated air army. Vasilevskii agreed with this estimate. Stalin at this point picked up his own map with the location of *Stavka* reserves displayed on it and studied it at length. Moving away from the table, Zhukov and Vasilevskii talked quietly between themselves in a corner, saying in effect that another solution would have to be found. Raising his head suddenly, Stalin asked: 'And what does "another" solution mean?' General Zhukov was apparently taken aback that Stalin had such sharp ears. Stalin continued: 'Go over to the General Staff and think over very carefully indeed what must be done in the Stalingrad area. Think about which troops and which areas they can be drawn from to reinforce the Stalingrad group, but at the same time don't forget the Caucasus Front. We will meet here at 9 o'clock tomorrow evening.'

Zhukov and Vasilevskii spent 13 September at the General Staff, examining the possibilities of this 'other' solution, an operation 'on a major scale' which would not fritter away fresh reserves and new equipment in partial attacks. It was plain that the outcome at Stalingrad must have a fundamental effect on future operations and it was obvious from the map that the German Sixth and Fourth Panzer Armies were being sucked into the all-out attack on Stalingrad on a narrow sector, with the long German flank on the Don guarded only by weakened satellite divisions. Just hours before Zhukov and Vasilevskii sat down to their investigation in the Soviet General Staff, General Paulus at Hitler's HQ emphasized the weaknesses of the German front at Stalingrad and pointed to the danger on the flanks: as far back as 16 August Hitler himself drew attention to what he called the '*Standard-Angriff*' mounted by the Red Army in 1920, the attack over the Don aimed at Rostov which cut the White armies to pieces. Hitler hoped that Stalin was not then recalling military precedents. While the German command approached the point where it must decide upon its objective – Stalingrad or the Caucasus – Zhukov and Vasilevskii had begun to conclude that neither was feasible, that the German army could not accomplish the 'strategic plan' for 1942: all the forces committed in the Caucasus and at Stalingrad had already suffered severe losses, nor was there any additional strength available for operations in the whole southern theatre. In one day Zhukov and Vasilevskii could not formulate a detailed operational plan, but both resolved to tell Stalin that any 'basic blow' must be directed against the flanks of German forces in Stalingrad, flanks then covered by Rumanian troops: a preliminary calculation showed that not before mid November could Soviet divisions and their equipment be ready and in position, a situation nevertheless offset by the fact that these strategic reserves included mechanized and tank forces equipped with newly produced т-34 tanks, thus permitting the Soviet command to assign them 'more significant tasks'.

In the evening (13 September) Zhukov and Vasilevskii returned to the Kremlin with instructions to call on Stalin at 22.00 hours. Stalin met them in his room and, with a rare gesture, shook hands with both officers. At first he spoke full of indignation: 'Tens and hundreds of thousands of Soviet men and women are dying in the fight against Fascism, but Churchill barters over a couple of dozen *Hurricanes*. And as for their *Hurricanes* – just rubbish, our pilots don't like them. . . .' This outburst may have been simply for effect – no particular dispute with Churchill was in the offing – since Stalin at once changed his tone, asking what Zhukov and Vasilevskii had to report, and who would submit the report. Vasilevskii pointed out that since both he and Zhukov shared a single opinion, it made little difference. Stalin than examined the map prepared by them: 'Is this yours?' Vasilevskii replied that indeed it was and that it showed the outline of a counter-offensive in the Stalingrad area. What did the concentration of forces at Serafimovich signify, Stalin asked. It signified, Vasilevskii pointed out, a new front, one which would have to be established in order to mount a massive blow into the 'operational rear' of German forces operating in the Stalingrad area. But the Soviet command did not dispose of sufficient forces for an operation on this scale, Stalin commented, whereupon Zhukov intervened to point out that according to calculations such an operation could be prepared and be really well fitted out within forty-five days. Stalin then raised another point: would it not be better to limit the scale of the operation with an attack from the north to the south and from the south to the north along the line of the Don? Zhukov disagreed: in that event the German command would be free to swing its armour speedily from around Stalingrad to block the Soviet attack, whereas with an attack by Soviet troops west of the Don the German command would be denied freedom of manoeuvre and the chance to move up reserves. To counter Stalin's reservations about moving the assault armies so far up, Zhukov and Vasilevskii explained that 'the operation' fell into two basic stages: first stage, breaching the enemy defences, encircling the German troops at Stalingrad and establishing a solid outer encirclement front to seal off these German divisions from other German forces: second stage, destroying the encircled enemy divisions and beating off attempts to break into the Soviet 'ring'. At this Stalin dropped further questions: the whole plan must be considered carefully and weighed against available resources.

The idea of the 'Stalingrad counter-offensive', which had just taken on its first real outline, also coincided with the onset of a major crisis in the defence of the city, the German attack which began on 13 September. As Stalin put down the Zhukov-Vasilevskii plan and remarked that the 'main business' at the moment was to hold Stalingrad and to stop the Germans striking in the direction of Kamyshin (north-east of Stalingrad and behind the Don), Poskrebyshev entered the room to report that Yeremenko was on the line from Stalingrad.

After listening to Yeremenko, Stalin told Zhukov and Vasilevskii that German
Panzer units were in action inside the city and that a new attack must be
expected the next day (14 September). Stalin instructed Vasilevskii to order
Rodimtsev's 13th Guards Rifle Division to start crossing from the eastern bank
of the Volga into the city: Zhukov was to telephone Gordov and Golovanov
with instructions to alert all aircraft, while Gordov would attack in the morning
in an effort to divert the German assault on the central sector in Stalingrad.
Both Zhukov and Vasilevskii were to return to the Stalingrad area, Zhukov
at once with instructions to 'study the situation' at Kletskaya and Serafimovich,
Vasilevskii in a few days also to study the situation on the left flank of the
South-Eastern Front: no mention must be made outside the Kremlin room
of what else had been discussed. Within one hour Zhukov's plane left for
Stalingrad Front HQ.

On the morning of 13 September two German assault groups, the first
comprising the 295th, 71st and 94th Infantry Divisions with 24th Panzer
Division, the second 29th Motorized and 14th Panzer Divisions, smashed into
the positions held by Chuikov's 62nd Army. Chuikov met this attack from his
HQ on the *Mamayev Kurgan*, smothered in the fire of German guns: bunkers
caved in or collapsed, killing their occupants and by late afternoon all communications with 62nd Army units were cut. After the day's fighting German
troops had made some gains, taking the station at Sadovaya, breaking into
outskirts of the suburb of Minin, and forcing a Soviet tank brigade back into the
factory settlements at *Barrikady* and *Krasnyi Oktyabr*, but for the moment the
attack was held. During the night Chuikov shifted his HQ off *Mamayev Kurgan*
into the old HQ occupied in August by the Stalingrad Front, the 'Tsaritsyn
bunker' with its lower exit leading to the river bed of the Tsaritsa and the upper
coming out on the street; this put 62nd Army HQ ahead of a number of
divisional HQs and even closer to German guns, though it afforded more secure
shelter for Chuikov's signallers. Yeremenko meanwhile ordered 62nd and 64th
Armies to counter-attack: Chuikov's men began their attack at 03.30 hours on
the morning of 14 September, only to be pinned down in most places by heavy
German fire, the prelude to the crisis which built up as the day advanced.

With the coming of the full day, many hundreds of German guns opened fire
on 62nd Army lines, which were also bombed for good measure, followed by
the assault troops and tanks. 'Lorry-loads of infantry and tanks burst into the
city' and by the afternoon German troops were attacking from several sides, in
the area of the *Mamayev Kurgan*, on the bank of the Tsaritsa, near the grain-
elevator and on the western edge of Upper Elshanka, with more attacks aimed
at Kuporosnoe, along the ravine of the Tsaritsa and through the *Aviagorodka*,
all with the object of chopping up the Soviet defences and trapping units one by
one there. The survivors of 62nd Army, 'snipers, anti-tank gunners, and artillery
men, crouching in houses, basements and block-houses', watched as 'drunken
German troops jumped out of their lorries, played mouth-organs, shouted their

heads off and danced on the pavements', then came bursts of fire and repeated
encounters fought out at close range. Block by block German troops fought
their way to the Volga: they took the crest of *Mamayev Kurgan* and near the
railway station *Stalingrad-1* occupied the engineers' house from which they kept
the central landing-stage on the Volga under heavy and accurate machine-gun
fire. To cover the Volga traffic the Russians laid down smoke-screens, but the
threat to the central landing-stage remained, a more dangerous development
than the appearance of German troops only 800 yards from Chuikov's HQ. To
hold the landing-stage Chuikov decided to commit his last reserve, a brigade
with nineteen tanks: Major Zalizyuk with six tanks had orders to block the
streets leading from the railway station to the landing-stage, Lieutenant-Colonel
Vainrub with three tanks went to wipe out the German machine-gunners in the
engineers' house.

On the eastern bank of the Volga, from which Soviet batteries continually
fired against targets in the city, Rodimtsev's 13th Guards waited to cross to the
central sector, having been assigned to 62nd Army strength by Yeremenko.
The division had moved down from Kamyshin by lorry to Srednaya Akhtuba
during the night of 10–11 September, but though up to full strength (10,000
men) it lacked weapons and ammunition: more than a thousand men had no
rifles. At 19.00 hours on 14 September Chuikov issued orders by radio for the
division to assemble on the eastern bank at Krasnaya Sloboda (facing the 'central
sector' of the city), form small parties and prepare to cross. Rodimtsev himself,
begrimed and dusty from jumping into shell-holes or diving into ruined
buildings for cover, had already arrived at Chuikov's HQ on the afternoon of
the fourteenth and received his battle orders: these were to leave his heavy
weapons on the eastern bank, bring the Guards over with anti-tank rifles and
mortars, clear the centre of the city with two regiments, retake *Mamayev
Kurgan* with another regiment, leave one battalion in reserve at Army HQ. First
to cross from 13th Guards was a lead group of the 1st Battalion of the 42nd
Regiment, reinforced with machine-gunners and anti-tank riflemen, commanded by Lieutenant Chervyakov. The men assembled in the gathering darkness, looking out over the blazing city with the silhouettes of separate ruined
buildings sharp against the glow of fires. A half-sunken barge blazed near the
crossing point, the flames illuminating the water for several hundred metres:
the burning barge served the German gunners admirably as an aiming point.
The small boats making the crossing had only to run towards the western bank
to be met with heavy fire: two rowing-boats tried for the mooring, were
spotted, machine-gunned and moved downstream a little, only to be raked by
more gunfire. The boats with the lead group moved off: the nearer the western
bank, the heavier the fire, with lines of tracer sweeping over the approach to
the central landing-stage. Without waiting for the boats to make fast the Guards
rolled into the water, struggled for the shallows and scrambled ashore, fighting
in the half-light with German infantrymen and machine-gunners, hacking,

stabbing and clubbing their way forward metre by metre to the north of the central landing-stage. Here Chervyalkov's men established a small bridgehead for 13th Guards.

For the rest of the night more Guards riflemen came ashore from small boats, tugs and barges, moving off the fire-swept landing-points into the shattered streets, only to be pinned in the daylight by *Stukas*, for in Stalingrad 'the Luftwaffe literally pounded into the ground anything that moved'. Rodimtsev's men, under constant aerial attack, could not form up properly and could not establish any real positions: straight off the streets they had to set about clearing the 71st German Infantry Division out of the railway station and away from the Volga landing-stage, as well as making preparations to dislodge the 295th Infantry Division from Height 102, *Mamayev Kurgan*, which at any cost the Russians had to retrieve. At the cost of a crack Soviet division, fighting in pieces as it came across the Volga, and with final expenditure of Chuikov's small but resolute reserves, the German onslaught against the centre of the city was choked off and 62nd Army won a few more precious hours.

In this wholly ruined and fire-blackened shell on the Volga, the defenders, with nowhere to retreat, faced the choice of fighting or being blotted out with the city, now a nightmare of rubble, sagging, shattered buildings, gaping burned-out shells with their corpses, where the noise never ceased by day or night. By day German planes hung in clusters in the sky, sweeping in to rake the streets, to unload more bombs on the ruined buildings or to fly across the city with their screamer-sirens wailing: at night, lit by fires, flares and the flashes of endless explosions, beside broken walls or in the grotesquely mis-shapen interiors of what once had been shops, offices, houses and factories hundreds of miniature but horrifyingly savage battles were fought for cellars, rooms, staircases and corners of walls. Lacking food and denied sleep, small units, the 'garrisons' of Stalingrad, went out to seek water and battled to death over drainpipes. The survivors of this heaving inferno, where survival seemed impossible, still elected to stay and fight, anchored in the fiery ruination of Stalingrad where 'the ground is slippery with blood'.

10

Transformation at Stalingrad:
Operation *Uranus*
(October—November 1942)

Late in May, when the Crimean Front had broken to pieces and those Soviet troops meant to attack from the Izyum bulge were now fighting desperately to hold off annihilation, Stalin abruptly switched his priorities in his dealings with his allies. During the night of 25–6 May he sent instructions to Molotov, then in London, to drop all the pressure upon the British to underwrite Soviet territorial demands in any post-war settlement; when Ambassador Maiskii saw the telegram with the new instructions so suddenly minted by Stalin, he was staggered. Stalin had decided to trade a little of the future for the present, to drop his territorial requirements in exchange for more urgent military relief. The campaign for the Second Front was mounted in deadly earnest, and rapidly generated blistering heat, throwing off accusations and reproaches not all of which could be kept from prying, gleeful enemy eyes.

By March, the British government in effect surrendered to Stalin's insistence and obduracy about the terms of a territorial settlement which would virtually guarantee Stalin all his gains under the Nazi-Soviet Pact, only the Soviet-Polish frontier being excluded from this package deal. During the Moscow talks in December 1941, Stalin had deftly slipped this under Eden s nose and made further discussions conditional upon the acceptance of the territorial demands. Back in London in mid January from his ambassadorial post in Moscow (to which he did not return), Sir Stafford Cripps discussed the terms and timing of the Soviet demands with General Sikorski: Cripps denounced the British Foreign Office for its failure to consider from the outset any 'general principles' relating to post-war frontiers in Europe, for in July (1941) when he was being flayed by the full effect of the German attack Stalin would have been obliged to negotiate. Now, with Soviet armies moving westward, that chance had vanished, and even with a German counter-offensive, German gains would be 'transient', Russia in the autumn would regain lost ground and would win the war – 'in 1942, in Berlin'. General Sikorski disagreed most profoundly: a German counter-offensive in the spring would change the situation, Stalin would be pressed and would make concessions, hence to sign everything away prematurely was a 'great error'.

Not much later (11 March) Churchill himself discussed the same question with Sikorski in London. Was Japanese restraint, asked the prime minister, due to German pressure for Japan to 'achieve an understanding between' Germany and the Soviet Union? This was the British nightmare, the prospect of a separate peace in the east. General Sikorski thought not, making the point (which few ever grasped) that 'both sides had burnt their boats'; Stalin was exploiting his present military successes and utilizing Allied weaknesses, especially in the Pacific; as for how the military situation might unfold, General Sikorski pointed to the likelihood of a German offensive 'in the Southern sector, in the direction of Rostov and the Caucasus' to be launched 'at the end of May or in June'. Much of this General Sikorski had elaborated in detail in his letter of 9 March to Eden, a letter which pointed out that Russian political pressure would slacken, that relief could be afforded a hard-pressed Russia by putting 'a single armoured division' on the European continent in 1942 where 'four-fifths of the German Forces are engaged on the eastern front', and that, though Russia would lose battles, she would not lose the war. A huge Soviet effort would be needed to defend the oilfields of the Caucasus, for the Wehrmacht would surely strike for Rostov; in the Far East, if the Japanese in the spring did not strike at Siberia, that meant they would launch themselves against India, possibly Australia. Then, with the allies struggling to defend the Caucasus, the Suez Canal, China and India – the loss of one vitally affecting the other – Stalin could no longer complain of 'the pretended isolation of Soviet Russia' in a common struggle. Stalin might 'insinuate' a threat of a separate peace, such as his Order of the Day for 23 February, but there could be no substance to it. For all this, however, London took that threat seriously and it was an open nerve upon which Stalin could drill as he wished.

It was perhaps no coincidence that the prime minister had brought General Sikorski's attention to the role of the Japanese. For all the verbiage of agreements, Germany and Japan were fighting almost self-contained wars: Germany kept its attack on Russia secret from the Japanese, who for their part hugged their Pearl Harbour plans to themselves. The 'Tripartite Commission', meant to be the brain behind Axis collaboration, was palsied from the outset, and ironically enough it was the Soviet-German war which cut all overland communication between the extremes of the Axis, Nazi Germany and Imperial Japan. The world was carved up between their armies by the agreement of 18 January 1942 (with Italy tagging on), though Japan might by agreement move out of these boundaries should the occasion arise. In the spring of 1942 this contingency appeared to come to life as Japanese warships hunted in the Indian Ocean and Japan was urged to strike for Madagascar. But in the Pacific, with the 'defensive perimeter' now in Japanese hands, the second phase of operations was about to begin, and it was here that Admiral Nagumo sped via Japan from the Indian

Ocean. The physical gap between these allies widened, never more to be closed, as Japan moved south-eastwards – away from Europe, and away from Russia.

In March (1942) the Imperial Japanese Navy discreetly conveyed to the German naval attaché in Tokyo that a negotiated peace was the only answer for Germany and the Soviet Union, and claimed that mediation would not be wholly unwelcome on the Soviet side. Such evidence as the Japanese Navy had for this assumption was flimsy in the extreme, but the German naval attaché readily conveyed this hint to Berlin. The net result was merely an explosion of Hitler's rage. Ribbentrop had meanwhile tried to engage Japan in hostilities against the Soviet Union: on 28 March he urged the Japanese ambassador Oshima to strike along with Germany whose 'crushing blow' was now in preparation. The German General Staff forwarded to their Japanese counterparts proposals for a possible Japanese attack against Vladivostok and in the direction of lake Baikal, complete with map studies. This evoked not a quiver of response from the Japanese soldiers (who in any event had in *Plan* OTSU some quite good map studies of their own). Meanwhile Japanese diplomats, whose contact with Moscow remained unbroken, tried their hand at 'mediation', though the hint they dropped in February 1942 fell on the stoniest of Muscovite ground. Flickers of 'peace' were in the air, but neither Hitler nor Stalin budged an inch from their pre-selected positions. The Japanese chased the phantom of 'mediation', not out of any concern for the Soviet Union but from fear that Germany might become ultimately and disastrously absorbed in the war in the east, and thus no real partner for Japan striking at the British and Americans; Germany sought not 'mediation' but a decision and therefore urged Japan to strike the one blow against Russia which would send her reeling from the war for ever. Neither prevailed successfully upon the other.

When at the end of March the British government finally agreed to discuss post-war frontiers with Stalin's emissaries, one of the reasons adduced for this concession was the possibility of a 'separate peace'; in fact, this was the slippery slope of offering 'compensation' for the failure to draw off German troops by attacking in the west. The cabinet had not come either easily or unanimously to this surrender to Stalin, and on informing President Roosevelt of the decision, learned to its discomfiture that the president contemplated negotiation of his own with Stalin. His first attempt to lure Stalin away from these territorial demands through conversation with Litvinov in Washington misfired. On 8 April, the cabinet, aware that President Roosevelt had agreed (albeit most reluctantly) to the British course, resolved to discuss a treaty with Molotov in London on the basis of the Soviet terms; almost at once President Roosevelt invited Stalin to send Molotov to Washington to 'discuss a very important military proposal'. When Molotov finally arrived in London he opened his discussions on 21 May by stating that he had come to discuss both a treaty and a 'second front', but the latter was more important. The next day, the prime minister, Attlee, Eden and the Chiefs of Staff explained in great detail to Molotov why landing a large force on the continent was out of the question, though Molotov had yet to discuss an 'important military proposal' with the president. As for the treaty, Molotov was not inclined to consider the 'alternative proposal' presented by Eden: this proposal specifically eliminated mention of frontiers and centred on mutual assistance over a period of twenty years. A talk with the American ambassador, Mr Winant, on 24 May nevertheless did much to modify Molotov's obduracy, for he learned that a treaty cast in the Soviet mould would scarcely rally American support; the next day (25 May) Molotov admitted an 'alternative proposal' for the first time and with astonishing rapidity obtained Stalin's assent to sign. For American goodwill, it was cheap at the price.

Once in Washington, where he arrived on 29 May, Molotov again broached the Second Front and the problem of 'drawing off' the forty German divisions which seemed to enter into all of Stalin's military mathematics. At his conference with President Roosevelt on 30 May, Molotov intimated that he had received no positive reply in London to his question. This President Roosevelt proceeded to rectify with a precision which, though it served admirably at the time, subsequently brought a deal of confusion and recrimination in its wake; having asked General Marshall whether developments were advanced enough for any positive answer to be given to Stalin, and having received an affirmative reply, President Roosevelt then told Molotov that he might inform Stalin that a 'Second Front' was expected this year. A little before his final meeting with Molotov (1 June) the president had to be dissuaded from mentioning August as the very month and General Marshall cautioned against mentioning even the year 1942 in the official statement. All the ammunition he had gathered in Washington Molotov now proceeded to fire off at his meeting on his return trip in London on 9 June, when he formally requested the British government to consider opening a 'Second Front' in 1942. The Soviet government would forgo some supplies due under the agreement: the American president was ready to sacrifice 100,000–200,000 men even if it brought a 'second Dunkirk'. Churchill responded with his famous *aide-mémoire* of 10 June which specified preparations for a landing in Europe in August or September (1942) but which specifically excluded a promise or binding undertaking to that effect. The essence of the British decision was that unless we intended to remain on the continent, no 'major landing' should be attempted in 1942: a rebuff would be an irretrievable disaster.

At the root of much dissension and discussion lay the wide divergences over just what a 'Second Front' implied. Early in February the British Joint Planners thought of it as 'Round-up', a cross-Channel attack against 'crumbling opposition' in 1942 or a straight and intended assault in 1943. A month later (10 March) the same planners made a brutally frank appraisal of the problem in terms of supporting the Soviet Union, whose armies were now largely halted in their westward rush: apart from the supply of war material, 'we are giving no direct help to Russia'. Late in February Major-General Eisenhower pressed in his paper for 'a definite plan' for operations 'against north-west Europe', designed to draw off German air strength and finally 'by late summer' more German ground troops. General Marshall himself in London during the April conference with the British chiefs of staff outlined a plan suggesting a landing possibly in May 1943, but which could serve at much shorter notice should either the Russian forces require speedy relief, a 'sacrifice attack' on our part, or if the Wehrmacht were tied totally in the east, or yet again if German military power appeared to crack. The cross-Channel attack plan enjoyed the president's greatest support and he hoped it would impress Stalin. Over 'Sledgehammer', the proposed attack plans, the prime minister and his senior officers entertained the gravest doubts concerning their feasibility for 1942 and sought for other diversionary enterprises (which raised not a few American suspicions): the ambiguities, however, were sufficient to explain the difference in the British and American approach to Molotov. As for Stalin, he seized upon these tentatives as a pledge: President Roosevelt's assertions about a 'Second Front in 1942' were turned into assurances, and there was General Marshall who pointed out the high level of preparations (though he had also pressed for the specific reference to 1942 to be deleted). In his *aide mémoire* of 10 June, the British prime minister had stated flatly: 'We can therefore give no promise in the matter. . . .'

The Soviet press at once delivered a unique and powerful salvo which drowned any note of disquiet or dissent: with the words '. . . 1942 must be the year of the enemy's final destruction', *Pravda* launched on 13 June a public display of Allied exchange as if all were signed, sealed and about to be delivered immediately. With German armour ripping the Red Army apart in the south, there was every need to stiffen morale; at the same time, a wall of German armies still stood beyond Moscow, clear of the capital but a threat none the less. When Stalin was about to loose his sternest warning on the Russians, there was compensation in the hope of relief from outside. The meeting of the Supreme Soviet in the Kremlin on 18 June was summoned to ratify the Anglo-Soviet treaty: Stalin attended in person, though Molotov presented the long report on the Anglo-Soviet Treaty bringing in his 'Second Front' conversations, but he touched one small – and chilling – note of caution. The 'complete agreement' over the Second Front emphasized by Zhdanov, himself much acclaimed by the assembly, rang a little hollow. And within a month, as the propaganda blast on the 'Second Front' theme continued undiminished, the explosion finally came, one which Ambassador Maiskii contrived to detonate (at least he claims as much).

In these ambassadorial skirmishes, Sir Archibald Clark Kerr (successor to Sir Stafford Cripps in Moscow) had on 4 July remonstrated with Molotov about the show of public certitude over a 'Second Front' in 1942: Molotov, who had earlier insisted that nothing short of 'a promise' had been given, replied that the 'government' well knew all the complications, but that 'the people' naturally fastened on the optimistic terms of the communiqué. In London, Maiskii touched another raw nerve over his questions about convoy sailings, whose runs through the hazardous 'northern route' had developed on a regular basis after October 1941. The convoy which had sailed at the end of May (PQ 16) had lost almost a quarter of its cargo and 7 out of 35 ships. On 27 June, PQ 17 which sailed from Iceland for Murmansk met a catastrophic fate: in addition to the German bombers and submarine packs which assailed these clusters of ships, the threat of the battleship *Tirpitz* had fallen over this convoy, which broke and scattered to its destruction. Only 11 out of 36 merchant ships made the Soviet port of Murmansk; more than 400 tanks, 200 planes and nearly 4,000 lorries had gone to the bottom. The Defence Committee decided to suspend convoy movement along the northern route, baleful news which the prime minister passed to Stalin on 17 July: the same message promised to divert ships to the southern (Persian Gulf) supply route, though the limited capacity of the ports and the lack of large-scale communications meant inevitably that a smaller volume of supplies could reach the interior of the Soviet Union.

Maiskii on 21 July had evidently submitted 'a plan' to Stalin to force the hand of the British government: in his dispatch to Moscow, Maiskii suggested that Stalin should take a very tough line over the convoys and over the second front, emphasizing that this was a critical hour for the Soviet Union. Without the relief of an attack in the west, the whole war might be lost or the Soviet Union so weakened that it might be incapable in the future of 'active participation' in the struggle. As Stalin sent off his signal, Maiskii would put the same pressure on MPs and the editors of British newspapers in an effort to break this 'British lethargy'. In short, Maiskii proposed to short-circuit the government and go straight for public opinion. When it came, Stalin's message (dated 23 July) was both blunt and biting: Soviet naval advisers found the British reasons for cancelling the convoys 'untenable', the deliveries via the Persian ports would 'in no way make up for the loss in the event of deliveries via the northern route being discontinued', and finally on the second front, 'I state most emphatically that the Soviet Government cannot tolerate the second front in Europe being postponed till 1943.' (For all its menace, the signal was milder than Maiskii had expected or hoped for.) A few days later, the Admiralty discussed the convoys with Maiskii and the head of the Soviet naval mission, Admiral Kharlamov, a furious interchange (as seen from the Soviet side), which ended with Admiral Sir Dudley Pound suggesting to Maiskii that he take command of the Royal Navy, though it brought the compromise of Maiskii forwarding to Moscow a request for heavier air cover (six bomber and four torpedo-bomber squadrons to 'make the Barents unsafe for the *Tirpitz*') in the north and the British agreeing to re-examine the convoy question. Maiskii, moreover, did not neglect very shortly afterwards to lay much of the unsavoury detail of this meeting before Lord Vansittart. At the end of the month, however, the prime minister signalled

Stalin that a new convoy, PQ 18, would leave for Archangel early in September; this concession was accompanied by a suggestion that both leaders might meet. By the same date (31 July), Stalin agreed to the meeting and proposed Moscow as the venue.

From London, Maiskii sent Stalin an immensely detailed report dealing with the prime minister's disposition, his manner of work and his foibles: in Moscow, Stalin set up a 'special commission' with the Marshals Voroshilov, Shaposhnikov and Colonel-General Voronov as members to handle the staff talks which were to take place at the same time. On 12 August at 7 pm, two hours after he landed in Moscow from Teheran, the British prime minister met Stalin in the Kremlin. At the outset, as Churchill crunched into the arguments why there could be no 'Second Front' in Europe in 1942, the meeting was tense and cheerless. Stalin was not disposed to accept the arguments and pressed a variety of alternatives: the capture of the Channel Islands, a feint at the Pas de Calais and the seizure of Cherbourg, landing six divisions on the Continent. Even at the prospect of 'Torch', the North Africa landing, Stalin emerged only slowly from his gloom. At the next encounter on the night of 13 August, Stalin, 'puffing his pipe, eyes half closed, emitting streams of insults', launched a savage attack, introduced by him handing over his own *aide-mémoire* formally rejecting the British arguments over the impossibility of a front in Europe in 1942. In a two-hour confrontation, Stalin charged the British with what amounted to cowardice and the Allies with regarding the Eastern Front as secondary, with a low priority for supplies. To all the jibes but one – that the British Army was afraid to fight – Churchill restrained himself, but at that he lashed out and finally the conversation ran into the calmer waters of technicalities. The following day the prime minister presented his formal counter to Stalin's charges of a breach of faith over a second front and that evening repaired to a Kremlin dinner: for Churchill, this was the end of the road, though on this occasion Stalin had circled him much more warily. Attempts at a form of mediation between the two leaders on 15 August seemed at first doomed to fail: the only response from the Kremlin was that 'Mr Stalin is out walking.' At 6 pm, Stalin stopped walking with great abruptness: he would see Mr Churchill that night, a meeting which adjourned to Stalin's private quarters and which ended in quietness and the spreading of a thin net of friendliness.

The staff talks proceeded in rather desultory fashion: the three Soviet officers did what they could to overturn the objections to a landing in Europe in 1942, insisting that a Second Front was both vital and feasible. In line with Stalin's remark to the prime minister about exchanging technical information, the British officers were taken to see a demonstration of the *Katyusha*. Voronov, however, was convinced that the British delegation had little faith in the ability of the Red Army to survive. He was also put about by the 'excessive inquisitiveness' of his visitors about the Caucasus. Stalin had assured Churchill that the mountain chain in the Caucasus would be held and maintained that the passes were fortified (which was in fact not true, and the Chief of the Imperial General Staff had seen only rudimentary defences from his aircraft flying between the Caspian and the mountains). At the British disclosure that what we meant by help in defending the Caucasus amounted to eight squadrons of aircraft – and those only after a turn for the better in North Africa – Soviet interest evaporated: the Soviet officers refused to consider any question of bringing in British aerodrome parties and ground staff. Having achieved little or nothing, the staff talks ground to a halt.

On the night of 16–17 August, at the final meeting when Stalin in his quarters turned on both domesticity and conviviality for the prime minister, Churchill learned more of the Soviet position: Stalin asked less for tanks than lorries, of which he had great need and also for aluminium. He apparently persuaded Churchill of the Soviet ability to hold out (an opinion which the CIGS did not come to share). Above all, Stalin let the prime minister into the immensely secret prospect of a vast counter-offensive (though the terrible day when the Panzer column tore through the northern tip of Stalingrad was still a week away). In the prime minister's view, Stalin now 'knew the worst', that in this 'most anxious and agonising time' there would be no external military relief: the Red Army (which some thought finished, a point which Stalin took great pains to flatten) would either have to fight it out or go under at Stalingrad and in the Caucasus. With the fading of the 'Second Front' whatever hopes Stalin had ever entertained of ending the war 'in the autumn, in Berlin' vanished outright. Much of the optimism of his May Day message was linked, publicly at least, with the 'Second Front' theme, and therein lay the sense of his formal disclosure in his memorandum of 13 August which emphasized that '. . . the Soviet High Command, in planning its *summer and autumn operations*, counted on a second front being opened in Europe in 1942.' For his part, Churchill was content to assure his colleagues formally that 'they', having lodged their protest, were 'entirely friendly': privately, he levelled harsh words over Maiskii and Molotov (and reportedly excoriated Stalin himself).

There was every compelling reason for Stalin to put up a bitter fight for a second front, to use private browbeating and public pressures. The bloody repulse of the Dieppe raid, coming as it did (19 August) straight on the heels of the Moscow confrontation, brought no abatement in these manoeuvres to mobilize public opinion: finally Maiskii had to be cautioned officially to play more softly on the public nerve. Yet for all the disastrous news from the battle-fronts (and fully aware now that he would have no help from outside), Stalin persisted with two observations: that Batum and Baku would not fall to the Germans, and that a 'counter-offensive on a great scale' was in the offing. When Stalin mentioned this, no specific plan for a 'counter-offensive' existed, if Zhukov's evidence is to be believed about the conversations in the Kremlin on 12–13 September. This, however, refers only to the 'other' solution proposed for Stalingrad. It is true that precisely at this time, when the talks took place, a considerable amount of armour was being drawn into *Stavka* reserve and large armoured formations were being built up, hence the need for lorries: nor did Stalin dissemble when he mentioned the high Soviet tank production. The Soviet General Staff had already arrived at the same conclusion that the German summer offensive, for all the terrible punishment it was inflicting, would not finally attain its objectives and must necessarily drain off German reserves. Above all, the Soviet gaze was being directed to the German flanks at Stalingrad, to the cordons of Rumanian troops holding lengthy sectors without reserves. But the 'practical' work of planning a counter-offensive at Stalingrad had yet to begin: for all his brave talk at the Moscow meetings, to judge by his comments immediately afterwards Stalin was a prey to secret but awful fears, that the Germans would break north-east over the Don, that Stalingrad might fall in one final, murderous rush, that the Germans might get to the oil of the Caucasus. What remained to be seen was whether the Red Army could stand the shocks of the next few critical weeks and whether Stalin could straddle this gigantic crisis: the burden of the meetings in Moscow, inconclusive and strained as they otherwise were, was that Stalin had announced that he could and would win out.

Contrary to German expectations, Stalingrad did not fall into their hands rapidly nor did Soviet armies fall back entirely to the eastern bank of the Volga. The attempt to storm into the centre of the city and on to the Volga itself was being held, though with only metres to spare. Each building in Stalingrad became its own battle-ground, with fortresses fashioned out of factories, railway stations, separate streets or small squares and finally single walls. Throughout August and well into September German successes flowed one after another, but none brought the attainment of any major objective. To the north of the Soviet-German front the offensive in the Leningrad area had died away: on the central sector German troops fought heavy defensive actions against Soviet units engaged in the dogged business of 'tying them down', day after day of bloody, apparently aimless fighting, or so it appeared to the Soviet divisions bearing the casualties: and while Army Group B closed in on Stalingrad, Army Group A in the Caucasus faced an enemy still unbeaten and still in possession of the mountain passes.

Grim as the fighting at Rzhev on the central sector was for Soviet troops, it produced dramatic results, even if at long range. Halder's insistence on adequate protective measures for the Ninth Army led at the end of August to a head-on clash with Hitler himself, and within a month Halder was ejected as Chief of the General Staff. While Hitler could no longer spread his armies even more widely, at least he could reshuffle the commands, implemented in earnest at the beginning of September. The lack of progress in Army Group A acted as the fuse to ignite the Führer's wrath: Hitler himself, after summoning Field-Marshal von List to the Vinnitsa HQ to offer an explanation, elected to assume personal command of Army Group A and to run it from his damp and stifling command centre in Vinnitsa, 700 miles behind the front. The Russians, so Hitler believed, were done and all but finished, an illusion to which Göring contributed in his report of 28 August at Vinnitsa that in Stalingrad the enemy no longer disposed of any significant force: Göring based his opinion on the personal inspection carried out by General von Richthofen of *Luftflotte IV* at Stalingrad. Gehlen at *Fremde Heere Ost* presented a different picture: Soviet reserves did exist (estimated by FHO at more than seventy rifle divisions and over eighty armoured formations) and they were being concentrated. Soviet output of weapons included large numbers of T-34 and KV tanks. All the while German armies were becoming fearfully dispersed between the Black Sea and the Caspian: Army Group B's flank on the lower Don was lengthy and but thinly screened (the specific observation made by General Paulus to Hitler on 12 September), while the northern wing of Army Group A, striking beyond Groznyi and to the Caspian, stood in urgent need of strategic flank protection along the lower Volga. The only successful preventive measure against any Russian 'initiative' on the lines of the 1920 attack – a thrust over the Don – was the rapid capture of Stalingrad, yet this 'solution' merely poured more German troops into an appalling battle of attrition which sucked in division after division.

On 13 September, on the eve of the savage German assault to break into the centre of the city and to the Volga, Soviet strength on the Stalingrad and South-Eastern Fronts numbered all of sixty-five rifle and four cavalry divisions, seven rifle, thirty-four tank and six motorized brigades, four 'fortified districts' (URs) and five military schools. The main body of the South-Eastern Front, 62nd, 64th, 57th and 51st Armies, held Stalingrad itself: the two armies in the centre of the battle, 62nd and 64th, comprised sixteen rifle divisions, eight rifle brigades, two tank corps and one 'fortified district', in all some 90,000 men, 2,000 guns and mortars, 120 tanks. The 'Stalingrad area', the 65-kilometre sector running from Rynok in the north to Malye Chapurniki in the south (57th Army sector), was held from Rynok to Kuporosnoe by Chuikov's 62nd, a 20-mile 'front' manned by about 54,000 men with 900 guns and mortars, 110 tanks (the best approximate strength figures for 13 September): 64th Army on its 12-mile front defended the line running from Kuporosnoe to Ivanovka, seven rifle divisions and two brigades. Chuikov's men, according to Soviet figures, faced twice their number of attacking Germans, five times their strength in tanks and twice the artillery strength of 62nd Army. Though nominally strong in divisions, these formations were mere shadows of former days, between 2,000 and 3,000 men and three, 87th, 98th and 196th, had now less than 800.

Between 13–14 September the German fist crashed full weight on 62nd Army in the fight for the centre of the city. By day and night battles roared round and through the Central Railway Station (*Stalingrad 1-i*), with the situation changing by the hour, recorded in 62nd Army war diary for 14 September:

07.30/hours/: Enemy in *Akademicheskaya ulitsa*
07.40   : 1st Battalion 38th Mechanized Brigade cut off
07.50   : Fighting near *Mamayev Kurgan* and at approaches to station
08.00   : Station in enemy hands
08.40   : Station recaptured
09.40   : Station retaken by enemy
10.40   : Enemy in *Pushkinskaya ulitsa* – 600 metres from Army command post.
11.00   : Up to two enemy companies with 30 tanks in support moving on 'specialists houses' [engineers houses]
13.20   : Station in our hands

Rodimtsev's Guards went into this fight as they came off the boats: during the night of 15–16 September more of 13th Guards Division was ferried across as the struggle for the railway station and for possession of *Mamayev Kurgan* intensified. Two German divisions, 71st and 295th, pushed into the centre, while a third infantry division, the 94th, with support from 24th and 14th Panzer divisions fought their way into Minin and towards Kuporsnoe, the southerly suburb where the flanks of 62nd and 64th Armies joined. Rodimtsev's men on the sixteenth cleared the area of the central landing-stage and the surrounding streets, and recaptured the central railway station – the fifteenth time it changed hands. At dawn on 16 September two Soviet regiments, the 42nd (13th Guards) and the 416th from Sologub's 112th Rifle Division, stormed *Mamayev Kurgan*: one regiment would take the northern and parts of the north-eastern slopes, the other the whole of the north-eastern side. After a ten-minute artillery bombardment, the Soviet regiments advanced in open order: the Guards battalion under Captain Kirin took the German positions on the northern slope, while the 416th fought its way up the north-eastern approaches to the summit, where a squad of thirty men under Lieutenant Vdovichenko cleared the German machine-gun pits with rifles, grenades and rifle-butts. Out of the thirty attackers, six were left and they at once faced a heavy bombing attack, followed by a counter-attack launched by German infantry with tank support. Fearful of hitting their own men, the German pilots bombed wide of the target; entrenched on the summit, the Soviet squad knocked out two tanks and broke up the infantry assault for the moment. But the Germans came back, not only that day but for many days after, with more tanks and more infantry: artillery and aircraft were used in attempts to blast the Soviet units off·the summit. The struggle for *Mamayev Kurgan* never slackened. Throughout the winter days no snow ever covered the slopes, for continuous shell-bursts melted it off.

On the morning of 17 September Chuikov sent a signal to Front HQ that 62nd Army badly needed reinforcement: Soviet reserves were expended, while fresh German forces appeared continuously. In a few days 62nd Army would 'be bled to death'. Chuikov asked for two or three divisions at full strength: he got two brigades, the 92nd Rifle Brigade (manned by marines of the Baltic

and Northern Fleets) and 137th Tank Brigade (from 2nd Tank Corps) equipped
with light tanks and 45-mm guns. Both brigades came over the Volga on the
evening of the seventeenth, the 92nd moving to the left flank of 13th Guards
Division (to check a German breakthrough on to the Volga along the Tsaritsa),
the 137th to the right flank, in the loop of the railway line which ran about 600
yards east of *Mamayev Kurgan*. Chuikov also received permission to change the
location of his headquarters, the 'Tsaritsa bunker' being too exposed to German
fire. The new HQ was sited about half a mile north of the *Krasnyi Oktyabr*
landing-stage; to reach it meant a laborious, dangerous journey by ferry to the
eastern bank of the Volga with a return journey to the new site, unappealing
as it was, lacking

... dug-outs of any kind of shelter to protect us even from bullets or shrapnel. Above us,
on the bare hillside, were oil-tanks and a concrete reservoir for crude oil. Piled up on a
spit of sand were lathes, motors and other factory equipment, put ready to be ferried over
the Volga, but left behind. A number of half-destroyed barges lay by the river bank. The
HQ staff established itself on the barges or just in the open. The Military Soviet and the
Chief of Staff were accommodated in hastily dug trenches, open to the sky.

Unaware that the oil-storage tanks above them were still full, the engineers set
about building bunkers and digging trenches: when German bombers subsequently hit the tanks, Chuikov was very nearly burned alive.

   The fighting for *Stalingrad 1-i* and *Mamayev Kurgan* continued throughout
18 September: the day began with the usual appearance of the *Stukas*, followed
by artillery and mortar fire, at which Soviet guns opened fire. The *Stukas*
headed in a swarm for the main railway station and for *Mamayev Kurgan* but
that morning, as the fighting built up round the station, the German aircraft.
suddenly veered off to the north and the sky over Stalingrad cleared of German
bombers. To the north-west of Stalingrad the left flank armies of the Stalingrad
Front, 1st Guards, 66th and 24th, were resuming their attacks, aiming as before
at Gumrak-Gorodishche with the object of relieving the pressure on Stalingrad:
Chuikov at 62nd Army received orders to prepare an attack to fight his way out
to meet the Soviet armies coming from the north. This was the attack General
Zhukov and Malenkov proposed in their joint letter of 12 September to Stalin;
then it was timed for 17 September. It came a day late on Zhukov's own orders,
since he had returned to the Stalingrad Front and supervised the preparations
for the attack. The cause of the delay rested with Moskalenko's 1st Guards, but
Moskalenko faced an almost impossible assignment, to prepare the offensive and
simultaneously to raise a new army. On 10 September, under Front Order
No. 00498/OP, 1st Guards handed its rifle divisions over to its neighbours, 24th
and 66th, exchanged sectors, and in turn received five rifle divisions and three
tank corps plus artillery and engineer units brought from *Stavka* reserve. The
24-hour postponement scarcely provided time to train the divisions and
regiments which sorely needed it. At 05.30 hours on 18 September, after a

preliminary bombardment, the two divisions of the left flank with two tank brigades attacked once more.

Moving towards the high ground held by the Germans, the Soviet infantry and tanks made up to 3,000 yards, even reaching the crest, when they were stopped in their tracks by a German counter-attack launched by infantry with armoured support: committing two Soviet tank corps failed to alter the situation, since these formations fielded mainly T-60 and T-70 tanks whose light armour could not stand up to the German guns. The majority 'burned like candles'. The German bombers came all too quickly, attacking in waves and bombing the Soviet units in groups of 30–40 machines. Burned-out or immobilized tanks lay in the wake of the Soviet advance, with infantry units effectively pinned by the sustained bombing and strafing. All Soviet movement in the rear lay exposed on the flat and monotonous terrain; with every move visible for a considerable distance the Soviet attack came as no great surprise to the German command, which hammered Moskalenko's men mercilessly. Towards the late afternoon the German bombers returned to Stalingrad, hanging once more in the sky over 62nd Army's head, a sure sign to Chuikov that things had gone badly to the north. Chuikov, exposed in his new-found HQ, was handling both the German assault on the centre and preparing to launch his own attack on the right flank, 62nd Army's contribution to the 'relieving attack' from the north. Yeremenko, South-Eastern Front commander, told Chuikov about the impending offensive only on 17 September, giving Chuikov less than twenty-four hours in which to make his own plans and also to bring over the rifle division from the eastern bank which he had been promised as reinforcement.

At 18.00 hours on 18 September Chuikov received his formal orders from Yeremenko, the Front Commander:

1 62nd Army Command, after creating a shock group of not less than three infantry divisions and one armoured brigade in the area of *Mamayev Kurgan*, will launch an attack towards the north-west outskirts of Stalingrad, with the aim of destroying the enemy in this area. The immediate task is to destroy the enemy in the city, firmly securing a line through Rynok-Orlovka-Heights 128.0 and 98.9, and the north-west and western outskirts of Stalingrad.

If Chuikov was annoyed at the few hours given him to ferry over a whole division and re-deploy his units already in Stalingrad, he was incensed at the preamble to this order which spoke of the enemy 'withdrawing a number of units and formations from the area of Stalingrad . . . transferring them north through Gumrak'. Only the German planes had left, and even they came back. The fighting raged in the city as before: Rodimtsev's riflemen, those still left alive, engaged the Germans in the main railway station, setting up their weapons in the ruins of the station outbuildings, in burned-out rolling stock or behind the platforms. The bombing and shelling on *Mamayev Kurgan* continued, with Sologub's men hanging on under the bombardment. Towards the southern boundary of 62nd Army lay the giant grain-elevator, in which Soviet and German troops fought for several days and nights for parts of the building: here Soviet marines from 92nd Brigade took position after landing on 17 September, holding off repeated assaults:

Enemy tanks and infantry, approximately ten times our numbers, soon launched an attack from the south and west. After the first attack was beaten back, a second began, then a third, while a reconnaissance 'pilot' circles above us. It corrected the fire and reported our position. In all, ten attacks were beaten off on 18 September.

. . . In the elevator the grain was on fire, the water in the machine-guns evaporated, the wounded were thirsty, but there was no water near by. This was how we defended ourselves twenty-four hours a day for three days. Heat, smoke, thirst – our lips were cracked. During the day many of us climbed up to the highest points in the elevator and from there fired on the Germans; at night we came down and formed a defensive ring round the building. Our radio equipment had been knocked out the first day and we had no contact with our units.

With his units everywhere engaged in this fighting at close quarters, Chuikov now had to rush his men and few tanks into position to attack to the north-west; this attack, timed for noon on 19 September, would unroll from *Mamayev Kurgan* 'in the general direction of the station' to cut off and destroy those German units which had penetrated to the centre.

The second attack launched by the Stalingrad Front with 1st Guards, 66th and 24th Armies, also timed for noon on 19 September, failed again. The German bombers duly turned away from Stalingrad, but by the early evening they gathered in their accustomed numbers over the city and Chuikov knew the worst. His own attack from *Mamayev Kurgan*, mounted by Sologub's 112th Division and two battalions from the reinforcement division still being ferried over, made some progress, but the German pressure on the centre did not relax: the *Stukas* effectively broke up the Soviet attacks in the north, which never once deflected the drive to split 62nd Army in two. On 20 September German bombers concentrated at first light to blow what was left of the railway station, *Stalingrad 1-i*, to pieces: 'After the bombing – an artillery bombardment. The station buildings were on fire, the walls burst apart, the iron buckled, but the men went on fighting . . .' The survivors, men of Chervyakov's unit from 13th Guards which had made the first crossing, moved out to the square facing the station and occupied part of a building – christened the 'nail factory' because of the stores of nails found there – on the corner. Chervyakov was wounded and evacuated over the Volga: Fedoseyev took command with the battalion being pressed back on three sides: 'The position with ammunition was serious, and there was no question of food or sleep. The worst part was the thirst. In our search for water, in the first place for the machine-guns, we fired at drainpipes to see if any water dripped out.' German tommy-gunners and snipers got behind the remnants of the Guards battalion: during the night the Germans blew up the wall separating the room holding the Russians from the rest of the

R.T.S.—O

building and threw in hand grenades. On 21 September the battalion was cut
in two, with the headquarters section trapped near the *Univermag*, the department store; inside the *Univermag* Russians and Germans fought a hand-to-hand
engagement, which ended when Fedoseyev and his HQ staff were killed. The
rest of the battalion pulled back yard by yard to the Volga, occupying its last
'position' in a three-storeyed building on the corner of *Krasnopiterskaya* and
Komsomolskaya streets, defended by forty men who held out for five nights:

> At a narrow window of the semi-basement we set up the heavy machine-gun with our
> emergency supply of ammunition – the last belt of cartridges . . . Two groups, six in each,
> went up to the third floor and the attic. Their job was to break down walls and prepare
> lumps of stone and beams to throw at the Germans. A place for the seriously wounded
> was set aside in the basement.

After five days that basement held twenty-eight seriously wounded men: the
girl nurse with the battalion, Lyuba Nesterenko, was dying from a chest wound:
there was no water, the only food 'a few pounds of scorched grain'. Finally the
heavy machine-gun joined the action, destroying a German column which all
unawares advanced along its line of fire; the emergency supply of ammunition,
the belt of 250 cartridges, was fired off in breaking up this attack. But soon
nothing of the building remained as the Germans used tanks: the walls crashed
down with a roar, burying the defenders alive. At night six Guardsmen, all
wounded, struggled out of the ruin. Stumbling off in the direction of the Volga,
they bumped into German patrols, their presence betrayed by the flares, but the
silent knifing of two German guards opened a route without the Russians being
discovered. Over the railway line, through a minefield, on to the Volga, these
scarecrow soldiers were finally rescued.

By 21 September, with both sides reeling under the toll of casualties, German
troops cleared the bed of the Tsaritsa, while a considerable force of tommy-
gunners supported by tanks positioned itself only a few yards from the central
landing-stage: in the built-up area behind *Stalingrad 1-i* railway station German
units spread out over a depth of about one mile square, trapping two Soviet
brigades and a regiment. The very lie of the streets in this quarter, running as
they did in a west-east direction towards the river, assisted the German attack,
for the Russian defenders soon discovered that German guns could 'pour' fire
down the streets from one end to another. German infantrymen set up fire-
points and road-blocks at the western end, then blasted their way to the other.
The infantry assembled for its attack with a few tanks in support; if the tanks
moved out the Russians rarely tackled them in isolation, preferring to let them
advance to within range of the dug-in Russian tanks. Only when the German
infantry moved up did the Russians open fire, but once located in their strong-
points the Russians had finally to face the tanks which used their heavier
armament to fire at close range and destroy whole buildings. For all their
protection, however, it was a hazardous job for the German tank-crews: once

in the narrower streets well-aimed anti-tank rifles or grenades could cripple the tanks if they burst through the thin armour of the rear deck or penetrated the engine grill. After each battle the Stalingrad streets bore the same look, great mounds of rubble sprouting single, half shattered walls with floors often still attached but hanging at one side in empty air, burned-out tanks surrounded by heaps of dead.

Chuikov learned to modify the system of 'divisions' and 'regiments', using his manpower in small, heavily armed 'storm groups', ideal for carrying out a lightning counter-attack on a recently captured building or strong-point. Tactics were increasingly dictated by urban geography:

City fighting is a special kind of fighting . . . The buildings in a city act like break-waters. They broke up the advancing enemy formations and made their forces go along the streets . . . The troops defending the city learned to allow German tanks to come right on top of them – under the guns of the anti-tank artillery and anti-tank riflemen; in this way they invariably cut off the infantry from the tanks and destroyed the enemy's organized battle formation.

But not always. On Chuikov's left flank, in the southern part of the city where 14th and 24th Panzer Division with 29th Motorized and 94th Infantry Division were operating, two Soviet brigades fought cut off from 62nd Army: Chuikov's left was in danger of being pushed in, though the German advance here was slowed by continued resistance, notably in the grain-elevator, from several strong-points held by Soviet 'garrisons'. Colonel Batrakov, commander of one of these brigades (42nd), was badly wounded and with him his staff in a German bombing attack on 23 September: 42nd Brigade combined with the 92nd, but the commander of the 'combined brigade' decamped, ferrying himself and his staff to Golodnyi Island (between the western and eastern banks of the Volga) from which they sent fictitious battle reports to 62nd Army HQ. Only on 25 September did Chuikov learn the truth when it was too late to do much: 42nd Brigade reported on 25 September 'Situation deteriorating in brigade area. Shortage of ammunition and food, also lack of men makes situation still worse.' The next day 92nd Brigade, now leaderless, disintegrated under the attack launched by 94th Infantry Division and 24th Panzer; the 92nd scrambled to safety across the Volga and 42nd Brigade eventually had to be pulled out.

The loss of the central landing-stage, however, brought immediate dangers and fresh difficulties to Chuikov: from here the Germans could observe the rear of 62nd Army and the Volga traffic upon which it depended. To repair his communication, Chuikov used the landing-stages at the *Krasnyi Oktyabr* factory and in the Spartanovka settlement to the north, with three additional landing-stages established on the eastern bank to deal with this re-routing, Even more serious, the Germans could be expected to push along the Volga bank north and south of the landing-stages, to slice 62nd Army away from its ferries. The incision made in 62nd Army was certainly deep and dangerous, though not

fatal: to prevent worse damage, Chuikov resolved to counter-attack using some
of the reinforcement he had just received. In the early hours of 23 September
Colonel Batyuk's 284th Rifle Division, manned by Siberians, was ferried over;
Rodimtsev's 13th Guards received a transfusion of 2,000 men. Chuikov proposed to attack on 23 September, clearing the Germans from the central
landing-stage, re-occupying the valley of the Tsaritsa and finally linking up
with the two Soviet brigades marooned in the southern sector of the city.

In the early hours of 23 September, Batyuk's Siberians crossed the Volga in
their barges and made for the western bank. Little of the darkness remained:
German aircraft dropped parachute flares, lighting up the river bank where the
284th was coming ashore. Near *Neftesindikat*, on the precipice overlooking the
river, German incendiary bombs hit oil containers which spilled blazing oil
towards the edge of the Volga and then set the river alight. German tommy-
gunners with tanks not far behind moved to within 150 yards of the bank,
firing at the Siberians as they came off their boats. One regiment fought its way
up the bank and broke up the German attack, moving on through the bombed
houses in the direction of the *Metiz* factory and the south-eastern slopes of
Mamayev Kurgan, where Goryshny's 95th Division was hanging on. At 10 am
in the morning Chuikov's counter-attack opened, by which time Batyuk's
regiments were fully engaged. The arrival of the Siberians helped to check the
German thrust northwards from the central landing-stage: together 95th and
284th Divisions pushed German units back in the centre towards the railway line
and even made ground towards the railway station, although to recover it was
beyond their strength. But still the Germans were not cleared from the Volga,
even if checked for the moment, and Soviet units on the northern side of the
Tsaritsa made no contact with those brigades pinned to the south of it.

Within twenty-four hours the fighting slackened in the centre of Stalingrad.
Chuikov, however, now faced an attack from both west and south: reconnaissance reported a strong German build-up at Razgulyayeva and Gorodische,
while the collapse on his left flank to the south – 92nd Brigade having disintegrated and 42nd almost destroyed – caused Chuikov to expect the German
command to swing its units here against *Mamayev Kurgan*. The main attack
was nevertheless being organized from Razgulyayeva-Gorodische, another
major thrust aimed this time at the factory settlements of Stalingrad lying to the
south of Rynok, the massive concrete blocks of the three great factories, the
Tractor Plant, *Barrikady* and *Krasnyi Oktyabr*. Paulus regrouped for this attack
in order to bring the greatest weight to bear on the centre and the northern
suburbs of Stalingrad. With its huge factories and blocks of workers' apartments,
the northern part of Stalingrad was studded with natural forts, the three large
factories, the chemical plant and the deadly meshes of the industrial railway
sidings, *der Tennisschläger*, the 'tennis racquet' as it was soon known to and
feared by German soldiers, the name derived from the looping shape of the
railway network.

Chuikov prepared both his front and rear. To bar the line of advance on the *Barrikady* factory and the Tractor Plant, 62nd engineers hurriedly prepared an anti-tank line running from the mouth of the river Mechetka, along its southern bank on to the beginning of the Vishnevaya gully, past a wood and along the northern rise of the Dolgi gully as far as the Volga. Divisional and brigade commanders received orders to lay down their own anti-tank lines, to pay special attention to anti-tank minefields and to have engineer squads ready with mines in the event of a German breakthrough to close off all roads and parks. Rearwards Chuikov reorganized his ferries, for without them 62nd Army could not survive. Strict orders went out over the handling of ammunition once it came off the barges on the Stalingrad side: on 18 September ammunition for 13th Guards had blown up on the bank, after which Chuikov issued an Army order enforcing the burying or concealment of all ammunition in trenches. The order of 25 September instructed all 62nd Army units to conceal unloaded ammunition, fuel and food in previously prepared caches located not less than 500 metres from the river bank. The supplies were at risk from the moment they moved towards the railway lines on the eastern bank of the Volga: German aircraft bombed rail traffic as it moved on the eastern bank, inflicting losses and bringing serious interruption in movement. Soviet fighters patrolled the lines, sixty sorties a day along the Krasnyi Kut-Astrakhan line and thirty along the Verkhnyi Baskunchak-Stalingrad line, and batteries of 85-mm and 37-mm guns, together with armoured 'AA' trains, provided what protection they could, but the air attacks continued, blowing up lines and smashing stations. The Russians tried to counter by unloading trains further from the base area, with lorries picking up the ammunition and supplies as far back as 150 miles and the infantry reinforcements left to march.

The 'ferries', some actual ferry-boats but mostly small cutters and barges, sailed under constant attack. German aircraft by day hunted down each boat and barge; if the aircraft missed them, as they drew towards the western bank the boats came under sustained and accurate fire. The Volga River Flotilla with its armoured gunboats, minesweepers and AA gunboats, came under naval command, Rear-Admiral Rogachev and his two brigade commanders. The Flotilla became operational on 10 July, affording Admiral Rogachev, who complained to his chief Kuznetsov earlier in 1942 at this appointment that it looked as if he might 'miss the war', one of the most arduous tasks laid upon a Soviet naval officer. In addition to helping with the ferrying, Rogachev's gunboats and monitors operated on the 'river flank' of the units in Stalingrad, as well as putting their sailors ashore to fight under Red Army command.

The civilian fishermen and river-men of the Volga manned the motley fleet of ferries, all of them skilled and demonstrably brave. At the end of August Rogachev took control of the Volga fishing fleet from *Narkomrechflot* (Commissariat for Fishing Fleets); the Lower Volga fishing fleet brought off more than 200,000 civilians after the end of August, using the *Krasnyi Oktyabr* and the Krasnoarmeisk landing-stages. In mid September, to centralize this traffic, the Lower Volga fishing fleet chief put his craft under the operational control of Major-General V.F. Shestakov, commander of the Volga crossings, though manning and servicing these boats remained the responsibility of the fishing fleet itself. The central landing-stage, latterly under heavy German fire, was not used to unload supplies after 15 September, though wounded were brought off until 26 September. Meanwhile Chuikov set up three new landing-stages and laid down precise orders for loading, evacuation and operating. The *Krasnyi Oktyabr*-Krasnaya Sloboda 'ferry' passed under the direct command of 62nd Army: the two motorized pontoon battalions, 44th and 160th, now came under the command of the engineer officer, 62nd Army. To regularize traffic, each landing-stage set up an 'operational group' with three officers, representing artillery supply, provisions and medical services. The chief engineering officer in 62nd Army was responsible for the maintenance and repair of ferry-boats, as well as supplying them with fuel and lubricants. Ammunition and food had priority for the Stalingrad side, wounded, sick and prisoners for the eastern bank. Cut off from all other Soviet units, surrounded on three sides and with the Volga at its back, 62nd Army divisions depended for their whole existence on the ferries.

After 25 September, in anticipation of the new German attack, Chuikov decided to regroup the 62nd, to reinforce on the Mechetka river sector and around *Mamayev Kurgan*. The soldiers moved by night through the gullies, ruined buildings and the mass of shell-holes or bomb-craters. Eleven German divisions were arrayed before 62nd Army, three Panzer divisions (14th, 24th and 16th), two motorized (29th and 60th), six infantry divisions (71st, 79th, 94th, 100th, 295th and 389th). The 16th Panzer Division was on Chuikov's right flank, the 389th Infantry Division, moved out of reserve, in the Gorod-ishche-Razgulyayeva area, 295th Infantry Division reinforced with armour near *Mamayev Kurgan*, 71st and 76th Infantry Divisions in *Stalingrad 1-i* and the central landing-stage, four divisions including 14th and 24th Panzer in the southern reaches of the city. For a new attack on the factory district the German command had also set about regrouping: the 71st Infantry Division, one of the crack divisions of the German Army, was to mount the attack on the *Krasnyi Oktyabr* factory settlement and the 100th *Jäger* Division was assigned to the attack on *Mamayev Kurgan*.

The situation on *Mamayev Kurgan* was giving rise to great concern at 62nd Army HQ. German troops already occupied the southern and western slopes of this hillock: another hundred yards and they would be in full possession of *Mamayev Kurgan*, looking down on the factory district. At six o'clock on Sunday morning, 27 September, Chuikov launched a spoiling attack to dis-locate the German preparations for the assault on the factory district and to relieve the pressure on *Mamayev Kurgan*: Shumilov with 64th Army received orders from Yeremenko to use 36th Guards Division to relieve Kuporosnoe.

At 8 am General Fiebig's *Stuka* squadrons and fighter-bombers pinned 62nd Army to the ground, breaking up units and bombing headquarters. Two and a half hours later the German bombers and artillery blasted away the Soviet strong-point on the summit of *Mamayev Kurgan*, where men from Goryshny's 95th Guards Division were dug in. Three German formations, 100th and 389th Infantry Division with 24th Panzer Division, struck out for the *Krasnyi Oktyabr* factory and for *Mamayev Kurgan*: 150 German tanks moved out from Gorodishche and Razgulyayeva, crashing through Soviet minefields and bringing infantry in their wake. By two o'clock German troops had reached the western edge of *Krasnyi Oktyabr* as far as the Banny Gully (*Bannaya ovraga*) and the south-western corner of *Barrikady*. By the evening Goryshny's men in regiments cut to shreds held only the northern and eastern slopes. Near Chuikov's HQ German bombing set the oil reservoirs alight, smoking out the command posts whose staff moved off to find units with whom they had lost touch.

On the left flank the situation worsened south of the river Tsaritsa: the 92nd Brigade disintegrated, 42nd Brigade was withdrawn (only to be brought back later to the western bank to take part in the fighting for the factory district) leaving the 272nd Regiment of Colonel Sarayev's 10th NKVD Division. The Germans broke through to the Volga in some strength south of Tsaritsa, occupying a five-mile sector of the Volga river bank. Shumilov's attack with 64th Army drew off some enemy strength, but it proved impossible to clear German troops out of Kuporosnoe, where they were jammed between 64th and 62nd Armies. Chuikov on 27 September appealed to South-Eastern Front HQ in desperation: his Guard units had been virtually blown to pieces on *Mamayev Kurgan*, up to eighty German tanks moved on the *Krasnyi Oktyabr* factory, his left flank was nothing but a bloody stump of broken regiments, the Stukas roared about Stalingrad with apparent impunity, and fresh German regiments waited to renew the assault. By the evening of 27 September German troops had made up 3,000 yards into his positions, leaving a trail of 2,000 dead men and some fifty blazing tanks. Chuikov urgently asked for air cover – even for a few hours a day – and for reinforcements. During the night of 27–8 September the remainder of Colonel Smekhotvorov's 193rd Rifle division was ferried over to Stalingrad (one regiment having gone to Chuikov on 22 September). Smekhot-vorov's men went ashore into another of those 'howling, screeching, bleeding nights' in Stalingrad, with companions blown overboard or mortared on the very banks of the river, leaping ashore under the searing light of the yellow-green flares, dragging weapons and infantry ammunition, moving along these monstrous streets with their sagging or disembowelled buildings brightly illuminated for a moment under some shell-burst or rocket, then plunged into the shadow thrown by the night. At 04.00 hours the 193rd was ashore, doubling under all its burdens to *Krasnyi Oktyabr* which loomed up in the half-light, the great bastion of the factory also lit by the flashes of the guns and the winking splashes of the reddish-yellow light sent out by small-arms fire. The 193rd took up positions near the big cook-houses which formed part of the factory, circling the bath-houses and School No. 5 occupied by the Germans. At night the Russians reclaimed much of what they had lost in the day, going out in fighting patrols or singly to knife and club in the darkness, sliding through sewers or across the weird bridges formed by the bombed buildings to unnerve the Germans. The Russians moved at night, sending their military traffic through the natural gullies and the artificial canyons formed from the flattened houses, streets which shone in the bluish light of bombardment or glistened under the parachute flares drifting across the city.

Day broke bright and hard, with fierce German infantry and tank attacks. Chuikov called for sustained artillery fire from the eastern bank on the summit of *Mamayev Kurgan*: mortars from 62nd Army fired their bombs towards the summit. German dive-bombers concentrated on Chuikov's own HQ, adding to the fire from the burning oil-tanks; they aimed for the ferry-boats on 28 September, knocking out five of the six larger steamers plying to the *Krasnyi Oktyabr* landing stage. On *Mamayev Kurgan* one regiment of Gorishny's 95th Division and two battalions of Batyuk's 284th, supported by the aircraft which Major-General Khryukin (commander of 8th Air Army) sent up over Stalingrad, made yet another effort to take the summit: fighting through the roar of continuous air and ground bombardment, these already depleted units reached the point of the height but failed to establish themselves on the summit. Neither side held the topmost ground which was swept by German and Russian guns. German dead lay all about the slopes of *Mamayev Kurgan*: Batyuk's 284th lost over two hundred to three hundred men and Gorishny's 95th, pounded by days of fighting, had lost most of its men. In the factory district the German assault continued throughout 28 September, breaking against the outworks of *Krasnyi Oktyabr* and crashing through the forward Soviet positions towards the south-eastern edge of the *Silikat* factory.

The next day, 29 September, fighting spread across Chuikov's extreme right flank into the 'Orlovka salient' which hung over the German formations in the Gorodishche area: this was the salient which the Stalingrad Front, attacking from the north with 1st Guards, 66th and 24th Armies, had tried to reach all through September. If the left wing of the Stalingrad Front and Chuikov's right ever connected, the German forces on the Volga at Latashanka would have been trapped and the whole German left flank imperilled. Some five miles long and two deep, with a frontage extending for twelve miles, the Orlovka salient was presently held by a 'composite battalion' of 250 men – all that remained of Sologub's 112th Rifle Division – and Colonel Andryusenko's 115th Rifle Brigade. To reduce the salient Paulus committed several regiments of 16th Panzer Division, 60th Motorized Division, 389th and 100th Infantry Divisions. The German offensive, unrolling in two directions from the west and north-east in a pincer attack, opened with a heavy ground and air bombardment. In the afternoon German infantry and tanks approached Orlovka from the north and from the south, over-running the 1st and 2nd battalions of Andryusenko's 115th Brigade. The 1st Battalion fell back to the northern outskirts of Orlovka, but Soviet troops west of the town were in danger of being trapped; the Orlovka 'corridor' had been reduced by half. In the city itself the fight for *Mamayev Kurgan* raged throughout 29 September, while Smekhotvorov's men were pushed back on the western edge of *Krasnyi Oktyabr*.

German troops redoubled their efforts to reduce the Orlovka salient on 30 September; shortly after noon German guns and aircraft hammered Andryusenko's units in the Orlovka area, where two Soviet battalions still held the northern and southern parts of the little town. To the east, however, the German pincers were almost closing, thus giving German troops passage along the 'Orlovka gully' to the giant Tractor Plant and to *Barrikady*. The threat to these two factories was now very real, with 14th Panzer and 94th Infantry Division brought up from the southern suburbs to join in the assault, which Chuikov had to face virtually without reserves. The *Stavka* late in September ordered three brigades of the 7th Rifle Corps to concentrate on the eastern bank: two tank brigades (84th and 90th) were rushed up from Saratov and two rifle divisions (87th and 315th) brought into immediate reserve. But Chuikov wanted troops on the western bank to fend off the attack on the factory district. Under cover of darkness on the night of 30 September–1 October, the 42nd Rifle Brigade was ferried back to the western bank and took up positions in the north-western corner of the city: the 92nd Brigade was also brought back to Stalingrad, taking over from the 23rd Tank Corps which had been reduced to seventeen tanks and little more than a hundred men. Major-General Stepan Savelievich Guriev's 39th Guards Division was simultaneously hurried over to the western bank, though its regiments were conspicuously under-strength: raised from the 5th Parachute Corps in August 1942, the 39th Guards had already taken part in the fighting at the approaches to Stalingrad and now, less than 4,000 strong, it occupied positions just west of *Krasnyi Oktyabr*, with a 'front' running from Kazachya Street to Banny Gully, backing up Smekhotvorov's 193rd.

Guriev's men arrived in the nick of time. German troops on 1 October severely dented Smekhotvorov's position, whereupon Chuikov ordered Guriev to set about fortifying the workshops of *Krasnyi Oktyabr* and turning them into a major strong-point. With this pressure on the factory settlements, Chuikov could send little or no help to the units fighting in the Orlovka salient; the German pincers closed at Orlovka on 1 October, trapping Andryusenko's 3rd Battalion – 500 men with two days' rations and 200 rounds per rifle – in the 'Orlovka gully'. East of Orlovka the two remaining Soviet battalions, reinforced with an anti-tank regiment (all Chuikov could presently spare), received orders to fight their way to relieve the beleaguered 3rd Battalion. In the 'Orlovka gully' where Andryusenko's men entrenched themselves German dive-bombers carried out repeated attacks, German guns fired one barrage after another and

German infantry tried without result to dislodge the defenders: cut off save for the occasional air-drop of supplies, the 3rd Battalion held the gully for a week, until the night of 7 October when 120 survivors broke out of encirclement. All through 1 October the Germans kept up their attacks on Smekhotvorov's division covering the *Krasnyi Oktyabr* factory and also intensified their pressure in the centre against Rodimtsev and Batyuk, with the aim of reaching the Volga and splitting 62nd Army in two. At first German parties tried to rush the gullies leading to the Volga, but Rodimtsev's men clubbed them to death or shot them down; the Dolgi and Krutoy gullies were strewn with German dead. During the night of 1–2 October about 300 men from 295th German Infantry Division, dragging their mortars along, crawled through the main drain which ran beside the Krutoy gully and came out on the Volga: once free of the drain, the German troops turned south into the rear of the 34th Guards Regiment and burst into the rear of other Soviet units. The raid through the drain coincided with an attack on the right flank of 13th Guards, held by the 3rd Battalion of 39th Regiment. Just before dawn a large body of German troops had burst into the rear and flanks of 13th Guards, with sharp and sudden encounters spurting at every corner. At 6 am Rodimtsev decided on a counter-attack to restore order within his divisional positions; after thirty minutes, with marauding German troops caught in cross-fire and ambushes, the situation was brought under control.

Attacks from the north (Stalingrad Front) by Soviet armies had so far failed to relieve the weight of the German attack directed against the city: the Orlovka salient was also practically in German hands. The *Stavka* decided to try diversionary attacks to the south, with 64th Army and the two armies (57th and 51st) on the extreme flank. The southerly attacks mounted by 51st and 57th Armies began on 29 September: at the beginning of October Shumilov with 64th Army, Chuikov's nearest neighbour, prepared to strike out with his right flank divisions towards Peschanka, a small village south-west of Yelshanka. During the night of 2 October Shumilov attacked with four divisions, 422nd and 36th Guards, 157th and 138th Rifle Divisions, but the attempt to drive north towards a junction with the 62nd failed. The gap between the 62nd and 64th was, if anything, widening. At the beginning of October Chuikov's 62nd held a twelve-mile front in Stalingrad with a depth varying from 250 metres to 2,500 metres: all movement in this dangerously compressed area was confined to the hours of darkness, regrouping was a hazardous affair now that the ferry traffic was so constricted, since the German seizure of parts of Stalingrad to the south from the Tsaritsa to Kuporosnoe and northwards to *Mamayev Kurgan* enabled them to look out over large stretches of the city and direct their guns against the ferries. One thousand yards of water, the Volga crossing, was raked by German gunfire and became the daily hunting-ground for German aircraft. Considerable sections of the northern and central parts of Stalingrad were in German hands: Yermanskii, Dzerzhinskii, *Krasnyi Oktyabr*, *Barrikady* and the Tractor Plant (STZ) regions, with the Orlovka salient including Orlovka itself sliced away, and

German troops pushing into Rynok and Spartanovka (though they never managed to capture these). Early in October great battles boiled and raged for the three great factories of the northern suburbs, *Krasnyi Oktyabr*, *Barrikady* and the STZ, the Tractor Plant, one of the biggest of its kind in the Soviet Union, where Soviet units offered yard-by-yard resistance. On the afternoon of 29 September more than 100 German aircraft bombed the Tractor Plant, setting outbuildings and workshops alight; Chuikov faced another burst of savage fighting in his dreadfully shrunken bridgehead.

Chuikov's own HQ came next on the German list of targets. On 2 October bombers racing along the bank of the Volga struck the oil-tanks on the bluff overlooking Chuikov's command post, setting them on fire and releasing a stream of blazing oil which rolled down the cliff towards the Volga, spread to the river and set the water alight. Surrounded by a sea of fire Chuikov and his HQ staff seemed in imminent danger of being burned alive, but the flames swept past the dug-outs, leaving dense clinging smoke in their path; the oil burned for several days, pouring more black smoke over the Volga bank and actually providing Chuikov with almost perfect camouflage, for the German pilots were persuaded that no one could live under this fiery, smoking pall. The attack on the three great factory fortresses, *Krasnyi Oktyabr*, *Barrikady* and the Tractor Plant meanwhile intensified. The walls of the assembly shops in the Tractor Plant stood out gaunt and blackened after the heavy German bombing: girders and roof-beams were twisted across the floor of the shops, piles of masonry heaped about the fittings which once held machines. The northern and north-western approaches were held by two brigades of Colonel Gorokhov's group and a regiment of the 10th NKVD Division: the western face was defended by the apparently indestructible 112th Division, subsequently joined during the night of 7–8 October by the remnants of Andryusenko's men who broke out of the 'Orlovka gully' and fell back on the Tractor Plant. During the night of 2 October yet another division, Colonel Gurtiev's 308th, waited to be ferried over the Volga: though only two regiments were in Stalingrad by the morning, Gurtiev's men moved up to the *Barrikady* factory and by noon were engaged in a fierce counter-attack which pushed German troops out of the north-western sector of the factory buildings as well as clearing part of the *Silikat* factory. Smekhotvorov's 193rd Division, its regiments reduced to a mere 100–150 men, fought off German attacks against the bath-house and the communal kitchens in the streets of the *Krasnyi Oktyabr* industrial estate, while Guriev's 39th Guards defended the factory itself.

Chuikov reckoned that five German divisions, three infantry and two Panzer, were fighting on a 5,000-yard front with the intention of smashing their way into the Tractor Plant: the reduction of the Orlovka salient was merely a diversion to distract Soviet attention from the assault on the factories. At the Front command Yeremenko supported this view and made one more division, Major-General V.G. Zholudev's 37th Guards, ready to cross into Stalingrad:

from 20.00 hours on 2 October 37th Guards passed under the command of 62nd Army, with orders to embark during the night 2–3 October and to take positions in the Tractor Plant not far from the north-western edge of the *Barrikady* industrial settlement. One of the tank brigades (the 84th) brought into reserve late in September was also destined for the western bank: the brigade had 49 tanks all told (5 KVs, 24 T-34s and 20 T-70s, light tanks). Zholudev's men did not begin crossing until the early hours of 4 October, but the shortage of ferry-boats meant leaving behind the divisional staff and the anti-tank guns. Chuikov's HQ, where the fire still lapped over the river bank and where German mortars were beginning to find the range, took over immediate command of 37th Guards, using headquarters officers to guide the regiments to their positions located between 112th and 308th Divisions.

The main German attack during the next twenty-four hours pressed forward from the *Barrikady* settlement towards the Tractor Plant as 37th Guards took up positions to block this advance. Nothing could be done to shift the heavier tanks of 84th Tank Brigade to Stalingrad but the light T-70s were brought over and moved into 37th Guards and 308th Division areas to act as stationary firing-points. During the hours of darkness, which kept the dive-bombers away, Soviet troops worked to fortify the streets in the workers' settlements, built block-houses along the walls of the factories and set about digging communication trenches: the detachments of armed workers, hitherto fighting independently, were formally put under Red Army command on 5 October and assigned to the divisions defending *Krasnyi Oktyabr*, *Barrikady* and the Tractor Plant. These men, who worked to the last minute repairing weapons and improvising a variety of devices for street-fighting, hung ammunition belts across their overalls, picked up grenades, rifles or anti-tank weapons and still in their working-men's flat caps took up positions in the firing-points or bunkers with Red Army men. On 5 October German dive-bombers came on in strength, making more than 700 attacks on the Tractor Plant and 2,000 raids over the whole factory area: 42nd and 92nd Brigades, with the 6th Guards Tank Brigade, were again cut off and German troops finally occupied the *Silikat* factory. Yeremenko at Front HQ ordered Chuikov to counter-attack on 5 October to clear the Tractor Plant and *Barrikady*, but this was wholly beyond the power of 62nd Army for its ammunition was almost exhausted.

On the evening of 5 October Lieutenant-General F.I. Golikov, deputy Front commander, crossed into Stalingrad to see the situation at first hand. During the day Stalin had prodded Yeremenko with an order demanding that Stalingrad be held:

The enemy is in a position to realize his plans, since he occupies the landing-stages for the Volga to the north, in the centre and to the south of Stalingrad. To eliminate that danger, it is necessary to slice the enemy away from the Volga and re-occupy those streets and houses in Stalingrad which the enemy has wrested from you. It is therefore essential to turn each house and each street in Stalingrad into a fortress.

Stalin concluded: 'I demand that you take every possible measure for the defence of Stalingrad. Stalingrad must not be taken by the enemy, and that part of Stalingrad which has been captured must be liberated.' Golikov, unlike Stalin, could see for himself how grim the position was. German mortar bombs were exploding at the entrance to Chuikov's HQ: the oil-tanks had burnt themselves out, but smoke from blazing pools of oil nearby drifted into the 'headquarters'. The singular 'traffic' of Stalingrad was already on the move, the reinforcements slipping into single buildings and strong-points, ammunition shunted forward through the gullies and the myriads of passages cut into the ruins, while hundreds of wounded dragged themselves or crawled to the landing-stages where the boats bustled to unload supplies and take on the battle casualties. The larger ferries came over the Volga with a varied cargo, troops, ammunition boxes, light weapons, any spare space filled with the carcasses of sheep or dry rations: the barges brought over the tanks, lashed to a platform, spare deck space also piled with ammunition. The first week in October, however, was a bad one for losses with the larger ferries, as the *Stukas* went on sinking the steamers which carried the bigger loads.

Unable for the present to mount a counter-attack from 62nd Army, Chuikov called on the artillery batteries on the eastern bank to bring down a heavy barrage to disrupt the German attack. Ammunition supply always presented great problems on both banks, for in one day a 'Front artillery group' would fire off 10,000 rounds. After a tense argument earlier in September Chuikov persuaded the Front command to leave 62nd Army artillery on the eastern bank: nowhere in Stalingrad could he deploy his guns, and it would need even more ferries to bring them ammunition. On 5 October Soviet guns on the eastern bank fired off a *kontrpodgotovka*, a 'counter-preparation' bombardment, selective but massive, aimed at German concentrations: more than 300 guns and heavy mortars fired for forty minutes, the artillery of five divisions and two brigades, the northern 'sub-group' of Front artillery and five regiments of *Katyusha* rocket-launchers fired over a three-kilometre sector. The opening salvoes lasted ten minutes, followed by twenty minutes of fire directed by observers on both banks and closing with ten minutes of final, smothering salvoes from all available guns. The weight of this massed fire fell on German assault units preparing to break through to the Volga between the Tractor Plant and *Barrikady*.

6 October proved to be 'relatively quiet', due in part to the punishment inflicted on the Germans by the previous day's bombardment. Throughout the day the German command resorted mainly to air attacks, conserving their armour and infantry for the moment. Yeremenko and his staff put another reading on this, arguing that the German Sixth Army was played out and that Chuikov at once ought to counter-attack, using Zholudev's 37th Guards. Chuikov resisted the idea at first, anxious as he was to bring his units up to strength and to derive maximum advantage from even a few hours respite in the ground attacks. Golikov remained at 62nd Army HQ, taking part in these

exchanges but recommending that Chuikov move his HQ quickly; this stretch
of the Volga bank had become very dangerous, with the dead and wounded
piling up at Chuikov's command post as the German mortar bombardment
intensified. Reluctantly Chuikov agreed to put in a counter-attack with parts
of two divisions on 7 October; less reluctantly he embarked on the quest for a
new HQ, finally lighting on Sarayev's dug-out further up the Volga bank and
nearer the Tractor Plant. Sarayev, commander of the 10th NKVD Division and
'garrison commander' in Stalingrad was being sent back to the eastern bank
with the remnants of his division to re-form, leaving only his 282nd Regiment
to fight on.

While Yeremenko pressed Chuikov to counter-attack, he was himself under
heavy pressure from the *Stavka* to safeguard his own Front. Early in October
the *Stavka* was increasingly impressed by the danger of a German assault on the
eastern bank of the Volga. On 6 October, while Chuikov argued about the
chances of a counter-attack by 62nd Army, Vasilevskii twice drew Yeremenko's
attention to *Stavka* instructions to prepare a timely defence plan for the islands
situated in the middle of the Volga, Spornyi, Zaitsevskii, Golodnyi and
Saprinskii, as well as the whole eastern bank. The *Stavka* suggested that Yeremenko locate artillery and AA guns on the mid-river islands: to expedite these
measures, the *Stavka* proposed to place a dozen special AA machine-gun regiments at Yeremenko's disposal, while Yeremenko was to submit a precise defence
plan to the *Stavka* by 7 October. The *Stavka*, obviously seized with the idea of a
German attack across the Volga, signalled on 7 October that it was making the
45th Rifle Division available for the defence of the mid-river islands, and four
days later Yeremenko received specific orders to deploy the 300th Rifle Division
for the defence of the eastern bank of the Volga along a sector running from
lake Tuzhilkino to the mouth of the river Akhtuba.

In Stalingrad itself Chuikov never mounted the counter-attack with
Zholudev's Guards: in mid-morning on 7 October two German divisions with
a powerful force of tanks launched a massive attack on the Tractor Plant. By
the end of the day, which involved 37th Guards Division in heavy fighting,
German troops occupied one whole block of the workers' houses and advanced
towards the sports stadium. Smekhotvorov's division defending *Krasnyi
Oktyabr* fought throughout the day for the bath-house, churned by repeated
German attack and Soviet counter-attack into a fire-swept no man's land.
Further to the north, on the sector of the river Mechetka, a German infantry
battalion began its attack in the early evening, only to be blown to pieces by a
well-placed salvo fired by the *Katyusha* rocket-launchers under the command of
Colonel Yerokhin, whose rocket-launcher trucks stood on the edge of the steep
Volga bank, backing over it with the rear wheels hanging in mid-air to fire the
hundreds of missiles at maximum range. Zholudev's 37th Division had blunted
Paulus's head-on blow at the factory districts; Chuikov had not been distracted
by the attack on the Orlovka salient, it was a timely movement which brought

37th Guards into a blocking position at the Tractor Plant and German attempts to rush the Soviet defences in an attempt to break for the Volga after 4 October had already failed. With four battalions and a score of tanks wiped out in the day's fighting on 7 October, Paulus now held his hand for a few hours.

At the end of September General Halder noted the 'gradual exhaustion' seizing the German Sixth Army at Stalingrad: companies were reduced to a strength of sixty men, the armour, also suffering heavy losses, was caught up in a 'dead *Schwerpunkt*' and burned to pieces in street-fighting for which it was totally unsuited. Colonel-General Kurt Zeitzler, successor to the dismissed Halder as chief of the general staff, recommended almost as his first act that the Stalingrad offensive be called off: Paulus, full of complaints about the shortages in Sixth Army and the resilience of the Russian defence, seemed to be in agreement, but a far from subtle hint to Paulus that great things awaited him – after the capture of Stalingrad – conveyed by the newly promoted Schmundt worked wonders on Paulus's flagging initiative. Paulus called for a reinforcement of three divisions; he got instead sapper battalions specially flown out from Germany to help in the house-to-house fighting which was killing off his infantry. Paulus envisaged no solution other than that of butting his way through the factory districts but any dissent he dealt with very brusquely, dismissing Generals von Wietersheim (15th Panzer Corps) and von Schwedler (4th Panzer Corps) for their criticism of his handling of the battle.

On 9 October, when the fighting slackened the Sixth Army prepared its 'final assault' and a four-day lull set in, Chuikov's 62nd Army estimated that it was facing 9 German divisions, with a main assault force of some 90,000 men, 2,000 guns and mortars, plus 300 tanks supported by *Luftflotte IV* with 1,000 aircraft. Chuikov, with 55,000 men, 950 guns and 500 mortars, 80 tanks and supported by 188 aircraft, mostly patched-up machines, of the 8th Air Army, held a perimeter at Rynok in the north, parts of the Tractor Plant workers' settlement (though German troops had driven up to the factory walls), the north-eastern slopes of *Mamayev Kurgan* and positions in the central railway station area. Soviet troops fought under constant air attack: Khryukin's 24 fighters, 63 dive-bombers and 101 bombers, all that 8th Air Army could muster, could scarcely fight off the aerial armadas the Luftwaffe put up day after day. For Chuikov, with a diminished bridgehead and reduced manpower, the problem was how to hold the three big factories and still defend what remained of the 'central sector', and so to strengthen the defences of the factories Chuikov regrouped his battered divisions.

With the Volga only some 4,000 yards behind the 'front line', Chuikov could not afford mistakes, though reconnaissance reports increasingly indicated an all-out attack on the Tractor Plant. Gorishny's 95th Rifle Division, with 3,075 men, moved off the slope of *Mamayev Kurgan* to the north-west, into the junction of 37th Guards and 308th Rifle Division defending the outbuildings of the *Krasnyi Oktyabr* factory: 42nd Brigade, reduced to 937 men, came under the command of the 95th Division. To strengthen the defences of the Tractor Plant Chuikov moved the 112th Rifle Division, 2,300 men in all, to the north-western sector of the factory settlement; the one remaining regiment of that division, the 524th, so far kept in reserve on the eastern bank, was ferried over on 12 October. Under orders from the Front command, Zholudev's 37th Guards Division, supported by a regiment from the 95th, now launched a spoiling attack from the western edge of the Tractor Plant. It was, as Chuikov admits, a risk to draw the Germans out on the attack, but only a part of 62nd Army was engaged and anything was better than sitting waiting to be battered by an enemy given every opportunity to prepare. Zholudev's Commando-Guards accustomed to fighting in small, heavily armed groups and with all the verve of a good Guards division did well, making up to 300 yards of ground; the regiment from the 95th also gained a couple of hundred yards, but all too quickly the Soviet units ran into the massed strength of the Germans, waiting to leap off in their 'general assault'.

That assault, bringing with it the most stupendous surge of fighting which Stalingrad would ever see, opened at 8 am on Monday, 14 October 1942: five German divisions, three infantry (94th, 389th, 100th *Jäger*) and two Panzer (14th and 24th), 300 tanks with mighty air support, moved off in one great wall of steel and fire to overrun the factory districts, to break through to the Volga in strength and to blot out the Soviet 62nd Army once and for all.

On the eve of the fighting in Stalingrad taking yet another savage turn within the gaunt and ruined factory district, where the steel ribs of the workshops stuck out amidst enormous mounds of rubble, tangles of girders and acres of shattered equipment ploughed into thousands of bomb-craters and shell-holes, a great and growing concentration of Soviet strength was piling up east of the Volga. Chuikov braced himself and his 62nd Army to meet the imminent 'general assault' on his mangled, blood-soaked, shrinking bridgehead at a time when the 'practical work' connected with launching the decisive Soviet counter-offensive was well advanced. With *Operationsbefehl Nr. 1* of 14 October, Hitler brought the German summer offensive to a close, halting all offensive operations save for Stalingrad and the Caucasus: a resolute defence of present positions and success in the 'winter campaign' would lay the foundation for the 'final destruction' of the Red Army in 1943. In view of their present grave weakness, the Russians could bring forward no great force in the coming winter, a view repeated in Zeitzler's elaboration of Hitler's order, the *Erganzung zum Operationsbefehl Nr. 1* (23 October) which stressed that the Russians 'were in no position to mount a major offensive with any far-reaching objective'.

The idea for a major counter-offensive at Stalingrad, proposed to Stalin on the evening of 13 September by Zhukov and Vasilevskii, envisaged 'two basic operational tasks: one, the encirclement and isolation of the main concentration of German troops operating directly within the city and second, the annihilation of this force'.* There was 'also no doubt' that the encirclement of the German armies must be achieved by 'powerful concentric blows on their flanks held by weak Rumanian troops', but the focus of Soviet attention must be to hold Stalingrad itself until the appointed hour of the counter-offensive: this meant 'the most earnest attention' to the defence of the city and further Soviet attacks to the north and south of Stalingrad to divert the German forces. To the Soviet command the situation of the German forces operating on the 'Stalingrad axis' looked distinctly and increasingly unfavourable: in Army Group B two German armies (Sixth and Fourth Panzer), Third Italian Army, Third and Fourth Rumanian Armies were stretched out over 400 miles, from Pavlovsk to Khalkut: some fifty divisions (nine of them armoured) formed a huge salient, its tip embedded in Stalingrad, the 'military impossibility' about which Halder had protested in vain. When German troops went over to the defensive they must do so with flanks only weakly held, with inadequate reserves and with their communications curving back to the west for hundreds of miles. Nor could the German command count on summoning fresh reserves from Germany or from other theatres: equally they would find it impossible to reinforce the southern wing with men moved from the western or north-western sectors of the Soviet-German front. But until such time as the Soviet counter-offensive opened, the bridgeheads in Stalingrad must be held by 62nd and 64th Army at all costs: Chuikov's 62nd, as Chuikov himself began to guess in October, was offered as live bait to the trap.

Both Zhukov and Vasilevskii left Moscow in mid September to carry out the inspections ordered by Stalin; the first idea for a strategic counter-offensive envisaged attacks from the right wing of the Stalingrad Front and the left wing of the South-Eastern Front, to slice through the flimsy Rumanian divisions at both of these extremities and thus strike at the German troops in the area of Stalingrad. Zhukov flew to the headquarters of the Stalingrad Front, from which he carried out his investigations of the situation north of Stalingrad, in particular the possibilities presented by the Soviet bridgeheads on the western bank of the Don at Kletskaya and Serafimovich. At Serafimovich the Soviet bridgehead was six miles deep on the southern bank, so that the river crossings could be exploited by Soviet units out of range of German artillery; the lack of natural cover was a disadvantage, but Serafimovich was a key position for manoevuring troops. At Kletskaya the Don bulged towards the south after looping through its 'little bend', thus presenting a chance to bear down on the enemy flank to the north-west of Kletskaya itself. But in addition to these bridgeheads, Zhukov's

* Marshal Zhukov in his account of 'the destruction of German troops in the area of the Don, the Volga and Stalingrad' (*Stalingradskaya epopeya*, Moscow 1968, p. 49), firmly scotches the idea that 'the counter-offensive plan' was nurtured as early as August 1942: the Marshal, criticizing the 'great vagueness' in post-Stalin discussions of the planning, emphasizes that discussions in August referred only to a 'counter-blow', *kontrudar*, designed to halt the enemy at the approaches to Stalingrad. He also dismisses the claim that Yeremenko and Khrushchev on 6 October 'submitted to the *Stavka* on their own initiative proposals for organizing and executing a counter-offensive'.

attention was presently fixed on the Don-Volga isthmus, from which the Stalingrad Front was about to launch another attack from the north aimed at relieving the pressure on Stalingrad, the operations promised by Zhukov and Malenkov in their letter of 12 September to Stalin; the Soviet attack would be launched from the station south of Kotluban towards Gumrak, to strike at the German forces committed in Stalingrad and to lock the flanks of the Stalingrad and South-Eastern Fronts. These two Fronts operated now as a joint command under Yeremenko, but were subject to the personal supervision and control of the *Stavka*, with Zhukov as its 'representative' and the State Defence Committee represented by Malenkov, hence the joint submission to Stalin. With Stalin's express permission, Zhukov invited Yeremenko to the HQ of 1st Guards Army on the Stalingrad Front, where Gordov, Moskalenko, Golovanov (commander of Long-Range Aviation) as well as Zhukov and Yeremenko conducted an 'investigation' of the position in the Stalingrad area. Unable to mention the possibility of a strategic counter-offensive, Zhukov confined the talk on this occasion mainly to problems connected with the reinforcement of the Stalingrad and South-Eastern Fronts, but Yeremenko asked specifically about the possibility of 'a more powerful attack'. Just what Yeremenko had in mind is not clear, but Zhukov turned the question for the moment by saying that the *Stavka* intended 'sometime in the future' to launch a counter-blow with considerably stronger forces, though at present there was neither a plan nor men available to execute it.

Meanwhile Colonel-General Vasilevskii inspected the left wing of the South-Eastern Front, the area south of Stalingrad held by the 57th Army and the right flank divisions of 51st Army. On the western bank of the Volga, south of Kuporosnoe, Soviet troops held the Beketovka 'bell', a bridgehead seven miles long and two deep, a danger which Fourth Panzer Army was only too anxious to eliminate but the divisions necessary to do this job were sucked one by one into the fight for the city itself. Rumanian units moved up to lace the flanks of Fourth Panzer which stretched down to the steppe and salt lakes further to the south. The lower edge of the Beketovka 'bell' (so christened for its bulging church-bell shape) was anchored on lake Sarpa, with two more lakes, Tsatsa and Barmantsak, lying below: here the Volga curved away in its bend to the south-west. Vasilevskii advised the commanders of 57th and 51st to prepare operations to seize the defiles between the lakes (Sarpa-Tsatsa, Tsatsa-Barmantsak), and having occupied them, to set up strong fortified positions.

Having established that from behind the undulating hills on the steppe from Tundutovo to lake Barmantsak south of Stalingrad (the left wing of the South-Eastern Front) and from the woods north of the Don (the right wing of the Stalingrad Front) Soviet forces could concentrate and then strike through the flimsy flank protection provided by Rumanian units into the great quivering body of German troops converging on Stalingrad, Zhukov and Vasilevskii returned to Moscow in the last week of September. Before reporting to the *Stavka*, both officers met to compare their findings on the flanks. Discussions at the *Stavka* on the whole concept of the proposed strategic offensive continued until the end of September; a few officers from the Operations Section of the General Staff, the *napravlentsy* (specialists in particular sectors), were called in to present their views on the practical problems involved in implementing the offensive, the selection of breakthrough sectors and lines of advance, requirements in manpower and armour, concentration areas and provisional timetables. The most immediate decision, however, affected the combined Stalingrad–South-Eastern Front and the disposition of Soviet forces in the area of Stalingrad; two autonomous Fronts were set up in the Stalingrad area, both directly subordinated to the *Stavka*. Yeremenko's South-Eastern Front officially became the Stalingrad Front on 28 September, the unwieldy Stalingrad Front was redesignated the Don Front and destined to be chopped in two, with a new Front, the South-Western, proposed for what had been the right flank of the old Stalingrad Front. For reasons of secrecy the existence of the new Front was not to be announced until late in October. The next step was to nominate commanders in the *Stavka* 'elections'; Stalin had already asked Zhukov for his opinion of Gordov, only to be told that while Gordov was a competent commander he failed to 'get on' with his staff and subordinate commanders. That eliminated Gordov as a candidate for a Front command. Zhukov, supported by Vasilevskii, put forward Lieutenant-General Rokossovskii as a candidate for the command of the new Don Front. Stalin agreed: Yeremenko remained in charge of his front, the new Stalingrad Front, with Major-General Varennikov as his chief of staff and Khrushchev the political member of the Front Military Soviet. Rokossovskii got Malinin as his chief of staff and Zheltov as political member. The new post, commander of the South-Western Front, went to Lieutenant-General N.F. Vatutin, currently commander of the Voronezh Front; Golikov, Yeremenko's deputy, was nominated for the command at Voronezh. To provide Vatutin with a Front staff it was proposed to use the officers of 1st Guard Army HQ, with Moskalenko transferred to the command of 40th Army; Stelmakh of the Volkhov Front was nominated as Vatutin's chief of staff.

This overhaul of the commands in the Stalingrad area was meant to assist both the deployment of the main strike forces designated for the forthcoming counter-offensive and also the defence of Stalingrad itself. Red Army forces deployed at the end of September on the 'Stalingrad axis' (the Stalingrad and Don Fronts) totalled 78 rifle divisions, 6 cavalry divisions, 5 tank corps and 18 independent tank brigades, in all 771,000 men, 8,100 guns and mortars, 525 tanks and 448 aircraft. The Front Rokossovskii inherited, with a strength of 39 rifle divisions, 3 cavalry formations, 3 tank corps, 9 independent tank brigades and 2 motorized rifle brigades, occupied positions along a 200-mile front from Pavlovsk in the north down to the Volga just south of Yerzovka; at the centre of this front lay the Soviet bridgeheads on the southern bank of the Don. The projected new Front, the South-Western, forming its junction with the Don Front at Kletskaya and running north along the Don to Verkhnyi Mamon, would take its basic composition from the two right flank armies of the Don Front (63rd and 21st) and a tank army drawn from the *Stavka* reserve; the main concentration of force would be in the bridgehead area west and south-west of Serafimovich. Once the new Front came into existence, the Don Front would run from Kletskaya to Yerzovka, with its bridgeheads over the Don at Novo-Grigorevskaya and Sirotinskaya while also closing off the Don-Volga isthmus. Yeremenko's Stalingrad Front ran along the Volga, from just north of Rynok in the upper reaches of the city itself, through Chuikov's bridgehead in Stalingrad, on to the Beketovka 'bell' thence southwards past the Volga bend to the steppe and the lakes – five armies, 62nd and 64th (committed within Stalingrad), 57th, 51st and 28th, the latter two covering also Maly Berbet and the sandy approaches to Astrakhan.

The basic idea of the counter-offensive plan was to mount two attacks, one from the middle reaches of the Don in a southerly direction, the other from the left wing of the Stalingrad Front, south of Stalingrad itself, to strike in a north-westerly direction towards the bend of the Don where the two pincers would meet. Both blows, to north and south, were aimed initially at the 'satellite' divisions holding the German flanks. South of Stalingrad, from Tundutovo to lake Barmantsak, the lower Soviet hook would slice through the Fourth Rumanian Army, covering the flank of Fourth Panzer. The final aim of the counter-offensive remained the encirclement and destruction of the two German armies, the Sixth and Fourth Panzer, more than 300,000 men pressed into the narrow Stalingrad salient. This plan, accepted by the *Stavka* in late September, embodied the basic principle of the Red Army's major counter-offensive, which under the code-name 'Uran' (Uranus) assumed its final and definite form in the second half of October. After these first full appraisals at the *Stavka*, Stalin wanted further investigations done over the actual ground: he instructed Zhukov to fly down 'to the front', to inspect once more the concentration areas for reserves and the jump-off zones on the Don, 'especially in the area of Serafimovich and Kletskaya'. Zhukov was also 'to take every possible measure to wear down and weaken the enemy still further'. Vasilevskii must go once more to the left wing of Yeremenko's front, south of Stalingrad, to 'investigate all the problems related to the proposed plan'. Again Stalin insisted on no disclosure of the whole concept of the counter-offensive, but wanted the Front commanders sounded out over 'future operations'.

On 29 September Zhukov flew south to the Stalingrad battle area, taking Rokossovskii with him in his Il-2 transport: immediately after landing the two officers went to the forward HQ east of Yerzovka. Rokossovskii had earlier spent some time at the *Stavka*, to which he was summoned from the Bryansk Front; he was briefed on the situation in the Stalingrad area and given details of a proposed attack – a 'counter-blow', *kontrudar* – to be launched from Serafimovich into the flank of German forces fighting in Stalingrad, for which the General Staff suggested the use of three armies (one on the spot, two to be moved from *Stavka* reserve) and 4–5 tank corps, 'a peach of an operation' to use Rokossovskii's own words, but one not immediately feasible since all available reserve divisions were about to be set on the move to Stalingrad itself.* A few days later Rokossovskii learned of his appointment to the command of the Don Front, where in the company of Zhukov (and with Galanin, the new commander for 24th Army) he arrived on the eve of his appointment becoming effective. It was a sombre introduction for Rokossovskii; that evening (29 September) the failure of further attacks by 1st Guards and 66th Army, aimed at breaking through to Chuikov to the north of Stalingrad along the Rynok-Akatovka sector, was brutally plain, with heavy losses but no breach in the German lines. Gordov berated and abused his commanders over the telephone, much to Zhukov's fury; in no uncertain terms Zhukov intimated that commanders ought to behave 'properly' towards their subordinates and not, like Gordov, hound them – an ironic scene, for Zhukov could wield the lash like no one else in the Red Army and Rokossovskii least of all needed lessons in how to behave like a good commander. Finally Zhukov gave Gordov permission to break off the attacks and returned with Rokossovskii to Front HQ.

Although he had just authorized Gordov to call off operations to the north of Stalingrad, Zhukov was emphatic in talking to Rokossovskii about his new command that 'active operations' must on no account cease, lest the German command pull out even more troops for the fighting inside Stalingrad; Yeremenko's Front must also help here by attacking in the southern reaches of the city, otherwise Stalingrad would fall to the Germans. About this Zhukov was dogmatic and immovable. The attacks to the north and the south must go on, regardless of cost. Rokossovskii pointed out, and justifiably so according to Zhukov, that the Don Front disposed of few resources, its divisions had suffered heavy losses in the recent fighting, which meant that no 'major objective' could be attained; he also maintained that not only could the Germans, disposing of considerable strength, fend off further Soviet attacks to the north of Stalingrad, but they might even launch attacks of their own and in more than one place. On the Don Front, 1st Guards Army had been pulled back into reserve; on the rest of the Front V.I. Kuznetsov's 63rd Army held a 100-mile front on the far right flank (with a small bridgehead on the southern bank of the Don at Verkhnyi Mamon): on the northern bank of the Don Chistyakov's 21st Army occupied a seventy-mile sector with bridgeheads on the southern bank at Yelanskaya, Ust-Khoperskaya and Serafimovich: in the fifty-mile 'neck' of the Volga-Don isthmus were three armies, Kryuchenkin's 4th Tank, Galanin's 24th

---

* In discussing the origin and development of the final plan for the Stalingrad counter-offensive, much confusion arises from the fact that the General Staff had worked out plans for a limited counter-offensive in the Stalingrad area, while Zhukov and Vasilevskii proposed a strategic counter-offensive on a much greater scale. This point does not become clear without reference to *Velikaya pobeda na Volge* (Moscow 1965), p. 220, the study edited by Marshal Rokossovskii, which is obliged to distinguish between these proposed operations, referring to the strategic counter-offensive as 'the three-front undertaking' involving the South-Western, Don and Stalingrad Fronts.

and Malinovskii's 66th. Rokossovskii thus had two armies stretched along the Don and three crammed into the isthmus. The present commitment of the Don Front remained unchanged – 'active operations' both along the Don and on the left flank to draw off as much German force as possible, also to break into the city from the north and link up with Chuikov. Yet without considerable reinforcement in armour and artillery the break-in was beyond the capabilities of the Front though the effort to relieve the pressure on Stalingrad had to be made; there was, Rokossovskii remarks, 'no other way out'.

On 1 October Zhukov flew back to Moscow in an aircraft piloted by Golovanov himself, who was forced to put the aircraft down due to heavy icing; Zhukov's own Il-2, following behind, also landed, picked up Zhukov and flew him to the Central Airport in Moscow. Once in Moscow Zhukov set about further examination of the plans for the strategic counter-offensive, as well as preparing orders for the relief attacks north and south of Stalingrad. Colonel-General Vasilevskii meanwhile continued his own investigations on Yeremenko's Stalingrad Front, accompanied this time by Colonel-General Voronov, head of Red Army artillery, and Lieutenant-General Ivanov, head of the Operations Section of the General Staff. The *Stavka* officers assembled at Yeremenko's HQ at Krasnyi Sad on the eastern bank of the Volga; here, as he had been charged by Stalin, Vasilevskii gave Yeremenko an outline of the *Stavka*'s 'general intentions', though Stalin also stipulated that Yeremenko must in no way be involved with the 'preparatory work' since his prime responsibility was the defence of Stalingrad itself. Vasilevskii gave Yeremenko twenty-four hours in which to 'prepare his observations' and at dawn on 6 October set out with Voronov, Ivanov and G.F. Zakharov (Yeremenko's deputy commander) for the forward headquarters of Trufanov's 51st Army, seventy miles away to the south-east of Stalingrad out on the steppe. For the past ten days (25 September–4 October) 51st and 57th Armies had carried out the limited attacks suggested earlier by Vasilevskii to seize and invest the defiles between the lakes Sarpa, Tsatsa and Barmantsak. These attacks, successfully accomplished, showed how speedily the Rumanians crumbled when two of their divisions (1st and 4th) screening the German flank sustained heavy casualties and lost all their artillery. During this inspection of the left flank the local Soviet commanders were told nothing, though Vasilevskii showed intense interest in the defiles and the enemy forces beyond them; Tolbukhin, commander of the neighbouring 57th Army, nevertheless had a shrewd idea that something big was brewing, for *Stavka* officers simply did not turn up on the open steppe by chance.

That same evening Vasilevskii returned to Yeremenko's HQ and took up a a further discussion of the basic idea of the counter-offensive: Yeremenko had already briefed his cheif of staff, Varennikov, and his arms commanders, Matveyev (artillery), Khryukin (air force) and N.A. Novikov (armour) on '*Stavka* intentions', so that all were in a position to contribute to the Front 'proposals' which Vasilevskii required for transmission to Stalin and the *Stavku*.

Yeremenko, Khrushchev and the select group of staff officers of the Stalingrad Front raised 'no objection in principle', but Yeremenko did draft a document on 'destroying the enemy in the Stalingrad area'.* Yeremenko admits that this document lacked 'technical detail', but it argued that the German lines must be broken on a broad front, so that by the evening of the first day of the counter-offensive a gap of not less than twenty-five miles would have been ripped in the German southern flank: faced with a breach of this size the German command would be unable to plug it with reserves, though tearing out 'a lump' of these proportions meant Soviet mechanized corps attacking concentrically, with every available force fused into one major blow with a depth of 15–20 miles.

Rokossovskii learned about the *Stavka*'s 'intentions' from Zhukov at the very beginning of October and knew 'the broad features' of the plan, though no specific date for the opening of the counter-offensive was mentioned. When Vasilevskii instructed Yeremenko to prepare his 'proposals', he also gave the same instruction to Rokossovskii on the Don Front. Between 6–9 October both Fronts prepared their reports for the *Stavka* and the formal report from the Stalingrad Front went to the *Stavka* on 9 October. According to Yeremenko, his Front 'submission' concentrated on the choice of strike axes, and argued that the blow from the north-west of Stalingrad must be mounted on a broad front, in great depth and should come from an area well to the north-west of Stalin-grad; shifting the attack further to the north-west would reduce possible resistance, since the German command could not counter from its main force, in particular to check the Soviet mobile units committed to the encirclement operation. In this way also a larger enemy force would be entrapped than any caught by only a 'shallow breach' of the enemy defences and by aiming only to hold the enemy troops engaged directly within Stalingrad or at its immediate approaches. This, in fact, was precisely the change worked in the September plan: the attack to the north-west of Stalingrad was shifted from the centre of the Don Front to an area south-west of Serafimovich, thus increasing the size and scale of the operation (as well as reversing the proposed roles of the Don and South-Western Front, with the latter mounting the main attack from the north). That modification of the first variant (derived in late September) was adopted in the second half of October.

Some of the men and machines destined for use in the three-Front counter-offensive were already on the move to their new stations. In September, on *Stavka* orders, the 3rd and 5th Tank Armies moved into special reserve; at the same time the *Stavka* re-formed the 43rd Army and through the special 'adminis-tration for forming new armies' rushed ahead with setting up five new reserve armies, as well as an appreciable number of tank, mechanized and cavalry corps,

* In his own memoirs, (*Stalingrad*, Moscow 1961, p. 325) Yeremenko claimed the 'idea' of the counter-offensive first came to him at the beginning of August and that his own staff, with Khrush-chev's help and participation, sent 'the plan' to the *Stavka* on 6 October. Marshal Zhukov dismisses this as nonsense and points to Marshal Vasilevskii's own evidence of his visit in early October to Yeremenko.

artillery 'breakthrough' divisions and independent tank brigades, regiments and battalions. Stalin himself culled the Fronts for more and more rifle divisions: on 7 September he had telephoned Voronezh Front HQ and ordered four rifle divisions to be sent south to 'Tsaritsyn' – here Stalin reverted to the old name for Stalingrad. Under a *Stavka* order of 1 October two tank corps, 17th and 18th, pulled out of the Voronezh Front and moved for re-fitting to the rear of the Don Front, to the railhead at Tatishchevo; the same day the *Stavka* ordered 4th Tank Corps on the Don Front to move back for re-fitting. The Don Front was due to receive seven rifle divisions from the 10th Reserve Army, all of them to be in position by 14 October; men of the 4th Reserve Army began to concentrate on the right flank of the Don Front in the area of Novo-Anninskii and Uryupinsk. In discussing the required scale of reinforcement, Yeremenko in his report from Stalingrad Front HQ had mentioned the need for two mobile formations, one mechanized and one cavalry; the *Stavka* drew 4th Mechanized Corps and 4th Cavalry Corps from their reserve for deployment on the Front (both went to the left flank, to Trufanov's 51st Army). Yeremenko also received a rifle brigade (143rd) and the 235th Flame-Thrower Tank Brigade; out of the armoured reinforcements sent to the Stalingrad Front, Yeremenko finally organized a fresh mechanized corps, the 13th. A cavalry corps, one rifle division and artillery regiments from the Voronezh Front were already earmarked for the new South-Western Front, in whose projected area a rifle corps was also forming up.

Reserve and newly raised formations had to be moved forward with both speed and stealth; with the new armoured formations, allotted 'a decisive role' in the forthcoming breakthrough operations, this presented difficulties of a special order. Old formations now loomed up again, refurbished after past battles and disasters. Major-General Volskii's spanking new corps, 4th Mechanized, was being raised at a furious rate on the Lower Volga; the battered 28th Tank Corps, which went down fighting at Kalach in July-August, and remnants of the 158th and 55th Tank Brigades formed the nucleus of the 4th Mechanized. Many of the tank-crews came straight from hospitals, their wounds now healed, thereby giving a fresh formation experienced men. The new corps possessed three mechanized brigades (36th, 59th, 60th), with a tank regiment to each brigade, as well as three independent armoured car battalions, an engineer and motor-cycle battalion, a fuel supply unit and a company of mine technicians plus one Guards mortar unit (equipped with *Katyushas*), in all a much more flexible and sophisticated instrument than the mechanized corps which went into action in June 1941. Major-General Volskii, no novice in tank warfare, had from the end of September until 20 October to raise and fit out his corps; by mid October, 4th Mechanized was in business, swelled with 20,000 men, bristling with 220 tanks, 100 armoured cars and more than 2,000 lorries. The corps moved south-west with its equipment hidden under tarpaulins and lashed to railway flat-cars; as air attacks intensified light AA guns or machine-guns were set up on the trucks moving into the battle zone. Finally the corps was almost opposite the Beketovka 'bell' and crossed the Volga bend at night; by day, 4th Mechanized remained absolutely immobile under its skilfully devised camouflage. Scores of formations and units moved in this fashion in October.

In September the General Staff estimated the requirement in tank strength for the counter-offensive at some 900 machines. Armour had a very special part to play but this also applied to the artillery. Colonel-General Nikolai Voronov, chief of Red Army artillery, had been in the Stalingrad area since September, taking part with Zhukov and Vasilevskii in the first 'reconnaissance' and then in the preliminary Front briefings for the counter-offensive. Voronov's primary task, in addition to preparing the artillery 'master plan', was to assist Front and army artillery commanders to plan the best use of their artillery resources: concealing the massing of artillery, especially heavy guns, and ensuring adequate supplies of ammunition proved to be difficult everywhere. On the Stalingrad Front there was the added complication of ferrying artillery over the Volga. On their first visit to the Don Front, Zhukov and Vasilevskii complained about the competence of some of the artillery officers: Rokossovskii was pleased when V.I. Kazakov, Bryansk Front artillery commander, came to the Don Front and Voronov was delighted, not only with Kazakov but also with Colonel Nadysev, the artillery chief of staff for the Don. The proper exploitation of Front artillery resources had to be planned, but Voronov found himself faced with deciding how to deploy the heavier guns drawn from the *Stavka* reserve; he settled this by referring to the First World War Instructions, 'Directions for breakthrough of fortified enemy zones' issued by the Imperial Russian Army. These were now re-issued to Front commands for their guidance in deploying heavy artillery.

The Red Army fired off more ammunition during the Stalingrad battles than in any other major Soviet operation during the entire war. It fell to the Main Artillery Administration (GAU), working with the State Defence Committee, to ensure the supply of both weapons and ammunition; the GAU, linked with the GKO, submitted its monthly requirements to the planners of *Gosplan* and *Sovnarkom* whose 'special industrial group' was controlled by Kirpichnikov and Borisov. The monthly ammunition production plan then went to the GKO, to the heads of the various People's Commissariats and to the chairman of the GKO (Stalin) for authorization. Now the GAU had not only to meet the requirements of the defensive operations but also to stockpile ammunition for the counter-offensive, as well as fitting out the fresh formations with infantry weapons, mortars and artillery. Weapons and ammunition came down to Stalingrad from GAU dumps and stores to Front depots; three main railway trunk lines, the Volga waterway from Saratov through Kamyshin and the roads on both sides of the Volga from Saratov were the principal supply routes. The rail traffic came under constant air attack; the roads north of Stalingrad were hit by bombing and the Volga was mined. On the Stalingrad Front ammunition trains with loads for Front depots might be halted for anything from two to seven days at the stations (Urbach and Baskunchak); to guard against loss by air attack, only small trains – half a dozen waggons – ran up to the individual Army ammunition dumps. Each Army had usually two main dumps sited a short distance from a railway track; convoys of 10–12 lorries moving by night shifted the ammunition from the dumps, a run of more than 100–200 miles in some cases. The men of Army Artillery Dump No. 2289 supplying Chuikov's 62nd Army worked in highly dangerous conditions, the dump itself located on the eastern bank and its 'forward section' in Stalingrad, set up after September in *Krasnyi Oktyabr*; German observers spotted this location and directed heavy fire on the dump. Twice during the first week in October direct hits exploded part of the ammunition.

The GAU was also responsible for the supply of weapons. Machine-guns and AA guns were in desperately short supply, and the dearth of AA guns left large areas of the Soviet rear zones vulnerable to air attack. In August there were only 123 AA guns in the entire Stalingrad area; throughout September and October this was raised to over 1,000. Half a million rifles, 80,000 automatic weapons, over 17,000 machine-guns, 16,000 anti-tank rifles and nearly 9,000 artillery pieces came from GAU depots to the Stalingrad Front, in addition to over 1,000 *Katyusha* rocket-launchers. The larger the concentration of armies and the greater the density of weapons, however, the more insatiable became the demand for ammunition. The GAU had to cope not only with rising demand but also the elimination of particular shortages, not least in 82-mm and 120-mm mortar bombs, 76-mm field gun ammunition, 122-mm howitzer ammunition and shells for 76-mm and 85-mm AA guns. Nevertheless, the steady rise after August in the *boekomplekty* (the ammunition norms allowed per gun per day) meant that the problem of ammunition supply both for the defensive action and for the planned offensive was being eased.

For all the shaping of the strategic counter-offensive, Stalin was a prey to increasing fears about the fate of Stalingrad itself. On 5 October he had sent special orders to Yeremenko, emphasizing the need to hold on in the bridgehead. The uneasiness in the *Stavka* about the defences on the eastern bank of the Volga led to a train of reinforcements being rushed to the south. Light AA regiments (mixed machine-gun and AA gun batteries) were sent down from the Moscow Defence Zone to stiffen the anti-aircraft defences of the islands in the Volga, followed by a full AA regiment (twelve 37-mm AA guns) and more heavy calibre machine-guns for use against aircraft. The islands – Spornyi, Zaitsevskii, Golodnyi and Sarpinskii – came under a special defence command (Popov's 2nd Tank Corps) early in October. By 12 October two cavalry divisions (61st and 81st) from 4th Corps, and a rifle corps (the 7th) had reached Yeremenko's Front; a fresh rifle division, the 169th, with the light AA regiments, also arrived. One further rifle division, the 45th, was drawn from the *Stavka* reserve and put under Popov's special command. Thus reinforced, Popov received orders to set up three defensive zones on the eastern bank, the first from the mouth of the

Akhtuba to Krasnaya Sloboda, Golodnyi and Sarpinskii, the third running north from the mouth of the Akhtuba.

In spite of its terrible battering, Stalingrad continued to function as an industrial city; the electric power station in the southern part, STALGRES, went on producing current, even though it was under artillery fire after 13 October. After the main buildings had been badly damaged, the power station workers could only operate their equipment by night, but the workshops busy repairing tanks needed electric power and they continued to get it. To increase power supplies, however, the plant went back to day working and the smoke from the chimneys again brought down heavy German fire. The slipways of the Stalingrad shipyard at Krasnoarmeisk continued to repair the gunboats and ferries of the Volga fleet, most of the work being done by hand since the local power plant had long since been destroyed. The shipyard workers also repaired tanks, tractors (used for pulling the boats to the shore), mortars and infantry weapons.

Civilians still lived even in the most heavily fought over parts of the city, though the Germans cleared their area of local inhabitants, sending them rearwards on a march which few survived. Large numbers of civilians, together with Red Army wounded, were huddled on the islands in mid-Volga amidst appalling conditions, lacking food, shelter and medicaments. The Stalingrad *gorkom* organized special brigades to bring rescue and relief. The Communist Party, which had frequently disgraced itself in 1941, buckled to in Stalingrad: as the GKO representative, Malenkov spent long weeks within gunshot and sat down with the senior commanders to wrest something from the pile of military wreckage. Andreyev, Mikoyan, Kosygin and Malyshev (Central Committee members) turned their hands to solving Stalingrad's problems: Z.A. Shashkov (Commissar for the Fishing Fleet), A.A. Goreglyad (Deputy Commissar for the Tank Industry) and A.G. Sheremet'ev (Deputy Commissar for Ferrous Metals) all worked on the spot. Goreglyad supervised the production of tanks in the Tractor Plant. Sheremet'ev the output of metal in the blast furnaces of *Krasnyi Oktyabr* which worked until the last possible moment. Even in August, when the factory was under artillery fire, the Tractor Plant turned out just under 400 tanks; after September the plant went over to repairing tanks and tractors, organizing an independent 'repair brigade' which salvaged Soviet tanks and tank-engines until it was incorporated into 62nd Army as a Red Army unit. Aleksei Chuyanov, first secretary of the Stalingrad *obkom* and chairman of the Stalingrad 'Defence Committee', kept the Party organization running and used it for a multitude of purposes – civil defence, welfare activities, militia mobilization, mobilization of skilled workers to maintain essential services as long as possible and what he himself called 'defence and economic-political matters'. Under heavy shelling and air attack a plenary session of the Party *obkom* and Defence Committee met on 3 October; the Party organized the mobilization of workers into 62nd and 64th Armies, men who knew their particular sections of the city like the back of their hand and who went into action as gunners, tank-drivers, reconnaissance troops and river-men, fighting literally in their own back-yards.

On 14 October the *Stavka* ordered Rokossovskii and Yeremenko to clear all civilians out of a twelve-mile zone leading to the front; the first to go must be civilians in Stalingrad itself and on the islands in the Volga, followed by those in the villages or settlements on the eastern bank of the Volga, as well as non-combatants in the Beketovka 'bell'. Chuyanov was put in charge of the evacuation. In the zones thus cleared the Don and Stalingrad Fronts were to set about building three defence lines and fortifying all villages, fitting them out to fight even in conditions of complete encirclement, and appointing experienced officers to take charge of the garrisons in these 'fortified districts'. This activity fulfilled a dual purpose, to set up defence works in the rear and also to persuade the Germans that the Russians had no purposes other than purely defensive; the movement of fresh units into the two Fronts could be screened under all this flurry of fortification and entrenching.

True to Zhukov's prescription that Stalingrad could not be held without 'active operations' by the Don and Stalingrad Fronts, the Don Front received orders to continue its operations, first with reinforced units on its left wing 'as from 11 October' to prevent any German regrouping increasing the pressure on Stalingrad, then (under the formal order transmitted on 15 October) to go over to the attack to try once again to link up with Chuikov in Stalingrad. The *Stavka* put seven reserve divisions at Rokossovskii's disposal, but in the frantic rush to prepare the attack only two could be brought into the line; the Don Front received orders to mount two attacks, a main thrust towards Orlovka and a subsidiary attack towards Rynok, with the right flank armies all the while holding fast to the Don bridgeheads. Rokossovskii proposed to use Malinovskii's 66th Army and the left flank divisions of the 24th; because Malinovskii's 66th faced the heaviest fighting, Rokossovskii assigned the seven additional divisions to him (though only two actually turned up). To the south of Stalingrad Yeremenko received corresponding orders to mount an attack on his far flank with 57th and 51st Armies in the Tundutovo-Tsatsa area. *Stavka* orders set 20 October as the date for Rokossovskii's attack leaving only very little time in which to prepare.

In the midst of issuing orders for this 'counter-blow', Stalin himself was seized on 13 October with the greatest alarm about the situation inside Stalingrad. On this occasion he vented his rage on Yeremenko, whom he considered to be not properly discharging his duties; instead of giving Chuikov all the help he could, Yeremenko was holding on the eastern bank troops Stalin had specifically assigned for the defence of the city. Stalin instructed Vasilevskii to order Yeremenko 'in the name of the *Stavka*' to go in person to Chuikov's HQ, to investigate the position – 'the true position', observed at first hand – and to weigh up what help Chuikov needed to defend those parts of Stalingrad still held by Soviet troops, and also to maintain a stubborn resistance right up to the moment when the Soviet counter-offensive opened. That would tie down substantial German forces and draw more into the vortex of the battle. Stalin's misgivings were far from unfounded. Battered as it already was, the 62nd Army in the Stalin bridgehead faced at dawn on 14 October a savage German assault and one mounted with 'unprecedented ferocity'.

At 8 o'clock on Wednesday morning, 14 October, three German infantry divisions and the regiments of two Panzer divisions launched an enormous battering attack along a four-kilometre front in the direction of the Tractor Plant and the *Barrikady* factory. The German infantry crouched in trenches or forward outposts, the tanks assembling behind them, as guns, mortars and *Stukas* bombarded the outbuildings, streets, and the remnants of houses held by the Russians. When the battle was fully joined in mid-morning, individual explosions no longer made themselves heard above the consuming roar of all-out bombing and shelling; the drifting smoke blotted out any sight of the pale autumnal sun inside Stalingrad and in the factory district visibility was reduced to no more than half a dozen metres in the murk of swirling dust coming from toppling walls and crashing houses, a yellow-grey fog lit only by the flashes of bursting bombs and shells. The Soviet dug-outs trembled, shook and started to collapse. Under their screen of fire German infantrymen leapt for the dead ground between the ruins, only to be met by rifle and machine-gun fire from behind stones or out of the chaotic mounds of rubble themselves; sheltering as best they could in slit trenches, parts of buildings or entrenched in the ruins, Zholudev's riflemen of the 37th and Gorishnyi's of the 95th Division fought off the advancing German tommy-gunners and assault engineers with grenades, small-arms fire and bottles filled with petrol. The remnants of the buildings between *Barrikady* and the Tractor Plant changed hands several times; round the Tractor Plant German and Soviet infantry fought for each floor and attic in every house, but shortly before noon a force of German tommy-gunners supported by nearly 200 tanks smashed a passage through Zholudev's lines, pushing on to the walls of the Tractor Plant and turning into the rear of the 112th Division. Yard by yard German troops ground forward with the tanks punching out Soviet strong-points one by one; the Stukas aimed for the regimental command posts, all of which stayed put, only to be blown to pieces along with the men in them. Late in the afternoon Zholudev's 37th and 112th Division were fighting in encirclement, while the right flank of 308th had been pounded to pieces; several explosions buried General Zholudev alive in his divisional command post from which he was finally dug out by the guard company. In Chuikov's own HQ below the bluff many officers and men were being killed by the German bombardment; to keep up communications with units inside Stalingrad, Army HQ transmitted messages to the eastern bank signal posts which then relayed them back into the city. Encircled Soviet units reported their positions by radio and continued to fight until their ammunition ran out;

after that there was only silence, the radios dead, every fighting man killed at his post.

By midnight German troops had surrounded the Tractor Plant on three sides; inside the walls of the plant Soviet troops and the factory militia fought hundreds of small, savage actions within the workshops. The approaches to the Tractor Plant were littered with the dead and dying, hundreds of Soviet wounded crawled to the Volga or waited in the night to be ferried on one of those ghastly journeys across the Volga; that night 3,500 wounded men were ferried to the eastern bank, the largest single tally in the whole of the defensive battle. The German tanks crashed into the Tractor Plant, grinding and roaring through the wreckage of the machine-shops, with more moving in the workers' settlements along the narrow streets where a single explosion followed by a blazing tank signalled a Soviet mine. Steadily widening their breach, German assault squads fought their way to the bank of the Volga while groups of tommy-gunners infiltrated the gaps torn out between Soviet units; flailing their way through the Tractor Plant German troops reached the Volga along a 2,000 yard front, thus splitting Chuikov's 62nd Army in two. Chuikov's right flank was now cut off from the main body of 62nd Army and pinned north of the Mokraya Mechetka; the German thrust to the Volga broke through 37th Guards Division, isolating the remaining men of the 112th Division, 2nd Motorized Rifle Brigade and three rifle brigades (115th, 124th and 149th). Colonel S.F. Gorokhov, commander of 124th Brigade, took control of these isolated right flank units and prepared to fight on, though nailed down on three sides by German forces (with the Volga at his back) and threatened with attacks from Latashanka in the north, from the west (along the valley of the Mechetka) and from the Tractor Plant itself.

Zholudev's division had been almost pulverized, lying as it did in the path of the main German attack, but it continued to fight in separate detachments, some in the Tractor Plant and others in Minusinskaya street; Gorishny's 95th and the 84th Tank Brigade, terribly thinned though they were, kept up their resistance and responded to Chuikov's order to 'fight and stay put'. In these shattered units, holed up in part of a ruined house, factory or workshop, the living took up the weapons of the dead, serving machine-guns, anti-tank rifles, machine-pistols in a frenzied effort to beat back the German infiltration. More and more men crammed in Chuikov's bunker, either for shelter or for orders; with his command post only 300 metres from the Germans, Chuikov on 15 October asked permission from Yeremenko to move part of his staff to the emergency HQ on the eastern bank, to ensure that the 62nd could fight on even if the eastern bank post was knocked out completely. Chuikov guaranteed that the Military Soviet of 62nd Army would stay in Stalingrad, even if some of his officers left, but Yeremenko refused this proposal outright. With his main artillery on the eastern bank Chuikov thought it better to have his Army artillery commander, Pozharskii, on that side of the Volga, and ordered him to go; Pozharskii, however, begged Chuikov to let him stay and Chuikov relented.

Throughout 15 October German units attacked Chuikov's isolated right wing units from two directions, from the north and from the west. Gorokhov's men held on and beat off the attacks with only small loss of ground. Zholudev's and Gorishny's divisions were practically finished, though the survivors of Zholudev's Guards still fired back doggedly from the ruins of the Tractor Pant. On the evening of 15 October Nikita Khrushchev telephoned Chuikov from the eastern bank; Khrushchev urgently wished to know what 62nd Army could do to hold the Tractor Plant. Chuikov replied that he could commit the whole of what was left of the 62nd to defend the Tractor Plant – and leave himself exposed on every other sector. Once trapped in the Tractor Plant, all of 62nd Army would be finally battered to pieces by von Paulus. Khrushchev agreed that other sectors must also be defended and promised to send what Chuikov most needed, more ammunition. Another rifle division was already on its way to the Stalingrad bridgehead, one regiment of Colonel Lyudnikov's 138th having crossed during the night and then fought throughout 15 October north of *Barrikady*. This single regiment got across the Volga that night but Yeremenko did not. Prodded by Stalin, Yeremenko set out to make his personal inspection of the situation but on 15 October German guns and aircraft paralysed the ferries on the Volga; no boat could get near the Tractor Plant landings which were lashed by German fire, and Chuikov's only contact with the eastern bank was by radio.

At 3 am on the morning of 16 October Yeremenko and his deputy, M.M. Popov, arrived at the forward HQ of the Volga River Flotilla and moved out in an armoured sloop from the mouth of the Akhtuba, making for the landing-stage at *Krasnyi Oktyabr*. Out on the Volga night turned to day under the flares and exploding bombs, the outline of the western bank loomed up and with it the grotesque shells of buildings heaped about with great mounds of rubble, the river bank itself alive with men on the move, the shuffling wounded, ammunition carriers, detachments changing positions, draft units scrambling ashore as Lyudnikov's remaining regiments landed from the barges. Chuikov and Gurov (divisional commissar of 62nd Army Military Soviet), alerted to Yeremenko's arrival, were out searching the river bank, moving amidst the hundreds of wounded crawling towards the landing-stage all under the unbroken bombardment of German six-barrelled mortars. In the half-light Yeremenko stumbled on to Chuikov's HQ, a mass of craters strewn with the wreckage of dug-outs and bunkers, timbers hurled aside, logs poking out of the ground and everywhere a shroud of ash. Krylov briefed Yeremenko and Popov until Chuikov's return; when Chuikov and Yeremenko finally met, unlike those reunions in Stalingrad when men who had been through so much managed a moment's talk, they did not fall on each other's shoulders. Yeremenko talked to the commanders of 138th and 95th Divisions, whose command posts were near by. Lyudnikov,

138th commander, had just taken up his post and was being briefed in the *Barrikady* bunker Chuikov occupied. Retreat, Yeremenko told Lyudnikov, was impossible because there was nowhere to retreat; the 138th would be deployed south of *Krasnyi Oktyabr*, with divisional HQ installed here in the *Barrikady* bunker. The devastation Yeremenko could see for himself and the attrition was exemplified in General Zholudev, who broke down in describing how his 37th Guards Division had been torn apart company by company until it was nothing but a bloody wreck, with only isolated detachments still fighting in the Tractor Plant.

With the dawn Yeremenko took his leave, promising Chuikov 'all he needed', including ammunition and the dispatch of reinforcements in small packets rather than whole divisions. The new day, however, brought fresh German assaults: the *Stukas* tried to blast a path southwards from the Tractor Plant to *Barrikady*, and German infantry, supported by tanks, began to turn south. This attack broke in great fury over 84th Armoured Brigade, directed by 62nd Army armoured commander Colonel Vainrub, on whose orders the T-34s were dug in to cover the road. At a range of 100 yards the Soviet tanks opened fire on Tramvaynaya street, blowing up a dozen German tanks and bringing the infantry to a halt; once the German columns were stalled and thrown about under fire from the tank ambush, Soviet guns on the eastern bank and *Katyushas* on the western bank battered the milling troops and the drawn-up tanks. After reinforcements moved up, the German infantry tried to storm the Soviet positions, only to have their ranks blown apart by *Katyusha* salvoes and more tanks crippled by the guns of the T-34s well-hidden in the rubble. Meanwhile Chuikov's men spotted preparations for a fresh attack on *Krasnyi Oktyabr*, all of which was confirmed by documents taken from prisoners serving with special assault engineer battalions; in the Tractor Plant, Zholudev's 37th Guards had all but disintegrated, with only a couple of hundred men left alive – 114th Guards Regiment had only eighty-four men left, 117th just thirty. All the divisional artillery, every 45-mm gun, mortar and anti-tank rifle had been destroyed, the artillery chief of staff Captain Pavlov, killed, together with most of the divisional staff.

When Lyudnikov's 138th Division came over in full strength during the night of 16–17 October, Chuikov resolved to put the fresh units in a blocking position at *Barrikady*, orders for which Lyudnikov received on the evening of 16 October:

16 October 1942. 23.50 hrs. Staff 62nd Army.

1 The enemy has taken the Stalingrad Tractor Plant, is developing an attack from the STP to the south along the railway line in an attempt to seize *Barrikady*.

2 62 Army continues to hold its positions, beating off fierce enemy attacks.

3 138th Red Banner RD from 04.00 hours 17.10.42 to occupy and stubbornly defend the line: south of the suburb Derevensk, Sculpturnyi. Under no circumstances to allow enemy to approach *Leninskii prospekt* and *Barrikady* factory.

650th Rifle Regiment/Major Pechenyuk: 138th Division/to take up positions in *Barrikady*, establish ring of fire-points and not to permit enemy penetration into the factory.

Signed: Lieutenant-General V. Chuikov

Divisional Commissar K. Gurov

Major-General N. Krylov

Lyudnikov's men were no sooner in position, digging weapon pits, siting machine-guns or anti-tank weapons and building fire-points when the German attack rolled over them, driving south from the Tractor Plant and south along the Volga bank to trap the Soviet troops. On the line of advance south of the Tractor Plant held by 84th Tank Brigade streams of German dive-bombers and fighter-bombers ploughed up the approach with bombs and bullets, setting everything ablaze until buildings, tanks and even the earth itself burned together, a hurtling mass of fire sweeping into the Soviet positions.

On 17 October fighting raged along the whole of 62nd Army's serrated 'perimeter'; Gorokhov's groups to the north continued to fight in encirclement, with German tommy-gunners breaking into the southern edge of the Spartanovka settlement, but the request by the Soviet brigade commanders to be allowed to fall back to Spornyi island (in mid-Volga) was refused by Chuikov who signalled that any move from the west bank would be treated as desertion. The preliminary German assaults on *Krasnyi Oktyabr* were beaten off for the moment but in the area of *Barrikady* German assault parties were moving along the railway line after punching a hole between 138th and 308th Divisions. The battle for the Tractor Plant was over, the battle for *Krasnyi Oktyabr* was only just building up, but it promised to be savage. During the early hours of 17 October in one of those howling Stalingrad nights Chuikov shifted his Army command post, moving first to Banny Gully where the staff officers, cluttered with papers and equipment, came under heavy machine-gun fire; Chuikov and his officers worked their way south for a further 1,000 yards until they came on a spot on the open Volga bank, not far from *Mamayev Kurgan*, where, bereft of any cover, 62nd Army HQ started functioning again.

Fighting south along the railway line German troops had already reached the north-west corner of *Barrikady*, where the heaviest fighting developed as the German attack rolled to the south: Height 107·5, *Mamayev Kurgan*, the outlets to the Volga in the Tractor Plant area as well as those near the Tsaritsa river were in German hands. Chuikov sent Lyudnikov defending *Barrikady* a categorical order to hold the 'line' against the German advance:

You are personally responsible for closing the breach with 308th RD, securing its right flank, establishing close contact; under no circumstances will you permit enemy penetration of *Barrikady* factory area and at the junction of 308 RD. You are responsible for the junction.

But by the evening of 18 October heavy fighting flared at the western edge of *Barrikady* where German infantry burst through the 'Tramvaynaya street line' and fought yard by yard along the railway. The factory militia now went into action fighting with the front-line troops, only to leave five men of the *Barrikady* militia detachment alive. On the right flank, where Gorokhov fought in virtual encirclement, Chuikov learned from Colonel Kamynin (the special liaison officer sent up to the right wing) that the situation had been restored; Gorokhov's men were holding the northern outskirts of Rynok, had beaten off the attack on Spartanovka and retained the landing-stage close by the mouth of the Mechetka river. The German tommy-gunners who had got as far as Spartanovka had been wiped out.

Gorokhov's men held an area of about eight square kilometres on the right flank: elsewhere all the territory held by 62nd Army was under heavy German artillery and mortar fire augmented by fierce bombing attacks, though the number of sorties flown over the Soviet positions by 18 October fell from 3,000 to 1,000 per day by 62nd Army's reckoning. Between 19–20 October, as fresh German units rolled on Stalingrad, the dwindling Soviet 'garrisons' beat off more German attacks on Spartanovka, *Barrikady* and *Krasnyi Oktyabr*; Chuikov's officers raked through all the rear detachments of 62nd Army on the eastern bank, trying to find more men for the rifle companies on the western bank. Still the bridgehead shrank, metre by metre: giant fires swept the streets and buildings: to screen the remaining landing-points on the Volga bank from machine-gun bullets walls piled up from shattered stones were quickly built and a little later the gullies, which afforded a passage for German tommy-gunners, were barricaded near the Volga bank. Although a wholesale German break-through to the Volga was still held in check, Chuikov's 62nd had taken fearful punishment between 14–19 October and the depth of the Soviet bridgehead on the western bank in Stalingrad now reached little more than 1,000 yards. On 21 October, with German units reinforced, heavy attacks were launched against *Barrikady* and *Krasnyi Oktyabr*; during the next forty-eight hours the reinforced 79th German Infantry Division supported by heavy tanks and dive-bombers flailed into the streets running to *Krasnyi Oktyabr*, moved along the railway line which once served the factory and by the evening of 23 October with a force of German tommy-gunners had penetrated the north-west corner of the factory. The next day German infantry fought their way into the central and south-western parts of *Barrikady* defended by 138th and 308th Divisions; at the north-western gates the factory militia and Red Army units were still holding off the German tanks and infantry.

Blackened with sweat and smoke, German infantrymen and tank-crews held their 'front' within flame-thrower distance of Russian positions at the edge of the advance; behind the forward assault groups German and Soviet squads were locked in protracted house-to-house fighting and wrapped in the 'heavy caustic stench' of hot metal, charcoal, burned brick and the dead rotting beneath the rubble. In each embattled house, the German dead lay strewn in the cellars and on the landings or were sprawled on the shattered staircases: inside the Russians held off the Germans with grenades, automatic fire, bayonets and fighting knives, every room turned into a small fort with weapons poking through firing-points, holes knocked in walls for observation or passage, a small stove glimmering in the middle. The Russians and Germans crashed into each other across a landing or through an attic in fierce spasms of hand-to-hand combat, usually shrouded in dust, bursts of fire and exploding grenades which brought down the plaster and timbers in cascades. If the Germans took part of a building by day, at night the Russians returned, feet bound in sacking to deaden the noise or swinging along the shattered roof-beams, grenades and light weapons at the ready; over the heads of the counter-attack party the German flares swayed to illuminate each corner and shattered coping, followed by intricately patterned, heavy machine-gun fire, forcing the Russian parties to hug the ground or else fall victim to stray bullets. Lightning counter-attacks or reconnaissance raids brought Russian and German squads into murderous collisions by day and by night; in the case of Sergeant Pavlov of 13th Guards Division a reconnaissance at the end of September near the ruined grain-elevator ended in turning the four-storeyed house (the object under scrutiny) into a small, heavily-armed fortress – 'Pavlov's house' into which Sergeant Pavlov finally crammed sixty men, mortars, heavy machine-guns, anti-tank weapons and a full complement of skilled snipers. 'Pavlov's house' covered the approaches to the whole square where Pavlov skilfully mined all the open ground leading to his 'fort'; from the third storey his observers detected any German ground movement, while tank attacks came to grief on the mines. Artillery fire, mortar fire and bombing finally wrecked a large part of 'Pavlov's house' but for fifty-eight days Pavlov beat off every assault.

'Pavlov's house', one of the landmarks of Stalingrad, stood towards the left flank of 13th Guards Division holding the central part of Stalingrad along a three-mile 'front' running from the railway line, the northern face of Dolgii gully, then southwards to *Neftesindikat* and curving in to the Volga bank not far from the central landing-stage; the depth of the divisional positions varied from 300–500 metres, but 34th Guards Regiment's 'front' was the high bluff itself, overlooking the Volga. With German outposts also on this high ground, the whole of Rodimtsev's divisional area, as well as the eastern bank, was under continuous enemy observation. German troops had also seized the main buildings in the centre including the 'L-shaped house', the Railwaymen's House and the 'specialists' house', all of which became powerful strong-points. Twice Rodimstev's regiments tried to recapture the 'L-shaped house' and the Railwaymen's house – impressive even in their ruins – but failed; Rodimtsev's men were desperately anxious to clear these German troops from a sector which allowed them complete domination of the Volga, but they were beaten back by German fire from formidable defences. Sergeant Pavlov, however, managed to take over his 'house', the 'four-storeyed house' on 9 January Square and this at least served the Russians well as a vantage-point. On 24 October a powerful counter-attack from 39th Guards Regiment (13th Division) lines did recover the *Voentorg* building on the corner of Solnechnaya and Smolenskaya streets; under cover of darkness the Guards moved up two 45-mm guns, which were used to knock out the four strong-points covering the building. A combined assault, covered by artillery, mortar and machine-gun fire put 39th Guards once more in possession of *Voentorg*.

Chuikov's 62nd Army depended not only on its skilful and tenacious riflemen committed to the house- and street-fighting, but also on its artillery deployed on both the eastern and western banks; Pozharskii, 62nd's artillery commander, disposed of 8–10 regiments of divisional artillery, five 'tank destroyers' artillery regiments as well as machine-gun and *Katyusha* regiments, all ranging in size from 82-mm mortars to 122-mm howitzers. Regimental guns (mostly 45-mm), were used with the infantry, sometimes from prepared positions but mostly firing over open sights at enemy infantry, tanks or strong-points. Divisional and Army artillery operated under centralized and local command as the situation demanded, with all divisional artillery coming frequently under Front command; for instance on 19 October, when Gorokhov to the north faced heavy German attacks, Yeremenko 'commandeered' 300th Division artillery firing from the mid-Volga islands to break up German infantry concentrations. Though Yeremenko refused to allow Chuikov to move a group of officers to the emergency command post on the eastern bank after 14 October, a Front order of 20 October set up an emergency artillery command post on the eastern bank which would operate under the deputy artillery commander (62nd Army) if communications were cut with the western bank. In mid October more heavy guns arrived on the eastern bank, enabling special 'Army artillery groups' for 62nd and 64th Army to be set up (in addition to Front artillery). Colonel-General Voronov suggested forming from the 'Trans-Volga Artillery Group', with its heavy 203-mm and 280-mm guns on the eastern bank, an 'independent heavy artillery division'. This greatly facilitated concentrated heavy fire and brought into existence the first 'heavy artillery division' in the Red Army once the *Stavka* approved.

Important though the artillery was, the primary role was played increasingly by 'small infantry groups, individual guns and tanks' – the 'storm groups' which 62nd Army developed with such rapidity. The core of the 'storm group' was the assault party, with 6–8 men lightly armed with machine-pistols, grenades, fighting knives and spades (the edges honed sharp for use as an axe in hand-to-hand fighting); the second component, the reinforcement party, which moved into the building once the assault party fired off its flare indicating a break-in, deployed heavier weapons, heavy machine-guns, machine-pistols, mortars, anti-tank rifles, crowbars, picks and explosive charges, with the necessary complement of sappers and snipers: the third element, the reinforce-ment section, supplemented the assault groups, secured the flanks and if neces-sary took up a blocking position. The actual assault was covered either by darkness or by smoke-screens, when 45-mm guns were often deployed to knock out enemy firing-points.

During the hours of daylight, when the bombers came and so much lay bared to German observation, movement was kept to a minimum; at night the city 'traffic' started up, moving along the fantastic circuitry of the slit trenches connecting rubble with craters, linking strong-points, fortified basements with supply points for food and water, basements with company and battalion headquarters. The Russian sappers pushed their communication trenches within grenade range of German positions to facilitate attacks on strong-points, or tunnelled beneath them to plant high-explosive charges. Where the men left off, the guns on both sides – and the Luftwaffe – laid on; German artillery smashed away at the upper storeys of buildings to wipe out the Soviet snipers, Russian artillery on the eastern bank fired to break up the preparations for German attacks, the gunboats of the Volga Flotilla fired off rapid, highly effective bombardments, the *Katyusha* regiments of 62nd Army – now on the very shore of the Volga – backed their rocket-launcher lorries into the water to get maximum reach from their weapons.

Chuikov's 62nd had survived its most critical day, 14 October, but the present situation with the 62nd Army split once again shrieked acute danger; the very shallowness of the remaining Soviet bridgehead seriously impeded the conduct of the defence. The Soviet defence ground down the Germans, but the defenders themselves were being torn to shreds. The *Stavka*, fearful after 14 October about the consequences of the German breakthrough into the Tractor Plant, once more ordered Yeremenko to look to the defences of the eastern bank and the islands in the Volga. Yeremenko ordered increased vigilance from 300th Rifle Division defending the shore and islands, alerted the 87th and 315th Rifle Divisions (from *Stavka* reserve) for action with 62nd Army and prepared to pull three broken divisions, 112th, 95th and 37th Guards (plus two brigades from Gorokhov's units on the right flank) over to the western bank to take in fresh drafts. During the night of 26 October the first battalions of Colonel V.P. Sokolov's 45th 'Shchors' Division were ferried over to Stalingrad, to take up positions between *Krasnyi Oktyabr* and *Barrikady* astride the German line of advance to the Volga and the ferries; to avoid useless losses, however, many more men already embarked in boats from Akhtuba had to be turned back since there was nowhere for them to land. The last ferry on the strip of the Volga between Mezenskaya and Tuvinskaya streets was under heavy German fire at close range on 27 October. Somehow Chuikov had to scrape up enough men to hang on for a couple of days until the whole of Sokolov's division came across to Stalingrad, though there was not a single reserve detachment left in 62nd Army; the HQ was almost without a guard company and the reserve regiment of 62nd Army had long ago been denuded save for the training battalion (turning out sergeants) but even this now went into the holocaust. Salvaging three wrecked tanks and taking a dozen men from the various headquarters, plus thirty riflemen recovered from their wounds in one of the Army aid posts on the Volga bank, Chuikov launched a counter-attack to beat the Germans back from a stretch of the Volga bank leading from Samarkandskaya street. With these patched-up tanks and rag-tag riflemen Chuikov won a whole day's respite after 27 October; the German radios crackled for hours with reports of 'Soviet tanks'.

Meanwhile north and south of Stalingrad Rokossovskii and Yeremenko had attacked in a fresh effort to draw off part of the German forces. On the morning of 22 October one corps of Shumilov's 64th Army, deployed south of Chuikov, attacked from the right flank in an attempt to break to the north-west towards Kuporosnoe-Andreyevskii-Zelenaya Polyana-Peschanka. Sweeping out on to the steppe Soviet units took the high ground at the approaches to the villages of Andreyevskii and Zelenya Polyana, only to be met by massed German artillery fire and a formidable armoured counter-attack. During the night more German reserves moved up, elements of 295th, 71st, 100th Infantry Divisions and 29th Motorized Division, and the next day rolled the Soviet corps back to its start-line. Rokossovskii's counter-blow with 24th and 66th Armies on the left flank of the Don Front, hammering away north-west of Stalingrad, also failed to make any ground. At 10 o'clock on the morning of 25 October Shumilov's right flank divisions attacked once again, precipitating a battle which lasted until 1 November; Soviet troops struggled fiercely to break into Kuporosnoe and succeeded in recapturing the southern outskirts, only to be halted by heavy and effective German resistance. Yeremenko claimed that this fighting on the flanks slowed down the German assault on the factory district in Stalingrad itself; for Chuikov, still fighting off heavy German attacks, these operations may have diverted German attention but they did not deflect the German blows aimed through Stalingrad straight at the Volga. Yet by the evening of 29 October the German onslaught, which had lasted full fifteen days, was slowly dying away; the next day passed in its entirety without any attack on the Soviet lines in Stalingrad. Both sides exchanged fire, both sides stood limp and exhausted from their murderous grappling in the mis-shapen, smoking ruins.

The Soviet 62nd Army had survived the terrible blasting of 14–18 October, even though the German Sixth Army at this time seized the Tractor Plant, smashed its way once more to the bank of the Volga, split Chuikov's army in two and lopped off its right flank. Still Chuikov's men continued to fight nor were they swept off the entire western bank of the Volga in the great fire-storm. What von Paulus had just done he could never again repeat on this fearful scale, using his army as a human battering-ram. To the world German propaganda trumpeted and bellowed over the triumph on the Volga; in truth von Paulus had impaled himself and his bone-weary soldiers, their senses numbed with the unending thunder, fire, smoke, dust and the countless agonies, on the spikes of Stalingrad. Through their mists of blood and screens of smoke Chuikov and his men also saw this; they had fended off catastrophe, admittedly with only metres to spare, but they knew at this point 'that Soviet troops were winning the battle'.

In the second half of October, as Chuikov was fighting off the maddened German attacks in Stalingrad itself, and as German intelligence reported Soviet deployment north of the Don, Operation 'Uranus' assumed its definitive form. The final fixative was the enlargement of the scale of the operation, so that the line for mounting the main attack north-west of Stalingrad was set now in the area south-west of Serafimovich. The counter-offensive was conceived as a single strategic operation involving a group of Fronts – Stalingrad, Don and South-Western: it would unroll simultaneously on a 200-mile front and would establish internal and external encirclements. The South-Western Front would mount its main attack from the bridgehead south-west of Serafimovich, destroy the Third Rumanian Army facing it, and developing a rapid drive on Kalach, would on the third day of operations link up with the troops of the Stalingrad Front, fighting to meet them at Sovietskii: thereafter, it was to encircle and in co-operation with Don and Stalingrad Fronts to destroy enemy troops. Elements of the right flank, South-Western Front, would attack simultaneously to secure the Front shock group, developing the attack south-westwards to the line of the rivers Kriv and Chir, thus establishing the outer encirclement. The Stalingrad Front would attack from the Sarpa lakes, destroy 6th Rumanian Corps facing it, and drive north-west on Sovietskii, link up with the troops of the South-Western Front, encircle and in co-operation with other Fronts destroy the German concentrations at Stalingrad; to secure the Front shock group, the left flank would also attack in the direction of Abganerovo and Kotelnikovo, thus establishing the outer encirclement. The Don Front would attack from the Kletskaya bridgehead and from Kalachinskaya, destroy the enemy forces facing it, and drive in the general direction of Vertyachi, to surround and destroy enemy forces in the small bend of the Don; co-operating with the South-Western Front in completing the basic task of encircling the enemy: thereafter, the Don Front would operate with Stalingrad and South-Western Fronts in destroying enemy forces. The Don and South-Western Fronts would go over to the offensive on 9 November, the Stalingrad Front on 10 November: the time differential allowed for the variation in the depth of the operations and the absolute necessity for having the shock groups from all Fronts in the Kalach–Sovietskii area simultaneously. To reach this objective, the South-Western Front would need to cover 60–70 miles in three days, the Stalingrad Front 50 miles in two days: once in the Kalach–Sovietskii area, Soviet troops were in the rear of the main German force driving for the Volga and would isolate them from their supply bases which were for the most part on the river Chir. In the plans for 'Uranus', the South-Western Front had a major role to play in securing the encirclement of the German and German-allied forces between the Don and the Volga: the Front assignments included an offensive operation to a depth of seventy miles, forcing the Don off the march, cutting enemy communications and completing the encirclement in co-operation with the troops of the Stalingrad Front.

As the Germans observed, both visually and by air reconnaissance, Soviet troops were on the move. At the end of August, *Fremde Heere Ost (I)* submitted a study on the possibilities open to the Soviet command, of which there were five by this reckoning; the reconquest of Stalingrad, a blow against the German Sixth Army's flank to strike on Rostov and thus cut off the Caucasus, an attack on weakly held German flank sectors from Serafimovich and Korotayak, an attack on Voronezh and finally an attack westwards from Astrakhan (ruled out for climatological and terrain reasons). On 13 October, *Fremde Heere Ost (I)* reported that no major Russian attack was likely before the mud came, but the first preparations for an offensive, *vermütlich gegen der Don-Front*, were already in train on the Soviet side. For the counter-offensive, the *Stavka* moved up to the area of the offensive operations a tank army (the 5th), ten rifle divisions, six rifle brigades, three tank, one mechanized and two cavalry corps, one tank regiment and some twenty artillery regiments; the reinforcement of the Fronts for the offensive meant that South-Western Front acquired five rifle divisions, three corps (1st and 26th Tank, 8th Cavalry), a tank brigade (13th), three tank regiments, 13 artillery regiments and six *Kaytusha* regiments, the Stalingrad Front two rifle divisions, six rifle brigades, three corps (13th Tank, 4th Mechanized and 4th Cavalry), three tank brigades, six AA regiments and two regiments of anti-tank artillery. In line with its more limited role, the Don Front got only three rifle divisions. Not all of this went unobserved, but the Russians made masterly use of darkness to hide as much as possible.

In mid October, the Don Front continued to fight on the left flank, repeating the attack which had failed so miserably less than a month before; Yeremenko's centre, 64th Army, was also attacking in the Kuporosnoye area to the south of the city in another attempt to relieve the pressure on Chuikov. Already substantial reinforcement had arrived for Yeremenko's Front: between 10–12 October two cavalry divisions (61st and 81st) of 4th Cavalry Corps joined the Front and were deployed to the south. Yeremenko had a new Front reserve in 7th Rifle Corps (93rd, 96th and 97th Rifle Brigades) which had completed its concentration at Dubovka. Rokossovskii and Yeremenko, in pursuit of the very precise orders to begin the construction of a twelve-mile 'defensive zone', were building no less than three lines of positions, in which every village or hamlet was fitted out for a protracted defence, even if fully encircled. These 'fortified hamlets' were placed under the control of experienced commandants, who would be responsible for all and any garrisons, the 'defensive zone' serving two purposes, to act as a final barrier and secondly to mask preparations for the counter-offensive. The limited attacks by the Don and Stalingrad Front, however, met with little success. Although the Don Front carried out that part of its orders which insisted upon the bridgeheads on the western bank of the

Don (in 63rd Army, 21st Army and 4th Tank Army areas) being held, it proved impossible to break into the northern part of Stalingrad – much as Shumilov's 64th Army in the south enjoyed only one day of success in seizing the southern part of Kuporosnoye.

Even as these attacks petered out, the Front staffs were engaged on detailed planning for their own operations in 'Uranus'. Lieutenant-General Vatutin took over the South-Western Front which was after 22 October officially operational with Zheltov as his political member and Stelmakh, who knew from hard experience on the grim Volkhov Front about breakthrough operations, as his chief of staff; the Front comprised the 63rd Army, 21st Army and 5th Tank Army, with the 17th Air Army. Both 63rd Army (shortly re-designated 1st Guards Army) and 21st Army had been components of the Don Front; 5th Tank came from the Voronezh Front, originally Lizyukov's much-bloodied formation on the Bryansk Front. Unlike many Fronts, which were 'raised' merely by expanding the administration of one formation, the South-Western was a collection of specially picked men. Vatutin had shown his paces at Voronezh; Stelmakh, in addition to being one of the best staff officers in the Red Army, was also an outstanding artilleryman. Lieutenant-General P.L. Romanenko, who commanded the 1st Mechanized Corps in 1941 and who had lectured the 'top brass' of the Red Army at the December 1940 meetings on shock armies, took over 5th Tank Army, a massive formation with two tank corps (1st and 26th), six rifle divisions (14th and 47th Guards, 119th, 124th, 159th and 346th), 8th Independent Tank Brigade, a motor-cycle regiment and twenty artillery regiments. Lelyushenko had the 1st Guards and Chistyakov the 21st Army, which had 4th Tank Corps attached to it, as well as 3rd Guards Cavalry Corps. Major-General Krasovskii commanded 17th Air Army (and finally the 2nd Air Army of the Voronezh Front was subordinated to the South-Western Front). 5th Tank Army commander had the 1st Mixed Aviation Corps subordinated directly to him. Krasovskii had commanded the Soviet air squadrons at Bryansk (and Voronezh); Vatutin had especially asked Stalin for him as air commander South-Western Front and Stalin agreed.

Throughout October the Fronts filled out. The nearer new commanders got to the Don, the more apparent did it become that 'something was up'. Lieutenant-General P.I. Batov, arriving to take command of one of the Don Front armies, had seen continuous movement by night, and by day tank units, artillery regiments and supply columns lying low under their camouflage. Once at Malo-Ivanovka, the Front administrative centre, Batov like everyone else could see away to the south-east the huge column of smoke by day and at night the red glow of fires – Stalingrad. Posted to take command of the 4th Tank Army, Batov asked his new chief of staff, Colonel Glebov, what was the 4th's present strength in tanks: he was told that there were exactly four tanks (currently guarding army headquarters), hence, added Colonel Glebov sarcastically, the designation – '*chetyretankovaya*', 'Four Tank [Army]'. Batov's force was speedily re-designated 65th Army, deployed on Rokossovskii's right flank, while Major-General I.V. Galanin's 24th and Major-General A.S. Zhadov's 66th Army held the centre and the left (the neck of the Don-Volga isthmus).

The movement of considerable quantities of material and large bodies of men put an enormous strain on the existing communications. Both the South-Western and Don Fronts had only one main railway line, the Povorino-Stalingrad line, which could serve them directly; the Stalingrad Front had also only one line, Urbakh-Baskunchak-Akhtuba. All these were under constant air attack and surveillance. The South-Eastern and Ryazan-Uralsk trunk lines brought the main quantities of equipment, ammunition, weapons and supplies to the three Fronts, South-Western, Don and Stalingrad. The rail traffic to the north of Stalingrad itself came under the immediate control of Major-General P.A. Kabanov and his railway troops, who had an enormous job on their hands controlling traffic and keeping it moving under constant air attack. In September, special 'columns', organized from the Communications Commissariat reserve, began to run high-speed, self-contained 'flyers' to slip supplies into the Stalingrad Front; from the 'columns' of locomotives fast trains of only a few trucks, fuelled and armed, would race to the very edge of the battle-front. Being independent of depots, these 'columns' could work on any sector. Meanwhile furious construction work expanded the rail networks, both in the rear and in the front areas; the GKO had already set up the GUVR (*Glavnoe upravlenie voenno-vosstanovitelnykh rabot*) a construction corps attached to the Communications Commissariat, 117,000 men who were placed 'as under service in the ranks of the Red Army'. To speed up trains, passing them along at the rate of one every 12–15 minutes, 'human signallers' were widely employed, screened from enemy observation and able to control the movement of trains in such a way as to have several on one track at once. One-way traffic was also widely used as a means of speeding up urgent traffic. In the Stalingrad area were also some 27,000 lorries, though the advent of the autumn mud slowed down their movements; nevertheless, by October, almost a dozen rifle divisions had been moved up more than 100 miles and lorries subsequently shifted 15,000 tons of food and ammunition just before the offensive began in the area north of Stalingrad. Stalin knew his own mind in asking Churchill for lorries. Tanks he had if not in abundance, then at least in quantity, for almost one thousand were being assembled in the armoured formations on the three Fronts (60 per cent of the armoured strength of the Red Army). Almost half the artillery reserve was shifted there, 75 artillery and mortar regiments; at the beginning of the operation, the Red Army deployed 230 of these regiments (including 115 'divisions' of *Katyusha* rocket launchers), 1,250 barrels or launchers. Twenty-five air divisions (101 regiments) were assembled, upwards of 1,100 planes (without the U-2 biplanes, the minute 'sewing-machines' used for every conceivable purpose).

South of Stalingrad, however, the Volga crossings presented a formidable problem, not least because the river was at least two metres higher than normal and the autumn ice would soon come. The Luftwaffe bombed the actual ferrying continuously; the ferries might take five hours in place of the usual fifty minutes. Red Army engineers set to building 'crossing zones'; on the Volga from Saratov to Astrakhan more than fifty pontoon bridges were laid, but in the vicinity of the city the ferrying came under the control of Vice-Admiral D.D. Rogachev of the Volga Flotilla. 'Ferries' included boats for carrying personnel and also the metal barges indispensable for shifting tanks and guns across the Volga. The armoured regiments destined for 57th and 51st Armies arrived only when ice was forming on the river; the pontoon bridges set up in the 'crossing zones' (Tatyanke, Svetlyi Yar, Kamenii Yar in the Volga bend) would not take heavy equipment in these conditions, so that tanks were ferried in *Barge No. 35*, lorries in the barge *Rzhavka* and the tank-crews and infantry in river steamers. Up to 15th November, the crossings were made at night, but after, because speed was essential, the barges and steamers charged over the Volga in daylight. North-west of Stalingrad, the Don and South-Western Fronts faced the Don; the South-Western Front had fifteen bridges capable of carrying loads from three to sixty tons, but preparations had to be made to build 'winter bridges'. Considerable masses of armour had also to be moved up to and within the Fronts; 5th Tank Army had already been moved into the *Stavka* reserve, and on 20 October began its rail movement to a railhead some sixty miles from its place of deployment on the northern bank of the Don as part of South-Western Front. The approach march proceeded only at night: by day, all units took to their camouflage. Night driving was done without headlights. The tank army finally installed itself in its bridgehead positions at Ust-Khoperskaya on the Don without enemy intelligence being unduly aroused. As much movement as possible was disguised as defensive work. Not all, however, could be concealed and disguised, but the main achievement was to conceal the area of the main concentrations and to conceal any sign of the direction in which attacks would develop.

With their formations flowing in, but never fast enough, Front commanders were engaged late in October in finishing their Front attack plans, in line with the revised plan for Operation 'Uranus'. Vatutin's South-Western Front was now to make a penetration of seventy miles into the German flank and rear; Vatutin proposed to mount his main attack with 5th Tank and 21st Armies from the bridgehead south-west of Serafimovich in the direction of Perelazovskii-Kalach. The defences of the Third Rumanian Army were to be pierced by the shock groups in two sectors, to tear a gap of some eleven miles, through which mobile forces would pass and drive south-eastwards; on the third day of operations, tank formations would link up at Kalach-Sovietskii with Stalingrad Front units. The left flank of the assault units would be fully secured by the right flank of the Don Front, but to establish an outer encirclement and to secure the assault from any attack from west or south-west, the left

flank of the South-Western Front would itself attack to the river Krivaya-
river Chir line and dig in there. Romanenko's 5th Tank Army (1st, 26th Tank
Corps, 8th Cavalry Corps, six rifle divisions), operating on the right flank of the
Front shock group, was to mount the main attack: the rifle divisions, in co-
operation with 21st Army, would encircle and destroy the Third Rumanian
Army between Bolshoi and Kletskaya, while the armoured corps were to break
south-east to be in the Kalach-Sovietskii on the third day of the offensive. The
8th Cavalry Corps was also to establish the outer encirclement. Chistyakov's
21st Army with six rifle divisions and two mobile corps (4th Tank and 3rd
Guards Cavalry) would also bite into the Third Rumanian Army, the two
mobile formations cutting off the Rumanian line of retreat to the south; on
the second day, the mobile corps would reach the Don at Rubezhnyi and Golub-
inskii, seize crossings and establish bridgeheads on the eastern bank. On the
third day, after forcing the Don, these forces would co-operate with 5th Tank
Army in taking Kalach. To consolidate behind the mobile formations, one
rifle division would move in lorries in the wake of 4th Tank Corps. Lelyushenko's 1st Guards Army with six rifle divisions would attack towards the rivers
Krivaya and Chir, thereby securing the flank and rear of the Front shock group;
for the remaining eighty miles of front, 1st Guards would go over to the
defensive.

With 1st Guards on the Chir, the external encirclement front would run for
some hundred miles, separated from the internal encirclement by intervals
which varied from twelve to fifty-nine miles; the Front was deployed in a single
echelon, the shock armies only with two echelons (second echelon having up to
a third of the rifle troops). Tank and cavalry corps were organized into 'exploitation' echelons (*eshelon ravitiya uspekha*). Artillery preparation was planned for
eighty minutes, five minutes for first salvoes, sixty-five minutes of destruction
bombardment, ten minutes for final salvoes. Krasovskii's 17th Air Army would
provide support for ground operations, and would itself be supported by 2nd
Air Army from Voronezh (under Major-General K.N. Smirnov).

From the south-east, below Stalingrad itself, Colonel-General Yeremenko
proposed to use three armies, 64th (Shumilov), 57th (Tolbukhin) and 51st
(Trufanov) to break the enemy defences on three sectors to a depth of some
twenty miles; mobile formations would be introduced through the breach on
the first day of operations to attack north-westwards and on the second day
reach Sovietskii-Kalach. Tolbukhin's 57th (two rifle divisions, 13th Tank Corps,
two tank brigades) was to attack at the very centre of the Front shock group
along a seventeen-mile front, applying its own pressure from the right flank
on an eight-mile front on a sector south-west of Tundutovo and south of
Solyanki: on the first day of operations, 57th Army was to secure the passage of
13th Tank Corps under Colonel Tanaschishin through the gap torn in the enemy
defences. Almost the entire strength of 57th Army was to be exerted on this
eight-mile sector; the remainder of the line would be held by three independent

artillery and machine-gun units. Trufanov's 51st Army (four rifle divisions) would attack through the defiles of the Tsatsa and Barmantsak lakes, break open the enemy defences on a six-mile sector and introduce Volskii's 4th Mechanized Corps, which was to 'demoralize' the enemy rear, avoid holding actions and strike north-west for Sovietskii-Kalach. On the second day of offensive operations 51st Army would also introduce with the coming of darkness 4th Cavalry Corps to attack south-westwards in the direction of Abganerovo, to secure the left flank of the assault formations. Shumilov's 64th (five rifle divisions) was to attack on its left flank and strike to the north-west for the line Nariman-Yagodnyi: this meant bursting out of the Beketovka 'bell'. Chuikov's 62nd Army, grappling with German attacks on the Stalingrad bridgeheads, was to 'activate' its operations the moment the Soviet offensive began, to prevent any German withdrawal of units engaged within the city. To the far south, the 28th Army would hold the Astrakhan defensive sector but would also be ready to attack the German 16th Motorized Division and seize Elista.

On Rokossovskii's Don Front, the main attack would come on the right flank in the direction of Vertyachii, penetrating enemy defences in two sectors, east of Kletskaya and south of Kachalinskaya, with concentric attacks converging on Vertyachii, thereby encircling enemy forces in the small bend of the Don. General Batov's 65th Army would therefore breach enemy defences on a three-mile sector at Kletskaya and to the east of it, then drive south and south-east to reach the line Verkhne-Buzinovka, Oskinskii-Blizhnaya Perekopka by the first day and then aim south-eastwards for Vertyachii, where 6th Army would link up with 24th Army (nine rifle divisions, the same strength as 65th) under Major-General Galanin. Galanin's formation had one tank corps (16th) attached to it, assigned to exploit the breakthrough south of Verkhne-Gnilovskii. Zhadov's 66th Army (six rifle divisions) was to fight a defensive action on the left flank and to contain as much enemy force as possible. Major-General S.I. Rudenko's 16th Air Army would cover Batov's assault divisions and would operate in small groups to provide maximum continuous air cover for ground operations.

From 25 October, the final 'practical work' for the offensive began. General Zhukov, Colonel-Generals Vasilevskii and Voronov were now detached by the *Stavka* to supervise the Front planning and to co-ordinate Front operations. Vasilevskii had already paid several visits to Yeremenko's HQ, for the Stalingrad Front had to make its preparations as the defensive battle in the city grew fiercer day by day. At the very end of the month, *Stavka* orders set the attack dates as 9 November (South-Western and Don Fronts) and 10 November (Stalingrad Front): Front commanders were instructed to bring assault units into their start positions. The strain, however, on communications and supply services was already proving too much. Galanin's 24th Army (Don Front) and Yeremenko's two assault armies (57th and 51st) urgently needed ammunition. Although enough diesel fuel for tanks was being moved up, 5th Tank Army, 65th, 24th and 57th Armies were short of petrol for lorries, with drastic consequences when units were moved far ahead of the Front bases – in the case of 65th Army, as much as 100 miles. Even if fuel was to hand, there was everywhere an acute shortage of lorries.

But even before the offensive opened, the Red Army had already won a famous victory, the re-establishment on 9 October under *Order No. 307* of 'unitary command', *edinonachalie*; the military commissars lost their control functions and upon the 'commander' (the term 'officer' had yet to be formally introduced) devolved 'responsibility for all aspects of work among the troops'. Unitary command was invested in all 'commanders', irrespective of whether or not they were members of the Communist Party; the 'commander-Party member' directed not only all political but also all Party work within the unit, the non-Party commander directed the political indoctrination – 'the political life' of the troops – but in theory continually 'leaned on' the Party organization. Under the new dispensations back came the *zampolit*, 'deputy commanders for political affairs'. At one stroke, though not without enormous pressure, the irksome restraint and the downright inefficiency of 'dual command' was swept away and the 'commander' was once more boss in his own domain. If the Red Army had to be restrained in retreat, then at least it was not to be curbed in attack. Accompanying this restitution of commanders' 'rights', at least from a military point of view, was a thorough revision of tactical training and an increase in operational effectiveness. At last armour was being freed from its infantry support role; in the past, the density of infantry support tanks had been increased by stripping the 'breakthrough' units, but for the forthcoming offensive at Stalingrad the mobile formations were to be used at full strength, their basic task being to complete the breaking of the enemy's tactical defence zone and to develop the success in depth – assigned to 4th Tank Corps (21st Army), or 13th Mechanized with 57th Army. Mauled though the Soviet armoured forces had been in the summer of 1942, when raw units came up against crack German Panzer divisions, the experience so dearly bought was not wasted. Tank armies were being formed, and at least one was to be used in the forthcoming offensive; on 16 October Stalin issued *Order No. 325*, a lengthy document to be studied down to company level, analysing the cause of previous failures and specifying new roles for all tank and mechanized units and formations. The Soviet command learned, though the study of German tactics did not result in mere blind imitation.

And even if no 'Second Front' had appeared to draw off those forty German divisions, the Soviet command could now reckon on the scales being tipped in their favour after the Wehrmacht had been mauled in the summer offensive and as its offensive slowed to a halt. Of 333 enemy divisions and 13 brigades, 258 divisions and 16 brigades (66 and 13 of them respectively belonging to the Axis 'satellites') were ranged on the Soviet-German front: the Soviet reckoning was that five million German troops were deployed against them. At the beginning of November 1942 the field armies of the Soviet Union numbered 6,124,000 men supported by 77,734 guns and mortars (excluding *Katyusha* rocket-launchers and 50-mm mortars), 6,956 tanks and 3,254 aircraft. On its Fronts the Red Army deployed 391 divisions, 247 rifles, independent armoured and mechanized brigades, 30 'fortified districts' (the UR garrisons), 15 tank and mechanized corps. (On the Fronts involved in the Stalingrad counter-offensive, divisional strengths varied; on the South-Western Front, the average divisional strength was 8,800 men, on the Don Front 5,580 and on the Stalingrad Front 4,000–5,000.) In reserve, the *Stavka* held 25 divisions, 7 rifle and independent armoured brigades, 13 mechanized and tank corps.

During the first week in November, when Soviet units began moving into their start-positions for the offensive on the three 'Stalingrad' Fronts and as Zhukov, Vasilevskii and Voronov carried out intensive, on-the-spot briefings and checks, Gehlen of *Fremde Heere Ost* (*I*) in an intelligence appreciation (6 November) submitted that Army Group Centre was the most likely target – '*Schwerpunkt kommender russischen Operationen*' – for any major Soviet offensive undertaking. Captured Russian documents tended to confirm this forecast: if the Russians required a 'decisive success', as indeed they did, then most logically they must seek it against Army Group Centre: the heaviest blows would most probably fall on Second Panzer: in the south, the situation was 'unclear', but it could be stated with confidence that given Russian resources, *two* major offensives were out of the question and it was on their Western Front that the Russians might most effectively win their strategic goals. Two days after Gehlen submitted his report, Soviet Front and army commanders in the south were signing their final attack orders.

There was no lack of warnings about the menacing situation on the German flanks; at 11 Army Corps in the great Don bend, reports flowed in about Soviet movement in front of Corps and the Third Rumanian Army which lay to the left of 11 Corps. Air reconnaissance tracked more movement. Behind General Dumitrescu's Third Army was 48 Panzer Corps (Lieutenant-General Heim), but this formation had only one Panzer division to its name (22nd) which was in the process of being re-equipped. The 1st Rumanian Armoured Division had about 100 Czech-built tanks (Type 38-T), but nothing to stand up to the T-34. Fourth Panzer Army, in addition to reporting considerable Russian troop movements to the east and north-east of Stalingrad, had evidence of wholly new Russian units present in the Beketovka 'bell'; something big was building up against the Rumanian 6th Corps (the Fourth Rumanian Army, under General Constantinescu) on this eastern flank away on the steppe to the south-west of Stalingrad. On paper, Army Group B was a multitude of armies; in the far south on the Kalmuck steppe was 16th Motorized – the 'Greyhound Division' – at Elitsa, then Fourth Panzer, Fourth Rumanian, Sixth Army under Paulus, Rumanian Third Army, Italian Eighth Army,

Hungarian Second Army and finally Second (German) Army. For reserves, Army Group B disposed of 48th Panzer Corps (effectively one weakened Panzer division) and one infantry division (that lodged behind the Italians). The 'Greyhound Division' was in the area of the Soviet 28th Army, holding a vast front with its sand and salt swamp; between 16th Motorized and Krasno-armeisk were Rumanian corps, holding extended lines with a weak and scattered defensive system, deficient in artillery and anti-tank guns. German formations laced up Stalingrad in an iron ring, but then once on the Don lay the Third Rumanian Army, with the Eighth Italian Army as its northern neighbour and farther along the Don, near Pavlovsk, was the Second Hungarian Army. The German Second Army held the line past Voronezh and on to Kursk. On 12 November, Gehlen at *Fremde Heere Ost* submitted his latest estimate of Russian intentions in the south: judging from what was known of Soviet order of battle (and allowing for the new Front, the South-Western, which had been recently established) the most likely eventuality was either limited operations against the Third Rumanian Army or operations over the Don on a larger scale against the Italian and Hungarian armies.

A vigorous, even mounting Russian propaganda campaign at the end of October and the beginning of November about 'large-scale operations' against the Wehrmacht brought no illumination to the German command; General Zeitzler, Halder's successor, was in no position to distinguish fact from fiction. The vaguely optimistic tone of the Soviet press was clearly intended to reassure the Russians at home, and on the night of 6 November Stalin made his anniversary broadcast commemorating the Revolution. In October, Anglo-Soviet relations had degenerated sharply but in November, Stalin did at least manage some faint cordiality towards his allies, though he did say that had a Second Front materialized, German troops would be fighting now at Pinsk, Minsk and Odessa in somewhat desperate straits. His comments about the British Army were ironical, fighting 'only four – yes, four German and eleven Italian divisions' in Libya. In his speech, Stalin insisted that the German objective in 1942 had been Moscow, to 'divert' the Soviet forces southwards and then to put Moscow at their mercy: 'This ... explains why the main German forces are now in Orel and Stalingrad areas, and not in the south.' Though chasing two hares at once – oil and Moscow – the German forces had nevertheless achieved formidable successes, due to the absence of a Second Front; assuming that sixty German divisions had been tied up in the west (Stalin's analogy was here with the First World War), then the German Army in the east would have been in dire straits.

Meanwhile Soviet troops moved up. On the South-Western Front the main task was to conceal the presence of Romanenko's 5th Tank Army, which first received orders to concentrate some 15–20 miles behind the front on the northern bank of the Don; towards the end of the first week in November, its formations began to move by night over the river on to the southern bank, though one corps, 1st Tank, did not manage to finish its crossing near Zimovskii under cover of darkness and was caught by German bombers. Once over the Don, the tank units were held back 5–10 miles from the front itself. On 3 November, Zhukov, accompanied by Vatutin arrived at Romanenko's head-quarters to go over in detail 5th Tank's assignment and operational plans with corps and divisional commanders; after reviewing the general plan and the role of each formation in it, the orders for 5th Tank were prepared at this lengthy briefing. The role of 5th Tank was vital since it was to mount the main attack at the centre of the Front on a five-mile sector with Perelazovskii as its first objective. By the evening of the first day of operations, the rifle formations should have reached a line running from Height 211-Karasev-Verkhne Cherenskii, 8th Cavalry Corps should have its forward elements near Pichugina and Pronin, 1st Tank Corps must be in the area Lipovskii-Gusinka, 26th Tank Corps in Perelazovskii-Zotovskii. On the second day, rifle formations would reach the line on the river Chir running from Bokovskaya to Chernyshevskaya thence to Kalach-Kurtlak and Perelazovskii; east of the Chir, 1st Tank Corps would seize the Don crossing at Verkhne-Chirskii, the railway station at Lozhki and cut the railway line; 26th Tank Corps would go for Kalach. On the third day, mobile formations would link up with the Stalingrad Front at Kalach. For its main attack, 5th Tank would use four out of six rifle divisions, two tank and one cavalry corps, one tank brigade and one tank battalion, and sixteen artillery regiments, supported by the 1st Mixed Aviation Division.

The next day Zhukov held a second planning conference at Serafimovich: present were Colonel-General Voronov from the *Stavka*, Rokossovskii as Don Front commander, Vatutin, Chistyakov of 21st Army, Batov of 65th Army, the two political members of the South-Western and Don Fronts, Zheltov and Kirichenko, as well as General Staff specialists. One of the main purposes of the meeting was to co-ordinate the operations of 21st (South-Western) and 65th Army (Don Front). There was a further review of the shock forces of the northern wing, the main striking force. For 65th Army, Batov reported on the strength and deployment of his formations and on the characteristics of the bridgehead he occupied; he also presented certain conclusions about the enemy deployment. Zhukov chipped in to say that he might by all means present the information, but he should leave the conclusion to them (the *Stavka*). Batov presented an interrogation report on a prisoner, which Zhukov read, at once connected himself with the *Stavka* by telephone and then spoke to Stalin: 'Your suggestions about the existence of a junction between two groups in the Kletskaya area have been confirmed. Batov's reconnaissance troops have taken prisoners from the 376th German division and 3rd Rumanian division.' For all this, Zhukov was far from pleased with Batov and berated him fiercely for his 'second mistake' (the first one being in the Crimea in 1941), though over lunch Zhukov talked at length about the proposed operations, questioning Batov extensively about his divisional commanders, about the disposition of his units and then enlarging on the peculiarities of deploying High Command Reserve artillery, night operations, and manoeuvre deep in the enemy's defensive zone, so that his earlier outburst was soon forgotten. Vatutin was planning to pour 500 tanks through the breach he proposed to rip in the enemy defences; 150 of them would be with 4th Tank Corps attached to Chistyakov's 21st Army and Pliev's 3rd Cavalry Corps. Batov's 65th had two tank brigades (91st and 121st) but very few tanks – 13 in one brigade, 11 in another; Zhukov roared his scorn when Batov proposed to attack with 'that force', but all that Batov finally got in the way of reinforcement for this flimsy force was two companies of tanks. Away to Batov's left Galanin of 24th Army had 16th Tank Corps with 105 tanks.

With the briefings finished, the attack troops were drawn up to their start-line and the attack orders were signed on 8 November, but during the night of 9 November Front commanders received a signal that the offensive was postponed for a week. Delays in troop movement and the shifting of supplies were chiefly responsible: not even Romanenko's 5th Tank Army was in position. Meanwhile Zhukov's next halt was at the HQ of Stalingrad Front, where he arrived on the day of the postponement, 9 November. A week earlier Yeremenko had summoned Trufanov and Tolbukhin, commanders of 51st and 57th Armies, to his HQ at Krasnyi Sad on the eastern bank of the Volga; here, for the first time (leaving aside any of Tolbukhin's shrewd guesses) both commanders heard details of Operation 'Uranus', but without being given any indication of attack dates were given eight days in which to prepare outline attack plans. All orders were passed orally at Yeremenko's HQ and both commanders were warned not to issue any written order or directive. For Tolbukhin, this was his third war: he had served after 1914 as a subaltern in the Imperial Russian Army, in the Red Army during the Civil War and had begun this war as chief of staff to the Trans-Caucasus Military District. Appointed to the south-east in 1938 as a brigade commander, Tolbukhin remained there until March 1942, when – running foul of Lev Mekhlis – he had been dismissed as chief of staff of the Crimean Front and made the scapegoat for the abortive Soviet offensive in March. Some, but not much of this he had been able to explain to Shaposhnikov. Now in command of 57th Army (a post he had held since July), he had a key command and he had also two things which were essential to success – great professional skill and a deal of experience. Assembling his officers for a dinner in honour of the anniversary of the Revolution, for two nights, 7 and 8 November, Tolbukhin at 57th Army HQ ran a series of war-games involving the army in attack; in repelling counter-attack and in introducing an armoured formation as a second echelon to exploit a breakthrough; present among the officers was Colonel Trofim Ivanovich Tanaschishin, commander of 13th Tank Corps. At 5 am on 8 November Tolbukhin was finished. Turning to his officers, he pointed out that 'we know no more than you' but that by 12 November divisional commanders should have played exactly the same war-game with their subordinates and no later than 14 November the same should be done with battalion and artillery division commanders.

The regiments for Colonel Tanaschishin's corps were only now approaching the Volga crossing and on 11 November moved over the river to the western bank at Tatyanka. Already an icy 'slush', *salo*, covered the Volga, followed by ice which made ferrying a dangerous business; a wind with a bite in it had now begun to blow as the temperature slipped down. In the area of Tatyanka and Svetlyi Yar, the crossing points (as yet under the control of 57th Army), large numbers of lorried infantry and tanks were stretched under their camouflage but never bombed. The evacuation of the civilian population of Stalingrad was proceeding with all its multifarious movement (and continued up to 15 November) which may have contributed to confusing the German pilots. Once on the western bank, 13th Tank Corps lay hid by day in the woods east of Krasnoarmeisk; 4th Mechanized and 4th Cavalry were to screen themselves by day about ten miles east of Tsatsa.

Even as these formations moved up, Zhukov held a major briefing at the HQ of 57th Army, about half a mile north-east of Tatyanka; the conference began on 10 November and went on through the night until 5 am. Yeremenko assembled all his officers and members of the Military Soviets: for the Front, Khrushchev, Zakharov and Popov (deputy Front commanders), Novikov, Matveyev and Khryukin for armour, artillery and aviation, the commanders and full Military Soviets of 57th and 51st Armies, the commanders of the armoured and mobile formations, Volskii for 4th Mechanized, Tanaschishin for 13th Tank and Shapkin for 4th Cavalry Corps, all commanders of divisions earmarked for assault roles, and finally engineers and signals commands. Unlike the South-Western and Don Fronts, the Stalingrad Front had to make its preparations while under heavy attack and with the prime responsibility for holding its bridgeheads in Stalingrad itself. Artillery units and engineers were hard pressed providing support for the city and much of their work was carried out under heavy German bombardment. The thirty-eight engineer battalions of the Stalingrad Front had to work like demons to carry out their array of orders: ferrying, transporting ammunition, shipping tanks over the Volga, setting up routes for the armoured formations, carrying out the 'engineering reconnaissance' of the breakthrough sectors. Divisional engineers were supporting infantry and artillery preparations, army and Front engineers the armour (with two to three sappers attached to each tank). In just under three weeks they shipped over the Volga more than 420 tanks, 111,000 men, 556 guns, 7,000 tons of ammunition. Khryukin's aircraft from 8th Aviation Army were to provide fighter cover for the assault divisions, bomb enemy defences and support the infantry and tank attacks on the battlefield; and special orders covered their co-operation with the three fast formations of tanks and cavalry. During daylight, 8th Air Army fighters would patrol the operational areas of the corps, and special radio signals were arranged for the tanks to call on air support.

All plans and preparations Zhukov scrutinized with that same rigour he had employed with the South-Western and Don Front commands. The employment of the armour came in for very detailed examination, and here Colonel-General Vasilevskii took 4th Mechanized more or less under his wing: Vasilevskii, unlike Zhukov, did not roar. To the chief of staff of 4th Mechanized, Colonel Poshkus, Vasilevskii gave the impression of being 'a clever general, with great talents' but he did not ignore those of other commanders. Volskii, 4th Corps commander, had only just received clarification of what his corps was meant to do; his earlier movement orders had merely stated that his assignment would be 'notified later'. After the Front meeting, he knew that 4th Mechanized was to link up with the South-Western Front; operating with 51st Army, his tanks were to provide support for the rifle divisions, for which purpose Volskii proposed to detach 55th and 158th Brigades, and then race through the gap in the defences. His main force he proposed to introduce when the defences had been pierced to a depth of 3–4 miles, when the infantry reached a line running from Height 87 to the village of Zakharov. Vasilevskii listened to the suggestions put forward by Volskii and Poshkus, then he examined their plans in minute detail; to speed through the gap, and to avoid one massive column of tanks, Volskii proposed to use three columns organized by brigades, though this solution was complicated since Volskii knew of only one road. Two brigades would operate across country making sure that they had carefully reconnoitred the terrain and interrogated people who had formerly lived there. The fundamental idea, however, was to avoid frontal engagements with powerful forces and avoid detaching forces to deal with enemy strongpoints or centres of resistance, merely outflanking them and leaving covering detachments behind. While Volskii and Poshkus planned and lectured to the officers, the corps had to be brought up to full fighting readiness; on 16 November, though the fuel barges coming up from Astrakhan had arrived, no one knew where they actually were and even a search by plane failed to locate them. Eventually the fuel was found after scouring the district, but then 4th Corps found itself short of winter lubricants (like the whole Front): only a telegram from Khrushchev to Mikoyan brought five hundred tons.

On 11 November Zhukov returned to Moscow to report to Stalin and the *Stavka*; he and Vasilevskii presented the operation on the completed General Staff maps and summed up the state of readiness, the state of Soviet forces and the chances of success:

1 According to the data supplied by the Fronts and confirmed by the General Staff, Soviet and German strength on 'the Stalingrad axis' was about equal. On the axes where the Soviet command proposed to mount its main attacks, thanks to *Stavka* reserves and stripping units from 'secondary axes' of the front, 'we will have a significant superiority over the enemy' which makes it possible to reckon on success. There are no signs of enemy reserves on any significant scale being moved from the rear towards Stalingrad. The deployment of German troops remains what it was before: their main forces, 6th

Army and Fourth Panzer, are being dragged into bitter fighting in the area of Stalingrad itself. On the flanks, the axes of our main attacks, there are Rumanian troops. In general, the relationship of forces in the Stalingrad area is such to favour successful fulfilment of the tasks assigned there by the *Stavka*.

During the course of operations it will be vital to concentrate on reinforcing Front aviation, on replacing losses in the armies, especially in the tank and mechanized corps and to send in fresh *Stavka* reserves to ensure a successful conclusion to present operations and the development of those to follow.

2 The concentration of forces and vital supplies assigned to the fronts by the *Stavka* has been due to the 'titanic work' of rail and river transportation workers and to those assignments additionally ordered by the GKO, especially the expansion of the front area railway network, finished with what is merely insignificant infringement of the stipulated timetable. As a result of the political work among the troops, morale is good and fighting spirit high.

3 Orders and assignments issued to all command staff down to regimental level are not only well and correctly understood but have also been worked out in practical terms on the spot. All questions of the co-operation of infantry, armour and artillery have been well worked out down to regimental level. Special attention has been paid to the problems of the tank, mechanized and cavalry corps.

In working out operational plans at first hand in the appropriate areas, no additional considerations bearing on deployment other than those envisaged in the Front command plans already approved by the *Stavka* have emerged. From the plan it is apparent that the basic role during the initial phase will be performed by the South-Western Front, which, according to our view and in the opinion of the Front command, has adequate forces for this purpose. The junction of the tank and mechanized forces of the South-Western and Stalingrad Fronts is to take place on the eastern bank of the river Don in the area of Kalach-Sovietskii, timed for the evening of the 3rd or 4th day of operations.

Envisaged in the plan are measures for establishing an external encirclement front, worked out with the commanders of Front forces and armies and under their direction, with the commanders of actual units involved.

There is now every reason for the offensive to be opened by the troops of the South-Western and Don Fronts on the nineteenth, and by the troops of the Stalingrad Front on the twentieth.

In conclusion, all the Military Soviets of Fronts and Armies on the Stalingrad axis and all commanders about to take part in this first extensive operation by our operational scales – and we ourselves – believe in its success.

What had been possibly timed as a simultaneous blow with 'Torch' (the North Africa landings which had gone ashore on 8 November) was now finally retimed by a little more than a week.

In discussing 'measures for establishing an external encirclement front', Vasilevskii had touched on a key point; this 'external front' ultimately became a massive new undertaking, though it was being examined at the end of the first week in November and received the code-name *Saturn*. *Saturn* had been originally a variant all of its own, whereby two Fronts, the Voronezh and South-

Western, should mount a very deep blow in the direction of Rostov (in fact, the 1920 plan which destroyed Denikin); the first stage of the operation would be the destruction of the Italian Eighth Army and an advance into the Kantemirovka-Chertkovo-Millerovo area. The attack would be made by the left flank of the Voronezh Front (6th Army) and 1st Guards Army (South-Western Front) reinforced by three tank corps, the 17th, 18th and 25th. The second stage of the operation would begin from the Chertkovo-Millerovo line to which *Stavka* reserves would be moved and then the South-Western Front would strike for Rostov, thus stabbing into the rear of the entire German forces in the south – into Army Group B and against Army Group A, shutting off its escape route. The Voronezh Front command had already prepared plans to destroy the Second Hungarian Army; on 13 November Golikov flew to Moscow to attend a *Stavka* session on the outlines of the Saturn plan.

At this juncture, however, even 'Uranus', the plan to encircle the German Sixth Army, appeared at risk as the final *Stavka* appraisal of plans and preparations coincided with a dangerous crisis in Stalingrad itself, where at 06.30 hours on 11 November German air and artillery attacks signalled a renewal of the furious assault to break through to the Volga and to break 62nd Army into pieces. That same morning, shortly before noon, in one great roar of artillery bombardment and *Stuka* attacks, German infantry and tanks reached the Volga on a 500-yard front, splitting Chuikov's bridgehead for the third time. South of the *Barrikady* plant, Lyudnikov's division was now cut off; much of the fearsome ruin of *Krasnyi Oktyabr* was in German hands. To the north, Gorokhov's shattered brigades were still hanging on, while the left flank was held by the remnants of Rodimtsev's force. But rammed right to the river edge was now a formidable German salient which left Lyudnikov trapped in a space 400 by 700 metres. Behind them was the river, but this highway of help was closing before their eyes; the Volga was freezing, the 'slush' packing into dangerous, floating ice. Rowing-boats had to take over from the 'ferries', for the little steamers and barges could make no headway; 20–25 rowing-boats would assemble by night to cross but they stood no chance once they came under German machine-gun fire or were shelled by light guns. Lyudnikov's regiments had been cruelly decimated: in his 650th Regiment only 31 men were left, while the 344th had 123 survivors. There was no more ammunition for the automatic weapons and no grenades; 20–30 rounds remained to each rifle. For each man, Lyudnikov had enough supplies for a daily ration of twenty-five grammes of rusks and five grammes of sugar. Soviet planes tried to drop bales of food and ammunition, but these either fell into the river, into the German lines, or burst on hitting the ground, damaging the ammunition. Worst of all, the wounded increased to nearly four hundred, lying soaked in the rain or snow drizzle without medical supplies or medical aid. None could be ferried out.

Chuikov's most powerful unit was 13th Guards Division with 1,500 men;

193rd Division had been ground down to just about 1,000 men. In all, 62nd Army numbered 47,000 men, with 19 tanks, split into three groups; about 1,000 men to the north under Gorokhov, holding out at Rynok and Spartan-ovka, Lyudnikov's 138th Division sealed off east of *Barrikady* with less than 500 men, and then to the south the burnt-out shells of 95th, 45th, 39th Guards, 284th and 13th Guards Divisions. Each corner of this immense rubble was turned into a strong-point: 'forts' were built out of shattered walls and slabs of stone. Fighting squads, armed with automatic weapons, knives, grenades and shovels, with a strength of 6–8 men, intersected and fought through each ruin, fighting for parts of houses or in the labyrinths of the wrecked factories. Lyudnikov's men continued to fight amidst their dead and dying; when seventy German tommy-gunners broke through to divisional HQ, Lyudnikov's staff officers, the twelve men left in the 179th Independent Engineer Company and the six remaining men of the HQ guard company fought a hand-to-hand engagement with the German assault troops and finally beat them off. Gorokhov, on 17 November, faced what looked like certain annihilation; 16th Panzer Division was about to roll over his dreadfully enfeebled garrison, the remnants of two brigades which had been mercilessly bludgeoned for weeks. Scraping up his last reserves – cooks, drivers and anyone from the rear services – Gorokhov put three hundred men in the line; in contact with Yeremenko and with Chuikov by telephone, Gorokhov received orders just to hold on – and in return he was promised 'the kind of help you have never dreamed of'. Chuikov nevertheless subsequently confessed that, 'we were at our last gasp [*my poistrepalis*], our ammunition was running out'. German assault troops and combat engineers were fighting for Stalingrad metre by metre, launching one more assault, fighting for one more yard, dragging assault guns into one more position, the men filthy, tattered and lashed now by wind and rain.

Upon news of the critical situation in Stalingrad, Stalin ordered Vasilevskii to fly there at once, to take over the preparations for the offensive so that Yeremenko would be able to devote his full attention to the defence of the city. Some of this time Vasilevskii spent inspecting the final attack plans drawn up by Volskii at 4th Mechanized. There was also the question of the shortage of artil-lery; to overcome this, 57th Army's barrage was so timed that the guns could be moved up to 64th Army sector to fire a second barrage in support of Shumilov's attack. On 17 November Vasilevskii had to face a new and quite sudden crisis which this time emanated from Moscow, though its origins lay in the Stalingrad Front; Stalin instructed him to return to the capital to attend a session of the State Defence Committee (GKO) which had before it a most extraordinary document, nothing less than a plea to Stalin to postpone the counter-offensive because it was doomed to fail. The author of this letter was none other than Volskii, commander of 4th Mechanized Corps and assigned a key role in the attack. Volskii wrote that the forces assigned for the opening of the counter-offensive were such that failure was practically inevitable, and that

he, Volskii, as an 'honest member of the Party' and knowing that many other
senior officers shared his views begged Stalin to call off the offensive, re-examine
the decisions which had been taken in connection with the planning, postpone
the offensive and then change it entirely. The GKO wanted Vasilevskii's opinion
on this hair-raising estimate: Vasilevskii pointed out that for the past two weeks
Volskii had been intimately associated with the planning and the preparations
for the counter-offensive, when never for an instant had he shown the slightest
reservation about the operation as a whole or the part his corps was to play.
On the contrary, at the vital meeting on 10 November in the company of the
Stavka officers and the Front command he had stated that his corps was ready
to carry out its orders. Vasilevskii (who had had a large personal share in
planning 4th Mechanized Corps operations and had discussed them in detail
with Volskii and Poshkus) reported that the corps was in full fighting readiness
and its men in excellent trim. In conclusion, Vasilevskii insisted that it was out
of the question to change anything in this operation which was now fully
prepared or alter the times set for its opening. At this, Stalin ordered Vasilevskii
to connect him by telephone with Volskii; the conversation was short and to
the utter astonishment of all those in the room by no means harsh. When it was
over Stalin advised Vasilevskii to pay no more attention to Volskii's letter.
Volskii would stay with 4th Mechanized since he had just given his word that
he would do everything to carry out his orders, but a final decision on him would
rest on the results of the first days of the operations, about which Stalin ordered
Vasilevskii to keep him specially informed. Meanwhile Vasilevskii was to
proceed to the Serafimovich bridgehead from which the decisive attack was to
be launched.

On the eve of zero-hour for Operation 'Uranus', Soviet forces on the
'Stalingrad axis' numbered 1,000,500 men, 13,541 guns (exclusive of AA guns
and 50-mm mortars), 894 tanks and 1,115 aircraft. The South-Western Front,
1st Guards, 5th Tank, 21st and 17th Air Armies, had 18 rifle divisions, 3 tank
and 2 cavalry corps, 1 tank and 1 motorized rifle brigade, 8 regiments of
artillery: the Don Front, 65th, 24th, 66th and 16th Air Armies, deployed 24
rifle divisions, 1 tank corps, 6 tank brigades, 52 mortar and artillery regiments:
Yeremenko's Stalingrad Front, 62nd, 64th, 57th, 51st, 28th and 8th Air Armies,
disposed of 24 rifle divisions, 17 rifle and motorized rifle brigades, 1 mechanized
and 1 tank corps, 7 tank brigades, 1 cavalry corps, 67 artillery or mortar
regiments (to be on their start-lines by 20 November). All three Fronts had
adopted a single-echelon deployment, dictated mainly by the shortage of
troops; this enabled Front and army commanders to introduce their armoured
and mobile forces as 'exploitation' echelons, but it nevertheless deprived the
command of any depth to those forces assigned to main attack roles. The
artillery density was still too low, which made long artillery preparation – up
to eighty minutes – inescapable.

For almost a week before the offensive opened the enemy positions facing the sectors marked for attack were reconnoitred by reinforced battalions and companies, to establish whether the main enemy forces were drawn forward or pulled back deep in the defensive positions; artillery reconnaissance aimed to avoid guns firing into empty ground. To conceal attack areas, the reconnaissance went on over wide sectors of army fronts. On the South-Western Front, reconnaissance showed that ahead of 5th Tank Army the forward positions were only lightly held but that the main positions were about half a mile to the rear; this enabled the start line for the armour to be advanced and artillery targeting to be corrected. Romanenko's 5th Tank carried out its reconnaissance up to 17 November, but in 51st Army area (Stalingrad Front) there had been only two reconnaissance raids, on 14 and 19 November; there was every possibility that enemy minefields might have been changed or the defences regrouped after the pre-assault surveys had been finished. The infantry and armour were on their start-lines; on 18 November commanders received notification of the final attack times, much like Chistyakov's orders:

To commander 21st Army   *Personal and urgent*

Artillery preparation to begin from 7 hrs. 30 min. 19.11.42
Infantry, artillery and tank attacks to begin at 8 hrs. 50 min. 19.11.42
Report every hour on progress of operations.

Commander SW Front
Lieutenant-General Vatutin

Member of Military
Soviet: Corps commissar
Zheltov

At midnight on 18 November Chuikov in Stalingrad was told to stand by for 'orders'. He was then told of the timing of the counter-offensive just at a time when 62nd Army's strength was fast failing and his request for reinforcements had not been met. Yeremenko had already moved his HQ from Krasnyi Sad to Raigorod, disguising his new command centre as an administrative centre; the Front Military Soviet had decided that when the offensive opened on the Stalingrad Front, Khrushchev and Popov (deputy commander) should go to 51st Army, Yeremenko and his armoured commander Novikov to 57th Army. At 65th Army on the Don Front Batov, in spite of the scepticism of the senior officers from the Front staff, had used the last day to take his officers through a final map-exercise, which proved its worth; on the eighteenth, his officers had dispersed to their units, and Batov was at his forward command post, at Height 90 on the right flank 2,000 yards from the forward positions, where he was due to be joined by the Front commander Rokossovskii and his staff, Rudenko, Orel, V.I. Kazakov. For the moment the view ahead of Batov's command post was clear; first the fields, then the Don itself already icing up under its 'slush', then the bank on the far side dotted with bushes whitened by the first snow flurries which had arrived on 16 November, on to the ridges and hummocks cut by enemy trenches, two lines of them. Behind them lay the bunkers and dugouts. Although the men in the Soviet divisions had received no orders as yet –

they were due to be read out three hours before the attack opened – most of them were well aware that 'something decisive' was afoot; in each division and unit there were the usual pre-attack huddles of Party meetings. On the South-Western Front, where Romanenko's tanks had moved into their jumping-off positions, commanders were finally alerted by the dispatch of a coded telegram at 16.17 hours, 18 November: 'Send a messenger to pick up the fur gloves' ('Infantry attack begins at 8.50 hours, 19.11.42.').

At midnight on 19 November, the snow clouds came: in the freezing fog and driving snow, as the temperature dropped sharply, visibility was reduced to zero.

At 07.20 hours, in the murk of Thursday morning 19 November, South-Western and Don Fronts issued the call-sign 'Siren', at which all guns, settled during the night in their firing pits or drawn up to their stations, were loaded; ten minutes later, the order to fire was given and eighty minutes of bombardment was signalled by the first salvoes from the RS-6 rocket-launchers. More than 3,500 guns and mortars, deployed along the three narrow breakthrough sectors which stretched altogether for some fourteen miles, joined in the bombardment after the first rocket salvoes. Although this great thunder rippled over the unsuspecting enemy, the thick fog and swirling snow made fire correction almost impossible for the Soviet gunners; instead of firing at selected targets, the guns were aimed and fired by quadrants, pounding away in the gloom at the Rumanian pill-boxes and bunkers. The guns firing over open sights, set about 400 yards from their targets, nevertheless fared a little better. The Rumanian defensive field was churned up in great columns of snow and mud. The infantry of 5th Tank Army, 47th Guards, 119th and 124th Rifle Divisions, moved up 300 metres to the edge of the Rumanian defences as the guns shifted to the centre of the enemy defensive field; at 08.48 the last salvo was fired and two minutes later the infantry, their support tanks also on the move, crashed ahead. Tanks carrying riflemen crouched on top of them loomed out of the mist driving for the wire and ditches. Chistyakov's 21st Army attacking from Kletskaya moved out, four divisions, 96th, 63rd, 293rd and 65th Rifle Divisions, in the lead; on the left flank, 76th Rifle Division on the orders of its commander, Major-General Tabartkeladze, went into the attack to the accompaniment of music blared out by the ninety-strong divisional band. Soviet tanks rolled out in parade order. Batov's divisions from 65th Army attacked at the appointed time; 304th Rifle Division, with 76th Division for neighbour, struck out for Melo-Kletskii but ran into a chalk cliff sixty feet high up which Batov's men had to clamber under heavy fire. By mid-morning the wind had begun to disperse the fog and Soviet aircraft so far grounded took off to survey the battlefield where Rumanian battalions, for all their pitiful equipment, were fighting it out manfully with the Soviet assault divisions.

At noon that same day the rout began. The rifle divisions in single echelon with too few tanks lacked the power to smash through the defences; 65th Army and the right flank of 5th Tank Army had come up against stiff resistance. Chistyakov of 21st Army and Romenanko of the 5th decided to loose the mass of their tanks; the mists closed in again as Major-General Kravchenko's 4th Tank Corps and Major-General Pliev's 3rd Cavalry Corps (both of 21st Army) were ordered to burst through the gap precisely at noon. Kravchenko's corps moved in two echelons and two columns on a four-mile front in the area of 76th and 293rd Rifle Divisions; behind the tanks came Pliev's 5th and 32nd Cavalry Divisions racing with the T-34s. At 12.30 hours, Romanenko issued personal orders for 1st and 26th Tank Corps to attack through 47th Guards, 119th and 124th Rifle Division sectors. Major-General A.G. Rodin's 26th Corps moved off in four columns with 19th and 173rd Tank Brigades in the lead, charging down on the surviving Rumanian and German batteries which fired over open sights through the gloom whenever the wall of tanks showed up; Major-General Butkov's 1st Tank Corps roared through 47th Guards sector and in the wake of both tank formations came 8th Cavalry Corps, flooding into the eight-mile gap which had been ripped in the defences. The tanks struck out south-east, steering by compass through the fog and snow while the infantry followed in their tracks, but even the reconnaissance tanks could find no easy way round or through the gullies and steep-sided ravines glazed with ice. Three Rumanian infantry divisions, 13th, 14th and 9th, began to disintegrate and fell back in confusion and panic, pursued by 47th Guards lifted on the back of the tanks of 8th Guards Tank Brigade, and by tank columns beginning to break out into the Don steppe. The whole of the Rumanian Third Army, outflanked from the west and the east, was lifted right off its hinges.

At Hitler's headquarters, the 'disturbing news' – '*alarmierende Nachrichten*' – of the Soviet attack brought immediate orders for General Heim's 48th Panzer Corps to counter-attack in an effort to hold this enemy offensive which the Führer had 'long foreseen'. Shortly before ten o'clock, Army Group B ordered Heim to attack to the north-east in the direction of Kletskaya; not much more than an hour later, with the realization that the Soviet objective was not Kletskaya but a much more dangerous drive, Heim's corps was swung against 5th Tank Army and ordered to move north-westwards, so that 22nd Panzer Division had to slither round in its tracks and set out to make contact with Romanenko; General Radu's 1st Rumanian Armoured Division would attack from north of Zhirkovskii towards the west, 22nd Panzer from Peschany to the north-east and 7th Rumanian Cavalry Division from Pronin also to the north-east. In the rapidly gathering darkness of the winter afternoon, with the vital wireless trucks in 1st Rumanian Division out of action, 22nd Panzer and 1st Rumanian lost touch; Radu's division never received the all-important order to swing south-west. Slicing south-eastwards through the dark, Rodin's tank columns came momentarily under artillery fire, switched off lights and engines at which the shelling ceased. To their left, Rodin's tank men heard a column sweeping north, straight into the Soviet rear with its mass of armour: this was the 1st Rumanian Armoured Division, 'going like mad'. Their ammunition and supply lorries at once drove slap into the columns of 26th Corps. At dawn on 20 November, as Radu's division went to its doom, Rodin's tanks sweeping south-eastwards surrounded Perelazovskii, traffic junction, supply dump and headquarters town, without firing a shot. Colonel Oppeln-Bronikowski's 22nd Panzer, unable to hold any of the Soviet tank thrusts, was falling back south-westwards to the Chir, at times holding a parallel course with advancing Soviet columns; the Rumanian Third Army, for all the desperate counter-attack attempts by General Lascar's infantry and Radu's old-fashioned tanks, broke in pieces and began to flee south away from the tanks which struck terror into them, five divisions reeling about on the Don steppe.

South of Stalingrad, Yeremenko's Front prepared to take the offensive on 20 November. On the evening of 19 November, Army Group B headquarters, alive now to the gravity of the situation on the deep flank of the German forces in Stalingrad, at 22.00 hours ordered Paulus at the Sixth Army to take 'radical measures', now that the Rumanian Third Army had caved in, to break off the Stalingrad attack and shore up the left flank, just as Soviet divisions were taking up their positions to smash in the right flank. Three hours earlier Volskii of 4th Mechanized received orders from Stalingrad Front HQ to move the main body of his corps to its start-line, a thirty-mile drive for some units; at 51st Army forward command post Khrushchev and Popov joined Trufanov, Volskii and Lieutenant-General Shapkin (4th Cavalry). Yeremenko and his chief of staff were at 57th Army, where Tolbukhin (a diabetic) was ill but insisted on supervising the attack. On the edge of the enemy positions, sappers in white camouflage capes set charges and checked mines; signallers buried cables lest the tanks sever them. Towards the dawn, however, the clear sky was obscured by mist which thickened by the hour. The guns were blinded and aircraft grounded.

From Moscow, the *Stavka* telephoned to ask whether Yeremenko would attack on time. Yeremenko replied that if the fog lifted he would open the barrage at the appointed time, exactly at 08.00 hours. At 07.30 hours, visibility was only two hundred yards and showed no sign of improving. The *Stavka* telephoned once and ordered a 'speedy start' to which Yeremenko replied that he was not sitting in his office but at a forward command post and he knew best when to start. At 09.30 hours Yeremenko gave orders to open fire in thirty minutes, and on the hour the first salvo from M-30 rocket-launchers was fired off. Forty-five minutes later the tanks and infantry of 57th Army, 13th Tank Corps in support, 422nd and 15th Guards Rifle Divisions, attacked from the southern edge of the Beketovka 'bell' and out of the defile between the lakes Sarpa and Tsatsa. To the south, 51st Army had opened its barrage on time; Popov, Yeremenko's deputy commander, had been unable to contact the Front commander, and failing a consultation about the weather and the timing of the operation decided to go ahead. Out of the defile between lake Tsatsa and Barmatsak, on a three-mile front, Trufanov's 126th and 302nd Rifle Divisions supported by the 55th and 158th Independent Tank Regiments of Volskii's corps attacked the 6th Rumanian Corps. Once the tanks got into the Rumanian positions, the Rumanians began to surrender, though five T-34s lay burning or blown up near Height 87. With 51st and 57th Armies on the attack, the guns from 57th Army were speedily hauled to new positions at Shumilov's 64th Army, and at 14.20 hours opened a second barrage in support of Shumilov's attack. To the south of the front the situation had developed favourably enough by noon for the armoured corps to be introduced.

At 14.00 hours, Tanaschishin's 13th Tank Corps was moved forward through 169th and 422nd Divisions, driving in two columns and striking out for Nariman in a northerly drive. The tanks could move fast enough, but the motorized infantry lacked lorries and had to march; while this march slowed Tanaschishin's corps down, it was abruptly halted when it ran into Leyser's 29th Motorized Division which had been ordered to race eastwards on a collision course with Tanaschishin. Leyser's artillery battalions ranged on both Soviet tanks and on infantry being rushed up by train. Volskii had meanwhile been slow to start with 4th Mechanized; although the order to move off from the start-lines was given at 11.20 hours, only at 13.00 hours were the first brigades moving, while the rear was jammed with lorries bringing in wounded or moving up fuel and ammunition. Only a third of the infantry in the motorized rifle groups had lorries (the Front command had earlier commandeered 150 lorries to shift supplies and these never found their way back to 4th Mechanized). Once out in the wind-swept, snowy steppe, brigade commanders lost their sense of direction; 60th Mechanized Brigade on the right wandered off the road, the two left flank brigades, 59th and 36th, careered into enemy minefields. All the brigades hugged one road (instead of the three routes planned) and churned it up into a morass. South-east of Tunguta, at Plodovitoe, Volskii's regiments literally ploughed into the 18th Rumanian Infantry Division as the main body of the corps drew up into this litter of smashed guns and lorries. The night drew on: 4th Mechanized had not reached its first objective, Verkhne-Tsaritsynsk, but Popov ordered Volskii to press on, to take the railway stations at Tunguta and at Abganerovo. Volskii, as he submitted in his report, wondered whether to go on: the icy, unknown steppe lay ahead, and God knew what threats in the depth of the enemy rear. The day's fighting had cost Volskii fifty tanks, and Leyser's 29th Motorized was hanging over his flank. During the night, Volskii's brigades continued moving though cautiously enough and by dawn were at Abganerovo station; Volskii was now concerned about his left flank. Much greater was Fourth Panzer's concern for the whole of its eastern flank, for its northern and southern wings had been ripped apart from Tundu-tovo (57th Army) to Abganerovo, a gaping hole more than twenty miles wide.

Fourth Panzer's HQ at Verkhne-Tsaritsynsk was directly threatened and hastily shifted to the hamlet of Buzinovka where the staff worked frantically as Volskii's tanks poked along westwards.

As Fourth Panzer headquarters pulled itself out of immediate danger, at another headquarters, that of Paulus at Golubinskaya on the Don, it was also on 21 November that the enormous danger of the present situation suddenly impressed itself. By the evening of the twentieth, the Soviet South-Western and Stalingrad Fronts were both fully on the attack, striking south-east and north-west, both more than twenty miles into the German rear; the deep flank of the Sixth Army and the eastern flank of Fourth Panzer had huge gashes torn in them through which more Soviet formations now began moving. Rodin's 26th Tank Corps seized Perelazovskii off the march and drove on for the Don during the twentieth; 4th Tank Corps, however, ran into some stiff fighting. The rifle formations of 5th Tank and 21st Army had outflanked several Rumanian divisions from east and west and were preparing to destroy them in encirclement near Raspopinskaya; left flank units of 21st Army and Batov's 65th were driving south-east and biting into the left flank of Paulus's Sixth Army. On 21 November, South-Western and Don Fronts struck on to the south-west and south-east. Vasilevskii had arrived at Chistyakov's headquarters where Colonel-General Voronov had been assisting 21st Army's operations; Vasilevskii was able to send Stalin an optimistic report. By the evening (21 November) 4th, 26th and 3rd Guards Cavalry Corps (South-Western Front) had driven sixty miles into the German rear and were racing for Kalach; Yeremenko's mobile formations on the Stalingrad Front had penetrated thirty miles and were on a line running north of Nariman to Zety.

At Zety, Volskii halted 4th Mechanized Corps; the corps concentrated here and took on fuel and ammunition. That evening deputy commander Popov spoke to Volskii by telephone and ordered him to get moving. To Yeremenko, Volskii's halt was 'inexplicable'. Popov and Yeremenko both had reports of stiffening German resistance and news that South-Western Front tank drives were being slowed down. Popov ordered Volskii to send him two-hourly reports on the situation of his units, which must be concentrated against possible German counter-attack. The early hours of 22 November began badly for Major-General Volskii; Yeremenko issued a 'grave warning' to him and at dawn an aircraft dropped a special signal from the Front commander 'categorically demanding' a resumption of the advance. As for his left flank, 126th Rifle Division would be advanced to Abganerovo to secure it; 4th Cavalry Corps and 302nd Rifle Division (51st Army) were moving north-east of Tunguta-Abganerovo to stiffen this flank still further. The blow from Fourth Panzer which Volskii quite properly feared nevertheless never came and 4th Mechanized moved off for Sovietskii; Volskii had issued immediate orders – twenty-five miles over a single road, with every prospect of having to fight for it with his right flank still open, since 29th Motorized had held off 13th Tank Corps from contact. Volskii picked Colonel Rodionov's 36th Mechanized Brigade to take Sovietskii; in the lead he proposed to throw Major Doroshkevich's 26th Tank Regiment with orders 'to ram ahead' to be at Sovietskii by noon on 22 November. In Doroshkevich he confided 'not only the honour of the brigade but of the whole corps'. With 26th's tanks in the lead, Rodionov set off; at 12.00 hours on 22 November, as Soviet motorized infantry tore into the town and Doroshkevich's tanks carried more infantry clinging to their sides, Sovietskii was cleared of German troops. After Yeremenko had presented his evening operations report, Stalin telephoned to seek confirmation of the capture of Sovietskii and the railway station at Krivomuzginskaya. Greatly pleased, Stalin added: 'Tomorrow [23 November] you can link up with the South-Western Front whose troops have taken Kalach.'

During the night of 22 November, 26th Tank Corps had begun to force a crossing of the Don; to seize the only useful crossing at Berezovskii Rodin formed a special squad of motorized riflemen and five tanks of 157th Tank Brigade and put it under Colonel Filippov's command. Soviet tanks had already appeared on the Don on the morning of 21 November, reaching the heights at Golubinskaya, where Paulus had his headquarters; Paulus had already flown to his winter headquarters at Nizhne-Chirskaya on the lower Don (and from there was flown back into Stalingrad, to a command post at Gumrak, a journey he made on Hitler's personal order). At Kalach lay the temporary bridge, fit for heavy traffic, which German engineers had built to replace those the Russians had blown up earlier in the summer; on the high ground near the Don was a German training school for anti-tank warfare, where captured Soviet tanks were used as targets. At 03.00 hours Filippov's detachment, lights switched on and travelling fast, approached the bridge and was taken for the usual traffic of captured tanks; three hours later Filippov's reconnaissance tanks crossed the bridge and signalled the column to follow. The bridge guard was shot down and later in the morning a German attempt to blow up the bridge failed. In the evening 19th Tank Brigade of 26th Tank Corps crossed to the eastern bank of the Don and concentrated in the woods to the north-east of Kalach; 4th Tank Corps was also moving down on Kalach and Sovietskii.

On the morning of 23 November, Volskii's reconnaissance units (36th Mechanized Brigade) reported that Kalach was still in enemy hands; in Plato-novka, between Sovietskii and Kalach, German tanks had been seen. Sporadic fighting flared in Sovietskii as German units put in counter-attacks but at 15.30 hours a column of tanks was reported to the north-west. Rodionov of 36th Mechanized decided to send out an armoured car carrying a flag. From the advancing tanks came one green rocket – Soviet tanks, those of 45th Tank Brigade, 4th Tank Corps. Part of Colonel Zhidkov's 45th Brigade had wheeled on Kalach to the north-east and linked up with 26th Tank Corps; the remainder had struck out for Sovietskii. When the brigades of South-Western and Stalingrad Fronts linked up at 14.00 hours, both brigade commanders, in the traditional Russian style, kissed three times. Two tank corps, 4th and 26th, and one mechanized corps, the 4th, had linked up in the area of Sovietskii-Marinovka; 13th Tank was not far behind. On both sides of the Don, east and west, a torrent of disorderly men, fleeing singly or bunched into columns fled to the bridge over the Don at Nizhne-Chirskaya or headed in the same precipitate flight for the temporary bridge at Akimovskii (in 384th Infantry Division area) where a cursing, heaving mob of disorganized units and panic-stricken rear service personnel clawed their way hurling the weak and wounded aside to the eastern bank towards Stalingrad and momentarily out of the clutches of the Soviet tanks which struck from the west.

On the basis of data supplied by the Don and Stalingrad Front staffs, Colonel-General Vasilevskii (and the Soviet General Staff) reckoned that as a result of the past 100 hours of offensive operations the Red Army had encircled between 85,000 and 90,000 enemy troops. The trap had been sprung, however, on more than three times that number of men, spread across an area running thirty-five miles from east to west and a little more than twenty miles from north to south – transformed by Hitler at the stroke of a pen into *Festung Stalingrad*; inside this 'fortress', from which the German commanders thought first of breaking out, were not less than five *Generalkommandos* (four infantry, one Panzer corps), fourteen German infantry divisions, with three motorized and three Panzer divisions, the elements of two Rumanian divisions (1st Cavalry and 20th Infantry), a Croat infantry regiment, specialist groups (engineers, artillery, signals, supply), a whole gamut of ancillary and auxiliary units ranging from police to men of the *Todt Organisation*: well over a quarter of a million men, 100 tanks, almost 2,000 guns and 10,000 trucks.

On the evening of 23 November, Vasilevskii reported from South-Western Front HQ to Stalin, who agreed that the most urgent task was to strengthen the outer encirclement and destroy German forces trapped in the ring; Yeremenko and Rokossovskii both supported an immediate attack on the encircled enemy and Vasilevskii had already issued verbal orders. During the night of 24 November, Vasilevskii prepared a formal directive to the Front commanders: on the South-Western Front Chistyakov's 21st Army would strike from the west eastwards, reinforced by the 26th and 4th Tank Corps, on the Don Front 66th Army would now attack from the north with 65th and 24th Armies, and on Yeremenko's Stalingrad Front 62nd, 64th and 57th Armies would bite into the encirclement area from the east and the south. All these attacks would aim for Gumrak, thus chopping up the German formations into small groups. On the outer encirclement, 1st Guards and 5th Tank Armies (South-Western Front) would build up a firm front on the eastern bank of the Krivaya and Chir rivers, and the line would continue along the railway to cover the Oblivskaya-Surovikino-Rychkovskii sector, to hold off German attacks from the west and south-west: to the south, 4th Cavalry Corps and rifle divisions of 51st Army would hold an outer line running from Gromoslavka to Umantsevo. These orders were effective from the morning of 24 November to be carried out without any regrouping or movement of reserves.

While Vasilevskii talked to Stalin on the night of 23–4 November and drafted the directives for the Front commands, the fate of the German Sixth Army pinned by the Soviet encirclement was being decided in a flurry of night messages between the Chief of the General Staff General Zeitzler and General von Sodenstern, Chief of Staff Army Group B (with its headquarters at Starobelsk); the Sixth Army had already agreed details of a break-out operation with Army Group B and now von Sodenstern learned that Hitler, after hours of argument, had finally come to accept a break-out and the abandonment of Stalingrad as the only means of warding off catastrophe. But on the morning of 24 November, almost at the hour when the Sixth Army was to receive its order to begin the break-out, Hitler radioed direct to von Paulus that the Sixth Army was to stand fast: the Führer would see that it was supplied and in due course relieved. At the heart of Hitler's 'personal assurance' to the Sixth Army on supplies lay Göring's 'personal assurance' to Hitler that the Luftwaffe could supply the encircled garrisons with 500 tons daily; as for the relief, neither OKW, OKH nor the Sixth Army in Gumrak had much notion how or where the relieving force would be assembled. That same morning, having issued orders for the 'chopping up' of the Stalingrad garrisons, Vasilevskii, Voronov and Novikov (Soviet Air Force Commander) gathered at the airfield near Serafim-ovich to fly north to Golikov's HQ on the Voronezh Front; the object of this mission was to discuss the new operation – 'Saturn' – to be mounted by the left wing of the Voronezh Front and the South-Western Front, aimed at Millerovo-Rostov. In the foul November weather, the transport plane had failed to turn up but Vasilevskii, conscious of Stalin's urging, decided to press ahead; Novikov brought in seven PO-2 bombers from 734th Night Bomber Regiment (262nd Aviation Division) to fly the *Stavka* officers northwards and briefed the crews himself. Once airborne, the bombers soon lost touch in the dense, unbroken cloud, flying singly in hazardous conditions and all but one crash-landed; Vasilevskii's plane came down at a collective farm near Kalach (Voronezh), and the Chief of the Soviet General Staff finally waylaid an army truck which took him to the nearest signals centre. In Moscow there was serious misgiving about the fate of the *Stavka* officers; Vasilevskii himself feared most for General Ruchkin's plane, since Ruchkin was carrying the secret operational papers (in fact, Ruchkin's was the only plane to land more or less on target at Buturlinovka, where Golikov's staff was waiting). The PO-2 pilots had no idea whom they were carrying. The *Stavka·* officers travelled without badges or rank and under assumed names: for these operations Vasilevskii was 'Mikhailov'. On 25 November, all the *Stavka* team, men and documents alike, finally assembled at the command post of Kharitonov's 6th Army, where the outlines of 'Saturn' were discussed.

The Soviet outer encirclement ran for some 200 miles, of which only 150 were covered by Soviet troops; for the moment, the distance between the 'inner' and 'outer' fronts was less than 10 miles on critical sectors, and varied along its length from 20–40 miles. West and south-west of Stalingrad, the open steppe was littered with the wreckage of broken divisions and units, whose survivors were bent on making for the refuge of Stalingrad itself. Overhead flew the first of the German transport planes escorted by fighters, making their way into the 'ring' where German troops now manned old Soviet fortifications or blasted positions out of the frozen earth. Chuikov's 62nd Army lay pressed into its 800-yard deep positions split into separate bridgeheads on the western bank of the Volga, though a Soviet relief force from the Don Front smashed its way to Gorokhov's beleaguered brigade in the northern tip of the city. The Volga had not yet frozen over and drifting ice in the river made supply by small boat impossibly dangerous even for the hardiest Volga watermen. Only in mid December did the ice crunch together into a solid mass; for many days 62nd Army lived precariously off air-dropped supplies with only sporadic loads delivered by boat when a channel was cleared through the ice. Some of Lyudnikov's wounded, as yet inevitably untended due to lack of surgical aid and supplies, were taken off in one such foray and a reinforcement of 200 men landed, all under heavy German fire.

Meanwhile five Soviet armies hemmed in Paulus's Sixth Army together with units of Fourth Panzer. The encirclement line ran from Kuroposnoe-Rakotino-Sovietskii (Stalingrad Front) on to Illarionovskii (north-east of Kalach)-Bolshenabatovskii (South-Western Front) thence to Golubaya-Panshino-south of Samofalovka-Yezovka (Don Front) – a very formidable captive with its twenty divisions, more than triple the '80,000–90,000 men to be reduced off the march' upon which the Soviet command then reckoned. In little more than a week it became unpalatably plain that the triumphant Red Army had caught a tiger by the tail.

Sources and References

This compilation is designed to furnish only main references and citations of primary source material, without extensive elaboration or additional commentary, save where the nature of the source itself requires it. Such a qualification applies particularly to *Soviet printed sources* where the several editions of monographs, memoirs and Party histories can result in substantial emendation, whether of the material itself or of the operational narrative so presented. Thus the same title may appear (and re-appear) but this can represent a work very heavily transformed; or again, it may be a question of seeking a few key alterations. One additional refinement with respect to Soviet military memoirs is that pre-publication extracts from them may have appeared in Soviet military journals and these extracts may not wholly correspond with the printed book. The all-important memoirs of Marshal Vasilevskii are a case in point: the printed volume – *Delo vsei zhizni* (Politizdat 1974) – took a pre-publication form of being presented in *Novyi Mir* (1973) as the serialization of several chapters, but both the printed volume and the *Novyi Mir* version are bereft of the major documents (*Stavka* directives, operational orders, exchanges with Stalin and so on) contained in the versions published in periodicals such as *Voenno-istoricheskii Zhurnal* and *Istoriya SSSR*. For that reason I have referred to the 'Vasilevskii materials' rather than to a single printed source. There may be a whiff of pedantry about all this, but the search for exactitude in Soviet sources requires no small amount of cross-checking and collation.

While exactitude over Soviet materials is one obvious requirement, the other which cannot be ignored is the compatibility (and the comparability) of Soviet and German sources. For this reason, wherever possible Soviet and German sources have been juxtaposed, which has meant calling to a large degree upon the captured German military documents (cited throughout as GMD: German military documents). I have relied on the GMD to establish operational narratives and timetables from the German side, though here I defer to Col. Albert Seaton and others in their analysis of German operational matters. Rather, my own concern amid the maze of captured German documents has been to extract from them a 'sub-archive' of captured Soviet materials or commentary on Soviet operational performance or military organization, prisoner-of-war interrogation and so into logistics, military equipment and all manner of personal papers (including captured letters in field post offices).

All this amounts to a form of double book-keeping, citing first the GMD provenance and then the Soviet document or item, thus giving Soviet materials the strange cast of having a German identification.

One German collection, of course, proved to be indispensable and that was the holdings of *Fremde Heere Ost* (FHO), the intelligence organization run first by Col. Kinzel and then by Gen. Gehlen, whose fame needs no advertisement, in spite of the sensationalism attached to his name. In all, there are some one hundred and fifty files which form a major item of intelligence on the Soviet Union, the Soviet military and Soviet intentions. The FHO files present a fascinating profile, with the decisive point coming after the late spring of 1942 when *Generalmajor* Gehlen assumed command of FHO after the none too precise bumbling of Col. Kinzel, who seemed to rely excessively on Balts, Russian *émigrés* and former Cossack officers. And to fill out this picture I turned also to the *Wehrmacht Propaganda-Abteilung* and to a wide range of German files, not the least illuminating of which proved to be those of the *General der Eisenbahntruppen* – railway troops do not promise much interesting material at first sight, but these files proved to be very extensive. None of this makes for light reading. There are, for example, the grimly repulsive studies from *Luftgau II* in 1941 on psychological studies of five captured Soviet Air Force officers. This is but the prelude to documents at once horrifying and pathetic which catalogue the dismemberment of the *Uhtermensch*, the Slav sub-human. Perhaps the most chilling aspect of military organization is not the ferocity of battle but the bureaucratism of these seemingly endless statistics. Here is all the zoology of war on the Eastern Front.

Finally, it remains to explain the context of 'personal holdings'. It is the inevitable lot of any historian working on the Soviet-German war to be the recipient of diverse private papers, diaries, single documents and personal accounts, many of which undoubtedly have their counterpart in the central archives even as they form part of cherished private holdings privately chronicling a grim and gruelling war. I must confess to having been surprised, not to say startled in the Soviet Union on seeing the extent and variety of these *lichnye arkhivy* – personal archives – held by men of varying rank, from the lowliest to the very senior. For all the plethora of official records and papers, there is no substitute for having the late Marshal Koniev – spectacles perched on nose – read from his own personal notebook, detailing operational orders, his own personal instructions to select commanders and his tally of Soviet casualties. And while on the subject of casualties, Marshal Koniev made it plain that, though such figures did exist, he was not prepared on his own authority to allow certain figures to be released for publication while a number of commanders were still alive. As for such figures as were published, I was assured by expert and thoroughly professional Soviet military historians that these were reliable, which is to say that they were the product of intensive and painstaking research. The comment upon them or the implications of the figures were presumably a different matter. It was all the more useful, therefore, to have the opportunity to discuss these findings with Soviet military historians, on the basis of their work with formal and informal sources.

Such material classified under 'personal holdings' ranges from small, even occasional items to massive compilations running to several hundred pages (such as the anonymous but authoritative report on the Vlasov movement compiled either by Vlasov's own German interrogator or by a senior German officer close to Vlasov and his movement).

It is impossible to dismiss items such as these as mere miscellanea, disparate though they may be: the discussion of their nature and scope may be disproportionate here, compared with the massive collective memories of the central archives, the commodious war diaries and the mountains of statistics, but they add a dimension all their own – marked maps, photographs, wartime propaganda leaflets, handbooks and bedraggled diaries.

I have eschewed the method of individual footnoting in favour of assembling a wide range of material relevant to each chapter, while attempting to identify the location of documents, reports and other original materials. It seemed apposite to identify not merely the source of specific items but also the broad range of materials from which the chapters had actually been fashioned.

INTRODUCTION: ON WAR GAMES, SOVIET AND GERMAN

References and documentary material

Conquest, Robert, *The Great Terror: Stalin's Purge of the Thirties* (London: Macmillan 1968), bk II.

Erickson, John, *The Soviet High Command 1918–1941* (London: Macmillan 1962), ch. 13 and ch. 14.

Leach, Barry A., *German Strategy Against Russia 1939–1941* (Oxford: Clarendon Press 1973), ch. 3 and ch. 4.

Seaton, Albert, *The Russo-German War 1941–45* (London: Arthur Barker 1971), pp. 50–60.

German

Halder, Col.-Gen. Franz, *Kriegstagebuch* (Stuttgart: Kohlhammer 1963) (ed. Hans-Adolf Jacobsen), 2, entries November and December 1940 (cited as Halder/KTB).

Kriegstagebuch des Oberkommando der Wehrmacht 1940–1945 (Frankfurt-am-Main: Bernard & Graefe Verlag 1965) (compiler: Percy E. Schramm), 1, dated entries, November and December 1940 (cited as KTB/OKW).

Warlimont, Gen. Walter, *Inside Hitler's Headquarters 1939–1945* (London: Weidenfeld & Nicolson 1962), pt III, pp. 135–9.

Auswärtiges Amt (Kandelaki Mission): Serial 1907H/Frame 429293ff.

Soviet

Anfilov, V.A., *Nachalo Velikoi Otechestvennoi voiny* (Moscow: Voenizdat 1962).

Anfilov, V.A., *Bessmertnyi podvig* (Moscow: Nauka 1971), ch. 5 and ch. 6.

Dashichev, Col. V.I., '*Sovershenno Sekretno! Tol'ko dlya komandovaniya*' (Moscow: Nauka 1967), ch. 3.

Proektor, Col. D.M., *Agresiya i katastrofa* (Moscow: Nauka 1968), pp. 144–9.

Stuchenko, A.T., *Zavidnaya nasha sudba* (Moscow: Voenizdat 1964), pp. 63–4.

Tukhachevskii, M.N., *Izbrannye proizvedeniya* (Moscow: Voenizdat 1964), II.

Zhilin, Lt.-Gen. P., *They Sealed Their Own Doom* (Moscow: Progress Pub. 1970) (Soviet translation), under 'Secrets of the German General Staff', pp. 102–22.

Bychevskii, Lt.-Gen. B., 'L.A. Govorov', *VIZ*, 9 (1963), pp. 66–9.

Gorbatov, Gen. A.V., 'Gody i voiny', *Novyi Mir*, 4 (1964), pp. 115–38 (see also *Gody i voiny* (Moscow: Voenizdat 1965), pp. 122–51).

Isserson, G., 'Zapiski sovremennika o M.N. Tukhachevskom', *VIZ*, 4 (1963), pp. 72–3.

I THE SOVIET MILITARY ESTABLISHMENT:
REFORMS AND REPAIRS (1940–1)

Berman, Harold J. and Kerner, Miroslav, *Soviet Military Law and Administration* (Cambridge, Mass.: Harvard UP 1955), pp. 45–9 (on Soviet disciplinary codes), p. 50 (on the obligatory salute and officers' Courts of Honour), pp. 72–85 (on 'military crimes'), pp. 55–7 (table of comparison of penalties in Disciplinary Codes for 1925, 1940 and 1946).

Erickson, John, 'Radio-location and the air defence problem: The design and development of Soviet radar 1934–40', *Science Studies*, 2 (1972), pp. 241–63.

Kilmarx, Robert A., *A History of Soviet Air Power* (London: Faber 1962), pp. 155–61 (on Soviet aircraft and aviation industry 1939–41).

Mackintosh, Malcolm, *Juggernaut: A History of the Soviet Armed Forces* (London: Secker & Warburg 1967), pp. 111–36 (on Soviet-Finnish war).

Milsom, John, *Russian Tanks 1900–1970* (London: Arms and Armour Press 1970), pp. 51–8 (Soviet theory and equipment, 1930s); pp. 102–5 (on 1940/1 tank programme).

Nowarra, Heinz J. and Duval, G.R., *Russian Civil and Military Aircraft 1884–1969* (London: Fountain Press 1971), pp. 117–21 (under 'Military Progress to 1941').

Seaton, Albert, *Russo-German War*, pp. 43–9 (German intelligence on the Red Army) and pp. 70–97 (on Soviet and German equipment, military organization).

Taylor, John W.R., *Combat Aircraft of the World* (London: Ebury Press and Michael Joseph 1969), pp. 571–84, 590–602, 624–5 (on Soviet aircraft 1930–41).

Documents: German-Soviet relations

Sontag, James Raymond and Beddie, James Stuart (ed.), *Nazi-Soviet Relations 1939–41* (henceforward cited as NSR) (Washington: Dept of State 1948), p. 167 (Schulenburg to German Foreign Office, 13 July 1940); p. 206 (Ribb ntrop to German Embassy, Moscow, 9 October 1950); pp. 207–16 (Ribbentrop letter and Stalin's reply); pp. 217–58 (Memoranda of Conversations, Draft Agreement); pp. 258–9 (Soviet reply/conditions of acceptance 26 November 1940); also pp. 260–4.

German Military Documents (GMD)

FHO Folder, 'Inhaltsverzeichnis zu den Akten D, Bewaffnung u. Ausrüstung (Fortsetzung): Microcopy T-78/Roll 488, frame nos. 6474151-351.

'Grosses Orientierungsheft Russland . . . Gliederung, Dislokation und Stärke der Roten Armee. Stand: 1 Februar 1939.' T-77/R794 5523750-827.

'Grosses Orientierungsheft Russland: Stand 1 März 1939.' T-78/R496 6483772-905.

Chef Ost/Russland (no other title): deployment table, with conclusion, dated 24 July 1940. Typescript (personal holding).

Soviet command appointments (1940): Gen. Köstring (Military Attaché, Moscow), report dated 24 October 1940. T-78/R464 6443404-443.

FHO: Photographs and brief description/Red Army manoeuvres/1940. T-78/R118 6043261-66 (text) and 6043339-69 (photographs).

Die Kriegswehrmacht der UdSSR. Stand 1 Januar 1941. *Auswärtiges Amt*. Serial 1891H.

FHO: *Taschenbuch Russisches Heer* (Januar 1941). T-78/R494.

Folder on Soviet weapons and military organization (no title). T-78/R502 6490073-263.

Finnish report on Soviet capabilities: FHO filed, dated 19 February 1941. T-78/R118 6043456-462.

FHO: 'Die russische Panzerwaffe', dated 20 April 1941 and 17 May 1941. T-78/R118 6043268-77 (description and diagram Soviet 'motor-mechanized corps').

Captured Soviet document

Order No. 001/26.6.40 (captured Soviet document): Bessarabia. T-78/R118 6043478-83.

Soviet official/Party histories

Istoriya Velikoi Otechestvennoi voiny Sovetskogo Soyuza 1941-1945 (Moscow: Voenizdat 1960), I. This is a six-volume history, compiled by collective authorship; cited as IVOVSS, with relevant volume number and publication date; IVOVSS, I, pp. 258-78 (on Soviet-Finnish war); p. 277 (on revised instructions for combat training, 1940); p. 450 (on Soviet Navy operational manual); p. 411-3 (re-organization of Soviet aircraft industry); pp. 436-51 (on Soviet military doctrine).

Istoriya Vtoroi Mirovoi voiny 1939-1945 (Moscow: Voenizdat 1973), ('Zarozhdenie voiny.'), pp. 256-72 (re-organization and re-equipment of Soviet armed forces). This is the first volume of a projected twelve-volume history of the war, issued under the general editorship of Marshal Grechko. This is presumably designed to supersede the previous six-volume history of the 'Great Patriotic War'.

50 Let Vooruzhennykh Sil SSSR (Moscow: Voenizdat 1968), pp. 234-5 (on command appointments, 1941).

Soviet military doctrine

Voprosy strategii i operativnogo isskustva v Sovetskikh voennykh trudakh (1917-1940 gg.) (Moscow: Voenizdat 1965), *passim*. This is a work of fundamental importance, covering pre-war Soviet doctrine.

Voprosy taktiki v Sovetskikh voennykh trudakh (1917-1940 gg.) (Moscow: Voenizdat 1970), *passim*. This is a basic work covering major arms and services.

Anfilov, V.A., *Bessmertnyi podvig*, pp. 124-9 (on turbulence in Soviet officer corps, shortcomings in combat training); pp. 128-37 (contemporary reports on combat training – Kurdyumov on Soviet infantry, Fedorenko on armoured forces, need to wait until October 1941 until new recruits trained); pp. 137-48 (December 1940 meeting and war games); pp. 149-60 (Soviet military doctrine and the image of a future war).

Kazakov, Gen. M.I., *Nad kartoi bylykh srazhenii* (Moscow: Voenizdat 1965), pp. 57-8 (on December meeting).

Kuz'min, N.F., *Na strazhe mirnogo truda (1921-1940 gg.)* (Moscow: Voenizdat 1959), pp. 184-5 (on 1940 military reforms programme).

Lobanov, Lt.-Gen. M.M., *Iz proshlogo radiol okatsii* Kratkii ocherk (Moscow: Voenizdat 1969), pp. 37-56 on *Burya* series, pp. 115-25 on *Redut* equipment (with photographs).

Meretskov, Marshal K.A., *Na sluzhbe narodu* (Moscow: Pol. Lit. 1968), pp. 175-90 (on Soviet-Finnish war); p. 196 (on Belorussian MD exercises, 1940); pp. 196-8 (on December 1940 meeting and report on combat training).

Petrov, Yu.P., *Partiinoe stroitel'stvo v Sovetskoi Armii i Flote (1918-1961 gg.)* (Moscow: Voenizdat 1964), pp. 325-34 (on deficiencies of command and political officers,

1940–1); p. 303 (on institution of military commissar and collective military Soviet control, May 1937); pp. 335–6 (on failures in Party-political work and deleterious effects of 1940 Disciplinary Code); pp. 326–7 (on retention in 1940 of 'dual command' and commissar control in corps raised in recently occupied Baltic states).

Matveyev, Navy Captain P. and Selyanichev, Col. A., 'Krasnoznamennyi Baltiskii Flot v nachale Velikoi Otechestvennoi voiny', *VIZ*, 4 (1962), pp. 36–7 February operational instructions, Fleet readiness (May–June).

Nosovskii, *loc. cit.*, 10 (1970), pp. 125–6.

Vannikov, Col.-Gen. B.L., 'Iz zapisok Narkoma vooruzheniya', *VIZ*, 2 (1962), pp. 78–86.

Vannikov, 'Oboronnaya promyshlennost SSSR nakanune voiny', *Voprosy Istorii*, 1 (1969), pp. 122–31.

Rotmistrov, Marshal P.A., *Vremya i Tanki* (Moscow: Voenizdat 1972), pp. 83–9 on reorganization of Soviet armoured forces, 1940–1.

Sandalov, Col.-Gen. L.M., *Perezhitoe* (Moscow: Voenizdat 1966), pp. 45–6; enlarged version, *Na Moskovskom napravlenii* (Moscow: Nauka 1970), pp. 40–1.

Shavrov, V.B., *Istoriya konstruktsii samoletov v SSSR do 1938 goda* (Moscow: Mashinostroenie 1969), pp. 470–521.

Sovetskie Voenno-vozdushnye sily v Velikoi Otechestvennoi voine 1941–1945 gg. (Moscow: Voenizdat 1968), pp. 10–25 (on Soviet aircraft 1940–1).

Shmelev, I.I. (ed.), *Soldaty nevidimykh srazhenii* (Moscow: Voenizdat 1968); see M. Kolesnikov on Yan Berzin (pp. 81–93) and R. Sorge (pp. 131–49).

Starikov, Col. I.T., *Miny zhdut svoego chasa* (Moscow: Voenizdat 1964), pp. 30–4 and 38–40 (on early preparations for partisan war and subsequent ban).

Timoshenko, Marshal S.K., *Shkola boevoi ucheby* (1940). Reprinted in *Voprosy taktiki*, pp. 123–8.

Voronov, Marshal N.N., *Na sluzhbe voennoi* (Moscow: Voenizdat 1963), p. 166 (on Kulik and artillery developments).

Yeremenko, Marshal A.I., *V nachale voiny* (Moscow: Nauka 1964), pp. 33–4 (on new Soviet mech. corps); pp. 36–40 (on December 1940 meeting; see also Ivanov, *VIZ*, 6 [1965]).

Zhukov, Marshal G.K., *Vospominaniya i razmyshleniya* (Moscow: Novosti 1969 and revised edn 1970); see 1970 edn, pp. 182–3 (on preparations for December 1940 military conference).

Articles/periodical literature

Chernetskii, Col. V., 'O nekotorykh voprosakh operativnogo iskusstva VVS nakanune Velikoi Otechestvennoi voiny', *VIZ*, 8 (1973), pp. 88–93 (pre-1941 Air Force doctrine).

Dorofeyev, Col. M., 'O nekotorykh prichinakh neudachnykh deistvii mekhanizirovannykh korpusov v nachal 'nom periode Velikoi Otechestvennoi voiny', *VIZ*, 3 (1964), pp. 32–6 (on pre-war organization).

Ivanov, Gen. V., 'O knige "V nachale voiny" ', *VIZ*, 6 (1965), pp. 72–4 (on Marshal A.I. Yeremenko's account of December 1940 meeting).

Kuznetsov, Admiral N., 'Vsya zhizn' Flotu', *VIZ*, 3 (1963), pp. 68–76 (on Galler and pre-war Soviet naval policy).

Nosovskii, Maj.-Gen. N.E., 'Nadezhnyi arsenal vooruzheniya', *Voprosy Istorii*, 10 (1970), pp. 116–27 and 11, pp. 116–29 (on Soviet artillery development 1938–40).

Ryzhakov, Col. A., 'K voprosu o stroitel'stve bronetankovykh voisk Krasnoi Armii v 30-e gody', *VIZ*, 8 (1968), pp. 105–11.

Stakhov, Lt.-Gen./Technical Troops N., 'Na voenno-avtomobil'nykh dorogakh', *VIZ*, 3 (1964), pp. 64–6 (on military motor transport).

Zakharov, Marshal M.V., 'Stranitsy istorii Sovetskikh Vooruzhennykh sil nakanune Velikoi Otechestvennoi voiny 1939–1941 gg.', *Voprosy Istorii*, 5 (1970), pp. 28–38 (on prewar planning and re-equipment plans).

2 'DON'T PANIC. THE "BOSS" KNOWS ALL ABOUT IT'

Bialer, Seweryn (ed.), *Stalin and his Generals*, Soviet Military Memoirs of World War II (New York: Pegasus 1969). This is an invaluable compilation of Soviet memoir material: see here part 6. 'Russia Prepares for War' (Vannikov, Voronov, Starinov, Yakovlev and Kuznetsov extracts), pp. 152–75; also from Starinov pp. 221–7 on western frontier alarms.

Churchill, Sir Winston, *The Second World War* (London: Cassell 1950), 3, 'The Grand Alliance', pp. 319–22 (warning to Stalin).

Van Crefeld, M., 'The German attack on the USSR: the destruction of a legend', *European Studies Review*, 2: 1 (January 1972), pp. 69–86. (Argues against the view that the German invasion of Greece and Jugoslavia delayed *Barbarossa*.)

Deakin, F.W. and Storry, G.R., *The Case of Richard Sorge* (London: Chatto & Windus 1966), *passim*.

Foote, Alexander, *Handbook for Spies* (London: Museum Press 1964), 'Prelude to War', pp. 76–7 (on 'Lucy''s information on impending German attack, June 1941).

Grigorenko, Maj.-Gen. P., *Der Sowjetische Zusammenbruch 1941* (Frankfurt/Main: Possev-Verlag 1969), *passim*.

Gwyer, J.M.A., *Grand Strategy*, 3 (pt 1) (London: HMSO 1964), p. 80 (Churchill's message to Stalin 3 April 1941; role of Sir Stafford Cripps), pp. 83–4 (Eden–Maiskii exchanges, June, also JIC assessments), p. 84 (Eden repeats warnings to Maiskii).

Halder/KTB, 2, *op. cit.*, p. 272, 5 February 1941; p. 313, 15 March 1941; p. 316, 16 March 1941; p. 319, 17 March 1941; p. 353, 7 April 1941.

Johnson, Chalmers, *An Instance of Treason: Ozaki Hotsumi and the Sorge Spy Ring* (Stanford UP 1964), *passim*.

Kilmarx, *op. cit.*, pp. 154–5 and 157–8 (on aviation industry re-organization and factory efficiency).

Leach, Barry A., *op. cit.*, pp. 159–75, 'Changes in the Operational Plan' (German planning and assessments of Soviet forces 1941).

Mader, Julius, *et al.*, *Dr. Sorge Funkt aus Tokyo* (Berlin: Deut. Militärverlag 1966), *passim*.

Philippi, Alfred and Heim, Ferdinand, *Der Feldzug gegen Sowjetrussland 1941–1945* (Stuttgart: Kohlhammer 1962), pt 1, 'Die Zeit der Vorbereitung', pp. 48–53.

Perrault, Gilles, *The Red Orchestra* (London: Arthur Barker 1968) (Trans. from *L'Orchestre Rouge* 1967), pt 1, pp. 44–6 (Leopold Trepper's intelligence of German attack).

Salisbury, Harrison E., *The Siege of Leningrad* (London: Secker & Warburg 1969), pp. 67–81, 'What Stalin Believed'.

Werth, Alexander, *Russia at War 1941–1945* (London: Barrie & Rockliff 1964), pp. 122–123 (version of Stalin's 5 May address to Soviet officers).

Whaley, Barton, *Codeword Barbarossa* (Cambridge, Mass: MIT Press 1973), pp. 37–40 (on role of Sam E. Woods); also discussion of discrepancies in American evidence on 'warnings', notes 48–57, pp. 277–8; pp. 190–8, 'The Soviet Intelligence System and its Perceptions'; pp. 39–40 (Sumner Welles–Umanskii exchange on intelligence of possible German attack – also detailed commentary. Notes 51–7, pp. 277–8); pp. 98–103 and notes 14–21, pp. 288–9 (on 'Lucy' – Rudolf Rossler – and intelligence communications to Moscow).

Woodward, Sir Llewellyn, *British Foreign Policy in the Second World War* (London: HMSO 1970), I, pp. 601–7 (on Churchill's message to Stalin; role of Sir Stafford Cripps); pp. 617–22 (further British estimates of German intentions, Eden–Maiskii conversations, British warning to Finland).

Documentary collections

Documents on Polish–Soviet Relations 1939–1945 (London: Heinemann/General Sikorski Historical Institute 1961), I, doc. 84, pp. 102–3 (Churchill–Sikorski conversation and memorandum, 23 May 1941); doc. 85, pp. 103–8 (Cripps–Sikorski conversation, 18 June, on possibility of German attack).

NSR, pp. 267–8 (Secret protocol on Lithuanian territory, 10 January 1941); pp. 318–9 ('Memorandum on the Present Status of Soviet Deliveries . . .', 5 April 1941); p. 326 (Tippelskirch on Soviet–Japanese pact, 16 April 1941); pp. 330–2 (Hitler–Schulenburg conversation, 28 April 1941); pp. 335–9 (Schulenburg on Stalin becoming Chairman of *Sovnarkom*, 7 May and 12 May 1941); pp. 345–6 (Schulenburg: Text of *Tass* statement, June 14).

German Military Documents (GMD)

OKH/Gen StdH·(operations):
  Chefsachen. Aufmarschanweisung 'Barbarossa': T-78/R335 6291235-819.
    Angaben über die Roten Armee 15 Januar 1941 (299–307).
    Lage der Roten Armee 15 Februar 1941 (Map) (316–17).
    Besondere Anordnungen für die Luftwaffe (336–42).
    Änderungen für *Barbarossa* 7 April 1941 (357–62).
    Kräfteübersicht (German OB) 12 Mai 1941 (389–419).
    Schematische Übersicht über die Verteilung der Heerestruppen zu Beginn *Barbarossa* (546–7).
    Total German strength (Ostheer), 20 Juni 1941 (688).
    Zeiten Barbarossa: 10 Juni 1941 (689).
Deutsche Heeresmission in Rumänien: Operationsbefehle mit Karten 3 April 1941–19 Mai 1941. 'Verteidigung der Moldan . . .' (Hubertus). T-501/R281; 000553-000587.
Allgemeine Weisungen für D.V.K.: D.V.K. 37. Nr 965/41 geh. v. 31 Mai 1941: 'Über Eigenarten der russischen Kriegsführung'. T-501/R28; 001042-45.
FHO Lagebericht Nr 1 (15 März 1941), Nr 2 (20 März 1941), Nr 5 (13 Juni 1941) (personal holding).
Feindbeurteilung (Stand 20 Mai 1941): estimated Soviet strength, deployment, operational intentions (personal holding).

Abschnittsstab Ostpreussen: Sabotage-Ansatz (*Abwehr* special group): 9 Juni 1941 (personal holding).

FHO/*Abschnittsstab Ostpreussen:* correspondence and orders relating to preparations for aerial, reconnaissance, sabotage, frontier security, *Regt. Z. b.v.800* (1940–1), T-78/ R482, 6466472–640.

Die Wehrwirtschaft der Ud.SSR. Teil II Stand: März 1941 (OKW printing). T-78/R479 6462171–292.

FHO *No. 945/41 geh.* Malenkov speech, 1st Party Congress and Soviet economic plan. T-78/R118 6043416–432.

FHO/*Gen. d. Pi. u. Fest:* Die Landesbefestigungen der Ud.SSR. Photographs, maps, description Soviet fortifications (personal holding).

German military map/Soviet order of battle/*Far East*/1939–40 (personal holding).

FHO Nr. 33/41 (15 March) and FHO Nr. 35/41 (20 March): Lageberichte (personal holding).

OKH publication: Denkschrift über die russische Landesbefestigung (Berlin 1942) (personal holding).

AOK 4, Ia (Operations) Beilage z. KTB Nr. 7: Grenzsicherung Bd. II. Measures against possible Soviet surprise attacks: 'Fall Achtung Bertha', March–3 June 1941, T-312/R136, 7672704–796.

AOK 4, Anlage zum KTB Nr. 7 u. 8. Aufmarschanweisung *Barbarossa* vom 14 Juni 1941. T-312/R162, 7704781–800.

AOK 4, Anlage zum KTB Nr. 7 u. 8. Vorbereitungen zum Angriff v. 1 Mai–21 Juni 1941. T-312/R162, 7704496–504.

VII Armeekorps: Korpsbefehl für den Angriff am B-Tage. 16 Juni 1941, T-312/R162, 7704511–19.

XXXXIII Armeekorps: Korpsbefehl ... (with maps) 15 Juni 1941, T-312/R162, 7704521–45.

AOK 17, Tätigkeitsberichte Ic (intelligence) vom Januar–December 12 1941. T-312/R674, 8308306–368.

AOK 17, Koluft: Stabsbildmeldung Nr. 1. Folder aerial photographs and interpretation, 20 April 1941; also folder dated 10 June 1941: see also maps 'Durch Luftbild gedecktes Gelände'. T-312/R683, 8318726–749.

Japanese materials/studies

Coox, Alvin D., 'Japanese Foreknowledge of the Soviet German War, 1941', *Soviet Studies*, 23 (April 1972), pp. 554–72. An important contribution based on Japanese sources.

Hayashi, Col. Saburo, *Study of Stategical and Tactical Peculiarities of Far Eastern Russia and Soviet Far East Forces, Japanese Special Studies on Manchuria.* 8, Dept of the Army (US), pp. 63–4 (Soviet troop strength, FE and westward movement).

Captured Soviet documents

Order Nr *008130*/Minsk, 26 March 1941: captured Soviet document (personal holding).

Baltic Special MD: orders on vigilance, security of documents, 'mobilizational readiness' (8th and 11th Armies), June 1941 (original documents), T-77/R1028, 6500549–579.

Soviet materials

Official documents and official/Party histories

Gosudarstvennys plan razvitiya Narodnogo Khozyaistva SSSR na 1941 g. SNK SSSR i Tsk

VKP (b): no. 127 (17 January 1941). (American Council of Learned Societies Reprint: Russian Series no. 30).

IVOVSS, 1 *op. cit.*, pp. 405–24 (on Soviet economy 1940–1), pp. 475–6 (Soviet tank production to May–June 1941); pp. 457–8 (re-organization Soviet Air Force, aviation logistics); pp. 477–8 (work on fortifications); pp. 471–5 (Soviet deployment frontier district armies).

IVOVSS, 6 (1966), p. 135 (Stalin's disregard of intelligence warnings, 1941).

Anfilov, V.A., *Bessmertnyi podvig*, pp. 146–7 (on January 1941 war-games); pp. 161–7 (fortification programme 1940–1); pp. 169–70 (details of *Plan Oborony gosudarstvennoi granitsy 1941*); pp. 164–6 (rate of construction on frontier fortifications); pp. 170–4 (general frontier defence plan and deployments).

Azarov, Vice-Admiral I.I., *Osazhdennaya Odessa* (Moscow: Voenizdat 1966), 2nd edn, pp. 8–10 (*Tass* statement 14 June, explanation to Black Sea Fleet personnel).

Bagramyan, Marshal I.Kh., *Tak nachinalas' voina* (Moscow: Voenizdat 1971), pp. 56–9 (Kiev MD order of battle and deployment, May 1941); pp. 68–70 (attempts to increase combat readiness, Kiev MD, mid-June).

Front bez linii fronta (Moscow: Novosti 1966), pp. 5–55 (on Sorge and intelligence data of German attack).

Golovko, Admiral A.G., *Vmeste S. Flotom* (Moscow: Voenizdat 1960), p. 7 (appointment to Northern Fleet).

Kalinim, Col. A., 'Podvig razvedchika', *KZ* (7 November 1964) (on Sorge's signals/intelligence data on impending German attack).

Karasev, A.V., *Leningradtsy v gody blokady 1941–1943* (Moscow: Akad. Nank 1959, pp. 26–7 (deficiencies in plans for defence of NW theatre and Leningrad).

Kazakov, *Nad kartoi*, pp. 62–7 (January 1941 war-games and debate).

Kolesnikov, M.S., *Takim byl Rikhard Zorge* (Moscow: Voenizdat 1965), *passim*.

Kuznetsov, Admiral N.G., *Nakanune* (Moscow: Voenizdat 1966), pp. 316–17 (discussions on security of Libaw and Tallinn); pp. 318–19 (signal from Naval Attaché Vorontsov).

Lobachev, Maj.-Gen. A.A., *Trudnymi dorogami* (Moscow: Voenizdat 1960), pp. 110–13 (on Gen. Lukin, Far Eastern armies); pp. 123–5 (movement of 16th Army to European Russia).

Na strazhe neba stolitsy (Moscow: Voenizdat 1968), pp. 61–7 (on 1st Air Defence Corps and 24th Fighter Aircraft Div.).

Nekrich, A.M., *1941 22 iyunya* (Moscow: Nauka 1965), pp. 123–4 (on Stalin's reception of Churchill's warning); pp. 124–5 (interview with Golikov on Soviet intelligence of German intentions).

Panteleyev, Vice-Admiral Yu.A., 'Na dal'nykh podstupakh k Leningradu', in *Voyuet Baltika* (Leningrad: Lenizdat 1964), pp. 49–50 (German reconnaissance observed, spring 1941); pp. 50–4 (Baltic Fleet movements and dispositions to mid-June 1941).

Peresypkin, Marshal I.T., *Svyazisty v gody Velikoi Otechestvennoi* (Moscow: Svyaz 1972), pp. 10–17 (on Signals Command 1939–41).

Petrov, *op. cit.*, pp. 334–5 (Zaporozhels on condition of fortified districts); pp. 335–6 (Zhdanov on shortcomings in propaganda, February 1941).

Pogranichyne voiska SSSR 1939–1941, Sbornik dokumentov i materialov, (Moscow: Nauka 1970) (frontier troops reports); pp. 216–24 (N and NW 1941); pp. 363–404 (Western frontier – Germany); pp. 478–94 (Rumania). Main Administration of Frontier Troops subordinated to NKVD since 1934.

Sandalov, L.M., *Na Moskovskom napravlenii*, pp. 60–1 (Soviet 4th Army intelligence of German OB), pp. 62–5 (Korobkov–Sandalov–Oborin exchange).

Starikov, *op. cit.*, p. 189 (quoting '*Bez paniki! Spokoistvie! Khozyain vsë znaet*').

Voennya svyazisty v dni voiny i mira (Moscow: Voenizdat 1968), p. 123, table 4 (Soviet radio equipment 1941); p. 124 (on Gapich).

Voronov, *op. cit.*, pp. 172–3 (on air defence measures, May-June 1941).

Yeremenko, *op. cit.*, pp. 45–9 (January 1941 war-games).

Zhukov, G.K., *Vospominaniya*, pp. 186–7 (exchanges over Soviet armoured forces); p. 214 (General Staff Ammunition production plan, March 1941); pp. 210–11 (discussion of Stalin's view of possible aims of a German attack); p. 211 (MP-41, 'Mobilization Plan-41'); pp. 211–14 (frontier fortification plans, General Staff directive, April 14 1941, instructions to Western and Kiev MDs); p. 218 (Stalin's permission for limited reinforcement under 'mobile training camps', spring 1941); p. 225 (Stalin's dismissal of Churchill's warning); pp. 226–7 (Stalin's 5 May address to Soviet officers); pp. 229–30 (Golikov's intelligence report to Stalin, 20 March 1941); p. 230 (Vorontsov intelligence report from Berlin); p. 231 (summary of Soviet strength in frontier MDs for Stalin, 1 June 1941).

Periodical literature

Dorofeyev, M., *VIZ*, 3 (1964), pp. 34–5 (deficiencies in Soviet mech. corps).

Matveyev, Navy Captain P. and Selyanichev, Col. A., 'Krasnoznamennyi Baltiskii Flot v nachale Velikoi Otechestvennoi voiny', *VIZ*, 4 (1962), pp. 36–7 (February operational instructions, Fleet readiness May-June).

Nosovskii, *loc. cit.*, 1970, no. 10, pp. 125–6.

Vannikov, Col. Gen. B.L., 'Iz zapisok Narkoma vooruzheniya', *VIZ*, 2 (1962), pp. 78–86.

Vannikov, 'Oboronnaya promyshlennost' SSSR nakanune voiny', *Voprosy Istorii*, 1 (1969), pp. 122–31.

3 THE SUNDAY BLOW: 22 JUNE 1941

Bialer, *op. cit.*, 'The Disaster' (22 June), pp. 179–264; extracts from M.I. Kazakov, N.G Kuznetsov, Tyulenev, Voronov, Starinov, Boldin, Bagramyan, Rybalko, Azarov.

Erickson, *op. cit.*, *Soviet High Command*, Pt. 6, pp. 587–97 (German attack, 22 June; Soviet order of battle table, pp. 589–92).

Erickson, 'The Soviet Response to Surprise Attack: Three Directives, 22 June 1941'; *Soviet Studies*, 23 (April 1972), pp. 519–53.

Gwyer, J.M.A., *Grand Strategy* III/I, p. 89 (Churchill broadcast, 22 June); p. 94 (Prime Minister's instruction to Chiefs of Staff to examine offensive action, Pas de Calais, 23 June).

Leach, *op. cit.*, pp. 192–5 (implementation of operational plan not fully prepared; military preference for direct thrust on Moscow after Dvina–Dnieper battles).

Salisbury, *op. cit.*, pp. 98–109 (German attack, 22 June, operations NW Front; Tilsit/Riga highway).

Seaton, *op. cit.*, pp. 98–115 (beginning of war, operations in north/west/Baltic MD); pp. 116–32 (early German success AG Centre; confusion in Soviet W MD).

Turney, Albert, *Disaster at Moscow: von Bock's campaigns 1941-1942* (London: Cassell

1970), pp. 41–2 (Commissar Order); pp. 48–53 (Army Group Centre operations 22–25 June).

Woodward, *op. cit.*, II, pp. 1–6 (Eden–Maiskii conversation, question of British aid to Soviet Union, appointment British Military Mission).

Documentary collections/War diaries

NSR, pp. 347–9 (Ribbentrop to Schulenburg, 21 June; text, German declaration); pp. 349–53 (Hitler to Mussolini, 21 June); pp. 355–6 (Schulenburg–Molotov exchange, 21.30, 21 June).

Halder/KTB, 2, *op. cit.*, pp. 459–61 (21 June entry, 'Gesamtstärken' German/Soviet).

KTB/OKW, *op. cit.*, p. 417 (21 June, 'OKW gibt in der Nacht 20/21.6 das Stichwort 'Dortmund' durch . . .); pp. 417–9 (entries KTB 22–5 June 1941).

German memoirs/monographs

Carell, Paul, *Hitler's War on Russia* (London: Harrap 1964), pt 1, 'Taken by Surprise', pp. 11–44 (opening of German operations). This is a translation of *Unternehmen Barbarossa: Der Marsch nach Russland* (Frankfurt/Main 1963).

Hossbach, Gen. F., *Infanterie im Ostfeldzug 1941/42* (Osterode/Harz: 1951), pp. 35–43 ('Am Bug'); pp. 44–61 ('Vom Bug zum Dnjepr').

Von Manstein, Field-Marshal Erich, *Lost Victories* (Chicago: Regnery 1958), pp. 179–80 (on *Kommissarbefehl*); pp. 180–3 (operations of 56 Panzer Corps; drive to Dvinsk).

Philippi and Heim, *op. cit.*, pp. 54–5 ('Einleitende Operationen . . .').

Warlimont, Walter, *Inside Hitler's Headquarters*, *op. cit.*, pp. 168–70 (on 'Commissar Order' [*Kommissarbefehl*].

GMD

These are not intended to cover German operations as such (see under German memoir/monograph sources), but have been adduced in relation to Soviet deployments and commitments.

Soldaten der Ostfront! (Adolf Hitler. Führer und Oberster Befehlshaber der Wehrmacht), 21/22 Juni 1941 (leaflet).

I

FHO: 1036/41. 21 Juni 41 *Lagebericht/OST* (typewritten) (personal holding).

Note des Auswärtigen Amtes an die Sowjet-Regierung. Berlin, den 21 Juni 1941. *Memorandum* (personal holding).

II

Soviet formations: Rifle Division number, first appearance at front. *Truppen—Übersicht und Kriegsgliederungen Rote Armee.* Stand August 1944. FHO (IIc) Nr. 7000/44 geh. Section A lists all Soviet rifle divs, with their 'first appearance' at the front (e.g. 100th Rifle/1st Guards, July 1941 facing Army Group Centre: see under Soviet Materials, I.F. Sazonov, *Pervaya gvardeiskaya*). I have used this compilation to check Soviet order of battle. T-78/R459 643754ff (under formation number).

III

Operationskalendar: sheets covering June 1941 (to 1943), divided into 'Deutsche Operationen'/Russische Operationen. Summary of operations in chronological order. T-78. R477 6460261-291.

IV
Select items, German divisional records
3 Panzer Division T-315/R137 (Frame sequence 000001-).
Feindnachrichtenblatt 16-29 Juni 1941. 1-13 (Soviet OB map, Kobryn-Brest-frame b).
Feindberühung (Enemy formations encountered): period 22-7 Juni (report dated 1 Juli 1941). 72.
Primernaya skhema svyazi komandnogo punkta strelkovo polka/batalona. (Two official Soviet diagrams: signal nets, regiment/battalion.) 75-6.
4 Panzer Division T-315/R206 (Frame sequence 000001-).
OKH: Die russische Panzerwaffe (17 Mai 1941, received 4 Panzer Div. 4 Juni 1941). 77-81.
Richtlinien für das Verhalten der Truppe in Russland 87-8.
Feindnachrichtenblatt Nr 1, 15 Juni 1941 (also map, Soviet OB). 94-7.
Artl-Nachrichtenblatt Nr 1-3, 13-17 Juni 1941 (panoramic views Soviet frontier positions). 112-38.
Soviet 22 Tank Division: translation, Order No. 1 on Signals Procedures (7 June 1941). 198-9.

Soviet materials
Official/Party histories IVOVSS, 2 (1961), p. 16 (Soviet air losses, 22 June; 1,200 aircraft to noon, 22 June, 800 of these on the ground); pp. 17-18 (Directive 07.15 hrs, 22 June); pp. 18-20 (German success, 22-4 June); pp. 20-1 (Soviet declaration of war, noon, 22 June).
p. 29 (General Staff *svodka* – operational digest – 22.00 hrs., 22 June); pp. 30-31 (*Directive No. 3*, all Fronts, evening 22 June and unsuccessful Soviet counter attacks, 23 June); p. 31 (serious position of 4 Army).
General military-operational chronology
SSSR v Velikoi Otechestvennoi voine 1941-1945, 2nd edn, Kratkaya Khronika (Moscow); Voenizdat 1970, pp. 11-19 (22-5 June; cited as *Khronika 1941-1945*. Daily dated items of main actions, command appointments, press announcements and releases. Moscow; Voenizdat 1964, 1st edn. All references here are to 2nd edn.

Bibliographies
Velikaya Otechestvennaya voina Sovetskogo Soyuza 1941-1945, Rekomendatel'nyi ukazatel' literatury (Moscow: Kniga 1965), *passim*.
Velikii podvig Rekomendatel'nyi ukazatel' literatury o Velikoi Otechestvennoi voine Sovetskogo Soyuza (Moscow: Kniga 1970), *passim*.

Memoir/monograph material

Anfilov, V.A., *Bessmertyni podvig*, pp. 181-2 (four fronts – N, NW, W and SW – envisaged; Odessa MD to form S Front); p. 182 (Politburo decision 21 June to form S Front; High Command Reserve on line of Dnieper under Marshal Budenny); p. 182 (Gen. Zhukov to direct SW and S Fronts, Gen. Meretskov – N Front); p. 185 (21 June Stalin's permission for Timoshenko and Zhukov to issue directive to take up positions and come to full combat readiness); p. 185 (Admiral Kuznetsov's operational orders to fleet commands 21 June); pp. 185-6 (Maj.-Gen. M.V. Zakharov's personal order, Odessa MD); p. 186 (Directive No. 1, transmitted 00.30 hrs, 22 June – text); pp. 190-1 (strength and deployment, Soviet armies, frontier MDs – 2,900,000 men, 1,540 modern aircraft, 34,695 guns and mortars, 1,800 heavy and medium tanks); p. 191 (German superiority); p. 197 (Signal 'GROZA' to w front HQ; 'red packets' and cover plan); p. 199 (Soviet air losses, 22 June); pp. 202–37 (frontier fighting, all fronts – detailed operational narrative, also Soviet declaration of war, noon 22 June; pp. 243–52 (operational narrative, Baltic/NW Front, 22–4 June); pp. 261–73 (operational narrative, w Front, 22–23/24 June); pp. 278–97 (sw Front, frontier battles, operational narrative). The latter sections (operational narrative) are based almost exclusively on Soviet archive materials.

Azarov, *op. cit.*, pp. 10–11 (Black Sea Fleet 21 June); pp. 12–19 (air attack on Sevastopol 22 June).

Bagramyan, *op. cit.*, pp. 83–4 (activation of 'Front administration', sw Front 19/20 June); pp. 87–95 (initial operations, 22 June); pp. 95–122 (Frontier detachments engaged, Zhukov's arrival, preparations for counter-attack).

Batitskii, Marshal P.F. (ed.), *Voiska protivovozdushnoi oborony strany*, Istoricheskii ocherk (Moscow: Voenizdat 1968), p. 48 (Voronov assumes official command PVO, 14 June); pp. 67–78 (initial operations, air defence order of battle, 22–7/8 June).

Berezhkov, V., *S. diplomaticheskoi missiei v Berlin 1940–1941* (Moscow: Novosti 1966), pp. 93–106 (22 June 1941, Soviet Embassy, Berlin).

Boldin, Col.-Gen. I.V., *Stranitsy zhizni* (Moscow: Voenizdat 1961), pp. 81–7 (22–3 June, w Front); pp. 87–95 (6 Mech. Corps counter attack); pp. 98–9 (Kulik visit).

Bor'ba Latyshskogo naroda v gody Velikoi Otechestvennoi voiny 1941–1945 (Riga: Zinatne 1970), pp. 94–9 ('Nachalo voennykh deistvii v Pribaltike').

Bor'ba za Sovetskuyu Pribaltiku v Velikoi Otechestvennoi voine (Riga: Liesma 1966), 1, pp. 54–81 (operations NW Front, Baltic area). This is a very detailed study, based on Soviet archives and of singular value for establishing the operational narrative.

Bug v ogne (Minski: Belarus 1965), pp. 15–21 (L.M. Sandalov on Brest defence); pp. 27–33 (A.P. Kuznetsov on Frontier Troops' action).

Bychevskii, Lt.-Gen. B.V., *Gorod-front* (Moscow: Voenizdat 1963), pp. 3–5 (15–21 June); pp. 7–12 (22–7 June, Leningrad and NW Front).

Edlinskii, S.F., *Baltiiskii transportnyi flot v Velikoi Otechestvennoi voine 1941–1945 gg* (Moscow: Morskoi Transport 1957), pp. 10–11 (sinking of *Gaisma*, 22 June).

Fedorov, A.G., *Aviatsiya . . . pod Moskvoi, op. cit.*, pp. 22–6 (Soviet aviation strength/ deployment, 22 June; losses, 22 June, 1,200 aircraft: 738 on w Front, 528 on the ground, 210 in the air).

Fedyuninskii, I.I., *Podnyatye po trevoge* (Moscow: Voenizdat 1964), 2nd edn., pp. 12–15 (20–1 June); pp. 15–18 (22 June); pp. 19–25 (24–8 June). Operations of 15 *Rifle Corps*.

Geroicheskaya oborona, Sbornik vospominanii ob oborone Brestskoi kreposti v iyune-iyule 1941g (Minsk: Gosizdat 1961), pp. 17–21 (Brest garrison, strength, deployment); individual accounts, *passim*; see also 2nd edn, 1963.

Geroicheskaya oborona (Minsk: Belarus 1971), 4th edn, *passim*; pp. 409–12, Combat report 28 Rifle Corps, beginning 22 June 1941; defence of Brest fortress.

Golovko, *op. cit.*, pp. 14–20 (diary entries 14–21 June); pp. 22–6 (22 June 1941); pp. 27–31 (23–7 June), narrative of operational orders and dispositions, N Fleet.

Grigorovich, D.F., *Kiev-Gorod geroi* (Moscow: Voenizdat 1962) pp. 10–13 (Kiev MD order of battle); pp. 13–15 (initial operations, Kiev mobilizes).

Kabanov, Maj.-Gen. S.I., 'Khanko', in *Voyuet Baltika, op. cit.*, pp. 141–4 (Hango, 19–22 June 1941).

Kolyshkin, Rear-Admiral I., *Submarines in Arctic Waters* (Moscow: Progress Pub. 1966), pp. 5–12 (submarine operations, N Fleet, 22 June 1941). See *V glubinakh Polyarnykh morei* (Moscow: 1964).

Kozlov, G.K., *V lesakh Karelii* (Moscow: Voenizdat 1963), pp. 19–28 (Frolov, 14th Army and 7th Army).

Kumanev, G.A., *Sovetskie zheleznodorozhniki v gody Velikoi Otechestvennoi voiny (1941–1945)* (Moscow: Akad. Nauk 1963), pp. 21–2 (halting exports to Germany, air attack on Soviet railways).

Kuznetsov, *Nakanune*, pp. 323–4 (alert orders, Baltic and Black Sea Fleets, 19–20 June); pp. 324–40 (22 June 1941).

Maiskii, I.M., *Vospominaniya Sovetskogo posla* Voina 1941–3 (Moscow: Nauka 1965), pp. 139–43 (22 June, Churchill's speech, Eden–Maiskii conversation).

Meretskov, *op. cit.*, pp. 209–14 (events 22 June); p. 214 (appointment to *Stavka* 23 June).

Moskalenko, Marshal K.S., *Na Yugo-zapadnom napravlenii* Vospominaniya komandarma (Moscow: Nauka 1969), pp. 25–36 (5th Army, SW Front operations 22–3/4 June).

Na strazhe neba stolitsy, pp. 79–80 (Moscow air defence – PVO – alert, 22 June).

Novikov, Chief Marshal/Aviation A.A., *V nebe Leningrada* (Moscow: Nauka 1970), pp. 43–53 (air operations, Leningrad and NW theatre, 23–5 June).

Ocherki istorii Leningrada (Leningrad: Nauka 1967), 5, pp. 13–28 ('V pervye dni voiny').

Peresypkin, Marshal I., *A v boyu eshche vazhnei* (Moscow: Sov. Rossiya 1970), pp. 53–8 (inspection trip 19 June, return to Moscow after war begun).

Piskunov, D.I., 'Na reke Prut', *Dorogoi bor'by slavy* (Moscow: Politizdat 1961), pp. 40–9 (95 Rifle Div. Sector, Soviet–Rumanian border).

Panteleyev, Admiral Yu.A., *Morskoi Front* (Moscow: Voenizdat 1965), pp. 31–44 (operational orders and commitment, Baltic Fleet, 21–5 June – 'Readiness State No. 1').

Platonov, Lt.-Gen., N.G., *Vtoraya mirovaya voina 1939–1945gg.* (Moscow: Voenizdat 1958), pp. 183–6 (NW Front operations); pp. 186–8 (W Front); pp. 191–3 (SW/S Front operations), for period 22–3/4 June. In spite of its age, this is still a valuable, informative and objective military analysis.

Platonov, Lt.-Gen. S.P., *Bitva za Leningrad 1941–1944* (Moscow: Voenizdat 1964), pp. 22–4 (22 June, opening phase of operations, crisis on NW Front).

Platonov, V.V., *Oni pervymi prinyali udar* (Moscow: Voenizdat 1963)', (on 9th Vladimir-Volynsk Frontier Tps Detachment); pp. 102–7 ('Na Sokal'skom napravlenii') (Capt. Bershadskii); pp. 19–20 (deserter Liskow, Maj. Bychkovskii reports to Gen. Khomenko).

Pogranichnye voiska . . . 1939–1941 (composite reports by Maslennikov, 19–21 June 1941).

Reportazh s frontov voiny 1941–1945 (Moscow: Politizdat 1970), pp. 11–17 (press writing/articles, 22–8 June 1941).

Rokossovskii, Marshal K.K., *Soldatskii dolg* (Moscow: Voenizdat 1972), 2nd edn, p. 9 (night 21/2 June); pp. 10–20 (opening engagements, tank battles after 23 June).

Sandalov, *Na Moskovskom napravlenii*, pp. 72–3 (night 21/2 June); pp. 74–109 (operational narrative, 4th Army, counter-attacks and loss of control).

Sazonov, I.F., *Pervaya Gvardeiskaya* Boevoi put' 1-i Gvardeiskoi Ordena Lenina strelkovoi divizii (Moscow: Voenizdat 1961), pp. 60–79 (operations, 22–3/4 June) 1st Guards was originally 100th O. Lenin Rifle Div., starting life as 45th Red Banner Rifle Div. in November 1923. This senior Red Army formation also became the first to be designated 'Guards' (*Gvardeiskii*).

Sevastyanov, Maj.-Gen. P.V., *Neman-Volga-Dunai* (Moscow: Voenizdat 1961), p. 5 (interrogation Lithuanian deserter, 21–2 June, 5th Rifle Div.).

Shtemenko, Gen. S.M., *General'nyi shtab v gody voiny* (Moscow: Voenizdat 1968), pp. 28–30 (operations Administration/GS, first days of war, movement of troops to w and sw).

Sovetskie Voenno-vozdushnye sily, pp. 29–36 (air operations 22–5 June).

Starikov, *op. cit.*, pp. 191–7 (22 June 1941, w Front 4th Army area); p. 197 (*svodka*, 23 June, on repulse of German attack).

Tyulenev, Gen. I.V., *Cherez tri voiny* (Moscow: Voenizdat 1960), pp. 140–1 (evening 21 June); pp. 141–2 (22 June, departure for Southern Front).

Vainer, B.A., *Severnyi Flot v Velikoi Otechestvennoi voine* (Moscow: Voenizdat 1964), pp. 21–4 (20–1/4 June, N Fleet readiness and initial operations).

Voronov, *na veonnoi sluzhbe*, pp. 175–8 (21–2 June). Memoir though it is, Marshal Voronov's book is one of the most valuable items for a study of the 1941–5 war. While in Moscow on one occasion I was discussing the behaviour of Stalin in these early days of the war with a prominent Soviet historian. In the course of this discussion the same historian pointed to a senior officer, identified him as Marshal Voronov and said, 'The Marshal was actually there – ask *him*', which seemed to be a logical course of action. What the Marshal said bears out his memoir, though with the addition of some personal details and a stark impression of the fearful strain and desperate work load.

Yeremenko, *op. cit.*, p. 56 (recalled to Moscow, 19 June); pp. 61–2 (German attack, 22 June).

Zakharov, Marshal M.V. (ed.), *Oborona Leningrada 1941–1944* (Leningrad: Nauka 1968), pp. 38–48 (Col.-Gen. M.M. Popov, GOC/Leningrad MD, operations, 22–6 June 1941); pp. 224–30 (N.G. Kuznetsov, Baltic Fleet commander, initial operations, 22–7 June).

Zhukov, *vospominaniya*, pp. 232–4.

Periodical literature

Arushnyan, B., 'Boevye deistviya 12-i armii v nachal'nyi period voiny', *VIZ*, 6 (1966), pp. 60–5.

Azarov, Vice-Admiral I.I., 'Nachalo voiny v Sevastopole', *VIZ*, 6 (1962), pp. 77–83 (alert Black Sea Fleet, air attack night 22 June).

Gapich, N., 'Nekotorye mysli po voprosam upravleniya i svyazi', *VIZ*, 7 (1965), pp. 46–55 (Red Army signals).

'Gitlerovskie diversanty', *VIZ*, 3 (1963), pp. 85–91 ('Regiment 800'/Brandenburg).

Grechko, A., '25 let tomu nazad', *VIZ*, 6 (1966), pp. 3–15 (Marshall Grechko – Soviet Defence Minister – completed his General Staff Academy examinations on 'operating art' on 19 June, posted to General Staff, served under Zhukov as officer in charge of compiling the operations map; sent to front as cavalry division commander, 3 July).

Korkodinov, P., 'Fakty i mysli o nachal'nom periode Velikoi Otechestvennoi voiny', *VIZ*, 10 (1965), pp. 26–34. This is a rare and significant analysis of the 'initial period' of the war.

Peresypkin, I., 'Svyaz General'nogo shtaba', *VIZ*, 4 (1971), pp. 19–25 (organization, equipment, High Command signals, first period of war).

Rybalko, N., 'V pervyi den' voiny na Chernom more', *VIZ*, 6 (1963), pp. 63–6 (Black Sea Fleet command, 21–2 June).

Smirnov, S., 'Taran nad Brestom', *VIZ*, 1 (1963), pp. 21–34 (air fighting over Brest, aerial ramming).

Tributs, Admiral V.F., 'Krasnoznamennyi Baltiiskii Flot letom 1941 goda', *Voprosy Istorii*, 2 (1969), pp. 125–9 (initial operations, Baltic Fleet).

4 THE DISASTER ON THE FRONTIERS: JUNE–JULY 1941

Bekker, Cajus, *The Luftwaffe War Diaries* (London: Macdonald 1967), ch. 7, 'operation Barbarossa' (general survey of Luftwaffe operations on the Eastern Front, summer/early autumn 1941).

Brereton, J.M. and Norman, Maj. Michael, *RTR, Russian T34* (Windsor: Profile Publications 1972), 47 (T34/76).

Dreisziger, N.F., 'New Twist to an Old Riddle: The Bombing of Kassa (Košice) June 26, 1941', *Journal of Modern History*, 44:2 (June 1972), pp. 232–42. The author argues persuasively that this was not some German-Hungarian 'plot', but most possibly a Soviet raid carried out on the authority of regional commanders on Kassa regarded as a *Slovak* – not Hungarian – target. Slovakia was already at war with the Soviet Union, but Hungary had not yet entered the war and Moscow hoped essentially for Hungarian neutrality.

Goure, Leon, *The Siege of Leningrad* (Stanford: Stanford UP 1962), pt 2, 'The German Advance', pp. 13–19; 'Leningrad at War', pp. 20–81 (mobilization, morale, evacuation, Party control).

Gwyer, *op. cit.*, III, pp. 85–8; pp. 89–93, German operational successes.

Pethö, Tibor, 'Hungary in the Second World War', *Hungarian Quarterly*, I:1 (1960), pp. 193–200 (p. 200, document on Kassa bombing).

Sherwood, Robert E., *Roosevelt and Hopkins, An Intimate History* (New York: Grosset and Dunlap 1950), pp. 325–48 (mission to Moscow, 27 July, meeting with Stalin 31 July).

Woodward, *op. cit.*, II, pp. 1–19 (German attack, British response and initiatives, Churchill–Stalin exchanges).

War diary

Halder KTB (vol. 3): entries 22 June–23 July 1941 (dated entries), pp. 3–107.

GMD

FHO (II): Lagebericht OST Nr 22: 7 Juli 1941 (Soviet deployment, losses, order of battle facing Army Group South); (typewritten) (personal holding).

Feindnachrichtenblatt: Stand 10 Juli 1941 (progress of German forces, all fronts; break into 'Stalin Line', operational value of Soviet defences). T-315/R44, 000777-779.

Feindnachrichtenblatt: 27 and 28 Juli: Soviet deployment, all fronts; reinforcements from Asia (*sic*): Soviet deployment facing 4th Panzer Army (22 July 1941). T-315/R206, 000267-272.

Vortragsnotiz über die Besetzung und Sicherung des russischen Raumes und über den Umbau des Heeres nach Abschluss Barbarossa (maps of special importance), July–August 1941. T-78/R336, 6292343-434.

AOK 4: KTB Nr 8 (Teil II), 1 July–26 July 1941. T-312/R159, 7700200-476. Almost illegible but useful operational record.

AOK 4: Anlagen zum KTB Nr 8: 25–8 June 1941. 77001244-1546. KTB Nr 8: 28–30 June 1941. 77001549-1821.

AOK 4: Luftbilder zum KTB Nr 8 (aerial photographs: Soviet positions behind the Dnieper, July 1941). T-312/R162, 7704955-996.

AOK 17: *Nachrichtenblatt* Nr 9/41, 11 July 1941 (Soviet formations encountered and identified since 22 June 1941) (Ukraine) (personal holding).

AOK 18: 'Propaganda-Anweisung des Armeekommissars der 8. russ. Armee von 15.7.41', (8th Army; NW Front). T-77/R1028, 6500470-475.

1 *Gebirgs-Division*: 11 July 1941, Bialystok–Minsk battle: 323,898 Soviet prisoners, 3,332 tanks, 1,809 guns captured. T-315/R44, 000784.

Captured/translated Soviet materials and documents: GMD

Ast Auswertungsstelle Berlin (Aus Ost-Russland), Reports of NKVD 'Special Section' (Osobyi Otdel: OO) attached to 19th Army: dated entries for July 1941, behaviour of Soviet troops. T-77/R1028, 6501087-092.

Announcement for all troops – of court-martial of Gen. Pavlov, Klimovskikh, 27 July 1941 (translation/Soviet document). T-315/R44, 000906.

To *GOC 6th Army* and *12th Army* (translation): uselessness of frontal attacks, lack of initiative in attacking flanks and rear, signed Budenny, 26 July 1941. T-315/R44, 000908.

Interrogation of staff officer, 13th Army (Capt. Narkievich), 13 July 1941; details of 13th Army (also 61st Rifle Corps). T-315/R206, 000226-228.

Order/Political Administration: NW Front, 20 July 1941, no. 0116: Directive on purging Red Army units of all 'unreliable elements', under signature of Stalin and Mekhlis (translation). T-77/R1028, 6500547.

General Kirponos (C-in-C: SW Front): criticism of poor reconnaissance, unsecured flanks, 12th Army. T-315/R44, 000905.

Select tabulations: Soviet losses (GMD)

Losses among senior Soviet commanders
June–August 1941

	Date	Rank/Name	Formation
i		*Taken prisoner*	
	July	Maj.-Gen. Yegorov	4th Rifle Corps
		Maj.-Gen. Sskutnyi	21st Army Corps
		Maj.Gen. Makarov	Not known
		Lt.-Gen. Karbyshev	Not known
	August	Maj.-Gen. Muzychenko	GOC/6th Army
		Maj.-Gen. Sokolov	Chief/Rear Services: W Front
		Maj.-Gen. Fedorov	Artillery Cdr/6th Army
		Maj.-Gen. Proshchkin	Cdr/58th Div.

Date	Rank/Name	Formation
	Taken prisoner	
August	Maj.-Gen. Sybin	Cdr/37th Rifle Corps
	Maj.-Gen. Snegov	Cdr/8th Rifle Corps
	Maj.-Gen. Abramidze	Cdr/72nd Rifle Div.
	Maj.-Gen. Ponedelin	Not known
	Maj.-Gen. Kirilov	Cdr/13th Rifle Corps
	Maj.-Gen. Tonkonogov	Cdr/14th Rifle Div.
	Maj.-Gen. Ogartsov	Cdr/49th Rifle Corps
	Maj.-Gen. Kirpitshnikov	Cdr/43rd Div.
	Maj.-Gen. Potaturshchev	Cdr/4th Tank Div.

ii		*Killed in action*	
	June	Maj.-Gen. Neujanis	Not known
	July	Maj.-Gen. Sushchii	Cdr/124th Rifle Div.
		Maj.-Gen. Shurba	Cdr/14th Rifle Div.
		Maj.-Gen. V.F. Pavlov	Cdr/23rd Motorized Div.
	August	Lt.-Gen. Kachalov	GOC/28th Army
		Maj.-Gen. Karpezo	Cdr/15th Rifle Corps (*sic*)
		Maj.-Gen. Versin	Cdr/173rd Rifle Div.
		Maj.-Gen. Karmanov	Cdr/62nd Army Corps

iii		*Court-martialled*	
	July	Army Gen. D.G. Pavlov	C-in-C/W Front
		Maj.-Gen. Korobkov	GOC/4th Army
		Maj.-Gen. Kossobutskii	Cdr/45th Rifle Corps
		Maj.-Gen. Klimovskikh	Chief of Staff/W Front
		Maj.-Gen. Grigor'ev	Chief/signals: W Front
		Maj.-Gen. Selikhov	Not known
		Maj.-Gen. Galaktionov	Cdr/30th Rifle Div.
		Maj.-Gen. Sudakov	Not known
		Maj.-Gen. Lazarenko	Cdr/42nd Rifle Corps
		Maj.-Gen. Oborin	Cdr/14th Mech. Corps
		Maj.-Gen. Chernykh	Cdr/9th Aviation Div.

T-78/R464, 6443384-386.

Losses in Soviet Tank Divisions Tabulation, no title;
period June–November 1941; identification by divisional number

Division	Area	Encountered	Remarks
1	Pleskau	June 1941/AG North	disbanded, April 1942
2	Kovno	July 1941/AG Centre	in Minsk battle
3	Porkhov	July 1941/AG Centre	disbanded, November 1941
4	Bialystok	June 1941/AG Centre	in Bialystok battle
5	Olita	June 1941/AG Centre	destroyed at Olita
7	Volkovysk	June 1941/AG Centre	destroyed on the Desna, July 1941

T-78/R494, 6481674-686.

Diplomatic correspondence/documents

Correspondence between the Chairman of the Council of Ministers of the U.S.S.R. and the Presidents of the U.S.A. and the Prime Ministers of Great Britain during the Great Patriotic War of 1941–1945 (Moscow: FLPH 1957; London: Lawrence & Wishart 1958), p. 11 (Churchill to Stalin, 8 July 1941); p. 12 (Churchill to Stalin, 10 July); pp. 12–13 (Stalin to Churchill, 18 July); pp. 13–15 (Churchill to Stalin, 26 July); p. 16 (Churchill to Stalin, 28 July). Cited as *Correspondence*, 1 (British–Soviet); 2 (American–Soviet, beginning August 1941).

Soviet materials

Official/Party histories

Kommunisticheskaya partiya v period Velikoi Otechestvennoi voiny (Moscow: Gospolitizdat 1961) (documentary collection), pp. 83–91 (party and government decrees on war footing, GKO, economic mobilization).

Kommunisticheskaya partiya v Velikoi Otechestvennoi voine (1941–1945), Dokumenty i materialy (Moscow: Politizdat 1970), pp. 37–50 (Central Committee and *Sovnarkom* decrees and ordinances, June–July 1941).

Velikaya Otechestvennaya voina Sovetskogo Soyuza 1941–1945, Kratkaya istoriya (Moscow: Voenizdat 1970), 2nd edn. Cited as VOVSS; p. 62 (creation of *Stavka Glavnogo Komandovaniya*, superseding *Glavnyi Voennyi Soviet*; pp. 62–3(W Front situation/command); pp. 63–4 (German thrust on Minsk); pp. 65–6 (defeat in frontier battles recognized); pp. 66–7 (Germans force Berezina); pp. 69–70 (causes of Red Army weakness).

IVOVSS, 2 (1961), pp. 21–2 (creation of *Stavka Glavnogo Komandovaniya*, 23 June; transition to war economy and war footing, Baltic, Belorussia, Ukraine, Moldavia); pp. 34–5 (disorganization and heavy losses in first echelon of Red Army; failure in frontier battles); p. 35 (creation of 'reserve armies group' under Budenny, 25 June); pp. 35–6 (crisis on NW Front); pp. 36–8 (disaster on W Front, end June; Timoshenko sent as commander; movement of reserve armies); pp. 39–40 (German approach to W Dvina and Dnieper); pp. 40–1 (Soviet counter-attacks, 6–9 July); p. 41 (S Front operations); pp. 41–2 (SW Front operations to mid-July); pp. 43–6 (summary, naval operations, Baltic, Black Sea, N Fleets); pp. 65–71 (battle for Smolensk; narrative of Soviet operations); pp. 79–83 (German advance to approaches of Leningrad); pp. 98–101 (SW Front operations to end July; operational narrative).

Memoir/monograph material

Anfilov, *op. cit.*, p. 237 (creation of *Stavka Glavnogo Komandovaniya* during night of 22/3 June); p. 317 (26 June, Timoshenko orders reactivation of defences on old pre-1939 frontier); pp. 318–19 (revised instructions to Budenny's Reserve Front command, 27 June); p. 319 (mobilization decree – TSK and SNK – 29 June); p. 323 (GKO established, 30 June); p. 324 (first partisan detachments); pp. 263–4 (attempted Soviet counter-attack/Grodno); p. 273 (Shaposhnikov at W Front; requests permission to withdraw; danger of Germans encircling main Soviet forces); pp. 383–4 (Yeremenko appointed W Front commander, 30 June, followed by appointment of Timoshenko as Front c-in-c, 1 July); pp. 430–4 (Tyulenev, S Front commander; opening of operations); pp. 246–50 (failure of Kuznetsov's armoured counter-attack, 12th and 3rd Mech. Corps); pp. 251–2 (difficult situation of 11th Army); p. 254 (11th Army ordered to fall back, 25 June); p. 259 (failure of signals network, NW Front – only infrequent use of radio); p. 332 (11th Army fighting in encirclement, 28 June; F.I. Kuznetsov reports death or capture of 11th Army staff; four rifle divisions – 5, 33, 188, 128 – out of contact); p. 332 (deployment of 5th Airborne Corps); pp. 332–3 (Berzarin's 27th Army deployed, 21 Mech. Corps moved in); p. 341 (Soviet concentration, Pskov/Ostrov); p. 343 (directive, 29 June, to defend Velikaya line, cover approaches to Leningrad); p. 352 (Luga operational group under Pyadyshev); pp. 355–6 (German armour approaches river Luga); pp. 363–7 (German thrust on Minsk, Soviet withdrawal and regrouping); pp. 368–9 (Timoshenko uses aircraft to stem German advance); pp. 374–9 (dangerous plight of 4th Army); pp. 381–2 (concentration of reserve front formations); pp. 385–6 (German encirclement of 3rd and 10th Armies, W Front); pp. 391–6 (Soviet counter-blow, 6 July; Timoshenko signal – 6 July 1941 – that Red Army to hold line of W Dvina and Dnieper); p. 395 (9 July, Soviet attacks broken off; heavy losses due to air attack); pp. 278–87 (mech. corps counter-attack, SW Front, 23–8/9 June); pp. 291–5 (operations 5th and 6th Armies); pp. 430–4 (S Front operations from 24 June); pp. 435–40 (S Front operations to first week July); pp. 405–26 (battle for the 'Zhitomir corridor'; struggle to win time for defence of Kiev – OB/operational orders); pp. 427–8 (resistance on SW Front better organized than on NW and W Fronts). See also earlier version, *Nachalo Velikoi Otechest. voiny* (Moscow: Voenizdat 1962). This first edn runs to only mid-July and follows a straight geographical plan – NW, W and SW Fronts, pp. 61–200 (followed by a penetrating conclusion, pp. 200–20). With this more cogent narrative, this first version is superior in a number of respects and there is little, if any, intrusion of secondary material. The second version does comment more liberally on Soviet performance in the field, though the actual addition of new material is small. It is also necessary to add that the first edn – ending in mid-July – also appears to be a more apposite study of the 'surprise attack' period, for by then 'surprise' had worn off.

Bagramyan, *op. cit.*, pp. 127–9 (Soviet armoured counter-attack June 24); pp. 129–38 (development of Vladimir Volynskii–Radzekhub–Dubno tank battle); pp. 138–9 (change in Air Force command – Astakhov replaces Ptukhin); pp. 138–41 (operational summary for 26 June; orders from *Stavka* not to fall back, to continue counter-attack); pp. 147–8 (Lukin's 16th Army, covering Ostrog); p. 148 (Kirponos's order, 28th June, to counter-attack enemy on Dubno–Ostrog axis); pp. 152–4 (Zhukov–Kirponos conversation, 1 July); pp. 165–7 (German threat to Ostrog and Rovno; revised orders from Moscow to SW Front, 30 June; planned withdrawal by 9 July); p. 171 (Zhukov–Purkayev conversation on withdrawal, 1 July); p. 175 (threat to Proskurov – SW Front forward HQ – and move to Zhitomir); pp. 181–2 (Zhukov – Kirponos conversation; Zhukov warning not to let 6th, 26th and 12th Armies be cut off); pp. 193–200 (preparations to defend Kiev); p. 233 (Stavka orders withdrawal of left flank armies, counter-attacks from the north, 18 July); p. 248 (Tupikov new SW Front Chief of Staff, Purkayev to *Stavka*); p. 255 (20 German divisions on approaches to Kiev, end July).

Barkov, Leonid, *V debryakh Abvera* (Tallin: Eesti Raamat 1971), pp. 61–9 (*Abwehr* on Soviet–German front); pp. 74–85 (*Abwehr* operations, Estonia).

Belyaev, S. and Kuznetsov, *Narodnoe opolchenie Leningrada* (Leningrad: Lenizdat 1959), pp. 11–50 (detailed analysis, formation of militia units); pp. 56–60 (first military actions).

Biryuzov, Marshal S.S., *Kogda gremeli pushki* (Moscow: Voenizdat 1962), pp. 14–17 (deployment of 132nd Rifle Division, assigned to 13th Army); pp. 25–8 (escape from encirclement); pp. 29–30 (river Sozh, death of Akhlyustin, GOC 13th Mech. Corps).

Platonov, Lt.-Gen. S.P. (ed.), *Bitva za Leningrad 1941–1944* (Moscow; Voenizdat 1964), pp. 22–4 (Baltic MD operations 22–9 June); pp. 27–30 (operations and deployment Soviet forces, 10 July; defence of 'Luga line'; re-organization of NW command); pp. 31–8 ('Luga operational group'; 11th Army operations); pp. 38–40 (8th Army operations to 23/5 July). This is an important work based exclusively on archive materials and presenting a close operational narrative. I found it also an advantage to discuss this work with Gen. Platonov himself, who had an impressive team of military historians involved: I.P. Barbashin, A.I. Kutnetsov, V.P. Morozov, A.D. Kharitonov and B.N. Yakovlev.

Boldin, *op. cit.*, pp. 90–4 (with 10th Army, orders from Pavlov); pp. 98–9 (visit of Kulik; Khatskilevich reports ammunition exhausted); pp. 107–11 (with isolated units in woods, Minsk area); pp. 111–12 (beginning of break-out attempt, dawn on 5 July).

Bychevskii, *op. cit.*, pp. 5–9 (operations 22–5 June, Leningrad command); p. 9 (Pyadyshev to command 'Luga group'); pp. 19–22 (manning 'Luga line', Kirov Infantry School Cadets); pp. 23–4 (fall of Pskov); p. 29 (visit to Luga); p. 31 (mining operations, Luga sector).

900 geroicheskikh dnei (Moscow/Leningrad: Nauka 1966) (documentary collection), docs 1–13, pp. 27–54 (mobilization in Leningrad, June–August 1941); doc. 13, pp. 51–4 (report on formation of militia divisions).

Fedyuninskii, *op. cit.*, pp. 25–31 (15th Rifle Corps operations, 28 June–7 July); p. 36 (report to SW Front command from 5th Army, summarizing operations, 9–16 July),

Inzhenernye voiska Sovetskoi Armii v vazhneishikh operatsii Velikoi Otechestvennoi voiny, Sbornik statei (Moscow: Voenizdat 1958), pp. 16–28 (V.A. Anfilov on engineers, summer 1941).

Isirlin, Col.-Gen. A.D. (ed.), *Inzhenernye voiska v boyakh za Sovetskuyu rodinu* (Moscow: Voenizdat 1970), pp. 77–91 (Red Army engineers; operations June–July 1941).

Kabanov, S.I., *Na dal'nykh podstupakh* (Moscow: Voenizdat 1971), pp. 127–44 (opening stages, defence of Hango); pp. 145–63 (defence of base to mid-July).

Karasev, A.V., *Leningradtsy v gody blokady*, pp. 35–7 (operational narrative, NW Theatre, 23 June–5 July); pp. 37–48 (Formation of militia divisions, Leningrad, end June–mid-July); pp. 63–6 (manning 'Luga line'; militia divisions moved in); pp. 69–70 (work on fortification to cover SW approaches to Leningrad); pp. 74–5 (Voroshilov's suggestion about designating militia formations 'Guards' – *gvardeiskii* – units).

Krivoshein, Lt.-Gen. S., *Ratnaya byl* (Moscow: 'Molodaya Gvardiya' 1962), pp. 48–60 (personal account of 25th Mech. Corps movement, operations, July 1941). Krivoshein was corps commander.

Kupriyanov, G.N., *Ot Barentseva morya do Ladogi* (Leningrad: Lenizdat 1972), pp. 34–50 (Frolov's 14th Army, operations at Petrozavodsk).

Kurochkin, Lt.-Gen./Signals P.M., *Pozyvnye fronta* (Moscow: Voenizdat 1969), pp. 114–134 (NW Front signals, June–July 41).

Kuznetsov, Maj.-Gen./Aviation, N.K., *Front nad zemlei* (Moscow: Voenizdat 1970) pp. 17–22 (Soviet Air Force operations, NW Front and Leningrad, June–July 1941)

Kuznetsov, Lt.-Gen. P.G., *Gvaudeitsy-Moskvichi* (Moscow: Voenizdat 1962), pp. 5–32 (1st Moscow Motor-Rifle Div. deployed, w Front); pp. 33–50 (operations with 20th Army; defence of Orsha; encirclement).

Lobachev, *op. cit.*, p. 131 (16th Army ordered to w Front, 26 June); pp. 133–4 (movement of 16th Army from sw Front; crisis at Shepetovka); pp. 139–40 (arrival in Smolensk area, 2 July); pp. 148–9 (beginning of evacuation of Smolensk); pp. 150–1 (Timoshenko's briefing, 13 July); pp. 153–4 (Timoshenko's orders from GKO to hold Smolensk); pp. 159–62 (rearguard action, Smolensk); pp. 164–5 (blowing up of bridges at Smolensk, arrest of Malyshev); pp. 170 (16th and 20th Armies link up, escaping encirclement, end July).

Logunova, T.A., *Partiinoe podpol'e i partizanskoe dvizhenie v tsentral'nykh oblastyakh RSFSR: iyul' 1941–1943 gg.* (Moscow: MGU 1973), pp. 8–33 (bibliographical survey); pp. 34–59 (first partisan units in central Russian region).

Loktionov, I.I., *Dunaiskaya flotiliya v Velikoi Otechestvennoi voine* (Moscow: Voenizdat 1962), pp. 11–49 (Danube Flotilla operations to end July 1941).

Maiskii, I.M., *Vospominaniya Sovetskogo posla* (Moscow: Nauka 1965), pt 3, pp. 139–47 (announcement of war); pp. 147–58 (Anglo-Soviet discussions, London); pp. 158–65 (Hopkins mission to Moscow).

Mazets, Maj.-Gen. P.S., 'Na Luzhskom rubezhe', in *Parol' – 'Pobeda'* (Leningrad: Lenizdat 1969), pp. 7–20 (first-hand account, manning the 'Luga line' and initial operations).

Nepokorennyi Leningrad, Kratkii ocherk istorii goroda v period Velikoi Otechestvennoi voiny (Leningrad: Nauka 1970), pp. 25–94 (early mobilization of city for defence).

Novikov, Aviation Marshal, A.A., *V nebe Leningrada* (Moscow: Nauka 1970), pp. 40–8 (air operations, 22–3 June, NW Theatre and Leningrad); pp. 67–8 (Novikov's order for deployment of aviation, 23 June); pp. 80–94 (German capture of Pskov, 9 July; operations 8th and 11th Armies; survey of Soviet air operations).

Partiino-politicheskaya rabota v Sovetskikh vooruzhennykh silakh v gody Velikoi Otechestvennoi voiny 1941–1945, Kratkii istoricheskii obzor (Moscow: Voenizdat 1968), pp. 21–31 (re-organization of political organs); pp. 31–62 (disciplinary measures, increasing steadiness of troops).

Perechnev, Yu. and Vinogradov, Yu., *Na strazhe morskikh gorizontov* (Moscow: Voenizdat 1967), pt 2, pp. 140–53 (coastal artillery, Baltic, defence of Libau and Tallin).

Popov, Gen. M.M., 'V boyakh za gorod Leningrad', in *Oborona Leningrada*, pp. 29–40 (defensive measures in NW Theatre and Leningrad; command personnel and duties, June 1941); pp. 41–7 (operations 22–6 June; entry of Finland into Soviet–German War); pp. 47–57 (German advance to 'Luga line'; Popov's command decisions mid/late July). See also in this volume: A.A. Novikov, pp. 75–101; Yu.A. Panteleyev, pp. 140–78; B.V. Bychevskii, pp. 179–85; N.N. Voronov, pp. 199–221; N.G. Kuznetsov, pp. 222–46. These accounts is this volume should also be related to the separate memoir/monograph studies. Nevertheless, *Oborona Leningrada* is a very significant work and covers not only the military but also the civilian aspects of the defence of Leningrad.

50 Let Sov. Voor. Sil., *op. cit.*, p. 256 (creation of *Stavka Glavnogo Komandovaniya*, 23 June – command function discharged for one day by Glavnyi Voennyi Soviet).

Rokossovskii, *op. cit.*, pp. 13–14 (concentration of 9th Mech. Corps); pp. 15–18 (operations, 24 June, tank battle Dubno); pp. 20–2 (9th Mech. Corps adopts 'mobile defence' end June, falling back with 5th Army); p. 22 (Rokossovskii assigned to w Front); pp. 25–6 (briefed on situation on w Front, 17 July, assumes command of 'Group Rokossovskii').

Sandalov, *op. cit.*, pp. 109–21 (on sw approaches to Minsk; 4th Army operations 24/5–7 June); pp. 121–4 (fall of Bobruisk, German breakthrough to Berezina, 28 June); p. 125 (visit of Shaposhnikov, Pavlov, revised orders for 4th Army); p. 130 (fall of Minsk, Pavlov and Klimovskikh relieved of commands by Stavka order, 1 July); pp. 131–2 (4th Army subordinated to Gerasimenko, 21st Army; orders to hold Germans from Dnieper).

Savchenko, V.N., *Gvardeiskaya Latyshskaya* (Riga: Akad. Nauka 1961), pp. 9–21 (Lativian units, nw Front, June–July 1941).

Sovetskie tankovye voiska 1941–1945, Voenno-istoricheskii ocherk (Moscow: Voenizdat 1973), pp. 20–34 (Soviet tank/mechanized operations to end July 1941).

Starikov, *op. cit.*, pp. 210–11 (present at arrest of General Pavlov, Klimovskikh and Klich, w Front command, 1 July).

Yeremenko, A.I., *op. cit.*, pp. 70–7 (summary of operations, w Front, 22–9 June); pp. 78–80 (Yeremenko assumes command, w Front 29 June); pp. 80–1 (discussions with Voroshilov, Shaposhnikov, Pavlov); pp. 83–4 (*Directive No. 14*, 1 July 1941: text); pp. 85–6 (improvisation of defences, anti-tank squads, partisan groups); pp. 87–8 (arrival of Timoshenko, deployment of 1st Moscow Motor-Rifle Div.; attempt to block Minsk–Moscow highway; pp. 94–100 (with 22nd Army, Soviet counter-attacks 6–9 July); pp. 104–5 (letter to Stalin requesting infantry-support tanks, 7 July 1941); pp. 108–69 (detailed operational narrative, 13th Army operations – 13A formed in early May 1941 – for period 22 June–end July 1941); pp. 208–13 (Koniev's 19th Army deployed on w Front); pp. 214–20 (Lukin's 16th Army deployed, w Front); pp. 220–3 (Soviet order of battle, strength, w Front, 10 July); pp. 224–5 (Soviet counter-attacks, 13–15 July); p. 225 (c-in-c, w Theatre – Timoshenko – signal to *Stavka,*·16 July).

Zhdanov, Col.-Gen. N.N., *Ognevoi shchit Leningrada* (Moscow: Voenizdat 1965), pp. 25–30 (organization of militia divisions, June–July 1941).

Zhukov, *Vospominaniya*, pp. 249–88.

Zhuravlev, D.A., *Ognevoi shchit Moskvy* (Moscow: Voenizdat 1972), pp. 23–43 (air defence of Moscow, June–July 1941).

Literature, literary materials

I have made limited use of such materials, the analysis of which is a specialized subject in its own right, so this is not any form of judgement on literary excellence (or the lack of it) as such: see Konstantin Simonov, *Zhivye i mertvye*, Sovetskii voennyi roman (Moscow: Voenizdat 1961); also Grigorii Baklanov, *Voennye povesti* (Moscow: Sov. pisatel 1967), pp. 5–182 ('Iyul' 41 goda'). See also *Literaturnoe nasledstvo*, 78 (Moscow: Nauka 1966), Sovetskie pisateli na frontakh Velikoi Otechestvennoi voiny, Book 1.

Periodicals

Baskakov, Lt.-Gen. V., 'Ob osobennostyakh nachal 'nogo perioda voiny', *VIZ*, 2 (1966), pp. 29–34.

Gapich, Maj.-Gen. N., 'Nekotorye mysli po voprosam upravleniya i svyazi', *VIZ*, 7 (1965), pp. 46–55 (Soviet signals).

Strizhkov, Lt. Yu., 'Boi za Peremyshl (22–27 iyuniya 1941 goda), *VIZ*, 6 (1965), pp. 51–6 (99th Rifle Div. operations).

Vaskilevskii, Marshal A.M.: The memoirs of Vaskilevskii have been published in instalments in *Novy Mir*, beginning with 4 (1973). The volume itself – *Delo vsei zhizni* – will be published by Politizdat. See here the first instalment, *Novy Mir*, 4 (1973), pp. 188–201 (on the Soviet high command and the General Staff); also pp. 201–8 (on Soviet operations to end-July).

5 TOWARDS THE EDGE OF DESTRUCTION

Carell, *op. cit.*, pp. 68–88 ('objective Smolensk'); pp. 103–15 ('Stalin's Great Mistake' – failure to interpret German intentions, Yeremenko's performance); pp. 116–28 (Battle of Kiev). Carell makes excellent use of German divisional histories and unit records, though his Soviet sources are less reliable; pp. 129–66 (Code Name 'Typhoon', German surprise, fall of Bryansk, German tally of Soviet losses, Tula and Kalinin).

Goure, *op. cit.*, pp. 90–135 (Battle of Leningrad, 20 August–25 September; also 139 ff. (on threat of complete encirclement).

Leach, *op. cit.*, pp. 203–7 (decline in German strength, logistics problems); pp. 207–14 ('abandonment of "Barbarossa" Plan', German directives end July, vacillation in selecting objectives).

Von Manstein, *op. cit.*, pp. 189–202 (56th Panzer Corps operations NW theatre; encirclement of corps mid-July; fighting round Luga; defeat of Soviet 38th (*sic*) Army).

Rohwer, Jürgen, 'Die sowjetischen U-Boot-Erfolge in Zweiten Weltkrieg', *Marine Rundschau* (December 1968), pp. 427–39.

Salisbury, *op. cit.*, pt 2, pp. 180–93 (Luga line and its collapse); pp. 214–20 (Stalin's interference with city defence committee and defence arrangements); pp. 221–32 (Tallinn disaster); pt 3, pp. 273–87 (German investment of city); pp. 316–26 (Zhukov in command).

Seaton, *Russo–German War*, pp. 104–15 (German intentions NW theatre, advance on Leningrad, Soviet military performance); pp. 126–32 (Timoshenko in command W Front; Smolensk battle); pp. 133–47 (German operations in Ukraine; capture of Kiev); pp. 171–91 (Directive no. 35 and Operation 'Typhoon'; Moscow defences and Soviet re-organization; destruction of the Bryansk Front and Vyazma encirclement; Zhukov takes over W Front):

Seaton, *The Battle for Moscow 1941–1942* (London: Rupert Hart-Davis 1971), pp. 70–89 (German plans for offensive against Moscow); pp. 89–113 (German break-through Bryansk/Vyazma; encirclement of Soviet forces; effect of *rasputitsa* on German movement; Zhukov in command W Front; pp. 118–30 (panic in Moscow, emergency defence measures, defence of Tula, German exhaustion at end of October). Col. Seaton's monograph presents a very clear operational narrative of the initial German encirclement operation and is especially useful for a description of the state of German forces late in October.

Turney, Alfred, *Disaster at Moscow: von Bock's Campaigns 1941–1942* (London: Cassell

1971), pp. 92–132 (Army Group Centre offensive on approaches to Moscow, Bryansk pocket and Vyazma encirclement, supply difficulties and impeded movement of German forces).

War diary (German)

KTB/OKW, 1, see *Tagesmeldungen der OperationsAbteilung des Gen Std H* (Auszüge), pp. 517–662 (10 July to 26 September); p. 661.

Diplomatic histories/materials

Churchill–Stalin Correspondence: Churchill, nos 4–16, pp. 13–29 (British aid to Russia; joint operations in Persia; Hopkins and Beaverbrook missions); Stalin, no. 3, pp. 12–13; no. 10, pp. 20–2; no. 12, pp. 24–5.

Gwyer, *op. cit.*, III: 1, pp. 105–10 (Harry Hopkins in Moscow, interviews with Stalin); pp. 139–62 (supply of military equipment and raw materials to the Soviet Union: Supply conference).

Maiskii, *op. cit.*, III, pp. 158–65 (Hopkins visit to Moscow); pp. 165–75 (question of British aid to the Soviet Union); p. 169 (Maiskii suggests that he persuaded Stalin to drop the pressure for a 'second front' and speak only of military-economic aid to the USSR).

Sherwood, *op. cit.*, pp. 333–41 (report of meeting with Stalin; Stalin's appreciation of military situation; Soviet requirements in war supplies).

Woodward, *op. cit.*, II, pp. 14–20 (Russian appeals for military action); pp. 28–35 (Russian demands for a second front, September 1941); pp. 35–40 (the Moscow conference).

Official/Party histories

IVOVSS, 2, pp. 63–247.

VOVSS, *Kratkaya istoriya*, 2nd edn, pp. 73–80 (Smolensk battle); pp. 80–8 (German advance on Leningrad); pp. 88–94 (SW and S Fronts, defence of Odessa).

VOVSS, 1965 edn, pp. 113–19 (German drive on Moscow; Bryansk Front collapses; Vyazma encirclement; Moscow placed on a siege footing). NOTE: p. 116 cites the figure of 90,000 men available for the defence of Moscow, though it is not clear whether this means before or after the limited reinforcement of 13 October. It could be assumed, none the less, that this was the strength left to the Soviet command after the massive encirclements had left their mark. VOVSS, 2nd edn (1970), p. 118 mentions the same figure and clarifies the point somewhat by referring to the four Soviet armies holding a 230-kilometre front covering Moscow.

Kratkaya khronika, pp. 27–95 (daily entries, July–end September 1941); pp. 94–111 (daily entries for October).

GMD

OKH: Op. Abt. (I): Weisung für die Fortführung der Operationen; see Anlage 1 (Feindlage) (Soviet intentions and strength, 27 July 1941). T-78/R335, 6291726–731.

OKH, GS: Op. Abt. (addition to Directive 1401/41 – '*Auffrischung*' of Panzer Groups 2 and 3, detailed operational tasks 31 July 1941). T-78/R335, 6291738–741.

OKH, GS: Op. Abt. to Army Group South, operations west of the Dnieper, 12 August 1941. T-78/R335, 6291745–750.

OKH, GS: Op. Abt. to Army Groups Centre and South, intention to destroy Soviet 5th Army, also 6th Army, 24 August 1941; subsequent instructions (to 30 August 1941). T-78/R335, 6291752-761.

Von Leeb, on deterioration of situation, Army Group North, Leningrad operations, 24 September 1941. OKH reply and instructions, same date. T-78/R335, 6291812-816.

OKH: Abt. Heeresversorg: '. . . Betreibstoff- und Kraftfahrzeuglage bei den neuen Operationen' (11 September 1941); fuel and vehicle stocks, also *Panzerlage*. Text, record of conversation with General Thomas. T-78/R335, 6291779-785 (see also 786-93, *Panzer-Nachschub Ost* before opening of AG Centre's operations, 15 September).

Gesamtzahl u. Typen der sowjetischen Panzerwaffe, 29 August 1941. A report liberally spattered with queries and question marks by higher authority. T-78/R481, 6465579-81.

Auffindung der Leiche des Generalobersten Kirponos, 24 September 1941 (discovery of body of Col.-Gen. Kirponos). 541-2.

Maiskii: report on conversation with Eden, unsure of Stalin's role in operations and command 6 August 1941. T-77/R1028, 6500477.

4th Army: air photos, Soviet positions behind the Dnieper, 13 July 1941 (Ia, *Luftbilder zum KTB Nr. 8*). T-315/R162, 7704954-995.

4th Army: Operations Branch (*Anl. zum KTB Nr. 8*) (daily reports, combat operations Moghilev–Smolensk–Orsha, 10–20 July 1941). T-312/R159, 7700478-568.

4th Army (Armeeoberkommando 4): army field orders (Operation *Taifun*, original order 26, September 1941). T-312/R150, 7689313-334.

4th Army: reports, orders, maps covering Soviet and German combat operations in central Russia, September–October 1941; list of important bridges; bridges round Moscow. 7689701-935.

17th Army: Soviet overall strength, Soviet forces encountered and identified by Army Group South (11 July 1941) (personal holding).

17th Army: *Bilder von Ermordungen in Lemberg* (Lwów massacre), photograph collection. T-312/R674, 8308287-96.

17th Army: *Schlacht von Uman* (Anlage 9 zum KTB Nr 1). T-312/R674, 8307884-99.

3rd Panzer Div.: *Feind-propaganda* (originals of Soviet propaganda leaflets, broadsheets, incitements to desertion). T-315/R137, 408-650.

4th Panzer Div.: *Feindnachrichtenblatt*, 10: 28 July 1941 total Soviet strength – 202 Rifle Divs, 50 armoured divs – Soviet strength facing 4th Panzer Army. 269-72.

Lagebericht Ost Nr. 40 (25 July 1941).

Lagebericht Ost Nr. 77 (31 August 1941), pp. 1-5.

Lagebericht Ost Nr. 79 (2 September 1941), pp. 1-6.

Lagebericht Ost Nr. 90 (13 September 1941), pp. 1-7.

Lagebericht Ost Nr. 91 (14 September 1941), pp. 1-6 ('Die Umfassung der russischen 21., 5., 37., 26., und 38. Armee ist nahezu vollendet'; identification of Soviet formations).

Lagebericht Ost Nr. 94 (17 September 1941), pp. 1-5 (encirclement of sw Front forces).

Lagebericht Ost Nr. 96 (19 September 1941), pp. 1-6 ('Kiev ist genommen': fall of Kiev, identification of Soviet formations).

Lagebericht Ost Nr. 98 (21 September 1941), pp. 1-6 (by evening 20 September, 170,000 PWs taken in Kiev encirclement; estimated 30 Soviet divisions broken; many captured weapons stamped '7.9.41 Tula'; AG Centre reports capture of Gen. Potapov, GOC 5th Soviet Army).

Lagebericht Ost Nr. 99 (22 September 1941), pp. 1–4 (AG South reports for period 11–22 September tally of 230,000 PWs, 340 tanks, 1,000 guns, 45 aircraft captured).

Lagebericht Ost Nr. 101 (24 September 1941), pp. 1–6 (AG South: tally of Soviet divisions destroyed between Dnieper and Desna – completely destroyed or effectively knocked out; rifle divisions, armoured divisions, cavalry and other units [including 207 Para. Brigade]).

'Aus den Erfahrungen der ersten Kämpfe mit den Deutschen': extracts (German transl.) from Soviet report on early combat experience (2 August 1941). T-315/R44, 1144-6.

Order No. 252 (31 July 1941) (Lt.-Gen. Khrulev on supply services and systems for Army groups/armies [German transl.].) T-78/R481, 6465718-24.

Order No. 270 (16 August 1941) (*Stavka* announcement that Gen. Boldin escaped from encirclement; officers who desert or remove rank badges to facilitate desertion to enemy will bring about arrest of their families in Soviet territory) (German transl.). T-78/R464, 6443282-3.

Interrogation of Senior Lt. Yakov Djugashvili (14th Howitzer Regiment), Stalin's eldest son (19 July 1941) (personal holding).

Diary of a military commissar: attached staff 45th Rifle Corps (22 June–27 July 1941) (extracts: German transl.). 342-6.

Order No. 03 (1 August 1941) (Soviet original of Gen. Khrulev on salvage/evacuation of equipment). T-78/R481, 6465877-8.

Mekhlis, revised instructions on propaganda and party-political work, instruction no. 81 (15 July 1941) (German transl.). T-77/R1028, 6500470-5.

Order No. 0098 (5 October 1941) (Gen. Zhukov [Leningrad] on discipline, indiscipline, dereliction of duty). T-78/R468, 6443370-3.

Collected captured documents (German transl.): No. 00207/sw Front to 12 Army, criticism of command (signed Kirponos); 27 July 1941 (list of punishments, Soviet senior officers [GKO announcement]); 26 July 1941 (to commanders, 6th and 12th Army, tactical instructions [signed Budenny]); 21 July 1941 (transmission of Mekhlis directive on organizing partisan/sabotage groups). T-315/R44, 902-10.

Interrogation of Maj. Kononov (436th Rifle Regt, 155th Rifle Div.) (24 August 1941). 393. See K. Cherkassov, *General Kononov* (Melbourne: 1963) 1, 'The history of one attempt'. Kononov went on to command a Cossack division fighting for the anti-Soviet 'Committee for the Liberation of the Russian Peoples', KONR.

Interrogation of Chief/Ops Section/Soviet 6th Army (6th Army OB, organization of break-out from encirclement, 7 August 1941). T-315/R44, 997-9.

Interrogation of Staff Maj., 266th Motorized Rifle Div. (12 September 1941); Commander, 219th Motorized Rifle Div. (15 September 1941). T-315/R206, 491-6.

Interrogation of Brigade-Commissar Kamenev (Staff, 5th Army, also with 9 Mech. Corps) (23 September 1941). 519.

Interrogation of Gen. Potapov (GOC, Soviet 5th Army; also Artillery commander, 5th Army, Gen. Ssotenskii) (22 September 1941). 509-10.

Order No. 04/00378, Soviet 19th Army (15 September 1941) ('Über die Formierung der Absperrabteilungen in den Divisionen') (signed: Lt.-Gen. Lukin). (German transl.) T-77/R1028, 6500731-3.

New location of People's Commissariats and government agencies (evacuation instructions)
Order No. 022: Khrulev (Rear Services) (5 November 1941). T-78/R464, 6443365-9.

GMD *Establishment of Soviet Rifle Divisions and Guards Rifle Divisions (1941-2)*

Order and date	Rifle Div.	Rifle Regt	Guards Rifle Div.	Guards Rifle Regt
04/400-17 5 April 1941	14, 454	3,182	—	—
04/600-16 29 July 1941	10,790	2,695	10,790	2,695
04/750-66 6 December 1941	11,907	2,957	11,907	2,957
04/200-13 18 March 1942	12,813	3,173	13,113	3,273
Revised 15 July 1942	13,534	3,380	13,834	3,480
04/300-16 28 July 1942	10,566	2,571	13,000	3,200
04/550-62 10 December 1942	9,354	2,443	10,585	2,758

(German military intelligence compilations: Soll-Kopfstärken)

NW, Leningrad and N theatre
Anfilov, *op. cit.*, pp. 332-474.
Bitva za Leningrad, pp. 31-97.
Bychevskii, *op. cit.*, pp. 29-106.
Fedyuninskii, *op. cit.*, pp. 41-60.
Karasev, *op. cit.*, pp. 50-141.
Kozlov, G.K., *V lesakh Karelii* (Moscow: Voenizdat 1963), pp. 19-32 (organization of Soviet 7th Army defences); pp. 32-61 (combat operations 7th Army, 1-30 July 1941, stemming German breakthrough to Rebola); pp. 75-90 (attempts to hold off German-Finnish junction; Meretskov assumes command 7th Army, with Gorelenko as deputy commander; 24 September, 7th Army directly subordinated to *Stavka* and re-designated 7th Independent [*Otdel'naya*] Army).
Kuznetsov, Admiral N.G., 'Osazhdennyi Leningrad i Baltiiskii Flot', *Voprosy istorii*, 8 (1965), pp. 114-16. This pre-publication extract 'reveals' that on 12 September Stalin discussed the 'abandonment' of Leningrad with Kuznetsov, to whom he gave orders for the possible scuttling of the Baltic Fleet. Kuznetsov refused to sign without the counter-signature of Shaposhnikov, pleading that since the Fleet was technically

under the command of the Leningrad Front, this was hardly a naval matter pure and simple. This proved to be a wise precaution, according to Kuznetsov, for a year later Tributs was accused by the NKVD of panic-mongering and of having laid premature plans to scuttle his own ships. Kuznetsov could at least explain the 'directive'.

In the event Stalin did not issue the Kuznetsov-Shaposhnikov directive to the Baltic Fleet command. That he, Stalin, was concerned over the fate of Leningrad cannot be doubted, for he said as much to Zhukov. But Kuznetsov insists that Stalin did entertain a notion to abandon Leningrad, though he goes on to say that he only wished to keep the Baltic Fleet out of German hands.

Ladoga rodnaya (Leningrad: Lenizdat 1969), see under N.D. Fenin (Commissar/Ladoga Flotilla), pp. 9–17 (operations to 25 September); Rear-Admiral V.P. Belyakov, pp. 18–26 (organization of Ladoga Flotilla); Vice-Admiral V.S. Cherokov (commander/Ladoga Flotilla), pp. 27–35 (flotilla command and organization).

Meretskov, *op. cit.*, pp. 220–8.

Nepokorennyi Leningrad, pp. 49–94 (labour mobilization, militia forces, mobilization of population for digging trenches, air raid precautions, air defence).

Novikov, *op. cit.*, pp. 104–65.

Oborona Leningrada, *see under* M.M. Popov, pp. 48–61.

    See under N.G. Kuznetsov, pp. 229–37.

    See under N.N. Voronov, pp. 202–12.

    See under Yu.A. Panteleyev, pp. 142–9.

Pavlov. D.V., *Leningrad v blokade (1941 god)* (Moscow: Voenizdat 1958); among several subsequent edns, see *Sovetskaya Rossiya* (Moscow: 1969), pp. 7–24 (military operations, NW theatre, June–August); pp. 24–5 (Stalin disbands Military Soviet for defence of Leningrad); p. 23 (GKO decision to split N Front); pp. 31–4 (Zhukov appointed new commander; Kulik in command 54th Army to E of lake Ladoga); pp. 42–3 (Zhukov leaves; replaced by Fedyuninskii, replaced by I.S. Khozin); pp. 51–9 (air and artillery bombardment, 8 September); pp. 59–69 (air defence, also artillery counter-battery operations under Voronov).

Pern, Lt.-Gen. L., *V vikhre voennykh let* (Tallinn: Eesti Raamat 1969), pp. 61–88 (2nd Rifle Corps operations, W and Bryansk Fronts, July–September 1941). This is an unusual book by an Estonian, a professional officer with the Red Army and latterly Estonian Corps commander. See criticism of Maj.-Gen. C.F. Zakharov, pp. 86–7.

Petrov, Yu.P., *Partizanskoe dvizhenie v Leningradskoi oblasti 1941–1944* (Leningrad: Lenizdat 1973), pp. 21–41 (organization of partisans, underground Party organs); pp. 41–8 (armed partisan groups, Luga district); pp. 48–55 (organization of partisan units, Leningrad and environs).

Tryll, I. (ed.), *Estonskii narod v Velikoi Otechestvennoi Voine Sovetskogo Soyuza* (Tallinn: Eesti Raamat 1973), I, pp. 128–89 (German attack; evacuation; military-operations, Estonia); pp. 240–87 (22nd Estonian Territorial Rifle Corps; operations July 1941).

Zhukov, G.K., *Vospominaniya*, pp. 312–17 (role in defence of Leningrad; assumes command, Leningrad Front, 10 September; first command decisions; attacks on Soviet 42nd Army; perimeter stabilized late September). This is a surprisingly brief and reserved account of one of Zhukov's major commands.

8th Army operations (June–July 1941): NW Front
See 'Oboronitel'naya operatsiya 8-i Armii v nachal'nyi period Velikoi Otechestvennoi voiny', *VIZ*, 7 (1974), pp. 75–84. Sobennikov's 8th Army was something of a phenomenon, thus meriting particular study: it disappeared and re-appeared and should by all the odds have gone under for good. This study by Col. N. Baryshev supplies some essential data on the Soviet 8th Army (including excellent maps).

Composition of 8th Army, June 1941
(The two sets of figures represent the formal establishment –
upper line – and real strength, lower line)

	10 Rifle Corps	11 Rifle Corps	12 Mech.Corps
Men	32,057	32,057	36,080
	25,480	23,661	30,436
Tanks	24	24	1,031
	12	17	651
Guns and mortars	600	600	358
	453	559	288
Armoured cars	26	26	266
	18	14	68
Lorries	1,900	1,900	5,165
	912	1,007	2,945

Total manpower 105,508 (including 9th anti-tank artillery brigade)
82,010
Tanks 1,079
680

Smolensk and the 'Moscow axis'
Biryuzov, *op. cit.*, pp. 33–47.
Lobachev, *op. cit.*, pp. 152–71.
Moskovskoe opolchenie, Kratkii istoricheskii ocherk (Moscow: Voenizdat 1969), pp. 18–57 (militia divisions created, Communist battalions and anti-sabotage/infiltration battalions).
Ordena Lenina Moskovskii voennyi okrug (Moscow: Voenizdat 1971), pp. 180–90 (organization of Moscow militia divisions); pp. 190–3 (Battle of Smolensk); pp. 195–200 (5 defensive sectors organized in Moscow, assigned to military academies; military schools supply reinforcements for front).
Rokossovskii, *Soldatskii dolg*, 2nd edn, pp. 24–50.
Sandalov, *Na Moskorskom naprarlennii*, III, pp. 154–96.
Sazonov, *op. cit.*, pp. 99–137.

R.T.S.—R

South-west, southern theatre

Anfilov, *op. cit.*, pp. 404–77.

Azarov, *op. cit.*, pp. 179–86 (*Stavka* directive on evacuation of Odessa).

Bagramyan, I.Kh., *Gorod-voin na Dnepre* (Moscow: Politizdat 1965), pp. 5–157. This is a highly personal narrative, opening in early July and ending with the September encirclement. It contains much documentary material, records of conversations, operational reports (though without specific references). I have found this a valuable small monograph and Marshal Bagramyan is by no means myopic or calculating in distributing blame – the roles of Stalin, Budenny and Shaposhnikov are quite carefully evaluated. In certain instances it is essential (or inescapable) to accept Bagramyan's evidence, as he was there with the Operations Staff. It would appear that this study was rushed out in the wake of the fall of Khrushchev to correct the over-simplification of the 'Khrushchev version', though this is speculation – born out none the less by the rapid publication dating.

Bagramyan, *Tak nachinalas' voina*, pp. 292–368. This section of the narrative opens on 16 August and proceeds to the German encirclement, closing with details of the belated Soviet break-out and the death of Kirponos. One of the most significant passages (pp. 332–8) deals with Bagramyan's visit to Timoshenko on 16 September, Timoshenko's *verbal* orders to pull sw Front forces back from the Dnieper and the refusal of Kirponos to act on anything but written orders, plus seeking Moscow's authorization and clarification of contradictory orders, signal of evening, 17 September (p. 338). *See also* under Moskalenko, Vasilevskii, Zhukov; also *Periodicals*.

Gorelik, Ya.M., *Boris Mikhailovich Shaposhnikov* (Moscow: Voenizdat 1961), pp. 84–7 (Shaposhnikov as cGs). This is very laudatory in tone, insubstantial in content, but one of the few works devoted to Shaposhnikov. (*See also* Col. Ya. Gorelik's letter to editor in *VIZ*, 9 (1965), pp. 112–13 – on the failure to recognize Shaposhnikov's contribution.

Krylov, Marshal N.I., *Ne pomerknet nikogda* (Moscow: Voenizdat 1969) ('Voennye Memuary'); *passim* (on the defence of Odessa). Transl. into English as *Glory Eternal*. Defence of Odessa 1941 (Moscow: Progress 1972).

Lisov, Lt.-Gen. I.I., *Desantniki (Vozdushnye desanty)* (Moscow: Voenizdat 1968), pp. 44–60 (use of Soviet airborne units in operations in the frontier battles, in Belorussia and the Ukraine; 4th Airborne Corps operations in Belorussia, July 1941; fighting on the Berezina and in Krichev operations; 10 July 1941, 3rd Para. Corps transferred from Odessa to Kiev area – 5th, 6th and 212th Airborne Brigades in defence of Kiev; Col. A.I. Rodimtsev in command 5th Para. Brigade in Kiev operations; at end August 3rd Para. Corps incorporated into 40th Soviet Army, fighting at Konotop; 3rd Para. Corps redesignated 87th Rifle Div., ultimately becoming 13th Guards Rifle Div. under Rodimtsev. NOTE: 212th Para Bde had already fought as ground troops in the Khalkin-Gol operations (1939), the first recorded use of parachute troops in this role. Many of the Soviet paratroopers were veterans of the 1939 Far Eastern operations.

Moskalenko, K.S., *Na Yugo-zapadnom napravlenii 1941–1943*, Vospominaniya komand-arma (Moscow: Nauka 1973), 2nd edn (1st edn: 1969), pp. 51–91 (sw Front operations, Kiev encirclement; encirclement of 6th and 12th Armies, early August; capture of Muzychenko and Ponedelin, Soviet army commanders; German attempt at rapid thrust on Kiev; Potapov fails to secure his right flank N of Chernigov; Moskalenko takes over 15th Rifle Corps, 3 September; Potapov's 5th Army breaks out of encirclement 10 September; 15th Rifle Corps forced to fall back, Potapov's displeasure; Moskalenko encircled, breaks out with improvised battle-group; escapes encirclement, 27 September; Soviet losses in Kiev encirclement not as great as German claims, only 452,000 men deployed in area; fate of Potapov); pp. 72–3 (survived captivity to serve in postwar army in Far Eastern MD; quotes von Schweppenburg on Potapov's behaviour under interrogation); pp. 74–91 (reconstruction of events leading to disaster on SW Front; Stalin–Yeremenko conversation, 24 August; Kirponos–Shaposhnikov conversation, 11 September); pp. 76–8 (Budenny's report to Stavka, 11 September); pp. 79–80 (Stalin–Kirponos conversation, 11 September; criticism of Stavka and Shaposhnikov); pp. 82–3 (Yeremenko unable to carry out his promise to hold German thrust; Timoshenko in command SW Front; basis for certain optimism); p. 84 (Kirponos report to Stalin, 13 September); p. 85 (Shaposhnikov criticizes Tupikov for 'panicky report'); p. 86 (Timoshenko gave *verbal* order to pull back troops, but Kirponos insisted on written confirmation and consulted Stavka – this his 'fatal mistake'); pp. 87–8 (Kirponos receives confirmation only during night of 18 September, and by then too late to escape full encirclement; biographical detail on Kirponos, death in action). NOTE: Marshal Moskalenko's study necessarily requires some commentary. It is both a personal memoir and a formal history based on archives and military records. In general it bears out all the testimony supplied by Bagramyan and all his writings (and supplies references to sources).

The key issue in looking into the question of responsibility for the SW Front disaster in September is Moskalenko's contribution on Marshal Timoshenko's views and actions; since Timoshenko swore himself to silence, the evidence of Bagramyan and Moskalenko must suffice. Moskalenko fills out the official record with a note of his own postwar conversations with Timoshenko. Here the two edns of Moskalenko vary slightly (see 1st edn, pp. 90–1 and 2nd edn, pp. 87–8), though the substance is essentially identical. Thus Marshal Timoshenko was prepared to 'go it alone' and pull Soviet forces back, issuing only *verbal orders* and hoping to persuade the *Stavka* – and Stalin – later. This is confirmed by Bagramyan (*Tak nachinalas'*, pp. 334–5), who visited the Marshal and was instructed to pass on to Kirponos *verbal* orders to fall back ('*Peredaite komanduyushchemu frontom moe ustnoe prikazanie: ostaviv Kievskii ukreplennyi raion . . .*'). Kirponos was to take up defensive positions on the Psël, having used his reserves to block off German forces penetrating his rear – if Kirponos 'got a move on' and attacked at Romny and Lubna, the Soviet armies might escape the trap.

Samchuk, I.A., *Trinadtsataya Gvardeiskaya* (Moscow: Voenizdat 1971), 2nd edn, pp. 5–24 (3rd Airborne Corps operations in defence of Kiev); pp. 24–39 (operations on River Seim, 3rd Corps concentrated at Konotop – incorporated into Soviet 40th Army).

Tyulenev, *op. cit.*, pp. 149–52 (S Front operations, first half July); pp. 152–4 (Tyulenev transfers troops to SW Front); pp. 154–6 (mistaken assessment of *Glavkom* SW Front; Tyulenev report, 4 August); pp. 158–9 (Tyulenev report, 6 August – plea for timely withdrawal); pp. 160–3 (withdrawal sanctioned, reserve armies moved up – but possessed neither anti-tank guns nor machine-guns).

Vasilevskii memoirs/materials, *loc. cit.*, pp. 203–17.

Vasilevskii, *Delo vsei zhizni* (Moscow: Gospolitizdat 1974), pp. 136–51 (on sw Front operations, early August to German encirclement, fall of Kiev). This account and its documentary material correspond very closely to the account presented by Marshal Zhukov. Marshal Vasilevskii puts the blame for the Kiev disaster squarely on Stalin.

Yeremenko, *V nachale voiny*, pp. 207–337. NOTE: See review by Gen. Ivanov, in *VIZ*, 6 (1965), for a swingeing attack on Yeremenko's version, with documentary support. This documentary material (e.g. Stalin–Yeremenko exchanges) is also cited by Marshal Vasilevskii. Gen. Ivanov sums up his argument in one sentence: '*Comrade Yeremenko above all else does not wish to confess that the forces of the Bryansk Front did not carry out their assigned mission: they did not destroy the enemy's Second Panzer Group and they did not frustrate his offensive into the rear of the forces of the South-West Front*'. See also Yeremenko, *Pomni voinu* (Donetsk: Donbass 1971), ch. 11.

Zhukov, G.Z., *Vospominaniya*, pp. 286–98. NOTE: Zhukov's version of the Kiev *débâcle* differs quite significantly from the 'Khrushchev version', (see IVOVSS, 2, pp. 106–10), though the principal blame still attaches to Stalin. Budenny's reputation rises a little, but Shaposhnikov seems to have played a dubious role.

In view of the complex and conflicting evidence bearing on responsibility for the *débâcle* on the sw Front and at Kiev, it might be useful to sum up what can be established with some degree of certainty:

i) Gen. Zhukov's strategic appreciation of 29 July proved to be absolutely correct and he seemed to be unique within the Soviet command in discerning German operational intentions;

ii) though much remains to be learned about Marshal Budenny's role, he was justified in proposing the reinforcement of the Central Front rather than its disbandment; Yeremenko erred seriously in overestimating the potential and the performance of his Front, and Stalin chose to believe all he said;

iii) as late as 11 September Timoshenko, having asked the General Staff to prepare a detailed study of the situation, seemed to believe that the situation was 'serious but not hopeless' and might be restored by 'firm and skilful leadership'. Some four days later he was evidently convinced that a timely withdrawal was essential and virtually conspired with Bagramyan to facilitate this, hence the *verbal* instructions to Kirponos to be passed on by Bagramyan;

iv) Shaposhnikov played a very dubious role, seeming to support the idea of a planned and timely withdrawal and yet trenchantly denouncing front-line senior officers, Tupikov in particular, for proposing such a step; Vasilevskii intimates that by the time the idea of a planned withdrawal had been accepted at the very top, it was too late to execute it;

v) should Kirponos have acted on Timoshenko's orders? The simple answer would appear to be that he should, but that still left him in an impossible situation – to hang on and pull out simultaneously – and one which was not clarified with any alacrity by the *Stavka*;

vi) while substantially to blame, Stalin was not the sole culprit; this is not exculpation, simply a recognition that the *Stavka*, the General Staff, theatre and Front commanders severally and army commanders individually all contributed to the catastrophe.

Operation 'Typhoon' ('Taifun'): Bryansk-Vyazma and the 'Moscow axis'

Most serious Soviet studies and no small number of memoir accounts acknowledge that the Soviet command was disastrously surprised by the onset of the German offensive along the 'Moscow axis' (Typhoon). Such candour has also been accompanied by some acrimony as to where responsibility really lay, with Marshal Koniev attempting to justify his own role and activity. I have concentrated here on the main Soviet accounts and both here and in subsequent passages I have relied on Marshal Sokolovskii's study of the battle for Moscow, which – though criticized – does incorporate a great deal of material on Soviet strength (or the lack of it) in all phases of the battle. Having talked with Marshal Sokolovskii, and his staff of military researchers, I can at least plead some subjective justification for relying on their compilation: as in most major Soviet studies, the *operational narrative* (chronology) and the *figures* (for troop strength etc.) are rigorously derived from archival records.

Besprimernyi podvig (Moscow: Nauka 1968) (material on conference convened for 25th anniversary of German defeat at Moscow, with foreword by Lt.-Gen. P. A. Zhilin); see Marshal Koniev, pp. 63–75 (in command of the Kalinin Front); Marshal Yeremenko, pp. 76–87 (on the sw approaches to Moscow); Marshal Zhukov, pp. 88–94 (the defensive battle); Col.-Gen. D.A. Zhuravlev, pp. 146–53 (air and anti-aircraft defence of Moscow); A.V. Zalevskii, pp. 358–69 (militia divisions in the defence of Moscow); I.M. Skachkov, pp. 409–24 (Mozhaisk Party organization in defensive battle). This is an informative volume but the memoir material is somewhat stylized and very conscious of the 'historical record'. Nevertheless, the material on the civilian mobilizations and the internal measures within the capital is often original and informative.

Bitva za Moskvu (Moscow: Moskovskii Rabochii 1958), 2nd edn; see in this memoir collection Marshal Koniev, pp. 35–62; Marshal Zhukov, pp. 63–96; General Artemeyev, pp. 111–27; Gen. Lelyushenko, pp. 128–50; Col. (later Marshal of Armoured Forces) Katukov, pp. 202–28 (on 1st Guards Tank in Moscow battle); Gen. A.P. Beloborodov, pp. 229–45 (on Siberian troops); also table of Front, army and corps commanders, pp. 624–9.

Biryuzov, *op. cit.*, pp. 49–67 (operations of 132nd Rifle Div. in Bryansk encirclement operations).

Boldin, *op. cit.*, pp. 139–58 (defence of Tula, military deployment and civilian defence arrangements). See also under *I.D. Klimov* (notes to Ch. 6).

Koniev, I. 'Nachalo Moskovskoi bitvy', *VIZ*, 10 (1966), pp. 56–67. Though limited to a single article, this personal account by Col.-Gen. Koniev – Western Front commander at the end of September – amounts to a defence of his actions and decisions at the time of the Bryansk-Vyazma encirclement. In the first place Koniev insists that the Front command was not taken by surprise by the German offensive: on 26 September he submitted a report to Stalin and to the General Staff on the signs of impending German attack, as well as sending out an alert to his army commanders. The day before he had emphasized the concentration of German aircraft and asked for a strike against these airfields, plus additional air reinforcement for his own Front. Koniev considers that the general *Stavka* directive of 27 September was issued much too late and in any event the measures it demanded were already in hand within his command.

As for the encirclement, Koniev again insists that he did everything possible to organize the escape of the trapped Soviet armies, but this was hampered by the fact that the Front disposed of only horse-drawn transport for its artillery: by 7 October sixteen divisions from three armies (19th, 20th and 32nd Armies), plus the remnants of divisions of 24th Army of the Reserve Front were trapped. The 30th Army, having taken the brunt of the German attack, had been shattered and was falling back eastwards on Volokolamsk. Koniev issued orders on 8 October for the encircled divisions to fight their way out in the direction of Ghzatsk.

Molotov, Voroshilov and Vasilevskii, with others, arrived at Koniev's HQ: Molotov demanded that Koniev get the encircled men out and directed on Gzhatsk, at the same time assigning 4–5 divisions to a *Stavka* reserve for deployment on the Mozhaisk line. Koniev could only say that he had already issued the requisite orders, both to free his armies and to provide for the reserve force. In the event only one division arrived at Mozhaisk.

Disposing thus of the charge of having been taken unawares by the German offensive, as well as explaining the complexity of the encirclement, Koniev presents his own reasons for the massive Soviet defeat:

1. German forces held the strategic initiative and had 'crushing superiority' in men and weapons;

2. superior German mobility, Soviet inferiority in aircraft and anti-tank weapons which ruled out attempts to check German movement;

3. lack of Soviet weapons, ammunition, insufficient manpower and thus too few reserves;

4. a single break-through on Vyazma from the north might have been localized, but German forces broke into the rear of the Western Front from the south and there were no reserves to fight against this danger.

Nevertheless, 28 German divisions were involved in clearing the trapped Soviet divisions and thus time was gained to organize Soviet defences covering Moscow.

Lelyushenko, D.M., *Moskva-Stalingrad-Berlin-Praga*, Zapiski komandarma (Moscow: Nauka 1970), pp. 32–63 (Lelyushenko transferred from post as Deputy Chief/ Armoured Forces Administration to field command; assigned to southern Soviet flank and Guderian's thrust, defence of Mtsensk, takes over new Soviet 5th Army, fighting at Borodino).

Moskovskoe opolchenie, pp. 58–74 (Moscow militia divisions deployed in front line, early October, and man defensive lines).

Moskva-frontu, Sbornik dokumentov i materialy (Moscow: Nauka 1966), pt 1, pp. 11–110 (organization of the defence of Moscow); pt 2, pp. 111–238 (militia divisions, military divisions, evacuation of civilian population). These documents are printed almost wholly from archival sources.

Muriev, D.Z., *Proval operatsii 'Taifun'* (Moscow: Voenizdat 1972), 2nd edn, pt 2, pp. 40–83 (Soviet operations in October: Vyazma, Bryansk, Kalinin and W Front operations on the 'Mozhaisk line'). This is a useful monograph, which utilizes some archival material. It is basically a textbook with some popular touches, but again, the figures and the operational narratives are useful.

Proval gitlerovskogo nastuplenie na Moskvu, with foreword by Marshal M.V. Zakhorov (Moscow: Nauka 1966). This is a reprint of memoir material, acknowledged in the footnotes to the essays.

Rokossovskii, *op. cit.*, pp. 51–61 (ordered to mount counter-attack in Yukhnov sector,

assigned finally to Mozhaisk sector and then ultimately to area of Volokolamsk);
pp. 62–72 (deterioration of situation on w Front, mid-October; Dovator's 3rd Cav.
Corps escaped encirclement; attack by Germans on Rokossovskii's left flank; continued pressure on Volokolamsk; Boldin escapes from encirclement but General
Lukin lost in the process – later taken prisoner; continued German pressure on left
flank threatening Volokolamsk–Istra road).

Samsonov, A.M., *Velikya bitva pod Moskvoi 1941–1942* (Moscow: Academy of Sciences
1958), pp. 67–123 (mobilization of Moscow as a front-line city). Also *Velikaya bitva
pod Moskvoi*, Kratkii istoricheskii ocherk (Moscow: Voenizdat 1961), pp. 57–101
(analysis of the battle on the 'distant approaches' to Moscow, October 1941).

Sokolovskii, V.D., Marshal of the Soviet Union, *Razgrom Nemetsko-fashistskikh voisk pod
Moskvoi* (Moscow: Voenizdat 1964), pt 1, pp. 33–47 (Soviet operations on the
'western axis', October 1941). A short, succinct operational narrative, depicting the
main operations, Soviet strength, changes in command; see also the index and the
map supplement.

Vasilevskii materials: see *Delo vsei zhizni*, pp. 152–61 (October military operations on
the 'Moscow axis', General Staff's failure to discern German offensive design,
Bryansk–Vyazma collapse).

Yeremenko, *V nachale voiny*, pp. 338–91 (German advance in operation 'Typhoon',
German superiority, Gen. Yermakov's group cut off, Bryansk Front War Diary for
October 1941 quoted, Soviet troops forced back, Yeremenko wounded by bomb
splinters, reports that Stalin visits him in hospital).

Za Moskvu' za Rodinu (Moscow: Moskovskii Rabochii 1964), pp. 25–47 (Telegin on the
organization of the Moscow defensive zone); pp. 177–92 (Sbytov on his air reconnaissance mission, disbelief at German breakthrough, interrogation by NKVD).

Zhukov, G.K., *Vospominaniya*, pp. 318–32.

Soviet naval forces

Achkasov, V.I. and Pavlovich, N.B., *Sovetskoe Voenno-morskoe iskusstvo v Velikoi
Otechestvennoi voine* (Moscow: Voenizdat 1973), pp. 56–64 (mine-laying, mine
barriers); pp. 65–112 (defence of naval bases).

Krasnoznammennyi Baltiiskii Flot v bitve za Leningrad 1941–1944 gg. (Moscow: Nauka
1973), see under V.F. Tributs, pp. 34–50 (defence of Tallinn); A.A. Sagoyan, pp. 65–
74 (naval artillery in defence of Tallinn); V.I. Achkasov, pp. 82–96 (withdrawal of
Baltic Fleet to Kronstadt); V.F. Tributs, pp. 149–83 (Baltic Fleet in defence of
Leningrad).

Tributs, V.F., *Podvodniki Baltiki atakuyut* (Leningrad: Lenizdat 1963), pp. 9–31, Baltic
Fleet operations in late summer/autumn 1941.

V'yunenko, N.P., *Chernomorskaya flot v Velikoi Otechestvennoi voine* (Moscow: Voenizdat
1957), pp. 44–83. A useful narrative of the role of the Black Sea Fleet in the defence
of Odessa.

Vainer, *op. cit.*, pp. 11–39.

Soviet Air Force operations

Fedorov, *op. cit.*, pp. 37–121.

Sovetskie Voenno-vozdushnye sily . . . *1941–1945 gg.*, pp. 29–64 (Soviet Air Force operations, July–September 1941). This is a sparse narrative covering all Fronts, giving
total number of sorties flown but little operational information.

Periodicals

(Unsigned), 'Pravda o gibeli General M.P. Kirponosa', *VIZ*, 9 (1964), pp. 61–70 (eyewitness reports and retrospective investigations of the death of Gen. Kirponos).

'42-ya Armiya v boyakh za Leningrad', *Istoricheskii Arkhiv*, 2 (1959), pp. 68–88 (publication of 42nd Army War Diary (Ocherk po istorii boevykh deistvii 42-i armii, 1941–1945 gg.), compiled in 1945 by Operations Section/42nd Army Staff).

Achkasov, Navy Capt. V., 'Sryv planov nemetsko-fashistskogo komandovaniya po unichtozheniyu Krasnoznamennogo Baltiiskogo Flota', *VIZ*, 1 (1964), pp. 36–46 (German attacks on Soviet Baltic Fleet 1941–2).

Achkasov, 'Operatsiya po proryvu Krasnoznamennogo Baltiiskogo flota iz Tallina v Kronshtadt', *VIZ*, 10 (1966), pp. 19–31 (detailed documentary study of the Soviet withdrawal from Tallinn, which brought out two-thirds of the ships and 18,000 troops but also brought heavy losses; the command charged with evacuating Odessa was ordered to study the mistakes of the Tallinn evacuation and avoid them).

Bagramyan, I, 'Zapiski nachal'nika operativnogo otdela', *VIZ*, 1 (1967), pp. 48–62 and 3 (1964), pp. 52–68 (a pre-publication extract from *Tak nachinalas voina*, to judge by the text).

Bagramyan, I., 'Geroicheskaya oborona stolitsy Sovetskoi Ukrainy', *VIZ*, 10 (1963), pp. 53–66. 20th anniversary essay on the liberation of Kiev.

Biryukov, N., 'V dni Smolenskogo srazheniya', *VIZ*, 4 (1962), pp. 80–8 (186th Rifle Div. operations).

Khrenov, Col.-Gen./Engineers A., 'Evakuatsiya voisk s primorskogo platsdarma', *VIZ*, 3 (1964), pp. 17–31 (details of the evacuation directive, organization within Odessa and its execution – though Khrenov does not agree entirely with the assessment of the role of the staff of the Coastal Army presented by Petrov in *VIZ*, 7 (1962), No. 7, *loc. cit.*).

Kuznetsov, Admiral N.G., 'Voenno-morskoi flot nakanune Velikoi Otechestvennoi voine', *VIZ*, 9 (1966), pp. 65–7 (on the organization of the Soviet high command in July–August 1941).

'Ladozhskaya ledovaya doroga (1941–1943 gg.)', intro. by M.I.Tyazhikh, *Istoricheskii Arkhiv*, 3 (1959), pp. 3–30 (report on and statistics of 'Ladoga ice road').

Lelyushenko, D., 'Na Mozhaiskom napravlenii', *VIZ*, 9 (1962), pp. 22–6 (formation of Soviet 5th Army, defence on 'tank dangerous' axes, Borodino and Mozhaisk).

Peresypkin, I., 'Svyaz Generalnogo Shtaba', *VIZ*, 4 (1971), pp. 19–25 (Marshal/Signal Troops Peresypkin provides much-needed information on the organization and state of signals facilities between the centre and field staffs).

Petrov, I., 'Kharakternye epizody perioda oborny Odessy', *VIZ*, 7 (1962), pp. 58–65 (Konstantin Simonov, the novelist, received these notes from Gen. Petrov, who had promised the author help in writing his novel about the war; whatever its uses to literature, it remains an excellent summary of the Odessa defence).

Polyshkin, M., 'Operativenaya oborona v pervom periode Velikoi Otechestvennoi voiny', *VIZ*, 6 (1971), pp. 14–22 (Soviet defensive tactics in early period of war); see also *Razvitie taktiki Sovetskoi Armii v gody Velikoi Otechestvennoi voiny 1941–1945* (Moscow: Voenizdat 1958), pt 3 on Soviet defensive tactics, with detailed diagrams and maps).

6 THE REAR, THE DEEP REAR AND BEHIND THE GERMAN LINES

There is not to my knowledge any general social history of the Soviet Union at war available in either Soviet or non-Soviet writing. Much the same has to be said for the administrative history of the USSR during the war years, while the wartime economic effort and industrial mobilization have received only patchy treatment. Such Soviet attention as has been given to these themes generally follows the pattern of the 'heroic myth', thus obscuring the details of actual performance and response. The political delicacy of the whole subject – popular response and performance – cannot be denied and it is complicated by the fact that for so long and over such vast areas the Soviet governmental machine along with Soviet 'presence' was almost wholly excluded. And paradoxically, any investigation of Soviet success (or failure) in military-Party-administrative activities (such as the Defence Councils or Local Defence Committees) depends on looking into not organization as such but rather personal abilities on the part of select individuals. This axiom holds good in spite of the formal arrangement whereby Party leadership and personnel dominated all organizations.

It would be presumptuous to suggest that the supporting and reference material assembled here can provide more than a mere profile of the problems involved in social response and performance, as well as the whole economic and industrial aspect (and the agrarian scene). The material itself makes peculiar demands, consisting as it does of a mass of political pulp literature (serried ranks of heroes and heroines), official government decrees, wartime regulations, the Party's own prodigious output, highly specialized monographs on social and economic aspects of the wartime scene (food-supply, the agrarian scene, skilled manpower, finances, labour mobility) and equally specialized articles in a number of academic journals (though *Voprosy istorii* has included several of these items). In addition there is the massive series of documentary publications or specialized monographs covering both regions (Belorussia, Trans-Caucasus) and *oblasts*, mainly documents drawn from the archives. To these must be added some select 'city histories', which illuminate the role of the Party, the populace and wartime urban administration.

These regional and *oblast* documentary records also throw light on the origins and organization of the partisan movement (for example, *Orlovskaya oblast*, published in 1960, is an important source for a study of the partisan concentrations in the Bryansk forests), though the partisan movement is a major theme in itself. It is linked with the Party, the NKVD, the role of escaped Soviet prisoners or those marooned behind the German lines. As far as possible I have utilized material that illustrates both organization and performance in the field. The much-vaunted memoir literature and the dramatic 'diaries' need fairly close inspection, for there have been hints that not a few armchair partisans, bent on securing or inflating their reputations, put pen to paper.

The captured German documents (GMD) also furnish a great deal of information on Soviet performance and attitudes, often through the analysis of captured Soviet materials, the collection of statistical records, the mountains of captured mail and the evidence provided by either interrogation or defection. But more often than not this was a brutalized business, connected as it was with ruthless economic exploitation, the mechanics of sheer conquest, the helot status to be forced on the *Untermensch* and, not least, the unrestrained savagery of *Bandenkrieg* – and the very designation given by the Germans to the partisan war suggests little but outlawry. I have made some use of these materials (particularly the statistics and interrogation reports) but I must otherwise defer to that one masterly study, Alexander Dallin's *German Rule in Russia, 1941–1945: A Study of Occupation Policies* (London/New York: 1957), which probes extensively into the reactions of Soviet citizens to the Germans.

There is of course a whole dimension missing – the social fabric, including the role of Soviet women, the social administration of the country, medical services, the press, radio, transport and so on – but a social profile of the Soviet Union at war would be a separate enterprise.

It is at this juncture also that I have included J. Stalin's own published war speeches as part of the official record of the war – it is a slender volume and one now largely banished from Soviet bibliographies.

Armstrong, John A. (ed.), *Soviet Partisans in World War II* (Univ. Wisconsin Press 1964), pt I, pp. 73–88 (first efforts at partisan organization); pt 2, Case Studies, pp. 399–410 (Yelnaya–Dorogobuzh area); pp. 458–62 (Bryansk area); also pp. 653–67 (Appendix on 'Selected Soviet Sources'); pp. 668–76 ('Soviet Directives to Partisans'); pp. 677–86 ('Partisan tactics'). This exemplary work is absolutely indispensable for any study of the Soviet partisan movement. The section on sources is excellent and the appendices are packed with primary material.

Gallagher, Matthew P., *Soviet History of World War II*, pp. 103–27 (Soviet writers and the war).

Hesse, Erich, *Der Sowjetrussische Partisanenkrieg 1941–1944 im Spiegel deutscher Kampf-anweisungen und Befehle* (Göttingen: Musterschmidt 1969), 2, pp. 38–71 (origins of Soviet partisan movement, Soviet government appeals, early Soviet organization); also 4, pp. 107–11 (organization of partisan groups, autumn 1941).

Howell, Edgar M., *The Soviet Partisan Movement 1941–1944* (Washington: Dept. of the Army, Pamphlet No. 20–244, August 1956), p. 47 (Partisan Combat Battalions and Diversionary units, 10 July 1941 – placed under 10th Department of Red Army Political Administration).

Rigby, T.H., *Communist Party Membership in the U.S.S.R. 1917–1967* (Columbia University 1968), pt I, pp. 250–7 (general levels of Party membership in Soviet forces); pp. 257–71 (Party membership in partisan units and in civilian organizations in Soviet rear).

Werth, *Russia at War*, pp. 189–97 (autumn visit to the Smolensk Front); pp. 198–201 (advance on Leningrad); pp. 213–24 (evacuation of industry); also pt 7, pp. 710–26 (Soviet partisan movement); pp. 225–42 (beginning of battle of Moscow; great panic in October in Moscow – '*bol'shoi drap*', 'the great skedaddle', as Mr Werth called it, after one popular description; accounts of these crisis days culled from Soviet eye-witnesses).

Captured German materials

OKW/Abteilung für Wehrmachtpropaganda, T-77/R 1028, 6500451–735 (for period July–December 1941). This is an important file crammed with variegated materials on 'Fremde Staaten – Russland', which is political (including captured documents) and 'Wichtige Meldungen aus die Ostgebiete' (economic information, attitude of the local population) which came under the OKW/Wehrwirtschafts- und Rüstungsamt (Wi Rü Amt): see 6500692-5 ('Nachrichten über Petersburg Nr 6', 31 October 1941, on the food-supply system in Leningrad); also 6500707-14, from Abwehr II bei Hr. Gr. Süd ('Stimmung und Lage beim Einmarsch der deutschen Truppen', 28 October 1941); also 6500635-80, Wi Rü Amt folders on important Soviet military-industrial regions (Leningrad, Donets, Azov sea region).

The second collection (beginning frame 6500735) runs into 1942 but is interesting for the light it sheds on the evolution of political programmes and platforms among Soviet PWS (cf. the Shigunov papers): for examples of this type of political writing, see '. . . über die Bildung einer politischen Gegenregierung in Sowjet-Russland gegen Stalin' (February 1942) and 'Plan zur Bekämpfung und vollständigen Vernichtung des Bolschewismus in der U.d.S.S.R.' (March 1942). Such is the scope of this material that it would be useful to undertake a study of Soviet PWS and how their political ideas evolved; note that much of this activity predates the 'Vlasov movement'.

Tables: aircraft, armour, gun production
FHO Flugzeug-Produktion. T-78/R479, 6462305-11.
FHO Panzer-Produktion. T-78/R479, 6462293-9.
FHO UdSSR Geschützproduktion. T-78/R479, 6462447-50.

Railway operations
OKH/General der Eisenbahntruppen. Soviet railway construction and operations: technical details, but much material on the supply of Leningrad (with excellent air photographs of bridges and rail lines built on ice). T-78/R119, 6044128-636.

German Foreign Ministry files (Auswärtiges Amt)

Serial 270/175713-176028 ('GPU Official Shigunov'). This substantial file contains the interrogation of and notes by Shigunov, starting in September 1941. Shigunov supplied extensive notes on his own career, with details of the counter-espionage organization of the NKVD (training courses, instructors, internal organization in the USSR), notes on military commissars and the commissars of the 'Special sections' (NKVD) attached to Red Army units. Shigunov also commented on the formation of partisan units and their early activities.

Shigunov's notes extend to his observations on the type of government to be set up in Russia following a German victory; as such, these passages provide an illuminating commentary on political attitudes and Shigunov was certainly not alone in toying with these ideas. The bulk of the file is taken up with Shigunov's own handwritten material, notes and diagrams.

Psychological profiles of Soviet Air Force officers
Luftgaukommando II, Posen, 19 December 1941: 'Gutachten und Sondergutachten Soviet PWS' (Air Force personnel) (biographies, photographs and psychological profiles of captured Soviet fliers). T-78/R 489, 6474650-65.
Der sowjetische Soldat (Prize essay, Reichsführer SS: SS Hauptamt, date undetermined. Political and psychological profile of the Soviet soldier.) T-78/R 498, 6486044-95.
(Personal holding)
Manuscript: '*Die Behandlung des russischen Problems während der Zeit des ns. Regimes in Deutschland*'. Teil A, '*Die deutsche Russlandpolitik . . . insbesondere 1941 bis*

1943 . . .'. *Teil B*, 'Die Aktion des Generals Wlassow . . .'. See under *Teil A* (II), 'Die ersten Wochen nach dem deutschen Einmarsch in Russland' (attitude of civilian population, German administration in occupied areas, the Church and nationalist movements).

Bibliographical references

IVOVSS (6), bibliography, pp. 560–3. ('documents and materials' published in the Soviet Union, covering the main wartime legal enactments; investigations of German war crimes; documentary collections of regions and *oblasts*, also industry and trade unions). Useful for tracing certain wartime and early post-war publications. See also pp. 574–85 (bibliography of Soviet writing on Soviet military operations and war effort, with some wartime material cited, though the bulk covers publication in the late 1950s and early 1960s).

Narodnoe khozyaistvo SSSR v gody Velikoi Otechestvennoi voiny (1941–1945), Bibilografi-cheskii ukazatel' knizhnoi i zhurnal'noi literatury na russkom yazyke (1941–1968 gg.) (Moscow: Nauka 1971): i) general material on Soviet war economy; ii) war economy in separate regions; iii) war economy also by regions; iv) state direction of wartime economy; v) food supply and rationing system; vi) labour and distribution/mobility of working class; vii) industry and shift to war footing; viii) agriculture; ix) wood and forestry; x) fishing industry; xi) hunting; xii) transport; xiii) communications and transport; xiv) state purchases; xv) trade; xvi) finances, budget and credit; xvii) urban economy, reconstruction; xviii) economy in occupied regions and restoration of economy. NOTE: this bibliography contains a 'bibliography of bibliographies', a very detailed name and collective work/official publication index, as well as an index of geographical names. It is exceedingly useful for main trends, though it is somewhat short on particular industries such as the electrical industry.

Government and Party decrees, regulations, Party mobilization, Party-political work, Komsomol

IVOVSS (6) (1965), pp. 41–143.

Kommunisticheskaya partiya v period Velikoi Otechestvennoi voiny 1941–1945, Dokumenty i materialy (Moscow: Gospolitizdat 1961), pp. 83–129 (government and Party decrees 1941–2).

Kommunisticheskaya Partiya v Velikoi Otechestvennoi voine (Iyun 1941 g–1945 g) (Moscow: Politizdat 1970):

i) Government decrees and regulations – declaration of state of war, mobilization decree, wartime working hours, Party and Soviet organizations in front-line *oblasts*, creation of State Defence Committee (GKO), compulsory civil defence training, penalties against rumour-mongering and spreading panic, organization of armed struggle in German rear, universal military training, creation of All-Union Committee for Aid to War Wounded (pp. 37–59).

ii) Announcements and speeches by Party and government leaders; Stalin's radio broadcast, 3 July 1941 (pp. 145–50).

iii) Activity of Party organizations at the front, in the rear and in German-occupied territory. Articles: 'Luchshie boitsy i komandiry vstupayut v Partiyu' ('The best fighting men and commanders join the Party'); 'Politotdel divizii v boevoi obstanovke' ('Division political section in a combat situation') (pp. 265–8).

iv) The Rear. Komsomol (Youth Organisation): the Komsomol and war work, 23 June 1941 (pp. 312–14). *Oblast, obkom, gorkom* Party committee resolutions on mobilization, Party's wartime tasks, defence measures in front-line areas, cities and towns (pp. 317–47).

Partiino-politicheskaya rabota v Sovetskikh vooruzhennykh silakh v Velikoi Otechestvennoi voiny 1941–1945 (Moscow: Voenizdat 1968), pp. 13–127. (Party political work in early weeks of war; role of commanders and political organs in reinforcing discipline; role of Party-political work in defence of Leningrad, Kiev and Odessa.)

Kirsanov, N.A., *Partiinye mobilizatsii na front v gody Velikoi Otechestvennoi voiny* (Moscow: Univ. Moscow 1972). A scholarly monograph on Party and *Komsomol* 'mobilizations' for front-line units and military organizations, including the militia divisions; the study is divided into two parts – general mobilizations and local Party mobilizations – with an informative section on Party and *Komsomol* involvement in raising 'national formations', the non-Russian nationalities – Armenian, Georgian and Azerbaidzhan divisions.

Petrov, *op. cit.*, pp. 341–63.

Ocherki istorii Moskovskoi organizatsii KPSS 1883–1965 (Moscow: Moskovskii Rabochii 1965), pp. 562–82 (placing capital on a war footing, mobilization of the Party and the population, autumn 1941).

Shpak, A.A., *Podvig yunosti* (Petrozadovsk: Kareliya 1969) (Karelian *Komsomol* in wartime).

Stalin, I.V. (J. Stalin), *O Velikoi Otechestvennoi Voine Sovetskogo Soyuza* (Moscow: Gospolitizdat 1953), 5th edn. Collected speeches.

Voropaev, D.A. and Iovlev, A.M., *Bor'ba KPSS za sozdanie voennykh kadrov* (Moscow: Voenizdat 1960), 2nd edn, pp. 189–222 (recruitment and training of command and political staff – officers and Party-political personnel – in wartime, as well as work of command/political training schools; also promotion of NCOs and rank-and-file soldiers).

War economy, industrial mobilization, industrial evacuation

IVOVSS (2), Soviet war economy, pp. 138–76 (new ammunition production plan, promulgated 6 June, put into effect 23 June; 30 June, national economic mobilization plan for 3rd quarter of 1941 activated; 4 July, GKO accepts recommendations of Voznesenskii's commission for full mobilization of national resources, including evacuation of major industrial enterprises to E and exploitation of fuel/raw materials base in E; 3 July, GKO – having accepted ammunition production plan – decided on transfer of armaments plants to Siberia and to Volga regions; provision for tank and tank-engine production in Siberia; 16 August, 4th quarter plan for 1941 and 1942 accepted for production schedules and quotas, Volga regions, Urals, W-Siberia, Kazakhstan and Central Asia; *Sovet po evakuatsii* under Shvernik, with Kosygin as deputy, established 24 June 1941; evacuation of Leningrad munition plants and personnel; 25 October, GKO decision to set up special Evacuation Commission under Mikoyan to supervise evacuation of factories from front-line regions; heavy demands on railway equipment caused GKO to set up special railway transit group headed by Mikoyan, with Kosygin, Voznesenskii and Khrulev as members; *Sovet po evakuatsii* disbanded and handed over to *Komitet po razgruzke* (transportation committee); 1,523 industrial plants evacuated to the E (1,360 major plants) in period July–November 1941; production started up again in E – 19 October, tank plant evacuated from Kharkov; 8 December, first batch of 25 T-34 tanks produced for front from newly established plant. Aviation industry: produced 15,735 aircraft in 1941 excluding naval aircraft. Tank production: Urals Heavy Machine Construction plant produced armoured chassis and by GKO decision went into serial production after 1 July; Chelyabinsk Tractor Plant produced heavy tanks and tank engines; in second half of 1941 Soviet industry produced 728 KVs, 1,853 T-34s and 1,548 T-60s, though production fell off sharply in November. Ammunition production: from August to November 303 plants put out of commission, with output reaching only 50–60 per cent of planned levels. New production plans for period November 1941–January 1942: annual average tank production to reach 22,000 machines and not less than 22–25,000 combat aircraft.)

Arutyunyan, Yu. V., *Sovetskoe krest'yanstvo v gody Velikoi Otechestvennoi voiny* (Moscow: Acad. of Sciences 1963), pp. 25–62 (effect of war/mobilization on peasantry; evacuation of population and grain stocks; Party-political work in villages) (2nd edn, 1970).

Boiko, Col. I., 'Tyl Zapadnogo fronta v pervye dni Otechestvennoi voiny', *VIZ*, 8 (1966), pp. 15–26. An important and detailed study of the logistics/supply position on the Soviet W Front early in the war, the decentralized 'rear services' – *tyl* – organization, repair and resupply facilities.

Chadayev, Ya. E., *Ekonomika SSSR v period Velikoi Otechestvennoi voiny (1941–1945 gg.)* (Moscow: Mysl 1965). A general outline, though with few references.

Dokuchayev, G.A., *Sibirskii tyl v Velikoi Otechestvennoi voine* (Novosibirsk: Nauka 1968), pp. 28–88 (Siberia on war-footing, reception of evacuated industry, new economic links).

Rabochii klass Sibiri i Dal'nego Vostoka v gody Velikoi Otechestvennoi voiny (Moscow: Nauka 1973), pp. 56–121 (economic mobilization, reception of evacuated industries, new fuels/raw materials discovered and exploited). These are two highly detailed, scholarly and invaluable studies on economic mobilization deep in the Soviet interior.

Eshelony idut na vostok. Iz istorii perebazirovaniya proizvoditel'nyk sil SSSR v 1941–1942 gg. (Moscow: Nauka 1966), pp. 15–30 (evacuation of population from war-zones); pp. 31–53 (movement of heavy industry); pp. 116–40 (railway operations). This entire volume is of great interest and utility.

Gladkov, I.A. (ed), *Sovetskaya ekonomika v period Velikoi Otechestvennoi voiny 1941–1945* (Moscow: Nauka 1970). It covers Soviet industry at large, industry at the republic level and its role in the war economy, labour mobility and labour forces, the agrarian sector, transport, trade and consumer goods supply in wartime, finances, health.

Istoriya Tul'skogo oruzheinogo zavoda 1712–1972 (Moscow: Mysl 1973), pp. 246–62 (the Tula arms works goes over to war-footing, evacuation of some industrial resources, Tula arms works under siege conditions).

Iz istorii Sovetskoi intelligentsii (Moscow: Mysl 1966), see under G.P. Veselov, pp. 39–82 (on Soviet professions and professional training for qualified personnel and specialists in wartime).

Khrulev, A.V., 'Stanovlenie strategicheskogo tyla v Velikoi Otechestvennoi voine', *VIZ*, 6 (1961), pp. 64–80 (on the Soviet 'Rear Services'/Logistics, which Khrulev commanded).

Kostyuchenko, S., Khrenov, I. and Fedorov, Yu., *Istoriya Kirovskogo zavoda 1917–1945* (Moscow: Mysl 1966), pp. 588–634 (organization of war production; production of arms in Leningrad Kirov factory; conditions under early onset of the blockade).

Kravchenko, G. (Col./Dr of Economic Sciences), 'Ekonomicheskaya pobeda Sovetskogo naroda ve Velikoi Otechestvennoi voine', *VIZ*, 4 (1965), pp. 37–47. A survey of the Soviet war effort.

Kumanev, *op. cit.*, pp. 30–95 (details of railway operation, organization, new line construction, supplying field armies and role in evacuation of industry to eastern hinterland).

Levshin, B.V., *Akademiya Nauk SSSR v gody Velikoi Otechestvennoi voiny* (Moscow: Nauka 1966), ch. 1 (wartime mobilization of the Academy of Sciences, including evacuation of institutes to the E); ch. 2 (scientific assistance to the Soviet armed forces and war industry); ch. 3 (work of Academy in surveying, assessing and exploiting new natural resources in the eastern hinterland – fuel, iron ore and also assistance to agriculture).

Nikitin, Col. A., 'Perestroika raboty voennoi promyshlennosti SSSR v pervom periode Velikoi Otechestvennoi voiny', *VIZ*, 2 (1963), pp. 11–20. An important article on the attempted conversion of Soviet industry to wartime requirements. The effect of evacuation on production and the loss of raw material bases; the author seems to have taken special care with his figures, especially ammunition and tank production figures for the latter half of 1941.

Voznesenskii, N., *Voennaya ekonomika SSSR v period Otechestvennoi voiny* (Moscow: Gospolitizdat 1948). This slender volume, also available in an American transl., is still useful and bears the name of the man who was the brains behind Soviet wartime economic and industrial mobilization, only to be shot as a result of the 'Leningrad affair' after the war.

Volkotrubenko, I.I., 'Boepripasy i artsnabzhenie v Velikoi Otechestvennoi voine', *Voprosy istorii*, 11 (1972), pp. 82–91 (small arms ammunition, artillery rounds, grenades and mine production; also gun-production). See also under GMD.

Partisan movement

IVOVSS (2), pp. 119–38. (29 June, *Sovnarkom* and Central Committee directive on partisan operations; 18 July, special instructions on partisan activity; 30 June, Ukraine sets up 'operational group' for partisans; formation of 'detachments', *otryady* in Ukraine under supervision of Party committees and Party organizations; Minsk 'underground Party centre' established by authority of Belorussian Party Central Committee; 1 July, Directive No. 2 from Central Committee on partisan operations: to set up partisan detachments in all occupied areas; partisan groups and shadow underground organizations set up in W *oblasts* – Smolensk, Moscow, Kalinin, Kursk, Orel and Tula; role of military soviets, 'operational groups' and partisan staffs; beginning of co-ordination of partisan operations with Red Army in the field; relations between partisans and population under German rule in occupied territory; German anti-partisan measures.) NOTE: this 'official history' is an unrivalled source for the chronology and organization of the partisan movement, that is, dates of directives or instructions and the role of the Party and military bodies, such as the military soviets.

Absalyamov, M. and Andrianov, V., 'Taktika sovetskikh partizan', *VIZ*, 1 (1968), pp. 42–55. One of the few studies of partisan *tactics* – ambush, lightning raids, etc.

Bogatyr, Z.A., *Bor'ba v tylu vraga* (Moscow: Mysl 1969), 2nd edn. This is intended to be a scholarly account of the Soviet partisan movement as opposed to the 'subjective' first-person memoirs and popularized histories, though the author was himself commissar of a major partisan unit.

Bychkov, L.N., *Partizanskoe dvizhenie v gody Velikoi Otechestvennoi voiny 1941–1945, Kratkii ocherk* (Moscow: Mysl 1965), pp. 41–112 (organization of partisan movement, partisan assistance to Red Army during early period of war).

Istochnikovedenie istorii Sovetskogo obshchestva (Moscow: Nauka 1964), see under A.A. Kurnosov, pp. 289–319 (review of personal memoirs by participants in partisan movement).

Kalinin, P., *Partizanskaya respublika* (Minsk: Belarus 1968), 2nd edn, pt 1, pp. 28–88 (details of organization of Belorussian partisan movement, initial organization and recruitment, role of the Party and NKVD).

Kalinin, Col. P., 'Uchastie sovetskikh voinov v partizanskom dvizhenii Belorussi', *VIZ*, 10 (1962), pp. 24–40 (very informative discussion by Kalinin, former chief of Belorussian Partisan Staff, of role of Soviet PWs and those marooned behind the German lines in Soviet partisan movement. It is noteworthy for a discussion of the double defector, Gil-Radionov, a Soviet colonel from 29th Rifle Div., a PW in 1941, who formed a pro-German anti-partisan battalion and then negotiated his return to the Soviet partisans from his 'SS Russian' regiment. See also on V.I. Nichiporovich).

Lesnyak, Col. T., 'Nekotorye voprosy organizatsii i vedeniya partizanskoi bor'by v pervye mesyatsi voiny', *VIZ*, 9 (1963), pp. 30–8. A concise but informative essay on the early origins of the partisan movement, from the first 'detachments' (*otryady*) and 'combat groups' to larger units with command and political staff; lack of communication and the isolation of separate small detachments led at first to heavy losses, but this was slowly remedied by co-ordination and brigading partisan forces; the figures for strength and distribution are taken from Party and military archives.

Logunova, *op. cit.*, ch. 1 (on the origins and early activities of the Party underground and partisan groups in the w/central regions).

Nepokorennaya zemlya Pskovskaya 1941–1944. Dokumenty i materialy (Pskov: Pskovskaya Pravda 1964), see under Documents, pp. 15–85 (collection of Party records, wall newspapers, partisan detachment diaries and operational notebooks – all original and presumably genuine).

Partizany Bryanshchiny, Sbornik materialov i dokumenty, 2nd edn (Tula: 'Priokskoe Knizh. Izd. 1970), pt 1, pp. 17–77 (organization of the Communist underground and partisan units 1941).

Petrov, *op. cit.*, ch. 1 and 2 (origins, early history of Leningrad *oblast* partisan movement).

Ponomarenko, P., 'Bor'ba Sovetskogo naroda v tylu vraga', *VIZ*, 4 (1965), pp. 26–36. A general survey of the Soviet partisan movement by the wartime chief of the Central Partisan Staff. Though an 'official history' of the partisan movement compiled by Ponomarenko was mooted and even mentioned in the mid-1960s, to my knowledge this study never appeared, though that is not to say that it does not exist in a classified version.

Rudakov, Lt.-Gen. M., 'Rol voennykh sovetov frontov i armii v rukovodstve boevymi deistviyami partizan v gody Velikoi Otechestvennoi voiny', *VIZ*, 7 (1962), pp. 3–14. (Traces the organization of special 'Partisan staffs' within the command structures of Military Soviets of Fronts and particular armies, starting with 'operational groups' and the supervisory work carried out by the Political Administrations in Fronts and armies; these same 'operational groups' also set up training schools and instruction courses; in 1942 these 'groups' became fully fledged 'Partisan staffs', by which time the entire partisan movement had its own Central Staff.)

Samukhin, V.P., *Volkhovskie partizany* (Leningrad: Lenizdat 1969), pp. 23–47 (organiza-tion of Volkhov partisans – *mestnye otrady* – local detachments).

Sovetskie partizany (Moscow: Gospolitizdat 1960 and 1963). Sixteen specialist studies, dealing with Soviet partisan and political activities in E Europe.

Voina v tylu vraga. O nekotorykh problemakh istorii sovetskogo partizanskogo dvizheniya v gody Velikoi Otechestvennoi voiny (Moscow: Politizdat 1974) (1 *vypusk*), pp. 98–114. On the organization of Soviet partisan forces.

Zalesskii, A.I., *V partizanskikh krayakh i zonakh* (Moscow: Izd. Sotsial.-Ekonomicheskoi lit. 1962), pp. 49–86 (creation of partisan regions and zones).

Zarozhdenie i razvitie partizanskogo dvizheniya v pervyi period voiny, 1941–1942 (Minsk: Belarus 1967) (vol. I of a three-volume series published by Belorussian CP and Historical Institute, Belorussian Academy of Sciences). An important collection of documentary material covering 1941-2, with useful name, geographical/district indexes and notes to the documents.

Social policy

IVOVSS (2), pp. 546–83 (evacuation of population, rationing and food-supply; 5,914,000 persons evacuated to rear areas by spring 1942; fall-off in consumer goods – 5,500 factories out of 10,400 under German occupation; food supply for workers under *Glavnoe upravlenie rabochego snabzheniya*, state aid to families of servicemen; education and public health policies; literature and art under wartime conditions). NOTE: this is one of the most comprehensive accounts of wartime social policies, ranging from food-supply to general welfare policies – family allowances, pensions and support for the families of servicemen, provision for orphans etc.

Soviet rations

Calorific value of foodstuffs for varying norms of supply (rations)*

Category of person (also types of additional supply)	Calories per day
dependants	780
officials receiving	
400g bread	1,074
or	
450g bread	1,176
workers receiving	
additional 500g bread	1,387
600g bread	1,592
workers supplied by	
'special list' and receiving	
500g bread	1,503
700g bread	1,913

Category of person (also types of additional supply)	Calories per day
workers supplied by special norms (foundry workers, heavy industry)	3,181
workers supplied with special high norms (underground miners, other physically demanding work)	3,460
miners supplied by special high norms and receiving cold breakfasts/midday meal	4,114
miners supplied with special high norms and receiving in addition a second hot meal	4,418

★ See U.G. Chernyavskii, *Voina i prodovol'stve. Snabzhenie gorodskogo naseleniya v Velikuyu Otechestvennuyu voiny 1941–1945 gg.* (Moscow: Nauka 1964), text, tables and bibliography.

Soviet women in wartime

Murmantseva, V., 'Sovetskie zhenshchiny v Velikoi Otechestvennoi voine 1941–1945 godov', *VIZ*, 2 (1968), pp. 47–54, Soviet women in front-line and auxiliary military service: in Red Army medical services 41 per cent of doctors, 43 per cent of medical/ nursing assistants, 100 per cent of nurses and 30 per cent of medical staff awarded medals and decorations were women; in anti-aircraft defence (PVO), in the special Moscow PVO force 30·5 per cent were women, and 34·5 per cent on the N Front serving as pilots and aircrew with the Soviet Air Force were 3 women's regiments (46th Night Bomber Regiment, 125th Day Bomber Regiment and 586th Fighter Regiment); women also served as snipers and tank crew with the Red Army, as well as manning offices, military traffic control, auxiliary services; labour in industry and agriculture; of all Soviet women on active service with the Soviet armed forces (including the partisans), 86 were awarded the decoration Hero of the Soviet Union.

V groznye gody (Petrozavodsk: Kareliya 1970), 2nd edn. A collection of documents dealing with the wartime achievements of the women of Karelia.

Medical

Ivanov, F.I., *Reaktivnye psikhozy v voennoe vremya* (Leningrad: Meditsina 1970), pp. 49–71 (on psychological disorder, illness, also depressive and paranoid forms).

Kuz'min, M.K., *Mediki – Geroi Sovetskogo Soyuza* (Moscow: Meditsina 1970) (biographies of Soviet military doctors and medical personnel who received the highest Soviet decoration).

Vyshnevskii, A.A. (Col.-General/Medical Services), *Dnevnik khirurga* (Moscow: Meditsina 1970, 2nd edn). Wartime notes and diaries of the present Senior Military Surgeon, Soviet Defence Ministry, with foreword by Marshal Zhukov.

Literature and the press

Denisov, N.N., *1418 dnei frontovogo korrespondenta* (Moscow: Voenizdat 1969). Wartime assignments of a war-correspondent with *Krasnaya Zvedzda*.

Pavlovskii, A., *Russkaya Sovetskaya poeziya v gody Velikoi Otechestvennoi voiny* (Leningrad: Nauka 1967), pp. 22–74 (early months of the war and poetry in relation to morale). I had the occasion to discuss this subject with Alexander Surkov, whose verse – often written on the side of a tank at the front – had a great impact.

Reportazh s frontov voiny (Moscow: Politizdat 1970), pp. 11–103 (reprints of wartime articles 1941).

Tvardovskii, A., 'Rodina i chuzhbina: stranitsy zapisnoi knizhki', *Znamya*, 11–12 (1974). This reconstruction of a wartime diary, which throws much realistic light on the social impact of the war, is quoted and analysed at length in Gallagher, *Soviet History, op. cit.*, pp. 113–18; also the case of Olga Dzhigurda's diary, 'Teplokhod "Kakhetia"; zapiski voennogo vracha', in *Znamya*, 1–2 (1948), defended for its realism by the famous partisan commander Vershigora – who was steadily downgraded from his partisan eminence for this and other spirited defences of realism and honesty; see Gallagher, pp. 118–25 on the Dzighurda diary.

Voennye byli (Moscow: Izvestiya 1969), pp. 151–235 (reprints of wartime articles from *Izvestiya* for 1941–2).

Zhukov, S.I., *Frontovaya pechat' v gody Velikoi Otechestvennoi voiny* (Moscow: Univ. Moscow 1968). A very useful study of front-line newspapers.

Soviet Far East: Japanese threat, movement of Soviet troops

Japanese Special Studies on Manchuria

Study of Strategical and Tactical Peculiarities of Far Eastern Russia and Soviet Far East Forces, XIII (Military History Section: Headquarters, US Army Forces Far East). See pp. 64–6, 'westward movement of Soviet forces'; pp. 64–6: redeployment of Soviet troops to the W began in March 1941, accelerated after the outbreak of war – by the end of 1941 more than half the divisional strength (15 rifle divs, 3 cav. divs) had moved to the European battle front, plus 1,700 tanks and 1,500 aircraft: distribution of forces moved: from Ussuri area 5 Rifle Divs, 1 cav. div., 3 tank bdes; from Amur area 2 Rifle Divs, 1 air div., 1 tank bde; from Trans-Baikal 7 Rifle Divs, 2 cav. divs, 3 air divs, 2 tank bdes; from Outer Mongolia 1 Rifle Div., 2 tank bdes.

In July 1941 the Japanese set in train the Kwantung Army 'Special Manoeuvres' which, after 2–3 months, had doubled Japanese strength in Manchuria: the Soviet Union also carried out local mobilizations in the Far Eastern regions to replace transferred troops and by December 1941 had raised 8 rifle divs, 1 cav. div, 3 tank bdes and 1 air div. Full mobilization of the Soviet Far East produced a manpower strength of 800,000 men, an increase of 100,000 over 1940 estimates and explained by war mobilization. See also: *Japanese Operational Planning Against the USSR*, 1 (Japanese Special Study on Manchuria); *Japanese Intelligence Planning against the USSR*, x (Japanese Special Studies); *Japanese Preparations for Operations in Manchuria (Prior to 1943)*, no vol. no. (Japanese Monograph no. 77).

Transfer of Soviet forces from Soviet Far East

See T-78/R486, 6470809-42.

FHO (IIa) Nr 668/43 g Kdos, Betr: Fernost. *Anlage 1* ('Gliederung der Fernost-Streitkräfte'), *Anlage 2* (movement of Soviet Far Eastern forces to European battle fronts).

This is a highly detailed and very useful report, which examines the Soviet Far East forces in detail; it also formed the basis of a German *démarche* to Japan, protesting at the Japanese attitude that allowed the Soviet Union a free hand in transferring troops westwards.

Savin, Lt.-Col. A., 'Podgotovka Yaponii k voine protiv SSSR v 1941 godu', *VIZ*, 6 (1971), pp. 38–47. Aims to prove that the Japanese used the Soviet-Japanese Neutrality Pact as a screen behind which to prepare war on the Soviet Union in 1941. The *Kantokuen* plan ('Special Manoeuvres of the Kwantung Army') was, in effect, a war plan envisaging the main Japanese thrust being mounted by the 1st Front's flank and prepared its own offensive against Zavitaya–Kuibyshevka. Hence the reinforcement of the Kwantung Army in the autumn of 1941. Japanese forces were poised for a lightning blow against the USSR in the late summer of 1941, but the confidence of the Japanese high command in a rapid German victory had waned by the end of July. None the less, even while preparing for war against the USA and Great Britain, the Japanese command intensified its war preparations against the USSR.

Soviet appraisals of wartime performance

Babalashvili, I., *Voiny-gruziny v boyakh za Ukrainu v gody Velikoi Otechestvennoi voiny* (Tbilisi: Izd. Sabchota Sakarvelo 1969), chs I–III (Georgian troops in military operations in the Ukraine and Crimea, 1941–2).

Burov, A.V. (ed.), *Tvoi geroi, Leningrad* (Leningrad: Lenizdat 1969), 2nd edn. A collection of biographies and the military records of those awarded high decorations during the defence and siege of Leningrad.

Geroi Velikoi Otechestvennoi Voiny, Rekomendatel'nyi ukazatel' literatury (Moscow: Kniga 1970); pp. 77–108, checklist of biographies of Soviet heroes (including intelligence operators, partisans and the Soviet underground in German concentration camps). More than 7 million members of the Soviet armed forces were awarded decorations; 11,000 received the decoration Hero of the Soviet Union, 111 were awarded that decoration twice and 2 Soviet Air Force officers – A. I. Pokryshkin and I. N. Kozhedub – received this award three times.

Golikov, S., *Vydayushchiesya pobedy Sovetskoi Armii v Velikoi Otechestvennoi voine* (Moscow: Gospolitizdat 1952). I have included this among 'official' publications, since it was an ossified and almost classic exposition, of the Stalinist line on the war.

Gor'kovchane v Velikoi Otechestvennoi voine 1941–1945 (Gorkyi: Volgo–Vyatskoe Izd 1970).

Istoriya Moskvy 1941–1965 (Moscow: Nauka 1967), pp. 14–73 (Moscow on a war-footing; also evacuation of the Soviet capital).

Klimov, I.D., *Geroicheskaya oborona Tuly* (Moscow: Voenizdat 1961). Useful account of the Tula Defence Committee.

Kondaurov, I.A., *Ratnyi podvig Kommunistov Prikam'ya 1941–1945* (Perm: Kn. Izd-vo 1970). Perm *oblast* contribution to Soviet war effort, including history of military units raised (see appendix, pp. 321–35).

Korkodinov, Maj.-Gen. P., 'Fakty i mysli o nachal'nom periode Velikoi Otechestvennoi voiny', *VIZ*, 10 (1965), pp. 26–34. A relatively rare critique of the initial period of the war, with reference to Soviet *performance* as a whole.

Radi zhizni na zemle (Voronezh: Tsentralnoe-chernozemnoe Izd. 1970). City of Voronezh, with valuable introductory essay by Marshal Vaskilevskii.

Sinitsyn, A., 'Iz istorii sozdaniya dobrovol'cheskikh chastei i soyedinenii Sovetskoi Armii', *VIZ*, 1 (1973), pp. 11–17, statistics of Soviet volunteer formations raised in wartime.

Telpukhovskii, Maj.-Gen. B.S., *Velikaya Otechestvennaya voina Sovetskogo Soyuza*

1941–1945 (Moscow: Gospolitizdat 1959). A work which teeters uneasily between a quasi-Stalinist line and the newer realism.

V plameni i slave, Ocherki istorii Sibiriskogo voennogo okruga (Novosibirsk: Zapadno-sibirskoe Kn. Izd-vo 1969), pt III, pp. 113–337 (Siberian military units on European battlefronts).

Voronezhskii dobrovol'cheskii (Voronezh: Tsentralnoe-chernozemnoe Kn. Izd-vo 1972). Reminiscences and combat record of 4th Guards Voronezh Rifle Div.

7 THE MOSCOW COUNTER-STROKE: NOVEMBER–DECEMBER 1941

Few would dispute that the historiography of the battle for Moscow – whether Soviet or German – is massive, controversial and in parts not a little confused. My concern here has been to work largely within the confines of the Soviet material, buttressing it where necessary with the substance of German war diaries and select German accounts. As for English accounts, I have deferred of necessity to Colonel Seaton's *Battle for Moscow*, which has thoroughly sieved the German material and which takes account of Soviet versions.

It was not until 1964 that anything approaching a definitive Soviet account of the battle appeared, in Marshal Sokolovskii's volume *Razgrom nemetsko-fashistskikh voisk pod Moskvoi*. The book was compiled by a group of generals and colonels (working presumably through the Military-Historical Section of the Soviet General Staff) and involving what appears to have been a thorough search of the military archives – the overwhelming majority of the references in the book consists of archival citations. Having seen such a group of officer-specialists at work, I can vouch for their professionalism and the rectitude with which such archival materials are handled, for which reason I repose a great deal of confidence in the Sokolovskii volume. There remains, of course, the problem of the memoir literature, not infrequently touched up to suit prevailing political fashions or to inflate personal reputations. The Party literature, if it can be called that, is naturally disposed and deployed to extol the fortitude and valour of the populace at large, as well as the all-important role of the Party itself.

Inevitably Stalin looms over this story, though he appears in several guises (again, not unconnected with political fashions). Zhukov shows him in several roles – arbitrary and interfering, iron-nerved, seized with doubts, the extraordinary military quartermaster who handed out '10–15 anti-tank rifles' only on being wheedled into it, a military Levantine who wanted a good return on the military loans he doled out. Oozing out of other accounts are descriptions of his extraordinary deviousness combined with what can only be called recklessness, 'doing deals' with individual commanders to ram the counter-offensive out as far and as fast as possible. Belov (whose description of Stalin Col. Seaton is inclined to discount as sheer contrivance) is less flattering. What is noticeable about the Belov account is its realism, as opposed to other literary posturing – tough, battle-hardened and almost cynically inured to the foibles of his political and military masters, Belov at least communicates the grimness of the situation. And there is other evidence to the effect that Stalin did not continually exude confidence.

The technical military analysis provides yet another dimension: the complicated tale of how clearing the Germans away from Moscow became a roaring and at times desperate counter-offensive, stripping the flesh off the Red Army, straggles out of the memoirs. But the same cannot be said for a study such as that by Col. Zhelanov (*VIZ*, 12 (1964), which is unrelenting in its analysis of this 'hand-to-mouth' counter-offensive. In the same vein the Sokolovskii volume identifies strategic blunders and tactical short-comings with cool professionalism. The same might be said, for example, about retro-spective appraisals of the Kerch–Feodosiya operation, and a number of others.

It is for this reason – the dichotomy (or the gulf) – separating the memoir material and the technical analysis of Soviet planning and operations – that I have divided them here, treating the memoirs first and assembling the analyses under a different heading. At times, however, the line is difficult to draw.

Carell, *op. cit.*, pt 1, pp. 167–341.

Preston Chaney Jr, Otto, *Zhukov* (Univ. of Oklahoma Press/Newton Abbot: David & Charles 1972), pp. 139–85 (battle of Moscow, using portions of Zhukov's memoirs published in *VIZ* and other extracts).

Goure, *op. cit.*, p. 202.

Hofman, Rudolf, 'The Battle for Moscow 1941', in *Decisive Battles of World War II: the German view*, ed H.A. Jacobsen and J. Rohwehr (London: André Deutsch 1965), pp. 137–78.

Von Manstein, *op. cit.*, pt 3, pp. 204–27 (the Crimean campaign; 17 September, assumes command 11th Army; composition of Rumanian forces; struggle for approaches to Crimea and breakthrough into Ishun; 16 November, all of Crimea except Sevastopol in German hands; first assault on Sevastopol; effect of winter weather; storming of heights and heavy fighting for pill-boxes; impact of Soviet landing on Kerch peninsula; no mere Soviet diversion but formidable threat due to weight of Soviet troops behind it; Soviet landing at Feodosiya; German 42nd Corps orders withdrawal from Kerch peninsula; Manstein countermands this order).

Philippi and Heim, *op. cit.*, pt 1, pp. 94–106.

Salisbury, *op. cit.*, pt 4, pp. 376–422.

Seaton, *Russo-German War*, pp. 192–241.

Seaton, *Battle for Moscow*, pp. 147–228.

Turney, *Disaster at Moscow*, pp. 128–66.

Werth, *Russia at War*, pt 2, pp. 243–328.

German war diaries (KTB)

Halder/KTB, III, entries 3 November 1941–31 December 1941, pp. 277–370.

OKW/KTB, I, Tagesmeldungen (Gen. St./op. Abt.), pp. 735–873 (1 November–30 December 1941); also under Appendices (D), *Chronik*, November–December, pp. 1235–43.

GMD and materials

Order No. 0089 (26 October 1941). Russian original of c-in-c/Crimea (Vice-Admiral Levchenko) on command appointments, reorganization Coastal Army, composition 'Crimea forces'. T-78/R464, 6443373–6.

OKH, op. Abt. ('Barbarossa Band 3') ('Beurteilung der Kampfkraft des Ostheeres', 6 November 1941; heavy losses in combat; sickness rate rising in infantry divisions; great shortage of equipment in Panzer regiments – an *effective* total strength of 65 inf. divs, 8 Panzer divs, 8 motorized inf. divs. This is to say that out of 136 formations in the order of battle, 83 alone are fitted for combat). T-78/R335, 6291878-80.

Lagebericht Ost (1–30 November 1941). Also *Einsatzberichten* and *Erfolgsmeldungen/ Verbindungsoffizier der Luftflotte 2* (November 1941). Also telephone/telegraph messages – AG Centre to corps and Panzer units. These are all interleaved with each other, but cover November 1941. T-78/R464, 646640-967.

OKH, Gen Staff/op. Abt (8 December 1941). T-78/R335, 6291885-913.

Auswärtiges Amt holding: *Die Kriegswehrmacht der UdSSR*
Stand Dezember 1941 (dated 1 December 1941). OKH: FHO, Nr 4700/41 geh. (signed Kinzel). Serial 1891H, 426125ff.

Diplomatic documents/memoirs

Churchill–Stalin Correspondence 16, p. 29 (Stalin to Churchill, 3 October); 17, p. 30 (Churchill to Stalin, 6 October); 19, pp. 31-2 (Churchill to Stalin, 7 November); 20, pp. 33-4 (Stalin to Churchill, 8 November); 21, pp. 34-5 (Churchill to Stalin, 22 November); 22, pp. 35-6 (Stalin to Churchill, 23 November).

Documents/Soviet–Polish Relations, I, doc. no. 112 (14 August), pp. 147-8 (Polish–Soviet Military Agreement); doc. nos. 113-14, pp. 149-53 (protocols of Polish–Soviet military conferences, 16 and 19 August); doc. no. 149, pp. 149-50 (record of conversation between Ambassador Kot, Stalin and Molotov on build-up of Polish Army, fate of Poles deported to USSR and release of Polish PWs, 14 November); doc. no. 159, pp. 231-44 (minute of conversation between Gen. Sikorski and Stalin on major problems of Soviet–Polish relations, 3 December); doc. no. 160, pp. 244-6 (Sikorski–Stalin conversation, with Lt.-Gen. Anders, 4 December); doc. no. 165, pp. 254-7 (Sikorski's letter to Churchill on results of his journey to USSR, 17 December).

Avon, Lord (Sir Anthony Eden), *The Eden Memoirs*, The Reckoning (London: Times Publishing 1965), pp. 263-303.

Gwyer, *op. cit.*, 3, pt I, pp. 193-325.

Maiskii, *op. cit.*, pt 3, pp. 165-218.

Woodward, *op. cit.*, II, p. 40-54.

Official/Party histories

IVOVSS (2), pp. 218-28 (summary of operations SW and S Fronts). Pp. 225-8 (Crimea). Pp. 229-68 (defence of Moscow, to early December), Pp. 277-98 (Soviet counter-offensive at Moscow). Pp. 298-304 (Tikhvin operations: planning of Soviet counter-blow, position of Soviet forces end November). Pt II, pp. 271-7 (planning and preparation of Soviet counter-offensive). Pp. 304-13 (Sevastopol–Kerch: Soviet defence of Sevastopol, repulse of German assault, end December).

NOTE: this volume is undoubtedly useful in establishing certain aspects of the chronology of the defensive battle for Moscow, together with details of the Soviet order of battle, but the account very carefully glosses over the problem of the scope and amplitude of the Soviet counter-offensive. For example, it is not clear that the first counter-stroke was designed simply to clear German forces from Moscow itself and it was upon this process that a much grander 'counter-offensive' design was imposed with particular features contrived by Stalin himself and imposed by simple *diktat*.

Soviet materials

i) *Memoirs and personal accounts*

Afanas'ev, D. and Badanin, B., 'O nekotorykh voprosakh inzhenernogo obespecheniya bitvy pod Moskvoi letom i osen'yu 1941 goda', *VIZ*, 12 (1966), pp. 11–20 (formation of uvps – *Upravlenie voenno-polevogo stroitel'stva* – with Reserve Front, subordinated to nkvd since military had no other resources available; work on field fortifications; also demolition plans in w approaches and suburbs of Moscow; diagrammatic map, p. 19). Col. Afanas'ev was chief of the uvps.

Antipenko, N.A., *Na glavnom napravlenii* (foreword by Marshal G.K. Zhukov) (Moscow: Nauka 1967), pp. 59–70 (role and function as a senior logistics – 'Rear Services' – officer with 49th Army, October 1941); pp. 71–8 (logistics of 49th Army in Moscow counter-offensive).

Artem'ev, P.A., 'Nepreodolimaya pregrada na podstupakh k stolitse', in *Bitva za Moskvu*, pp. 111–27 (describes activity of the Moscow Military District during operations at the 'distant approaches' to the capital, followed by the relationship between the Moscow MD and the MZO. Cf. this account with N. M. Mironov in *Besprimernyi podvig*, pp. 114–30.

Bagramyan, *op. cit.*, pp. 405–35. NOTE: this appears to be the most detailed account of the Rostov operation and certainly provides a very detailed picture of Marshal Timoshenko as sw Front and 'sw theatre' commander, though it is necessary to take the text as it stands.

Batov, P.I., *V pokhodakh i boyakh* (Moscow: Voenizdat 1966), 2nd edn, pp. 5–145 (*Perekop*, an enlarged first chapter in this 2nd edn which deals with the operations of 51st Indep. Army, the Soviet defensive plan for the Crimea, the Soviet withdrawal and the evacuation of Kerch); pp. 146–8 (summoned to General Staff, 21 December; talk with Shaposhnikov, who was anxious about lack of means to effect rapid manoeuvre in present Soviet offensive operations; Batov not under a cloud for operations in Crimea; assigned to 3rd Army Bryansk Front; meets Ya. T. Cherevichenko – cavalry man, the 'dashing attack', *likhaya ataka*, his forte but little idea of modern mobile operations). Though it is bereft of references – save for an extensive acknowledgement to his fellow commanders in compiling the revised chapter on the Crimea in 1941 – I have drawn extensively on Gen. Batov's book, having had the opportunity to talk with him and discuss a number of these actions, not least his part in the Stalingrad operations. It did not seem that there was any great discrepancy between what he had written and what he recounted, so at least Gen. Batov had not been 'edited' out of all recognition.

Baurdzhan, Momysh-Uly, *General Panfilov* (Alma-Ata: Kazakhskoe Gos. Izd. Khudozh. Lit 1963). Memoir of Gen. I.V. Panfilov, commander 316th Rifle Div. – 8th Guards Panfilov Div. – killed in action November 1941 in defence of Moscow by one of his associates.

Beloborodov, Gen. A.P., 'Sibiryaki v velikoi bitve za Moskvu', in *Bitva za Moskvu*, pp. 229–45.

Belov, P.A., *Za nami Moskva* (Moscow: Voenizdat 1963), pt 1, pp. 33–54 (2 Cav. Corps moved to Moscow zone; composition of 2 Cav.; assigned to w Front 9 November; Zhukov indicates deployment and assignment; Belov accompanies Zhukov on visit to Stalin, 10 November; Stalin looked much aged, Zhukov seemed to be in command; plan for limited counter-blow; promise of air support discounted by Belov); pp. 54–69 (takes offensive, 15 November; return to defensive, 21 November; threat of German concentration at Tula; Belov's insistence that 2 Cav. Corps counter-attack at Serpukhovo significant – though 49th Army mentioned only in this context); pp. 70–106 (defence of Kashira; Belov assigned personal responsibility for town; Stalin promises weapons and reinforcements; report to Zhukov; initiative passes to 2 Cav. Corps, 27 November; Guards designations for corps – 1st Guards Cav. Corps); pp. 107–25 (attack plans; attack on Mordves, 30 November; operated by night to avoid Luftwaffe; operations to 9 December); pp. 126–47 (operations in Tula offensive; drive on Kashira; Belov's corps to break into rear; German 4th Army aiming at Yukhnov; Belov's attempt to get his former men back from field hospitals or rear; ordered to take Odoevo for Stalin's birthday; results of 1st Gds Cav. Corps operations, 6–22 December).

NOTE: This account by Col.-Gen. Belov (who died before the book was published) is a strange mixture of direct personal comment, extracts from operational orders and material extracted from official archives. It is valuable precisely for this reason, plus the postscript by Col. Malakhov (pp. 327–31). There is certainly little 'stylized heroism' here and a hardbitten attitude towards all and sundry.

Eliseyev, Vice-Admiral I., 'Pervye dni oborony Sevastopolya', *VIZ*, 8 (1968), pp. 51–60.

Eroshenko, Rear-Admiral V.N., *Lider 'Tashkent'* (Moscow: Voenizdat 1966), pp. 114–30 (Commander Eroshenko commanded the flotilla-leader *Tashkent* 1941–2; describes supply runs to Sevastopol and part in Kerch–Feodosiya landings).

Fedyuninskii, 2nd edn, *op. cit.*, pp. 65–88.

Getman, Gen. A.L., *Tanki idut na Berlin (1941–1945)* (Moscow: Nauka 1973), pp. 10–32 (beginning of war in Soviet Far East, chief of staff to 30th Mech. Corps; posted to European theatre as commander of 112nd Tank Div. which forming up; assigned to Belov's 'operational group', 14 November; 25 November, ordered to move 112nd Tank Div. to support Kashira and electric power station alongside Belov's cavalry corps; operated with 50th Army and 2nd Cav. Corps, holding sw approaches to Kashira; few tanks left; assigned to 50th Army in counter-offensive; southerly drive from Tula; 17 December, assigned to special 'mobile group' under Popov for drive on Kaluga; recapture of Kaluga after heavy street fighting on 30 December; 112nd Tank Div. taken into reserve).

Golikov, F.I., *V Moskovskoi bitve, Zapiski komandarm* (Moscow: Nauka 1967), pp. 5–11 (assumes command of 10th Army; reserve force presently being assembled, end October); pp. 18–23 (difficulties in finding manpower, weapons); pp. 25–9 (concentration of 10th Army in Ryazan area); pp. 42–6 (attack orders, 2 December; Zhukov's explanation of general plan); pp. 46–51 (final orders from w Front command – text – 5 December; shortage of artillery, mortars; no armour); pp. 51–76 (10th Army offensive operations, 8–13 December). NOTE: Soviet order of battle is detailed in numerous footnotes, which include some texts of orders and directives.

Kalyagin, Lt.-Gen./Engineers A., 'Na dal'nikh podstupakh k Moskve', *VIZ*, 11 (1970), pp. 73–8 (role of engineer troops in building field fortifications, mine-laying and demolition work, Bryansk Front and right flank sw Front).

Katukov, Marshal M.E., 'l-ya Gvardeiskaya v boyakh pod Moskvoi', in *Bitva za Moskvu*, pp. 202–28.

Katukov, Marshal M.E., 'Gvardeitsy-tankisty v Moskovskoi bitve', in *Proval gitlerov. nastupleniya*, pp. 178–200.

Koniev, I.S., 'Na Kalininskom Fronte', *Besprimernyi podvig*, pp. 63–75. Operational narrative, with figures pertaining to Soviet strength in manpower and equipment, from mid-October to mid-December 1941.

Lobachev, *op. cit.*, pp. 210–36.

Meretskov, *op. cit.*, pp. 228–58.

Meretskov, 'Na Volkhovskikh rubexhakh', *VIZ*, 1 (1965), pp. 54–70 (Volkhov Front operations from decision – 10 December 1941 – to establish Front to offensive of January and on to disaster of summer 1942; the editorial comment from *VIZ* speaks for itself – Marshal Meretskov is describing events which 'so far have been little studied and require further research', that is, the whole tragedy of the 2nd Shock Army).

Mironov, Lt.-Gen. N.M., 'Rol Moskovskoi zony oborony v ragrome Nemtsev pod Moskvoi', *Besprimernyi podvig*, pp. 114–30 (12 October GKO decides on defence zone directly within Moscow's region; Staff of the Moscow Reserve Front becomes the staff of the Moscow Defence Zone – MZO; 3 defence lines declared by order, 21 October, of Moscow garrison; 28 October, Moscow Military District and MZO work out defence plan for city covering all approaches; MZO reserve consisted of 2nd Moscow RD, naval detachment, an HQ guard battalion, 1 cavalry squadron and 3 armoured trains, plus the NKVD troops under Maj.-Gen. K.R. Sinilov, who was also city commandant.

Lelyushenko, *Moskva–Stalingrad–Berlin–Praga*, pp. 70–119.

Voronov, N.N., *Oborona Leningrada*, pp. 199–221.

Odintsov, G.F., pp. 102–7 (Chief of Staff/Artillery and Artillery Commander 54th Army; composition of Soviet artillery, including ship-mounted guns of Baltic Fleet; plans for counter-battery fire).

Pavlov, *op. cit.*, pp. 79–107 (food supplies in Leningrad, need to provide rations for 2,544,000 people – which included some 400,000 children – plus 343,000 others within city limits and caught in blockade; September ration levels; cuts in rations; substitute food experiments; need to maintain strength of working force and yet not expend meagre stores of food); pp. 109–25 (food distribution August–December 1941; fixing of food supply norms; rise in numbers of 'lost' ration cards and rigorous methods to stamp out cheating; types of ration cards issued [p. 122] and table of changes in rations [p. 122]; Party measures to prevent speculation and illegal dealing); pp. 127–43 (military rations; table of rations for front-line and rear units [p. 131]; table of fall in military rations, 1 October–20 November [p. 135]; soldiers and sailors also received 20g makhorka or 10g tobacco daily; to conserve tobacco, exchanging tobacco ration for chocolate or sugar encouraged – 300g tobacco for 300g sugar or 200g chocolate – but scheme failed to work; also need to include spices in diet to maintain appetites – not field tactics but the organization of supply became the key to any kind of success).

Perventsev, Maj.-Gen. G., 'V boyakh za stolitsu nashei Rodiny', *VIZ*, 3 (1963), pp. 58–68 (173rd Rifle Div. operations).

Rokossovskii, *op. cit.*, pp. 62–77 (deployed on Volokolamsk sector mid-October; meeting with Panfilov and Dovator; defence of wide frontage; appeals to Zhukov for artillery, 25 October; Skirmanovo offensive blow by 16th Army; ineffectiveness of partial offensive launched on 16 November; onset of renewed German offensive); pp. 78–97 ('nowhere to retreat' – *otstupat nekuda*; German attack towards Volokol-amsk–Moscow highway; death of Panfilov; Zhukov refuses to allow 16th Army to pull back to Istra line; Rokossovskii appeals to Shaposhnikov; Shaposhnikov agrees and Rokossovskii assumes that Stalin has approved; deployment on the Istra line; Zhukov countermands order to fall back – 'I am the Front commander ... and order you to defend the lines you occupy without retreating one step'; Rokos-sovskii's defences penetrated; crisis at Solnechnogorsk; w Front HQ orders Rokos-sovskii to clear Solnechnogorsk; failure of hastily organized attack; heavy losses in Dovator's cavalry corps; friction between Rokossovskii and Zhukov as Zhukov 'asserts his will'; Zhukov's brusqueness with Stalin; Stalin's softer attitude to Rokossovskii; 16th Army takes brunt of main German attack; crisis at Kryukovo); pp. 98–103 (offensive operations; penetration of Istra sector; effective artillery support; heavy fighting in Volokolamsk sector; heavy losses in 16th Army – by end December divisions down to 1,200–1,500 men). NOTE: this is a useful, if terse account, marked by its mild but unmistakable criticism of Zhukov.

See also *VIZ*, 11 (1966), pp. 46–55 and *VIZ*, 12 (1966), pp. 50–61. These two accounts cover the 'Volokolamsk axis' and defensive operations on the N approaches to Moscow. They are both annotated and are more properly military narrative and analysis, as opposed to the 'memoir' tone of *Soldatskii dolg*. In the second instalment (12, p. 53) the editors of *VIZ* had approached Marshal Zhukov for his explanation of that countermanded order over the withdrawal of 16th Army behind the 'Istra line' – Marshal Zhukov argues here that not only the interests of 16th Army were at stake but those of the entire front; hence his refusal to countenance Rokossovskii's planned withdrawal, which would have threatened the right flank of 5th Army and uncovered the approach to Perkhushkovo, w Front command centre. In this version, however, Marshal Rokossovskii does not include his criticism of Zhukov's person-ality and his treatment of subordinates.

In general, comparison of the extracts published in *VIZ* (and occasionally *Istoriya SSSR*) and the actual printed volume of memoirs for wide circulation shows that documentary material, archival references and technical military detail is presented in *VIZ*, while the personal slanging-match is much reduced or suitably adjusted for a professional military readership. None the less, this presents difficulties in deciding upon the authoritativeness of any given version.

Rotmistrov, Marshal P.A., '8-ya tankovaya brigada v boyakh pod Moskvoi', in *Proval gitlerov. nastupleniya*, pp. 161–77 (began war as C-of-S to 3rd Mech. Corps in Baltic, in autumn 1941; Ya.N. Fedorenko – Deputy Defence Commissar for Armoured Forces – proposes that Rotmistrov become C-of-S to Red Army Armoured forces, but Rotmistrov requests front command; assigned to 8th Tank Bde on NW Front – fully equipped with 22 T-34s, 7 KV heavy tanks and 32 light tanks – and rushed to Kalinin on Kurochkin's orders with express approval of *Stavka*; Vatutin takes over special operational group to hold Kalinin, 12 October; 8th Bde wins time for Koniev to stabilize situation, in defence of Klin and Rogachevo; end November, withdrawn into second échelon of 30th Army to re-equip; operates with 30th Army in Moscow-counter-offensive; recapture of Klin; 16 December transferred with 30th Army to Kalinin Front; great praise for Koniev's conduct on the battlefield; 8th Tank Bde becomes 3rd Guards Bde and is used to form 7th Tank Corps). NOTE: this is a highly detailed account – including tactics, organization, operations – of 8th Tank Bde, without references but bearing many of the hallmarks of Marshal Rotmistrov's strictures on tank warfare, as well as being demonstrably a pro-Koniev piece.

Sandalov, *op. cit.*, pp. 227–45 (assigned to Tula end October, interviewed by Vasilevskii; repulse of German assault; attempts to outflank Tula, mid-November; assigned to sw Front with liquidation of Bryansk Front; recalled to Moscow, 28 November); pp. 245–69 (conversation with Shaposhnikov, evening 28 November; appointed c-of-s newly formed 20th Army – commander Andrei Vlasov, recently escaped from Kiev encirclement; preparations for Moscow counter-stroke; drive on Solnechnogorsk; Vlasov and Zhukov's reprimand; capture of Volokolamsk; preparations for general offensive on all fronts; interview with Sokolovskii). NOTE: this is one of the very few current references to Gen. Vlasov's 20th Army command in Moscow counter-offensive.

Surchenko, A., 'Likvidatsiya proryva v raione Naro-Fominska', *VIZ*, 12 (1962), pp. 49–57 (operations of 18th Indep. Rifle Bde, 33rd Army, sealing off German breakthrough, early December).

Telegin, Lt.-Gen. K.F., 'Moskovskaya zona oborony' in *Proval gitlerov. nastupleniya*, pp. 58–82 (the third, political member of the Military Soviets of the Moscow MD and the Moscow Defence Zone, MZO, assigned end June 1941 as commissar and chief of political administration of Moscow MD; work with raising Moscow militia divisions; July, decisions on outer defence lines for city; October crisis; location and manning of defensive sectors; 12 October, decision to form MZO on basis of Moscow Reserve Front; main task of MZO to organize defence on the outskirts of the city and within it; MZO report on 19 October results in declaration of state of siege; MZO takes active part in military operations – Klin in particular – also Rogachevo; 27 November, formation of 'northern operational group' under Col. Lizyukov; later incorporated into 20th Army; forces available to MZO formed the second échelon of the Moscow defence; MZO responsible for fitting out and deploying *Stavka* reserves; responsibility for air defence forces; even after German forces thrust back from Moscow *Stavka* required Moscow MD and MZO to hold defences in full operational readiness). This is a much more detailed and documented account than that presented by Mironov in *Bitva za Moskvu*.

Timoshenko, Marshal S.K., 'Yugo-zapadnyi front v bitve za Moskvu', in *Bitva za Moskvu*, pp. 97–110. A rare appearance of Marshal Timoshenko – or at least an account bearing his own name – in the memoir literature. This is a straight, unadorned military narrative of sw Front operations, both in the tense defensive actions and in the first phase of the Moscow counter-offensive, with a very terse explanation of why sw Front offensive operations slowed in pace between 25 December 1941 and 8 January 1942.

Vasilevskii memoirs/materials, *Delo vsei zhizni*, pp. 152–78 (General Staff's failure to comprehend German plans – 'Typhoon'; grave weakening of Soviet forces due to Bryansk–Vyazma encirclement; sent to Gzhatsk–Moshaisk with GKO delegation; assisted by L.A. Govorov; situation mid-October and Soviet order of battle; promoted Lt.-Gen. by Stalin, end October; illustrates Stalin's contradictory behaviour from anger to generosity; recognition of inevitability of renewed German offensive; change in 'balance of forces', beginning December – Red Army had 4·2 million men, 22,000 guns and mortars, 583 rocket launchers, 1,730 tanks, 2,495 combat aircraft, while German Army had 5 million men, 26,800 guns, 1,500 tanks, 2,500 aircraft; arrival of Soviet reserve armies; idea of a counter-offensive first mooted at *beginning November*; postponed and brought up again end November with Shaposhnikov and General Staff working on definite plan in *last week* November; concern over situation at Tikhvin; Vasilevskii's close co-operation with Sokolovskii; conversation with Koniev, 1 December; with staff of Kalinin Front; Stalin's personal interference with operations and attack plans; Soviet errors and shortcomings; effect of shortage of ammunition, tanks, aircraft; genesis of plan for general offensive on all fronts). NOTE: much seems to be left unsaid in this passage from Vasilevskii, which is more or less a general narrative, the only detail concerning his assignment to the Kalinin Front. Again the unpredictability and irregularity of Stalin's behaviour is much emphasized.

Voronov, N.N., *Na sluzhbe voennoi*, pp. 204–10 (assigned to Leningrad in November, reports to *Stavka* on munitions production in Leningrad; arranges to air-lift guns and ammunition to Moscow sector); pp. 211–15 (refuses to consider taking over command of Leningrad Front, as suggested by Zhdanov, pleading that is Chief of Red Army Artillery; criticism of Kulik's handling of 54th Army); pp. 215–23 (planning of counter-battery operations in Leningrad). NOTE: this represents a very questionable phase in Voronov's wartime service, when he did work in Leningrad but seems to have helped to strip the city of its weapons – shipping out ammunition and guns – only to have ammunition production fall to almost zero within weeks, and also parrying the suggestion that he take over the Leningrad Front command.

Zhavoronkov, V.G., 'Geroicheskaya oborona Tuly', *Besprimernyi podvig*, pp. 131–45. Personal account by chairman of the Tula Defence Committee; composition, competence and activities of this Committee.

Zhukov, G.K., *Vospominaniya*, pp. 332–60 (battle of Moscow, Soviet counter-offensive: Stalin suggests military parade, 7 November; Zhukov foresees no major German action but proposes strengthening air defences; Stalin issues order for Soviet attack at Volokolamsk and Serpukhov; Zhukov disagrees but overridden; German preparations for renewal of thrust on Moscow; assaults on Klin and Volokolamsk; Stalin inquires of Zhukov, 'Are you convinced that we shall hold Moscow?' [p. 338]; Zhukov confirms this but needs two more armies and 200 tanks; Stalin promises 2 reserve armies but no tanks for the moment; Zhukov–Vasilevskii agree to assign 1st Shock Army to Yakhroma, 10th Army to Ryazan; defence of Tula–Kashira, crisis with 16th Army Solnechnogorsk; Stalin orders Zhukov to recapture Dedovsk; Govorov assigned to this task – pointless and due to mistaken information; reason for German failure to take Moscow not weather conditions but miscalculations in manpower and *matériel*; 29 November, calls Stalin and reports 'enemy bled white', but need for w Front to acquire 1st Shock Army and 10th Army to eliminate dangerous German penetrations; 30 November, w Front HQ submits attack plan to throw enemy as far as possible from Moscow; Stalin promises aircraft but still no tanks; Soviet offensive opens, 6 December; Stalin's great optimism as offensive developed and idea of a *general offensive* along entire Soviet–German front; Stalin's role in battle of Moscow – 'through his unrelenting exactingness he was able to achieve, one could say, the near-impossible' [p. 360]).

NOTE: memorable though the 'battle for Moscow' was (and Zhukov insists that it is engraved on his mind out of all the wartime operations), this is a pallid and even uninformative account. Its chief feature is the dogmatic insistence on the correctness of Zhukov's own appraisals and actions – witness the statement that 16th Army retreated at Solnechnogorsk *tout court* – and it is clear that this chapter is but a small portion of all that passed between Zhukov and Stalin. See also *VIZ*, 10 (1971), pp. 58–67 and 12 (1971), pp. 44–52. These are shortened extracts from Zhukov's memoirs dealing with the battle for Moscow. One significant difference in 12, p. 52 is the fulsome praise lavished on Stalin – his unyieldingness, his strategic prescience and his ability to undertake major strategic operations with a full grasp of the situation: 'He was, in all truth, a worthy Supreme Commander'. This eulogy, possibly intended for military readers, is missing in the printed vol., in both 1st and 2nd edns.

This raises the question of what exactly *are* the 'Zhukov memoirs' (see J. Erickson, 'Marshal Zhukov and the meaning of Soviet Military Memoirs', *Problems of Communism* (November–December 1973), pp. 71–4); now a 2-vol. version of the memoirs is promised, even after Zhukov's death. The political purposes can be readily guessed at, though this must mean further dilution of the text. The original Zhukov manuscript (or notebooks) does exist, but some doubts must arise over these constant emendations.

ii) Studies and analysis

Barbashin, I.P. and Kharitonov, A.D., *Boevye deistviya Sovetskoi Armii pod Tikhvinom v 1941 godu* (Moscow: Voenizdat 1958), *passim*. A small but very useful study which has not been so far superseded.

Bitva za Leningrad, pt 1, pp. 97–116 (military situation, October 1941; attempts to thicken Leningrad defences with anti-tank obstacles but great shortage of explosives; defensive operations at Tikhvin; Soviet counter-stroke at Tikhvin; correct delineation by *Stavka* of Soviet objective and proper timing for operation). NOTE: this remains the most authoritative and objective account, based as it is largely on Soviet military records and archival materials. For those who have seen him at work, the ed. (the late Lt.-Gen. Platonov) was highly professional and very exacting, if somewhat peppery and I found it an advantage to have been able to discuss this study with him. It was one in which he took justifiable pride, for it does establish a reliable guide to both the military chronology, comparative strengths and timetable of decisions on the Soviet side.

Evstigneyev, V.N. (ed.), *Velikaya bitva pod Moskvoi* (Moscow: Voenizdat 1961), pp. 131–69 (military narrative of defensive operations, November 1941); pp. 170–215 (Soviet counter-offensive; operational planning; destruction of northern German assault forces; w and Kalinin Front pursuits, first half December; destruction of the s German group; Soviet offensive operations in Tula region; w Front operations on central sector to line of river Nara; sw Front operations on 'Yelets axis').

Frunze Academy, *Sbornik materialov po istorii Sovetskogo voennogo iskusstva v Velikoi Otechestvennoi voine 1941–1945 g.* (Moscow: Voenizdat 1956) (vol. 4 of a 4-vol. study, ed. Lt.-Gen. V.F. Vorob'ev), pp. 22–88. This volume, which bears a Soviet security classification, consists of reprints from contemporary and immediate postwar accounts of battle of Moscow. See Lt.-Gen. E.A. Shilovskii, pp. 46–50 (from Gospolitizdat publication, 1943); Maj.-Gen. P. Korkodinov, pp. 51–5 (from

Voennaya Mysl, 19 [1951], pp. 9–13); N. Talenskii, pp. 55–6 (from *Bol'shevik*, 23–4 [1942], p. 45).

Geroicheskaya oborona Sevastopolya 1941–1942 (collective authorship) (Moscow: Voenizdat 1969), pp. 33–49 (defensive preparations in Sevastopol, land-based and seaward defences); pp. 50–131 (repulse of first German offensive, 30 October–21 November 1941; withdrawal of Coastal Army on Sevastopol; reinforcement of Sevastopol defence; first engagement at naval base; organization of SOP [*Sevastopol'skii oboronitel'nyi raion*]; role of 'rear services' in providing support for defence; Crimean partisan activity; positions held on sectors 1–4 by Soviet troops on 30 November); pp. 132–96 (German plans for reduction of Sevastopol; *Stavka* subordinates SOR to its own direct command, 19 November); pp. 163–88 ('days of decisive engagements, 22–31 December; reinforcements stem German thrust to N Bay; 24 December, P.E. Petrov relieved as commander of Coastal Army and replaced by Lt.-Gen. I.S. Chernyak. *Stavka* responds by leaving Petrov in command of Coastal Army and making Chernyak 'assistant commander SOR for land-based defence'; night of 31 December, Petrov convenes extraordinary session of Coastal Army Military Soviet, reads Stalin's order to hold, demands no further retreat; 31 December, directive of Trans-Caucasus Front commander that SOR mount *offensive* on morning 31 December to hold German forces at time of Kerch–Feodosiya landings, but SOR almost bled white – artillery had fired off almost all ammunition, 241st Rifle Regt had only 100 men left alive, 8th Naval Inf. Bde and 40th Cav. Div. wiped out to a man, only 2,000 men left in 345th RD); pp. 188–96 (Kerch–Feodosiya operation: Soviet operational plan; assembly of assault landing force; effect of bad weather; Azov Flotilla under Rear-Admiral Gorshkov; lands men of 51st Army; 23,000 men landed at Feodosiya, plus 734 tons ammunition during 30/1 December in night landings; Sevastopol also supplied by sea, late December; operations meanwhile centred on Kerch isthmus); pp. 335–63 (list of commanders – down to regiments and individual ships – involved in defence of Sevastopol).

    NOTE: this must be regarded as the authoritative account of the defence of Sevastopol, based as it is on original records and archival materials, as well as un-published accounts (listed pp. 6–7) and first-hand interviews.

Kazakov, Marshal of Artillery K.P., *Vsegda s pekhotoi, vsegda s tankami* (Moscow: Voenizdat 1973), 2nd edn, pp. 27–70 (artillery in battle of Moscow); great shortage of all types of artillery in defensive phases of battle – even museum pieces pressed into service; 260 old French and British guns, 1,600 Vickers and Browning heavy machine-guns [p. 42]; artillery in Soviet counter-offensive suffers from ammunition shortages, especially for 76mm and guns of heavier calibre [p. 55]).

Karasev, *op. cit.*, pp. 120–90.

Klimov, *op. cit.*, pp. 37–97.

Koval'chuk, V.M., 'Iz istorii oborony Sevastopolya vo vremya Velikoi Otechestvennoi voiny (Zashchita kommunikatsii)', *Istoricheskie zapiski* (Moscow: Nauka 1965), 75, pp. 26–43 (detailed study of seaborne supply runs to Sevastopol).

Malakhov, M.M., *Udar konnogvardeitsev* (Moscow: Voenizdat 1961), pp. 20–70. A formal military narrative and analysis of the operations of Belov's 2nd Cavalry – 1st Guards – Cavalry Corps, November–December 1941.

Muriev, D. Z., *Proval operatsii 'Taifun'*, pp. 83–157.

Muriev, D.Z., 'Nekotorye voprosy sovetskoi voennie strategii v Moskovskoi bitve',

VIZ, 12 (1971), pp. 11–19. An important study that deals in detail with the deployment of Soviet reserves.

Muriev

Composition/deployment W Front armies (10 field armies), 5/6 December 1941

Formation	Frontage (km)	Depth of objective (km)	Composition Rifle/Cav. Divs	Gun/mortars	Tanks
30th Army	80	40	10	586	35
1st Shock Army	30	50	6	358	50
20th Army	30	40	3	311	54
16th Army	20	30	7	643	125
5th Army	60	30	8	425	90
33rd Army	35	20	6	158	40
43rd Army	35	20	5	225	50
49th Army	70	30	5	330	40
50th Army	140	30	11	526	—

Ocherki istorii Leningrada (Leningrad: Nauka 1967); *Leningrad v Velikoi Otechestvennoi voine*, 5: see pt 2, A.V. Karasev and G.L. Sobolev, pp. 170–220 (on the winter famine 1941–2) and A. L. Fraiman, pp. 221–59 ('Doroga zhizni', the Ladoga 'ice-road').

Ordena Lenina Moskovskii voennyi okrug, pp. 225–50. General account of the Moscow Military District in the battle of Moscow.

Safronov, G.P., *Vozdushnye desanty vo vtoroi mirovoi voine* (Moscow: Voenizdat, 1962), pp. 36–8 (Soviet parachute battalion dropped; Kerch–Feodosiya operation; reconnaissance parties dropped for 8 days before main landing from the sea).

Sazonov, *op. cit.*, pp. 163–86 (1st Guards RD assigned to right flank of SW Front early December; awarded Guards Banner; operations with Gen. Kostenko's mobile group, December 1941).

Sokolovskii, *op. cit.*, pp. 48–203ff.

Sokolovskii

1. Comparative strengths, 'W strategic axis' at beginning of Soviet counter-offensive

		Soviet*	AG Centre
manpower	approx.	718,800	801,000
guns and mortars		7,985	14,000
tanks		721	1,000
aircraft		1,170	615

* Includes Kalinin, W Fronts and right flank SW Front; excludes troops in 'Moscow defence zone'.

2. Comparative strengths: W Front, 6 December 1941

	Soviet	German
manpower	approx. 558,800	approx. 590,000
guns and mortars	4,348	7,440
tanks	624	900
aircraft	199*	—

* Not including Moscow air defence aviation and High Command Reserve aircraft; also used in supporting Red Army operations.

3. Comparative strengths: flanks of W Front, 6 December 1941

i) *Right flank*

	Soviet	Left flank AG Centre
manpower	222,400*	135,000
guns and mortars	1,673	approx. 2,000
tanks	290	over 400

* After reinforcement with two reserve armies – 1st Shock Army and 20th Army – and additional strength for 30th Army.

ii) *Left flank*

	Soviet	Right flank AG Centre
manpower	approx. 210,800	approx. 200,000
guns and mortars	1,436	2,740
tanks	140	approx. 300

4. Comparative strengths: Kalinin Front, 1 December 1941

	Soviet	German 9th Army
manpower	approx. 100,000	approx. 153,000
guns and mortars	980	2,198
tanks	67	60
aircraft	83	—

5. *Comparative strength: right flank SW Front, 6 December 1941*

		Soviet	Left flank German 2nd Army
manpower	approx.	60,000	59,000
guns and mortars		388	745
tanks		30	up to 40
aircraft		79	—

Tamonov, Col. F., 'Primenenie bronetankovykh voisk v bitve pod Moskvoi', *VIZ*, 1 (1967), pp. 14–23 (strength of Soviet tank units; tactical employment in defensive fighting; use in offensive operations; significance of the 'mobile groups').

Ternovskii, G.V., *Voennye moryaki v bitvakh za Moskvu* (Moscow: Nauka 1968), pp. 69–108 (Soviet naval infantry units – 'independent naval brigades' – in defensive fighting in Moscow battle, October–November; also in Moscow counter-stroke).

Voiny stal'nykh magistralei, pp. 115–28 (Soviet railway troops in battle for Moscow); pp. 128–30 (railway troops during siege of Leningrad and blockade).

Zemskov, Maj.-Gen. V., 'Nekotorye voprosy sozdaniya i ispol'zovaniya strategicheskikh rezervov', *VIZ*, 10 (1971), pp. 12–16 (organization and deployment of strategic reserves 1941 and early 1942 based on published sources): in summer–autumn 1941 campaign *Stavka* moved from its reserve 291 divs and 94 bdes to the front – 70 divs from internal military districts, 27 from Soviet Far East, Central Asia and Trans-Caucasus, 194 divs and 94 bdes being freshly raised).

Sovetskie tankovye voiska 1941–1945, pp. 35–52 (general account of Soviet tank units in defensive and offensive operations; battle of Moscow: importance of role of several 'mobile groups' set up for counter-offensive, leading to decision to re-establish larger mobile formations with more tanks and more lorried transport).

Tamonov, F.I., 'Nekotorye problemy nauchnoi razrabotki istorii velikoi bitvy pod Moskvoi', in *Besprimernyi podvig*, pp. 189–96.

Literary works

Bek, A., *Volokolamskoe shosse* (Moscow: Voenizdat 1959 and Mol. Gvardiya 1964). Much-acclaimed novel of defence of Moscow on Volokolamsk sector, depicting Panfilov and the Panfilov div.

Ehrenburg, I., 'Lyudi, gody, zhizn', *Novy Mir*, 1 (1963), pp. 88–9 (talk with Zhukov on Stalin's role in Moscow battle; Zhukov's comment – 'That man has iron nerves'; Zhukov telephoned many times for permission to throw Germans back, twice a day sometimes on direct line to Stalin; but Stalin insisted that must wait, that in three days' time necessary reserve divs would arrive, in five days anti-tank weapons; Stalin kept notebook in which he scrupulously listed divs and equipment on move to Moscow region; only when Zhukov intimated that Germans were moving up heavy artillery to shell the capital did he relent and gave his approval for counter-offensive to go forward).

8 STALIN'S FIRST STRATEGIC OFFENSIVE: JANUARY–MARCH 1942

Though the main outlines of the Red Army's general offensive in the winter and early spring of 1942 are well enough known and clearly established, the term *maloissledovannyi* – under-researched – recurs consistently in accounts of particular aspects of the Soviet offensive. While that is technically correct and applicable in some contexts, it would be truer to say that *maloissledovannyi* connotes deliberately ignoring or avoiding sensitive subjects – the Volkhov Front's operations and the beginning of the martyrdom of the 2nd Shock Army (not to mention the eventual fate of Gen. A.A. Vlasov) being a case in point. No doubt this circumstance has helped to impart to much of the material on this period the curious quality of being half subjective personal memoir, half formal military narrative and analysis. It is for precisely that reason that I have not attempted (as with the classification of Soviet material for the previous chapter) to separate memoirs from analysis as such. At this point also the memoirs of both Marshal Zhukov and Marshal Vasilevskii are conspicuously informative, both senior officers casting themselves in the role of a military Pontius Pilate. There is perhaps some justification for this, since at almost every juncture the figure of Marshal Shaposhnikov obtrudes – or rather the opposite, for Shaposhnikov, with his cleverness and undoubted acumen, could see that there was no point in arguing with Stalin and made no attempt to do so. Col. Seaton puts it very neatly in stating that Shaposhnikov was to Stalin what Jodl was to Hitler. The latest consensus, however, suggests that no one man or any single institution can be blamed for the Soviet offensive falling short of its very ambitious objectives. While the overweening optimism of Stalin or the fumbling of the *Stavka* could be blamed for specific failures, lack of experience in conducting large-scale offensive operations and the acute shortage of tanks, artillery, aircraft and ammunition, to mention only the basic items, precluded success on the scale or within the time-span envisaged by Stalin and the *Stavka*.

Particular interest, therefore, attaches to the *Stavka* directives, which I have tried to track both for their timing and their content. It is here that the point about the fusion of memoir with formal narrative is most pertinent. Captured German documents can also be called into play here, for though they do not relate directly to high-level Soviet command decisions – this was to become Gehlen's forte when he took over *Fremde Heere Ost* in the late spring of 1942 – they do nevertheless illuminate Soviet order of battle, reinforcement and command changes. Finally I have included the materials on Soviet airborne operations under a separate heading, not only because the operations themselves command considerable interest but also by virtue of the nature of these works – once again, part memoir and part formal analysis.

Armstrong, *op. cit.*, pt 2, Case Studies (Gerhard L. Weinberg), pp. 389–430 (Yelnaya–Dorogobuzh area; Soviet partisan movement end 1941; Red Army breakthrough and organization of large-scale partisan movement; German response and attempts to destroy Soviet partisans; operation 'Munich').

Carell, *op. cit.*, pt 4, pp. 342–66 ('south of Lake Ilmen'; opening of Soviet NW Front offensive; operations at Staraya Russa; Yeremenko's Shock Army; capture of Toropets and Andreapol); pp. 366–90 (Model takes over German 9th Army; destruction of Soviet 29th and 39th Armies; operation Sukinichi; Rzhev held); pp.

390–408 (Soviet operations on Volkhov Front, German attempts to discern Soviet intentions; supply route of Soviet 2nd Shock Army cut; 'Demyansk pocket'; German air supply to Demyansk; crucial importance of Kholm; role of 'Combat Group Scherer'; Kholm pocket supplied by freight gliders; organization of defence of Kholm).

Von Manstein, *op. cit.*, pp. 227–33.

Philippi and Heim, *op. cit.*, 'Der Feldzug des Jahres 1942', I, pp. 107–20 (crisis engendered by the Soviet winter offensive, operations in AG Centre area, AG North, AG South; by mid-February German command could reckon that gravest crises were past; German counter-moves and counter-blows; in March Soviet offensive largely tamed – 'kommt unter deutsche Kontrolle').

Seaton, *Russo-German War*, pp. 230–41 (extension of Soviet counter-offensive at Moscow; Soviet winter offensive against AG Centre; Soviet and German operations); pp. 242–254 (flanks of Soviet winter offensive, Volkhov Front).

Seaton, *Battle for Moscow*, pp. 237–63 (German retreat January–February 1942; Soviet and German operations); pp. 264–80 (improvement in situation of AG Centre, though still 'potentially dangerous', early February; condition of German and Soviet armies mid-March; destruction of Soviet 33rd Army and death of Yefremov; AG Centre and Soviet armies on defensive; end April 1942). NOTE: Once again this work is most valuable for its delineation of German plans and operations.

German War Diaries

KTB/OKW, *op. cit.*, II (1942). See *A. Einführung*, IV, pp. 38–46 ('Die Situation im Winter 1941/42'); B. Kriegstagebuch 1942, das erste Quartal (1 Januar bis 31 März 1942), pp. 181–311; also das zweite Quartal (1 April bis 30 Juni 1942), pp. 313–31 (for April 1942); C. Dokumenten – Anhang zum Kriegstagebuch 1942, under 2) 'Führerbefehl vom 8 January 1942 betr. Verteidigung aller Stellungen (Auszug)' (pp. 1264–5); 5) 'Führerbefehl an die H. Gr. Mitte vom 15. Januar 1942 zum Rückzug auf die Winterstellung' (pp. 1268–70); 6) 'Führerbefehl vom 1. April 1942 betr. weitere Kampfführung der H. Gr. Mitte' (p. 1,270).

Halder/KTB, *op. cit.*, 3, pp. 371–429.

German Military Documents (GMD)

OKH Gen Std H OQU IV – Fremde Heere Ost, January 1942; *Die Kriegswehrmacht der UdSSR* (Auszug), Soviet military organization, Front commanders, Army commanders, 'aufgetretene Truppenteile'. This is a revision of earlier handbooks and takes account of improvements in Soviet organization and performance, significance of stocks of weapons and supplies and the effectiveness of Soviet improvization. It was evidently a somewhat chastened Col. Kinzel – head of FHO – who was responsible for this report. See T-78/R501, 6489388-520 (the order of battle data runs from pp. 112–250 through formations and units, including divisional and artillery regiments).

FHO, 'Russischer Kräfteeinsatz Stand 25 Februar 1942'. Total of Soviet formations committed since 1 December 1941 continued to climb until 10 January 1942 – putting 4·62 million men in the field. This figure was maintained until 1 February 1942, when it began to fall slowly.

Übersicht über zahlenmässige Entwicklung der russischen Kräftestandes 1.12.41–28.12.41. T-78/R494, 6481137-9.

FHO holding, OKH Abt. K. Verw (Qu 4 B/Kgf) 24 April 1942, 'Kriegsgefangenenlage im Operationsgebiet und Rumänien'. T-78/R489, 6475047-86.

FHO Auswertegruppe, 'Russischer Kräfteeinsatz Stand 28.2.42'. Including some tables for late February and March on Soviet reinforcement and deployment, including tank brigades. T-78/R462, 6441661-71.

FHO (II), 'An die Front zugeführte, neue russ. Verbände Januar–Juli 1942'. See T-78/R486, 6470347ff.

FHO, including 'Verzeichnis der russischen Kommandeure, 9.4.42'. T-78/R464, 6443285-301.

FHO, file on Soviet commanders, promotions and posts (press analysis, intelligence data), January–February 1942. T-78/R464, 6443319-64.

Soviet 33rd Army, captured materials, order of battle Soviet w Front (dated 30 May 1942 for period cited '8.12.41 bis 7.4.42'. T-78/R464, 6443261-3.

FHO file AOK 9 Abt. IC/AO. Notes on leading Soviet commanders, 7 April 1942. T-78/R464, 6443302-6.

Official/Party histories

IVOVSS (2), pt 2, pp. 315-62. (Offensive, January–April 1942: Soviet strategic and operational intentions; destruction of German forces at Leningrad, w of Moscow and in s, the main blow to be mounted against AG Centre with final encirclement in the region of Rzhev–Vyazma–Smolensk carried out by w and Kalinin Fronts in co-operation with NW and Bryansk Fronts); p. 318 (*Stavka* issues 10 January special instruction on methods of organizing and conducting offensive operations; recommended 'shock/assault groups' for main attacks; mass use of artillery and co-operation of all arms right into depth of defences; organization of front-line training courses for officers; five such courses on w Front; February 1942, creation of special '*Komsomol*-youth sections' to train anti-tank squads, machine-gunners, snipers; 27 of these battalions operating in winter 1941-2, with 15,400 young men selected by local *Komsomol* committees).

a) pp. 319-32 (Soviet general offensive on 'Western axis', *zapadnoe napravlenie*: strength of AG Centre; Soviet offensive opens in severe weather conditions; German aim to keep Rzhev–Vyazma–Bryansk rail link open and to hold strong points; difficulties for Soviet Air Force as no airfield servicing units to maintain planes as troops moved westwards); p. 320 (*Stavka* directive, 7 January 1942, prescribing Kalinin, w, Bryansk Front assignments, also NW Front; decisions of Front commanders; most spectacular progress made by Yeremenko's 4th Shock Army/NW Front; 16 January, take Andreapol, advance of up to 80km and frontage doubled; 3rd Shock Army slower pace; 4th Shock Army captures Toropets, 21 January; NW Front attacking in two directions – NW and SW – so that its s armies, 3rd and 4th Shock, handed over to Kalinin Front; 22nd Army, Kalinin Front in wide NW outflanking movement; 39th Army at Sychevka and in rear of German forces holding Rzhev; 10 January, right flank w Front attacks 'assault force' of 20th Army and elements of 1st Shock Army; 13 January, enemy line broken and Pliev's 2nd Guards Cavalry Corps introduced; German reinforcements from France; AG Centre falls back on Rzhev, Gzhatsk and Orsha; drastic measures to hold on; *Stavka* fails to grasp significance of this and even orders 1st Shock Army into reserve, 19 January; also elements of 16th Army taken from right flank w Front; 20th Army unable to capture Gzhatsk late January; 5th and 33rd Army operating at centre, capture Mozhaisk, also Vereya, 19 January; 43rd and 49th Armies outflank German forces at Yukhnov; Zhelane airborne operation; 20 January, Zhukov orders 33rd Army into breach N of Yukhnov and with 1st Guards Cavalry Corps to capture Vyazma; 10 January, left flank forces w Front capture Mosalsk, outflank German forces at Yukhnov from sw; 50th Army outflanks from s of Yukhnov; Tula *oblast* cleared; 1 February, conditions appear favourable to complete encirclement of AG Centre; 27 January–1 February, 4th Para. Corps dropped, but only 8th Para. Bde actually on ground; 1 February, *Stavka* re-establishes 'w theatre command'; Zhukov appointed; fresh *Stavka* instruction to complete encirclement AG Centre; German grip on Vyazma, counter-attacks on 33rd Army; attacks w of Rzhev; 33rd and 39th Armies half-encircled; alarm in *Stavka*; instruction of 16 February to w and Kalinin Fronts to utilize all forces; *Stavka* reinforcements moved up; Koniev pulls out 29th Army – only 6,000 men left; completed by 28 February; struggle s of Vyazma as 1st Guards Cav. Corps tries to break through northwards to link up with 11th Cavalry Corps; 49th and 50th Armies take Yukhnov but unable to link up with 33rd Army; 20 March, *Stavka* directive orders w and Kalinin Fronts to reach assigned line by 20 April; end March/first half April one more attempt to destroy Rzhev–Vyazma German groups and to link up with Soviet forces NW and SW of Vyazma, but no success).

b) pp. 332–8 (offensive on 'NW axis'): p. 333 (*Stavka* instructions to Volkhov and Leningrad Fronts; main role for Volkhov Front; reinforcement of Volkhov Front [2nd Shock Army and 59th Army]; decision on further evacuation from Leningrad, 22 January; 7 January, Volkhov Front offensive opens; drive on Lyuban, outflank German forces from s and sw, but no major success in gaining Lyuban; German counter-blow and 2nd Shock Army encircled; thaw halts movement; great concern over 2nd Shock Army; NW Front attack, 7 January, on Demyansk and Staraya Russa; 34th Army outflanks Demyansk from E and s; *Stavka* assigns 1st Shock Army to speed encirclement operation; 20 February, 7 divs of German 16th Army encircled at Demyansk; *Stavka* directive, 25 February, puts Demyansk operation under unified command of NW Front; German air supply for trapped garrison; weakened 34th Army fails to stop German concentration s of Staraya Russa; German deblockading operation; 21 April, Soviet ring broken with 'corridor').

c) pp. 339–43 (offensive on 'sw axis' and Crimea: sw theatre command plan to mount 2 operations in January–February, first with Bryansk Front forces to effect deep outflanking of German forces in Moscow region and exit on Bryansk–Sevsk line, second with s Front/left flank sw Front to liberate Donbas and come to Dnieper line, requiring capture of Kharkov to provide N cover; Timoshenko request for 500,000 men, plus 10 rifle divs, artillery, armour, tanks; *Stavka* refused and offensive plans scaled down; revised offensive plan and front assignments [p. 340]; Bryansk Front offensive, 7 January; sw Front, 1 January; Maslov's delay with 38th Army; surprise lost, heavy fighting for Oboyan, Balakleyz and Slavyansk; 26 January, *Stavka* directive to cut German lines of communication Slavyansk–Chistyakovo; German reinforcements block s Front advance; lack of transport and tractors slows artillery and ammunition supplies, seriously slowing offensive; Kerch peninsula:

2 January, *Stavka* approves Caucasus Front plan for offensive to liberate Crimea; *Stavka* instruction to speed preparations; 15 January, Germans attacked in direction of Feodosiya; 51st and 44th Armies withdraw to Ak–Monai positions; *Stavka* directive, 28 January, ordered help for defenders of Sevastopol; troops in Kerch to attack towards Karasubazar, w of Feodosiya; to break into rear of German forces investing Sevastopol; operation began only on 27 February; badly organized, unable to break through German defences, no success in March and April).

d) pp. 345–56 (partisan operations; role of Party underground organizations; 'detachments' organized into partisan brigades – 227 'detachments' in Belorussia formed into 19 brigades [1942]; reconnaissance role of partisans and usefulness to Red Army, partisan raids).

e) pp. 356–62 (summary of results of winter offensive: German losses – 50 divs; severe weather hampers Soviet offensive; insufficient production of weapons and ammunition; serious errors by *Stavka*, Front and army commanders; armies drawn into reserve piecemeal and no major reserve to commit on decisive 'w axis'; reinforcements thrown too hastily into battle; 16 March, GKO issues new regulation that reinforcements must receive some preliminary training; lack of mechanized and tank formations; ineffective use of artillery and need for 'artillery offensive' rather than merely preliminary barrage or bombardment; effectiveness of German use of armour in 'compact groupings', hence *Stavka* order of 22 January to commit tank brigades in full strength in co-operation with infantry, aviation and artillery, with *mandatory* reconnaissance and commander going over the ground; deficiencies in command and control of aviation).

See also table, p. 361: war production January–March 1942.

	January	February	March
mortars (all calibres)	17,581	18,235	20,136
artillery pieces	3,427	3,971	5,971
tanks	1,564	1,607	1,690
aircraft	1,039	915	1,647

Soviet materials

Bitva za Leningrad, pt 1, pp. 133–56.

Belov, *op. cit.*, pt 1, pp. 165–300.

Basistyi, Admiral N.E., *More i breg* (Moscow: Voenizdat 1970), pp. 73–120 (naval support for Kerch–Feodosiya operations).

'Direktivnoe pis'mo Stavki Verkhovnogo Galvnokomanddvaniya ot 10 yanvarya 1942 goda', *VIZ*, 1 (1974), pp. 70–4 (extracts from *Stavka* instruction of 10 January 1942 on tactics and organization, reprinted from *Sbornik boevykh dokumentov Velikoi Otechestvennoi voiny*, Vyp. 5 [Moscow: 1947], pp. 8–9). See also *Razvitie taktiki Sov. Armii*, pp. 165–7.

Fedyuninskii, *op. cit.*, pp. 89–109.

Galkin, Maj.-Gen./Technical Services F.I., *Tanki vozvrashchayutsya v boi* (Moscow: Voenizdat 1964), pp. 3–77 (Galkin was in charge of tank repair services, assigned to the Kerch/Crimea operations in the winter and early spring of 1942). This account is useful for its picture of the internal disposition of the Soviet forces as well as the series of observations on Mekhlis, who in his usual fashion managed to make life intolerable for engineer as well as command officers. Much more sympathetic is the portrait of V.T. Volskii, one of the first commanders of the Red Army's early tank formations in the early 1930s and now Inspector-Gen. of Soviet Armoured Forces, assigned to the Kerch/Crimea operation specifically at the request of Mekhlis.

Ignatova, A.A. and Vinogradov, A.P., *Geroi-komandarm* (Moscow: Voenizdat 1967). Biography of Lt.-Gen. Yefremov. See pp. 150–94 for operations with 33rd Army, encirclement and death.

Khozin, Col.-Gen. M., 'Ob odnoi maloissledovannoi operatsii', *VIZ*, 2 (1966), pp. 35–46 (Khozin commanded Leningrad Front October 1941–June 1942 and this study deals with Leningrad–Volkhov Front operations in 1942, beginning with *Stavka* directive of 17 December 1941 [p. 36 for fn extract from directive]).

Khrulev, Gen. A., 'V bor'be za Leningrad', *VIZ*, 11 (1962), pp. 27–36. Account of attempts to supply Leningrad through blockade, with details of 'ice-road' and loads delivered; fns supplied by the eds of *VIZ* either amplify Khrulev's account or provide some corrections to the figures quoted.

Kuznetsov, Lt.-Gen. P.G., *Dni boevye* (Moscow: Voenizdat 1964), pp. 65–142 (NW Front operations; drive on Lovat; Soviet operations at Demyansk and 'Ramushevo corridor'). NOTE: this is a modest but informative account of offensive operations in the Staraya-Russa/Demyansk area, complete with useful maps.

Lobachev, *op. cit.*, pp. 278–301.

Meretskov, *op. cit.*, pp. 266–82.

Moskalenko, *op. cit.*, pp. 132–71.

Rokossovskii, *op. cit.*, pp. 104–14.

Semenov, Maj.-Gen. V., 'Iz opyta organizatsii i vedeniya operatsii na Severo-Zapadnom napravlenii', *VIZ*, 9 (1967), pp. 40–50. Analytical study by former Chief of Operations 54th and 23rd Armies/Leningrad Front and Operations Staff/Volkhov Front on geographical, operational and tactical features of Soviet operations in 'NW theatre'.

Sokolovskii, *op. cit.*, pt 3, pp. 309–75.

U Chernomorskikh tverdyn Otdelnaya Primorskaya armiya v oborone Odessy i Sevastopolya (Collection of memoirs) (Moscow: Voenizdat 1967), see under Col.-Gen. (Arty) N.K. Ryzhi, pp. 139–70 (artillery in defence of Sevastopol); Lt.-Gen. (Engrs) E.V. Leoshenya, pp. 232–43 (engineers and defence works in defence of Sevastopol).

Vasilevskii memoirs/materials: *Delo vsei zhizni*, pp. 173–4 (transition to general offensive beginning January 1942; importance of *direktivnoe pis'mo* of 10 January issued by *Stavka* – though initiative Stalin's – on conducting offensive operations; yet reinforcements needed to carry out assignments laid down by *Stavka* and time needed to mobilize these); pp. 179–86 (Soviet reserve armies – 9 at disposal of *Stavka* – scattered across several Fronts; general offensive expends reserves so carefully built up in late autumn and winter; Stalin's view that German reserves would be exhausted by spring 1942 not borne out by facts; question of spring operations; situation in N – Murmansk and Karelia – stabilized; blockade of Leningrad unbroken; German garrison at Demyansk encircled but undefeated; German still holding Rzhev–Vyazma *place d'armes*; General Staff and *Stavka* troubled over situation on sw Front – Soviet salient w of Izyum but here sw and s Fronts halted and in Crimea Soviet troops tied down in Kerch peninsula; by April fronts on defensive; Soviet General Staff considering summer operations; conviction that temporary turn to strategic defensive essential; main attention fixed on 'central theatre'; also need to complete evacuation of industry to hinterland; reinforcements consisted largely of fresh recruits, hence General Staff suggestion to bring back combat units for rest and training, filling them with fresh men, thus helping to train field reinforcements; need to improve 'rear services', re-organization of rifle divisions, tank corps being reformed and first two tank armies; 30 rifle corps HQ staffs and administrations established; Stalin did not believe in possibility of large-scale operations in early summer but wanted 'active defence'; limited offensives in Crimea, Kharkov region, Kursk and Smolensk axes, Leningrad and Demyansk; Shaposhnikov believed that broad offensive operations impossible at this time; Zhukov supported this but advocated destruction of German forces at Rzhev–Vyazma; in mid-March General Staff had assembled all data for operational plan for spring and early summer 1942, with aim of implementing 'active strategic defence', filling out Soviet reserves and then embarking on decisive offensive operations; Shaposhnikov presented plan to Stalin and work on it continued; *Stavka* involved but with proposal from Timoshenko for major offensive operations with Bryansk, sw and s Fronts; thus Stalin did accept the plan – a turn to strategic offensive but with limited offensives: intelligence data on German intentions and preparations for offensive in s largely ignored, while Soviet reserves were for most part drawing up in region of Tula, Voronezh; Vasilevskii's comment that basic weakness of Soviet plan was intention to attack and defend simultaneously; comparative strengths – *Soviet* 5½ million men, more than 4,000 tanks, 43,000 guns and mortars, 3,000 aircraft; *German* 6·2 million men, more than 3,000 tanks, 43,000 guns, 3,400 aircraft).

See also 'Nekotorye voprosy rukovodstva vooruzhennoi bor'boi letom 1942', *VIZ*, 8 (1965), pp. 3–6 (interview between editorial staff of *VIZ* and Marshal Vasilevskii, material already written for *VOVSS Kratkaya istoriya*; *Stavka* and General Staff in error in thinking that fresh German offensive would be aimed at Moscow; General Staff firmly of opinion that Red Army must go over temporarily to strategic defence; Stalin accepts but opts for limited offensives; criticism of S. Zlobin's *Propavshie bez vesti* (1964); role of General Staff not properly understood; General Staff officers not 'making careers' but closely involved with Fronts and front-line operations).

See also Saltykov, Maj.-Gen. N., 'Predstaviteli General'nogo Shtaba . . .', *VIZ*, 9 (1971), pp. 54–9 (on the organization of General Staff, use of General Staff 'representatives' on various fronts in command and co-ordinating posts).

Vladimirov, Lt.-Gen. B., '140-ya otdel'naya strelkovaya brigada v Lyubanskoi operatsii', *VIZ*, 12 (1968), pp. 84–93 (140th Ind. Rifle Bde in Lyuban operation, March–May 1942; this bde was part of 4th Guards Rifle Corps/54th Army).

Yeremenko, *op. cit.*, pp. 392–420 (24 December talk with Stalin, who asked if Yeremenko knew Sklyanskii; Yeremenko to serve under Kurochkin, command of 4th Shock Army, NW Front; strength and composition of 4th Shock Army; difficulties with supply and rail links; incorrect data on German positions, concentration of army required 7–10 days; growing shortage of food supplies – quotes *Zhurnal boevykh deistvii voisk 4-i udarnoi armii*, war diary [p. 406]; differences with Front commander Kurochkin; weakening of 4th Shock Army; operational plans; Yeremenko assembles his commanders, 8 January, 4th Shock Army offensive deployment and plans in detail; great variation in ages of men in the several divisions; divisions move to start-lines); pp. 421–44 (offensive opens on 9 January; penetration of German defences; Andreapol taken 16 January; advance on Toropets; capture of town assigned to Tarasov's 249th Rifle Div.; Yeremenko wounded in forward observation post; 10.00 hrs, 21 January, Toropets cleared; no reinforcements forthcoming from Front command, yet new offensive operations pending); pp. 445–75 (4th Shock Army transferred to Kalinin Front, objective to reach Rudna by 29 January; thus 'Toropets operation' led without pause to 'Velizh operation', fruitless attacks on Kresty; Yeremenko orders units to bypass it; beginning 4th February Shock Army forced to split forces along 3 axes; use of captured motorcycles to provide mobility to staff; 2 tank battalions attached – 62 tanks, 30 of them light tanks; 13 February, successful conclusion to both Toropets and Velizh operations; Yeremenko handed over 4th Shock to Lt.-Gen. F.I. Golikov in order to have hospital treatment).

Zhelanov, Col. V., 'Iz opyta pervoi operatsii na okruzhenie', *VIZ*, 12 (1964), pp. 21–24 (this is a very important study of the attempt in the winter of 1942 to encircle and destroy the German 16 Army at Demyansk), outline of the Soviet plan for an offensive on all fronts December 1941, danger of dispersing Soviet forces too widely including NW Front, command and strength of NW Front under Kurochkin, *Stavka* Directive 18 December for NW attack operations, joint operations with Kalinin Front envisaged, scale of operation did not correspond to forces available to NW Front, assignment 'nereal'nyi', difficulties of NW Front terrain, Front commander inhibited in his choice of offensive sectors since he was bound by the *Stavka* directive, Front could only operate with a single echelon due to lack of troops, offensive opens 7 January 1942, 3 Shock Army attacks 9 January, also 4 Shock Army under Yeremenko, 17 January Kurochkin reports to Stalin and proposes to effect encirclement at Demyansk, but under-estimation of German resilience, 19 January *Stavka* orders Kurochkin to hand over 3rd and 4th Shock Armies to Kalinin Front, NW Front to receive 1st Shock Army from W Front, decision to hand over 3rd Shock Army to Kalinin Front correct in circumstances in order to strengthen drive on Orsha–Smolensk and Rzhev–Vyazma but withdrawal of 3rd Shock Army severely weakened left wing of NW Front, need to co-ordinate operations against Demyansk largely ignored in spite of Kurochkin's pleading with *Stavka*, *Stavka* underestimates capacity of German troops at Demyansk, deterioration in situation of 1st Guards Rifle Corps end January, *Stavka*'s dissatisfaction 3 February, much weakened 1st Shock Army attacks south of Staraya Russa 13 February, difficulties with inner and outer encirclement operations, 25 February, *Stavka* disquiet at slow progress of Demyansk encirclement and lack of co-ordination; 'Group Ksenofontov' ordered to NW Front; 9 March, *Stavka* orders broadening of Soviet offensive front and suggests splitting up German forces at Demyansk; Bulganin's interference in military operations; NW Front command insufficiently experienced in offensive operations and scattered Soviet troops over several sectors; also shortage of ammunition, fuel and fodder; mid-March, situation on NW Front changes in favour of German 16th Army; NW Front command does not discover concentration of German forces s of

Staraya Russa in time and hence takes no measures to block German counter-blow; German troops smash Soviet encirclement ring; 29 March, all Soviet troops operating on inner encirclement line brought under Vatutuin's command; Kurochkin to attend to outer encirclement troops; *Stavka* reinforcements of AA guns and AT guns; 21 April, German forces complete deblockading operation and link up at Ramushevo; assessment of Soviet operations in Demyansk encirclement.

Zhidilov, Lt.-Gen. E.I., *My otstaivali Sevastopol* (Moscow: Voenizdat 1963), 2nd edn, pp. 109–77. Personal account of defence of Sevastopol by Col. Zhidilov, who was at that time – winter and early spring 1942 – commanding 7th Naval Inf. Bde.

Zhilin, Lt.-Gen. P.A. (ed.), *Na Severo-Zapadnom fronte 1941–1943* (Moscow: Nauka 1969): see under P.A. Kurochkin, 'My srazhalas na Severo-Zapadnom fronte', pp. 13–52 (short outline of history of NW Front).

See also F.Ya. Lisitsyn, 'l-ya Udarniya nastupaet', pp. 76–93 (1st Shock Army operations with NW Front, February–March 1942). Lisitsyn was a senior political officer with 1st Shock Army.

Zhorov, Dr./Senior Surgeon I., 'V tylu vraga pod Vyazmoi', *VIZ*, 2 (1965), pp. 57–65. Personal account by Red Army military doctor, senior surgeon in 33rd Army, of operations behind German lines in Vyazma area.

Zhukov, G.K., *Vospominaniya*, pp. 350–60.

Soviet airborne operations

Lisov, *op. cit.*, pp. 102–52.

Sofronov, G.P., *Vozdushnye desanty*, pp. 14–27.

Starchak, Col. I.G., *S neba-v boi* (Moscow: Voenizdat 1965), pp. 113–44. Personal account by former chief of Parachute/Air-Landing Service (*nachal'nik parashyutno – desantnoi sluzhby*) w Front of operations in German rear, January 1941.

9 HIGH SUMMER AND THE ROAD TO STALINGRAD

Though elsewhere and at other times there is a general consonance between the German and Soviet records, allowing for some disparity in numbers or estimates of intentions, in the late spring and early summer of 1942 this congruity vanishes. The intentions and capabilities of each side as seen by the other proved to be a source of confusion, error and ferocious dispute. Courier aircraft straying wildly off course or falling to enemy defences delivered to Germans and Russians alike a haul of captured plans, which further confused the situation. Hitler smelled plots combined with military incompetence; Stalin refused to believe the evidence laid before him, partly because it contradicted his own assessment of German objectives and partly out of suspicion that here was 'disinformation' on a grand scale. And all too soon the mighty shade of Stalingrad fell over both contestants, ironically enough an objective that the German command had never specifically delineated in its plans for a mighty reach into the southern reaches of the Soviet Union – designed to eliminate Soviet *Wehrkraft* once and for all – and which the Soviet leadership had at first to defend in desperate and improvised fashion.

Like the hapless men involved in the disasters in the south, reputations were scythed down on the Soviet side: Mekhlis was momentarily disgraced, but this was nothing compared with the fate meted out on the battlefield to Kostenko, Bobkin and Podlas, all killed in action. The survivors went on to fight for their honour in the postwar battle of the memoirs: Vasilevskii defends the high command and the General Staff, Rokossovskii the Front and field commanders who carried the brunt of the fighting; Moskalenko blames his own Front command for ignoring what all the army commanders in the south-western theatre knew by bitter experience; Chuikov with barely concealed savagery lashes out at the incompetence, muddle and dispiritedness among Soviet commanders during the early stages of the Stalingrad battle; Yeremenko, with Khrushchev in his wake, elaborates upon what is virtually a personal myth – and in contemporary terms, in the terrifying days of 1942 itself, the Party and even the nation came to blame the army for the train of disasters. Two small enigmas also fill out the picture – the attitudes adopted towards that regimental ramrod soldier Gordov and the mystery that still clings to Vlasov.

In terms of formal historical narrative and analysis I have come to rely heavily on A.M. Samsonov, Corresponding Member of the Academy of Sciences, with whom I had extensive conversations, all of which confirmed the depth of research in his major work on Stalingrad. Otherwise the battle of the memoirs is difficult to disentangle, though there can be no gainsaying the powerful impression that resulted from a personal encounter with Marshal Chuikov – whose tactical genius was displayed at Stalingrad, though that abstraction scarcely conveys the brooding sense of the agony of the experience. For that reason I have held to the first edition of his book, which seems so naturally and so effectively permeated with this experience. It is perhaps best summed up by saying that all who were involved in the Stalingrad battle were each in their own way branded irrevocably by it. That same observation also holds good for the German combatants.

Carell, *op. cit.*, pt 6, pp. 439–63 (Soviet disaster at Kerch; encirclement of Soviet armies s of Kharkov); pp. 464–76 (reduction of Sevastopol); pp. 476–87 (Operation 'Blau'; circumstances and consequences of capture of Maj. Reichel's documents; opening of 'Blau'); pp. 502–25 (German advance on Caucasus; capture of Maikop; into mountain passes. Pt 7, pp. 541–51 (opening of Stalingrad operation; fighting for Kalach; Soviet–German tank battles in Don bend; German armoured thrust on Stalingrad; the first engagements on outskirts of Stalingrad); pp. 552–60 (German attack on Spartakovka; German bridgehead on Volga bank and Soviet attempts to dislodge it; great danger from 4th Panzer Army and threat to Soviet 64th Army; Soviet response to this threat). NOTE: in his account of the Soviet operations at Stalingrad Carell relies heavily on Yeremenko and (not unnaturally) lavishes considerable praise on him.

Cookridge, E.H., *Gehlen. Spy of the century* (London: Hodder & Stoughton 1971), chs. 4 and 5 (Gehlen's rise; assumes command of *Fremde Heere Ost*; methods and organization); also ch. 6 ('Stalin's secrets', Gehlen takes over Kinzel's agents – including 'Ivar'; Minishkii affair; Operation 'Flamingo'; Gehlen and battle of Stalingrad; Operations 'Graukpf' and Schamil in Caucasus; BERGMANN composed of Caucasian defectors). Col. Kinzel, who was abruptly displaced as head of FHO on 1 April 1942, was dispatched to regimental command at front; Gehlen 'eased Kinzel out within a week' rather than allowing Kinzel the month allotted for handing over his duties. Maj.-Gen. Kinzel finally committed suicide at the end of the war.

Craig, William, *Enemy at the Gates, The Battle for Stalingrad* (New York: Reader's Digest/ Dutton 1973), *passim*.

Doerr, Maj.-Gen. Hans, *Der Feldzug nach Stalingrad, Versuch eines operativen Überblickes* (Darmstadt: E.S. Mittler 1955), *passim*; see also Soviet transl., G. Dërr, *Pokhod na Stalingrad* (Moscow: Voenizdat 1957).

Foote, Alexander, *Handbook for Spies*, pp. 138–9 (interrogated after war on 'Kharkov disaster' – messages that 'cost us 100,000 men at Kharkov and resulted in the Germans reaching Stalingrad').

Görlitz, Walter, 'The Battle for Stalingrad 1942–3', in *Decisive Battles of World War II: the German View*, pp. 219–34 (the course of the German offensive to end September).

Von Manstein, *op. cit.*, pp. 231–59.

Philippi and Heim, *op. cit.*, Pt 1, 'Der Feldzug des Jahres 1942', pp. 125–46.

Schröter, Heinz, *Stalingrad*, transl. Constantine Fitzgibbon (London: Michael Joseph 1958), *passim*.

Seaton, *Russo-German War*, pp. 255–65.

Steenberg, Sven, *Vlasov*, transl. from German Abe Farbstein (New York: Alfred Knopf 1970), pp. 16–28 ('Stalin's favourite': Vlasov's assignment to 2nd Shock Army and capture).

Strik-Strikfedlt, Wilfried, *Against Stalin and Hitler*, Memoir of the Russian Liberation Movement 1941–5, transl. from German David Footman (London: Macmillan 1970), pp. 69–81.

Werth, *The Year of Stalingrad*, An historical record and a study of Russian mentality, methods and policies (London: Hamish Hamilton 1946), II, pp. 72–83. NOTE: this is Alexander Werth at his brilliant best, combining comment with his on-the-spot wartime diaries together with his observations on the mood and disposition of the populace, not to mention his unique relations with Soviet writers.

Werth, *Russia at War*, pt 4, pp. 410–28.

Official/Party histories

IVOVSS (2), III, pp. 397–423 (the German Army renews its offensive, spring/early summer 1942; Soviet and German forces and deployments; Soviet plans to conduct limited offensives in area of Leningrad, Demyansk, along 'Smolensk axis', Kharkov region; fortified lines set up at Voronezh, Rostov, Saratov, Stalingrad; concentration of reserves in May; disbanding of W Front *Glavkom*, Kalinin and W Fronts subordinated to *Stavka* command; *Stavka* controls Bryansk Front; 'N-Caucasus theatre' established in April; Soviet intelligence confirms southerly direction of coming German offensive but *Stavka* clings to view that main German offensive will be aimed at Moscow and central industrial region; meanwhile Red Army still lacked 'technological superiority' over enemy).

a) *evacuation of Crimea and loss of Sevastopol*, pp. 404–11 (German offensive against Kerch; Soviet command unable to take effective counter-measures; poor Soviet deployment; incompetence of Kozlov and Mekhlis; *Stavka* relieves Mekhlis of command; 18 May, General Staff warns Sevastopol to expect major assault; German concentration for final assault; artillery preparation; final Soviet reinforcements; difficulties in supplying Sevastopol; 30 June, evacuation orders; fighting continues until 9 July; deterioration of situation in Black Sea and on S wing as a whole).

b) *battle of Kharkov*, pp. 411–17 (plans for limited offensive; *Stavka* cuts down scale of Timoshenko's proposed operation to capture of Kharkov only; Timoshenko's plan for this offensive; weaknesses in Soviet forces; preparations for offensive – operation 'Fridericus'; Soviet offensive opens first on 12 May; Kleist's operations threaten to encircle Soviet forces in Barvenkovo *place d'armes*; Timoshenko plans to halt offensive on Kharkov and regroup, but *Stavka* overrules him; Khrushchev appeals directly to Stalin; *Stavka* finally agrees to Soviet withdrawal, but much too late; Kostenko takes command of 6th and 57th Armies; Timoshenko attempts to organize Soviet breakout; Soviet offensive on Kharkov ends in loss of 3 armies; German forces regroup for fresh offensive; 38th and 9th Armies cut off; Barvenkovo salient eliminated; Red Army's loss of valuable bridgeheads and heavy losses in men and equipment; Germans hold strategic initiative).

c) Soviet defensive operations at Voronezh and in the Donbas, pp. 417-23 (German thrust on Stalingrad and N-Caucasus; operation 'Blau'; 2 German blows on concentric axes; aim to link up at Kantemirovka and encircle SW Front; German strength; Soviet deployment – Bryansk, S, SW and N-Caucasus Front; *Stavka* reinforces Bryansk Front, 28 June; critical situation Voronezh axis, early July; Vasilevskii sent to Bryansk Front; German threat to rear of S and SW Front; 7 July, *Stavka* splits Bryansk Front, beginning of Soviet withdrawal to escape German trap; German attempt to cut off Soviet forces in middle Don region; attempt to encircle S Front forces at Rostov, but by 24 July Soviet armies fallen back over Don; from 28 June to 24 July Bryansk, S and SW Fronts had fallen back 150-400km and abandoned Donbas; German forces in Don bend and threatening both Stalingrad and N-Caucasus).

See also pp. 424-41 (defence of Stalingrad:
a) fighting on approaches to Stalingrad; *Stavka* regroups and reinforces; defence works in and round city; deployment of Soviet armies; German ground and air strength; counter-blows by Soviet tank formations/Stalingrad front; Stalin's order No. 227, 28 July – 'not a step back'; Chinkov's 'operational group'; Vasilevskii in Stalingrad; 13 August, Yeremenko takes over Stalingrad and SE Fronts; German pressure to reach Volga.

b) operations on inner approaches, pp. 435-41, German bombing attacks, breakthrough into N sector of Stalingrad; drive to Tractor Plant; German drive in direction of Astrakhan; evacuation of civilians from Stalingrad; 3 September, *Stavka* directive to Zhukov at Stalingrad Front HQ; 62nd and 64th Armies in defence of Stalingrad; in mid-September 62nd Army had 50,000 men; many defence lines and field fortifications still not complete; networks of high ground and hillocks – *kurgany* – enabled Germans to overlook city and the Volga crossings).

See also pp. 454-67 (defence of N-Caucasus:
a) German plans and assigned forces; Soviet forces covering 'Caucasus axis'; small and badly equipped armies of S- and N-Caucasus Front holding enormous lines, and in July *Stavka* orders S Front to eliminate German bridgehead on Don and hold up German drive on Caucasus; Germans breakthrough; end July, 37th, 12th and 18th Armies to hold new line and Kagalnik river line; 28 July, *Stavka* unifies S- and N-Caucasus Front under Budenny, deputy commander Malinovskii; evacuation of Armavir, Krasnodar and Maikop, end July; first half August German attempt to drive on Tuapse; Soviet attempt to win time to mobilize reserves and establish a firm front on Terek–Baksan line; defensive positions built in rear; fight for mountain

passes begins 18 August; inadequate Soviet defences; organization of 'Alpine-rifle detachments'; defence of Novorossiisk; operations of Grechko's 47th Army; 2 September, German troops force Terek in Mozdok area and penetrate Soviet positions; Germans unable to break out of Terek bridgehead in direction of Grozny; fighting for Tuapse and operations of Petrov's 'Black Sea Group'; Black Sea fleet support; 25 October, fall of Nalchik and German drive on Ordzhonikidze; Maslennikov's blunders with 37th Army; German offensive finally halted.

b) pp. 468–76, operations on other sectors: operations of Soviet N Fleet; destruction of 2nd Shock Army – Volkhov Front – and capture of Vlasov; Soviet and German forces prepare offensives; operations of 'Neva operational group' and drive along 'Sinyavino axis'; attempts to improve food and fuel supply for Leningrad; NW Front operations May–June to destroy 'Demyansk pocket'; W Front and Kalinin Front operations on 'W axis'; encirclement of 39th Army and loss of bridgehead SW of Rzhev; 5–12 July, 10th, 16th and 61st Armies/W Front operations on 'Bryansk axis' against German Second Panzer Army; 30 July, W and Kalinin Front offensive to eliminate German-held Rzhev salient; 6–17 August, 6th Army/Voronezh Front offensive, 2nd Hungarian Army s of Voronezh).

German war diaries

KTB/OKW, II (1942) (1. Halband).

See A 'Einführung', IV (2–4), 'Der östliche Kriegsschauplatz 1942', pp. 46–50 ('Planung und Vorkämpfe zur Offensive 1942'); pp. 50–72 ('Der Sommerfeldzug nach Stalingrad und zum Kaukasus'); pp. 72–9 ('Die Kämpfe im mittleren und nördlichen Abschnitt der Ostfront, April bis November 1942').

See B 'Kriegstagebuch 1942: 2. 3. Quartal, Mai 1942–September 1942', pp. 331–707 (daily reports and summaries, plus documentary extracts; 'Lagebericht OKH', preceded by 'KTB der Kriegsgeschichtlichen Abteilung des OKW'). See esp. p. 571 ('Gliederung der Ostfront am 12. August 1942') and p. 592 ('15 August 1942 [Aufzeichnung Greiners] Zahl der russischen Heeresverbände einschliesslich Finnland, Kaukasus, Iran und dem Fernen Osten' [Table]: total 789 formations with combat capability equivalent to 593 formations; of these 418 formations committed on Ostfront (combat capability equivalent to 222 formations), 245 formations in reserve, 126 formations on other fronts – total, 593 formations to be reckoned on in terms of combat capability'.

See also pp. 596–7 ('Aufzeichnung Greiners zum 16 August 1942' – 'Der Führer ist in Sorge, dass Stalin den russischen Standard-Angriff von 1920 wiederholen könnte, nämlich einen Angriff über den Don etwa bei und oberhalb Serafimowitsch, in der Stossrichtung auf Rostow, wie ihn die Bolschewiken im Jahre 1920 gegen die weissrussische Armee des Generals Wrangel unternommen. . . . Er fürchtet, dass die an diesem Don-Abschnitt sichernde italienische 8. Armee einem solchen Angriff nicht standhalten würde. . . .'

See C 'Dokumenten-Anhang zum KTB 1942': no. 9, pp. 1273–6 ('Beurteilung der Gesamtfeindlage an der Ostfront . . . FHO vom 1 Mai 1942'); no. 14, p. 1282 ('Führerbefehl vom 13. Juli 1942 betr. Fortsetzung der Operationen der H. Grn. A und B); no. 19, pp. 1287–90 ('Aufzeichnung des Botschaftsrat vom 8. August 1942 über Vernehmungen von kriegsgefangenen sowjetischen Offizieren, u.a. General Wlassow).

Halder/KTB, 3, pp. 435–522 (dated/daily entries for period 3 May 1942–14 September 1942 (excerpt from entry 16 August 1942, p. 506: '9. Armee: Sehr gespannte Lage bei Rshew. Schwer absuzehen, wie das enden soll').

German Military Documents (GMD)

OKH GenStdH. Op. Abt.

OKH GenStdH. Operationsabteilung m. *'Barbarossa Band 4': 11 März 1942–19 Juli 1942.* T-78/R336, 6291960–2175.

OKH GenStdH. Operationsabteilung Gruppe I/N. Chefsachen: 11 Army operation 'Georg' (destruction of enemy forces on Finnish Front) and AG N preparations for 'Nordlicht'; cancellation of 'Nordlicht'. T-78/R337, 6293336–587.

OKH GenStdH. Operationsabteilung II. Folders, 'Studie Kaukasus' ('Operation aus Nord-kaukasien über den Kaukasus und Nordwestiran . . .', compiled late 1941; 'Anlagen zur Studie Kaukasus' and 'Kaukasus' file of background material for 'Unternehmen Kaukasus'. T-78/R336, 6292476–501; 501–83; 583–end, for these 3 items.

FHO 'Teil A Zusammenstellung der in der Zeit vom April 1942–Dezember 1944 in der Abteilung fremde Heere Ost abgefassten Beurteilungen der Feindlage . . .'
See 1) 'Russische Operationsmöglichkeiten' 10 April 1942, also 2) 1 May 1942; 3) 15 July 1942 – reporting meeting of the 'Militarrät' in Moscow on 13 July, with Shaposhnikov, Molotov, Voroshilov and English, American and Chinese Military Attachés; 4) 14 August 1942. T-78/R466, 6445876–92.

FHO (II) Folder 'Angriff-Charkow Chi-Abwehrmeldung', date of first entry 18 May 1942: listing of information received, date and source for period 12 February 1942–18 June 1942; monitoring of Tass announcements and Moscow radio; analysis of foreign news items; telegram from Major G. Baun to FHO citing *Abwehrstelle* report of 13 April on Central Committee member Nossenko's comment to ed. of *Pravda* that *Politburo/Stavka* session had decided on Soviet pre-emptive attack to wrest' initiative from German Army and likeliest date would be 1 May (4102). T-78/R496, 6483905–4110 (documents run in reverse order, from May–February).

FHO (II) Folder 'Gliederung von Stäben' on Soviet command and military organization. See table on Soviet order of battle opposed to AG S, 9 May 1942. T-78/R483, 6468102.

'Gefechtsvorschrift für die Infanterie der Roten Armee, 1942': Teil I (Schütze, Gruppe, Zug), *Dienstvorschrift*; also Teil II (Bataillon, Regiment). (Soviet Field Service Regulations/Infantry, revised 1942). T-78/R498, 6485856–6044 and 6530–731.

FHO (II) File labelled 'Kürze – 15 September 1942'; copies of 'Kürze Beurteilung der Feindlage' (first item is for 15 September 1942, but situation reports run backwards to April 1942, with sudden jump to December and then back to April); each 'Kürze Beurteilung' (or simply 'Beurteilung') sets out main data on Soviet operations in area of specified German Army Groups or individual armies, plus information on Soviet movement and Soviet reserves. See T-78/R467, 6446576–7103 (running from end August 1942 to 4 April 1943).

Die Behandlung des russischen Problems . . . (ms.): see under Teil A (v) 6, pp. 91–4 ('Die erste Wlassow-Aktion'–'Wer ist Wlassow', with brief biographical details; enigma of Vlasov; his role in defence of Moscow; his assignment to Volkhov Front and 2nd Shock Army – his friends aver that he was given this well-nigh impossible task in order to ruin his reputation as one of 'true saviours of Moscow', if not *the* saviour –

and, finally, report that 200 Soviet parachute troops standing by to go into 'Volkhov pocket' to ensure Vlasov's safety and escape.

Cf. K. Cherkassov, *General Kononov*, p. 105.

Soviet sources and materials

Anan'ev, Col. I., 'Sozdanie tankovykh armii i sovershenstvovanie ikh organizatsionnoi struktury', *VIZ*, 10 (1972), pp. 38–47 (organization and structure of first Soviet tank armies – 3rd and 5th – formed May–June 1942, followed by 1st and 4th, 5th and subsequently 2nd; 'mixed establishment' with rifle divisions as well as tank/mechanized corps, also 'homogeneous' tank army with only tank/mechanized formations).

Biryuzov, *op. cit.*, pp. 73–7 (appointed chief of staff 48th Army; preparations to carry out attack plans for offensive on 'Kharkov axis', 48th Army assigned important role, though this army still existed 'only on paper' and would have to be formed from scattered units or reserve troops; new army commander Samokhin not yet arrived at his post; Samokhin's aircraft lands by mistake on German aerodrome at Mtsensk – carrying details of the *Stavka* directive; hurried alteration of 48th Army assignment to offensive aimed at Orel from N of Livny).

Bitva za Stalingrad (Volgograd: Nizhne-Volzshkoe Kn-Izd 1969), collective authorship; see under Golikov, Yeremenko. NOTE: the Volgograd publishing house retains the traditional name for the battle – Stalingrad.

Chuikov, V.I., *Nachalo puti* (Moscow: Voenizdat 1959; 2nd edn, 1962; 3rd edn, Volograd: Nizhne-Volzhskoe Kn-Izd. 1967). I have relied primarily on 1st ed., though also using the 2nd and 3rd. See also *The Beginning of the Road*, trans. Harold Silver (London: MacGibbon & Kee 1963), for an excellent translation derived from 2nd edn.

See also from 1st edn, pp. 8–103.

See also shortened version, *Vystoyav, my pobedili*, Zapiski komandarm 62-i (Moscow: Sov. Rossiya 1960).

Dvesti ognennykh dnei (Moscow: Voenizdat 1968), see under Vasilevskii. See also Soviet transl., *Two Hundred Days of Five* (Moscow: Progress Pub. 1970).

Ehrenburg, Ilya, *Lyudi, gody, zhizn*, pp. 90–1. Reports interview with Vlasov in March 1942, when he spoke of Suvorov, and a longer conversation in which he described experiences at Kiev in 1941; Stalin's telephone call to him; Stalin's thanks to him for his successful operations with 20th Army; though Vlasov had many criticisms – 'We are badly trained' – he did mention Stalin's telephone call to him with his appointment to 2nd Shock Army, emphasizing that 'Stalin has shown great trust in me'. Ehrenburg did not conduct this interview himself, but comments on Vlasov as an interesting, vain but brave man, neither a Brutus nor a Prince Kurbskii. His motive was vanity, for if Germany had won in the E, he would have been War Minister in a Russia ruled by Hitler.

Geroicheskaya oborona Sevastopolya, pp. 245–322. (German plans for final assault on Sevastopol, Soviet defensive measures and dispositions to fight off assault; last-minute German preparations; fighting for main defence line between 7–20 June; difficulties of supply-running; curtailment of runs due to German air attacks and short summer nights; civilian transports sunk, leaving only Soviet warships; use of submarines from 1st and 2nd Bdes/Black Sea Fleet; *Tashkent* disabled by German dive-bombers; throughout June Soviet ships land 23,500 men, 11,300 tons of ammunition plus fuel and food, evacuate 25,157 wounded or civilians, fighting in Sevastopol itself, 20–30 June; the final phase of defence – on 30 June commander of SOR had expended all his reserves; 1,259 shells left for medium artillery but none for heavy guns, permission for Sevastopol commanders and 200–50 key personnel to be flown out; 4 July, final Soviet resistance on the Kherson spit).

Golikov, 'Nezabyvaemye vstrechi', in *Bitva za Stalingrad*, pp. 75–95.

Grechko, A.A. (Marshal: Soviet Defence Minister), *Bitva za Kavkaz* (Moscow: Voenizdat 1969), 2nd edn, pt 1, pp. 45–171 (Soviet and German operations in Don and Kuban steppe; opening of battle for Caucasus; operational situation and comparative strengths N–Caucasus Front; Stavropol axis, Krasnodar axis, Maikop axis; operations in foothills of Main Caucasian Range; Soviet defence measures; *Stavka* reinforcement for N–Caucasus and Caucasus Front; Mozdok and Novorossiisk; operations in mountain passes). NOTE: this detailed history based on Soviet military records (and information derived from senior commanders) must be regarded as the standard work, completely replacing A. S. Savyalev and T. I. Kalyadin, *Bitva za Kavkaz*. Incidentally, it illuminates the roles of Grechko, Brezhnev and Gorshkov.

Gulyaev, Maj.-Gen. V.G., *Chelovek v brone* (Moscow: Voenizdat 1964), pp. 107–12 (Feklenko relieved of command of 17th Tank Corps and recalled to Moscow; Parsegov relieved of command of 40th Army and 3rd Tank Corps – 17th, 18th and 25th – re-assigned to 60th Army); pp. 113–23 (Antonyuk summarily relieved of command of 69th Army by Stalin; Chernyakhovskii assumes 60th Army command; Col. Polyuboyarov takes over 18th Tank Corps from Korchagin – Chernyakhovskii had originally assumed command of 18th Tank Corps on 13 July and Korchagin was momentary replacement).

Kazakov, Marshal K.P., *Vsegda s pekhotoi, vsegda s tankami* (Moscow: Voenizdat 1973), 2nd edn, pp. 71–90 (artillery in defensive battle; Soviet deployment and operational practices at Stalingrad, w and E bank of Volga; see diagrammatic map [p. 83] for deployment of rifle units and artillery, 62nd Army, 13 September).

Kazakov, M.I., *Nad kartoi bylykh srazhenii*, pp. 99–135.

Kazakov, M.I., 'Na Voronezhskom napravlenii letom 1942 goda', *VIZ*, 10 (1964), pp. 28–44 (formal military narrative and analysis of Bryansk Front operations and covering 'Voronezh axis'; failure of General Staff intelligence to discern coming German attack and Stalin's rejection of evidence relating to Operation 'Blau'); pp. 32–3 (Vasilevskii's criticisms of Golikov and handling of tank formations, 1 July), pp. 36–7 (failure of 5th Tank Army counter-attack; 4 July, Vasilevskii informs Kazakov of establishment of Voronezh Front and of appointment of Golikov as commander).

Krupchenko, Maj.-Gen. I., 'Marshal bronetankovykh voisk Ya. N. Fedorenko', *VIZ*, 10 (1966), pp. 45–50. Biography of Marshal Fedorenko, head of Armoured Forces Administration. In 1942 particularly, senior Soviet commanders tried to blame the disasters on the shortcomings of the Soviet tank arm, even demanding the punishment of tank army and corps commanders, but Fedorenko 'beat off' these attacks on his tank officers.

Ksenofontov, P. and Samoshenko, V., 'Bitva pod Stalingradom i memuarnaya literatura',

VIZ, 11 (1967), pp. 94–7. Review of the memoirs dealing with Stalingrad, drawing attention to inaccuracies in writings of Yeremenko and Voronov.

Kuznetsov, Lt.-Gen. P. G., *General Chernyakhovskii* (Moscow: Voenizdat 1969), pp. 66–74 ('*Komandarm*' – Chernyakhovskii takes over 60th Army, Voronezh Front).

Loktionov, I.I., *Volzhskaya flotiliya v Velikoi Otechestvennoi voine* (Moscow: Voenizdat 1974), pp. 10–35 (composition and organization); pp. 36–90 (Flotilla operations in defensive battle to end September).

Meretskov, *op. cit.*, pp. 289–98.

Moskalenko, *op. cit.* 2nd edn, pp. 168–213.

NOTE: this detailed narrative, interspersed with Moskalenko's own analysis and not a little conjecture, places the blame for the disastrous outcome of the Kharkov offensive on the sw theatre and Front command, whose estimate of German strength and Soviet capability was woefully wrong, combined with the failure to see the danger looming up even when the *Stavka* pointed it out in no uncertain terms. Thus this account squares with that of Marshal Zhukov and does not spare either Timoshenko or Bagramyan.

Pshenyanik, Maj-Gen. Aviation, G., 'Soveteskaya aviatsiya v boyakh na Tereke', *VIZ*, 10 (1972), pp. 31–7 (Gen. K.A.Vershinin's 4th Air Army in support of Maslennikov's 'N Group'/Trans-Caucasus Front, also 50th Bomber Division/ADD, August–October 1942).

Rokossovskii (ed.), *Velikaya bitva na Volge* (Moscow: Voenizdat 1965), pt 1 (17 July–18 November 1942), pp. 26–90 (the battle in the great bend of the Don, 17 July–10 August; German conviction that capture of Stalingrad would be both swift and easy, Soviet defensive measures to cover Stalingrad; Stalingrad Front created and sw Front wound up, 12 July; Gordov in command, 27 July; Front assignment; Stalingrad Front strength [p. 28], also German strength on 'Stalingrad axis'; Soviet defensive tasks defined in *Stavka* directive no. 170495, 12 July; 62nd and 64th Armies to fight w of Don; defence works to be constructed round Stalingrad; role of Stalingrad Party *obkom* in defensive preparations after 15 July).

a) Stalingrad Front defensive preparations: pp. 32–6 (Stalingrad Front command decisions; 63rd, 38th, 62nd and 64th Army assignments, also 8th Air Army; Front commander disperses available armour to separate armies); pp. 36–8 (operational decisions of V.I. Kuznetsov, 63rd Army, Moskalenko, 38th Army, Kolpakchi, 62nd Army and Chuikov, 64th Army); pp. 38–40 (deployment and strength of artillery, armour and aircraft); pp. 40–1 (engineers and construction of defence lines); pp. 41–4 (intelligence, anti-tank and anti-air defence); pp. 44–6 (communications, hoop control measures); pp. 46–7 (rear services); pp. 47–9 (Party-political work); pp. 49–53 (Soviet forces regroup, 17–22 July; forward elements from 62nd Army on river Chir in contact with German advance units, 17 July; German attempts to capture Kalach and Don crossings along shortest route to Stalingrad); pp. 53–8 (commitment of main forces; German 6th Army strength; *Stavka* commits reinforcements to Stalingrad Front; 22 July, *Stavka* redesignates 38th Army 1st Tank Army with 2nd Tank Corps, 1 rifle div., 1 tank bde; 28th Army redesignated 4th Tank Army – see table [p. 57] and footnote [p. 58]).

b) fighting in great bend of Don, 23–31 July, pp. 58–73 (attempts to seal off German breakthrough, 62nd Army heavily engaged, 24 July; German forces press gains on right flank of 62nd Army; several divisions of 62nd Army encircled and

Col. Zhuravlev flown in to command this force; 26 July, *Stavka* orders 62nd Army to restore situation and push Germans back to river Chir; German attack now directed against 64th Army; caught 64th Army in unfavourable position; 26 July at 20.30 hrs front commander – with *Stavka* consent – decides on frontal attack on German forces crushing right flank of 62nd Army; 1st and 4th Tank Armies to play main role; attack orders for Moskalenko's 1st Tank and Kryuchenkin's 4th Tank, also 21st Army attack orders; Soviet tank armies not ready for full-scale operations; heavy Soviet losses and situation of 62nd Army continues to deteriorate; Soviet 1st Tank Army brought to halt by end July; Stalingrad Front command plans counter-attack to take pressure off 64th Army; end July, German forces broken Soviet 62nd Army's right flank and reached Don NW of Kalach; on Soviet 64th Army's right flank German units had also broken through to Don, all of which increased German threat to Stalingrad from W; Stalingrad Front now deploying 23 divs and 2 bdes; German command now commits 4th Panzer Army to operate against Stalingrad from the SW; great weaknesses in Soviet anti-tank defence; fruitless use of armour; poor co-operation between formation and units; *Stavka* interfered in arbitrary and damaging fashion – issuing even *tactical* instructions and thus impeding work of front command in making timely and effective decisions).

c) holding German drive on Stalingrad from SW, 30 July–10 August, pp. 74–85 (Soviet command forced to deploy forces against 4th Panzer and prevent thrust from SW on city; preparation of fresh German offensive, hence momentary lull in area of 64th Army; concern of front command at situation on left flank, where 4th Panzer might quickly overwhelm Soviet 51st Army, thus threatening left flank and rear of Stalingrad Front; Chuikov's 'operational group' to shore up left flank 64th Army; early August, two operational axes on Stalingrad Front – to NW and SW – with 8 Soviet armies deployed; 5 August, Stalin splits Stalingrad Front and establishes SE Front in addition; Yeremenko nominated to SE Front command; responsibility for defence of Stalingrad itself fell to 62nd Army; *Stavka* directive of 5 August detailing Stalingrad Front tasks; masses German air attacks, role and importance of Volga flotilla; continuous *Stavka* reinforcement – from 17 July– 5 August, dispatched 18 rifle divs, 1 tank corps, 1 motor-rifle bde, 6 independent tank bdes, 1 anti-tank bde and artillery/mortar reinforcements; 6 August, 4th Panzer broke through to Abganerovo–Tingut area, whereupon *Stavka* demanded *immediate* counter-attack without regard for time factor; 64th Army counter-attack mounted and by 9–10 August forced 4th Panzer to halt).

d) Stalingrad Front effort to hold bridgehead in great bend of Don, 1–8 August, pp. 86–9 (German breakthrough to Don endangered situation of Soviet 1st Tank Army and 62nd Army, as well as right-flank forces 64th Army holding bridgehead w of Kalach; attempts to expel German forces from Verkhne–Buzinovka, but in early August Soviet tank corps had only 15–20 tanks left; 1st and 4th Tank Army attacks badly co-ordinated and heavy losses resulted; German attempts to encircle and destroy 62nd Army, 8 August, 16th Panzer Div. broke through to Kalach; Verkhne–Buzinovka battle lost and these forces not available to support 62nd Army; German units moving to outer face of city and Stalingrad Front armies on defensive).

e) conclusion, p. 90 (*Stavka*, though fully realizing implications of German plans once German armies had broken through on S wing of Soviet–German front, miscalculated quite seriously in attempts to seal breach; failed to appreciate German advantages on 'Stalingrad axis'; time factor not properly considered in concentrating reserves; deployment and concentration lines not properly or realistically organized; decisions of the *Stavka* and General Staff corresponded more to wishes rather than to what was feasible; units committed too hastily and piecemeal, while *Stavka* interference prevented Front commanders acting independently and in conformity with situation on ground: 'Had it not been for all these miscalculations, the enemy would scarcely have succeeded in reaching the Volga').

Pp. 91–162 (fighting on the immediate approaches to Stalingrad, 15 August– 12 September: German and Soviet operational plans; defence of Stalingrad environs; Zhukov and Vasilevskii sent to Stalingrad; Stalingrad and SE Front forces and deployments; forces engaged by 15 August).

a) Operations NW of Stalingrad, 15–29 August, pp. 112–45 (4th Tank Army operations in small bend of Don; attempts of 4th Tank Army and 62nd Army to check German advance failed; further *Stavka* reserves – 15 rifle divs and 3 tank corps from 1–20 August; Soviet aviation committed in full strength; Stalingrad front to hold German 6th Army and SE Front to fight off 4th Panzer, Yeremenko's serious mistake with 63rd and 21st Army; overestimated combat capability).

b) Offensive in Serafimovich area, 20–8 August, pp. 128–31 (63rd, 21st and 1st Guards Army capture bridgehead on w bank of Don).

c) Kotluban counterblow, 23–9 August, pp. 131–41 (23 August, critical situation in Stalingrad; German units penetrating NW suburbs of city; operational sector established in Tractor Plant area; heavy German bombing; German units establish a corridor to Volga; 24 August, *Stavka* orders this to be eliminated; second command point set up 26 August/Stalingrad Front under K.A. Kovalenko; failure of Soviet counter-attacks; barricades to be constructed inside city).

d) 62nd Army operations at Kalach, 23–9 August, pp. 141–5.

e) Fighting on SW approaches to Stalingrad, 17 August–2 September, pp. 145–61 (4th Panzer Army offensive begins 17 August; sector defended by 64th Army; German breakthrough in area of 57th Army SW of Stalingrad; heavy attacks on left flank 64th Army, 23 August; 4th Panzer Army checked on this approach).

f) 64th Army operations, 29 August–2 September, pp. 150–3 (4th Panzer regroups; 62nd and 64th Armies fall back to new defensive positions; V.F. Gerasimenko – commander of Stalingrad Military District – ordered to defend Astrakhan defensive region; these forces become 28th Army; mobilization of local communists to reinforce Soviet troops holding the Tsaritsa river line, 29 August; barricades to be built round each factory; withdrawal of 62nd and 64th Armies from outer to middle defence line delayed 2–3 days to enable front command to collect reserves and establish middle defence line).

g) Operations N of Stalingrad and SE Front operations on the inner defence line, 3–12 September, pp. 154–61 (German forces on inner defence line, 2 September; SE Front's heavy losses; German air superiority; *Stavka* commits 24th and 66th Armies; 1st Guards Army finishing its concentration; 16th Air Army assigned to Stalingrad; Soviet attack on German flank; begins 3 September; little Soviet progress and 12 days of attacks fruitless; poor organization of this left-flank counterblow; inefficient use of Soviet tanks and effectiveness of German air power; heavy fighting on inner defence line; urgent reinforcement for 62nd and 64th Armies; threat of German breakthrough to Volga along Kalach–Stalingrad railway

line and actually forcing river measures for defence of E bank; artillery support for
Stalingrad from E bank; German units in suburbs; Chinkov appointed commander
62nd Army, 8 September; right wing of SE Front forced back into city itself).

h) Conclusion, pp. 161–2 (defensive battle between Don and Volga lasted
from 15 August to 12 September; Soviet troops succeeded in manning city defence
line; withdrawal of left flank of 62nd Army and German breakthrough to Volga
on right flank of 64th Army meant that Stalingrad pierced from the NE and SW;
full German assault directed against city itself and much-weakened 62nd Army
unable to hold it; desperate need to win time to regroup; organize the defence of
Stalingrad and move up reserves).

NOTE: this very detailed history bearing the imprint of Marshal Rokossovskii is
demonstrably highly critical of the *Stavka*, the General Staff and Stalin himself –
though Stalin is mentioned by name only once throughout the entire volume, being
otherwise identified as 'the Supreme Commander' – and seeks to justify the Front
and formation commanders, the men on the spot who were doing the fighting. Like
Marshal Sokolovskii's volume on Moscow, this is a terse military narrative based
almost entirely on archival materials. Like the Sokolovskii volume there is a comprehensive map supplement. Both volumes were intended for 'generals and officers of
the Soviet Army' and both were approximately the same size of edition (Sokolovskii,
10,000; Rokossovskii, 14,000).

Rok: *Comparison of Soviet and German forces on the
'Stalingrad axis': situation on 22 July 1942*

	German forces	Soviet forces
divs	18	16
manpower in divs	250,000	187,000
guns and mortars	7,500	7,900
tanks	740	360
aircraft	1,200	337

Rok 109: *Comparison of Soviet and German forces on the
Stalingrad Front: 15 August*

	Along entire 480km front		Along axis of main German blow (50km/front)	
	Soviet	German	Soviet	German
divs	26	28	5	10
manpower	414,700	427,735	39,132	129,635
tanks	200	440	113	275
guns and mortars:	1,969	5,270	556	2,105
mortars/82mm calibre				
and over	350	1,610	170	395
field pieces	845	2,275	169	795

Rok III: *Comparison of Soviet and German Forces* SE *Front: 15 August*

	Along entire 320km front		Along axis of main German blow, 35km front	
	Soviet	German	Soviet	German
divs	16	12	4	7
manpower	163,270	158,200	134,490	90,760
tanks	70	595	70	440
guns and mortars:	1,390	2,110	990	1,210
mortars/82mm calibre and over	370	470	230	260
field pieces	520	1,040	390	590

Rok 155: *Comparison of Soviet and German forces in operational area of Soviet 62nd Army: 3 September*

	Soviet 62nd Army	Enemy forces committed against 62nd Army
manpower	44,970	80,240
guns (76mm calibre and over)	85	630
mortars (82mm calibre and over)	150	760
tanks	108	390

Rok 210: *Soviet war production, 1942: comparison of output for first and second half of 1942*

	January–June 1942	June–December 1942
Aircraft		
fighters:	3,871	5,973
MiG–3	12	36
LaGG–3	1,766	970
La–5	—	1,129
Yak–1	1,578	1,895
Yak–7 and Yak–9	515	1,943
Il–2 *shturmoviki*	2,629	5,596
bombers	1,641	1,867

	January– June 1942	June– December 1942
Tanks		
heavy	1,663	890
medium (T–34)	4,414	8,106
light	5,100	4,272
Artillery		
anti-tank	8,957	11,142
AA guns	2,368	4,120
76mm	11,052	12,257
122mm	2,240	2,597
152mm	1,008	766
Mortars		
50mm	66,802	36,511
82mm	45,485	55,378
107mm and 120mm	10,183	15,164
Infantry weapons		
machine carbines	524,473	952,332
light machine-guns	71,923	100,183
medium machine-guns	16,011	40,544
heavy machine-guns	1,864	5,478

Rok 166: *Comparison of Soviet and German forces on*
'Stalingrad axis': 13 September

	Soviet	German
manpower	590,000	590,000
guns and mortars	7,000	10,000
tanks	600	1,000
aircraft	389	1,000

Rudenko, Marshal/Aviation S., 'Aviatsiya v bitve za Stalingrad (Oboronitel'nyi period –
iyul-noyabr 1942 goda)', *VIZ*, 7 (1972), pp. 27–33 (Khryukin's 8th Air Army began
air operations in Stalingrad battle; 16th Air Army – commanded by Rudenko –
committed in September; continuing shortage of fighters, Soviet air units having
suffered 'considerable losses'; Khryukin combined all his damaged but airworthy
machines into one air group; long-range aviation – ADD – also used in immediate
front-line area; one singular feature of Stalingrad air operations was number of

sorties flown at night; Gen. A.A. Novikov, c-in-c of Soviet Air Force, co-ordinated air operations at Stalingrad, acting also as *Stavka* representative).

16-ya vozdushnaya, Voenno-istoricheskii ocherk o boevom puti 16-i vozdushnoi armii (1942–1945) (Moscow: Voenizdat 1973), pp. 16–42 (16th Air Army operations in defensive battle at Stalingrad).

Samsonov, A.M., *Stalingradskaya bitva* (Moscow: Nauka 1968), 2nd edn, pp. 81–182. NOTE: the 2nd edn of Professor Samsonov's work must be regarded as virtually the standard work on Soviet operations at Stalingrad, drawing as it does on a wealth of Soviet military records, primary material from participants and a discriminating use of secondary sources. Inevitably I have relied heavily on Professor Samsonov's study, as well as his personal comments in dealing with Soviet materials.

Samsonov, A.M. (ed.), 'K 20-letiyu bitvy na Volge (Postanovleniya Gorodskogo komiteta oborony oktyabr 1941–iyul 1942)', *Istoricheskii Arkhiv*, 2 (1963), pp. 3–56. Documents on work of Stalingrad city defence committee.

Sandalov, L.M., *Pogorelo-Gorodishchenskaya operatsiya* (Moscow: Voenizdat 1960) (20th Army/w Front operations, August 1942). A detailed operational analysis intended for 'generals and officers of the Soviet Army'.

Sharipov, A., *Chernyakhovskii*, Povestvovanie o polkovodtse (Moscow: Voenizdat 1971), with a foreword by Marshal V.I. Chuikov, pp. 144–63 (Chernyakhovskii takes over 18th Tank Corps, assigned to command of 60th Army on Stalin's orders; Gen. S.S. Varentsov and others concerned at appointment of such a young officer to army command).

NOTE: General Varentsov's fears were groundless, for Chernyakhovskii proved to be one of the most brilliant and successful commanders of the war, though his career was terminated in February 1945 by a shell splinter which killed him; by this time he was a full General and a Front commander.

Shtemenko, *op. cit.*, pp. 47–62.

'K 30-letiyu Stalingradskoi bitvy', *VIZ*, 11 (1972) (30th anniversary articles): see under Marshal N. Krylov, pp. 31–6 ('Volzshkaya tverdynya: account by Chief of Staff of 62nd Army); N. Mazunin, pp. 55–60 ('Volzhskaya voennaya flotiliya v boyakh za Stalingrad': Volga Naval Flotilia – under Rear-Admiral D.D. Rogachev – operations to secure Volga waterway, clear mines, provide fire support for Soviet troops in Stalingrad, transport of troops into Stalingrad and evacuation of wounded; in all, 35,400 runs into Stalingrad, 122,418 men transported to w bank, 627 lorries ferried over, 4,323 tons of assorted military supplies); A. Galitsan, pp. 61–3 ('Komanduyushchii Stalingradskim frontom' – on Yeremenko).

Utenkov, Col. F., 'Nekotorye voprosy oboronitel'nogo srazheniya na dal'nykh podstupakh Stalingrada', *VIZ*, 9 (1962), pp. 35–48. An important and detailed study of the battle on the 'outer approaches to Stalingrad'.

Vasilevskii memoirs/materials. See *Delo vsei zhizni*, pp. 186–202.

See also 'Reshayushchie pobedy sovetskogo naroda', in *Radi zhizni na zemle* (Voronezh: 1970), pp. 21–32.

See also 'Pobeda, ne merknushchaya v vekakh' in *Dvesti ognennykh dnei*, pp. 11–28.

See also 'Vospominaniya ob istoricheskoi bitve', in *Stalingradskaya epopeya*, pp. 73–120, here pp. 73–82.

Yeremenko, A.I., *Stalingrad*, Zapiski komanduyushchego frontom (Moscow: Voenizdat 1961), pt I, pp. 50–138.

NOTE: written as much to bolster Khrushchev's 'military image' as Yeremenko's own reputation, this account is not wholly reliable and is somewhat one-sided, with almost no attempt at corroboration or identification of documentary items quoted. See also 'Odin iz 200 ognennykh dnei', in *Bitva za Stalingrad*, pp. 63–73.

Zhukov, G.K., *Vospominaniya*, pp. 366–95.

Literature

Grossman, V., *Zapravoe delo* (Moscow: Voenizdat 1959).
Nekrasov, V., *Front-line Stalingrad* transl. David Floyd (London: Harvill Press 1962).
Simonov, K., *Dni i nochi* (Moscow: Voenizdat 1955).

I am much indebted to Alexander Werth for being able to draw on all his unique insights into wartime literature, contact engendered while discussing his own book.

IO TRANSFORMATION AT STALINGRAD: OPERATION 'URANUS'
(OCTOBER–NOVEMBER 1942)

In Marshal Zhukov's own words, 'After Stalin's death the question as to who was the architect of the plan for a counter-offensive [at Stalingrad] . . . was not made altogether clear.' That is putting it mildly, to say the least, even if the Marshal adds that the question is 'not of any great particular importance'. Perhaps apportioning praise is not so important, but what does command attention is the need to distinguish between the *kontr-udar* (a limited two-front counter-blow N and S of Stalingrad) and the grand design of the *kontrnastuplenie* (the counter-offensive proper involving 3 Fronts – SW, Don and Stalingrad). There were, of course, the myths, such as that propagated by Yeremenko, who also linked Khrushchev with this grand design nurtured within the bosom of this Stalingrad Front itself; but such fanciful accounts have been almost wholly discredited. To judge by Soviet reviews, it is also necessary to proceed cautiously in appraising N.N. Voronov's recollections, though they are far from detailed. Quite the best review of both the plans and the associated memoirs is to be found in A.M. Samsonov's study on the Stalingrad battle, though in the final analysis he rests much of his case on the writings of Marshal Vasilevskii, who at least adduces substantial documentary evidence.

Adam, Wilhelm, *Der schwere Entschluss* (Berlin: Verlag der Nation 1965), pp. 153–84 (*Gegegnoffensive und Einkesselung*: Soviet counter-offensive and encirclement of 6th Army).
Carell, *op. cit.*, pt 7, pp. 568–75.
Clark, Alan, *Barbarossa*, The Russo–German Conflict 1941–1945 (London: Hutchinson 1965), 2, pp. 273–82 (entombment of 6th Army; last days of defensive fighting in Stalingrad and the final German assault; development of the Soviet counter-offensive).
Craig, *op. cit.*, pt 2, pp. 179–214.
Doerr, *op. cit.*, see under C: 'Die russische Gegenoffensive I. Akt', pp. 62–9 and pp. 69–76.
Görlitz, Walter, 'The Battle for Stalingrad', in *Decisive Battles of World War II*, pp. 235–41.

Philippi and Heim, *op. cit.*, pt 2, 'Stalingrad', pp. 177–84.
Seaton, *Russo–German War*, pp. 300–5.
Werth, *Year of Stalingrad*, III, pp. 266–346.
Werth, *Russia at War*, pt 5, pp. 475–91.

Diplomatic materials/memoirs

Stalin–Churchill Correspondence, no. 41, p. 45 (received 25 April 1942, Churchill to Stalin on Molotov's visit to London); no. 43, pp. 45–6 (Stalin to Churchill, 6 May: urges speedy sailing of convoys); no. 44, pp. 46–7 (Churchill to Stalin, 11 May: difficulties in convoy traffic and urgent need for greater cover from Soviet naval and air forces); no. 45, p. 47 (Stalin to Churchill, 12 May: promises greater Soviet naval/air support but these resources limited); no. 46, p. 48 (Churchill to Stalin, 20 May: 1 convoy already sailing but heavy losses expected without Soviet bombing of German long-range airfields); no. 47, pp. 48–9 (Churchill to Stalin, 24 May: report on conversations with Molotov); no. 51, p. 50 (Stalin to Churchill, 28 May: signing of new treaty); no. 53, p. 51 (Stalin to Churchill, 20 June: desirability of joint operations in N but when and on what scale can British forces participate?); no. 56, pp. 52–5 (Churchill to Stalin, 18 July: suspension of convoys to Russia; Persian Gulf supply line; transfer of Polish troops in USSR to Palestine; impact of 'preparations now going forward on a vast scale for Anglo-American mass invasion of the Continent'; no. 57, p. 56 (Stalin to Churchill, 23 July: protest at suspension of supply convoys to Russia); no. 58, p. 57 (Churchill to Stalin, 31 July: proposes meeting with Stalin); no. 60, p. 58 (Stalin to Churchill, 31 July: Stalin invites Churchill 'on behalf of the Soviet Government'); no. 65, pp. 60–1 (Stalin's memorandum to Churchill, 13 August: commitment by US and UK to Second Front); no. 66, pp. 61–3 (Churchill's *aide-memoire* to Stalin, 14 August: US–UK plans for 'Torch' and refutation of argument that any 'promise' broken over Second Front).
Documents on Soviet–Polish Relations, I, see doc. no. 176, pp. 269–71 (conversation between Gen. Sikorski and Sir Stafford Cripps on territorial claims put forward by Soviet government, 26 January 1942; Cripps recommends accepting Soviet terms; Sikorski adopts very guarded position and believes that importance of Soviet military victories is presently overrated – Sikorski discerns that Stalin's policy with regard to the Polish frontiers means 'to push Poland from E to W'); doc. no. 191, pp. 295–9 (Sikorski–Churchill conversation, 11 March 1942: Churchill asks whether Japanese restraint due to German influence and Japanese interest in achieving understanding between *Reich* and Soviet Union; Sikorski of opinion that both sides had 'burnt their boats'; Sikorski predicts German offensive in Russia on S sector in direction of Rostov and Caucasus at end of May or June; importance of keeping good relations with Turkey; warns British government of danger of Soviet territorial claims – which must also mean encirclement of Poland by Russia; deadlock in organization of Polish army in Russia; 'notorious Russian cunning' would try to exclude Britain from Polish–Soviet negotiations; Churchill asks Sikorski not to publish 'Red Book' on conditions in USSR); see also doc. no. 211, pp. 336–40 (Sikorski–Churchill–Cripps talk, 26 April: Churchill reveals that 'political treaty with Russia will be concluded' in spite of various oppositions, accepting terms that represent the 'lesser evil'; Churchill's deep doubts about 'Soviet loyalty'; the Czech problem; Churchill discloses that 'in current year Great Britain

would limit herself to air-force action . . . without any attempt at invasion'); see also doc. no. 193, pp. 301–10 (Stalin–Lt.-Gen. Anders discussion of evacuation of Polish troops in USSR, 18 March 1942).

Butler, J.R.M., *Grand Strategy*, III, pt 2, pp. 583–663.

Churchill, Winston S., *The Second World War*, IV, The Hinge of Fate (London: Cassell 1951), pp. 425–51 (Prime Minister's visit to Moscow, August 1942; explains N-African landings to Stalin; problem of 'Second Front'; Stalin's attitude and behaviour).

Israelyan, V.L., *Antigitlerovskaya koalitsiya* (Moscow: Mezhdunarodnoe otnosheniya 1964), pt I, pp. 153–74 ('Vtorogo fronta v 1942 godu ne budet' – 'no Second Front in 1942'; Anglo-American discussions of strategy in 1942; British return to 'old plan'; landing in N-Africa; Dieppe losses used as '*the* argument' against early opening of Second Front in NW Europe; United States underwrites 'Torch'; Churchill's visit to Moscow to diminish the unfavourable impression caused by postponement of Second Front; Soviet objections forcefully stated; Anglo-Soviet talks in Moscow in August conducted in strained atmosphere; difficulties over delivery of war supplies to the Soviet Union – convoy PQ 17; forceful Soviet protests at suspension of Russian convoys; drop in quantity and quality of supplies to Russia; Soviet complaints at inferior quality of combat aircraft delivered to USSR).

Jones, F.C., Borton, H. and Pearn, B.R., *The Far East 1942–1946* (RIIA, Oxford UP 1955), pp. 104–5 (on Japanese interest in mediation in Soviet–German war 19 April 1942, Weizsäcker interview with Oshima, also report from Persian sources of Soviet fear of a Japan sea attack; in March 1942 Japanese Naval Staff sent emissary to sound out German naval attaché in Tokyo – Japanese naval view that only negotiated peace could save Germany from bleeding to death in Russia and Japanese Navy inclined to view that Soviet Union would not repulse any approach on mediation; this duly reported to Admiral Raeder and thus came to Hitler's attention, provoking only outburst of rage). See also H. Kordt, *Nicht aus den Akten*, pp. 418–19. (At end of June 1942 General Staff of Imperial Japanese Army through Lt.-Col. Tsuji proposed mediation, with Tsuji making contact with Kordt via an intermediary; Japanese proposed special Japanese mission, headed by Japanese gen. and 1 special member of Japanese cabinet, to travel to Berlin to discuss a possible Soviet–German peace – whole enterprise being disguised as mission engaged on discussing greater prosecution of war. Note also that Oshima intimated that from Japanese side there was no final refusal to consider an attack on Soviet Union, which might come in autumn of 1942 or in spring of 1943).

See also Shigenori Togo, *The Cause of Japan* (New York: 1956), p. 240, on mediation.

Maiskii, *op. cit.*, pp. 238–89.

Woodward, *British Foreign Policy*, II, pp. 236–44.

Official/Party histories

IVOVSS (2), pt 3, pp. 441–53 (fighting in inner city, Stalingrad, mid-September–mid-November: 14 September, extract from combat report on fighting for station; fighting for *Stalingrad 1-i*; by 27 September, German troops holding city from river Tsaritsa to Kuporosnoe; also seizure of *Mamayev Kurgan*; breakthrough to Volga in centre of city; Tractor Plant still producing – supplies 170 tank-turrets with guns and machine-guns; 28 September, *Stavka* reorganized Fronts into Don and

Stalingrad Fronts; 5 October, special *Stavka* orders on holding Stalingrad reinforces 62nd Army with 6 rifle divs – fall of Stalingrad would be signal for Japan and Turkey to attack the USSR; crisis of 14 October with massive German attack; extracts from Chuikov's operational diary, 15 October [p. 445]; Germans take Tractor Plant and cut off 62nd Army; Don Front counter-blow N of Stalingrad, 19 October; in November stage of defensive fighting 62nd Army holding sectors N of Tractor Plant; Barrikady and NE corner of central district of city; 64th Army holding S approaches to city; vital role of Volga Flotilla).

IVOVSS, 3, 'Korennoi perelom v khode Velikoi Otechestvennoi voiny (Noyabr 1942 g.-dekabr 1943 g.)' (Moscow: 1961), pt 1, pp. 17–26 (preparation of Soviet counter-offensive: reorganization of Front command, end September – Don, SW and Stalingrad Fronts; intensification of work on counter-offensive, early October; 6 October, Yeremenko and Khrushchev send suggestions to *Stavka* for conduct of counter-offensive operations; Vasilevskii to Rokossovskii, 7 October; 9 October, detailed submissions by Stalingrad Front; emergence of outlines of 'Uranus', 3-Front operation to unroll over 400km front; provisional fixing of attack dates; great attention to tank and mechanized formations, 60 per cent of entire armoured/mechanized forces concentrated here; air reinforcement; movement of supplies and ammunition; instructions on secrecy and Vasilevskii's special orders, 25 October, to SW and Don Front commanders – movement only by night, heavy AA cover, radio silence mandatory; collective farms deliver food supplies, such as 23 million *pud* bread, 3½ million *pud* meat; civilian population mobilized to build roads and aerodromes; Zhukov's command briefings, 3 November and 4 November, 21st Army; 10 November, command briefing Stalingrad Front; by mid-November preparations generally complete; SW Front armoured army in position and in receipt of attack orders; Don and Stalingrad Front deployments complete; German strength on 'Stalingrad axis' amounted to 35 infantry divs, 5 tank, 4 motorized and 4 cav. – in sum, 50 divs, of which 26 German, 18 Rumanian and 6 Italian – table of comparative strength [p. 26]:

	Soviet	German/Axis
tanks	894	675
guns and mortars	13,540	10,300
aircraft	1,115	1,216
manpower	1,005,000	1,011,000

NOTE: this version of the planning of the counter-offensive hints unmistakably at the 'initiative' of Yeremenko and Khrushchev in 'suggesting' ideas to the *Stavka*, an interpretation since scotched.

IVOVSS (3), pp. 32–41 (SW and Don Front go over to offensive, 19 November; SW Front operations with Romanenko's 5th Tank Army and Chistyakov's 21st Army; Germans reinforce Kletskaya; success of 26th Tank Corps; German 48th Panzer Corps in difficult situation; 26th Tank Corps drives on SE to link up with Stalingrad Front; Germans fall back on Don; 23 November, capture of Kalach; Maj.-Gen. Kravchenko's 4th Tank Corps driving for Sovetskii and link-up with Stalingrad

Front; 21st Army moving behind mobile formations widening breach; encirclement and surrender of Rumanian formations; Stalingrad Front offensive opens 20 November; 57th and 64th Armies attack in morning and afternoon; 51st Army penetrates enemy defences on 20 November; 4th Mech. Corps introduced into breach; 57th and 51st Armies destroy Rumanian divisions; 4th Mech. Corps driving for Sovetskii and link-up with sw Front; Stalin telephones Yeremenko, 22 November, and expresses pleasure at imminent link-up with sw Front; sw and Stalingrad Front tank units link up at Sovetskii, 23 November and exchange recognition signals – green rockets).

German war diaries

KTB/OKW, II (Erster Halbband), see Introduction, p. 65 ('Am 13.9. begann der systematische Angriff auf Stalingrad, seit 16.9. unter alleiniger Führung des Armeeoberkommandos 6.'); p. 66 (12 September 1942, von Weichs and Paulus on threat to flanks of Army Group B); pp. 67–8 (Hitler's disbelief in any major Soviet attack; see also Order of Day, 17 November 1942, to capture all of Stalingrad); p. 70 (Operationsbefehl 1, 14.10.42' – 'Der Russe selbst ist durch die letzten Kämpfe sehr geschwächt und wird im Winter 1942/1943 nicht mehr die Kräfte wie im vorhergehenden aufbringen'; also 'Ergänzung zum Operationsbefehl Nr. 1 23.10.42' – 'Der Russe ist z. Z. wohl kaum in der Lage, eine grosse Offensive mit weiträumigem Ziel zu beginnen . . .'); see also pp. 72–9 (operations in central and N sector of E Front April–November 1942).

For daily entries OKW, 13–30 September 1942, pp. 719–80.

See also Band II (Zweiter Halbband) ('Das vierte Quartal', daily entries 1 October–24 November 1942, pp. 781–1018. See under C Dokumenten-Anhang, no. 26, pp. 1301–4 ('Operationsbefehl Nr. 1 vom 14. Oktober 1942 btr. weitere Kampfführung im Osten'). See no. 27, pp. 1305–6 ('Beurteilung der Feindlage vor Heeresgruppe Mitte vom 6. November 1942 . . .'. See also under GMD. See no. 28, pp. 1306–7 ('Kurze Beurteilung der Feindlage . . . 12. November 1942'), FHO (1) (possible Soviet intentions; notes build-up opposite 3rd Rumanian Army; imminence of attack across Don to cut off Stalingrad, but threat from flank to s of Stalingrad is *not* mentioned). See no. 29, p. 1307 (Führerbefehl vom 17. November 1942 btr. Fortführung der Eroberung Stalingrads durch die 6. Armee).

German Military Documents (GMD)

FHO (II) 'Decree on abolition of military commissars . . .' (German text) ('Bekanntgegeben, Moskau den 10.10.42 8.00 Uhr'), T-78/R491, 6478370–4.

Order no. 325, Defence Commissariat/Defence Commissar 16 October 1942 (German text) (signed J.V. Stalin) (on eradication of mistakes in use of tank formations – tank regiments, bdes and corps; also mechanized bdes and corps – and revised instructions to be followed. T-78/R491, 6478335–43.

FHO (1) 'Beurteilung der Feindlage vor Heeresgruppe Mitte, 6.11.42'. T-78/R466, 6446307–12.

FHO (1) 'Beurteilung der Feindlage vor Heeresgruppe Mitte 6.11.42': 'Vor der deutschen Ostfront zeichnet sich mit zunehmender Deutlichkeit *im Bereich der Heeresgruppe Mitte der Schwerpunkt kommender russischer Operationen* ab. Ob der Russe daneben eine grössere Operation über den Don zu führen beabsichtigt, oder ob er – im Glauben, aus Kräftegründen nicht an *zwei* Stellen die Entscheidung suchen zu können – seine Zielsetzung im Süden begrenzt, ist noch unklar' (italics as in original). T-78/R467, 6447054-9.

FHO (I) 'Aussagen über russische Angriffsabsichten am 7.11.42' (annotated map). T-78/R467, 6447118-19.

FHO (I) 'Kurze Beurteilungen der Feindlage'

'Beurteilung' for 24 November	6447285-6
23 November	7289-91
22 November	7292-5
21 November	7297-9
20 November	7300-302
19 November	7305-7

(For Beurteilungen for November, to 1 November 1942, see 7308-87.) See 6447360 for Beurteilung of 6 November reporting on a conference held by Stalin on 4 November. This conference was reported by an agent to have considered winter operations and concludes '. . . zur Zeit keine grossen Angriffsoperationen mit weitreichenden Zielen zu erwarten sind'.) T-78/R467, frame numbers supplied as above.

FHO (IIa) 'Übersicht über die Entwicklung der neuen sowjetischen Angriffsgrundsätze . . . Stand 20.11.42'. T-78/R491, 6478318-32; see also 6478333 (diagram, 'Schematische Darstellung der Kampfform der roten Infanterie im Angriff nach Stalinbefehl Nr. 306').

'Anlagen zu Op. Abt. (IIa) vom 4.4.42. Die Möglichkeiten für ein militärisches Eingreifen Japans gegen die U.d.S.S.R.'. T-82/R158, 0295479-86 (Operation Wladiwostok/ Operation Baikalsee).

Soviet materials

i) *The defensive battle: Stalingrad, to 18 November*

Chuikov, V.I., *Nachalo puti*, pp. 161-243.

Chuyanov, A., *Stalingradskii dnevnik 1941-1943* (Volgograd: Nizh.-Volzhsk. Kn-Izd 1968), pp. 244-86 (diary entries for period 14 October-18 November; final stages of defensive battle and preparations for Soviet counter-offensive; Chuyanov's role as first secretary of Stalingrad *obkom* and *gorkom*); p. 255 (22 October meeting with Yeremenko on planning of counter-offensive operation); p. 256 (138th Rifle Div. and defence of *Barrikady*); p. 257 (creation of SW Front under Vatutin), p. 281 (under entry for 18 November details of Lyudnikov's position; very heavy casualties and little food; 138th Div. cut off from 62nd Army).

Elin, Maj.-Gen. I.P., 'V tsentre goroda', in *Bitva za Stalingrad*, pp. 199-207 (42nd Rifle Regt ferried into centre of Stalingrad mid-September; Chuikov orders regt to hold Height 102 with remnants of 112th Rifle Div. and to hang on until arrival of 39th Guards Rifle Regt; fighting for railway station; defence of 'Pavlov's house'; counter-attack on 'G-shaped house' and railway workers' apartments – from which German troops could observe and bring under fire Volga crossings).

Kuznetsov, Admiral N.G., 'Voennye moryaki v Stalingradskoi bitve', in *Stalingradskaya epopeya*, pp. 401-19 (20 Naval Infantry Bdes formed winter 1941-2, many used as reinforcement in Stalingrad fighting).

Kuznetzov, Lt.-Gen. P.G., *Marshal Tolbukhin* (Moscow: Voenizdat 1966), pp. 52–67 (Tolbukhin in command of 57th Army).

Lyudnikov, Col.-Gen. I.I., *Doroga dlinoyu v zhizn'* (Moscow: Voenizdat 1969), pp. 22–47 (Lyudnikov's 138th Rifle Div. in fighting for *Barrikady*, October).

See also 'Na zashchite volzhskoi tverdyni', in *Dorogoi bor'by i slavy*, pp. 197–214 (defence of *Barrikady*, October–November; 138th Rifle Div. surrounded, 11 November; food and ammunition exhausted – Division War Diary for 14 November 1942 quoted [p. 205]).

Moskalenko, *op. cit.*, pp. 336–46.

Ot Volgi do Pragi (foreword by Col.-Gen. M. Shumilov) (Moscow: Voenizdat 1966), pp. 26–37 (defensive operations of 64th Army – later 7th Guards Army – September–October).

Peresypkin, Marshal/Signals Troops I.T., *Svyaz v Velikoi Otechestvennoi voine* (Moscow: Nauka 1973), pp. 126–48 (organization of signals during defensive phase of Stalingrad fighting and in counter-offensive: plan of 62nd Army signals net, 15 September [p. 133]; also Stalingrad Front signals net – *Bodo* equipment, ST-35 sets, telephone links [p. 143]).

Petrov, *op. cit.*, pp. 374–7.

See decree of 9 October 1942 in *KPSS o vooruzhennykh silakh Sovetskogo Soyuza*, Dokumenty 1917–1968 (Moscow: Voenizdat 1969), pp. 318–19.

Rodimtsev, Col.-Gen. A.I., '13-ya Gvardeiskaya strelkovaya divizyá v boyakh za Stalingrad', in *Stalingradskaya epopeya*, pp. 321–36.

Rogachev, Rear-Admiral D.D., 'Udary s Volgi', in *Bitva za Stalingrad*, pp. 277–83.

Rokossovskii, *Velikaya pobeda na Volge*, pt 1, pp. 163–204.

Samchuk, *op. cit.*, pp. 99–151.

Samsonov, *Stalingradskaya bitva*, pp. 183–211.

NOTE: this whole narrative enlarges very considerably on V.I. Chuikov's account by utilizing much archival material and unpublished military records.

Smekhotvorov, Maj.-Gen. F.N., 'Vrag k Volge ne proshel' in *Bitva za Stalingrad*, pp. 169–73.

Smekhotvorov, F.N., 'V boyakh za Stalingrad' in *Stalingradskaya epopeya*, pp. 337–46.

Yakovlev, Marshal N.D., 'Artilleriiskoe snabzhenie v bitve na Volge', in *Stalingradskaya epopeya*, pp. 421–42.

Zhukov, *Vospominaniya*, pp. 383–90.

ii) *Planning and preparation of the counter-offensive: 'Uranus'*

Batov, *op. cit.*, pp. 162–89.

Kazakov, Marshal V.I., *Na perelome* (Moscow: Voenizdat 1962) (appointed to Don Front, October; interview with N.N. Voronov on artillery requirements for this command; difficulties with ammunition supply on Don Front; strong forces on Don Front – 6 armies with 39 rifle divs, 102 artillery and mortar regts, in total some 3,000 guns/mortars and 218 'Katyusha' rocket launchers; Rokossovskii informs Kazakov of visit of Zhukov, Vasilevskii and *Stavka* representatives; Kazakov's discussions with Voronov on changes in artillery command of Don Front; right flank of Don Front regrouped; operational planning to strike at flanks of enemy forces; on 24 October 65th Army conducts limited attack to invest Kletskaya and gain Don bridgehead; beginning November, Don Front artillery fully up to strength and in operational order; final artillery deployment; 6 November, command meeting and discussion of 'artillery offensive').

Krasovskii, Aviation Marshal, S.A., *Zhizn' v aviatsii* (Moscow: Voenizdat 1968), 2nd edn, pp. 156–62 (newly established 17th Air Army to be attached to sw Front; aviation servicing and repair units transferred from 16th Air Army; importance of co-operation between Soviet air and 5th Tank Army; briefings by Zhukov, Vasilevskii and Novikov).

Rokossovskii, *Velikaya pobeda na Volge*, pt 2, pp. 207–59.

Rokossovskii, *Soldatskii dolg*, 2nd edn, pp. 140–55.

Samsonov, *Stalingradskaya bitva*, pp. 339–74.

Samsonov, *Ot Volgi do Baltiki*, Ocherk istorii 3-go Gvardeiskogo mekhanizirovannogo korpusa 1942–1945 gg. (Moscow: Nauka 1973), 2nd edn (1st edn 1963), pp. 11–23 (4th Mech. Corps – later 3rd Guards Mech. Corps – forms up from 18 September to 20 October; 3 mechanized bdes; 3 tank regts and supporting units; V.T. Vol'skii in command – one of first armoured commanders in Red Army; in 1930 commanded first 'mechanized regt' and then first 'mechanized bde'; 4th Mech. Corps fully fitted out by middle October; 20,000 men, 220 tanks made ready for rail transport to forward area).

Varennikov, Lt.-Gen. I.S., 'Shtab Stalingradskogo fronta v dni podgotovki i razvitiya kontrnastuplemiya', in *Stalingradskaya epopeya*, pp. 489–500 (Varennikov assigned on *Stavka* orders as Chief of Staff to Stalingrad Front early October; serious situation on 62nd Army front in Stalingrad; planning for counter-offensive already begun; arrival of Vasilevskii; Varennikov and Maj.-Gen. A.M. Dosik – chief of operations/Stalingrad Front – alone privy to operational planning; difficulties of moving and concealing troops; important role of Maj.-Gen. D.I. Gustishev – commandant/Volga crossings; in these movements, Yeremenko's command conference with army commanders in November; with corps and divisional commanders, 10 November; Zhukov oversees these meetings; difficulties caused by fog on morning of Soviet counter-offensive; 2-hour delay in opening artillery barrage; importance of the work of signals troops under Lt.-Gen. I.F. Korolev).

Vasilevskii memoirs/materials: See *Delo vsei zhizni*, pp. 219–25 (9 October introduction of 'unitary command' into the Soviet armed forces; Stalin's great preoccupation with raising authority of Red Army commander; *Stavka* aware of heavy losses to German 6th and 4th Panzer Armies as well as lack of significant reserves that would inhibit their defensive capacity; decision in mid-September to mount Soviet counter-offensive that would not merely alter situation in Stalingrad but radically transform position on entire wing; this now transferred into operational planning terms involving attacks from NW of Stalingrad – Serafimovich – and s of Stalingrad – the passage between the Tsatsa and Barmantsak lakes – to link up at Kalach; strict injunction from Stalin over need for secrecy; end September, outlines of operational plan 'Uranus' presented to *Stavka* and GKO; decision to establish sw Front kept secret until end October; important role for mobile formations and Stavka despatch of 900 tanks to Stalingrad area; detailed operational planning now handed over to General Staff; Zhukov to supervise on sw and Don Fronts; Vasilevskii assigned to Stalingrad Front, 25 October, sw Front officially established; bad autumn weather slows up rail movement of supplies and reinforcements; German intelligence reports that any major Soviet attack would come on central sector; early November most preparations complete and counter-offensive timed for 'not later than 15 November'; 3 November, Zhukov's command briefing on sw Front, 4 November on Don Front and 10 November briefing with 57th Army and Stalingrad Front command; 13 November, final plan inspected by Politburo and *Stavka*; attack dates fixed at 19–20 November for sw and Don Fronts, 20 November for Stalingrad Front; Zhukov assigned to supervision of offensive operations planned for Kalinin and Bryansk Front; Vasilevskii to Stalingrad zone); pp. 226–7 (growing crisis in Stalingrad defence; 11 November, renewed German attack; 62nd Army faced with grave situation as Volga begins to ice up; Vasilevskii recalled from Stalingrad area, 18 November, by Stalin, to look into 'one matter' related to offensive; Volskii's letter to GKO about shortcomings in and possible failure of forth-coming Soviet counter-offensive; Stalin speaks not unreasonably to Volskii by telephone; Volskii gives word to do all he can to carry out mission and Stalin leaves him in command of 4th Mech. Corps; Vasilevskii returns to Serafimovich).

See also 'Nezabyvaemye dni', *VIZ*, 10 (1965), pp. 18–25.

See also 'Vospominaniya ob istoricheskoi bitve', in *Stalingradskaya epopeya*, pp. 82–90.

Voronov, *Na voennoi sluzhbe*, pp. 255–81.

Yeremenko, *Stalingrad*, pt 2, pp. 325–37.

> NOTE: This tendentious version, designed to give the impression that the counter-offensive plan originated with Yeremenko–Khrushchev, has now been entirely displaced and dismissed.

Zhukov, *op. cit.*, pp. 396–407.

iii) *The Soviet counter-offensive: 19–23 November*

Chistyakov, Col.-Gen. I.M., 'Doblestnaya 21-ya', in *Bitva za Stalingrad*, pp. 361–73.

Popov, M.M., 'Yuzhnee Stalingrada', in *Stalingradskaya epopeya*, pp. 641–59 (Popov, deputy commander of the Stalingrad Front; Stalingrad Front forces to be directed against Sovetskii as main objective; original attack date set as 10 November; Stalingrad Front proceeded with offensive preparations after 21 October; many difficulties in concentrating attack formations on Volga bank; need for anti-freeze and winter lubricants; *Stavka* fixes final attack date as 20 November; 4th Mech. and 4th Cav. Corps take up final positions; fog impedes initial artillery bombardment; Volskii commits 4th Mech. Corps after initial hesitation; Yeremenko dissatisfied with progress of mobile formations; Volskii ordered to submit reports every 2 hours; 36th Mech. Brigade in Sovetskii and Soviet units already in contact with Kravchenko's 4th Tank Corps from sw Front; urgent requirement to force 4th Mech. Corps forward to strengthen the encirclement front; firm link-up of sw and Stalingrad Fronts on 23–4 November).

Rokossovskii, *Velikaya pobeda na Volge*, pt 2, pp. 260–84.

Rokossovskii, *Soldatskii dolg*, pp. 156–60.

Samsonov, *Stalingradskaya bitva*, pp. 374–410.

Samsonov, *Ot Volgi do Baltiki*, pp. 34–54.

Vasilevskii, *op. cit.*, pp. 228–32.

Yakubovskii, Marshal I.I. (c-in-c Warsaw Pact), 'Surovoe nachalo boevogo puti', in *Bitva za Stalingrad*, pp. 513–19.

Yeremenko, *Stalingrad*, pt 2, pp. 338–52.

　　See also A.I. Yeremenko, 'Stalingradskaya epopeya', in *Dvesti ognennykh dnei*, pp. 103–10; also 'Velikii perelom' in *Stalingradskaya epopeya*, pp. 142–6.

Zheltov, Col.-Gen., 'Yugo-Zapadnyi front v kontrnastuplenie', in *Stalingradskaya epopeya*, pp. 443–52.

Index